Research Methodology

Author
Dr. Harshna Agarwal
Dr. Arvind Rathore

Sakshar Bharat

Research Methodology

ISBN : 978-93-81951-93-4

Price : 2795/-

First Edition : 2015

Sakshar Bharat
57, Second Floor, Natani Bhawan,
Mishra Rajaji ka Rasta,
Chandpole Bazar, Jaipur - 302001
email:saksharbhratjpr@gmail.com

Printed by
Thomson Press, Jaipur

CONTENTS

Chapter - 1

Introduction

Doing a review of a body of literature is often seen as something obvious and a task easily done. In practice, although researcher do produce what are called reviews of the literature, the quality of those reviews varies considerably. Many reviews, in fact, are only thinly distinguished annotated bibliographies.

Quality means appropriate breadth and depth, rigor and consistency, clarity and brevity, and effective analysis and synthesis. In other words, the use of the ideas in the literature to justify the specific approach to the topic, the selection of methods and demonstration that this research contributes something new to the society.

The originality of a research work often depends on a critical reading of a wide ranging literature. The nature of this concerns, on one hand, immersing oneself in the research topic to avoid the shallowness of quick and dirty research and, on the other, there is the need to identify the key ideas and methodologies from which some contribution to knowledge might be made.

Without a systematic search and critical reading of the literature it would be very difficult to judge how academic research project could make new application of a methodology or contribute in some way, on matter how small, to knowledge.

It is very important to study in detail already available information at first stage as it prevents from duplicating the research study that has been done before. It helps to find out what others have learned and reported on the research problem to be studied. This may giver in refining the statement of the research problem. It also provides with convincing arguments for why the particular research work is needed. It helps to become more familiar with the

the various research approaches that might be used in the proposed research work.

Redman and Mory define research as a "systematized effort to gain new knowledge". *"Research comprises of defining and redefining problems, formulating hyporthesis or suggested solutions; making deductions and reaching conclustions, and at last carefully testing the conclusions to determine whether they fit the formulating hypothesis or not".*

According to Webster Dictionary, research is to search or investigate exhaustively. It is a careful or diligent search, studious inquiry or examination especially investigation or experimentation aimed at the discovery and interpretation of facts, revision of accepted theories or laws in the light of new facts or practical application of such new or revised theories or laws, it can also be the collection of information about a specific subject.

Importance of Research: Research gives a base for our sound decision-making.

There are following three important parts involved in any of our systematic finding:

1. Implicit question posed
2. Explicit answer proposed
3. Collection, analysis, and interpretation of the information and data from the question to answer.

Major Characteristics of Research

(a) ***Systematic Approach*** : Each and every step must of our investigation be so planned that it leads to the next step. Planning and organization are part of this approach. A planned and organized research project saves our time and money.

(b) ***Objectivity*** : It implies that true research work should attempt to find an unbiased answer to the decision-making problem.

(c) ***Reproducible*** : A reproducible research project procedure is one, which an equally competent researcher could duplicate, and from it deduces approxmately the same results. Precise information regarding samples-methods, collection etc., should be specified.

(d) ***Relevancy*** : It avoids collection of irrelevant information and saves time and money and compare the information and data to be collected with researches criteria for action. It enables to see whether the research work is proceeding in the right direction or not.

Exploratory & Experimental Research

Some times a decision maker is grappling with broad and poorly defined problems. If we attempt to secure better definitions by analytic thinking, it may be the wrong approach and may even be counter productive in the sense that this research approach may lead to a definitive answer to the wrong question.

Exploratory research technique uses a less formal approach. It pursues several possibilities simultaneously and in a sense it is not quite sure of its objective.

Experimentation will refer to that process of research technique in which one or more variables are manipulated under conditions, which permit the collection of data, and information which show the effects. Experiments will create situation so that we as a researcher can obtain the specific data needed and can measure the data accurately.

Experiment techniques are artificial in the sense that the situations are usually created for testing purposes.

This artificiality is the essence of the experimental technique, since it gives us more control over the factors we are studying. If we can control the factors, which are present in a given situation, we can obtain more conclusive evidence of cause and effect relationships between any two of them.

Problem Definiation

First of all one should be clear as what exactly the research problem is. If we are working in a company, the problem is assign by the top management; usually we get broad ideas regarding the problem. Then with the broad concept from the top officers we define the specific problem statement. Or it we are doing some research project then we have to identify our research problem statement of our own. Remember our problem statement should be specific.

Research Proposal :

Research proposal are necessary for all types of research, it may be the internal research proposal or it may be the external research proposal. But research proposal is also required in case of research studies for P.hd., or paper presentation as concerned. A research proposal is known as a work plan, prospectus, outline, statement of intent, or draft plan. The research proposal tells us what, why, how, where, and to whom it will be done.

The proposal of research is:

1. To present the top officer questions to be researched and its importance.

2. To discuss the research efforts of others who have worked on related research project.

3. To suggest the data necessary for solving the research questions and how the data and information will be gathered, treated, and interpreted.

Major Errors in Research Process:

There are following two types of errors in research process :

(a) Sampling error

(b) Non-sampling error

Sampling error is the difference between sample value and corresponding population value.

Non-sampling errors are errors in the different stages of research work such as :

(a) Defective problem design
(b) Defective population definition
(c) Frame set
(b) Surrogate information error
(e) Non response error
(f) Measurement error
(g) Experimental error
(h) Poor questionnaire design
(i) Interview bias
(j) Data processings error
(k) Data analysis error
(l) Interpretation error

Factor Analysis : Factor analysis is a very popular technique of research analysis to analyze interdependence. In factor analysis studies entire set of interrelationships without defining variables to be dependent or independent is done. Factor analysis combines variables to create a smaller set of factors.

Mathematically, a factor is a liner combination of many variables. A factor is not directly underlying structure among the different variables. The techique identifies underlying structure among the variables, reducing the number of variables to a more manageable set. Factor analysis groups different variables according to their correction. The factor loading can be defined as the correlations between the factor and their underlying variables. A factor-loading matrix is a key output of the factor analysis. An example of matrix is shown below:

	Factor 1 Factor 2	Factor 3
Variable 1		
Variable 2		
Variable 3		
Column's Sum of Squares		

Conjoint Analysis : The conjoint analysis is a powerful research technique for determining consumer preferences for product attributes.

Cluster Analysis : Market segmentation usually is based not on one factor but on multiple number of factors. Initially, each variable represents its own cluster. The challenge is to find a way to combine variables so that relatively homogeneous clusters can be formed. Such clusters should be internally homogeneous and externally heterogeneous. Cluster analysis is one way to accomplish this goal. Rather than being a statistical test, it is more of a collection of algorithms for grouping objects, or in the case of marketing research, grouping people.

Cluster analysis is useful in the exploratory phase of research when there are no a-priori hypotheses.

Major steps in Cluster Analysis

Formulate the research problem, collecting data and choosing the variables to analyze. Choose a distance measure. The most common is the Euclidean distance. Other possibilities include the squared Euclidean distance, city-block (Manhattan) distance, Chebychev distance, power distance, and percent disagreement. Choose a clustering procedure linkage, nodal, or factor procedures.

Fix the number of clusters. They should be well separated and ideally they should be distinct enough to give them descriptive names such as professionals, buffs, etc. profile the clusters.

Examine the Validity of the Clustering

The format of the marketing research report varies with the needs of the business organization. The report often contains the following sections:

- Authorization letter for the research,
- Table of contents,
- List of illustrations,
- Executive summary,
- Research objectives,
- Methodology,
- Results,
- Limitations,
- Conclusions and recommendations.
- Appendices containing copies of the questionnaires, etc.

Data is then processed in order to summarize the results of research. It seeks to determine how units covered in the research project respond to the items under investigation. It could be:

- Univariate
- Bivariate
- Multivariate

"Research comprises defining and redefining problems, formulating hypothesis or suggested solutions; making deductions and reaching conclusions; and at last carefully testing the conclusions to determine whether they fit the formulating hypothesis".

On evaluating above definition we can conclude that research refers to the systematic method consisting of :

- Enunciating the research problem,
- Formulating a hypothesis,
- Collecting the facts or data,
- Analyzing the facts and
- Reaching at certain conclusions either in the form of solutions towards the concerned problem or in certain generals for some theoretical formulation.

Research has become an important part in management decision-making. Marketing research is a critical part of such market intelligence system; it helps to improve management decision making by providing relevant, accurate, and timely information. Every decision poses unique needs for information gathered through marketing research.

Thus, we can say that marketing research is the function that links the:

- Consumer,
- Customer, and
- The public to the marketer through information

Following information used to identify and define marketing opportunities and problems;

- Generate,
- Refine, and evaluate marketing actions;
- Monitor marketing performance: and
- Improve understanding of marketing as a process.

In the nut-shell we see that marketing research specifies following :

- The information required to address these issues,
- Designs the method for collecting information,
- Manages and implements the data collection process analyses,
- Communicates the findings and their implications

Intelligent use of research tools is the key to success and achievement :

There are following three parts involved in any of our systematic finding:

1. Implicit question proposed
2. Explicit answer proposed
3. Collection, analysis, and interpretation of the information leading from the question to answer.

Example: Consider the following statement :

"We recommend that Model X-42 of music system be priced at Rs. 20,000/-" Marketing Research Manager forwarded this recommendation to Marketing Vice-President.

Implicit Question: What should be the selling price of model X-42?

Explicit Answer: The explicit answer is Rs. 20000/-.

The third part deals with the collection, analysis, and interpretation of the information leading from the question to the answer of Rs. 20000.

Research is a systematic approach to gather information required for sound decisions.

Research is not synonymous to common sense. The difference lies in the methods and procedures used to reach a conclusion.

Major Characteristics of Research

(a) Systematic Approach : Each step of our investigation so planned that it leads to the next step. Planning and organization are part of this approach. A planned and organized research saves our time and money.

(b) Objectivity: It implies that true research work should attempt to find an unbiased answer to the decision-making problem.

(c) Reproducible: A reproducible research procedure is one, which an equally competent researcher could duplicate, and from it deduces approximately the same results. Precise information regarding samples-methods, collection etc., should be specified.

(d) Relevancy: It furnishes following three important tasks:

• It avoids collection of irrelevant information and saves time and money.

• It compares the information and data to be collected with researcher's criteria for action.

• It enables to see whether the research work is proceeding in the right direction or not.

(e) Control: Research is not only affected by the factors, which one is investigating but many other extraneous factors also. It is impossible to control all the factors. All the factors that we think may affect the research study have to be controlled and accounted for.

For Example, suppose we are studying the relationship between incomes and shopping behavior, of university teachers of Jaipur city without controlling for education and age, it will be a height of folly, since our findings may reflect the effect of education and age rather than income.

• All the factors, which are under control, must be varied as per the research study demands.

• All those variables beyond the control should be recorded the structure of research work.

Most research works share the same general struction. We might think of this structure as following the shape of an hourgless. The research process usually starts with a broad area of interest, the initial problem that the researcher wishes to study. For example, the researcher could be interested in how to use computers to improve the performance of students in accountary. But this initial interest is far too broad to study in any single research work (it might not even be addressable in a lifetime of research).

The researcher has to narrow the question down to one that can reasonably be studied in a research work. This might involve formulating a hypothesis or a focus question. For example, the researcher might hypothesize that a particular method of computer instruction in accountary will improve the ability of elementary school students in a specific city. At the narrowest point of the research hourglass, the researcher is engaged in direct measurement or observation of the question of interest.

Once the basic information is collected, the researcher begins to try to understand it, usually by analyzing it in a variety of ways. Even for a single hypothesis there are a number of analysis a researcher might typically do. At this point, the research begins to formulate some initial conclustsins about what happened as a result of the computerized accountary program.

Finally, the researcher often will attempt to address the original broad question of interest by generalizing from the results of this specific research to other related situations. For example, on the basis of strong results showing that the accountary program had a positive effect on student performance, the researcher might conclude that other school districts similar to the one in the study might expect similar results.

Importance of Research in Decision

The importance of research has greatly increased in the field of business and economy as a whole. The study of research methods gives the knowledge and skills we need to solve the problems and meet the challenges of today's modern pace of development following three factors stimulate the interest in a scientific research to decision making.

(i) The society's increased need for more and better information.

(ii) The availability of improved techniques and tools to meet this need.

(iii) The resulting information overload.

The usefulness and contribution of research in helping decisions is so crucial that it has given rise to the opening of a new field altogether called 'market-research'. Market research is basically the systematic gathering, recording and analyzing of the facts about business problems with a view to investigate the structure and development of a market for the purpose of formulating efficient policies for purchasing, production and sales of a specific product or Service.

Research with regard to demand and market factors has important utility in business. Market analysis has become an integral tools of business policy. Once sales forecasting is done, the Master Production Schedule (MPS) and Material Requirement Planning (MRP) can be efficiently done within the limits of the projected capacity based on the MPS Budgetary control can be done more efficient, thus replacing subjective business decisions with more logical and scientific decisions.

Modern trade and with its large-scale operations tends to create alig gulf between the customer and the manufacturer. Particularly when business is too big and operations are too far-flung, one cannot depend upon casual contacts and personal impressions.

Research methodology has been developed as the tool by which we keep in touch with our society. If an entrepreneur has to make sound decisions, he must know who are his customers and what they want. To a find extent he relies on his salesmen and his dealers to supply him with market information but in recent years, more and more firms/executives have turned to research methodology as a medium of communication between the customer and the company.

Research is the link between the manufacturer and the consumer and the means of providing consumer-orientation in all aspects of the business function. It is the instrument of obtaining the knowledge about the market and consumer through objective methods, which guard against the manufacturer's subjective bias.

Many researchers define research as gathering, recording and analyzing of all facts about problems relating to the transfer and sale of goods and services from producer to consumer.

Research methodology is a major prerequisite for consumer oriented marketing. It is necessary for developing the marketing strategy where in factors under the control of the business organization, viz., product distribution system, advertizing, promotion and price can be utilized so as to obtain maximum results in the context of the factors outside the control of the business organization viz., economic environment, competitor and laws of land.

Major Application of Research

Following are a number of examples on the applications of modern research. They clearly bring out how research has been helpful in resolving business problems or in identifying opportunities or the development of new products.

1. A pharmaceutical orgaziation carried out a study on the prescription behavior for a major brand on account of its declining sales. The study brought out interesting and even startling findings on many of aspects such as the relationship between the sales and the age of the brand, its regular promotion, its core therapeutic emphasis and the role or retailers in servicing prescriptions. Prior to the study, all these aspects had been only a matter of conjecture all the

while. On the basis of findings of the research, the organization changed its marketing strategy. This enabled it to regain the lost market share of its brand.

2. N.K Publishers, which is India's largest publication group, has recently launched a monthly women's magazine in Hindi, Vibha. While launching this magazine, the management observed that it was convinced through market research that there was a huge vacuum in the Hindi magazine segment. This new magazine Vibha has been positioned as a partner and friend that the modern women can identify with.

The first print run of Vibha was one lakh copies. Indications are that within a short time it may become one of the popular Hindi magazines.

3. Kapil India Limited launched Picnic from its international portfolio in February 2000. It is wrapped in vibrant colors of red, blue and yellow in conformity with its international packaging. Earlier, Kapil India Limited commissioned a consumer research study in Delhi. The results of this study were encouraging and showed that the Indian youth is always interested in experimenting with new food options.

4. Procter and Gamble (P&G) launched Menthol, an international vibrant of Head and Shoulders. This joins the extra-conditioning anti-dandruff shampoo of the same brand. The organization conducted a market research prior to its launch. The findings of the research indicated a distinct need for a menthol-based shampoo. The study showed that in hot and humid conditions as in India, consumers prefer a shampoo which not only removes dandruff but also gives a cool and tingling sensation to the scalp.

5. Another example from P&G shows how marketing research is used to field new opportunities in the marketplace. The company was getting a lot of information on Vicks-Vaporub. The analysis of such data revealed that the most common symptom of cold was a headache and that majority of adults typically take a pill to cure it. This shows an opportunity for a product that can treat the headache as well as the other symptoms. The organization thus launched Vicks Action 500. It not only treated headache but also gave relief from blocked nose. Research can therefore lead to the development of a new product.

6. Pepsi Foods know importance to marketing research. Through research it gets systematic information about its markets and its customers. All its research is done by the IMRB. Research studies done for Pepsi Foods fall in the following three areas:

(i) Studies done on a continuous basis like marketing tracking studies and audies.

(ii) Research that are commissioned for specific marketing problems faced by the organization.

(iii) Research done from time to time as per the requirement of the company such as a study to find the effectiveness of an ad campaign.

All above three types of research studies have tremendously helped emphasis on modern research. In this company, every activity, strategy and decision is based on data collected through the research process. It believes in planning research in advance though it is rather difficult. It strives to have a meaningful dialogue with the consumer in order to know his real opinion about its goods, what difficulties he experiences and what suggestions he has to offer.

Information thus received proves to be quite useful to the orgaziation in modifying its goods or in evolving new ones. Whirlpool has gained an insight into the different segments in the market. In India, it has segmented the market on the basis of the different stages of the product life cycle.

On the basis of the functions we can state some of the general objectives of Research:

- Decision-making objectives
- Economic and business objectives
- Policy objectives
- Product development
- Profit objectives
- Human Resource Development objectives
- Market objectives

1. Innovation objectives
2. Customer satisfaction objectives

- Promotional objectives
- Corporate change objectives

Uses of Research in Important Areas

Through research, a business can quickly get a synopsis of the current scenario, which improves his information base for making sound decisions affecting future operations of the company. The following are some important areas in which research plays a key role in making effective decisions.

Marketing

Marketing research is undertaken to half the marketing function. Marketing research stimulates the flow of marketing data from the consumer and his environment to marketing information system of the enterprise. Market research involves the process of

- Systematic collection
- Compilation
- Analysis
- Interpretation of relevant data for marketing decisions

This information goes to the concerning executive in the form of data. On the basis of this data the concerning executive develop plans and programmers.

Advertising research, packaging research, performance evaluation research, sales analysis, distribution channel, etc., måy also be included in research. Research tools are applied effectively for studies involving following :

1. Demand forecasting
2. Consumer buying behavior
3. Measuring advertising effectiveness
4. Media selection for advertising
5. Test marketing
6. Product positioning
7. Product potential

(i) ***Product Research*** : Assessment of suitability of goods and sarldiers with respect to design and price.

(ii) ***Market Characteristics Research (Qualitative)***: Who uses the product and sarldier? Relationship between buyer and user, buying rates, units in which product is purchased, customs and habits affecting the use of a product, consumer attitudes, shopping habits of consumers, brand loyalty, research of special consumer groups, survey of local markets, basic economic analysis of the consumer market, etc.

(iii) ***Size of Market (Quantitative)***: Market potential, total sales quota, territorial sales quota, quota for individuals, concentration of sales and advertising efforts; appraisal of efficiency, etc.

(iv) Competitive position and Trends Research

(v) ***Sales Research***: Analysis of sales records with state wise.

(vi) ***Distribution Research***: Channels of distribution, distribution costs of goods and reviews.

(vii) ***Advertising and Promotion Research***: Testing and evaluating, advertising and promotion of goods and reviews.

(viii) New product launching and product positioning.

Production : This type of research helps a company to decide in the field of production on:

- What to produce
- How much to produce
- when to produce
- For whom to produce

Some of the areas we can apply researches are:

- Product development
- Cost reduction
- Work simplifiction
- Profitability improvement
- inventory control

Materials

The materials department uses research to frame suitable policies regarding purchase and storage.

Various types of researches, e.g., market research, operations research and motivational research, when combined together, help in solving many complex problems of business and industry in a number of ways. These techniques help in replacing intuitive business decisions by more logical and scientific decisions.

Government and Economic System

Research helps our government and economic system decision maker in a number of ways, e.g., it can help in examining the consequences of each alternative and help in bringing out the effect on economic conditions of a country. Many examples can be quoted such as problems of big and small industries due to various factors-up gradation of technology and its impact on lab or and supervisory deployment, effect of government's liberal policy. WTO and its new guidances, ISO 9000/14000 standards and their impact on our exports allocation of national resources on national priority basis, etc. Research lays the foundation for every Government Policies in our economic system.

We all are aware of the fact that research is applied for bringing out union finance budget and railways budget every year. Government also uses research for economic planning and optimum utilization of resources for the development of the country. For systematic collection of information on the economic and social structure of our country we need research. Such types of information indicate what is happening to the national economy and what changes are taking place.

Social Relationships

Research in social relations is concerned with both-knowledge for self and knowledge for helping in solving immediate problems of human relations. It is a sort of formal training, which helps an individual in a better way, e.g.

- It helps processionals to earn their livelihood in better way.
- It helps students to know how to write and report various findings and suggestions.
- It helps philosophers and thinkers in their new thinkings and ideas.
- It helps in developing new styles for creative work.
- It may help researchers, in general, to generalize new theories in every find of sciences and arts.

******

Chapter - 2

Types of Research

On the basis of the fundamental objectives of the modern research, we can classify research into following two important types:

1. Exploratory Research

Many times a decision maker is grappling with broad and poorly defined problems. If we attempt to secure better definitions by analytic thinking, it way be wrong approach and may even be counter productive. Counter productive in the sense that this type of research approach may lead to a definitive answer to the wrong question.

Exploratory research uses a less formal type of approach. It pursues many possibilities simultaneously and in a sense it is not quite sure of its main objective.

Exploratory research is designed to give a background, to familiarize and, as the word implies, just "explore", the general subject.

A part of exploratory research is the investigation of relationships among variables without knowing why they are selected for studied. It borders on an, idle curiosity approach, differing from it only in that the investigator thinks there may be a pay off in the use some where in the forest of questions.

Following three important typical approaches in exploratory research are:

(a) The literature survey,

(b) The experience survey, and

(c) The analysis of "insight-stimulating" examples

The literature search is fast, economical way to develop a better understanding of a research problem, in which we are investigating and have limited experience and knowledge. It also familliarizes us with past research results, data sources, and the type of data available.

The experience survey concentrates on persons who are particularly knowledgeable in the specific field. In this type of research project representative samples are not desired. A covering of widely divergent views is better.

In this type of researchers are not looking for conclusions; these are looked for ideas.

The analysis of specific examples is a sort of case study approach, but again, researchers are looking for some fresh possible divergent views.

2. Conclusive Research

Exploratory research gives rise to many hypothesis, which we will have to tasted for drawing definite conclusions. These conclusions when tested for validity paydown for the structure of our decision-making.

Conclusive research is followed for this purpose of testing the hypothesis generated by exploratory research. Conclusive research can further be classified as following :

- Descriptive
- Experimental.

(a) Descriptive Research

Descriptive research as the name suggests is designed to define something. For example, the characteristics of users of a given product or service; the degree to which product use varies with income, age, sex or other characteristics; or the number who saw a specific television commercial.

To be of maximum benefit, a descriptive study must only collect data and information for a definite purpose. Our objective and understanding should be clear and specific.

Descriptive research studies very in the degree to which a specific hypothesis is the guide. It allows both implicit and explicit hypotheses to be tested depending on the research problem.

For example, a cereal company may find its sales declining. On the basis of market feedback the company may hypothesize that teenage children do not eat its cereal for breakfast. A descriptive research study can then be designed to test this hypothesis.

(b) Experimental Research

Experimentation will refer to that process of research work in which one or more variables are manipulated under conditions, which permit the collection of data, which show the effects.

Experiments will create situation so that we as a researcher can obtain the particular data needed and can measure the data accurately.

Experiments are artificial in the sense that such situations are usually created for testing purposes only.

This artificiality is the essence of the experimental method, since it gives us more control over the factors we are studying for our research project. If we can control the factors, which are present in a given situation, we can obtain more conclusive evidence of cause and effect relationships between any two of them.

If our objective is to validate in a resounding manner the cause and effect relationship among variables, then undoubtedly experiments are much more effective than descriptive technique of research.

Thus, we can conclude that:

- Research methodology minimizes the degree of uncertainty involved in management decisions. Research study lays the structure for decision-making.
- Research is not synonymous with common sense in any way.
- Research study is characterized by - systematic, objective, reproducible, relevance, and control.
- The role of research study in the important areas of management has been briefly covered. The areas include marketing, production, banking, materials, human resource development, and government.
- Research process involves the five important steps problem: definition, research design, data collection, data analysis, and interpretation of results. All these steps have been explained in detail with their key elements.
- We have dichotomized the types of research into - exploratory, and conclusive.
- While exploratory research work enables the researcher to generate hypotheses, these are tested for validity by the conclusive research work.
- Conclusive research work could be further divided into-descriptive, and experimental.
- While the descriptive research procedures merely test the hypotheses, the experimental research establishes in a more effective manner the cause and effect relationships among different variables.

Basic and Applied Research

Basic research is intended to expand the body of knowledge in a field or to give knowledge for use of others applied research used for solving a particular social problem or guiding a specific decision.

Basic Research

1. The U.S. Bureau is the world's largest fact gathering agency. All its data are for use by others including economist, politicians and socialist of the whole word.

2. The research of an advertising agency studies the result of use of coupons versus rebate as demand stimulation tactics, but not in a specific example or in relation to a specific client's purpose.

• A research study conducted by too professors measuring differences between high level and low performing sales representatives, relative to their job satisfaction and their job turnover. Resets were published in an article available to anyone with a problem to which research findings were relevant.

We can classify research in following three categories:

1. Exploratory research
2. Descriptive research
3. Causal research

These classifications are done according to our objective of the research project. In some cases the research will fall into one of these categories, but in other cases different phases of the same research project will fall into different categories.

(1) Exploratory Research

Exploratory research work has the goal of formulating research problems more precisely, clarifying concepts, gathering explanations, gaining insight, eliminating impractical ideas, and forming hypotheses. Exploratory research work can be performed using a literature search, surveying certain people about their experiences, focus groups, and case studies.

When we will be surveying people, exploratory research studies would not try to obtain a representative sample, but rather, seek to interview those who are knowledgeable and who might be able to provide us the insight concerning the relationship among different variables.

Case studies can include contrasting situations or benchmarking against a modern business organization known for its excellence. Exploratory research work may develop hypothesis, but it does not seek to test them. Exploratory research work is characterized by its flexibility.

(2) Descriptive Research

Descriptive research work is more rigid than exploratory research and seeks to describe users of a product or service, determine the proportion of the population that uses a goods, or predict future demand for a goods or describes the happening of a specific phenomenon.

As opposed to exploratory research work, if we are doing descriptive research work we should define questions, people surveyed, and the method of analysis prior to beginning data collection.

In other words, who, what, where, when, why, and how aspects of the research work should be defined. Such preparation allows us the opportunity to make any required changes before the costly process of data collection has been started by researcher.

There are following two basic types of descriptive research:

(a) Longitudinal Studies: Longitudinal research studies are time series analysis that make repeated measurements of the same individuals, thus allowing us to monitor behavior such as brand switching. However, longitudinal research studies are not necessarily representative since many people may refuse to participate because of the commitment required.

(b) Cross-sectional Studies: Cross-sectional research studies sample the population to make measurements at a specific point in time. A special type of cross sectional research analysis is a cohort analysis, which tracks an aggregate of individuals who experience the same event within the same time interval over time. We can use cohort analysis for long forecasting of product or service demand or supply.

(3) Causal Research

Causal research study seeks to find cause and affect relationships between different variables. It accomplishes this goal through laboratory and field experiments.

Important Step of Research Process

Step 1: Problem Definition

The first important step in any research project is to define the research problem. In defining the problem, we should take into account : the purpose of the study, the relevant background information, the information needed, and

- How it will be used in decision making.
- Problem definition involves discussion with the decision makers.
- Interviews with subject experts.
- Analysis of secondary data and
- Perhaps, some qualititative research, such as focus groups.
- Once the problem of research investigations has been precisely defined, the research can be designed and conducted properly.

Step 2: Development of an Approach to the research Problem

Development of an approach to the research problem includes:

- Formulating an objective or theoretical framework,
- Research questions, and hypothesis and identifying the information needed for research.

This research process is guided by :

- Discussion with management and industry experts,
- Analysis of secondary data,
- Qualitative research, and
- Pragmatic considerations

Step 3: Research Design Formulation

A research design is a framework or blueprint for doing the research project. It details the procedures necessary for obtaining the required information, and its purpose is to design a research study that will test the hypothesis of interest, determine possible answers to the research questions, and provide the information required for decision making.

Conducting exploratory research work precisely defines the variables, and designing appropriate scales to measure them are also a part of the research design.

The issue of how the research data should be collected from the respondents (for example, by conducting a research survey or an experiment) must be addressed. It is also necessary to design a questionnaire and a sampling plan to select respondents for the research study.

More formally, formulating the research design includes the following important steps:

1. Definition of the information needed
2. Secondary data analysis
3. Qualitative research work
4. Methods of collecting quantitative data (survey, observation, and experimentation)
5. Measurement and scaling procedures
6. Questionnaire design for research
7. Sampling process and sample size of research work
8. Plan of data analysis for research work

Step 4: Fieldwork or Data Collection

Data and information collection involves a field force or staff that operates either in the field, as in the case of personal interviewing (in-home, mall intercept, or computer-assisted personal interviewing), from an office by telephone (telephone or computer-assisted telephone interviewing), throught mail (traditional mail and mail panel surveys with pre-recruited households), or electronically (e-mail or Internet). Proper selection, training, supervision, and evaluation of the field force help minimize data-collection errors in our research project.

Step 5: Data Preparation and Analysis

Data or information preparation includes the editing, coding, transcription and verification of data. Evary questionnaire or observation from is inspected or edited and, if necessary, corrected. Number or letter codes are assigned to represent each response to each question in the questionnaire. The data from the questionnaire are transcribed or key punched into magnetic taps or disks, or input directly into computer. The data are analyzed to derive information related to the components of the research problem and, thus, give input in to the management decision problem.

Step 6: Report Preparation and Presentation

The whole project should be documented in a written report that addresses the specific research questions identified, describes the research approach, the research design, data collection, and data analysis procedures adopted, and presents the results and the important findings. The findings of research should be presented in a comprehensible format so that management can readily use them in the decision making process. In addition, an oral presentation should be made to management using tables, figures, and graphs to enhance clarity and impact.

Responsibility to the Research Supplier :-

Unless the research work is sole sourced (the client directly approaches the supplier and does not deal with anyone else), it is normal practice to ask suppliers to bid on a research work. The buyer should inform the supplier that others are also biddings and even disclose their names :

Give as much information as possible regarding the research project, the support that will be provided, information that may already be available, timelines and budget considerations that will allow the supplier to make an informed decision about whether to bid or not; and

Important direction on the research methodology :

All of this information would be part of the Request for proposal (RFP)

If the research project needs to be terminated early for whatever reasons, the buyer should follow due process and/or compensate the supplier for the time spent and costs incurred. Payment for work completed is normally stipulated by a payment schedule agreed upon as part of accepting the research proposal from the supplier.

Research Supplier's Responsibility to the Research Buyer (Client) :-

All data contracted and paid for becomes the assets of the client unless otherwise stipulated as part of contract, and should be delivered to the buyer. As part of this commitment, the methodology outlined as part of the research proposal must be followed and the supplier would fined appropriate quality control techniques to ensure that the work was carried out according to instructions, particularly if fieldworkers or sub-contractors were used and it becomes important that many different people administer a research survey in the same way.

Estimate the precise costs of the research work to be done can be quite difficult and the supplier should take great care in calculated all potential cost since the buyer is not obligated to pay any unanticipated costs unless these were incurred at the buyer's specific request.

The supplier should also carefully estimate the time required since completing the research project in time is another key responsibility.

The supplier should give the buyer with advice regarding the most appropriate and cost-effective methodology for the problem at hand.

Lastly, but perhaps most important, the supplier should provide the buyer with an interpretation of the data that is useful in managerial decision-making. This requires not only a description of the detailed methodology and its limitations as well as assumptions made as part of the study, but also comments on the reliability of the results and their implications.

Buyer's and supplier's Responsibility with Respect to Respondents :

Ethical behavior when dealing with respondents is perhaps the most important ethics in research, and codes of ethics tend to rule many research-oriented organizations today. For example, Ryerson's ethical guidelines bind all of its faculty as well as students working on research with them. Be sure to check out the other ethical guidelines under "reference".

It tends to be common practice to ensure respondents that their identity will remain anonymous and their responses confidential. This means that their names cannot be used for any purposes, and indeed that they cannot be contacted for further research unless they were specifically asked and agreed to it.

Respondents should be given with sufficient information to allow them to decide whether they wish to part of the research or not. Furthermore, they must be allowed to withdraw from responding at any point in time.

The identity of the client as well as the researcher should be made clear to the respondent. If there is concern that this might bias the response, the information should be given at the earliest opportunity, but certainly before the survey or interview is completed.

Respondents have a right of privacy which includes not only the hours when they are contacted, but also the use of tape recorders, cameras and/or two-way mirrors, as are used in focus groups, for instance.

If respondents were promised a summary of the research project's results or payment or other incentives for their time, these must be respected.

The respondents' safety is another important area of increasing concern. With food allergies on the rise, for example, taste tests must inform the respondent about ingredients.

Research on children is even more stringent and generally not only needs the parents' consent, but often also their presence or at least proximity so that they might pull their child out of a situation that they find unsafe.

Case Study : Suppose we are asked to carryout research to find out knowledge, attitude and practice of customers towards soft drinks after knowing pesticides resides being used.

How shall we carry out this research work? Here we explain with suitable research instruments, illustrations assumptions and examples.

Ans : The two global majors Pepsi Co and Coca-Cola companies dominate the soft drink market in India. Coca-Cola, which had winded up its India operations during the introduction of the FERA regine, re-entered India 16 years latter in 1993. Coca-cola bought local brands-Thums up, Limca and Gold spot from Parle Beverages and soft drink brands crush, Canada Dry and Sport Cola from Cadbury Schweppes in early 1999. Pepsi started a couple of years before coca cola in 1991 has bought over Mumbai based Duk's range of soft drink brands. According to NCAER survey 91% of the total consumption of soft drinks in our country is by lower, lower middle and upper middle class people. Per capita consumption in our country is amoung the lowest in the world at 6 bottles per annum compared to 80 bottles in Thailand and 800 bottles in U.S.A. Delhi market has highest per capita consumption in our country with 50 bottles per annum.

Problem's Solution:

An exploratory research work has to be carried out to know the consumers attitude towards pesticides being found in soft drinks. It can be used in formulating research problems more precisely, clarifying research concepts, gathering explanations, gaining insight, eliminating impractical ideas, and forming hypothesis. Exploratory research work can be performed using:

A literature search work

Surveying some people about their experiences when surveying people, exploratory research work would not try to obtain a representative sample, but rather, seek to interview those who are knowledgeable and who might be able to give insight concerning the relationship among different variables.

Sampling

A research survey has to be conducted for finding out knowledge, attitude and practices of customers towards soft drinks after knowing pesticides residues being used.

The cities that can be selected for survey are : Delhi, Mumbai, Kolkata, Hyderabad, Chennai, Banglore, Ahmedabad, Lucknow, Jaipur, Patna, Pune, Indore, Ludhiyana, Chandigarh, Kota and Kochi.

Number of respondents from each city can be 600, divided in male and female respondents. The age profile has to taken care of.

Hypothesis

1. Consumption of soft drinks has been reduced after knowing pesticides residues being used.

2. Consumption of soft drinks is increasing as usual in youth generation.

Data Collection

There can be three ways of administering this research survey, including, telephone, online surveys, personal in home survey, personal mall intercept survey etc. The major brands that can be included in the research work are :

Pepsi, Coke, Thumps up, Maaza, Limca, Fanta, Sprite, Miranda and 7up.

Data Analysis

Following data analysis techniques can be used : univariate analysis like mean, frequency charts, histograms. Bivariate analysis like correlation, regression analysis. ANOVA to find differences between means, chi-suqare test to find any differences between observations and expectations, factor analysis to identify factors affecting attitude and practices, multidimentional scaling can also be use to understand the consumer perceptions in our country.

******

Chapter – 3

Pure and Applied Research

Research in art, commerce and other sciences has been class field into the following two types:

1. Fundamental or Pure Research: Pure research is the research concerning principles or laws or rules. In social research, pure research includes fundamental principles and laws concerning social life. Pure research aims at the achievement of knowledge. It is not concerned with the utility or use of the conclusions of any research work. Thus, pure research is done only for the attainment of knowledge and truth.

Besides the research for new principles, pure research verifies the old established principles and laws. With the change of time and space it often becomes necessary to make a change in the fundamental principles concerning them. This need is also pointed out by pure research. Principles are purified by constant and repeated research upon them. Sometimes the scienntists start doubting some prevalent principles. To verify the doubts and to remove them, pure research is carried on concerned principles and laws are modified according to the conclusions and results of pure research.

Thus pure research is concerned with the theoretical aspect of a science. It aims at the attainment, increase and verification of knowledge. It tries to find out cause-affect relationship in social phenomena. For example, the relationship between crime and economic status is a proper subject of pure research. Again, pure research aims at finding out the laws working behind the observed phenomena. It is a postulate that a phenomenon is governed by some definite laws. These always are discovered by pure research. The sociologists organise pure research in order to find out laws governing social phenomena. Thus, pure research is the fundamental basis of the progress and evolution in different sciences. It is also the basis of the evolution of necessary concepts and technical terminology. The process of standardization of these is based upon pure research.

2. Applied Research: Applied research is related with the solution of particular problems. While pure research discovers principles and laws, applied research discovers their application in order to solve some social problems. Thus applied research is concerned with the applied aspect of life. In sociology, it is generally carried out in the field of social, semi-social economic, socio-psychological and socio-anthropological problems. In the field of social planning, social legislation, social hygiene, religion etc. are known as applied research. For example, research in the field of family planning aims at certain applications of some principles. Similarly, administrative plans need applied research gives complete and valid information about the many facets of social problems. In order to solve socio-pathological problems, applied research is carried on to gather all sort of information about the social maladies.

Applied research is thus concerned with actual life. It discovers the what, how and why of actual social life. Pointing out the importance of applied research Stouffer has rightly pointed out that if sociology has to increase its importance, it should lay emphasis upon the applied aspects. For example, if the sociologists could point out as to how a guidance system may be useful in public school, its social influence will increase and so also the social sanction for its study. Thus applied research is concerned with research for amelioration of social problems. It removes so many prejudices, preconceptions and false ideas. It suggests ways for the solution of social problems.

Role of theory in Research

In this perceptive analysis of the interrelationship between theory and research, Robert K. Merton has discussed following five ways in which sociological theory influences research :

1. By providing general orientation: According to Talcott Parsons, "The alternative for the scientist in the commerce management or any other field is not as between theorizing and not theorizing, but as between theorizing explicitly with a clear consciousness of what he is doing with greater opportunity that gives of avoiding the many subtle pitfalls of fallacy, and following the policy of the ostrich, pretending not to theorize and thus leaving one's theory implicitly and uncricized, thus almost certainly full of errors?" Theory points of variables and helps in the selection of cases, facts and data. The researcher is guided by the relevance of variables to the logical structure of theoretical scheme. This role of theory in research has been however, rejected by other. Homans calls it presumptuous and argues, "There are few cases in research in which a developed deductive system has actually guided research. The reason is that there are few such deductive systems and still fewer among 'general' theories. Let the researcher feel guilty about that if he likes, but not about the fact of theoretical guidance. It makes sense to have theory guide research only if there is some reason for having confidence in the theory, and the theorist's own assertion is not sufficient reason. In the absence of such confidence, the researcher should feel free to do anything he pleases, so long as he studies men. Indeed, he could do worse than indulge in mere data collection." M.F. Abraham rejects Homan's position as an extreme. According to him, Homans claim is debatable. General agreement among research theory for social research Abraham points out, "Theoretical consideration also enables the researcher to narrow the range of inquiry by pinpointing potentially significant and relevant variables, thereby saving time, money and other resources." Therefore, according to Abraham, "The reciprocal relationship between theory and research may be summarized thus : theory guides research, research guides theory."

2. By Developing Concepts : Theory may be further useful in research by developing research concepts. Pointing out the close relationship of facts and concepts, McClelland has written, that a concept is, "A shorthand representation of a variety of facts. Its purpose is to simplify thinking by subsuming a number of events under one general heading." Therefore concepts are needed to formulate a research problem as well as to design ways of solving it. Pointing out the importance of concepts in science, Abraham Kaplan has said, "These important terms of any science are significant because of their semantics ....(they) reach out to the world which gives the science its subject matter. The meaning of such terms results from a process of conceptualization of the subject matter. In this process the things studied are classified and analysed; several things are grouped to together and particular things assigned to the several groups to which they belong." Examples of the use of sociological concepts in empirical research way be found in Person's pattern variables which have been effectively utilized in the empirical analysis of the process of modernization. While Durkheim defined different types of social integrations conceptually, the empirical researchers used it for construction of different indices to measure it.

3. By furnishing post factum research interpretations : In research the data are first collected and then interpreted. Explanations consistent with the particular set of observations, are advanced for interpretation. According to Homans, this function of theory in social research may be called codification or the 'stratery by which deductive systems are inductively arrived at. This helps in organizing and systematizing empirical findings. The process of codification centres around **ex-post facto** explanation. According to Homans, "All science begins with **export facto** explanations and without them could not get off the ground."

4. By formulating empirical generalization : An important role of theory in research is performed by formulating empirical generalizations. In the words of M.F. Abraham, "A major function of research theory in empirical research is to summarize observed uniformities of relationship between variables and to synthesize them with reference to existing conceptual schemes." The sociologists must present an interpretative synthesis by comparing the new findings with the prevailing theories. As Alfred Marshall points out, "The most reckless and treacherous of all theorists is he who professes to let the facts and figures speak for themselves." Therefore, Talcott Persons maintains that no scientifically oriented empiricist is 'content to state bald, discrete facts'; According to Parsons, "It is stated not merely that the steam railroad was developed and certain kinds of industrial development took place, but that without the invention of the railroad these developments could not have taken place that the inventions of the railroad was a causal factor in industrial development. Now I with to assert that such an imputation of causal relationship cannot be proved without reference to generalized theoretical categories. If it is asserted, the assertion is logically dependent on these categories whether they are explicit or implicit."

5. By further development of theory : One of the most important functions of theory is the provision of conceptual framework. As Merton puts it. "By providing a rationale, the theory introduces a ground for prediction which is more secure than more empirical extrapolation from previously observed trends....The theoretic empiricist would have no alternative, however, but to predict on the basis of extrapolation."

The researcher starts with a set of propositions derived from a theory. He gather data in order to form a hypothesis. But the researcher may also start from the data itself and examine relationships between different variables to arrive at generalizations or even a general theory. However, it is admitted that this function of research theory makes our research more precise, determinate, testable and enhances the like lihood of approximating a crucial observation of experiment. As Abraham points out, "Successive exploration of new leads in empirical inquiry and resultant modification of initial theories as well as 'formalized derivation' and 'codification' make empirical studies more theory-oriented and substantive theories more empirically sound."

Impact of Empirical Research on Theory

John McKinney has summarised the impact of empiricism on theory in these words, "First, the refreshing contrast of empirical research with the a priorism of the classifical writers discredited the completely speculative approach. Second, empiricism established the necessity of controlled observation and research design as components of scientific investigation. Third, the necessity of keeping theory in touch with evidence and relating it to the bedrock of accumulative fact is basically an empirical contribution. Fourth, empiricism made an outstanding contribution of the procedural rules of research. It is the empirically oriented who to a great extent have codified the research rules and practices. Fifth, the empiricists have accomplished an enormous amount of investigation, much of it trivial but most of it arduous."

Accounting to Robert Merton, "bearing of empirical research on sociological theory" may sumarised as follows:

1. **Initiation of theory by the serendipity pattern** : Serendipity pattern means the unanticipated, anomalous and strategic datum. This pattern exerts pressure for initiating sociological theory. Unexpected new turns are given to theorising. Exploration of new leads results in the development of new theory as well as the extension of the existing ones. Hyman lays great stress on serendipity patterns and even advocates 'a programme of training for serendipity' which he believes will enable the research worker to experience serendipity weight greater frequency and stimulate him to new and better theorizing.

2. **The recasting of theory** : The recasting of theory means the elaboration of new conceptualist scheme resulting in re-evaluation and even a substantial revision of the existing theory. In the words of Merton. "Where as the serendipity pattern centres in an apparent inconsistency which press for resolution, the reformulation pattern centres in the hitherto neglected but relevant fact which process for an extension of the conceptual scheme."

3. **The refocusing of theoretic interest** : This means that the new methods of empirical research exert pressure for refocussing of theoretic interest. It invents new procedures and techniques, facilitating the collection of new and pertinent facts stimulating fresh hypothesis. With the help of new techniques old theories are tested and attention is focused on 'areas in which there is an abundance of pertinent statistical data.'

4. **The classification of concepts** : An important bearing of empirical research on research theory is in the form of classification of concept. Theretical discussion clarifiese the conceptual scheme which is necessary for progress of research.

Reciprocal Relationship of Theory and Research

M.F. Abraham has pointed out the following points showing reciprocal relationship between theory and research:

1. Suggestion of Problems and Hypotheses. While empirical research contributes by means of investigation, a theoretical system suggests a number of problems and hypotheses which may be investigated.

2. Guidance and facilitation: Theoretical considerations guide and facilitate research by means of selection of key-variables and relevant cases. They delimit the scope of inquiry by pin pointing significant facts.

3. Validations and repudiation of theory: While sociological theories present hypotheses, empirical inquiry helps in testing, validating and repudiating theories. In the words of Hyman, "Methodologists reduce the danger that theorists will waste their time building plausible theories out of fallacious findings or will reject a fine theory because of apparently contradictory, but fallacious, findings."

4. Help in theory building: Not only sociological theory suggests hypotheses but even empirical findings may suggest new hypotheses and relationships leading to the formation of new theories and modification of the existing ones.

******

Chapter – 4

Research Design

A research design is a plan of action, a plan for collecting and analysing data in an economic, efficient and relevant manner. A research design could be constructed either to test a hypothesis or to give a cause-effect relationship to a specific situation. Whatever be the nature of the design, the following four general rules should be followings in planning a design : 1. Define the nature and scope of the problem. 2. Specify the related variables. 3. Exclude the variables not relevant to the research study. 4. Start from logical hypothesis.

Steps in Research Design

However, a further understanding of the components of a research design elicit the following important steps:

1. Selection and definition of a research problem : The problem selected for research study should be defined clearly in operational terms so that the researcher knows positively what facts he is looking for and what is relevant to the present study. Since human behavious, as an interaction pattern, is the result of various forces it is best to delimit the scope of one's study which reaps ample benefits during the actual course of data and information collection. Now besides the operational definition of the problem, the problem selected should be practicable in costs of time and money. If the criteria of validity and reliability of results are to be fulfilled, such problems as are unmanageable by the researcher should both be selected for the design.

2. Sources of data : Once the research problem is selected it is the duty of the researcher to state clearly the various sources of information such as library, personal documents, field work, a particular residential group etc.

3. Nature of study : The research design should be expressed in relation of the nature of study to do be undertaken. The choice of the statistical, experimental or comparative type of study should be made at this stage so that the following steps in planning may have relevance to the proposed problem.

4. Object of research study : Whether the design aims at a theoretical understanding or presupposes a "welfare" notion must be explicit at this point, stating the object of the study aids not only in clarity of the design but also in a sincere response from the respondents.

5. Social-cultural context : As one would rightly remember, a research design is always set to a context which has a social and cultural bearing on the individuals. For example, in a research study of the fertility rate in a people of "backward" class, the context of the so called "backward" class of people and the conceptual reference must be made clear. Unless the meaning of the term is clearly defined, there tends to be a large variation in the study because the term backward could have religious economic and political connotations.

6. Temporal Context : The geographical limit of the design should also be referred to at this stage that the research related to the hypothesis is applicable to particular social groups only.

7. Dimension : It is physically impossible to analysis the data collected from a large universe. Hence the selection of an adeuqate and representative sample is the byword in any research. Depending upon the dimension of the proposed research study, such a sample of the large population can be selected to facilitate a practical design.

8. Bases of Selection : Now can an adequate and representative sample be selected. The mechanics of drawing a random, stratified, purposive, double cluster or quota sample when following carefully will produce a scientifically valid sample in an unbiased manner.

9. Techniques of Data Collection : Relevant to the research study design a suitable technique has to be adopted for the collection of required data. The relative merits of "Observation", "Interview" and "Questionnaire" when studied together will help in the choice of suitable technique. Once the collecting of data is complete analysis, coding and presentation of the report naturally follow.

Forms of Research Design

1. The classical design: The classical design of proof can be diagrammatised as following.

	Before	After	Comparison before U.S.
Experimental Group	X	X^1	After
Control Group	X_1	X	Difference X_1-X
			Difference X_1-X^1

Concerning the impact of a film on soldier attitudes, Stouffer aptly remarks "one of the troubles with using this careful design was that the effectiveness of a single film when thus measured turned out to be slight. Much more "satisfactory", results were obtained when only the after groups were selected. Thus the soldiers who remembered the film were the ones most affected by it."

2. Successional Experimental design : Frequently, social researches use only the experimental group.

Experimental Group	X	X_1	Difference X_1-X

In this case the technique would be to have a preliminary observational period to measure 'control' of usual behaviour and there upon introduce the stimulus.

It may be called a successional experiment. For example, the series of relay assembly experiments in the Hawthorne study. The first period was one of intensive observations of the relations of production and behavioural norms. The variables were gardually introduced at intervals. The weakness of this design is that we have no control group for comparison.

3. Before and after measurement : The before and after comparison is adequate for a simple measurement of changes such as panel study.

X	X_1	Difference X_1 - X

In panel study the after group is an entirely different sample. There are many implied limitations of this design since the sample are entirely different. Stouffer and other used this model for the study of army personnel. Since they could not get the same people over an interval of time, they collected matched samples of men.

4. Comparison of two after groups : A very common pattern in social research is to compare two "after" groups in this fashion.

Experimental Group	X	X^1
Control Group	X_1	X^{11}

In this case one tries to assume the before phase. However, one uses statistical techniques to naturalise the variables. This design is frequently used when we are faced with a situation which is already existing and an after situation for two or more groups which differ at least in the important experimental variable.

For example, there are school districts cutting through a slum area. However here one cannot test the effect of the experimental variable upon the situation.

5. Single all design : Perhaps an equally common design is the "single all."

Experimental Group | X |

This is actually a report on what exists at the time of the study for example, the young are more literate than old.

What is sociometry?

About 15 years after the appearance of the earliest Bogardus scales, S.L. Moreno and H.H. Jennings applied a measure of social distance which was radically different from the Bogardus approach. The main divergence of this usually called sociometric method, from the earlier techniques lay in the fact that it was concerned with attractions and repulsions between individuals within a small group and with the group structure as defined in these terms. Jennings described sociometry thus: "Stated briefly, sociomatry may be described as a means of presenting simply anad graphically the entire structure of relations existing at a given time among members of a given group. The major lines of communication, or the pattern of attraction and rejection in its full scope, are made readily comprehensive at a glance."

Main Aresa of Application

Sociometric technique has been applied in such widely diversified situations as informal groups, school classes, prisons and other organisation and industry. In the words of Jennings, "The form of the sociometric test as applied up to the present has had 3 characteristics:

1. A specific number of choices is allowed varying according to the size of the groups tested.

2. A specific criterion for choices is used, varying with the functional activity of the group.

3. Different levels of preference are designated for each choice.

Moreno's Sociometric Test

The "Sociometric test" was applied by Moreno to a public school. It involved study of the children's choices of others from the group. These choices were allowed to each child, and the *situation* was difined as one in which the criterion for selecting other children in the class was "liking to work with them on a study committee." *The levels of choice* were designated by asking the children to designate the number 1 to the child they would most like, their second choice with 2, and the 3rd choice with 3.

The important point to note here is the fact of designating the choice situation in such a way as to be meaningful in this case, by asking the children to name others with whom they would like to associate in committee work. Obviously there is an infinite number of ways in which situation can be structured. The important thing there is 1. that the situation must be a real one to the group being tasted and also, 2 that it must fit the sort of sociometric structure being studied.

To return to the research study of the school children, the next step was the tabulation of data. A very useful form for this is the nXn cross tabulation of individual attitudes known otherwise as the "sociometric matrix."

Another method of analysis, however, used the scalogram whose function is to make clear the network of acceptance and rejections in a graphic way.

These and other variants of sociometric techniques offer rather simple methods of ranking individuals on a continuum of "acceptability" or "outgoingness" on the part of the group members. Where their use is justified they may be powerful research tools, since they meet the general problems of scaling very well. It is also used in the statistical techniques of indexes and scoring devices.

Classical Experimental Design

The classical experimental design or the 'method of differences' as Mill calls it can formulated in a simple manner. If there are two or more cases, and in one of them observation Z can be made while in the other it cannot, and if factor C occurs when observation Z is made and does not occur when observation Z is not made, then it can be asserted that there is a causal relationship between C and Z . Such relations are studied by way of constructing an exprimental design, defining controlled groups or series and "experimental series or groups."

Problems of Classical Experimental Design

There are following important problems inherent in the above design :

1. **Recognition and Control of Variables**: The first problem is recognising and controlling the variables which are of importance in the research. "Control" may mean actual manipulation i.e., changing the values of the variables. Usually, however, manipulation is confined to the experimental variable. 'Control', then means that the values of the variables are know, or that their efforts are deliberately minimised by equating them in the experimental and control series which can be achieved by various statistical techniques, such as factor analysis, partial correlation or analysis of convenience. For usually, the two groups are equated by (a) Precision matching, (b) Matching by frequency distributions or (c) Randomisation.

(a) *Precision Matching*: In precision matching, for any individual in the control series there will be one in the experimental series, with exactly (or almost) the same features. Thus to ascertain whether changing the living pattern in a home for elderly people from a central building with all facilities in it to a cottage system, would increase the integration of the group, we might wish to control such factors as these when comparing the two series of homes, age and sex structure, number of visits from relatives, economic independence of individuals, health, etc., in one series we would find a comparable in the other. Actually, this is difficult.

(b) ***Matching by frequency distributions:*** Consequently, one solution is to "match frequencies" instead. Thus, in the case used for illustration (which is complicated by the fact that we have to match homes with homes, and individuals with individuals), if the experimentral group averages 70 years of age, we would try to design out control group so that its average age would be about the same. Frequency matching is thus less precise but easier than previous matching. All that we seek is to have equal representation of the relevant factors.

(c) ***Randomisation:*** An apparently less precise but more trustworthy technique or in combination with the frequency matching pattern. Since in modern research we frequency have large population, and since the precision and frequency matching pattern have the weakness that there may be important factors other than those we have chosen to control, randomisation is the best alternative. This means simply choosing which individual shall be the experimental and which shall be in the controlled group. We can thus arrive at the conclusion that half of those possessing a important characteristic will fall into each group, even though we way discover only later that a certain variable is significant.

2. Confused causal relationship : The second problem in classical experimental design is that the causal relationship may not be clear:

A	B	C	Produce	Z
A	B	C	Produce	Z on Z
		C	Produce	Z

In the above illustration it was stated that C was the cause of Z. The direction of this relationship is not made clear by the experimental design. In fact the possibility of the following relationships should be considered :

1. C is the cause of Z.
2. Z is the cause of C.
3. C and Z are both caused by another and unknown variable.
4. A or B may also be a cause of Z, but this is obscured by other unknown factors.
5. C may cause Z but only in the presence of other and unknown factors.
6. C does not cause Z because this is simply in accidental or fortuitous occurrence.

It is not a wonder, therefore, that many scientists prefer to aviod the term"cause" altogether and say simply that one event leads to another. The fact that the concept of causation always involves time brings up any other problem in the logic of proof.

3. Confusion of results due to time : The 3rd major problem is that the element of time may confuse experimental results in social science. Any social variable requires time to affect social behaviour. In those cases where the time span is long, cases may be lost through moving. Even if they are not lost, they may have on experimental stimulus. If, on the other hand, they are tested immediately after the stimulus, it may not have had enough time to effect any significant changes. The sociologist cannot develop pleasing mathematical equations until his methods achieve the elegance of the other sciences. However, he can take the problem of time into account in three ways: (a) By 1st learning how powerful and continuing stimuli affect social behaviour over longer periods, instead of attempting to trace very intermittent or minor stimuli. (b) By studying the inter-relationships of both minor and major stimuli within manageable time limits. (c) by attempting to locate and measure subsystems such as decision making adjustment to crisis, etc., of related variables, at definite moments of time.

4. Proof of simplest form: The 4th major problem is the proof that the classical design is stated in simplest form. For the purposes of simplification, the classical design is presented in an all or nothing form. It states, that "given event C, event Z follows." It is thus in a qualitative form. The event Z however, may be a quantity. Thus the sociologist uses probability theory, however, statistical techniques allow the possibility of determining whether event Z expressed as a quantity is likely to be a consequence of event C. It is possible to compute the increase in the proportion disliking "Wops" as neighbours, over the proportion disliking Italians as neighbours, in which it would be required to prove that the difference in the labels Wops and Italians, actually had an effect.

Research design and its problems :-

The classical experimental design of J.S. Mill is development from both the positive and negative canons. It attempts to avoid their weakness. In a simplified form Mill called in the "Method of difference." For example, it may be stated that there are two or more cases and in one of them the observation Z can be made while in the other it cannot and if factor C occurs when observation Z is made and does not occur when observation Z is not made then it can be asserted that there is a causal relationship between C and Z.

To develop the classical research design of proof one needs two series of observations, one set is the control series where the cause is not present and another set is the experimental series where the causative factor is present. For example, if it is assumed that a boy gets unsatisfactory grades in courses where he had not done his homework and gets satisfactory grades in some courses where he has done his homework, then the matter of the boy's doing his homework is the causative factor and is present in the experimental series. Formulating experimentally it can be stated :

Situation X

A	B	C	Produces	2

Situation Y

A	B	Non C	Produce	Non 2

∴ | C | Produce s | 2 |

Thus in a research study on treatment of malaria two series of groups of persons are watched in all other health factors while one group is administered with atabrine. The control series is left on its own. If Malaria gets cured in the experimental group then atabrine is thought up as a cure for Malaria.

✶✶✶✶✶✶

Chapter – 5

Scientific Methods of Research

The uniques and most distinctive feature of the scientific method is its ability and capacity to obtain definite, general and verifiable knowledge, discover causal relationships between diverse and scattered facts and to predict future. According to Encyclopedia Brittanica, "Scientific method is a collective term denoting the various processes by the aid of which the sciences are built up. In a wide sense any method of investigation by which scientific or any other impartial systematic knowledge is acquired, is called a method." This definition underscores the unique quality of scientific methods which is acquisition of systematic and impartial knowledge. The science, by hypothesis, confines to the study of definite and limited subject matter; and the study of limited subject matter must naturally be systematic. All constituent elements of scientific method, namely, observation, experimentation, classification and explanation also exhibit their systematic nature. It is this feature which of marks the specific method of all other human devices and methods.

According to Lundberg, "Scientific method consists of systematic observation, classification and interpretation of data. The main difference between our day to day generalizations and conclusions usually recognized as scientific method lies in the degree of formality, rigorousness, verifiability and general validity of the latter." This definition rightly stresses the fact that compared with common sense thinking, the scientific thinking is more formal, strict, empirical and goal-directed. Therefore, it yields conclusions which have far greater reliability than the counsels of common sense. The scientific method observes, classifies and interprets data according to rigorous test of verifiability. The belief in causal relationship existing in natural and social phenomena is the backbone of the scientific method. Accordingly the primary task of scientific method is the discovery of causal relations in the diverse facts under it and to generalise about these. If is to the credit of the scientific method that it can predict about future.

Important froms of Scientific Method

There are many popular scientific methods if we consider their main forms as well as sub-forms : but substantially speaking, there are only six primary forms of scientific methods and all merely variations of same forms. The primary forms are the following :

1. **Induction**: The movement of knowledge from particular facts to a general rule of principle is known as induction. An example of induction is; a, b, c, d... are things and they occupy space; therefore, all things are extended.

2. **Deduction**: A movement in knowledge from a general rule to a particular case is called deduction. The classic example of deduction is; Man is mortal and Ram is a man; therefore, Ram is mortal.

3. **Historical**: Historical method is a backward movement in knowledge to trace the antecedent cause or causes of a phenomenon. Darwin's theory of evolution and Karl Marx's law of economic determinism are examples of this method.

4. **Comparative**: Analysis and comparison of two contemporary phenomena is known as comparative method. For example, studies of two or more constitutions, governments or political systems. The comparison is always undertaken in order to discover new facts or relations.

5. **Structural**: A research study of what a thing is, what are its outlines and significant features is a structural study. Anatomy is a structural study.

6. **Functional**: In contrast to the structural method, functional method studies the process and their causes, that is, 'how' and 'why' of a thing. Physiology is a functional study.

The above mentioned research methods are used nearly in all types of sceinces. Induction and deduction are, of course, the two foundation pillars of every science. All generalisation and framing of rules is made possible through induction and by means of deduction the rules are made to apply in particular cases. Not only in limited spheres. The limited sphere of philosophy, wherein the use of induction and deduction is made is known as Logic. Logic, too, is counted as science, because logic in the words of eminent philosopher John Dewey, is coextensive with scientific methods; the two are synonymous. The historical method has proved fruitful not only in social sciences but also in physical sciences. The comparative method is used in zoology, botany, chemistry, etc. in the sphere of physical sciences and in sociology, anthropology, psychology etc. in the share of social sciences. The structural and functional methods are, as a matter of fact, complementary to each other and are used in almost every science. Thus we learn about one more important feature of scientific method, namely its use is common to all sciences. It aims at the study of facts, verification of hypothesis, classification and analysis of facts in order to draw general conclusions thereform. The sciences method involves not only the discovery of new facts but also tests the practical validity of ideas and theories. For the test of a theory, the facts relative to it are collected and examined to see if they really are what theory assumes and that what is caused according to theory is caused in fact as well. If the facts confirm our theory, it is accepted as true and it attains the status of a scientific rule or law, and if facts refute the theory, the theory has either to be suitably modified or rejected altogether, depending upon the nature and kind of refutation.

What is Technique

In the words of W.J. Goode and P.K. Hatt, "Techiniques are thought of as comprising the specific procedure by which the sociologist gathers and orders his data." If we substitute the term science in place of sociology, the definition will be applicable to science. The techniques are those special procedures by which a scientist collects and orders data in the field of this specialization. It is obvious that in different specialized branches of science the problems have certain peculiarities which demand certain variant procedures which will fit in those peculiarities and unique feature. Therefore, every specialized branch of science uses certain important techniques which, though not fundamentally different, very considerably from one specialization to other. For example, introspection is techniques peculiar to psychology, whereas survey is a technique used in the social science of sociology. The method of experiment is common to all sciences, but whereas its use is maximum in physics and chemistry, its use in sociology is marginal only. The method of observation is the main stay of all scientific methods and this is used both in social and physical sciences. Besides these methods, certain important techniques are used in social research which are peculiar to it and have special importance for it. These techniques are the dynamic study of historical material, the case study techniques, mailed questionnaire and schedule and techniques of interview. As the study in a particular field progresses, the techniques used in it also undergo refinement and new, more sophisticated techniques are developed.

Methods and Techniques

There are following main distinctions between methods and techniques.

1. **Essential difference**: Both methods and techniques are made use of in the various sciences; and because of certain affinities the essential difference between them is over looked and the terms method and technique are used interchangeable. But strictly speaking, this is not permissible. The indiscriminate use for the terms method and technique for observation, experiment, survey etc., can be highly confusing. The two terms are different

and must be applied carefully. The difference becomes crystal-clear if we compare their respective definitions. A scientific method is a systematic study of a limited and definite subject matter; on the other hand, by techniques we mean the actual procedure of collecting and ordering the data. For example, in social research, the method of data collection is the same as in physics or any other science, namely, induction; but the techniques may be Questionnaire, Schedule or interview.

2. A method is common to all sciences, but technique is not: A scientific method is common to every science. It has five phases; observation, noting, classifition, generalization and verification. In every science the same order is following. First we observe, then make notes and then divide up the data into various classes. Thereafter we venture to draw a conclusion, which eventually, is tested or verified. But the techniques are not common to all sciences. For example, in archeology, we use the technique of carbon analysis for the determination of data of any thing; but in social research we have no use for this particular technique. Again, in no science except social research, the use of mailed questionnaire is made. It can obviously, have no value for physics or chemistry; and by the same token, the techniques or microanalysis and telescopic observation have no place in social research. Therefore, whereas a method is common, technique is uncommon to various sciences.

3. Methods are definite, technique are indefinite: Every research method has a fixed outlay and follows scheduled steps. As we observed just now, every method passes through five definite phases in a fixed order. It is never the case that classification can be made before collection of data or verification can be made prior to generalization. On the other hand, the techniques keep changing. For example in modern social research, taking down of notes has been replaced by the use of tape-recorder and naked eye observation is giving way to photo and movie camera.

4. Method is underived but techniques are derivate: As we just saw the observation is the phase number one of scientific method. Now the various research techniques of observation follow from the fact that observation is part of the scientific method. We may observe through naked eye, or with the help of microscope. Therefore we can say that the method is indepednent of techniques; but the techniques are dependent upon the method.

5. The difference of Aim: The aim of a scientific method is systematic knowledge of a certain subject matter; but the aim of technique merely collection and ordering of facts. The research technique's aim is subservient therefore to that of method. The aim of the method includes within it the aim of the technique but the aim of technique is limited and does not include the wider aim of the method.

6. Difference of Kinds. The main scientific method are : 1. Induction, 2. Deduction, 3. Comparison, 4. Historical, 5. Structural, and 6. Functional. The main techniques of social research are: Observation, study of Historical Documents, Questionnaire; Schedule and Interview etc.

Scientific method gives the framework and defines the field of social research. Scientific procedures provide the outlines for planning social research. Scientific techniques of observation and interviews provide the required social data. Sampling reduces the field of social study and increases its quality. Statistical techniques increase the precision of study.

Scientific techniques can be successfully used in small scale studies and social surveys. By studying and analysing scientifically we can provide probable explanations of a greater degree of precision about social phenomena. Scientific technique is being successfully used in criminology, prison reforms, child behavior, social pathology, counseling etc. Scientific social research supplies us with many clues in understanding the otherwise incomprehensible social phenomena. However, the use of scientific techniques, and their successful application depends upto the objectivity of the research and the repeated occurrence of the phenomena. Scientific method can only succeed in fields where one may categories his data as regards listed characteristics such as students and their study habits. The use of scientific method implies some basic knowledge about the subject of study even among respondents and their free cooperation.

Empirical Method

The power of science lines in the fact that its results can proved by experiment. The proofs of science are collected through human sense organs. What we see, hear, know by tough, smell or taste, whatsoever we know through our sense organs is true. Ninety per cent proofs proved by experiments are based on sight, or observations. Anything that the individual sees and describes can be seen and tested by another individual. The explanation of a phenomenon must be valid after verification. One must not believe something simply because it is stated and heard. Hence empirical observation is the basis of scientific method.

In empirical research studies ideas are subject to real test and such experiments are made available by which he ideas can be re-examined. It also creates new methods of testing ideas more reliable. Empirical methods of research emphasize the necessity of keeping the study free from the research worker's personal ideas and values. Efforts are made to know how a particular phenomenon occurred. What the phenomenon should be has no place in the empirical study. The facts or data collected through empirical method must be so true that anybody may verify their truty by using the same or other means.

Strength of Empirical Study

Data obtained through empirical methods have firmness or certainly about them. These are quite clear. The proofs of empirical method have a kind of firmness about them and offer the same meaning of different readers. The conclusions reached through empirical method are also certain and firm like its proofs. Anybody can verify the conclusions drawn by some-body else. Similarly its faults may also be pointed out. In empirical method the research worker sees his subject-matter exactly as it is. There is no place for saubjectivity in this method. The entire study is objective and it is based on objective facts.

Even a small amount of subjectivity may affect the conclusions. A research worker may always discover the faults of the earlier research workers.

Stages of Empirical Method

First of all, the research worker selects a subject for his research study. Then, he examines the studies conducted carrier in the same field. He tries to evaluate the methods used in the earlier studies. Now, after selecting the subject and examining the related studies a working hypothesis is framed. This hypothesis may be verified and its truth may be established. Now, the goals and scope of the study are also determined. The research worker clearly knows what facts to examine and collect. Through these facts he may get information about the truth of the hypothesis. Suitable means are used according to the situation to collect the facts. Facts may be obtained from historical sources as well regional sources. Facts are then classified so that they may be interpreted and their mutual relationships established.

Effort to determine the truth of the hypothesis is made by classifying the facts and understanding their relationships. Now, conclusions can be drawn from the detailed description of the subject of the study. These conclusions may be compared with the conclusions of previous studies.

Historical Method

In modern times, a number of researchers have made extensive historical studies of various institutions. An eminent example of this type of study is Westernmark's *History of Marriage,* in which the gradual evolution of the institution of marriage has been studied historically. The method of historical study in social sciences has had great impetus from Darwin's studies of biological evolution. Another instance of social study being done on exclusively historical basis is Oppenheimer's *The State* in which it has been shown how the institution of state has developed in the course of human history. Many famous and influential social scientists have popularized the historical method by using in it their studies of social, political and cultural development; Karl Marx, Max Weber, C. Wright Mills, Raymond Aron, to mention only few of the stalwards of historical method.

What is historical method? The research scientific who have used this method seem clearly to have been influenced by Hegal's philosophy of history and Drawn's theory of biological evolution. The historical method is primarily concerned with the origin and development of social institutions and cultural forms and the progress of their evolution is charted. The historical method studies a particular institution in the background of entire human history. August Comte, Herbert Spencer and Hobhouse studied the main social institutions in the light of and in connection with other institutions; the entire history formed a back-ground in their studies.

Some research have vehemently opposed the extension of Herbert Spencer's methods. According to them the various treatises claming to trace the origin and development of various social institutions were in fact no more than blind historical descriptions. As the theory of evolution was fashionable in the 18th and 19th centuries, every social scientist wished to base his studies on evolutionary basis and follow the pattern of simple to complex form, as is the case with Darwin's theory of evolution. But this extension of biological methodology to social science is considered illegitimate by many modern sociologists. To follow the biological method of simple forms to complex forms blindly in research science tantamounts to fill in material in dyes already cast. This makes the research study superficial and artificial. Still we cannot condemn the contribution of evolutionary method in social science.

Bases of Historical Method

Historical method is based upon historical facts. Historical facts are collected from various sources. The first sources include those documents, relics and historical materials that are kept in archives and museums. Historians reach their conclusions by study of this material. Data about cultural history are provided bystone inscriptions, coins and articles obtained from excavations. Reliable observes provide reliable information about phenomena. Ancient books and relics have contributed towards understanding ancient society. Travelogues have proved helpful in understanding society.

Strength of Historical Method

One can know with the help of historical method the circumstances in which a particular phenomenon or institution was possible. What was the nature of change is economy? What were the reasons that caused them? How did the altered phenomenon change further? What were the reasons behind these changes? Thus, one comes to know systematically about the altered conditions of an institution through a long period of time. It also shows how a particular institution attained its present form.

A scientific evaluation of the past may be given through this method. It helps in studying the rites and rituals, practices, ideals and values of traditional society. While attempting such evaluation, it is necessary to keep in mind the historical background. It is essential to adopt an objective point of view otherwise them scholar may reach subjective conclusions. It is improper to evaluate an ancient society on the basis of modern values since values are created in the real conditions of a society.

Historical method is helpful in the understanding of not only the past but also the present. It unravels the social values and relationships over which the present social values and relationships are mounded. One also comes to know the changes and the organisations which give society its present form. Society's past is responsible for its present. The historical method acquaints us with the social forces of the past responsible for the changes. Sociologists have special interest in change. Change in social conditions and social institution leads to change in various social units and social organisations. Historical method proves very helpful in studying these changing forms.

Limitations of Historical Method

However, historical method has its own limitations. In the historical method it is necessary to obtain reliable facts. But collecting reliable facts is a difficult task particularly where ancient books are concerned. Every country has an institution which hunts archaeological relics on the national level. It is necessary to arrange these ancient books and facts in order. Computers give scientific help in collecting and arranging data. Such material is available in large quantity in National Archives. The research worker however, has to hunt other museums too.

Again, historical facts and phenomena cannot be subjected to experiment. These phenomena cannot be repeated in the same circumstances. Hence statistics is not of much use in this method. It is not possible to measure these phenomena.

Max Weber is the modern researcher to make extensive use of historical method. Though critical of many Marxian principles, Weber folow the historical method in his study. He has appreciated Marx's emphasis on economic factor in history. As a matter of fact, modern sociologists are not in favour of wholesale application of historical method and the study of institutions in the background of entire human history. They are however, not opposed to the study of particular institutions in their evolutionary aspect. Max Weber has studied capitalism, modern government and religions in the light of economic determinism, that is he has tried to see the role of economic factors on these. For these studies of popular institutions, it is essential to study them in connection with other institutions. The historical method has proved useful in the research study of particular human institutions.

Comparative Method

The most eminent example of the application of comparative method in research is to be found in Durkhim's *The Rules of Sociological Methods.* According to Durkhim various social institutions are interconnected and interacting. Some are causes and some are effects. To determine which is cause and which is effect a comparative study of various institutions has to be made. In physical sciences the method of controlled observation in used to study two things comparatively; but in social sciences such control is not feasible. Durkheim thinks that the use of comparative method in sociology is inevitable. He has called it indirect that it is not easy to pin-point facts which can be definitely said to be "cause" and facts which can be determined to be "effect", still by the use of comparative method we can succeed at least in determining thew antecedents and consequents of a phenomenon.

The comparative method has been successfully and fruitfully used in various fields of research. Hobhouse, Wheeler and Morris Ginsberg have studies the primary social institutions of primitive societies by comparative method. The various societies were classified according to their differential economic patterns and then it was studied as to what difference does the religious, patterns. In recent years, The International Society for Social Research has studies the correlation of social status and social mobility in the industrialized society of America, by means of comparative method. Another example of successful use of comparative method is S.M. Lipset's *Social Mobility in Industrial Society* and *Political Man*.

While the comparative method has been used to study different societies, it has also been used to study social changes within a particular society. The example of the former is the well-known study *Suicide* by Emaile Durkheim. He has analysed various social groups to find out the relative incidence of suicide in them and their causes. The studies of later type are into relief significant facts. Sociologists have studied by this method the correlation between divorce and juvenile delinquency in a given society, the correlation between the size of family and social mobility and the relation between social and educational levels.

In the 19th century the comparative method was used to study various civilized societies; but latter on the use of this method was extended to the study of social events in a particular society. These days again the trend is towards the study of different societies by comparative methods.

The comparative method has also been subjected to severe criticism by many researcher. According to Radcliffe Brown, "The comparative method alone gives you nothing. Nothing will grow out of the ground unless you put seeds into it. The comparative method is one way of testing hypotheses." This criticism of comparative method brings into relief an important fact, often ignored by zealots, that the comparative method can fructify only if we have a prior hypothesis in mind. Another limitation of this method is that it is not quite possible to study whole societies comparatively; and the various institutions in different societies may be common only in name, their contents may radically very. For example, Indian Education System and that of American Education are so diverse that a comparative study of the two makes little sense and same is the case between Indian capitalism and American capitalism; the two are very much different. The comparative method can be used in the study of social institutions in a particular sociaty. Its use in limited sphere is highly productive and useful. This method can be used to study social groups having same socio-economic levels and it can also be used to study social events of a given time in a given society.

To conclude : comparative method has undergone change in the course of sociological history. Whereas in the beginning its use made for studying different societies, now it is more used to study institutions and social phenomena in a limited sphere in a particular society.

Limitations of Comparative Method

Speculations are necessary in order to use comparative method. No comparison can be successful without speculations. If these speculations are not direct and clear, the comparison of phenomena cannot be adequate. It is necessary to know what are the units on which the speculations of comparative research study.

One more problem involved in the comparative method is that one has to compare the whole society. While it is very difficult to compare two societies in their totality, it is easier to compare social institutions than societies as a whole. Hence this method is useful in comparing small institutions of another society. Hence, it is possible that apparently similar institutions may not be so in reality. Again, it is also necessary to study social institutions in their social context otherwise the comparison, which belong to similar societies. The comparison must have more or less similar environments, economics, political systems and religions. By using comparative method, Wheeler and Ginsberg made a systematic study of the social institutions of primitive societies. They studied the economic systems of these societies. They discovered the relations among the political systems, social stratification, and various economic systems of the societies. Comparative studies have also been systematically made about social stratification and social mobility in industrial societies. Major among these are the studies by Lipset and Bendix. Sociologists like Durkheim, Lipset, Freeman and Moore have all praise for this method but Malinowski has criticised it.

Difference between Deductive method and Inductive method

Two method are used generally in studying the social phenomenon: induction and deduction. Induction is the method by which we observe, watch and assess a phenomenon for relevant facts. We separate these from other and collect and classify them in order to discover causal connections which enable us in drawing a conclusion. A conclusion is a generalization from multiplicity of facts. Whether the conclusions are valid or invalid can be determined only by applying the conclusion to particular cases. The process of applying a generalization to specific case and thus verifying it is a deductive progress. Therefore, induction and deduction are both used to study the social phenomena. These will now be dealt briefly.

1. Induction Method

Induction is a movement in knowledge from particular to the general. According to Joyce, "Induction is the legitimate derivation of universal laws from individual cases." For the purpose, we have to observe the relation of agreement between a multiplicity of facts, because similar facts must be expressions of the same law, therefore, a single principle or rule can account for them. If we find that various objects in a group have a common circumstance we form a hypothesis about it on this basis of agreement. For example, if a doctor finds that all cancer patients he has come across are heavy smokers, he easily concludes that smoking is the cause of cancer. The other method of induction is disagreement. If a conclusion is supported by the methods of agreement as well as disagreement, its validity becomes almost certain. For example, in a party two types of food are served: vegetarian and non-vegetarian. Now if some guests are taken ill on eating the food while some others are quite well, the obvious question will be, did the sick and nonstick eat different foods. Now if sick ate meat and non-sick did not eat meat then both agreement and disagreement confirm that meat must be the cause of illness. The third method used in induction is called concomitant variation. For example, if we find that with the rise in the prices of wheat, the incidence of crime shows upward trend, and with the falling of the prices, it shows downward trent, then the price rise is the cause of crime. This we learn by the fact that variation of prices have corresponding, proportionate effect on the incidence of crime. In social studies we observe that the children coming from broken home tend to be delinquent. Now if by further research we can establish that children of happy homes are not delinquent, we shall succeed in establishing the family disturbances as the cause of delinquency.

Another illustration of the use of inductive method in modern research is the following. The cases of violence exhibit psychology of frustration. The induction method will work in the following manner :

A, B, C, D, are cases of violence.

A, B, C, D, are cases of frustration.

∴ The cases above conclusion to be valid, it is necessary, that A, B, C, D should be both representative and sufficient. That is, the above cases must represent all individuals of a group and the number of examples must be enough to warrant derivation for conclusions. To give a concrete example, the cases of violence must not be of sexual violence only, they should include other violent acts also.

If we look to the fabric of social science we would discover that most to the sociological theories and principles have been derived through the means of induction. But one thing which must be remembered in this connection is that the theories based on induction cannot, in the nature of things, be certain. They are probable only. For example, if we find that prostitutes carry on their profession not for the sake of repeated and concentrated sexual pleasure but in order to fill up their bellies, we may conclude that prostitution is due to economic factors alone. But our conclusion cannot be certain because it is not possible to examine and interview each and every prostitute and, therefore, it is quite possible that we may have missed in our study those prostitutes who are votaries of bodily pleasure and who enjoy the dominant position which their good looks and sexual finesse endows upon them. Therefore, we must emphasize that the conclusions reached through induction are probable only.

2. Deductive Method: In complete contrast to inductive method is the method of deduction, in which we proceed from general rules to particular cases. For example, if we have a hypothesis that drinking leads to accidents, our hypothesis can be deductively verified if we find that all major accidents occurred in a particular town were due to drinking.

Induction and deduction are two full-fledged scientific methods. In both the use of hypothesis, generalization, inference, comparison and classification is made. The techniques are concerned with collection and ordering of facts and methods and aim at systermatic knowledge of facts.

The value of hypothesis both in induction and deduction can not be overestimated. Induction's first phase is observation; but as a matter of fact, there can be no scientific observation unless we know what to observe and what not to observe. A doctor examining a patient suffering from fever, sees his pulse rate, eyes, nose, throat, chest and heart etc., because fever can be due to influenza, typhoid, malaria etc. He does not as a rule examine the genital organs. In venereal diseases, on the other hand, the doctor examines skin because venereal disease expresses itself on skin and not in fever form. Thus we see that the doctor examines a patient with a tentative idea or hypothesis about the condition of the patient. Similarly a researcher observing juvenile delinquency does not go to a prison house, because he knows that juvenile criminals are not kept in ordinary jails. Thus we see how important it is to have a hypothesis even at the beginning of a study. Sometimes it is not possible to examine particular instances because they are rare. Here wwe have to form a probable theory about them and check its validity when these facts occur. For example, many social scientists were interested in speculating about the future of India after Nehru. Obviously, observation and other inductive means were of no avail. Only a hypothesis could be entertained and this could be checked when the event took place.

Another example is that a book carrying some defamatory remarks about a religious prophet leads to agitation and violence in India. This is a sociological reason why Government of India tries to restrict freedom of expression and proscribe objectionable books.

Most of the research scientists make use of both deduction and induction in their researches.

In sciences when we wish to reach a conclusion on the basis of some facts, we use the inductive method. When we wish to test a certain theory or hypothesis, we use deductive method. The deductive method is also used when we wish to explain a future phenomenon. The relation between induction and deduction is very close. They are complementary methods.

According to Charles Beard, "It would b interesting to find an assumption of promise that is not in some way entangled with experiences and method of inference from particulars.

To conclude, we may observe that though the main business of science is discovery of facts, and therefore, scientific investigation involves induction, on facts can ever be discovered without the use of some hypothesis. Besides, the business of research is not merely colligation of facts, but the perceiving of significant relations and connections in facts. As a matter of fact deduction and induction are not opposed to each other, though descriptions, general to particular and particular to general suggest as if they were mutually exclusive, they are twin processes of reasoning and each complements the other.

Structural Method

The structural method aims at the analysis of the form, shape and other statistical features of a phenomenon. As the name clearly suggests, it studies relatively static and stable aspect rather than the dyamic aspect of a thing. The use of structural method is made in social science to analyse the shape of a society or group and the fixed features in it, the structural analysis always precedes the functional. Before knowing the function of anything we should know that it is. For example before studying the function of a state, we analyse its structure and say that every state has land, population, government and sovereignty. These elements are to be found in every state. But the functions of a state may vary considerably. A welfare state has more functions than other states. The structural method provides the basis of the definition of society, group, community etc. According to some the important element is group. According to Simmer, sociology should concern itself not with the actual behaviour of individuals but with the processes of socialization, human interaction and other social processes like competition, domination, submission, limitation and division of labour. The structural method can discuss the relative significance of various elements in society : but its discussion naturally runs into functional aspect of society though as a matter of fact the structure and function are two sides of the same coin.

Functional Method

The functional study of society is based on the biological assumption that society is an organism like human body. As the various limbs do their respective work in a human body, the various constitutions of society play their respective roles in society. Herbert Spencer made us of this method in his *Principles of Sociology;* but its most perfect use was made by Emile Durkheim in his *Division of labour in society* and the *rules of sociological methods.* According to Dhurkhein the needs of a social being in relation to social institutions are the functions of social institutions. He has distinguished between the normal and pathological functions of a society.

The functional method in sociology was a reaction from the historic-evolutionary method prevalent in sociology in the 19th century. The functional researcher criticized the use of both historical and comparative method. Accordingly, the theory of evolution may hold good for animal life: but it can certainly not be extended to the entire warp and woof of human society. However, the very assumption to functional method has come under bad weather. There are so many points of crucial differences between the human organism and the social organism that the two cannot be said to be one. For example, the various limbs of human body do not have the self-consciousness, but the constituents of society namely, human beings are all self-conscious. What is more, society as a whole cannot be said to possess self-consciousness which a human being has. Furthermore, human organism in centrally governed, whereas, society does not control human beings in any such manner. Nevertheless functional method has played creditable role in the study of human society; in particular, the rural society has been fruitfully studied with the help of this method. Malinowski's studies are worth mentioning in this connection though Malinowski has criticized the functional method's assumption that there is functional integration of human functions in a normal society. This method is now not in much vogue in social studies. Its use is confined to a limited sphere and there too lots of precautions are indicated.

Prevailing Postulates in Functional Analysis

Functional anaylsis have adopted three interconnected postulates. These are as follows :

1. **Postulate of the Functional Unity of Society**: Radcliffe Brown characteristically puts this postulate in explicit terms on the concept of function as follows. "The function of a particular social usage is the contribution it makes to the total social life as the functioning of the total social system. Such a view implies that a social system has a certain kind of unity, which we may speak of as a functional unity. We may define it as a condition in which all parts of the social system work together with a sufficient degree of internal consistency, i.e., without producing persistent conflicts which can neither be resolved nor regulated."

But social usages or sentiments may be functional for some groups and dysfunctional for others in the same society. For example, by the functional interpretation of religion deriving from Durkheim's orientation which was based largely upon the study of non-litegrative consequences of religion an neglect its possibly disintegrative consequence in certain types of social structure. Some facts are as given below :

(i) When different religions co-exist in the same society, there is often deep conflict between the several religious groups. In what sense then, does religion make for integration of "the" society in the numerous multireligion societies?

(ii) Human society achieves its unity primarily through the possession by its members of certain ultimate values and ends in common. But what is the evidence indicating that "non-religions" people, say, in our own society less often subscribe to certain common "values and ends" than those devoted to religious doctrines?

(iii) In what sense does religion make for integration of the larger society, if the content of its doctrine and values in at odds with the content of other, non-religious values help by many people in the same society?

Such functional analyses show that religions provide integration of those who believe in same religious values. But it is unlikely that this is meant since it would merely assert that integration is provided by a consensus on any set of values.

In non-literate societies, there is but one prevailing religious system, so apart from individual deviants, the membership of the total society and the membership of the religious community are virtually co-extensive. In this type of social structure a common set of religions values may have as one of its consequences the reinforcement of common sentiments and of social integration. But this generazation cannot be applied to other types of society.

2. Postulate of Universal Functionalism: The items of culture must be recognised to have multiple consequences, some of them functional and others perhaps dysfunctional. This postulate holds that all standardardized social or cultural forms have positive functions. Malinowski advances this in Anthropology in its most extreme form when he says. "The functional view of culture insists therefore upon the principle that in every type of civilization, every custom, material object, idea and belief fulfils some vital function."

The postulate of universal functionalism of the course the historical product of the fierce, barren and protracted controversy over survivals which raged among the anthropologists over the question that a custom cannot be explained by its present utility but only becomes intelligible through its past history. But the evolutionary theory of culture make rethinking on it necessary.

This postulate also faced criticism from a range of non-functional consequences of existing cultural forms. Present cultural forms have a net balance of functional consequences either for the society considered as a unit or for sub-groups sufficiently powerful. This formulation at once avoids the tendency of functional analysis to concentrate on positive functions and directs the attention to other types of consequences as well.

3. Postualte of Indispensablility: This postulate shows that every cultural item satisfies some vital need of society, and cannot be substituted by any other item. Malinowski advances this in Anthropology in this form. "In every type of civilization, every custom, material object, idea and belief fulfils some vital function, has some task to accomplish, represents an indispensable part within a working whole." Again, he points out, "Thus magic fulfills an indispensable function within culture. It satisfies a definite need which cannot be satisfied by any other factor of primitive civilization."

The account of the role religion by Davis and Moore seems at first to maintain that it is the institution which is indispensable. "The reason why religion is necessary....religion plays a unique and indispensable part in society." It is the function of religion but not the institution of religion, which is regarded as indispensable.

The postulate of indispensability contains the following assertions :

(a) It is assumed that there are certain functions which are indispensable in the sense that, unless they are performed, the society will not persist. This then, sets forth a concept of functional prerequisites, or preconditions functionally necessary for a society.

(b) It is assumed that certain cultural and social forms are indispensable for fulfilling each of these functions. This involves a concept of specialized and irreplaceable structure.

In contrast to this concept of indispensability of cultural forms, there is then the concept of functional alternatives or functional equivalents, or functional substitutes. Just as the same items may have multiple functions so may the same functions be diversely fulfilled by alternative items.

So in this postulate the indispensability of functions gives rise to the concept of functional necessity, and the indispensability of institutions gives rise to the concept of functional alternatives.

Premises and Propositions of functionalism

According to Abrahamson, "Functionalism...requires the prior conceptualization of a system before its "exmlanatory imagery" makes any sense." According to Martindate the organic system is the fundamental explanatory model of functionalism. Thus the following are the premises and propositions of functionalism:

1. **Functional analysis involves emphasis on the primary of the system**: In the words of Martindale, "The distinctive property of functional analysis is the utilization of some concept of system as primary for sociological analysis. The first requirement of a comprehensible analysis is the clear definition of the system presumed. Nothing will render a functional analysis ambiguous more quickly or completely then uncertainty as to just what, in the particular case, constitutes these system. Once one has isolated the system, the next task is to identify its components. And once the components have been identified, the relation between these components becomes primary."

2. **Functional Interrelation between the elements**: Functionalism is based upon the premises that the elements of system are functionally interrelated just as the part of an organism are internally interrelated. In the words of Talcott Parsons, "On the one hand, it includes a system of structural categories which must be logically adequate to give a determinate description of an empirically possible, complete empirical system of the relevant class. One of the prime functions of system on this level is to insure completeness, to make it methodologically impossible to overlook anything important, and thus explicitly to describe all essential structural elements and relations of the system. On the other hand, such a system must also include a set of dynamic functional categories. These must articulate directly with the structural categories, they must describe processes by which these particular structures are maintained or upset, the relations of the system to its environment are mediated."

3. **Contribution of every element to the system**: The functionalists believe that every element of a system contributes to it, positively or negatively. While the positive contribution is known as eufunciton the negative function is known as dysfunction.

4. **Integrated configuration of elements**: In the words of Parsons, "functionally specialized or differentiated sectors or living systems stand in some

kind of an order of cybernetically hierarchical control relative to each other. This is quite a fundamental principle of ordering such systems and, as such, is an enormous aid to the solution of a wide variety of theoretical problems."

5. Built-in-mechanisms for self regulation: Functionalists believe that every society has a built in mechanism for self regulation. Parsons has explained this self regulating principle by means of homeostasis. He says, "The maintenance of relative stability, including stability of certain processes of change like the growth of an organism, in the face of substantially greater enviromental variability, means that......there must be "mechament." Self regulation, however, does not mean maintenance of *status quo.* Functionalists believe in the concept of dynamic equilibrium meaning a minimum of integration of a net balance of an aggregate of consequences. In the words of Vanden Berghe, "Although integration is never perfect, adjustive responses to outside changes tend to minimize the final amount of change within the system. The dominant tendency is thus towards stability and inertia, as maintained through builit-in mechanisms of adjustment and social control."

6. Shared goals and values: Pointing out the value of shared goals and values in a social system, Talcottt Parsons wrote, "This integration of a set of common value patterns with the internalized need-disposition structure of the constituent personalisties is the core phenomenon of the dynamices of social systems. Thus the stability of any social system except the most evanescent interaction process is dependent on a degree of such integration may be said to be the fundamental dynamic theorem of sociology. It is the major point of reference for all analysis which may claim to be a dynamic analysis of social process." In the words of van den Berghe, "The most important and basic factor making for social integration is value consensus i.e., underlying the whole social and cultural structure, there are broad aims or principles which most members of a given social system consider desirable and agree on. Not only is the value system (or ethos) the deepest and most important, source of integration, but it is also the stablest element of socio-cultural systems".

7. Dominance of stability and consensus: Thus society is based upon stability and consensus. To quote, Van Den Berghe, "Dysfunctions, tensions and 'deviance' do exist and can persist for a long time, but they tend to resolve themselves or to be 'institutionalized' in the long run. In other words, while equilibrium or integration is researched, it is the limit towards which social system tend.

✶✶✶✶✶✶

Chapter – 6

Case Study and Social Surveys

The case study approach to research in social sociences is a popular method for understanding why an individual acts in a certain way and how he is likely to act in the future or it is an intensive examination of some single unit. The unit for the business researcher is likely to be a business organization, a single unit, a department or even an event taking place in the organization. The case study is a holistic approach to the understanding of events, people and incidents and differs from the survey method which is simpler and more elementary.

The basic assumption that underlies the case study method is that people's attitudes and behaviour patterns emerge from their experiences and how they tackle events. These attempts to tackle events mould their behaviour and act as the 'turning point' in their lives.

The case study method is used in a vast specturm of social sciences. It is also used in business research e.g. to make a selection of persons for appointment or promotions.

Case study : The Methodology.

Although the step involved in the case study method are not so specific that they have to be followed everytime. The general procedure that is followed includes the following steps:

Step 1

Determining the Present stutus :

This would lead to an understanding of where the problem lies and finding out the extent of the problem.

Step 2

Date Collection :

A number of techniques are used to gather information for the case study method. Most commonly used are-depth, interviews, observations spread over a time period, documents such as letters and diaries and recording of significant events etc.

Step 3

Testing suggested Hypotheses :

The research problem identified is constructed into hypothesis and the data collected is organized, summarized and the information is interrelated to test the hypothesis.

Step 4

Stating the Recommendations and suggestions and conclusions.

Step 5

Instituting Remedial Action

The recommendations are put into action and then a follow up is made to see if the corrective programme was successful.

Major Advantages of the Case Study Method :

(1) It can serve as a guide to future research on large sample.

(2) It adds to our knowledge and is of immense use in the areas of behaviour and attitudes, values etc.

(3) It is essential for exploring completely new fields where very little information is available.

(4) It requires an indepth analysis of a single unit, organization, person or event and is an excellent method of studying change management.

(5) Case studies are flexible enough to allow the focus of the study to extend to any dimension of the studied.

Major Disadvantages :

(1) It can only be used to say something about a very similar person, unit, organization or unit. Larger generalizations will not be reliable.

(2) Since it is detailed study, the orientation of the researcher may introduce bias in the form of his own pre-set ideas.

(3) It is difficult to limit the scope of the study and lay down boundaries as to where to stop collecting data !

(4) It depends too much on the recall of others' experiences or knowledge regarding past events.

(5) Often case studies involve problem cases or exceptional cases. As such, some factors may be over-emphasized or under-emphasized and may not apply to the general population.

Social Surveys

The word survey literally means "oversee". It become a widely used technique of research.

It may be defined as a **comparative effort** which used the **scientific method** in the study and treatment of **current problems and conditions** within a certain **geographical** and **time** frame. Its **purpose** is to generate such facts, conclusions and recommendations that will support intelligent coordinated action.

Purpose of Research Survey :

(1) Collect information on a certain problem.

e.g. The growth in the percentage of older people in problem.

(2) Surveys are used to give a detailed description of a phenomenon.

e.g. To describe the culture prevalent in an organization.

(3) To explain the interrelationships between variables.

e.g. A survey may be carried out to find out the relationship between the age of the audience and the genre of the movie, outside a movie theater.

Thus, a survey may be general or specific, it may be utilitarian or may have some academic importance. The fact is that it is one of the most widely used method to carry out research.

Subject Matter of Research Surveys :

Surveys are used for a variety of purposes but their subject matter is related to-

(1) Demographic characteristics-Like age, marital status, type of family-nuclear or joint, educational background etc.

(2) Social and Economic Factors. e.g. occupation, income, family relations etc.

(3) Social Activities-e.g. behavioural data and actions of the respondents.

(4) Opinions and Attitudes-e.g. attitudes towards and social, economic or political events, policies or incidents, the motives and expectations of people etc.

Types of Surveys :

(1) **General or Specific surveys** : when a survey is conducted for collecting general information without any particular object, it is known as a general survey. Specific surveys are carried out to test the validity of some theory or hypothesis.

(2) **Regular and adhoc surveys** : Regular surveys like the population census is carried out every 10th year whereas, Adhoc surveys are a one time survey usually to test a hypothesis or add missing information to a research study.

(3) **Preliminary and Final Surveys** : Preliminary surveys are like pilot studies and preced the actual survey or the final survey.

(4) **Census and sample surveys** : In a census; survey every single unit in the universe is to be studied while a sample survey shall only study a sample chosen for this purpose.

Major Advantages of the Survey :

(1) It is field study so there is direct contact with the respondents.

(2) This method permits greater objectivity.

(3) Survey results often bring to light actual problems that cannot be discovered in the purly theoretical manner.

(4) Surveys record actual experiences of respondents.

(5) Survey method has applicability in all social sciences and the body of knowledge thus grows with its universal appeal.

Major Disadvantages of Survey :

(1) It is an expensive proposition that involves field staff and their training etc.

(2) It is a time-consuming process large and elaborate surveys take monumental effort of the part of the researcher.

(3) The reliability of the data depends upon the honesty and efficiency of the field staff.

(4) A survey must be fairly extensive to give valied results.

(5) Many surveys fall trap to problems of sampling and if the sampling error is too large, the results lose their reliability and validity.

******

Chapter – 7

Hypothesis and its Confirmation

The word hypothesis is a compound of two words 'hypo' and 'thesis' and literarlly hypo means under or below and thesis means a reasoned theory or rational viewpoint. Accordingly, hypothesis would mean a theory which is not fully reasoned. In other words, hypothesis is a theory entertained in order to research study the facts and examine the validity of the theory.

Mill has defined hypothesis as "any supposition which we make (either without actual evidence, or an evidence avowedly insufficient) in order to endeavour to deduce conclusions in accordance with facts which are known to be real under the idea that if the conclusions to which the hypothesis leads are known truths, the hypothesis itself either must be or at least likely to be true." According to Coffey, "A hypothesis is an attempts at explanation: a provisional supposition made in order to explain scientifically some fact or phenomenon." And, according to Cohen and Nagel, "A hypothesis directs out search for the order." It is not essential for a hypothesis to be necessarily true. In fact, hypothesis is not a claim for truth. Hypothesis is a bridge in the process or inquiry or search which begins with some felt difficulty or problem and ends without the resolution of the problem. In the words of Cohen and Nagel, "The function of a hypothesis is to direct our search for solution to the problem. Whether they are, is the task of the inquiry." There truth of hypothesis involves observation, imaginative thinking, anticipation and deductive verification, these will be studied in this chapter.

Steps in Hypothesis

1. **Observation**: Observation is a pre-condition of formulation of hypothesis. Unless we perceive a difficulty or problem and do not feel the inner goading for solving it, we do not reflect. Therefore, observation is the first stage of hypothesis making.

2. Reflection: Having felt a difficulty and needs for a solution we consider the problem by perceiving the relevant facts. For example, we see a sea in high tide and also find clear moon above. Now we anticipate a relation which is based upon an experience, namely whenever there is high tide there is full moon and never otherwise as far as our experience goes. Having established a relation between two facts we now formulate an answer for the why of this relation. This answer is a hypothesis.

3. Deduction: The third and the last step in this process is examination of hypothesis for various deductions possible from it and their mutual compatibilities and correspondence with already known facts. In the words of Chohen and Nagel, "From the analysis we may conclude that the deductive elaboration of a hypothesis must follow its formulation. We can discover the full meaning of a hypothesis, whether it is relevant and whether it offers a satisfactory solution of the research problem, only by discovering what it implies." For example, if we have a hypothesis that madness increases with increasing complexity of civilization, it will follow from this that there are more mad persons in London today than in Delhi today. Now this is in fact not true. Therefore, our hypothesis is defective because certain facts which follow from it are false. Thus deduction is extromely useful in rejecting ill-formed hypothesis.

4. Verification: Actually, verification is post-hypothesis formulation and, therefore, is not a step in its formulation, but as much as our interest in making hypothesis is not purely academic or theoretical, we wish to solve our difficulty; and this difficulty can be solved if we actually test our hypothesis.

Importance of Hypothesis

The success and effectiveness of induction depends crucially upon the elimination of unnecessary and irrelevant facts and picking out of relevant facts. Now, this elimination and selection of facts hinges upon our hypothesis. Although Newton has said "I do not make hypothesis", he fully recognised the importance of hypothesis for scientific discovery. T.H. Huxely makes this significant observation. "Those who refuse to go beyond fact rarely get as far as fact. Almost every great step (in the history of science) has been made possible by the anticipation of Nature, that is, by start with." According to Charles Darwin that means no observation is possible if we do not have some hypothesis in mind. He says, "How odd it is that any one should not see that all observation must be for or against some view, if it is to be of any service."

Origin of Hypothesis

According to Cohen and Negel, "No rules can be stated for hitting upon relevant hypothesis. It follows that the valuable suggestions for solving a problem can be made only by those who are familiar with the kinds of connection which the subject matter under investigation is capable of exhibiting." There is no particular method of forming hypothesis. The choice of hypothesis depends upon the researcher's range of knowledge and his native abilities. James Watt formed an idea of railway engine on seeing boiling kettle. There are, however, certain aids to hypothesis making. These are :

1. Induction by Simple Enumeration: We see that all roses, irrespective of color and size, are sweet-smelling and from this observation we form the hypothesis that rose is a sweet-smelling flower.

2. Method of Agreement: If we find that different objects in a group have a common circumstance we form a hypothesis about it on this basis. For example, if a doctor finds that all cancer patients he has come across are heavy smokers, he will easily conclude that smoking is a cause of cancer. Similarly, if all guests in a marriage party feel giddy and sick after taking food, we shall conclude that food must be poisoned. In the words of Cohen and Nagel, "A hypothesis is believed to be relevant to a research problem if it expresses determinate modes of connection between a set of facts, including the fact inverstigated; it is irrelevant otherwise."

3. Analogy: If we observe some common features among different things then we form a hypothesis on this basis. For example, if we find that some hill people we came across are very simple we shall suppose that other hill people are also simple, because they are inhabitants of hills. This hypothesis about hill people on analogical reasoning.

4. Concomitant variation: Sometimes we form hypothesis about two phenomena by observing certain relationship between them. For example, if we find that medicines in attractive containers sell more than those in simple containers, we may form a hypothesis that all medicines presented in attractive containers will sell more than before.

Formal Conditions of a Good Hypothesis

The following are the major formal conditions of a good research hypothesis:

1. Non-contradictoriness: A research hypothesis must first and foremost be self-consistent and the conclusions derivable from it deductively must not contradict. For example, it will be self-contradictory to believe that all philosophers are university professors. However, a belief which may appear false or ridiculous but against which we have no positive evidence cannot be considered self-contradictory. Copernican belief that earth revolves around the sun and not vice-versa may have appeared ridiculous when it was first suggested. Similarly, the belief that earth is round is apparently false but in fact, true. Therefore, only that belief is self-contradictory against which we have positive evidence. In this also comes the fact that a hypothesis should not contradict any established truth. However, since scientists regard their theories as no more than hypothesis, any hypothesis contradictory to an accepted scientific theory need not be rejected.

2. **Definite and Clear**: A research hypothesis must not be vague. When its meaning is ambiguous its truth cannot be verified .

3. **Verifiable**: How important verifiability is for research hypothesis can be gauged from the following quotation by Carveth Read; "Except the condition of verifiability and definiteness for the sake for verifiability, without which a proposition does not deserve the name of a hypothesis, it seems inadvisable to lay down rules for a legitimate hypothesis." At the same time a hypothesis is developed, it way be impossible to verify it actually due to of practical or technical difficulties. But while a hypothesis is frequently incapable of immediate verification, it must be verifiable, that is, its consequence must be stated in terms of determinate empirical operations. A research hypothesis may not be fully verifiable because universal propositions cannot be demonstrated; but it will be regarded verifiable if we know the evidence which will be disproved if there is a man who defies death and nothing can kill him.

4. **Simplest**: As a rule the simplest is the best research hypothesis. Simplicity, however, does not mean familiarity. It means simplicity of system. It means generality. In the words of Cohen and Negel, "One theory will, therefore be said to be more simple or general than another if the first can, while the second cannot, exhibit the connection it is investigating as special instances of the relations it takes as fundamental."

Kinds of Research Hypothesis

1. **Explanatory or Descriptive Hypothesis**: A research hypothesis may be about the cause of a phenomenon or about the law of which it is a example. A hypothesis about cause is explanatory whereas a hypothesis about law is descriptive.

2. **Tentative Hypothesis**: When a phenomenon cannot be fully understood because of technical difficulties we make tentative hypothesis about it and see how far this is successful in explaining. Sometimes we simultaneously test two or more hypotheses. The famous hypothesis about propagation of light, namely wave theory and corpuscular theory of light both explain the phenomenon of light but none of them is final. These are tentative.

3. **Representative Fictions**: According to Bain, "Some hypotheses consist of assumptions as to the minute structure and operation of bodies. From the nature of the case, these assumptions can never be proved by direct means. Their only merit is their suitability to express the phenomenon. They are "Representative Fictions". Einstein's formula $E = MC_2$ is an instance of representative fiction.

The research hypothesis is based upon imaginative reasoning and it primarily involves thinking without the help of concrete instances. This is why hypothetical reasoning is abstract.

A hypothesis which proves to be correct becomes a theory or law. The law of gravitation was a hypothesis in Newton's mind, but when it proved to be true it became a law.

Confirmation of Research Hypothesis

A research hypothesis may be directly or indirectly confirmable. It is confirmed directly if some observation or experiment can test it. The hypothesis that coffee taken at night makes a man sleepless can be tested by giving coffee at night to a number of people a number of times and observing its effect upon them. Where are cannot confirm a hypothesis directly we may test it indirectly by verifying the consequences derivable from it or we may examine the validity of its opposite consequences. This will be made clear by an example. The law of gravitation is not directly observable, but if it is true, heavy things must fall. An aeroplane does not fall. But an aeroplane uses some special device to stay in air; therefore, the law of gravitation is true. Again, if we want to know what is the effect of moral education upon man, and we have a hypothesis that more education produces induction, we will have to see how a man without moral education acts in comparison with a man with moral education when confronted with a chance of premarital sex adultery, taking job etc.

According to Cohen and Nagal, "A study of what is involved in making observation will enable us to offer the *coup de grace* to the utterly misleading view that knowledge can be advanced by merely collecting facts. The following difficulties or shortcomings observation make it unreliable for confirmation of hypothesis :

1. Observation itself requires research hypothesis for interpretation of sensations and perceptions.

2. The research hypothesis may be erroneous.

3. The hypothesis which directs observation also determines in large measure what factors in the subject matter are noted. Therefore, the observation is unreliable and even worthless unless its conditions are known.

4. Since scientific observations are carried on by the aid of instruments, the nature and limitations of such instruments must be known.

The function of research hypothesis is to search fact, where the term fact "denotes those existing in space or time, together with the relations between them, in virtue of which a proposition is true. The above limitations of observation are equally applicable to experiment though to a lesser degree. As regards the claim of what is known as crucial experiment to verify a hypothesis, Cohen and Nagel have pointed out, "Crucial experiments, we must conclude, are crucial against a hypothesis only if there is relatively stable set of assumptions which we do not wish to abandon. But no guarantee can be given, for reasons we have stated, that some portion of such assumptions will never be surrendered.

******

Chapter – 8

Problems and Areas of Research

Defining the origin of problem, says F. L. Whitney, "The problem comes out of a situation in which there is a recognition that something is the matter, that unsolved difficulties exist." Pointing out the multiplicity of research problems says, R. A. C. Oliver, "The unsolved problems of research are so numerous and so varied that it is necessary to simplify a survey of them by using some rather arbitrary classification." The research problems can be classified under various stages of research such as Infant Education, Primary Education, Secondary Education and University Education. It may include different kinds of education such as General Education, Technical or Vocational Education, Moral Education, Physical Education etc. It may be classified on the basis of various educational aspects, such as Curriculum, Text books and Syllabuses, Organization, Administration, Equipment, Methods of Teaching, Socio-Economic Conditions, Teacher Education and the like. To quote International Bureau of Education, "Let us confine ourselves to setting out, in order or frequency, the subjects which most often give rise to research : language teaching (problems of bilinguism etc.); teaching of mathematics, science, history and geography, the influence of environment on school adaptation, new educational techniques, (programmed learning, television, audio-visual aids); popular education and literacy teaching; School drop-outs, pupils who repeat the same class or fail in school; highly gifted and less gifted children; teaching about nutrition and the improvement of health; comparative education."

Problems of Research

1. **Curriculum** : The question of what to teach at various levels of education, to various types of pupils, needs intensive research. It is only after a decision has been reached as to what is to taught that one can discuss intelligently the plan of the school building, the kind of equipment necessary,

the form of organization, the qualifications of the teacher and the methods to be used.

Curriculum must change with the world of matter as well as ideas, to which children have to be introduced. Teaching material must be, constantly or periodically under review. What subject matter is to be taught-how much and in what form-these are questions which need to be satisfactorily answered. They give rise to innumerable problems of research. Introduction and teaching of foreign languages, various concepts in mathematics, science, social studies, art and craft, are fields in which considerable research has to be undertaken. The question for minimum essentials for the needs of the community and the individuals comes under this field.

2. Text Book's and Syllabi: Allied to the formulation of suitable curricula is question of prescribing the right type of syllabi and text books. The suitability of the existing textbooks and syllabuses need to be verified. There is also a need for investigation into the best types of syllabuses and textbooks. The textbooks and syllabuses need to be changed with changes in the aims and methods of teaching a subject, or in the population of students. For example, the justification for rejecting grammar and translation, and for introducing a structural syllabus in the teaching of English has to be established before the change is adopted on a large scale and textbooks written accordingly. Vocabulary content, printing and illustration of textbooks are also important problems inviting our attention.

3. School Organization: The organization of school presents innumerable problems in education system. It includes issues such as the age of entrance to school, the proper size of a class for the teaching of different subject, the relative efficiency of collective and individual teaching, different aspects of examination, promotion and wastage, co-education, comprehensive or multi-purpose schools.

4. Educational Administration: Problems of educational administration call urgently for consideration. These include problems both in the financial and educational side of administration. The financial problems include the relative contribution of local and national funds to educational expenditure and the costs of administration. The distribution of freedom and responsibility among students, teachers and the Head of institution and the Directorate or Department of Education is a controversial subject which need appropriate research. In these institutions there is the very important problem of promoting good human relations in educational institutions.

5. Child Development: The development of the pupil is the central focus of every educational research. This is created by the practices of the school. Therefore, developmental studies constitute a major area of educational research. The physical, mental, moral and personality development of children offers situations which pose numerous important questions requiring research. Researchers should find out the conditions that lead to or hamper a full and harmonious development of a child's personality and the step by which schools promote favorable conditions. They should find out how can schools develop among children certain desirable traits, interests and attitudes, what provision is to be made for individual differences among children, how should backward children be educated, how best can be rehabilitated the maladjusted or delinquent children. These problems concerning child development demand attention of modern researchers.

6. Skills: Handwriting, reading and spelling, etc. are skills which have to be developed through proper educational means. In the field of handwriting there is much scope for research in speed, legibility, fluency, in standardizing tests and scales, and in diagnostic work. Again, in the field of reading there is scope for research in vocabulary, comprehension, speed, in basic reader and supplementary readers, in interests and habits. In the field of spelling much worthwhile research as well as diagnostic and remedial work has been done.

7. Guidance and Counseling: The value of guidance programmers has been recognized after the study of individual differences as well as the educational and vocational choices required to be made. This needs an equitable distribution of aptitudes, interests and abilities on the one hand and of educational and vocational facilities on the other. Guidance services in schools are necessary for the nation's future citizens. Therefore, there are problems of diagnostic and prognostic research in the field of educational and vocational guidance. Proper guidance to the children needs adequate tools to diagnose their abilities and aptitudes. These may be prepared and their values and limitations tested. Construction of proper attitude scales, personality inventories and intelligence tests is a worth-while field of research in India.

8. Educational Measurement: Teachers and educators are concerned with educational result in the form of acquisition of attitudes, behaviors and skills. It has to be ascertained periodically and in a systematic way, how much a student has gained in these respects during a specific period of time. This needs valid and reliable tools for measuring educational values. Questions such as shortcomings of essay type examination, how can they be removed, alternative types of tests more appropriate for the purpose, the techniques of constructing such tests and how are they to be used, these and other questions require research in the field of educational measurement. Therefore, a critical evaluation should be made of the existing forms of tests, the construction and standardization of more valid and reliable instruments for measuring the educational outcomes of teaching specific subjects and of different educational activities. Examination reform calls for intense research work in the present Indian education system.

9. **Educational Aids and Equipment**: Designing and engineering of equipment for educational institutions is an important field of research and development. Research is needed in the designing of proper buildings, chairs, desks, tables, lockers, toilets and other college furnishings. The new mechanical devices offer sufficient scope for research which may facilitate learning - their construction, utilization and evaluation, the effectiveness of mass-media like the cinema, radio and television and of excursions and other audio-visual aids, should be explained before having to make these popular. Experiments should be conducted about the value of illustrations, charts and diagrams, in teaching a subject.

10. **Methods of Teaching**: The effectiveness of the structural approach to the teaching of a foreign language like English, can be compared, through experiment, with that of the traditional grammar-translation approach. The effectiveness of the discussion method of teaching a topic can be compared to that of the lecture method. According to R. A. C. Oilver, "Methods are legion and most of them could be tested by experimental investigation." In order to improve class room teaching it is necessary to construct experiments on and evaluation and criticism of particular methods of teachings. The comparative and critical evaluation of any two or more methods of teaching the same subject is necessary for improvement in class room teaching.

11. **Teacher Education**: Teacher education is a comparatively productive field of education. It is open to many kinds of research project. For example, research may be conducted into the goals of teacher-education, the ways of teaching those goals in terms of curriculum, syllabus and activities. Research may be done into the methods and sources of educating teachers. Assessment may be made of the relative merits of the one or two year professional training after general education or else of the concurrent general and teacher-education courses. In the West, research has been undertaken in the field of the analysis of the personality pattern of successful teachers and its relation to teacher-education courses. Job analysis and aptitude for teaching are very fruitful topics for research in the field of education.

12. **History of Education**: The value of a study of the history of different aspects of education is necessary for the planning of future education. Every aspect or kind of education may end itself to historical research. One may trace the beginnings and development of Basic Education in our country. One may study historically the development of nursery, primary, secondary, university, or teaching of English in India. In the use of certain audio-visual aids in

teaching, or in other specific areas of academic interest, historical research may be usufully done.

13. Philosophy of Education: Philosophy of education, old and new, past and present, popular and otherwise are subjects of endless controversy and discussion. Theory is at the basis of every aspect of education, every type of education, every method of education. Soundness of the theoretical bases of education, past or present, must be examined so that future plans of education produce sound results. Objective examination of the suitability of educational theories to the prevalent circumstances and conditions at a place has always been a very highly significant and fruitful field of educational research.

14. Psychology of Education: Psychological conditions conducive to learning, memory, worthwhile responses, reading and writing etc. are subjects with which a researcher is as much concerned as a teacher. Researches in psychology have solved some problems in these and allied fields. However, teachers are, still confronted by situations which do not always get solved by the psychological solutions. These and such other problems confront researcher can devote and unravel psychological factors.

15. Socio-Economic Conditions: Socio-economic conditions influence educational processes and results. These factors have their impact on the educational philosophy of a school system and population of a school. These offer various subjects for research. Their research may be of broad application in the field of education. Therefore, socio-economic conditions influencing education are important subjects of research.

16. Comparative Education: Geographical, cultural, socio-economic and political conditions influence educational systems of different countries according to local differences. Comparison of the educational systems of different countries may be made by a variety of methods of treatment. These must be objective and scientific. At times emphasis may be laid upon the countries. Socio-economic or geographical or cultural forces moulding them may be studied. Researches may be conducted on the levels of achievement reached or aimed at.

In the words of Travers, "The areas of research may be likened to areas on a map that have been roughly circumscribed to show gross differences in terrain. Some penetration has perhaps been made with the border of these areas, but most of them remain unexplored. Explorers of the future will provide broad knowledge of those general areas and then must come the developers who will exploit the resources that each domain has to offer. The boundaries which have been set up are artificial, for each one of the areas of the educational research fuses into the other."

Problems of Research in India

In India, the students, teachers, supervisors, educationists and even laymen are faced with innumerable problems and unsolved difficulties, in almost all the fields of our life. This shows the urgent need for research as the best means to solve such problems. However, while the problems are numberless, personnel and resources to tackle them scientifically are extremely limited in India. Therefore, when planning for research one has to arrange the problems in order of priority. Due to different viewpoints and varied ideas about education, there is no order of priority in the study of these problems. Different educationists in India may draw their own orders of priority.

P. S. Naidu, gave the following order of priority to educational problems for research in India -

1. The Philosophical Problems: Aims of Indian National Education.
2. (i) The Sociological problems.
   (ii) Educational Surveys.
3. The Psychological Problems.
4. The Technological Problems.

Though one may not agree with this order of priority, he will not disagree with the neccessity for research in the above fields.

According to **J. Lahiri**, the main fields in which educational research is needed are :

1. Psychology in the Classroom.
2. Empirical Child Study.
3. Secondary School Curriculum.
4. Examination System.
5. History of Education.
6. Philosophy of Education.
7. Educational Administration and Organisation.
8. Moral Education.
9. Methods of Teaching.

The Sub-Committee in the Seminar on Promotion of Research in Training Colleges identified the following problems of educational research in India :

1. Experimental Work in Curriculum Construction.
2. Organisation and Administration.
3. Teaching Personnel (e.g. the teaching load).
4. Improvement of Instructional Techniques and Methods.
5. Psychology of the India Child (e.g. backward, gifted, and delinquent).
6. Testing and guidance
7. Educational Sociology

V. V. Kamat in his article "Can a Teacher do Research?" published in Teaching, No. XXX. No. 1, September 2013, listed the following educational problems for research in India.

1. Vocabulary of children of various age groups in different mother-tongues.
2. The public schools of India.
3. Errors committed in learning languages.
4. Voluntary activities of boys and girls of various age groups.
5. Heights, weights and other physical indices of boys and girls of various age groups.
6. Self-government in schools.
7. Methods of Teaching Geography and History.
8. Reading Interested of Boys and Girls.
9. Education of superior children.
10. Education of backward children.
11. Administrative practices.
12. Group methods of teaching in primary school.
13. L. E. A's in the State of Bombay.
14. Educational contribution of various educationists in India.
15. Hobbies of boys in various age-groups in secondary schools.
16. Hobbies of girls in various age-groups in secondary schools.
17. Voluntary schools in primary education.
18. Educational qualifications of primary school teachers.
19. Differential attainment of children of urban and rural areas.
20. Comparison of attainments of children who have attended nursery schools and those who have not.

In the Sixth Conference of All India Association of Training Colleges held at Bangalore in June, 2014, Prof. M. Varma said, "Stress should be laid on the development of basic tools and to direct research activity towards the solution of problems which have a fundamental and functional importance in education." The following list of problems was suggested for research in the field of education, in this conference.

1. Educational and Development Psychology.
2. Indian Philosophy.
3. Educational Administration.
4. Educational Evaluation and Measurement.
5. Educational and Vocational Guidance.
6. Methodology of Teaching Various School Subjects.
7. Syllabuses, Text-books of Teacher's Training.

The Central Institute of Education, Delhi organised a Seminar in 2013 to promote educational research through interdisciplinary collaboration. It was sponsored by the University Grants Commission. The participants included eminent professors in different Indian Universities belonging to different disciplines like Economics, Education, History, Philosophy, Psychology, Political Science and Sociology. In their notes and discussions these seminarians searched for problems in the field of education which needed interdisciplinary approach and support.

******

Chapter – 9

Kinds and Sources of Data

Research is based upon various types of information, it is not possible withtout different kinds of information. Justs as a building requires bricks and mortar for its construction, similarly every research requires concerned information. These informations giver knowledge concerning social phenomena. Now, in order to carry on research successfully, information should be gathered from proper sources. The more valid is the sources of information, the more reliable will be the information received which, in its turn, will lead to correct and reliable conclusions. Therefore, research presupposes a knowledge of kinds and sources of information. Different types of researches require different types of information. This requires a wide knowledge of kinds and sources of information.

Kinds of Data

Different kinds of information are required in our research. This can be classified into the following two types of information:

1. Primary Data : Primary data are the actual information which are received by the researcher for social study from the actual field of research. These data are obtained by means of questionnaires and schedules. In some field primary data are collected through interview and observation method. The observation method, for collecting primary data, may be both participant and non-participant. Such data are known as primary because they are attained by the researcher from the field of research directly and for the first time. Primary data are generally attained through two sources. The primary source of primary data are the facts of living person's lives. The other source is the connected events known through observation such as the life of the group, traditions and customs and different aspects of daily life. Participant observation sometimes unravels such primary data which can not be known by any other means.

2. Secondary Data: Secondary data are the informations which are attained indirectly. The researcher does not attain them himself or directly. Such data are gatherally from published and unpublished material. Secondary data are gathered from informations collected from the individuals and institutions through personal diaries, letters and survey documents etc. The secondary data again, are gathered through two types of sources. The first source are the personal documents such as books, manuscripts, records, census reports of surveys by private institutions and various informations published in news papers and magazines. According to Lundberg, the information achieved from inscriptions on stones and objects of excavations may also be included in secondary data.

Sources of Data

The sources of information are generally classified as - primary and secondary. Different sociologists have classified the sources of informations differently. Of these some more important view are as follows :

1. Acccording to P. V. Young, the sources of information can be classfied into - documentary sources and field source. While the first includes books, manuscripts, diaries and letters, the second includes the information given by individuals.

2. According to W.A. Bageley, the sources of information in the field of research, may be classified into primary sources and secondary sources. Primary sources include the actual informations received from the individuals directly concerned with the problems of research study. It also includes social pohenomena by observing which some information and facts may be discovered. The secondary source of information includes all types of published and unpublished, public or private documents and other such types of information.

3. According to G.A. Lundberg, the sources of information may be include sources and field sources. The historical sources include sources representing the past incidents. For example, some inscriptions on stones of the ages of Ashoka the great, can be authentic sources of information about his time. Historical sources give information about the conditions and incidents which can be known through observation or any other means of information. Thus historical sources include documents, papers and stone inscriptions concerning past, as well as the articles discovered through excavations. The field sources include informations received from concerned persons and also through the observation of their behaviour.

Primary or Field Sources

On the basis of the above mentioned views the sources of information may be classified as primary or field source and secondary or documentary source. These sources may now be discussed in some more details. Primary sources are those from which information is gathered for the first time. This information is gathered by the researcher himself. The sources of such information are the individuals and the incidents around them. Generally, primary source information is gathered through direct observation, questionnaires, schedule and interview methods.

1. **Direct observation**: The chief primary source of information concerning social phenomenon is direct observation. This method needs that the social-researcher should personally and directly observe the conditions and incidents of his field of study. Direct observation is the most reliable method for gathering information concerning the life, status, conduct, behaviour, language, festivals, customs and traditions etc. In this observation, the observer should be absolutely detached and objective in gathering facts. Direct observation, again, has been classified into participant observation and non participant observation. In participant observation, the observer lives in the groups or community as a member of it and participates in their life. On the contrary, in non-participant observation, the researcher does not participate in the group life but only observes as an external spectator.

2. **Questionnaire**: Questionnaire include questions concerning different aspects of the subjects of research study. It is used in such cases where the subject of study is very wide and direct observation is not possible. It is also used about such things which can not be known through direct observation such as the ideas, intentions and motives of the persons concerned. Sometimes the questionnaires are delivered by hand and at other times they are delivered through posts. Questionnaires may be sources of information only when the informers are well educated and prepared to co-operate with the research worker.

3. **Schedule**: Schedules are a particular type of questionnaires. The main distinction between questionnaires and schedules is that whereas in the former the informers themselves reply to the question, in schedules this is done by the researcher himself. He questions the informers and records the replies in the proper places specified in the schedules. The main advantage of a schedule is that it may be used even in the case of uneducated informer. However, it can be used only in a limited field, as compared to the questionnaire method.

4. **Interview**: In an interview, the researcher meets people and discusses his problems with them. During the course of this discussion, he gathers facts. An interview is different from a schedule. A schedule includes some predetermined

questions asked by the researcher in a definite order without change. But the interview has no such definite form or order of questions. The researcher may ask any question on the basis of his insight into the problem.

Secondary or Documentary Sources

The sources of information through documents concerning individuals and institutions are known as secondary or documentary sources. The secondary sources represent incidents, conditions and systems. Informations received through secondary sources are sufficient and useful. They also give information concerning the past which is not possible through any other source. In order to gather complete information concerning some present social custom, it is generally necessary to know its historical background. This historical background can be known through secondary sources. Besides, secondary sources supply information concerning difficulties, precautions and methods of study. Documentary sources include books, survey scripts, memories, letters and diaries along with historical inscriptions and material published in news paper and magazines from to time. To facilitate study, secondary sources have been further classified into personal documents and public documents.

1. Personal documents: Personal documents include all the published and unpublished information documented by the individuals for different purposes. Personal documents are not written in scientific style nor have an objective basis. They generally represent some ideas, ideals, values and feelings etc. In spite of being subjective and unscientific, personal documents have been very much useful in modern research. They provide important information about contemporary social circumstances, system, customs, ways of life etc. The personal documents of notable persons are very useful sources of information concerning their social attitude. The causes of writing personal documents are generally as follows :

(i) In order to prove the validity of some activity.
(ii) In order to accept one's mistake.
(iii) To achieve the satisfaction of ordered description.
(iv) To achieve the pleasure of literary presentation.
(v) For research in personal documents.
(vi) To get relief from mental tension.
(vii) To attain riches, money or fame etc.
(viii) To fulfil some assigned job.
(ix) To provide clinical information and description.
(x) To exhibit and express one's abilities and capacities.
(xi) To support some theory or ism.
(xii) Due to motivation for social service and social welfare.
(xiii) To attain immortality.

Personal documents have been classified into four types - biographies, diaries, letters and memories.

(i) ***Biographies:*** Biographies are generally autobiographies. Some great political leaders, social reformers and eminent persons write their autobiographies. These autobiographies are not mere collections of the incidents of their life. They provide useful information concerning the social, political, religious and cultural conditions and incidents of their time. Some autobiographies unravel some things which could not be known from any other source of information. This is particularly true about the autobiographies of eminent political leaders.

Autobiographies again, may be of different types. Some autobiographies may be written in order to preserve specific feelings and incidents of the writer's life. Such autobiographies have sufficient objectivity. Some other autobiographies are written in order to be published to gain financial advantage or popularity. These autobiographies have less reliability. They are often full of exaggerations and under-estimations. They are full of deliberate distortion of facts. Some other biographies include life histories of some eminent persons written by some biographies. The objectivity of some biographies very much depends upon the purpose and personality of the biographies. Very few of such biographies are reliable, as most of them are written to achieve certain advantages.

Whatever may be the kind of biography, it is important source of information about social conditions and incidents. Some biographers have elabortely described the evils of contemporary society and also suggested reforms. They also exhibit the social attitude of the subject of biography. An autobiography are more simple than historical books. And yet they have certain limitations. For example, a good number of authors have tried to exaggerate or underrate so many incidents and feelings of their life with different intentions. They delibertely hide facts which show their personality in unfavourable perspectives. All this makes the biographies less valid.

(ii) *Diaries* : Many of the more educated persons have a habit of writing diaries concerning their relationships and life incidents. Similarly, some other persons daily write diaries to include programme of the day. Then, some other persons do not write diary daily but write only important incidents and deeper feelings and observations.

Diaries are written with different intentions. Some persons write diaries to remember important incidents of their life. Some other persons write diaries to note things which they can not tell any one. This releases their mental tension. Some other persons review their lives from time to time and note it in diaries. These informations are very useful in modern research. Diary writing is a confidential and private performance. Most of the diary writers have no intention to publish them. Therefore, generally it is expected that information recorded in diary will be reliable. Hence diary forms an important source of valid informations in social research as a personal document.

However, inspite of the above mentioned advantages, diary, as a source of information, suffers from the following limitations :

1. In a diary the incidents of life are generally described in a dramatic and exaggerated form. It entirely ignores the normal, non-dramatic incidents.

2. Diary writing is mainly personal. Therefore it does not include detailed and complete description of incidents but a very sketchy and rudimentary form of the same. It does not record the context in which an incident has taken place. This makes it difficult to interpret incidents and understand their real meaning.

3. Sometimes some persons aim at publishing their diaries. They give them to be read by their friends. In such conditions the diaries become artificial.

4. Diaries written irregularly lack connection in information. It is very difficult to connect different incidents and feelings described in them.

(iii) ***Letters*** : Letters are often used by researchers as evidenced in the study of the Polish Peasant. The authors Thomas and Znaniecki analysed 754 letters exchanged between the Pole in the U. S. A. and those in Poland. Most of the educated persons write a number of letters during the course of their livers. Letters are the medium of expressions of the feelings, likes and dislikes, plans, attitudes, desires, emotions, ambitions and also important incidents of life. Letters are personal and very reliable. Therefore, they constitute one of the most reliable sources of information about interrelationships, such as friendship, love, marital affairs, family tensions and divorces etc. In sprite of so many advantages, letters have limitations, which are as follows :

1. It is difficult to collect private letters. In the first instance, many people do not preserve their letters for a long time. This is particularly true about those letters which consist of important secrets. Secondly, no one can pass off his personal or confidential letters to any other person easily.

2. The letters do not give detailed and complete description of incidents.

3. If letters of only one person are secured, they hardly provide scientific data since no comparable information is available.

4. It is difficult to imagine as to how much reliablity may be expected in a letter. It may be absolutely false and deceptive. For expected love letters are generally full of ortificiality, hypocracy and deceit.

(iv) *Memoires.* Some persons are interested in writing down memoires of their travels, participation in wars, hunting expeditions, excavations, explorations and mountaineering assaults, etc. Such memoires provide useful information in social research. Some historical memoires have given very useful description of the contemporary time and circumstances. Such were the memories of Magasthnes, Fahiyan and Ibnebatuta, etc. in India. They have been acclaimed as very reliable historical documents concerning contemporary social, political and cultural conditions. However, memories have certain limitations. They are seldom scientific. They are full of subjective ideas and feelings. They are full of exaggeration particularly concerning author's own achievements. This is particularly evident in the memories of eminent army generals and political leaders. Therefore, memoires should not be considered as absolutely reliable.

Importance of Personal Documents

The description concerning the importance of various types of personal documents, shows that they are very important sources of information in modern research. While providing information in objective conditions they also throw important light upon the subjective conditions of the author. Therefore, apart from sociological data they are very impoortant sources of information for psychological analysis. Their information is relatively more reliable particularly when they have not been prepard with the intention of publication.

Limitation of Personal Documents

Inspite of the above mentioned importance, personal documents suffer from the following limitations, as sources of information :

1. **Difficulty in collection**: As has been already pointed out, it is difficult to collect more important and confidential personal documents. They are rarely recorded, and more seldom preserved. They are generally destroyed after a short time. Again, as the personal documents involve the author's emotional attachment the seldom likes to share them with other persons. Therefore, the collection of important personal is very difficult.

2. **Reliability of data**: It is very difficult to assess correctly the reliability of personal documents. There is almost no criteria to judge their validity since they are written from subjective view point, coloured by personal ideas, ideals, likes and dislikes. They are full of distortions and exaggerations. Therefore, their reliability is always questionable and rarely established.

3. **Difficulty of definite conclusions**: It is not easily possible to arrive at some definite conclusions about a research problem on the of personal documents. Personal documents do not represent contemporary social conditions objectively. They never utilise scientific methods. Then, most of the authors of personal documents are abnormally sensitive and emotional. Therefore, not much reliable information can be secured through their personal documents.

Suggestions for use

Inspite of the above limitations the modern researcher has to make use of personal documents particularly in such subject which are intimately concerned with personal feelings, attachments, emotions, likes and dislikes of men and women such as marital tension, extra-marital and pre-marital relationships, divorces, sexual behavior, etc. Therefore, the social researcher has to judge the validity of the information supplied by personal documents. Gottschalk lists five kinds of information's state is truthful.

(a) When the truth of the statements is a matter of indifference to the witness, he is likely to be unbiased (this might possibly have impaired his observation or memory).

(b) When the statement is prejedical to the infomation or his interest, it is likely to be unusually truthful.

(c) When the facts at issue are so much the matters of common knowledge that the information would be unlikely to be mistaken or to lie about them.

(d) When the part of the statements of primary interests to the investigator is both incidental and intrinsically probable.

(e) When the information makes statements which are contraty to his expectations and anticipations as assessed by the investigator's knowledge of his thought patterns and preconceptions.

Many of the documents are recorded by the investigator himself, particularly when the informations are illiterate. In such cases, so many distortions are commited by the investigator himself. He may put some questions which may not be relevant and clear to the information. However, whatever may be the limitations and disadvantages of personal documents, they may be used in modern research by observing certain precautions. Some suggestions, in this direction, may be as follow :

1. The investigator should seek the cooperation of a representative cross section of the population.

2. Most of the documents should be purchased at reasonable prices.

3. Anonymity of personal document should be guaranteed to the information by the investigator.

4. Large samples should be gathered to achieve more reliability.

It may be remembered that working on these suggestions eminent researcher have conducted important research with the help of personal documents. Thomas and Znaniecki used a number of fragmentary autobiographies, large number of letters and considerable collection of records, newspaper accounts etc. In his study of gang. Thrasher supplemented his main techniques by persuading a number of gang members to write their life stories.

Public or Official Documents

In the secondary source of information in modern research the public or official documents occupy an important place. A public document is the information gathered from some government or non-government institutions.

Public documents are of two types. Some documents generally remain unpublished such as reports of big companies, confidential records of government departments and non-government institutions. These are generally unpublished. Some other public documents are published in the general interest of the public. Such documents may be prepard by government or non-government departments. Some more important public documents are know as follow :

1. **Records**: Records occupy the most important place among public documents. Most of the governmental and non-governmental departments preserve many types of records consisting of important information. For example, every police department keeps a record of its activity. Each police stations keeps a records of criminals living within its field. Besides, private companies keep different kinds of records. All these records are important source of information for modern research. Informations received through them have a high degree of reliability. It is however, difficult to collect such records, particularly those which are never published.

2. **Published Data**: Public documents include data published by government and non-government institutions from time to time. Such institutions conduct periodical survey concerning population, rate of mortality, birth rate, annual production, average annual income, foreign trade, marriages and divorces etc. A very important example of published data in India is *India*, published by government of India every year. It includes all types of data concerning almost all the departments of every part of government of India and the states under it.

3. **Letters and Magazines**: Journals and magazines are important public documents including a wide veriety of informations which can be usefully utilised in social research. Most of these informations are very much reliable. Letters to the editors published in various magazines and journals are in an important source of information.

4. **Newspapers**: Newspaper publish news, discussion on contemporary issues, reports of meetings and conferences, essays and articles on living controversies and the letters of the readers to the editors. All this is an important source of information for different kinds of social research. The reliablility of such information is very high at least in the case of renouned newspapers, circulated among millions of persons. However, some of the newspapers, particularly those of different political parties, serve vested interests and therefore have low reliability. A comparative study of several newspaper, will give the investigator an insight into regorous government control and without much freedom of press, however, represent the views of party in power and therefore do not give much useful information. However,

as the freedom of press in most of the democratic countries is respected, newspapers today supply very reliable information to social investigator.

5. Other Documents: Besides the above mentioned public documents, film, television, radio, and public speeches etc. are other important sources of information. They supply useful informations about contemporary issues. The research investigator, however, should be capable of sorting out the reliable material and distinguishing it from the unreliable meterial advanced by these sources.

Utility of Documentary Sources

The informations received through the secondary sources are easy to obtain but difficult to use in social research. It requires a keen insight and a capacity to distinguish between reliable and unreliable data, to make use of documentary informations. Therefore, such information should be carefully judged before utilising it. This verification requires attention towards reliability and adequacy of facts.

1. Verification of reliability: Reliability of facts should be verified before using them in any social investigation. First of all, information should be attained about the experience, honesty, ability, methods and tools of the investigator himself. Then the method of collection should be rigorously scrutinized. This method should be objective and scientific. It should be verified whether the sample made for social research is representative or not. Then, the organisation for collection of data should bescrutinized. The reliability of the method and tools of study and the techniques of analysis should be verified. The sociometric scales utilised for measurement, the investigator should select some facts and verify them, so that he may have some idea about the reliability of total secondary data.

2. Verification of adequacy: Besides reliability, the adequacy of facts should be judged before utilizing them in our research. In this connection, it should be remembered that whatever secondary data is collected should have an aim identical with the aim of social investigation. It is then alone that relevant data will be collected. Secondly, the units of available data should be verified so that adequacy of facts may be observed.

Census Reports and Statistics

One very important sources of data collection for our research are the census report, the annual digest of statistics and statistical reports of various state departments and national bodies. These reports are prepared by experts and therefore their data are highly reliable. The data collected by these reports are arranged according to the administrative aim. Thus, the health department collects statistics concerning birth and death rate ect. Public and private economic organisations collect and publish data on wages, hours of work, productivity, absenteeism, strikes and lockouts etc. Education department collects statistics concerning various aspects of education. Similar is the case about all other departments of the government. These reports have been widely utilized by sociologists for different purposes. K.M.Landis based his study *'Segregation in Washington'* exclusively on the analysis and interpretation of available statistical data, e.g. census reports official health statistics, employment data, police statistics etc. Similarly, Leo Srole in his study of 'Status and Prestige' in the *'Yankee City'* series of investigation by Warner and associates utilized a rather unusual source of data relevant to his problem - the cemetery records.

The use of available statistics should be guided by the principle the research investigator should keep himself flexible in respect of the form in which research questions are asked, for example, Durkheim's study on suicide provides a classical example of how the superior flexibility of a genius resulted in the testing of a social theory by available statistics. He started with the hypothesis that the causes of suicide are to be found in the social conditions. To test this theory he studied statistics of suicide in certain European countries. He relied on the analysis of data collected for purposes other than those of the particular research study. In other studies such data are used in conjunction with other procedures. Thus, in the *Hawthorne Electrical Studies* by Roethlisberger and Dickson, it was found that changes in such conditions as illumination, rest periods and hours of work could not account for a consistently rising rate of productivity in experimental groups over a period of time. It was concluded that changes in social organization of work-groups and their relationship to management were responsible for a rise in productivity. Again, available statistics may be used for other purposes in a study. For example, in the study of the psychological impact of long-term unemployment in an Austrian village by Jahoda, Lazarsfeld and Zeist, the 'shock' effect of unemployment was checked against such records as the accounts of the local grocer.

Precautions in the use of modern statistics: In order to use statistical data usefully, the investigator must observe the following precautions:

1. The definitions of categories used in available statistical data frequently do not coincide with those used in our research. Therefore, the investigator should ascertain the precise definition on which the statistics are based.

2. It is not enough to know merely what the original collector of data aimed at, it is also necessary to enquire into his methods. The investigator, should therefore, ascertain about the aims as well the authenticity of the method of data collected.

3. The degree of inaccuracy instatistical data may be negligible from the point of view of the research scientists, and yet there may be grave methodological errors. Therefore, the investigator should scrupulously check the method of collection of data. To sum up in the words of A.L. Bowely, "It is never safe to take published statistics at their face value, without knowing their meaning and limitations, and it is always necessary to criticise arguments that are based on them, unless one is able to trust implicitly the knowledge and good falsify lessons which numerical statements should teach. The actual use and appreciation of statistics are ultimately a matter of intelligence, special knowledge and common-sense......".

Statistics in India

In Indian constitution, special provision has been made for collection of statistical data. Such sources were not available in preindependence time. Another important reason for the absence of sufficient statistical data is the lack of finance. Sometimes collection of data is considered a wastage of money and energy. However, as has been already pointed out, after independence, Indian constitution made provision for collection of statistical data. According to section 246 of Indian constitution, it is the responsibility of the central government to collect and preserve data concerning railway, defense, banking, currency, population and foreign trade. The state government collect data concerning agriculture, animal husbandry, forests and education. Thus in the public sector the collection of statistical data in India has been considerably widened. Besides the government source, statistical data are collected by non-government and individual sources. All these three sources will now be described in details:

1. Government Source

In every developed country, it is necessary to collect statistical data concerning economic and social development. In India, attention has been paid in this direction in recent years. The chief government sources of collection of statistical data are as follows :

(i) ***Census of India:*** Census in India is undertaken once in every decade. The last census was conducted in 2011. The next census falls due in 2011. Census data collection is supervised by the Home Ministry. Data is gathered from all over the country. It includes data concerning population traits such as age, sex, profession, income and religion etc. On the basis of these data conclusions are deduced in different fields of life.

(ii) ***Directorate of Economics and Statistics:*** This department is an important source of statistical data. It is under Central Agriculture and Food Ministry. Data is Collected in the whole country. The publication of these data is done through the following important magazines - *Agricultural Statistics in*

India (Monthly), *Abstract of Agricultural Statistics* (Annual), *Agricultural Wages in India* (Annual).

(iii) *Reserve Bank of India:* This institution works under Finance Ministry. It preserves data concerning credit and finance etc. through publication in th following magazines *Statistical Supplementary* (Weekly), *Statistical Statement Relating to Cooperative Movement in India* (Annual).

(iv) *Ministry of Commerce and Industry:* This department collects and preserves data concerning trade and commerce. This data is published in *Indian Trade Journal.*

(v) *Ministry of Labour:* This department collects statistics concerning average income, average working hours, employment and unemployment of skilled and unskilled labour in the country. All these data are published in *Indian Labour Gazette,* a monthly journal.

(vi) *Ministry of Railways:* Ministry of Railways collects data concerning annual income and expenditure, accidents, thefts and travel without ticket in railways etc. All these data are published in *Monthly Railway Statistics.*

(vii) *Transport department:* Transport department collects Statistical data India level and published them in *Traffic survey.*

(viii) *Ministry of Education:* This department collects Statistical data about different aspects of education and publishes in the *Annual Journal of Education in India.*

(ix) *Ministry of Information and Communication:* This department has been collecting data concerning a wide variety of social life in India, since 1953. These data are annually published in *India - A Reference Annual.* This book includes data concerning Indian land and people, national symbols, social patterns, government, defence, education, cultural activities, scientific research, health and hygience, social welfare, communication, economic development, agriculture, irrigation and hydroelectricity, trade and commerce, transport, labour, housing etc.

(x) *Central Statistical Bureau:* This department performs the important function of systematizing and coordinating the statistical data collected by various government departments. It also publishes them through different journals, magazines, booklets, etc.

(xi) *Directorate of National Sample Survey:* This was established in 1950. Its main aim is to help planning commission in the formulation of five year plan. It collects data concerning five year plans, throughout the country. Such data include information concerning families, form of expenditure, condition of housing, trends of unemployment and the states of agricultural labourers etc.

(xii) *Ministries of state government:* The responsibilities of collecting statistical data within the state falls upon Ministries of State Government. Thus, they collect data concerning health, education, unemployment, condition of labourers, housing, social security, crime etc. The function of systematisation and coordination of the data gathered and published by different ministries has been entrusted to State Statistical Bureau.

2. Non-Government Sources

The non-government sources of collection and preservation of statistical data in India, are as follows :

(i) ***University Institutes:*** Today in India every big university has established some centers or institutes for collecting and preserving various types of statistical data published time to time. Some notable university institutes are - gokhale Institute of Politics and Economics, Indian Institute of Social Sciences, Agra Institute of Social Sciences, Delhi School of Social Work.

(ii) ***Trade Chambers:*** Different trades have their independent chambers which collect data concerning their particular trade. Besides such limited trade chambers, All India Chamber of Commerce and Industry also collects and publishes various types of Statistical Data.

(iii) ***Special Annual Numbers:*** So many Magazines and Journals and Weekly papers publish Annual of periodical special numbers including data concerning different aspects of some particular problem. Such special numbers are very important sources of statistical data.

(iv) ***Newspapers, Magazines and Journals:*** Newspapers, Magazines and Journals regularly publish reliable informations and statistical data concerning their particular areas, or about the country as a whole.

3. Personal Sources

Some eminent scholars have also published reports of their researches including important statistical data in different fields. Among the most important such personal sources of statistical data may be mentioned *Attitude towards family planing in India* by S.N. Agarwal, *Nutrition in India* by C.G. Pandit and *Studies in Indian Public Finance* by M.H. Gopal, etc.

Defects of Indian Statistics

Inspite of the above mentioned efforts for collection and preservation of statistical data Indian Statistics suffer from the following major defects :

1. Inadequacy: In India the social and economic data collected from various sources are still far from sufficient. They do not represent their particular field of information. Besides, no data are available about so many aspects of life. The reasons for the inadequacy of data are - lack of sufficient finance and other means, lack of interest, lack of scientific attitude etc.

2. Obsolete-informations: Most of the publications in India include obsolete informations. This is particularly due to the fact that the speed of survey and data collection is very slow. Therefore, till the stage of latest information is available. For example, the statistics concerning census are available some years after actual census survey.

3. **Unreliability**: The reliability of Indian Statistics gathered from government and non-government agencies is very much doubtful. On many occasions, the government agencies deliberately change and modify statistical data to present a rosy picture of the state of affairs to again popularity. Besides, informations are suppressed and modified in the name of public interest such as the data concerning communal riots, crimes, defence, foreign trade and economic development, etc. In these fields the data published by govt. agencies are not is reliable.

4. **Lack of order**: In actual circumstances data are collected in villages, districts, states, etc. In order to have a wider picture on state level or national level, the data collected by smaller units have to be properly ordered. This is however, not done with sufficient care in this country. Therefore, no overall picture is available.

5. **Inadequacy of sufficient magazines and journals**: There is great dearth of journals and magazines in different areas in India to publish data concerning various aspects of social life. Therefore, even if data are collected by some private agency, it is seldom published in time. For example, the data collected in field researches by the research students in different universities in India, mostly remain unpublished or when they are published, they are already obsolete. As a general rule, few field researches get an opportunity to be published anywhere in India. Thus a lot of labour in data collection is unnecessarily wasted.

Suggestions for Improvements

It is clear from the above discussion that Indian statistics suffer from many major disadvantages. All these defects may not be removed but much improvement is possible by following the suggestions given below :

1. **Increase in efficient**: Most of the defects of Indian statistics are due to inefficiency of the workers of the concerned departments. Most of the workers do not complete a job in time and go on postponing it indefinitely, with the result that the publication of data becomes very late. Besides, in the absence of proper control, the salaried workers do not perform their functions sincerely. All this requires suitable control over concerned workers in different government departments.

2. **Encouragement to research**: Statistical data very much depend upon private and organisational research activities. In order to obtain reliable and latest data, research should be encouraged. It is only in stimulating environment that new data may be obtained by continued research work.

Encouragementg to the research students of social sciences in the universities will prove to be very much beneficial.

3. Establishment of coordinating agencies: Lack of order and coordination is a grave defect of Indian statistics. Generally, the collected data are not coordinated with the result that definite conclusions are not arrived at. In order to remove this defect it is necessary that agencies may be organised on All India level which may coordinate the data obtained and collected in different fields.

4. Establishment of laboratories: Reliable data are generally obtained from the laboratories. Such laboratories should be established everywhere in the country with the government aid. Besides conducting research and providing training in research, these laboratories should collect data, analyse and coordinate it.

5. Reform in the means of survey: In order to make statistical data reliable, the means of social survey and research should be reformed. As the means become more scientific the conclusions become more reliable. By the use of more and more mechanical devices in the collection of data their objectivity may be increased. For example, the use of taps recorder, photo camera and movie camera etc., is very advantageous.

6. Arrangement for early publication: Every type of statistics are constantly changing. Therefore, if they are published in time, their importance becomes obsolete. Hence in order to use social statistics properly, in time and by a wider circle of persons, social statistics should be published at the earliest opportunity. Arrangement may be made by the government for the early publication of social statistics.

7. Verification of reliability: Generally, social statistics suffer from the defect of unreliability. In order to remove this defect the data may be verified before publication. Standardised methods may be used for verification of the reliability of social statistics.

Importance of Census Data in India

In India today there is no proper arrangement for collection and publication of statistical data. Therefore, decannial census survey is very much important. It is a cheaq source of collection of data on all India levels. The data supplied by census are multiple and valuable. They include population statistics, size and types of families, religious communities, languages, professions, education, birth and death rate, age groups, sex groups etc. They show many social problems in their details. For the purpose of study the importance of census statistics in India may be classified as follows :

1. Political importance: Census survey is very much important from the administrative and political view point. It provides population statistics about the whole country. This information helps the government in formulating various plans and policies. It shows the increase or decrease and tends of population. It is on its basis that the government may formulate policies concerning different aspects of population. For example, it is on the basis of census survey that the present government has made it a policy to propagate the objective of small and limited family. Social statistics concerning education may be the most suitable basis for educational reforms, educational expansion and establishment of various types of educational institutions. Data concerning different languages are also the basis of so many policies. Census reports also provide help in the development of backward groups, scheduled castes and scheduled tribes.

2. Economic importance: Economic planning of the country is based upon population statistics. Census survey provides data concerning income and expenditure of individuals in different areas. It is on the basis of this data that attempts are made to reform economic conditions. Besides, help is given to different classes for economic development. The census survey discloses the average income, the minimum income and the maximum income in the country. It is on the basis of this data that additional texts are imposed on some classes and taxes are reduced on other classes in order to maintain a socio-economic balance in the country.

3. Sociological importance: Census survey is particularly valuable from the sociological view point. It show social conditions, social evils, customs and traditions etc. It is on the basis of the social statistics that plans for social research and social survey are formulated. For example, the census report points out the incidence and areas of child marriages. On the basis of this information the social evil of child marriage may be reformed and eradicated. Besides, census survey provides information concerning social events on the basis of which attempts may be reformed and eradicated. Besides, census survey provides information concerning social events on the basis of which attempts may be made for social amelioration and social change.

4. Commercial importance: It is necessary to formulate plans and policies before running a commercial enterprize efficiently. The formulation of such policies and plans needs different types of informations and statistical data. This is very much supplied by census report. For example, it shows the quantity and quality of population in different area of country.

******

Chapter – 10

Data Collection

Indian business firms specialize in non-customer facing, processes. In the coming years, countries like the Philippines and other Asian countries might take that away from us. Indian companies have to be prepared for this and work on building their comparative advantage.

Retail is on a boom and outsourcing has provided Indian businesses unprecedented filliep. In such a scenario, what role does market research play?

Ugam Solutions, provider of research and analytics services, is focused on serving the marketing information needs of global business enterprises.

Providing outsourced services to the global market research and product information industry, Ugam is among India's key providers of outsourced services to the global market research industry.

It has its second International Centre for Research and Analytics in Malad and it plans to have an employee strength of 3000 by 2015.

Sunil Mirani, CEO, Ugam Solutions, who is responsible for longterm vision and strategy, business development and human resources, shares some insight into how the Indian research scenario is shaping up and the global trends.

Latest Trends in Market Research Worldwide

The market research industry worldwide is seeing a lot of action. The trend of consolidation from the previous year will continue. Last year alone, there were around 88 mergers and acquisition (M&As) in the industry. These were greatly driven by the need for market research firms to get a global footprint.

India has also seen a huge growth in market research. With companies consolidating their business across the globe, there is a growing need for market research companies to expand their businesses across counties and continents.

Multi-mode research (via telephone, online and face-to-face) is another area of focus for market research companies. Along with global coverage, companies are needed to study specific markets, topics, and countries. As a result, market research companies are actively acquiring companies with similar additional capabilities across the world.

Consider the example of cell phones. Due to the availability of cheap phones, mobile penetration has singnificantly increased. Now we have more people buying phones; this in turn increases the size of the overall market. In a similar way, if the cost of market research decreases, more companies will do research and the overall market will grow.

Market research firms are increasingly being forced by their clients to not just give data but also to give insights - more of consulting, modelling and prediction, which was earlier the domain of the consulting companies.

The marketing practice within a consulting company is comparable to a market research company, as it offers research as well as consulting. A multinational FMCG company would go to such companies for consulting on how to build a better brand.

Till date, market research companies were thought to be very good at collecting data and doing surveys, which gives us a very good indication of the past, but based on the data analysis they were not able to offer any predictions or trends for the future. Increasingly, companies are looking at insights, predictions or future trends.

Market research companies are expanding their set-up and upgrading their skills to be able to go up the value chain. Interestingly, we are also seeing changes in their senior leadership. Market research companies are hiring leaders from the client side or from consultants or from the technology side.

This fresh guidance will definitely boost the image of these companies and equip them with better skills. In order to shed the image that they are merely a data collection outfit, market research companies prefer to off-load non-core functions of the research cycle. This in turn will have a positive impact on outsourcing and is good for players like us.

The India market grew at 16 per cent and last year; we crossed the $100-million mark. Out of the total market of $23 billion worldwide, $100 million is in India. But the point worth-noticing is that India is growing at 16 per cent, whereas the average worldwide growth is only 15 per cent, and this is significant for us.

India being a different market compared to global markets, MNGs want to study and understand the market before they set up facilities in India. This is further propelling the growth of market research in India.

Even with Indian companies, market research has become an integral part of the marketing budgets. In any country, increasing competition is one of the most important factors that drives market research. The one who understands the consumer the most is able to offer the latest products - better, cheaper and faster.

Market research is one of the ways which can help us to get better customer understanding. It is needed not just for foreign companies wanting to enter into India but also Indian companies that are fighting for market share in our country.

In 2010, the amount spent on market research in India was around $50 million, and today it is $100 million. We have doubled in size in four years, which shows the tremendous pace of growth in India.

Per capita spend is also a good way to assess the maturity of the market. The average worldwide per capita spend is about $3.6. Per person spend on market research in the UK is $36, in North America it is $25, in Europe it's $13, and in APAC it is $0.9.

Coming to India, the amount spent on research per person is as low as $0.09. The world average is pulled down because of regions like APAC, Central America, West Asia and Africa which have higher population but have low research spends on a per capita basis.

New avenues where market research is being used and can be used in India

In India, what may happen, which may be different from the rest of the world, is: while other countries are moving from fact-to-face to other methods like telephonic and online, in India we might just jump the telephone phase and go directly to online, SMS research and other new-age methods. Worldwide, it is typically the FMCG and medicine sector that is using market research extensively. India by far mirrors what is happening to other parts of the world, as a lot of MNCs are getting into India. All industries, from telecommunications and media to infrastructure and IT, can draw on such services.

To give an example, market research can do wonders for the growing retail sector in India. The retail sector in India has come a long way from small family-owned retail outlets to organized retailing businesses. Large business houses including the Reliance, Tata, and RPG are setting up retail stores across the country.

Serious investments by such giants have made the retail business very competitive. Companies now need to conduct customer satisfaction surveys, demand analysis, brand research and a host of other market research activities relating to advertising and market segmentation.

Exposure to global clients and research involves handling multi-country, large, complex data and far more complex research.

And as partners serving them we have to significantly upgrade our skills. As this talent did not already exist in India, we were forced to train and significantly upgrade the kind of skills available in the market.

What can India do to stay ahead?

Globalization has increased pressure on market research companies. They now feel the need to have global delivery centers for their MNC clientele. The increasing pressure on market research agencies to provide more value has made them outsource non-core operations.

Apart from the work like data collection and processing, project management is also being outsourced to us. Our clients what us to take complete charge of the back-end rocesses. We mostly compete with South American countries like Costa Rica, Dominican Republic and the Philippines for the CATI (Computer Aided Telephone Interviewing) market and Europe for data processing work.

We specialize in non-customer facing, that is data processing and analytics processes. In the coming years, countries like the Philippines and other Asian countries might take that away from us. Indian companies have to be prepared for this and work on building their comparative advantage.

Where do us fell the market will be in the next 10 years? What are our basing our predictions on?

The market research industry has a size of $23. About 58 per cent of this comes from the top 25 companies, and 66 per cent from the top five countries in market research - the US, the UK, France, Germany and Japan.

The industry has grown by 5 per cent in the past four years. But if you look closely, clearly there are some countries that have grown rapidly, and all APAC countries can be accounted in this. China grew by 27 per cent last year, India by 16 per cent and certain other East European countries have also shown rapid growth.

The $23 billion figure consists of the revenues of all market research firms put together.

There could be research that is done by companies directly (e.g. market research done by P&G directly is not be accounted here). While the developed countries are dominating, growth is also taking place in the developing countries.

Introdution

In search of scientific enquiry, the marketing research process attempts to collect and analyze the relevant information. If secondary information is inadequate and inconsistent, the research has the only choice to gather information from the primary source. Respondents are a major source of primary information, thus the researcher himself or by hired agency gathers the first-hand information by asking questions from the people (respondents). This chapter is confined to the means of obtaining marketing information from the primary source i.e. respondents.

A research method comprises a tool or technique which is used by the researcher to elucidate the information from the respondents. The techniques or tools are part of the marketing research process which deal with collection of information only. It is important to note that the techniques in all types of the researches are not the same but choice of techniques depends upon the nature of research problem. Many research techniques have been developed and are in use.

Data Objectives

The research objectives were derived from the decision objectives. That served as a basis of understanding to assure the client of relevant findings. That does not though suffice to direct the project's planning. The statement tells the nature of the nature of the results expected from the study, what it should enable the client to conclude or predict. It states the particular marketing actions (in pricing and composing) whose effects are to be measured (in general terms, which can be defined more sharply). It does not tell what data are to be obtained, or from whom to make the predictions. And it fails to specify the methods to be employed. The data objectives are derived from the research objectives and comprise what we have observed to be lacking in example. Their determination rests mainly on the researcher, to translate what the decision maker wants into a specific description of the needed data.

Let us first look at the general qualities that should be required of the data :

The measurements will be relevant to the decisions faced and will guide their key aspcets. The data will be accurable in both :

1. **Validity**, that is, they will measure what they are supposed to, and

2. **Reliability**, that is, repeating the same methods would produce the same results.

3. **Quickly and at Affordable cost,** that data can be obtained quickly enough and at an affordable cost.

Those principles are obviously generalities, but they are essential. As the researcher words towards precise data objectives, those that are tailored to the client's particular decisions, the task becomes more difficult. When clients have clearly described their perception of the task, it becomes more difficult. When clients have clearly described their perception of the problems and their decision methods. The researchers in turn can put the data objectives on target for the client's use.

Besides considering decision requirements, the researcher should consider the personal objectives and decision-making style of the clients. Unless these needs are met, clients may lack confidence in study findings and reject them. Sometimes researchers are too fascinated with sophisticated methods and novel concepts to recognize what the client really wants.

Data Types

A nearly endless variety of data now exist or can be obtained, but only a few types are relevant to each study's data objectives, Researchers have a substantial task a selecting the prices types of data to acquire. To be able to make this selection efficiently, one should sift through a number of data types to focus one the suitable once. For that reason, we now will describe numerous data classifications that indicate something of that background. It may seem tedious to read still more lists, but recognize that they are here as examples and not as things to memorize.

We will just indicate what is done during it and first give clues to specifying data by describing two types of classification :

1. The data's nature and
2. Its function in the ultimate interpretation and analysis.

Nature of the Data

We are categorizing data here in general terms of their meaning. There are distinct differences among the meanings of facts, knowledge, opinions, intentions, and motives.

Facts include the measurements of anything that actually exits or has existed. Usually, facts describe tangible things. Although they can be intangible as long as they can really be determined. It may be a fact that Smith and Sons sold 417 new Plymouths last year and that this bettered the previous year by 55 units. It may be a fact too that Joe Smith dominnaties the partners who own the firm, but this fact might defy measurement. Facts are ideal in the sense of possible measurement accuracy. The interpretations we place on real facts, through, may be inaccurate. We must beware of the danger that what we are dealing with the "quasifacts": as we would call them which are seemingly facts or reality. We are often learning that long-accepted truths were never valid. Many "facts" too are based on estimates or on samples that have a degree of unreliability.

These later may be used in research. But should not be treated as absolute truth. Some of our fundamental data (like the gross national product) have to be based on quasi-facts.

It helps data specifications also to recognize that facts have many sub-types, and the relevance to us are those descriptive of people. We will mention four of them;

1. Demographic : These are facts that describe the population to which the data refer, and in marketing, much of our description is economic, for example, that a family responding in a survey has an annual income of $21,700. The composition and age of family member or of one person also would be a form of demographics.

2. Sociological : These data describe how people are organized in and relate to society, for example, groups or churches to which they belong.

3. Psychographics : Facts that describe the lifestyle of an individual of a group, in some respect pertinent to the study. For a hypothetical example, automobile sales people tend to live in apartments rather than in single homes (more often than average U.S. adults). That might be quantified that 69 percent of them rent.

4. Behavioural : What people do, how they actually behave, are facts of high importance in many marketing studies. If a large proportion of new car buyers visit three to five dealers, all with the same make of car; this could be very significant in a dealer's decision on how to treat them. Knowledge (that is, what people know) also may be desired data, since that information (be it true or false) may be a determinant of what they do. Consumers' knowledge or awareness of products or brands in an example that is an indicator of the effectiveness of past communication, when setting goals or deciding the scale of future advertising.

Opinions are how people perceive something what they believe about it and what those beliefs signify. The most potent form of opinions tends to be attitudes, which are mental sets or predispositions to act in some manner (e.g., to decide in advance not to accept the trade-in offered by the first dealer visited). Another form is images of what something is like are significant, of course, as they affect behaviour, and attitudes exert a general and consistent influence.

For example, Mrs. R believes that her balanced diet supplies plenty of vitamins and that she has no need to pay a premium price to obtain them in breakfast cereal. As a result, her behaviour is to buy those cereals with the lower prices per ounce. Intentions are the acts that people have in mind to do, expectations of their behaviour. The extent to which people intend to commit a particular marketing behaviour and changes in these intentions may be key information. If Union Motors Corporation learns from a monthly data service that 14.1 percent of consumer families intend to buy a new car within the next 12 months, as against 14.4 percent in the previous report, it may receive its production plans. Motives are the internal forces that cause people to behave as they do. Marketers would dearly like to have accurate data on the motives that impel buyers' actions relative to the marketer's product categories. Many motives are quite obvious or are subjects about which people will speak freely. The basic causation of behaviour instead may lie deeply and be difficult to draw out. We will meet some techniques, that may motivational data. That often cannot be done, so the researcher needs to select other kinds of data with which the motives might be inferred.

Functions of the Data

Also relevant in specifying data needs is to have it classified in terms of how it will be utilized, at the stage of analysis, when the researcher brings together various bits of data and synthesizes conclusions from them. As that implies, one needs to anticipate early the future analysis and synthesis of the data and how it would function in that process. This takes time and it is challenging. But it avoids wasted time and money gathering redundant data while making it likely that the collected data will fit the decision needs.

Let us begin by thinking about a simple experiment, in which one hypothesis (or possible cause) is to be measured in terms of its effects. If we have one cause (x) and one effect (y), this hypothesis a simply expressed as Y=f (X)

To make this determination, the reader needs to conceive of and specify just two kinds of data: the causation (X) and the effect or payoff (1). These are our two first functional categories. The researcher in Union Motors wants to find out whether taking a demonstration ride (the cause) affects whether a car is bought (the payoff).

Considering this example further, we may recongize that the character of the person of family buying a car may have significant effects on the payoff. That is, some kinds of people or those in certain circumstances may be more affected by the causal variable than others. Therefore, the researcher needs to obtain an adequate description of them with certain data. These comprise our third functional classification of data description. This category of data is needed also to describe the sample or cross-section of the population that the study has covered.

As an example, consider again the proposed study for Union Motors. For interpretation purposes, an important factor might be whether the subject(s) in each car buying incident was an individual man or women or some combination of two or more people. To check the sample, may be the researcher wants to know the make of car(s) now owned by the shoppers(s). Thus, descriptive data would play important functions and must be specified to be gathered. There is still a fourth function to be served by the data; that of identification of the person who obtained an interview or made observations, the name or address of the subject, or the location where the data were obtained.

Identification data for the Union Motors, study could be the date and the place of obtaining the information (e.g., at Smith and Sons on March 18, 2014) and the field staff member who made the interview.

To summarize our terminology for functional classifications of data, they are these four :

1. Causation
2. Payoff
3. Description
4. Identification

Sources of Data

There are numerous possible sources of data, and again we cannot list them in detail. Anyway, this is a determination that is special to each project. A step towards that determination is having, first, general classification of sources, which we now offer in many dimensions.

Secondary sources should first be considered, which refer to those for already gathered and available data (in contrast with primary data). There may be internal sources within the client's company. Externally, these sources may include books or periodicals, published reports, data services, and computer data banks.

Primary data may be obtained from individuals, from families' representatives, or from organizations. There is increasing use of panels, which are groups of people (usually with some factor in common) that supply information. These may be one time or ad hoc panels that are utilized for just one occasion. There are also more or less permanent panels that are used repeatedly, which tends to make the information more comparable over time. This also avoids the costs of recruiting new sets of people for each data gathering, valuable also for repeated measurements. Location of the data sources is another option to be considered. Traditionally, there have been three common types of locations :

1. Where the subject lives (at home),
2. Where the subject, their congregating in shopping malls has been a boon to gathering information.
3. Mail intercepts in which people are importuned in shopping malls to participle in a study (typically in a small facility that a research agency maintains) have rapidly increased in usage.

As these many kinds of options suggest, today's marketing researcher has a variety of sources possibilities. This also must be stipulated in the data specification. Next we will discuss a different data decision: By what means of communication should it be obtained?

Communication Approaches

In deciding on which of the various means of communication to choose, a researcher has much to consider. We introduce this subject with a simple division of communication media into two broad types : observation and questioning.

Also we well consider the meters of whether to use structure and disguise. After that, each of the main media will be discussed and then their merits will be compared.

Through perceiving situations or actions, one can records and measure some descriptive facts. Observation includes both human means of perception and recording, which might be termed manual, and human means or mechanical. Manual is carried out by personal observations who see or hear the phenomena specified in the study.

Observation Method

A number of mechanical means of observation are in use today, some quite ingenious. Some have been around for many years, including attachments placed on television sets to record the time and channels when turned to telecasts. Tape recorders, traffic counters, and photography have long been used in marketing studies. An example of the last is the eye camera. Set up in laboratory to records the gaze motion of the eyes of a subject who is looking at an advertisement. A very notable development, in observation, stemmed from the adoption by food manufactures of the Universal Product Code (UPC) and its symbols (each one unique for a product) printed on labels. This was accompanied by electronic recognition devices of "read" or scan those codes at retail checkout counters. Projection of growth in scanners, by A.C. Nielsen Company, is that about 14,000 supermarkets will be using them when this book appears all of them sources of quick and exact data on movement through supermarkets.

Another important innovation, in observation methods, has been devised to "cut into" cable television reception of selected homes. With this, a commercial under test may be substituted for the scheduled commercial being transmitted to the rest of the homes on that cable service. This created data for determining the tested commercial's effects. One drawback has been that homes not hooked up to the cable were excluded. A more recent electronic creation enables commercials also to be cut into non-cable households.

In this Nielsen service, both forms of scanning (of supermarket purchases at checkouts and of home viewing of commercials) are combined with a third observation measurement that uses a 2500-member consumer panel who present an identification card when they purchase at the supermarket checkouts. With this, their particular purchases can be specifically identified in the UPC and can be linked with the scanning of their TV viewing. Other variables in the sales environment, observed by the agency's field personnel, are gathered that measure the promotional variables in each supermarket (e.g., displays, special pricing, and store advertisting). These variables are reported along with the scanner information, enabling them to be analyzed for their effects on sales (for any segment of the consumer panel).

The Nielsen service was chosen as our example, but other agencies offer similar service. This illustrates the amazing innovations that are changing marketing research. Also it shows the extent of information and analysis that can be gained from observation alone.

Means of Obtaining Marketing Information

Primarily three types of methods are broadly used for collection of primary information. These are observation, experiment and communication.

Observation Method

Observation is one of the methods of collecting data. It is used to get both past and current information. For example, instead of asking resepondents about their current behaviours, we may observe it and record our observation. Although it is not possible to observe past behaviours, we may observe the results of such behaviour. In a way, secondary data reflect the result the results of the past behaviours of people as also of past occurrences.

In marketing research, the observational method in not used frequently. All the same, as is used especially in marketing experimentation, a brief discussion is provided here.

At the outset, let us go through a faw examples indicating how observation may be used in marketing research. One of the factors influencing the sale of a branded product is how readily it is kept in stock. An interested manufacturer may send some observers to a sample of stores to find out how frequently the product is out of stock. Likewise, sales are also influenced by its display position in a store. A prominently displayed product will receive greater attention of the people visiting the store as against another product displayed in an obscure corner. Here, too, a manufacturer can ascertain from observers what sort of display his product is getting in selected stores and with what results.

- In order to ascertain what prices competitors charge, a manufacture may depute some observers to go round the stores.
- Today, certain mechanical devices are used for observation, for example, the eye camera, the pupilometric camera and the motion picture camera. A device known as the audiometer is attached to radio sets for recording automatically the station to which the redio set is turned. This is supposed to give an idea of the size of audience for a particular programme. Similarly, the size of audience watching a particular television programme can be ascertained through mechanical devices, which enable the manufacturer, who has sponsored that programme, analyzes whether it has been viewed by a sizeable

number or not. Furthermore, he can ascertain the reaction of those who actually viewed the programme by interviewing a sample of them. Thus, the observation method in conjunction with interviewing the respondents provides very useful information.

There are some advantages of observation as a method of collecting information. To being with, the direct observational technique enables a researcher to record behaviour as it occurs. In contrast, other techiniques record the data mostly retrospectively on the basis of the respondent's report after the event. Another merit of direct observation is that it can be used regardless of whether the respondent is willing to report or not.

In a field survey, if an enumerator comes across an unwilling and hostile respondent, he cannot collect the desired information. But, this problem does not arise at all in the case of direct observation. Yet another advantage of observation is that it can be used even when it pertains to those who are unable to respond such as infants and animals.

There are, However, following limitations of this method :

• Firstly, only the current behaviour nor can one observe a person's future behaviour because the act of observation takes place in the present.

• Secondly, observation does not help us in gauging a person's attitude or opinion on a certain subject nor his knowledge of the same.

• Thirdly, the observational method is very slow and as such when a large number of persons are to be contacted, it becomes tedious because of the long time required for this purpose.

Apart from these inherent limitations of observation, there are certain difficulties too.

Difficulties in Observation

Following difficulties come in the way of accurate observation and cause it to become distorted.

These difficulties arise on account of :

(i) Inadequacies of our sense organs,

(ii) Interdependence of observation and inference, and

(iii) Effects of interaction between the observer and the observed.

The first set of difficulties arises on account of inadequacies of our sense - organs, which "operate in a highly variable, erratic and selective manner." Several studies, conducted by psychologist, how that the perception of a man depends on several factors such as his freshness, interest, and freedom from interruption. The more favourable the conditions, the more receptive the person will be to outside impressions. Further, objects that are large or clear and sounds that are repetitive are likely to receive greater attention of the person.

Other difficulties arises on account of the interdependence of observation and inference.

All perception, arise on account of the interdependence of observation and inference.

All perception, after the first weeks of life, is compounded to the immediate experience and of the stored experience. Anything that impinges on our senses conveys a meaning to us largely to the extent that we relate it to what we already know.

Observation and inference are inspirable

This means that whetever an observer sees he tries to explain or interpet it on the basis of his past experience. Thus, the observer inference problem is the main difficulty in as much as the observer can draw wrong inferences from observations. The third set of difficulties crops up because of the effects of interaction between the observer and observed. This may have two distinct dangers. First, persons being observed may become self-conscrious of the observation and this may influence their normal behaviour. Second, observation may get distorted merely because one more person, the observer, is present and people are conscious of his presence.

To Goode and Hatt, science begins with observation and then one has to finally return to observation for verification of truth. This method is used to get the current information of events happening around the respondent. The researcher observes and records the current behaviour of the respondent instead of asking questions. Though it is not possible to observe the past behaviour of respondents, the result of past behaviour occurring at present can be observed.

In marketing research, observation method may be used as a sole means of gathering data or it may be used in conjunction with other means of data collection, whenever there is need to gather the information on current behaviour. This method can suitably be applied with less cost and more accuracy. However, in some research problems of specific circumstances, observation is the only means of gathering relevant data. For example, to know the competitive price of a product, the researcher will have to observe the price behaviour of competitor's products by shopping and observing the same. The alternative methods may not reveal the information accurately. Because the respondents generally do not report even remember the brand names. Brand usage reports of reputed brands generally show a 'hale effect', on upward bias reflecting the prestige the respondents feels by being associated with that brand.

Green and Tull have classified the observation method into different categories like audit, recording devices and direct observation as discussed below.

Audit

Audit is an assessment of activities of the level of distributors and consumers which is performed frequently with certain time intervals. Other research agencies may also give audited estimates regarding market size, market share, market dispersion, purchasing pattern, results of promotional efforts, impact of pricing etc. This facilitates second-hand information; therefore, salesforce is generally 'employed' by the manufactureres to perform their own audits to obtain first-hand information. Besides, it ensures that salespersons regularly check inventories and prices as a routine activity. The whole process of audit at the level of distribution/retailer is called Distribution Audit.

On the other hand, when audit is performed at the end of consumer to take our inventory of brands, quantities and package sizes it is called Pantry Audit. This activity is relatively costlier in terms of other reporting systems. In pantry audit, inconspicuous labels are generally attached on package of the products depicting the date of putting them into the inventory. When the audit is combined with questioning of the consumer, an estimate of usage can easily be made.

When carrying out retail audits are :

- In-store availability of product/brand;
- Types of outlets (by owner, location, specialty);
- Sales volume cross-tabbed with type and location;
- Pricing of product/brand cross-tabbed with type/location of outlet;
- Display value;
- Customer demand;
- Resulting market share and rank/position of product/brand.

It must be noted that there are no readily available retail universe data. The design of a retail audit is critical to the success of the project. The data obtained from the retail audit is useful for carrying out:

- Identification of market opportunities
- Trend analyses and forecasting
- Studying market structure
- Prioritization of markets
- Conducting analyses of competitions
- Product portfolio analysis
- Understanding changes in distribution
- Pricing trend analysis.
- Consumer Panel

There's nothing (consumer) panel data can tell us that we don't already know from scanner data. Consumer panels are a unique tool that can enable a clever researcher to examine dynamic longitudinal changes in behaviours, attitudes, and perceptions. Consumer panels can also be an overly costly, excessive generator of unused data.

Consumer Panels

There are two basic kinds of consumer panels.

In the first kind, respondents report essentially the same information repeatedly over some period of time. The chief examples of these kinds of panels are the syndicated purchase panels using store and home, termed as, continuous panels.

The second kind of panel offer can be measured through a before-and-after design, using a panel approach. Thus, a sample of families might be interviewed initially to gather information on their purchases of soft drinks, possibly over several weeks to obtain a good idea of their "steady state" purchasing patterns. A special deal for a particular brand is then introduced, and the purchases of the same sample are monitored for perhaps every week for three months. In this way, sampling variation is minimized and both short-term and long-term effects of the deal are obtained. Topics, termed as discontinuous access panels.

Both kinds of panels come in all different forms. Panel studies can involve data collection at widely different intervals varying anywhere from a day to several years between waves of interviews. Panel operators are continuously faced with the decision about how often panel members should be contacted and asked to report. Contacting the panel either too frequently or too infrequently may lead to reduced cooperation.

The benefits of continuous consumer panels

1. The effect of a special offer can be measured through a before and after design using a panel approach. Thus, a sample of families might be interviewed initially to gather information on their purchases of soft drinks, possibly over several weeks to obtain a good idea of their "steady state" purchasing patterns. A special deal for a particular brand is then introduced, and the purchases of the same sample are monitored for perhaps every week for three months. In this way, sampling variation is minimized and both short-term and long-term effects of the deal are obtained.

2. A static consumer panel of families with young children might be set upo to monitor the acceptance of new lien of toys. In this case no type of experimental treatment is involved. Rather, information is obtained, say, every month on the toy purchases of the families. In this may, data are compiled on the types of families that are buying any of the new toys, how soon the toys are purchased after they have been placed on the market, and how many of the toys are purchased by each family.

3. A dynamic consumer panal might be used to keep track of the purchases of frozen foods of one brand in relation to other brands. By obtaining such data every week for several years, very detailed information can be obtained on what sorts of families are purchasing each major brand and on thew change in market shares of the different brand over time amoung different groups of consumers. Also estimates can be derived of the extent to which purchasers remain loyal to different brands.

4. Diary method,

5. Internet as a sources of data,

6. Interviewing.

7. Questionnaire

Recording Devices

Many electro-mechanical cad gets have been in use of marketing research to observe the behabviour of respondents. These devices are meant for recording the behaviour in natural as well as controlled laboratory settings. Important recording devices - an eye camera, pupitometric cemera, psycho galvanomether, motion picture camera, andiometer etc.

For laboratory studies, the eye-camera is an aid to record the eye movements in relation to the specific location of material on a page. The pattern of eye movements through which the advertisement is seen or read by the respondents is recorded by the eye-camera. On the basis of analysis it can be identified as which part of the advertisement attracts, attention and takes greater time for rading the message by a viewer. This device is largely confined to the prestesting of advertising. Another important device for laboratory studies is pupilometric camera which photographs eye movements which identifies the correlation between the interest aroused and the visual stimulus responsible for the same on the basis of dilation and restriction of the eye pupil. There are proved indications that the extent of pupil dilation can depict the degree of interest shown by the respondent in reading or seeing an advertisement. The psychogalvanometer is another device to measure the extent of the respondent's immediate reaction to the advertisement. It measures the role of perspiration of the body when there is an excitement as a result of stimulation of advertisement. All these devices facilitate detailed observations of behaviour that could not be made otherwise. It also provides the permanent records of the behaviour of respondents which can be used for further reference. Observation in laboratory situation is helpful to control the extraneous variables causing the behaviour of people.

However, when the behaviour of people outside the laboratory is different in natural situation, the aforesaid devices may predict irrelevant and inaccurate results. Therefore, different devices are applied to record respondent behaviour. Hidden motion camera is a device which is used to record the movements and actions of buyers in the real situation. The subject is unaware of the application of this camera to measure his movements. For example, the analysis of photographs of the camera reveals that the buyers spend fairly more time and are more careful to see the information on the label, the television set is turned on and off and the channels to which it is fixed up. It is installed in the television sets of a panel of selected families. It helps to chalk out the programme to position the T.V. commercial aids on the basis of greater viewship.

Questioning

Attractive as observation may be as the medium for gathering data, it is very limited in its uses and its data. In the majority of research problems, the required information can be gained only by asking for it. This is done mainly by interviewing, but also data may be obtained through self administered questionnaires distributed by main and other ways. There are several means by which questioning can be carried out, which we will categorize as personal, telephone, and mail. Each will be discussed under separate headings.

Direct Observation

When the behaviour of a person is observed as and when it occurs it is called direct observation. The shopping behaviour of people is observed which may determine the relative, effects of different variables such as displays, availability, attention of sales assistent, reliance on salesperson advice, quantity purchased, brand chosen etc. Direct observation helps to determine the inventory level, waiting line, product line, location of the shop. Another mode of direct observation is participant observation in which the observer actually participates in the shopping activities of a group under study.

The observation methods have been classified differently as given below :

(i) **Simple Direct Observation**: Where the observer acts and appears like a shopkeeper and observes the regular customers without acknowledging the customers.

(ii) **Structured Observation** is used when the research problem has been formulated in very clear words and if the observer has been told specifically as what is to be observed.

(iii) **Unstructured Observation** refers to the situation in which the observer is placed in a particular place and asked to observe those activities whichever he thinks appropriate.

(iv) **Contrived Observation** refers to an appropriate situation which is established for observation so that observation is made in a more effective manner.

(v) **Indirect Observation** implies the observation of effects rather than behaviour of the respondents. The observer looks for physical traces of behaviour. For example, to observe the consumption of certain products, the observer may see the empty packages of the same as is done in pantry audit.

Advantages

It enables the observer to record the behaviour as it occurs which reduces the bias to a greater extent.

There is no need of seeking co-operation of the respondents as needed in the survey method. It helps in gathering information accurately within time framework.

It is very useful method for different spread out conditions like

(i) when no other technique can supply the desired information

(ii) when the accuracy of information is doubtful through other techniques and

(iii) when a high degree of accuracy is urgently needed.

The gathered information are more objective and correct.

Disadvantages

1. The observation method measures the current behaviour and ignores the past or future behaviour of respondents.

2. The observer will have to be present for recording the current events which takes more time that too uncertain.

3. The negligence or prejudices of the observer may give wrong results of the observation.

4. It does not help to elicit the respondents' attitude, opinion or knowledge on certain subjects.

Experiment Method

This method is used in the laboratory setting when the researcher goes for testing various alternatives frequently in controlled situation. After analysis of the tested alternatives he may advise as to which is the best in terms of profitability. A retailer decides to establish new point of purchase to see how it words, the marketer offers a new incentive package for sales of certain items, an advertising agency compares print media advertising with T.V. advertising etc. are some of the example of experiment method of gathering information.

The experiment methods involves the manipulation if one or more variables by experimenter to measure the effects on one or more other variables. Experimental method is a special type of investigation which is used for determining how and what form the variable being related to one another. A variable being manipulated is called independent variable. A variable that will reflect the impact of the independent variable is called dependent variable. The point of purchase (POP) display of retailer is an independent variable whereas the impact of the pop display in the form of increased sales turnover is dependent variable in the above example. This experiment is sought to establish the extent to which particular displays would cause a change in sales. Thus experiment is oriented towards establishing and measuring causal relationships among the variables under consideration.

Experiments are defined as studies in which implementation involves an intervention by the observer beyond the requirements for measurement. Basically, the experimentation can be of two types such as laboratory experimentation which is introduced in an artificial or laboratory setting and field experimentation which is conducted in the field. Laboratory experiments are used in the initial testing of new products, package designs, advertising theory and copy. Laboratory experiments isolate the research in a physical situation apart from the routine of ordinary living and by manipulating one or more independent variable under rigorously specified, operationalized and controlled conditions. This isolation allows the researcher to be sure that the same experimental procedure will produce the same results if repeated with similar subjects.

Field experiments are characterized by a high degree of realism which is obtained in the market place where the researcher does not have control over extraneous variables. This lack of control reduces internal validity of field experiments. However, this setting tends to increase their generalizability.

A marketing researcher uses this method of data collection for identifying numerous marketing strategies such as training method for sales personnel, the best incentive methods, the appropriate pricing panel, the best advertisement programmer etc.

Advantages

- This method is convenient and useful in test marketing.
- This method helps in sales forecasting under controlled environment.
- This method facilitates to solve the problems which cannot be tackled by any other technique.
- It is helpful in decision-making regarding the product and promotion mix elements.

Disadvantages

- This method cannot work independently therefore it is essential to use other techniques for better results.
- It is more expensive and time consuming.
- The experimentation may not claim actual happening as experiment is help under controlled variables which may not be prevalent in practice.

Communication or Survey Interview Method

Communication method involves the questioning of respondents to obtain the desired information with the help of questionnaire. In other words, it can be termed as 'interview technique' or survey method. In marketing research, the correct solution of marketing problems depends upon the availability of adequate and appropriate information. Hence, survey method is the approach which seeks information from the respondents by questioning. Survey research is the most common method of gathering primary information for marketing solutions as they provide adequate and appropriate information on attitudes, feelings, belief, past behaviour, knowledge, personal characteristics and other descriptive information.

Survey method is concerned with interviewing techniques specially with administration of questionnaires. Survey research studies the universe (population) by selecting and studying samples chosen from the same to discover the relative incidence, distribution and interrelationships of related variables.

There may be different name of this method like survey, communication, interview or questionnaire but the process is the same. Hence, finally survey research is the systematic gathering of information from respondents for the purpose of understanding and/or predicting some aspect of the behaviour of the population of interest (Tull and Hawkins). Therefore, the survey researcher, to get adequate and approapriate information, must be concerned with sampling, questionnaire design, questionnaire administration and analysis.

Types of Interviews

Interviews can be classified by their degree of structure, disguiseness disgracers of the questionnaire, directions of directions of awareness to the respondents and disguisenses of purpose of the interviewer. According to Tull and Hawkins, the interviews can be classified as under :

(i) Structured Direct Interview: is generally conducted to obtain descriptive information by using a formal questionnaire consisting of non-disguised questions to gather the facts. It is a simple prespecified set of direct questions. The interviewer will be expected to ask the questions in the order given in the questionnaire. Therefore, the exact wording of the questions can be worded out carefully to reduce the misunderstanding and maintain uniformity in interpretation of questions by the respondents, pretesting should always be done for such an interview. This type of interview requires extensive pre-preparation at the initial stage but needs less highly trained interviewers and interpreters. Editing, tabulation and analyzis of information is easier as the questions are standardised. Hence, it is less costlier. If the preparation of questionnaire design is thorough, this type of interview it can gather the required information. Hence, it is most commonly used type of interview in marketing research.

(ii) Unstructured: Direct interview is conducted by the interviewer who is given certain general guidelines on the nature of information to be gathered. The interviewer is not free to specify the wording and order of questions in the questionnaire. This type of interview is useful in developing a clearer understanding of the marketing problem at a preliminary stage. The firm interested in joining a new product manufacturing may be interested in information of consumers' attitudes, suggestions and experiences which can be elicited through pilot interviews. Pilot interviews are unstructured and direct which may identify the areas to be included in the questionnaire. Further, it will focus upon in depth interview in which the interviewer will ask all the relevant questions from all aspects to gather information regarding the particular product until he is satisfied with its adequacy. The interviewer frames the questions with inherent flexibility to ensure that the respondents understand fully. The questionnaire is administered to seek maximum information. It requires high degree of knowledge and skill in the interviewer to frame the questionnaire and conduct the extensive and intensive interview. Further, editing, tabulation and analysis become more complicated as a result of varied order of interviewing.

(iii) Structural Indirect Interview: It is psychiatrists' approach to gather maximum information. It is believed that the target respondent does not respond to direct questions correctly therefore, there is need to employ disguised techniques to extract the relevant information. This approach relies upon the fact that the more unstructured, disguised and ambiguous a stimulus, more temptations will be there for the respondent to reveal his hidden emotions, needs, motivation, attitudes and values. The ambiguity will compel the respondent to reveal his own alternatives and interpretation which otherwise would have not been told. The revealed interpretation through these projective methods is supposed to be more accurate and realistic. Because it is a matter of fact that individual's unstructured stimulus situation is indicative of his basis perceptions of the phenomenon. The description involves a complete projection of characteristics of personality to the situation prescribed.

Structured indirect interview or projective techniques can be administered through various techniques such as word association, sentence completion, story writing etc.

(a) Word Association

Word association tests are simple and easy to understand and conduct. Here the respondent is asked to give the first word that comes into his mind. The test words are sometimes dispensed throughout the list and are intermixed with some control words to conceal the purpose of the study. In this way, the respondent may be asked to add the immediate word coming to his mind. Single word association tests are invariably useful in choosing the brand name, brand memory and brand loyalty. On the basis of frequency of researcher may reach to a conclusion for naming brand for a particular product or pepresenting of a particular brand.

(b) Sentence Completion

The researcher asks the respondent to complete the incomplete sentences in the sentence completion tests. It is generally administered to uncover the emotional responses to the marketing situations. These incomplete sentences must be able to disclose the model attitude of the respondent to the product or marketing situation. The following are the illustrations of sentence completion tests :

- I like Lahar Pepsi because ....
- People who smoke Wills cigarette feel that ....
- I changed my Maruti car because ....
- I use Nescafe coffee because ....

The respondent is instruced to write the first reaction fo complete the sentences, when a respondent completes such sentences he discloses some emotional values and tension. In order to trace the true emotions, the expert in the field of clinical psychology should be appointed/hired.

(c) Story Writing

The respondent is asked to write a story on the basis of a picture given to him. This pictorial interpretation may reveal the perception of individuals which builds the basis for decision-making in the marketing areas. These decisions must address to the perception created by the respondents. It is a common form of Thematic Apperception Test (TAT) to describe the pictorial situation. Cartoon is another form for which the respondent may be asked to describe the same. Some of the descriptions related to cartoons may be interpreted as below:

On seeing the low price tag on a product, it may be interpreted that the quality of the product is poor or the buyer is interested in buying the same.

On seeing the high price take on a product, it may interpreted as the product is of good quality which the buyer may or may not be in a position to buy the same and so forth.

The researcher may analyze and interpret the association of price and quality for the product.

(d) The Paired Pictures

In this technique, paired pictures are shown to the respondents to gather their preceptions. For example, one picture shows a child eating fast food of a popular brand (say, Maggi) and another shows a similarly dressed child eating fast food of and another brand (say, Top Raman). The respondents are then asked to say any story which comes to their minds about these pictures. The difference in interpretation of these pictures is occasioned by different attitudes they have towards the fast food.

(iv) Unstructured : Indirect interview is seldom used in marketing research. In this interview, the respondent is encouraged to talk about whatever is of interest to him. The interviewer probles into the process occasionally to keep the respondent on the main track. This is attempted to secure the advantages of disguised approach to elicit subconscious and hidden motives and attitudes.

Surveying Media

Survey is the widely used method of obtain information in marketing research due to its flexibility in use. There is also a fear of bias if not conducted properly. One should not get confused that survey is different from the interview techniques. In fact, it is a part of communication approach of gathering information. With the help of a questionnaire, interviews are conducted as a part of survey technique to gather information. The following types of interview techniques are generally used:

(a) Personal Interview: In a personal interview, the interviewer asks the questions to the respondent in a fact-to-face meeting. Personal interview can be conducted at the respondent's home or at central location or at shopping point. The interviewer introduces himself to the potential respondents and attempts to ask certain questions framed or unframed in the questionnaire. These responses may be recorded by taking notes or recording on taps recorder. This techniques is widely used and considered most successful in India as it provides critical types of information such as knowledge, intentions, demographic characteristics, attitudes, opinions and life styles. It also provides the opportunity to reach virtually all the sample units to obtain a better representation. Apart from more flexibility for adopting and interpreting questions as the situation requires, it also gives the opportunity to obtain maximum information through lengthy discussions.

(b) Telephone Interview: Telephone interview is a presentation of questions to the respondent and gathering the responses on related questions by telephone. It is used to gather the quick responses. It has become more popular in the countries where tale-communication network has spread well. In India also this technique is emerging gradually. Computer Assisted Telephone Interviewing (CATI) is a new system which involves programming a survey questionnaires directly into the computer in which the interviewer asks the questions through television sets adjusted with CATI and records the same on the terminal key boards. Telephone interview provides a number of advantages in addition to speed and economy. It is frequently easier to get the cooperation of people over the where the respondents have to spare some time on telephone out of their busy schedule which is perhaps not possible in personal interview.

Important disadvantage of telephone interviews are the sampling errors and bias which can't be detected on telephone. Further, the inability to include non-subscribers in the sample may not give adequate representation ultimately affecting the findings.

(c) Mail Interview: The mail interview involves collection of information through questionnaires sent by post along with instructions and self-addressed envelope. The respondents fill up the mail questionnaires and return duly filled at their own convenience. Mail questionnaires provide a greater degree of variability at relatively low cost. There is no scope of interviewers bias to influence the respondents. In case of desire to maintain anonymity the respondents' identity can be kept secret. The serious disadvantage of mail interview is non-response from indifferent respondents. To counteract this bias, it is necessary to contact a sample of the non-respondents by other means. Besides, it is time consuming due to mailing process and it is difficult to ensure the understanding of questions by the respondents.

Using Diaries in Social Research

Biographers, historians and literary scholars have long-considered diary documents to be of major importance for telling history. More recently, sociologists have taken seriously the idea of using personal documents to construct pictures of social reality from the actors' perspective (see Plummer's book *Documents of Life*). In contrast of these 'journal' types of accounts, diaries are used as research instruments to collect detailed information about behaviour, events and other aspects of individuals' daily lives.

Self-completion diaries have a number of advantages over other data collections methods. First, diaries can provide a reliable alternative to the traditional interview method for events that are difficult to recall accurately or that are easily forgotten.

Second, like other self-completion methods, diaries can help to overcome the problems associated with collecting sensitive information by personal interview. Finally, they can be used to supplement interview data to provide a rich source of information on respondents' behaviour and experiences on a daily basis. The 'diary interview method' where the diary-keeping period is followed by an interview asking detailed questions about the diary entries is considered to be one of the most reliable methods of obtaining information.

The Subject Matter of Diary Surveys

A popular topic of investigation for economists, market researchers, and more recently sociologists, has been the way in which people spend their time. Accounts of time use can tell us much about quality of life, social and economic well-being an patterns of leisure and work. The 'time-budget' involved respondents keeping a detailed log of how they allocated their time during the day. More qualitative studies have used a "standard day" diary, which focuses on a typical day in the life of an individual from a particular group or community.

One of the most fruitful time budget endeavours, initiated in the mid-60s, has been the Multinational Time, Budget, Time Use Project. Its aim was to provide a set of procedures and guidance on how to collect and analyze time-use data so that valid cross-national comparisons could be made.

Two other major areas where diaries are often used are:

- Consumer expenditure and
- Transport planning research.

Other topics covered using diary methods are social networks, health, illness and associated behaviour, diet and nutrition, social work and other areas of social policy, clinical psychology and family therapy, crime behaviour, alcohol consumption and drug usate, and sexual behaviour. Diaries are also increasingly being used in market research.

Using Diaries in Surveys

Diary surveys often use a personal interview to collect additional background information about the household and sometimes about behaviour or events of interest that the diary will not capture (such as large items of expenditure for consumer expenditure surveys). A placing interview is important for explaining the diary keeping procedures to the respondent and a concluding interview may by used to check on the completeness of the recorded entries. Often retrospective estimates of the behaviour occurring over the diary period are collected at the final interview.

Diary Design and Format

Diaries may be open format, allowing respondents to records activities and events in their own words, or they can be highly structured where all activities are pre-categorized. An obvious advantage of the free format is that it allows for greater opportunity to record and analyze the data. However, the labour-intensive work required to prepare and make sense of the data may render it unrealistic for projects lacking time and resources, of where the sample is large. Although the design of a diary will depend on the detailed requirement of the topic under study, there are certain design aspects, which are common to most. Below are sets of guidelines recommended for anyone thinking about designing a diary. Furthermore, the amount of piloting requireed to perfect the diary formal should not be underestimated.

1. An A4 booklet of about 5 to 20 pages is desirable, depending on the nature of the diary. Disappointing, as it might seem, most respondents do not carry their diaries around with them.

2. The inside cover page should contain a clear set of instructions on how to complete the diary. This should stress the importance of recording events as soon as possible after they occur and how the respondent should try not to let the diary keeping influence their behaviour.

3. A model example of a correctly completed diary should feature on the second page.

4. Depending on how long a period the diary will cover, each page denoting either a week, a day of the week or a 24 hour-period or less. Pages should be clearly ruled up as a calendar with prominent headings and enough space to enter all the desired information (such as what the respondent was doing, at what time, where, who with and how they felt at the time, and so on).

5. Checklists of the items, events or behaviour to help jog the diary keeper's memory should be printed somewhere fairly prominent. Very long lists should be avoided since they may be off-putting and confusing to respondents. For a structured time budget diary, an exhaustive list of all possible relevant activities should be listed together with the appropriate codes. Where more than one type of activity is to be entered, that is, primary and secondary (or background) activities, guidance should be given on how to deal with "competing" or multiple activities.

6. There should be an explanation of what is meant by the unit of observation, such as a "session", an "event" or a "fixed time block". Where respondents are given more freedom in naming their activities and the activities are to be coded later, it is important to give strict guidelines on what type of behaviour to include, what definitely to exclude and the level of detail required. Time budget diaries without fixed time blocks should include columns for start and finish times for activities.

7. Appropriate teminology or lists of activities should be designed to meet the needs of the sample under study, and if necessary, different versions of the diary should be used for different groups.

8. Following the diary pages it is useful to include a simple set of questions for the respondent to complete, asking, among other things, whether the diary-keeping period was atypical in any way compared to usual daily life. It is also good practice to include a page at the end asking for the respondents' own comments and clarifications of any peculiarities relating to their entries. Even if

these remarks will not be systematically analyzed, they may prove helpful at the editing or coding stage.

Data Quality and Respones Rates

In addition to the types of errors encountered in all survey methods, diaries are especially prone to errors arising from respondent conditioning, incomplete recording of information and under-reporting, inadequate recall, insufficient cooperation and sample selection bias.

Diary Keeping Period

The period, over which a diary is to be kept needs to be long enough to capture the behaviour or events of interest without jeopardizing successful completion by imposing an overly burdensome task for collecting time-use data, anything from one to three-day diaries may be used. Household expenditure surveys usually place diaries on specific days to ensure an even coverage across the week and distribute their fieldwork over the year to ensure seasonal variation in earnings and spending is captured.

Reporting Errors

In household expenditure surveys, it is routinely found that the first day and first week of diary keeping shows higher reporting of expenditure than the following days. This is also observed for other types of behaviour and the effects are generally termed "first day effects". They may be due to respondents changing their behaviour as a result of keeping the diary (conditioning), or becoming less consientious than when they started the diary.

Recall errors may also extend to 'tomorrow' diatires. Respondents often write down their entries at the end of a day and only a small minority are diligent (and perhaps obsessive) diary keepers who carry their diary with them at all times. Expenditure surveys find that an intermediate visit from an interviewer during the diary keeping period helps preserve 'good' diary keeping to the end of the period.

Literacy

All methods that involve self-completion of information demand that the respondent has a reasonable standard of literacy. Thus the diary sample and the data may be biased towards the population of competent diary keepers.

Participation

The best response rates for diary surveys are achieved when diary keepers are recruited on a face-to-face basis, rather than by post. Personal collection of diaries also allows any problems in the completed diary to be sorted out on the spot. Success may also depend on the quality of interviewing staff that should be highly motivated, competent and well briefed. Appealing to respondent's altruistic nature, reassuring them of confidentiality and offering incentives are thought to influence co-operation in diary surveys. One research company gives a 10 pound postal order for completion of their fourteen-day diary and other surveys offer lottery tickets or small promotional items.

Coding, Editing and Processing

The amount of work needed to process a diary depends largely on how structured it is. For many large-scale diary surveys, the interviewer while still in the field does part has the editing and coding process. Following this is an intensive editing procedure, which includes checking entries against information collected in the personal interview. For unstructured diaries, involving coding of verbatim entries, the processing can be very labour intensive; in much the same way as it is for processing qualitative interview transcripts. Using highly trained coders and a rigorous unambiguous coding scheme is very important particularly where there is no clear demarcation of events or behaviour in the diary entries. Clearly, a well-designed diary with a coherent pre-coding system should cut down on the degree of editing and coding.

Relative cost of Diary Surveys

The diary method is generally more expensive than the personal interview, and personal placement and pick-up visits are more costly than postal administration. The interviewers usually make at least two visits and are often expected to spend time checking the diary with the respondent. If the diary is unstructured, intensive editing and coding will push up the costs. However, these costs must be balanced against the superiority of the diary method in obtaining more accurate data, particularity of the recall method gives poor results. The ratio of costs for diaries compared with recall time budgets are of the order of three or four to one

Computer Software for Processing and Analysis

Probably the least development area relating to the diary method is the computer storage and analysis of diary data. One of the problems of developing software for processing and manipulating diary data is the complexity and bulk of the information collected. Although computer assisted methods may help to reduce the amount of manual preparatory work, there are few packages and most of them are custom built to suit the specifics of a particular project. Time budget researchers are probably the most advanced group of users of machine-readable diary data and the structure these data allows them to use traditional statistical packages for analysis. More recently, methods of analysis based on algorithms for searching for patterns of behaviour in diary data are being used. Software development is certainly an area which merits future attention.

For textual diaries, qualitative software packages such as The ETHNOGRAPH can be used to code them in the same way as interview transcripts.

Archiving Diary Data

In spite of the abundance of data derived from diary surveys across a wide range of disciplines, little is available to other researchers for secondary analysis (further analysis of data already collected). This is perhaps not surprising given that the budget for many diary surveys does not extend to systematic processing of the data. Many diary surveys are small-scale investigative studies that have been carried out with very specific aims in mind. For these less structured diaries, for which a common coding scheme is neigther feasible, nor possibly desirable, an answer to public access is to deposit the original survey documents in an archive. This kind of data bank gives the researcher access to original diary documents allowing them to make use of the data in ways to suit their own research strategy. However, the ethics of making personal documents public (even if in the limited academic sense) have to be considered.

Internet as a Sources of Data

The expansion of the internet over the decade has provided the researcher with a range of new opportunities for finding information, networking, conducting research, and disseminating research results.

Through the use of tools such as online focus groups, electronic mail, and online questionnaires, the internet opens up new possibilities for conducting research. It offers, for example:

1. Shorter time-frames for collecting and recording data : e-mail messages can be saved and analyzed in qualitative data packages, for example, while online surveys can be captured directly into a database.

2. The possibility of conducting interviews and focus groups by e-mail, with realted savings in costs and time.

3. New "communities" to serve as the object of social scientific enquiry.

4. Opportunities for including mixed multiple media in questionnaires.

On the other hand, these opportunities also raise new challenges for the researcher, such as:

- Problems of sampling.
- The ethics of conducting research into online communities.
- Physical access and skills required to use the technologies involved.
- Accuracy and reliability of information obtained from online sources.
- The changed chronology of interaction resulting from asynchronous communication.

Internet is a useful media to get valuable information and resrults of various surveys. Access to computer-led data becomes handy in solving many complex mysteries, related to the market place. The 10 C's outlined here, provide criteria to be considered while evaluating internet resources :

1. Content

What is the intent of the content? Are the title and author identified? Is the content "juried?" Is the content "popular" or "scholarly", satiric pr serious? What is the date of the document or article? Is the "edition" current? Do you have the latest version? (Is this important) How do you know?

2. Credibility

Is the author identifiable and reliable? Is the content credible? Authoritative? Should it be? What is the purpose of the information, that is, is it serious, satiric, humorous?

Is the URL extension .edu, .com, .gov or .org? What does this tell about the "publisher"?

3. Critical Thinking

How can we apply critical thinking skills, including previous knowledge and experience, to evaluate internet resources? Can we identify the author, publsher, edition, etc. as we would with a "traditionally" published resource? What criteria do we use to evaluate Internet resources?

4. Copyright

Even if the copyright notice does not appear prominently, someone wrote, or is responsible for, the creation of a document, graphic, sound or image, and the material falls under the copyright conventions. "Fall use" applies to short, cited excerpts, usually as an example for commentary or research. Materials are in the "public domain" if this is explicitly stated. Internet users, as users of print media, must respect copyright.

5. Citation

Internet resources should be cited to identify sources used, both to give credit to the author and to provide the reader with avenues for further research. Standard style manuals (print and online) provide some examples of how to cite internet documents, although these standards are not uniform.

6. Continuity

Will the internet site be maintained and updated? Is it now and will it continue to be free? Can we rely on this source over time to provide up-to-date information? Some good. edu sites have moved to .com, with possible cost implications. Other sites offer partial use for free, and charge fees for continued or in-depth use.

7. Censorship

Is our discussion list "moderated"? What does this mean? Does our search engine or index look for all words or are some words excluded? Is this censorship? Does our institution, based on its mission, parent organization or space limitations, apply some restrictions to internet use?

Consider censorship and privacy issues when using the internet.

8. Connectivity

If more than one user will need to access a site, consider each users' access and "functionality." How do users connect to the internet and what kind of connection does the assigned resource require? Does access to the resource require a graphical user interface? If it is a popular (busy) resource, will it be accessible in the time-frame needed? Is it accessible by more than one internet tool? Do users have access to the same internet tools and applications? Are users familiar with the tools and applications? Is the site "viewable" by all web browsers?

9. Comparability

Does the interest resource have an identified comparable print or CD ROM data set or source? Does the interest site contain comparable and complete information? (For example, some newspapers have partial but not full text information on the internet.) Do we need to compare data or statistics over time? Can we identify sources for comparable earlier or later data? Comparability of data may or may not be important, depending on our project.

10. Context

What is the context for our research? Can we find "anything" on our topic, that is, commentary, opinion, narrative, statistics and our quest will be satisfied? Are we looking for current or historical information? Definitions? Research studies or articlses? How does internet information fit in the overall information context of our subject? Before we start searching, define the research context and research needs and decide what sources might be best to use to successfully fill information needs without data overload.

Conclusion

This part of course has discussed the means of obtaining information from the respondents viz. observation, experiment and communication-directly with the respondetns through different interviews techniques. In the same part, surveying media such as personal telephone and mail interview have been discussed in brief. It is important to note that every technique of information collection has its application to the related area depending upon availability of resources, time urgency, nature of respondents, type of marketing problem and so on. Therefore, depending upon the requirements of marketing situation, the researcher must choose the technique of obtaining information from other respondents.

Case study

Product Testing on the Internet

Procter & Gamble (P&G) is offering a number of different products and/or product versions over the internet that we can't buy at our local retail store. But a consumer can go the Procter & Gamble Website (wwp.gcom) and under 'Sevices and offers' a consumer can click on Try and Buy'. Then, for a number of products, P&G will offer us a free sample, a cents-off coupon, or the ability to purchase the actual product online. If the purchasers of a new item offered on the Website give it great reviews, then P&G will consider making the product available in retail stores.

Although P&G only began testing products online in 1998, the company already is doing 40 present or its 6,000 product tests and related research projects online. One successful new product that was launched as a result at online testing is Crest Whitestrips, a home tooth-bleaching kit. Despite its $44 retail price, P&G was able to sell 144,000 whitening kits online over an eight-month period, thereby providing evidence that the public would not balk at the product's rather steep price. When the product was finally introduced nationally into retail stores, consumers spent almost $50 million on kits in the first three months.

What personality traits do we believe many of the consumers who buy try products found on the Protect & Gamble Website might share in common?

******

Chapter – 11

Interview

The method of interview is used very used very extensively in every field of modern research. In interview, a research scientist or some one authorised by him for the purpose meets individuals to interrogate them about various things. An interview is a direct method of enquiry. The purpose of interview, however, is not to collect superficial details about the interviewee, but is rather to problem into the inner life of the interviewee. Therefore, the method of interview is direct as well as depth study. Emphasizing this point, Mrs. P.V. Young has observed, "The interview may be treated as a systematic method by which a person enters more or less imaginatively into the inner life of a comparative strange." In an interview a rapport is established between the interviewer and the interviewee. Not only is physical distance between them annihilated, the social and cultural barrier is also removed; and a free mutual flow of ideas to and fro takes place. Both create their respective impressions upon each other. The interview brings them both on the same level and an emotional attachment supervenes between them. This signal quality of bringing the scientist and layman into personal, emotional and intellectual contact marks research. In the other methods a formality and remoteness and data obtained by other methods with the result that the information and data obtained by other methods can never have the seal of reliability characteristic of the interview. In interview all formalities are laid down and the gate is opened for delving into the intellectual, emotional and subconscious stirrings of the interviewee. It is the sterling qualities of interview which enable a psychoanalyst to unravel the "depth" of man and go to the very bottom of his emotional pool.

However, in contrast to Mrs. Young's views, some modern scientists consider interview to be merely a formal affair. According to them there is no vital difference between writing down of responses or report by the respondents, and dictating them to someone in front of them, basically both are same. But the majority of modern scientists accepts the informal character of the interview. If an interview has to be formal, the interviewer approaches the respondents with a set of well defined questions and notes down their answers. He does not deviate at all from his belief and makes no effort to ask supplemental questions for classification. On the other hand, in an informal interview, the interviewer has the freedom to change the order of questions, explain their meaning and even rephrase them for better understanding. W.J. Goode and P.K. Hatt have observed that "Interviewing is fundamentally a process of modern interaction." In the interview two persons are not merely present at the same place, but also affect each other emotionally and intellectually. According to Vivien Palmar, "the interview constitutes a social situation between two persons, the psychological process involved requiring both individuals mutually respond though the social research purpose of the interview call for a varied response from the two parties concerned."

Major Aims of Interview

The foregoing discussion about the interview brings into relief the following aims of this methods :

1. **Direct Contact**: The first and the foremost aim of the interview method is to bring the scientist and the layman into direct contact so that both may know each other and understand the respective needs of each other. Furthermore, by direct contact the scientist is able to perceive imaginatively the social under currents and the personal dispositions of his respondents.

2. **Eliciting Intimate Facts**: There are many facts of personal life which a person does not like to reveal. All other methods are helpless in goading him to pass an information which he does not want to share. It is the aim to the interview not to waste time on facts which can be easily known by other methods. An interviewer concentrates on knowing the unique facts about a person. He can also persuade him to tell many intimate facts of his life.

3. **Establishing Hypothesis**: Sometimes the interviewee reveals such facts about the background of his peculiar attitudes, outlooks, aspirations and behavior as are not already in the comprehension of the scientists. These new revelations help him in forming new hypothesis about personal and social behaviour. For example, generally it is supposed that a man in whom the sex urge is very strong may seek its gratification outside the bounds of his marriage; but there are numerous cases, unravelled by depth interviews, in which the cause of straying outside marriage is not the powerful sex impulse but, most surprisingly, the sexual inadequacy. An unsatisfied person seeks satisfaction by various means available to him. Accordingly, now-a-days the usual hypothesis about Don-Juanism and nymphomania is not over-active sex

glands but the feeling of sexual inadequacy. The interview also helps or disprove the hypothesis of the scientist.

4. **Verification of Unique Ideals:** This is as a matter of fact a corollary of the foregoing point. When a psychologist or a sociologist entertains a novel idea about certain types of behaviour, it is always desirable to hold interviews with the persons concerned and see how far the ideas entertained are borne out by actual facts. For example, if a psychologist believes that sexual behaviour is unaffected by moral values and that every person, if given opportunity, would try homosexual, heterosexual and multiple sexual contacts, he must make a deep study of a large number of persons differing in cultural values, and see if his idea really is borne out by facts.

From the above discussion, it becomes evident that the purpose of interview is to obtain specialized information rather than study the general facts. The interviewer steps in to help in cases where other methods are inadequate. In the words of Dr. Lundberg, "The researcher is interested in the objective data secured from the interview such as income, number of children, their ages etc. and also in the personality of the information-his attitudes, prejudices, likes and dislikes as revealed by his verbal behaviour, including the subtle gestures that accompany it such as facial expression, tone of voice and so forth." Explaining the nature and purpose of the interview, Mrs. Young has rightly observed that interview is not an independent tool of research but is supplemental to other methods. Whereas the case studies can be prosecuted by interview, it can help to scrutinize and test the informations obtained by other methods of modern research.

Types of Interview

The types of interview have been classified by modern scientists differently from various points of view. The chief types of interview are the following –

1. **Classification according to formalness:** The formed classification of interview gives us two main types –

(i) Formal interview: In this type of interview the interviewer presents a set of well defined questions and notes down the answers of informant in accordance with the prescribed rules.

(ii) Informal interview: In contrast with the formal interview, the interviewer has full freedom to make suitable alterations in the question to suit a particular situation, in formal interview. He may revise the order or paraphrase the questions to suit the needs of the respondents.

2. **According to the number:** Another classification of interview is according to the number of persons taking part in it. Following are its types :

(i) Personal interview: In personal interview a single individual is interviewed. The personal interview helps to establish close personal contacts

between the interviewer and the interviewee and by its means detailed knowledge about intimate and personal aspects of the individual can be had. According to Bogardus, "Attitudes and changes in them may best be secured by the personal method *i.e.,* interview".

(ii) Group interview: As the name makes it plain the group interview is the opposite of the personal, because in it two or more persons are interviewees. The first is aimed at probing into the inner life and feelings of an individual, the group interview is suited for gathering routine information. Whereas the former is uneconomical of time and money, the latter economises both time and money, but compared with the former, the knowledge gained through the latter is very superficial and routine like.

3. **According to purpose**: The interviews have also been classified by the purpose for which they are help. Following are the types of this classification :

(i) Diagnostic interview: As the name makes clear, this types of interviewers, try to understand the cause or causes of a malady. In clinical psychology and psychoanalysis, the preliminary interviews with the patients are help with a purpose to grasp the nature and causes disease.

(ii) Treatment interview: If the cause of a psychological malady is diagnosed as non physical, further interviews help to bring to fore-conscious of the patient that his malady is due to this or that mental complex or faulty style of life. These interviews are christened 'Treatment interviews'.

(iii) Research interview: These interviews, as help to gather information pertaining to certain problem. The questions to be asked to gather the desired information are pre-determined and by asking them of the informations the data is collected. In as much as this data is gathered for the purpose of research into a problem, these are called 'Research Interview'.

(iv) Interviews to fulfil curiosity: These interviews, as the name implies, are help to satisfy some question lurking in the mind of a scientist. For example, if a scientist gets an idea that good lectures are delivered extempore, he has to interview some reputedly good lecturers whether they take extensive notes for delivering a lecture or not.

4. **According to the period of contact**: The different types of problems require different amount of time for contact with the respondents. The time can be short or long. According, two according to time are as follow :

(i) Short-contact interview: For filling-up schedules etc., single sitting of small duration suffices. Therefore, in researches of this types short-contact interview suffices.

(ii) Prolonged contact interview: In contract with research by schedule, the case-history method requires prolonged interviews. In these, establishment of close personal relations between the interviewer and interviewee is very likely.

5. **According to subject-matter**: The classification of interviews according to subject-matter gives us the following three types –

(i) *Qualitative interview:* The qualitative interviews are about complex and non-quantifiable subject-matter. For example, interviews held for case studies are qualitative, because the interviewer has to range over past, present and future to know enough about a case.

(ii) *Quantitative interview:* The quantitative interviews are those in which certain set facts are gathered about large number of persons. The census interviews are its example.

(iii) *Mixed interview:* In certain interviews both types of data-the routine and speciatlized- is sought, some of it is quantifiable while some is not. Therefore it is known as mixed interview.

6. **According to role**: Mrs. P. V. Young, while recognizing the above-mentioned categories of interview, has attached special significance to the classification of interviews according to the role assumed by the interviewer and the interviewees during the interview. Following are the types according to this classification :

(i) Non directed interview: This is also known as free or unstructured interview. This is a types of interview in which the interviewer exercises no control, provides no direction and has no brief or pre-determined set of questions to ask. The interviewer merely engages the interviewee in talk and encourages him to tell about his experiences and feelings. The informant is left free to narrate as well as explain his experiences. When the interviewee has discussed his experiences elaborately and offered their explanation, the interviewer rounds off the interview by summing it up and raising the remainder questions in the interview guide.

This type of interview is used in very special circumstances, particularly, when the researcher wishes to assess the amount of awareness a person has about certain problems and the manner in which he views them. The information thus gathered is made use of in preparation of schedule. Therefore, this type of interview is a preliminary study for a schedule. By gathering the impressions and attitudes of various persons towards a particular problem, it becomes possible to know the important aspects of the problem, and the ways in which these are viewed by the people. All this information is a *sin qua non* for a good schedule. This type of interview is also very useful in discussing the problem of social disorganization, the problem of divorce and other of marital discords. Again, this is the only method by which adequate information about underground activities can be obtained. This is an eminently suitable method for studying sexual deviations.

(ii) Focussed Interview: This type of interview has been employed by Robert K. Merton and his associates for studying the socio-psychological effects of mass media like Radio, Television, Cinema etc. They have enumerated four special features of focused interview which distinguish it from other types. These are :

(i) This type of interview takes place when the interviewees are in a specialized concrete situation. For example, when they have seen a particular film or heard a particular radio broadcast or are-witnesses of a social situation, under these circumstances they can give information about these things.

(ii) This type of interview is possible in those concrete circumstances which have been analyzed before hand, that is prior to the beginning of the interview.

(iii) The interview is taken on the basis of an interview Guide in which the field of inquiry and hypothesis are clearly stated.

(iv) In an interview of this the inner feelings and emotional attitudes of the interviewee vis-a-vis a given problem or situation are given particular attention.

The specialty of the focused interview is that by its means the personal reactions, emotional and intellectual orientation of the persons to be interviewed towards specific issues can be studied. Therefore, the focussed interview focusses attention on the background of emotional and intellectual atmosphere of the problem rather than its apparent features. The peculiar and unique quality of the focussed interview is that the interviewee cannot successfully conceal his reactions and sensibilities because the interviewer knows fully well before hand the reactions and responses likely to be made by the interviewees. He has analyzed these before undertaking the interview. Therefore, as soon as an interviewee tries to dodge or side track the issue he is pulled up. This type of interview has proved very useful in the study of situations of social tension. At times this type of interview serves to verify hypothesis. For example, it has been observed that the fear complexes which develop in human beings as a result of specialized propaganda affect their thinking and emotional tone vis-à-vis those situations. For example, if as a result of concerted propaganda, a particular community thinks of the other community in consistently hostile terms, the vary mention of that community or presence of its members would ignite hatred in the hearts of members of other community.

(iii) Repeated Interview: This type of interview is made when we wish to study the development process of a social psychological situation. According to Mrs. Young this type of interview is eminently suited to trace the development of process and to determine the factors or attitudes which are behind a given behaviour pattern or situation. Paul Lazarasfield and his associates have used

this method to study the voting behaviour of U.S. people in the successive American Presidential Elections. Though the repeated interview is very expensive of time and energy, we cannot study the developmental side of an issues by any other method.

Preparation for Interview

Before undertaking an interview, the researcher has to arm himself with knowledge of certain things and also make other necessary preparations. If he is not thus prepared, he will waste much time in unnecessary and irrelevant issues at the time of interview and will fail to make maximum use of the time available to him. The organisation of interview should be flexible and must leave room for new and unexpected developments. Before the interview the interviewer makes a tentative list of replies and reactions he expects of interviewees. He also notes the point requiring emphasis and the direction which must be provided to interview from time to time in order to minimise the detraction and maximize the eliciting of relevant informations. The pre-arrangement and prognostication about interview help to keep the interviewee in check and prevent his straying into dark and blind alleys. The preparedness also makes the interviewer alert and this alertness or his part gets transmitted to the interviewee who realizes that the interviewer means business.

The major stages of prior preparation for interview are the following :

1. **Anticipation of Responses**: The more complex issues involved in an interview are studied before-hand, and questions about these formulated. But the important thing is not writing down the questions before hand, because this is rather easy, but to guess the nature of replies. If an interviewer is able to make correct guesses about the replies, he has not to pause again in the interview and this if he is getting natural answers and that he is not being cheated.

2. **Knowledge of the subject matter**: The interviewer should be well appraised of the theoretical aspect of the interview. That is, he must have all literature available to him on the subject of research. For example, if he is studying the causes for rise in the incidence of divorce, he should know fully well the role that sex, money and status play in marriage. He should know every thing about sexual deviation, the kind of subliminal facilitation going on in society due to current mass media etc.

3. **Knowledge of the daily routine of the interviewee**: It is of crucial significance that an interviewer make right initial approach to the interviewee. In this connection the most important things is that the interviewee should be approached at a time when he is free and relaxed. To expect cooperation from him when he is busy and tense is foolish. In order not to disturb him at

unwanted hours, it is desirable to gather before band the knowledge about his daily routine.

4. **Introduction card:** Before starting the interviewer full introduction about himself. In this matter introduction slips given by the research organization are not very helpful; but a letter of introduction from some one well-known to the interviewee can be of great help.

5. **Interview of leaders:** Prior to interviewing the members of a group it is desirable to interview the leaders of the group, because they represent in outlook and culture their group and because their ideas are better formulated, the interview with leaders makes the interview of others very simple affair. Mrs. Young, in her study of molokans, first approached the leaders of that group.

6. **Selection of the respondents:** For the success of any research project it is essential to know who can be most helpful, who know most about the problem and who are likely to cooperate. Taking these factors into account, a selection of the respondents should be made. It is neither possible nor desirable to interview each and every member of a group.

7. **Fixation of time and place:** After preparing the list of interviewees or respondents, a decision regarding time and place of the interview should now be made. An advance information about this to the respondents is very essential. In fixing the time and place of the interview, the primary consideration is the mutual convenience.

Process of Interview

After the preparatory stage, the actual process of the interview begins.

1. **Introduction:** On meeting the interviewee, the interviewer should first of all introduce himself. The preparation of written letter of introduction is better than the verbal introduction. The letter induces confidence about the genuineness of the interviewer. The letter of introduction should be printed on the paper bearing the printed or embossed name and address of the research organization. The letter of introduction should be signed by a senior official of the organisation and besides introducing the interviewer it must make an earnest appeal of cooperation. The letter should be polite and couched in a language of gratitude. It should not take the interviewee for granted. It on reading the letter of introduction, the interviewee wishes to know more about the interviewer or the research project, his curiosity should be fully satisfied. On being fully satisfied the interviewee becomes ready for cooperation. At times the interviewee wishes to know why he has been selected out of so many persons of similar status, he may be told that his choice means that research organisation greatly values his cooperation and thinks him better placed to do the job than others. If the interviewee is called in the office of the research

organisation the process of introduction is completed at the time of fixing interview and there is no need for further introduction at the time of actual interview.

2. **Elucidation of the purpose of Interviewer:** Once the formality of introduction is over the interviewer must now explain to the interviewee in clear and intelligible terms the nature of the research project and what is expected to be achieved by it. How will it affect the interviewee? Does he stand to benefit by it any direct or indirect way? The questions like these must be plainly and honestly answered. The interviewer should not tell a lie or exaggerate the value or worth of the project. This may make the interviewee more cooperative: but his response may also suffer from the corresponding exaggeration or he may find it difficult to believe that mere interview can bring about such revolutionary changes.

3. **Beginning of Interview:** In the beginning of an interview the mood of seriousness has to be induced. If the atmosphere becomes light-hearted, the concentration of both interviewer and interviewee would sag. Therefore, the interviewer should begin asking question in full seriousness, and having asked the question must patiently wait for, and listen to the answer. The temptation of interfere in the middle should be curbed. Or when the interviewee has had his say should the interviewer make his comment, if necessary.

4. **Free talk Atmosphere:** Once the interview has begun in a solemn atmosphere, certain amount of relaxation may be allowed to encourage the interviewee to open. He should be encouraged to talk without any fear of inhibition. The relaxation in the atmosphere is particularly necessary when subject-matter of interview is sexual behaviour. The interviewee would be reluctant to talk about his marital life, extra-marital affairs etc. If the atmosphere is relaxed and the interviewer can create confidence in the interviewee, he is likely to reveal his secreats. It is a good rule to remember that a secret lies heavily on one's heart. Therefore, proper approach and honesty and integrity of the interviewer can win over the interviewee to tell what he normally would not.

5. **Help in recall:** Something the interviewee falls dead silent. He tries hard to remember; but something has blocked his memory. At such delicate moments, an appropriate hint form the interviewer can be of a great value. It can join the broken link in the memory chain.

6. **Research value questions:** It has been found in actual experience that the interviewee wishes to skip over certain questions. He does not like to reply to them. This is often the case if the questions pertain to early sexual experience, income sources and marital behaviour. Under these circumstances the interviewee must be assured that it is not the purpose of interviewer to

propel his life to demean his character or harm him in any way. Actually the questions are asked purely in the interest of research and may even prove a factor in liberalizing rigid codes of society.

7. **Encouragement:** In order to maintain sustained interest in the interview, the interviewee should not be allowed to feel discouraged on account of certain incoherence in his talk or pauses of long silences. He should be from time to time given a shot in the arm to boost his morale by the interviewer. He should be told that he is giving very valuable information for which the world of science is indebted to him and that whenever matters of momentous importance are discussed, certain amount of hesitancy is worry on this account. However, while encouragement is necessary and desirable, it should not degenerate into flattery. The interviewee should not be given the impression that he is a prophet whose every work, however disjointed, is a revelation for science. An intelligent interviewer tries for balance between the two extremes of flattery and rebuff.

8. **Providing direction:** Sometimes the interviewees indulge in orgy of talk. If they are telling about their personal experiences they tend to reproduce everything in details in and garnish it with their imagination as well. Therefore they indulge in the orgy of non-stop talking. Under these circumstances, the task of bringing them back on track is extremely delicate. As they are in a high state of tension any direct interference will offend them and they may walk out. Therefore, the interviewer should bear them patiently and wait for opportunity to turn the direction of talk in the desired course. This job requires great grace and tact.

9. **Note-taking:** As it is not desirable to rely upon memory exclusively and make notes of the interview after it is over, certain jottings have to be done simultaneous with the process of interview. This, however, is likely to interfere somewhat with the progress of the interview. Here also a balance has to be struck between continuous noting and no noting. It is, of course, undesirable to take notes while the interviewee is talking; only when he has finished his talk notes while the interviewer take an abbreviated note and go on with next questions. Therefore notes should be taken between brief pauses between two questions. Some scientists have a very good memory and defer the task of noting till the end of interview. However, most persons do not have so good memories and besides, memory is proverbially a cheat, it is recommended that brief jottings in long or short hand should be made during brief pauses in the interview. However, with advancement of the modern techniques of research the use of tape-recorder is ideal for making notes. The use of taps-recorder is ideal, if the room of interview is bugged and the wires are concealed and the tape is at a reasonable distance hidden from the view of the interviewee. This

avoids the whizzing and whirring of the machine which certainly distracts and produces self-consciousness.

10. Concluding the Interview: If an interview cannot be completed in one sitting or its purpose requires more sittings, it is desirable to break off the interviewee at such time when there are visible signs of fatigue in the interviewee. The interviewee should be called again and in the revised sitting he should be given a resume of previous day's interview. But if one sitting is enough for the interview, the interviewer should ask the interviewee at the end if he has anything more to tell. It should also he seen that nothing essential has been left uncovered. Sometimes the interviewer feels uneasy because he thinks that he has passed on some secret information which may prove detrimental to his interest. For example, one in the course of his discussion on marital discord divulges that before marriage he loved a girl whom he, however, did not marry. Now she has gone to town as a married women; and he has resumed his liaison with her. This is the reason for if his wife learns of secret liaison she may seek divorce and make scene. Under these circumstances, the interviewee should be given a firm assurance that his interview is strictly confidential and, under no circumstances, would his wife or his friends learn about the contents of the interview. This will help to allay his secret fears.

11. Report: Immediately after the conclusion of the interview, the report about it should be committed to writing; other deferment of this would increase the probability of errors. As we know there is considerable forgetting soon after a matter is learnt. The report should be full and detailed. It should not only contain a summary of the interview, but also the mental of the general physical conditions-room, lighting, temperature etc. of the interview and also any incident which may have occurred in the course of the interview. The preparation of the report is an expert job which requires great skill of observation and writing.

Causes of Errors

Having prepared the report, the interviewer has to re-check everything to detect possible errors. It has to be tested for reliability so that it may be determined how far one may go in drawing conclusions on its basis. Following are the main causes which render an interview invalid.

1. Often interviewees, under emotional spells, embellish their accounts with high-flow imagination and exaggerate their accounts in order to satisfy their vanities an create impression.

2. Sometimes there is communication gap between the interviewer and interviewee with the result that interviewee says one thing and the interviewer understand something else.

3. Some interviewee deliberately try to mislead the interviewer and make fool of him. For example, a college student may graphically describe the blue films he has seen, and how he and his friends have had sex with girls, married women, prostitutes, college lecturers etc. and say sneakingly, am I not a healthy and moral young man? The interviewer must be mature and experienced enough to tell off and rebuff such fake interviewees.

4. Sometimes an inexperienced interviewer is offended by the behaviour of interviewees and in a revengeful mood distorts the facts in his report.

Means of avoiding errors

Dr. Komarovsky has suggested following precautions to maintain the validity of a research interview :

1. The interviewer tries to obtain extensive facts about important issues. This information works as test of reliability for the facts obtained though the interview.

2. He examines data obtained through other sources.

3. Generally he tries to learn about the relations of the interviewee and his changing attitudes towards them. Dr. Komorovsky in his study of the unemployed make tried to learn about the reactions of sons and daughters during the period of their father's unemployment.

4. He critically examines those aspects of the interview in which the relationship of cause and effect seems to hold. This helps to determine whether the causes are always present or not when certain effects appear. In his study of parental authority, Komarovsky tried to see the effect of unemployment on this authority and also tried to find the circumstances in which the parental authority remains undiminished inspite of unemployment.

By the above methods suggested by Dr. Komarovsky the validity of the interview can be examined.

Having examined the validity of the interview, the researcher can draw conclusions with assurance. He also knows the limits to which he may go.

Interview Guide

In modern research, a printed or cyclostyled Handbook of Instructions for Interview is made use of whenever the research is done through the method of interview. According to Mrs. Young; the Interview Guide helps in four ways. These are :

1. Focuses attention on the main issues of the research project.

2. To maintain uniformity in interviews of different interviewers and thus help in the comparative study.

3. In collecting same type of units for analysis and examination of hypothesis.

4. Accumulating specific concrete details as a basis for quantitative studies of life histories.

The interview Guide serves best when its various details are well imbibed by the interviewers and they are in a position to vary its detail to suit particular situation. That is, it is wrong to follow the guide literally. It is not essential to allow the serial order of guide in asking the questions. It should be borne in mind that the guide is not an oral questionnaire. The guide becomes a hinderance, instead of aid, if too much attention is paid to it. When too many questions are asked from the guide and fixed replies are expected, the atmosphere of interview becomes chocked and free self-expression vanishes and everythings becomes artificial. These defects are not to be traced to the guide by an interviewer, defects are meant to show the general outline, it can not become a substitute for specific concrete situations. Therefore, the guide must be taken as a highly flexible tool and one should handle rather than allow himself to be handled by.

Moreover the use of guide does not mean that the interview is a 'directed on'. The guide only mentions the topics to be discussed and directions to be followed. It does not indicate the contents of the discussion.

The Interviewer

In the method of interview, the interviewer occupies as pivotal role. He gathers, tabulates and classifies the research material. The success of research depends largely on his proficiency and expertise. In the words of G.A. Lundberg, "An amount of preliminary preparation will serve as a substitute for fact and spontaneous insight in a concrete situation regardless of interview." In the interview a personal relationship emerges between the interviewer and the interviewer, both affect each other. Therefore, the personally of the interviewer of the crucial significance. It is the personal character and development is of the interviewer which either encourages the interviewee to open up and reveal his heart or discourages him and makes him reticent and evasive in replies. A men of charming manners and shrewd intelligence can easily create confidence in others; whereas a shabby and ill-mannered person is difficult to bear what to say of trust and confidence.

It is the constant vigil and alertness of the interviewer which can ensure that facts about a case become known and that fake information is not given. It is again the skill of the interviewer which keeps the interviewee on track. As a rule the interviewee tends to digress and, worse still indulges in irrelevant long talk just to satisfy his vanity. A note of encouragement given by a careless interviewer may start the interviewee on a high speed to heap personal memories and revelations and he may expect of hearing from the interviewer how great a man he is! These pitfalls are avoided by proficient interviewer;

otherwise the research material will become a tower of babble. Again, only a shrewd and sympathetic interviewer can study a problem like venereal disease. Most of the interviewees will pretend innocence about the cause of their affliction; few will admit promiscuous sex. Yet an intelligent, shrewd and sympathetic interviewer will learn all about their sexual habits.

To conclude: The interviewer is the centre from which all information disseminates. Therefore, he occupies a most vital role in the research by interview.

Means of Eliciting Correct Responses

The main concern of the researcher employing the method of interview is to get correct and to the point answers on the topic of research. A research can be less expensive and economical only if the entire concentration of everybody involved in it is on the topic and if deviation from the main line of approach is checked. The aim of research is success with minimum effort and this is possible if we scrupulously follow the above mentioned suggestions. According to Bogardus, in order to ensure correct responses the interviewee should be given maximum freedom of self-expression and should be allowed to describe his responses. Normally, the veracity of responses depends upon the skill and tactful approach of the interviewer and no rules can be framed in this connection. Still the following points should be kept in mind :

1. **Narrative Style**: For allowing maximum opportunity of self-expression to the interviewee, he should be allowed to tell his experience in the story from. That is he may narrate his experiences in connected and sequential form.

2. **Freedom of Description**: The interviewee should be allowed to describe whatever he thinks worthwhile. Even if some irrelevant facts are being described, the interviewee needs not be checked. As long as he remains within reasonable limits of the main topic in question, he should not be pulled up.

3. **Alert Direction**: Though maximum freedom of self-expression is desirable, this can only be within the scope of the problem being discussed. If there is total digression from the problem and what is being said has no bearing on the problem, the interviewee must be politely reminded to keep himself within bounds. This requires alertness and direction at the suitable occasion.

4. **No Harshness in Direction**: However, there should be no abruptness and harshness in providing the direction. Under no circumstances can an interviewer afford to offend the interviewee. Good humour is the essence of successful direction.

5. **Interested Hearing**: The interviewer must hear the interviewee with full interest. Nobody should be able to guess from his expressions that he is bored or his mind is somewhere else.

6. **Normal Emotional Attitude**: Whatever may be the content of descriptions being given by the interviewee, the interviewer must keep his cool and remain self-composed. For example, if an interviewee describes murder in all its gory details, the interviewer should not become pale and if he describes the sexual acrobatics in a blue film the interviewer should not get excited. A successful interviewer must possess a good deal more of self-restraint than others.

7. **Winning the confidence of Interviewees**: For the narration of facts fully and frankly the interviewee must confidence in the interviewer. Therefore, the interviewer must try his best to win be confidence of his interviewees.

8. **Appreciation of interviewees**: If an interviewer can convince the interviewee that he appreciates his cooperation and greatly values the information given by him, this word of encouragement has salutary effect on the interviewee, who then gives correct responses.

9. **Care in Dealing with Emotional Issues**: If the interviewer has to ask questions about the personal habits, likes and dislikes of the interviewee, he must do so skillfully. He must not appear to be interested in probing the secrets of the interviewees and he should ask them in the context where their value for research is clear.

10. **Objective Attitude**: The comments, wherever necessary, must not smack of personal views, likes and dislikes of the interviewer. He must remain objective and should not let his personal feeling interfere. He must at all cost avoid criticism of the interviewer. He must remain objective and should not let his personal feeling interfere. He must at all cost avoid criticism of the interviewee's behaviour. For example, if an interviewee tells him that the rich people stock so many things in their houses that they are unlikely to notice if some small things is missing, and when they come to know of it they would not bother, therefore he steals books, stationary etc., from rich people's houses, there is strong temptation to say, "your conduct is blameworthy even if it seems to hurt nobody"; but a wise interviewer would avoid such comments.

11. **Care for Convenience of Interviewee**: This is as a matter of fact *sine qua non* of the whole process of interview. Nobody can hold an interview by issuing threats ti interviewees or making them uncomfortable. In social research, the interviewee is an honoured person without whom the business of research would grind to a halt. Therefore, full care to his convenience has to be taken.

12. **Adverse Effect of Quick Report**: Sometimes that interviewees get into mood and begin narrating the adventures ad infinitum and ad nauseam. There is strong temptation under these circumstances to rebuke them and tell them to

shut up. But this privilege can be ill-afforded. We cannot alienate an interviewee permanently, because he has lost his balance temporarily.

Major Merits of Interview

As compared with order research methods, the method of interview possesses some unique qualities. These are :

1. **Direct research**: In the interview method, the social scientist has not to confine himself to the external aspects of human behaviour; but can probe into the internal aspects as well. Further more in the interview the barrier between the scientist and the layman is annihilated and they know each other directly.
2. **Deep research**: This characteristic follows from the above mentioned fact that the interview studies the internal aspects of the behaviour, which are inaccessible to other methods. Accordingly, in comparison with other methods, the interview method is a method of deep research.
3. **Knowledge of past and future**: By an interview the scientist, particularly psychoanalyst, is able to unravel the hidden memories of past affecting man's present behaviour. In interview we also learn about the outlook, aspirations and future goals of human beings and their present abilities. Accordingly, by interview we unravel the hidden past and prognosticate about the future.
4. **Knowledge of special features**: By an interview we learn about the unique qualities of human beings; the secret motivation and hidden desires and incentive working on human beings.
5. **Mutual encouragement**: In an interview there is inflow and outflow of ideas between the interviewer and the interviewee. This exchange proves encouraging for the researcher and the layman.
6. **Supra-observational**: An interview gives us knowledge of facts which are inaccessible to observation. The emotional attitude, secret motivation and incentives governing human life come to surface in an interview though these are unobservable. Therefore interview has a quality which may be called supra-observational.
7. **Knowledge of historical an emotional cause**: In social psychology there are many problems, the understanding of which requires knowledge of history and the emotional background of the problems. This becomes available in interview only.
8. **Examination of known data**: The informations given by the interviewee, if suspect, can be tested through cross-examination of the interviewee. Moreover, the emotional expressions accompanying the response give clue to the interviewer about the veracity or otherwise of the answer being given.

Major Limitations of Interview

Inspite of the above-mentioned unique features and merits of the method of interview, it suffers form certain important defects which limit its scope and value. These defects or limitations are :

1. **Misleading information:** There are certain maters which can be written in privacy but about which one does not speak before others. If these matters are to be revealed in an interview, the likelihood is that only a garbed version of these will be presented. Again, there are people who are temperamentally unable to discuss things though they are powerful writers. These persons are also unlikely to express their true thoughts and feelings in an interview.

2. **Defects due to interviewee:** If an interviewee is of low level intelligence and is emotionally unbalanced he is unfit to give correct information. Some persons are in the habit of talking in slangs and abuses and it is impossible to decipher what they say.

3. **Prejudices of interviewer:** The prejudices of interviewers are as much subversive for research as are the stupidities of the interviewees. If the interviewer is unable to suppress his prejudices, his understanding and interpretation of the material given in interview will be defective.

4. **Difference in the mental outlook of interviewer and the interviewee:** It there is very wide gap in the thinking and outlook of the interviewer and the interviewee, the discussion in the interview will be at cross-purpose. One will fail\to understand what the other says : For example if an old-fashioned person is to give his view on the effects of films on society, he will go on asserting that there is no redeeming feature in films and that actors and actresses are prostitutes and they pollute morals. Obviously, under these circumstances there can be no gain for research; only time is wasted.

5. **One-sided and incomplete research:** In the interview, certain aspects of human behaviour get over-emphasized at the expense of others. There is a tendency to give too much importance to personal factors and minimize the role of the social factors. For these reasons, the research by interview is liable to suffer from one-sidedness.

6. **Art rather than science:** Another limitation of interview method is that its procedures cannot be standardized, there is too much room for improvision. The success of an interview is more due to skill and tact than due to knowledge. It is believed that if a study or method is scientific, a man of mediocre intelligence can handle it. But as we have had occasion to note, the success in interview depends exclusively on the intelligence and skill of the interviewer. Therefore, the method of interview is more an art than science.

7. **Emotionalism**: The interview is liable to cease being objective and becoming emotional. In the current of emotionalism all objectivity is swept aside.

8. **Difficulty in Persuading the interviewee**: Many people are unwilling to participate in interviews. Even if persuaded, they refuse to answer many questions. Under these circumstances, the first problem before the interviewer is to persuade the prospective interviewee to extend his cooperation for the research project and agree for being interviewed. It has also been noticed that the points which prove most trying for the interviewee are the very sources of concealed facts. By tapping these sources, the skilful interviewer is able to gather significant information.

From the above discussion of the interview method as a research tool, it becomes clear that the success in the use of this method depends largely in the personal qualities of researcher. It needs intelligence, shrewdness, tact and charm of style and manners. Besides, certain intuitive power and psychological insight is essential for efficient use of the interview method. If we carefully look into the above mentioned limitations of the interview method, we shall perceived that almost all these limitations are due to lack of some or the other quality in the interviewer or the interviewee. Another reason for the lack of success in the interview is due to lack of clarity about the aim of the research. In these circumstances, the interviewee wastes away time by narrating his personal views and the interviewer wastes his effort by asking pointless questions. Many social scientists have made useful suggestions for ensuring success in interview. According to Mrs. P. V. Young, The limitations of the interview can be partially overcome by :

1. Employing non-directive techniques in probonged free-flowing interviews.
2. Using carefully constructed questions in which the subject matter is consistent with research objectives.
3. Standardizing the ways of asking questions.
4. Standardizing the ways of recording data.
5. Supplementing interviews with projective techniques, that is, using procedures in which the respondent is given an opportunity to interpret freely certain selected materials or situations and to give overt expression to his hidden conflicts, strivings and anxieties." The sources of an interview depends upon successful communication between the interviewer and the interviewee.

From the above discussion it is clear that by making concerted efforts the limitation of interview method can be overcome. The interviewee is not only a provider of useful informations but also is the touchstone for verifying the information. According to Goode & Hatt, "Interviewing has become of greater importance in contemporary research because of the reassessment of the qualitative interview." On account of many sterling qualities in the interview method, its use is most widespread in the modern research.

Precaution in Interview

Like all other research activities, interviewing has many facets. There are many types and purpose to it. Although interviewing is easier for some than for others, everyone can improve this technique by learning to avoid certain type of errors by developing an alertness to ambiguities and deceptions, and by becoming aware of the purpose of the interview, as well as the interaction between interviewer and respondent. It is of particular importance that the modern social investigator develop this skill; errors at any stage any stage may weaken or destroy the validity of the investigation. Yet the interview is the foundation upon which all other elements rest for it is the data-gathering stage.

Its importance is further seen in the gradual recognition, location and control of the interviewer's bias, since the interview is really a tool or instrument. As interviewer may not penetrate the rush of refusal which a potential respondent offers. Another may receive a cordial reception. Important difference may be found in the interviewers which raises the question of interview's reliability.

1. **Structured:** A qualitative interview would be an in-depth study for a shrewed, careful interviewer but it is basically unstructured. To effect standardisation in an interview the interviews should be structured which however sacrifices depth to gain standardization. Sampling of the responses of the respondents is thus made possible.

2. **Insight in cues:** In the research process of interviewing, the student of social sciences has to necessarily develop an insight of picking up cues which the respondent might offer consciously or unconsciously. To create this insight he must (1) develop an alertness to the fact that there are many subliminal cues, and that one can learn to 'read' them. (2) He must attempt to bring these cues to a conscious level, so that comparisons can be made with the hunches of other observers. (3) He must systematically check the predictions made from these hunches, to see what is correct.

3. **Alertness:** The interviewer must become alert to what he is bringing to the interview situation-his appearance, his facial and manual gestures, his interaction, his fears and anaxieties, his obtuseness and his cleverness. The interviewer's actions, gestures, speech and dress should divert attention from himself, in this situation it is the respondent who is important. Just as extreme dress will arouse attentions, so will exaggerated mannerisms and over practised speech.

These externals are not matters of the individual's personality and taste but are the indices by which the respondent himself will make preliminary judgments. Congruently, they may determine the case whether the interview be obtained at all.

4. **Rapport**: Several research studies have indicated that when the interviewer is closer to the class and ethnic position of the respondents, a greater range and intensity of attitude are more likely to be expressed. This follows from the general notion that the resonant also has an insight. He judges the interviewer by his external characteristics both gross and subtle. A common response to a request for an interview is a housewife's, "Oh I'm much too busy right now. Come back some time latter." The interviewer then must learn to "read" this situation carefully before accepting her claim. He must be able to decide whether the respondent is really too busy or is merely using this claim to avoid the interview. In most cases the interviewer is bound to have prior contact with the friends or relatives of the potential respondents so as to get background material for his work. Here also his approach should be gainful and elicit co-operations from the persons so as to obtain clue about the potential respondent and not meet with an once-operative "I don't" reply. A state of rapport exists between the interviewer and respondent when the latter accepts research goals of the interviewer, who asks to help him to obtaining the necessary information. Mere friendliness between the two is not sufficient in all cases. The best way to achieve this result may usually be a warm and sympathetic-approach. The goal is to obtain the facts the extent that the respondent is capable for presenting them therefore, in may situations even the friendliness must be broken, or suspended in order to obtain these facts.

5. **Confidence**: The interviewer must approach the interview with some confidence. The cock-sure approach is likely to arouse antagonism and refusals more often than even a timid, shy and awkward approach. The interview is not simply a conversation. It is rather a pseudo-conversation. In order to be successful it must have all the warmth and personality exchange of a conversation, with the clarity and guidelines of the scientific searching. The interviewer must introduce himself as though beginning a conversation but from the beginning the additional element of professional competence should be maintained.

6. **Reassurance**: Even after the interviewer has been cordial and warm in his introductory greeting, some respondent will fell ill at ease because they are afraid that they will have to answer difficult questions. They do not wish to be embarrassed by being unable to answers questions about international relations, impending legislation, and so on. Usually, however this type of anxiety can be easily assailed by re-assuring the person by such easing words,

"this is just a survey you know, there are not any right or wrong answers and this is not a quiz. We are simply trying to find out how you feel about". He will sympathise with the personal problems of the respondent. He will adjust to them in every possible way except in ways which would weaken the interview.

7. **Easy Conversation**: The types of interviews to be used in social research may vary from extremely lengthy and intensive interviews which probe into the most intimate aspects of the respondent's life, to the voting poll which merely obtains basic information about age, sex, occupation etc. Carrying the interview forward, in a single dimension some precautions may be taken in any interview. The interview which is developed in an easy, natural fashion, approximating a conversation in its effect on both participants, stimulates the interviewer himself to a better effort. In some cases the situation is more of a psychoanalytical nature when the emotions of the respondent come into play.

8. **Probe question**: Probe questions are warranted for a clearer and deeper understanding for the two people in the situation. In some cases the respondent will reflect the enthusiasm or annoyance of the moment. He will answer in terms of questions only. Other times the interviewer is not able to answer a particular question. Hence more probing ones are warranted to clarify the situation.

Recording the interview is of utmost importance. The utmost precaution is to be taken to see that the interviewer makes his detailed report immediately after the interview so as to get the full implication of it on the paper. Similarly, how he takes leave of the interviewee should be a point of courtesy and warwth for the total success of his interview process.

Factors Governing Merits & Demerits

The word 'questionnaire' in general refers to a device for securing answers to questions by using a form which the respondent fills himself. Thus any one who has filled a job application has had experience of answering a questionnaire. "Schedule" is a set of questions which are asked and filled in by an interviewer in face-to-face situation with another person. These forms have much in common. In both cases the working of the questions is the same for all respondents. 'Interview' is a face to face conversation type study. Though conducted on an open-structured scale, it is more limited in its application. Being a self administered one the questionnaire, unlike the schedule and interview guide, had been in popular use in sociological studies. However, the advantages and disadvantages of using either of these methods depend on various factors the most important of which are as follows :

1. **Difference in the type of information required**: Very extensive bodies of data cannot be obtained through the use of questionnaire. An extensive

survey type problem suggests the need for such a wide range of data that personal participation and depth interviewing is required. Again, the questionnaire is effective only when the respondent is able or willing to express his reactions clearly. A considerable controversy has prevailed among social researchers as to whether the answers from the anonymous questionnaire are franker or given with greater openness, because there is less fear when there is no immediate listener. The frankness has been contrasted with the interview situation since it is claimed that the interviewer may inhibit the answers somewhat.

A good questionnaire can elicit frank answers on almost all subjects. On the other hand it is equally true for the interview. When good questionnaires are compared with good interviews, it is likely that in the score of simple lying or frankness there is little to choose. The interviewer has the advantage of seeing the evasion, while in questionnaire the person who answer the questionnaire may feel less constraining in telling the truth.

2. **Different in Depth**: The difference between the two is not in the dimension of frankness but in that of depth. On this matter there is little doupt that the good interview can prode more deeply than the best questionnaire. The complexities of a question can be better understood in an interview situation. On the other hand, the questionnaire has to indulge in a series of minor questions and referents if a clarity is to be obtained. The active work of the interviewer is required to stimulate the respondent to express the deeper levels of motivation, desire etc. It is not that in the interview it is possible to obtain a better report with the respondent, although it is likely that the interviewer can get and hold the emotions of the respondent somewhat better. Rapport is the not most important element in this comparison, but it is rather that fact that the respondent is not able to give the necessary answers without help.

3. **Emotional different**: The questionnaire fails when its questions place an emotional burden on the respondent. This is met by the mental alertness of the interviewer, who probes when the answers are vague, meaningless, irrelevant or contradictory. However, the fact-to-face interview offers the emotional support of a sympathetic listener, in addition to a purely intellectual help.

4. **Difference in the type of respondent reached**: The questionnaire cannot be used a representative sample of the entire population Emphasis has been placed on the fact the a substantial segment of the population cannot answer the questionnaire because of lack of the minimum amount of unity reading knowledge. In addition, exists another group of "will not" respondents to the questionnaire. It has been found that a questionnaire is more successful in an educated population than otherwise. This restriction is not necessarily

imposed on the interview technique. Thus the questionnaire is applicable not to any but to a highly selected group unlike the interview. Hence it has to be chosen for data collection only in studies where relevant sections of the population are concerned.

5. **Differences in accessibility of respondents:** It is certain that when the group of respondents is widely scattered, the costs will be less if the questionnaire is use. 'Costs' pertain to both time and money. For example, if the researcher wished to poll the membership of the Janta Party, transportation costs would be considerably reduced if the Questionnaire is chosen an also cost in terms of man-hours spent on interviewing the population. This is not a blanket statement that the questionnaire is cheaper only that it can be cheaper under certain circumstances. 'Costs' should be computed in terms of the amount of usable information secured and not on the basis of number of questionnaires or interviews.

6. **Difference in the precision of the hypothesis:** The more closely focussed the hypothesis the more effective the questionnaire. At such stage, the interview is equally application. However, the interview is effective even with a vaguely explanatory hypothesis. Indeed the testing of the questionnaire must utilise the interview. The meaning of each question can be adequately tested only by flexible probing questioning of those who are representative of the final respondent group. This type of test cannot usually be done by the use of the questionnaire alone. As a consequence it is only when the hypothesis has been rather sharply focussed that the questionnaire is most effectively used.

******

Chapter – 12

Schedule

There are two important ways in which the response to a questionnaire may be secured. In the first, it may be sent by post to various individuals; and in the second the researcher may himself present the questionnaire to the individuals whose responses are desired. The first method is collect the mailed questionnaire, while the second method is called schedule. In the words of Thomas Carson Macormic, "The schedule is nothing more than a list of questions which it seems necessary to test the hypothesis or hypotheses." A schedule, therefore, is a list of questions formulated and presented with the specific purpose of testing an assumption or hypothesis. For example, if a research scientist believes on the basis of his general experience that women do not enjoy good status in a joint family, he will so formulate his questions that the actual state of affairs may come to surface in responses to those questions. A sample of questions is :

1. Do you often go out of your house?
2. What is the usual purpose of your outside visits?
3. Do you often entertain your friend at home?
4. Do you receive an allowance for personal expenses? etc.

According to W. J. Goode and P. K. Hatt, "Schedule is the name usually used to a set of questions which are asked and filled by an interviewer in a face success in the use of schedule is largely determined by the ability and tact of the interviewer rather than by the quality of the questions and notes down the answers all by himself, the quality of question has not any great significance. The list of a single item thoroughly. Emphasizing this, G.A. Lundberg observes, "The schedule is a device for isolating one element at a time thus intensifying our observation."

From the above discussion, it is quite clear that in the schedule method, interview occupies a central place and place and plays a vital role. As a matter of fact success in the use of schedule is largely determined by the ability and tact of the interviewer rather than by the quality of the questions posed. Because the interviewer himself poses the questions and notes down the answers all by himself, the quality of question has not any great significance. The list of questions is merely a formal document intended to maintain uniformity in the questions asked by different persons. C. A. Moser has pointed out his fact is the following words: "Since it is handled by interviewers, it can be a fairly formal document in which efficiency of field handling rather than attractiveness is the operative consideration in design."

Characteristics of Schedule

From the above-mentioned definition, following salient points about schedule emerge :

1. The schedule is presented by the interviewer. The questions are asked and the answers are noted down by him.

2. The schedule of questions is a mere formal document; it need not be attractive.

3. The schedule can be used in a very narrow sphere of social research.

Major Objects of Schedule

P. V. Young has laid emphasis on the following objects of the schedule. According to her, a researcher "makes the schedule a guide, a means of delimiting the sense of his enquiry, a memory tickler, a recording device." These may now be discussed pointwise :

1. **Delimitation of the topic**: A schedule is always about a definite item of inquiry; its subject is a single and isolated subject-item rather than the subject in general. The interviewer presents questions about one item and notes down answers about it. Therefore schedule delimits and specifies the subject of inquiry.

2. **Aids memory**: In an interview the choice question is left entirely to the interviewer; he may ask any question. In this there is always a chance of some important points being left. Therefore, in the schedule the list of questions is preplanned and noted down formally. The interviewer is always armed with the formed document detailing the questions. Accordingly in the schedule method an interviewer is not dependent upon the memory.

3. **Aid to classification and analysis**: When the interviewer obtains replies to the questions given in the schedule, these replies are classified and analyzed. Many different tables are used in the schedule; and the questions are also of many types. Some need only yes/no answer; other require choosing one of the alternatives given or arranging them in order of preference; still other require certain amount of thinking and can be answered in small sentences.

Therefore, all the varieties of replies are sifted and classified under various heads. This helps in the analysis of the replies.

The above aims of schedule method have been discussed by Mrs. Young in the following words: "An observation usually serves several purposes simultaneously :

1. It is a specific memory tickler.
2. It is an objective recording device which makes possible accurate accumulation of large quantities of data.
3. It is a standardizing derive; and
4. It aids to delimit to scope of the study and to concentrate on the circumscribed elements essential to the analysis.

Important Types f Schedules

P. V. Young has described following four types of schedules. These are to be discussed now :

1. **Rating schedules**: In the field of business guidance, psychological research, and social research, the rating schedules are used to assess the attitudes, opinions, preferences, inhibitions and other like elements. As evident from the term "rating", in these schedules, the value and trend of the above mentioned qualities is measured.

2. **Documents schedules**: The schedules of this types are used to obtain data regarding written evidence and case schedules, those terms are included which occur frequently in documents and are too generally found in case histories. For example, in the field of criminology, rating schedules are used to gather data to be found in crime studies, the different kinds of crime, their incidence, the nature of earlier crime and the personal data on criminals like school-leaving age, the age at the time of employment, the level of economic and social status and other sundry facts about crime and criminals.

3. **Institutional survey forms or evaluational schedules**: The use of these schedules, as is evident from the name, is made to gather data about specialized institutions ore agencies. The form and the size of evaluational schedules is determined by the nature and the complexity of the problems of an institution; more complex the problem, bigger the size of the schedule. To study the problems of American Public Organization for health services, a schedule running into as many as 3 pages, was used.

4. **Observation schedules**: In these schedules, observer records the activities and responses of an individual a group under specific conditions. The observation schedules may need one or more research work to be completed. The main purpose of an observation schedule is to verify information.

5. **Interview schedules**: A fifth form of schedules is sometimes treated independently and at other times considered included in the 4th type. In an

interview schedule, an interviewer presents the questions of the schedule to the interviewee and records their responses on blank spaces.

Of all the above-mentioned types of schedules, the observation schedule depends of blank spaces.

Major Characteristics of Good Schedule

Mrs. Pauline Young has enumerated following two characteristics of a good schedule. These are :

1. **Accurate communication**: If a respondent is unable to understand the meaning of questions in schedule, the schedule is defective in design. Therefore the first and foremost quality of a good schedule is that it must communicate. That is a respondent should be able to understand the meaning of question on reading them. Whatever meaning the researcher wishes to communicate to the respondent should be grasped by him. If this does not happen the researcher and the interviewer all work at cross-purposes. Accordingly, the language of the questions should be simple and free from technical jargon; it should also be free from ambiguity and circumlocution. In this as much as the aim and purpose of a schedule is to obtain accurate data, it is of utmost significance for the researcher that the language and style of his questions should be transparent so that the respondent can see clearly the meaning of the questions by all himself.

2. **Accurate response**: Next in order, but equal in importance, is the second quality of schedule, that is, ability to elicit accurate response. For making accurate response, the respondent should be motivated and made to feel the importance of his cooperation. The schedule should be so constructed that it is easily understood by the respondent and that he realizes the value of his accurate response. The schedule should avoid all possible irritants – technical jargon, misleading and too intimate questions; otherwise the respondent would feel no compunction or guilt in giving inaccurate responses. For example, if the respondents are asked. Do you make fruitful use of your spare time? Most of them would not know what the interviewer means precisely by "fruitful use." Some may consider that fruitful use means monetary gain, whereas others may have different ideas. At times, the respondents willfully misleads by giving wrong responses, therefore the researcher must closely scrutinize the data made available in the schedule. He should test its veracity by every available means before drawing conclusions based on the data.

From the above discussion it is evident that a schedule can be considered good only if it has following features :

1. Attractive form and style;
2. Direct, simple and unambiguous questions;

3. The questions should not be so intimate that the respondent may be reluctant to make replies;

4. The questions must be directly related to the specialized problem being explored;

5. And the responses should be such as are classifiable and amenable to statistical treatment.

Formation of Schedule

The difference between a questionnaire and a schedule is due to their structures. Therefore, in order to understand the schedule, it is necessary to know the how of its structure, i.e., what is the method of its formulation. A schedule has two aspects: internal and external. Accordingly, in the formulation of a schedule, both internal and external aspects have to be considered. With regard to the internal aspect, it has to be seen that all the questions included in the schedule should be subservient to the main purpose of the schedule and that there should be included in it no question which does not have direct bearing on the subject matter which is being investigated. To ensure this, the problem or the subject matter should consult the experts in subject to further sharpen the outlines and gather all the necessary information. If the problem is regional in character, people living in the region can prove very helpful in the formation of the schedule.

A. The internal aspect of the schedule

1. The Sorting various Aspects: In constructing a schedule, the first step is sorting out of the various aspects of the schedule. For this the problem should be considered from all possible points of view. For example, if we wish to study the effects of Hindu Code Bill on the Hindu family, we have first of all to determine the aspects or elements of Hindu family which have been affected by the aforesaid Bill. Moreover, we should distinguish between the elements which have been directly influenced by the Bill from those which have been indirectly influenced. That is, we must prepare a list of primary effects and anther of secondary effects. By preparing such exhaustive lists, the problem can be studied most effectively.

2. Determination of essential information: Having determined the different aspects of a problem, the next point which needs to be determined is the kind of information needed on these aspects. For this purpose, the various aspects may be subdivided. The subdivision presumes, of course, thorough knowledge of the subject. To illustrate this point by the above-mentioned example of the Hindu Code Bill, an investigator whose knowledge of either the clauses of the Bill, or of the complex structure of Hindu family in its historical aspect is deficient can hardly be expected to prepare an efficient schedule about this problem.

3. **Formation of questions**: After taking decision about the different aspects of the problem, with their respective subdivisions, to be studied, the next step is formation of questions to elicit information of each subdivision of each aspect. The distinguishing feature of the question is communicability, i.e., they should convey the intended meaning. Therefore, the use of idiomatic, technical, ambiguous, indefinite, imaginative, private and inferential terms should be strictly avoided. Unless the words are simple. Clear, univocal and unambiguous, they are liable to varying interpretations. And if the respondents understand the questions differently, their responses will not be to one and the same questions but to the different senses of one question. This will make the confusion worse confounded. Besides the fact that questions should not be liable to different interpretations, another important consideration in the formulation of questions is that they should be such as can be easily answered by the respondents themselves, without either external help or sense of shame. For example, if there is a question: Do you have normal blood pressure, pulse rate and heart beat? Obviously, the question cannot be answered without consulting a doctor. Again if the question is: Do you remain celibate during your wife's absence? The question is too intimate to be answered.

4. **Serialization of questions**: In order to obtain well organized formation, it is necessary that the questions should be presented to the respondents in a well-ordered serial. It has been experienced in various field studies that the change in the order of questions affects the answers adversely. Therefore, it is of crucial significance that while formulating the questions, these should be so placed in the schedule as to be serially concerned. If any particular question upsets the respondent, its effect is likely to be carried over to later questions must be followed.

5. **Test of reliability**: The success a schedule is to be measured by the fact that it elicits natural responses and that the answers given are not artificial. In order to counteract and forestall the possibility of misleading answers being given, the schedule must be tried on a sample group. If there is some lacuna in the schedule it must be removed and the schedule tried again. This process has to go on till the time all the questions are shown to be easily intelligible and there is no trace of artificiality left in them. If a particular question continues to be confusing inspire of modifications, it should be removed from the schedule. In this connection it has to be borne in mind that the sample group on which the schedule is tried must be drawn from individuals who are actually to be interrogated.

B. The External Aspect of the Schedule

After taking care of the internal aspect of the schedule, the external aspect must also be attended to. In the external aspect, following elements are studied :

1. The form and size of the schedule,
2. Organisation of units, and
3. The material used.

The external aspect of the schedule is known as form or structure of the schedule. As has been noted above, if the structure is unattractive the chances of its success are very limited. Therefore, the structure must also be given adequate attention. In this connection, following things are to be considered :

1. **Material used**: The paper used for printing should be of high quality, the letters printed on it should stand out visibly and must not be broken, furthermore the ink should not spread. If the paper is rough, the letters printed will be poor in visibility and are liable to be broken due to crumpling of the paper; moreover when the interviewer fills it by ink, the ink may spread. The paper must be both tough and pliable; otherwise, it may break on collapsing. Even if it means more expenses, the paper and printing must be of excellent quality. Undue economy in this respect may prove very costly.

2. **Form of Schedule**: In the determination of form and size of the schedule, a number of things should be taken care of. The schedule should not be unduly long or wide test repeated collapsing and folding affect it adversely. The size of the schedule is, of course, to be determined by the number and length of question, the two following sizes are generally adopted. These are 81/2" X 11" and %" X " or 21 cm. X 28 cm. and 18 cm. X 21 cm. Normally printing is done only on one side of the paper in the schedule.

3. **Length of schedule**: As a matter of fact the length of the schedule varies with the nature of the problem, but it should not be so long as to take half an hour or more. Most of the respondents do not want to spend such a long time in filling up the schedule. Therefore, as a rule, the length of schedule should be such as to take less than half an hour in filling it up.

4. **Organisation of units**: The units of a schedule are comprised of titles, sub-titles and columns. A proper arrangement of these helps in making the schedule well-ordered. The questions should be strictly within the context. By taking this precaution the length of the schedule can be kept within reasonable limits.

5. **Marginal space**: The marginal space on the should be about ½" or 1 cm. and on the right it should be ½", or ½ cm. This lends attraction to the schedule. Besides, the researcher takes marginal notes in the marginal space. In the absence of margin, the schedule cannot be field, because punching it will destroy some words, and moreover, part of the writer is concealed.

6. **Spacing**: In between the questions, titles, subtitles and columns, there should be reasonable space for noting of responses.

7. **Printing:** A printed schedule is definitely more desirable as printing makes it attractive; but if the number of respondents is small, or economy is desired, cyclo-styled or type written schedule may be used; but in both cases the schedule must be neat and free from over-writing etc.

8. **Use of Pictures:** It has been found by the researchers that the insertion of appropriate pictures in the schedule increases their present ability and that the respondents taken greater interest in making responses. Therefore it is desirable to insert suitable pictures, whenever possible. For example, if in a schedule the questions pertain to different professions like engineering, law, teaching and medicine, the representative pictures of an engineer, a lawyer, a teacher and a doctor may be inserted at appropriate places.

Outlines of a Schedule

In a schedule, following three aspects seem distinct :

1. **Prefatory:** In this opening part, following data with regard to inquiry and the respondents are sought :

   i. Name of the survey and the surveyor with address.

   ii. Reference number.

   iii. Name of respondent, his address, age, sex, education, profession etc.

   iv. Place of interview.

   v. Time and date of interview.

2. **Main schedule:** It includes titles, sub-titles, columns and the questions.

3. **Direction of field worker:** In this part, the workers who have to present the schedule, hold the interview and collect the data. They are given elaborate instructions regarding the reading and presenting of schedule and the method of the interview. In the absence of these instructions there is a probability of arbitrariness which will surely vitiate the purpose of research. The researchers are given detailed instructions about the use of words in recording the responses. Every other detail is explained in order to ensure uniformity of recording the responses.

Pilot Study

Before the formulation of the schedule, a preliminary survey of all connected questions is made. A general knowledge about the problem is gathered first of all in order to know the nature and different aspects of the problem. Moreover, an idea about the difficulties involved in the problem comes to light. In the preliminary research study, no hypothesis about the problem is formulated. The preliminary study is made on a small sample; but it is necessary that the individuals of the sample should be from the actual group to be studied. That is they should be respondents who would act as representatives of the entire group of respondents. From this study an estimate about the extent of response likely from the group can be made and an idea about possible problems to be encountered is formed. For example, if the problem is the study of women labour force of a particular region, a small group of women from this force is chosen and their problems enquired into by interview. This preliminary study would go a long way in formulating the schedule; many a time certain facts undreamt of by the researchers come to surface. From the preliminary study the researcher gets an idea about the nature and extent of the problem, the primary elements in it and their important phases.

Value of Preliminary Testing

Having made the preliminary study, the schedule is prepared. But before submitting it to respondents at large, a select group of respondents drawn from the whole group is used to test the intelligibility and reliability of the schedule. The preliminary test gives the researcher an idea as to how far the schedule will succeed in achieving its purpose. Furthermore, the preliminary testing is liable to be left out, or some question will turn out to be either unintelligible or objectionable. The popular adage that only the shoe wearer knows where the shoe pinches, applies in case of schedule as well. As no amount of craftsmanship and care of the shoe-maker can turn out the shoes which will give discomfort to no one, in the same manner no amount of industry and ingenuity can prepare a perfect schedule. Even if the schedule is technically fool proof, it may prove a hard nut if the level of intelligence of the respondents is quite poor. Accordingly, to avoid ultimate loss and failure, every schedule is tested on few individuals belonging to the group to be studied. This gives the researcher an idea about errors in the schedule and also difficulties due to intelligence-level. If the sample group shows its inability to grasp the content of the questions, these will have to be modified and restructured and this process will be completed only when the restructure schedule has become intelligible to the group. The answers like "don't know", "can't tell", "makes no sense" clearly indicate that the respective questions need to be drastically modified. Again, if a question elicits contradictory and paradoxical response, the indication is that the concerned question is ambiguous over univocal. If the respondent hesitates in reply to a particular question, this may be due to emotional reasons. There are matters which may cause no emotional storm in one group but may cause great upset in some other group. For example, if a schedule is to be tried in U.S.A. the question, do you kiss your wife before leaving home, is quite unemotional; but in Indian respondents this will cause blush. To conclude, preliminary test is a *sin qua non* of the success of a schedule.

Organisation of Research Study

After having made the preliminary test, the planning and organisation of research study may begin. The research study using schedule can be of two types. One is called observation and the other interview. If the research is done through observation, the researcher merely presents the schedule to the respondents and makes note of their behaviour. He put no questions. If the researcher employs the methods of interview, the researcher personally asks the questions and himself records the replies in the appropriate spaces in the schedule. Generally, however, the method of interview is used in research by schedule. Mere observational schedule research is rare. Accordingly, we find the following phases or steps in the organisation of research.

1. **Selection of respondents**: Having prepared the schedule and having tested it for intelligibility and reliability, the next step is the selection of respondents how are to be interviewed and to whom the schedule is to be presented. Either each and every member of a group may be interviewed, in which case there is no selection, or some of them may be chosen for the purpose. The first method where there is no selection is known as census method, whereas the second, involving selection, is known as simple method.

2. **Selection of field workers**: A major factor in the success of research project is the selection of able and competent observers or field researchers. This is a step which needs maximum attention. In the selection of field workers the following consideration must be kept in mind.

(i) *Honesty*: The most single quality that a field worker must have is honesty. An honest worker is dedicated to his work. He carries out the instructions faithfully, works hard and asks the questions and fills up the answers scrupulously. On the other hand, a dishonest worker is careless, slovenly and shirks hard work. The schedules filled up but him are more liable to mislead than to provide reliable information. In as much as a researcher is dependent for the data on the field workers, he is to make sure that the field worker is an honest, hardworking and conscientious individual.

(ii) *Intelligent and Devoted*: Besides the quality of honesty, the field worker should also be intelligent and interested in research. He must not be a mere mercenary who works in any position for money, but must be convinced of the value and worth of research. A merely honest worker is not enough and a merely intelligent worker is also not enough. Both the qualities must coexist in a good field worker. An honest but unintelligent worker will carry out the instructions so faithfully that even where slight modifications are indispensable for carrying on research, he will refuse to make them and let the cause of research suffer. Similarly, if a worker is intelligent but dishonest, he will understand everything, and because of greater imaginative ability, will be persuaded to fill up the schedules all by himself without bothering to hold the interview. Even when he actually holds the interview he is liable to ignore the answers given by the respondents and substitute them by his own. A worker

who is both honest and intelligent will be able to handle practical situations imaginatively and avoid ugly scenes and still not allow the cause of research to suffer.

(iii) ***Patience***: Another quality essential for a field worker is patience, because he has to encounter all kinds of situations. There are some very difficult moments. For example, a respondent may abuse the worker, upset his furniture and tear the schedules if he is asked a question which hurts some feelings of his. Under these circumstances the field worker must maintain his cool, must not lose his head or temper. He must handle the situation tactfully and this is only possible if the possesses the quality of patience.

(iv) ***Tactfulness***: Sometimes the respondents make a joke of the interview and become too light and facetious in their responses. For example, when asked, are you married or single, a respondent may say – No doubt I am single yet I am more married than married ones or worse still may use obscenities in his answers. These difficult cases require great tact wisdom in him. If some questions annoy the respondent, he can be told that he should not take it in any personal sense. The aim and purpose of research is not to judge morals but to obtain objective and true information. By such counsels, his annoyance may be overcome. However, it is not possible to frame rules for handling each and every practical problem; only the innate tact and wisdom of the field worker can help.

(v) ***Alert and Agile***: A worker must be alert and agile. These qualities add to his personality and help to create favourable impression on the respondents. Moreover, an alert and agile person is more tactful and can easily persuade the indifferent and hostile respondents to lend cooperation.

(vi) ***Scientific outlook***: A field worker must have a scientific approach to the research. He must not have any strong likes and dislikes: must note entertain some per theories about social events. He must be open-minded and prepared to see things in their proper perspective and should also be free from all kinds of prejudices and predilections. If he has some preconceived strong notions, he is liable to distort the information to suit his ideas. Accordingly objective and scientific outlook is very essential for a good field worker.

(vii) ***Cautiousness***: Though a worker should not be cynical and skeptical about all information he gathers from the respondents, he must not also he gullible and believe everything told by the respondents. A middle-of-road attitude, that is cautiousness is necessary to a good worker. If he is able to persuade by this practical tact and wisdom to cooperate in research, this provides no guarantee that the respondents may not wittingly or unwittingly pass or take information. A field worker must be very cautious and constantly guard against such eventualities.

(viii) Experience: Practical tact and mental alertness and a determination not to be cheated are the qualities which a man gains through practical experience. Therefore, before allowing the field workers independent jobs they should well apprenticed and trained.

(ix) Knowledge about respondents: The field workers have to encounter individuals of diverse cultures and traditions and unless he will cut a sorry figure. For example, it is customary and deemed an honour, to entertain guests by providing them women companions, by the natives of Polynesia. A mission-choice between two lovely damsels. Not understanding the native language, the missionary gestured refusal. The king was annoyed but he maintained his cool-headness; he offered the missionary both damsels because he could not possibly conceive that any body would spurn a lovely damsel and therefore, thought that the missionary was not satisfied by having only one beautiful girl. This example clearly brings out the crucial point that as a teacher should know both Latin and John, the research worker, must know his schedule as well as his respondents. It, due to innocence of culture, the research worker insists on knowing the name of the husband of a rural women, he is likely to forfeit all his good-will. Worse still, if he ask a rustic woman, is the faithful to her husband ? Or does she know the use of contraceptives? He is likely to be thrashed and hounded out of village as an immoral man and a corrupter. The knowledge of the dialects of the respondents is very useful. This helps to establish rapport with the respondents. Sometimes innocence of culture and language proves helpful, because the field worker concentrates on the essentials and is not distracted. However, as a rule, the knowledge of culture and language is essential for successful research.

While selecting the research workers, the above points should be borne in mind. In order to tap these qualities, various tests are given to the prospective researchers. Some persons become professional researchers. In the West there are many organisations and sociological laboratories which help in providing able and competent research workers. These workers are professionally mature and approved by authorities but to recruit new workers; many objective tests have to be administered. In the West, mostly professional researchers having considerable experience are used in research. The sociological bureaus or laboratories are told the nature of research and kinds of workers needed. These bureaus then send professional researchers having the abilities demanded by the research organization or the individual doing the research.

3. Training of field workers: For different types of modern research, different set of qualities and specialized knowledge of particular field is required. If a worker has not had some previous experience of the kind of research which he is now to undertake, not much efficiency and faithful work can be expected. Therefore now-a-days, the workers are given training after recruitment. The nature and the period of training, differs in different is most commonly used. The social researchers participate in various conferences and they are given specialized knowledge and training in these conferences. In the first conference, and in subsequent meetings they are trained in reading the schedule and noting the responses. They are also explained in detail, the content and meaning of each question. If some technical words and symbols are used in the schedule their interpretation is made clear to the research workers. If some code words and numbers are used in the schedule, their values and purpose is clearly explained. The use of codes economizes the time in filling up the schedule and this gives the field worker almost uninterrupted time to talk to the respondents. Besides this formal training, the workers are given training in the interview technique and are also acquainted with the culture and language of the group under their charge. They are also fore warned about the possible difficulties they are likely to encounter and given hints to overcome these. Normally, when a worker approaches the respondents he is asked many questions about the aim and purpose of research. An idea of these questions about the aim and purpose of research. An idea of these questions becomes available during the preliminary testing. The worker is told about information which must be given to the respondents before undertaking actual interview work. After general training, the worker is also given practical training. For this purpose he is sent to some persons for getting the schedule filled up. If some mistakes are noticed, the worker is pulled up and told to rectify them. If some workers fails to improve he is dismissed.

4. The Interview Technique: After making selection of the field workers and imparting them the necessary training, the next step, in the social research by the schedule method, is to determine the method of interview to be employed. This is the most vital link in the process of schedule method research. At this stage a strategy is planned for approaching the respondents, making them interested in the research and the ways and means of obtaining the correct information and closing of the interview. An efficient and well mannered worker is able to impress the respondents easily agree to extend cooperation. However, some try to avoid cooperation by pretending to be over-busy or disinterested. Instead of just insisting that they should cooperate and that it is their civic or social duty to help research, the field worker must make an indirect approach. He should try to know the cause and point of their resistances. He should break these tactfully. He should make it clear that he in no way wishes to impose any thing on them: that they are intelligent and conscientious citizens who can make their own decision and must inform them thoroughly to be able to make a right decision. Besides, an intelligent worker would arm himself about some preliminary facts about his respondent and approach him when he is free and relaxed. If adequate attention is paid to the study of causes of resistance among the respondents, a way can be usually found to break it.

Reluctance in Cooperation

Following are the main causes of reluctance to cooperation in modern research :

1. **Business:** One of the major factors for refusal to cooperate in responding to the schedule is preoccupation. Most persons when they are approached for filling up the schedule, if they are engaged in some personal activity refuse point bland to listen to the research worker but saying – Sorry ! you see I am very busy. However, no person is busy all the twenty-four hours of the day. There area always some spare moments. Therefore, instead of demanding time straight way, it is better to know when the respondent is free and fix appointment at that hour of the day. Usually the evenings are most suitable for this purpose because in the evening most people are relaxed after day's work. When a respondent is free and relaxed he must be found out by the field worker either through a reliable person or by asking the resonant personally on telephone or otherwise. If an appointment is made the respondent is mentally ready to cooperate with the interview at the fixed hour. The meeting by appointment also solves the problem of initial hesitancy during the first meeting. Sometimes the field worker carries a letter of introduction from influential friends of the respondents, this ensures good response and warm reception. However, under these circumstances the respondent refuses to answer the question which may divulge information likely to be against him by his friends. Therefore, the letter of introduction procedure is not a very appropriate approach in this matter. While going to meet a respondent, the worker must scrupulously observe all courtesies and decencies of behaviour.

2. **Evasiveness:** Some respondents do not wish to bothered by research workers. They avoid them and consider them a nuisance. The reluctance of such persons can be overcome by explaining to them the aim and purpose of research and convincing them how worth while their contribution is and how much will it be appreciated.

3. **Fear:** Fear is important factor inhibiting response and cooperation. If the respondent feels that certain information that he gives in responses to certain questions may be used to injure his interests, his fear and reluctance are quite natural. For example, if the question is : Do you have some other source of income than your regular employment, the disclosure of the source may attract adverse attention of Income Tax Department or his employer. Under these circumstances the respondents will cooperate only if they are convinced

that their replies will be strictly confidential and would not become available to any one other than the genuine researcher.

4. **Skepticism**: Some respondents do not appreciate the worth and value of the research. They consider it to be social nuisance rather than social research. Such persons are opinionated and do not easily listen to others. To disabuse these persons of their faulty notions requires yeoman courage and tact. By his correct approach and upright manners, the field worker can succeed in breaking resistance in these people.

5. **Suspicion**: Sometimes the social researchers are mistaken as government agents or the agents of some private detective agency. The suspicion can be removed by showing identification cards and cogent explanation.

6. **Introvert nature**: Some people by nature like loneliness and keep themselves aloof from drum of world. Such persons are temperamentally disinclined to participate in public activities, it is really difficult to persuade these persons to make some concession in their generally averse attitude. It needs great tact and wisdom to tackle such persons. They may soften a bit if told that their indifference to social matters is a boon, because it helps them view the social goings on in their proper perspective and that their observations are truly acute and perspicacious. Therefore, their help is of exceptional value for the social research.

7. **False Prestige**: Some people are in the habit of feigning over-business and do not agree to do anything unless repeatedly requested or approached through highly influential persons. They usually remark, "We are so awfully busy; not a moment to spare, have reluctantly turned down so many invitations for which ordinary person craves. However, we shall give you time because we deem it out duty to favour a person whom our bosom friends recommended." Such persons are actually suffering from false prestige and wish to be humoured.

Accordingly a field worker should try to get to the causes of respondent's refusal to cooperate and should try to remove the cause. Once a man is persuaded to cooperate he will give the necessary information. However, one must be ever alert and cautions about the replies. If he has reason to doubt the validity of an answer he should immediately cross examine the interviewer. The success of an interview depends upon correct communication and correct response. The respondent must understand the real content and meaning of the question and must respond naturally. These two qualities make for success of the interview.

8. **Scrutiny of answers:** After interview and filling up of schedules, the next step is the scrutiny of answers. For this purpose, few schedules are examined at random for any possible errors. While checking the replies, it has

to be remembered that the particular replies to particular questions are determined by the outlook traits of the respondents, the surrounding atmosphere and the outlook traits of the interviewer. An alteration in any of these factors results in change in the replies. Therefore, the time gap between the interview an scrutiny of answers should not be unduly long: otherwise the given replies may appear invalid.

9. Editing of Schedules: The field workers and interviewers fill up the schedules and also make a check on the validity of answer. After this, the schedules are submitted to the researcher for editing. The editing involves following phases –

(i) After receiving the schedules, the editor checks their quantity to ensure that all the schedules are in. The schedules submitted by each field worker are kept in separate files and on each file are noted the total number of respondents unavailable etc. Generally, these statistics are given by the field-worker himself. If, on checking some discrepancies are noted in the above mentioned statistics, these are noted down on the file.

(ii) Checking entries: A schedule contains a large number of questions. The field worker has to enter replies for each of these after making the interview. After checking the number of schedule the next editorial task is to check the number of actual entries in a schedule and the number of those which are filled-up and also the number of unfilled entries. There are some questions which are not replied and the entry is left blank. If checking reveals that entries have not been properly filled-up in certain schedules, these should be returned to the worker for necessary action. If some entries are unwittingly left blank, these can be got filled up. The editor has to ensure that the entries of a schedule are properly filled up.

(iii) Illegible schedules: If due to bad hand or writing pencil or writing in abbreviations or other such things, a schedule's entries cannot be read, the labour is wasted. These have to be got refilled by a different worker if the original worker's hand is very poor; otherwise he can be asked to use ink only and write in full.

(iv) Coding: For the purpose of classification, the received data are properly coded. Firstly, all replies are broken up into various classes and each class is given a set code of numbers. With it the counting by statistical methods become possible. Sometimes the workers are told the code numbers and they themselves fill-up the appropriate codes in these entry spaces. Though this saves a lot of time, it yet is quite a risky procedure. The worker can fill in wrong codes due to carelessness or forgetfulness and this would vitiate the whole effort. Accordingly, it is more advisable to do coding at the editing stage.

The last stage in research is the classification and description of data by means of statistical methods. Now the conclusion of the research becomes available.

Kinds of Questions

A schedule contains different kinds of questions. The different types of questions are framed by the social scientist in order to elicit different types of informations on various aspects of a problem. Following are the main types of questions used in schedules-

1. **Structured questions**: These are the most simple of all types of questions. A structured question is that in which the possible alternative replies can be pre-determined and these are noted against the question. The respondent chooses one of the alternative that suits him and the interviewer either encircle all alternatives or crosses out all others that are inapplicable. Following examples will help understand the structured question form.

(a) Your marital Status: Married/unmarried, widower/ widow/separated/divorced.

(b) Your Economic Status: Low/Low-middle/High-middle/ Rich/Very Rich.

2. **Open end Questions**: In these questions, the respondents are given no alternative answers. They have to make replies on their own after due thinking. These are the types of questions where the possible alternative replies cannot be exhausted and, therefore, cannot be pre-determined. Following are examples of this types :

(a) What, according to you, are the causes of communalism in India?
(b) How can the virus of communalism be removed in your opinion?
(c) What measures would you suggest for National integration?

3. **Dichotomous Questions**: These are the questions which admit of only two alternatives, a positive, and a negative, the example of dichotomous questions are :

(a) Are you employed – Yes/No.
(b) Do you think present government is socialistic – Yes/No.
(c) Do you think India will break-up like Pakistan – Yes/No.

4. **Multiple Choice Questions**: In these, various alternatives are given. The respondent has to choose one of these.

An example – Which profession do you like most -

(i) Agriculture
(ii) Business or Commerce
(iii) Government service
(iv) Private Service
(v) Engineering
(vi) Medicine

(vii) Teaching
(viii) Law
(ix) Journalism
(x) Any others.

A care should be taken to include all possible alternatives in the multiple choice questions.

5. **Leading Questions**: These are the questions where the preferred answer is hinted. Though it is not necessary that a respondent would choose the suggested alternative, there is a strong bias in its favour. These questions are suited to determine if the respondent is of independent or servile nature. The examples of this types are :

(a) Is it not desirable that teachers must keep themselves free from politics?

(b) Will it not be better if girls are given education suited to make them good house wives?

(c) It is not desirable that women should be denied employment in government and private services so that more men may be employed and the problem of unemployment be reduced?

(d) Is it not desirable to give total sex freedom to young boys and girls to eradicate the lure of pornography, pot-smoking and juvenile crimes?

6. **Ambiguous Questions**: Sometimes questions are included in the schedule as can be interpreted in more than one way. Such questions are detective and undesirable to be included in the schedule. Following are the examples of this type :

(a) Do you play with yourself?
(b) Do you give lectures?
(c) Do you take tonic foods?

The question (a) may mean playing the game of patience or seeking self-gratification. The questions (b) may be understood to mean whether you are a teacher or a public speaker. Similarly (c) may be understood to mean medical tonics or it may mean apples, milk, eggs etc.

7. **Ranking Item questions**: In these questions various alternatives are given; but unlike the multiple choice question where one alternative had to be picked-up; here the various alternatives are to be arranged in order of your preference. For example which o the following professions you like best? Give them in order of your preference; putting the most-liked on top and the least-liked on bottom-

1. University Professor
2. I.A.S. officer
3. Advocate in Supreme Court

4. Director of Research Institution
5. Physician or Surgeon
6. The General Manager
7. Chartered Accountant

Defective Questions

Following types of questions must not be included in the schedule as these will impede or injure the cause of research. The questions are defective.

1. **Long or Circumlocutory Questions**: If a question is very long or put in a roundabout way, it is difficult to apprehend its meaning. It should either be broken into parts or the unnecessary expressions should be removed.

2. **Complex Questions**: A complex question is also difficult to understand. For example, the question, would you deem it worth your while to develop in you worthiness and ability to exercise your right to vote? Actually, the question merely is, Do you vote? By contrast, we can appreciate how difficult it would be to grasp the meaning of the first question.

3. **Presumptuous Questions**: It is undesirable to include those questions in which the answer is presumed or suggested.

4. **Personal Questions**: Most of the respondents do not like to answer very intimate questions which probe the secrets or privacy of their lives. For example, no one would like to answer a question like this – Have you ever felt important with you wife? What do you think was the cause of your importance? Obviously, such questions may not be included in the schedule.

5. **Questions Regarding Social and Moral Ideals**: Even when one flouts in private life the moral and social ideals of a society, one would not like to publicly express his disapproval of these. Therefore, a schedule must not have questions about the validity and desirability or mores and social norms prevalent in the society. If such questions are put, only artificial answer can be expected. For example, the questions – Do you favour abolition of marriage? Would you like sexual relations depicted in individual arts? – cannot be answered in proper manner; therefore these must be ruled out of the schedule.

6. **Unrelated Questions**: As we remarked earlier only strictly topical questions ought to be included in a schedule. There is no place in it for out of context and unrelated questions.

7. **Unnecessary Questions**: As the time at the disposal of interviewer is limited, such questions, whose answer can be known by ordinary observation, must not be included in the schedule.

8. **Upsetting Questions**: Such questions as – Do you avoid tax payment? or do you sleep with women other than your wife? – merely upset the respondent and serve no useful purpose in research. Accordingly, such questions may find no place in the schedule.

Questions Worth Inclusion

The foregoing discussion gives us an idea about the questions unworthy of inclusion in the schedule. Form them it is possible to infer the kind and nature of questions which will be worth of inclusion in the schedule, because the questions having qualities opposite to the worthy will obviously be considered unworthy. It is not possible to frame rules about worthy questions; this has to determined by the nature of inquiry and the nature of respondents. However, following are the qualities which are to be connected in questions fit for inclusion in the schedule.

1. **Simple and Clear Questions**: The questions included in the schedule must be simple and clear, that is, they must be easily intelligible.

2. **Suitable to Respondent's Intelligence level**: Even a most complex and circuitous question may be grasped in a second, by some individuals, and, on the other hand, most simple questions may appear humdrums to them. Therefore, it is impossible to determine the intelligibility of questions in abstract. This has to be done with reference to the intelligence level of the respondent. This is why the preliminary test is so crucial in the formulation of the schedule.

3. **Relevant**: Relevance is a high water mark of the worth and suitability of any question. The questions of the schedule must strictly be related to the problem in hand.

4. **Indirect Questions**: There are certain matters in which it is inadvisable to ask a direct question, because it causes embarrassment, whereas the desired information can be easily elicited by putting an indirect question. For example, instead of asking name of the political party for whom you would vote, we may ask, which political party, do you think, has most dedicated leadership?

5. **Serial Order**: The questions pertaining to single item should not be scattered all over the schedule, but should find place together.

6. **Classifiability**: The questions included in a schedule must be divisible in certain sets or classes. It should not have questions which are completely unrelated, i.e., each is a class in itself. If this happens no classification will be possible and this will make the task of research insurmountable.

7. **Verifiable Question**: The questions in a research schedule should be seen as can be verified.

8. **Impersonal Questions**: From the fact that the questions of intimate nature probing the personal lives of the respondents are unsuitable for a schedule, it follows that the questions included in the schedule should be impersonal in character.

9. Unambiguous Questions: The research schedule should have only those questions which can be interpreted in one way alone and have no ambiguous or doubtful expression in them.

10. Answerable in few words: One should not include in the research schedule the questions which can be answered in long essays alone. The time at the interviewer's disposal is limited and so is the space in which the answer are to be entered. Therefore, as far as possible, only questions which the answer which can be answered in few words should be included.

11. Questions regarding causes of sentiments: The questions related to sentiments and opinions of the respondents should be supplemented by questions enquiring into the causes of these. This will reveal the background of the opinions, ideas and sentiments of the respondents.

From the above discussion regarding the fitness of questions to be included in the schedule, one fact which emerges clearly is that the form and style of the question play a great role in making the questions intelligible. The language of the questions must be simple and unadorned, the use of metaphor, rhetorics and other adornments should be strictly avoided as these may, no doubt make the language beautiful, the meaning is surely veiled by these embellishments. As per style, circumlocution, terseness and flouridity should be eschewed. The literary embellishments are out of place in the scientific language, because the function of literature is to veil the real meaning and the function of science is to make the meaning transparent.

Moreover, the technical and unfamiliar expressions should be eschewed as far as possible. The relative expressions like little, more, some, almost all, often etc., tend to confuse the meaning and therefore, these should be replaced by definite expressions. Instead of "little", it is better to mention the actual value in quantitative terms like 5%, 1/10, 2 to 11 etc.

Important Rules Regarding Serial Order

Besides the language and style of questions, the order of the questions is of vital importance for the good schedule. Following rules are to be followed to determine this order-

1. **Natural subject order:** The order of questions should be such that the succeeding question should appear to follow naturally from the preceding, that is, the subsequent question may assume something to the earlier questions; but the earlier question should not contain things which are better explained in later questions.

2. **Integral wholeness of schedule:** The question in a schedule should be so connected with each other that the entire schedule should appear to be a connected whole where nothing is out of place or unconnected.

3. **Title-wise order:** The various aspects of the problem should be sifted and separated. Firstly, the order of title should be determined and then questions under each title should be inserted.

4. **Order by attractiveness:** Another method determining the order is to determine the appeal and attraction of the questions, and thereafter the questions may be arranged putting the most attractive question on the top and least attractive on the bottom.

5. **Simple to complex order:** Still another method of arrangement of questions, is to determine the range of simplicity of each question and, thereafter, placing the most simple question on the top and follow the descending order, that is, placing the least simple or most complex question at the bottom of the list. This appears to be an eminently suitable procedure of arrangement because if the interview starts with simple questions, the respondent will be encouraged to cooperate; but if he begins with tough questions, the respondent will be discouraged.

Merits of Schedule

Whereas in the questionnaire method the list of questions is dispatched to respondents by post and they are requested to fill it up and return it by post, in schedule method, the research worker goes to the respondents and presents them the list of questions and fills-up the replies in the schedule himself. As compared with questionnaire the schedule has following advantages-

1. **Higher percentage of responses:** It can be easily appreciated that the return of the questionnaire depends exclusively on the goodwill of the respondents. If they have slightest doubt or suspicion they would not respond and they cannot be persuaded nor their suspicions removed, since no one is present to allay their doubts. In the schedule, a research worker is present and he can explain, persuade, even cajole the respondent to make response. On account of this, it is small wonder that the percentage of responses of schedule are much higher than those of questionnaire.

2. **Personality-factor:** In as much as the research worker is entrusted with the job of getting the schedule filled up, he tries by all the means available to him to get the job done. Since he is well trained and informed about respondents' habits etc., he is able to approach them in a way that they are influenced by his personality and charm. A person who knows his job well, behaves well and also appears well. This is a common observation.

3. **Personal contact:** In the schedule method there is personal contact between the respondent and the respondent and the field worker. The behaviour, character and intelligence of the field worker succeeds often in winning the confluence of respondents. This obviously facilitates his task.

4. **Human touch**: Sometimes reading a thing does not impress so much as when the same is heard or spoken by experts. They are able to lay right emphasis. This greatly helps better response.

5. **Removal of doubts**: In the questionnaire, if the respondents is unsure about the meaning of a question he either leaves it blank or fills in any imaginary answer. But in the schedule, in case of doubt the meaning is made clear by the field worker. Moreover if a respondent is afraid that certain information may be used against him, his doubt can be allayed by the worker by telling him that the schedules are strictly confidential, and if need be, allow the respondent to remain anonymous. Furthermore, the presence of the field worker acts as a deterrent against giving artificial replies because there is fear of cross examination and being found out.

6. **Knowledge of Defect**: If there are some defects in questionnaire it is liable to remain unnoticed; but in the schedule method such defects easily come to notice and rectified.

7. **Filling up of Schedules by Research Workers**: In as much as the research workers who are socially trained fill up the schedules, the likelihood of errors and defects is much less compared with questionnaire where the responses are filled by respondents.

Limitation of Schedule Method

Inspire of above mentioned merits of the schedule method, it also has, like all other methods, some difficulties or limitations. The discussion of the schedule method cannot be completed without mention of these :

1. **Costly and Time-consuming**: As compared with questionnaire, schedule method is generally container and more time consuming. But this factor becomes a serious limitation when the respondents are not found in a particular region but are scattered over a wide area. To approach them all is prohibitively costly, besides involving excessive time.

2. **Requirement of a large number of well-trained field workers**: The schedule method requires very large number of well trained and experienced field workers. An ill-trained and inexperienced worker is a liability. Therefore if becomes very difficult, if not impossible, to hire a large number of experienced workers. It involves great cost and sometimes so many workers are not easily available and one cannot depend upon inexperienced hands.

3. **Adverse Effect of Personal Presence**: Whereas the personal presence proves helpful in assuring the respondents, removing their doubts, it also becomes an inhibiting factor. Many people can note down certain facts on papers but cannot say them in others' presence.

4. **Organisation Difficulty**: In the field of research is sprawling, it becomes difficult to organize research. To gather workers who are well-

acquainted with various geographical regions and different types of people is a herculean task. Though not beyond achievement, it is certainly difficult.

From the above discussion about merits and demerits of the schedule method, it is clear that the schedule methods can be well used in a limited region and on limited number of respondents.

✶✶✶✶✶✶

Chapter – 13

Case Study Method

Defining the case study method, Mrs P. V. Young writes: "Case study is a method of exploring and analyzing the life of a social unit, be that a person, a family, institution, culture, group or even entire community." Its aim and goal is to know precisely the factors and causes which explain the complex behavioural patterns of a unit and the place of the unit in its surrounding social milieu. Goode and Hatt define the case study method as "a way of organising social data so as to present the unitary character of the social subject being studied. Expressed somewhat differently, it is an approach which views a research scientist, "Case study method may be defined as a small inclusive an intensive study of an individual in which the investigator brings to bear all his skills and methods, or as a systematic gathering of enough information about a person to permit one to understanding how he or she functions as a unit of society." Biesanz and Bieasanz have defined case study method as "a form of qualitative analysis involving the very careful and complete observation of a person, a situation or an institution."

Characteristics of Case Study

1. Study of a Unit: The case study method studies a subject matter which forms a cohesive whole and may be treated as a unit. It is not necessary that this unit must always be a person. It can be an institution or a group or even a community, provided these are cohesive and homogeneous and may be studied as integral wholes.

2. Intensive or Depth Study: The quantitative methods study only those aspects of a subject which it shares in common with other similar subjects. Therefore, they study a subject in its particular aspect and not in its entirety. But the case study method, on the contrary, deals with every aspect of the subject and studies it both intensively and extensively. Thus each element is studied deeply and no element is left untouched.

3. Knowledge of Behaviour Patterns: The case study method deals with both what and why of the subject, that is, it tries to describe the complex behavioural pattern of a unit and, having done this, tries to discover the factors which will rationally account for them. In brief, case study method aims at description as well as explanation of the unit it studies. It also explains the place and role of a unit in its surrounding social milieu.

4. The Study of the Whole Unit: The case study method tries to perceive the unitary forces of the subject matter and organizes it into an integral whole. According to Goode and Hatt the case study method is a means of organizing and intergrating the social material by which its integrity and wholeness can be preserved. In other words, it is a viewpoint which sees the social phenomenon as an integral unit having unifying bond of thread binding all of its diverse elements. Accordingly, this method treals man.

Aids to Integral Study

From the above description of the case study it is quite clear that the primary need in this method is to know the manner and technique by which the subject matter appears as an integral whole. For this purpose following points are to be borne in mind :

1. Extension of Matorial: In the case study method an extensive collection of the relevant material is made and this helps in getting an overall view of the problem.

2. Material regarding every aspect: The sole means of achieving success in case study method is to collect material about each of the aspects in a unit. For example, while studying a human person, the information about his social status and situation is primary but equally important is to gather all information regarding his biological, economic, political, psychological and philosophical including religious, ethical and spiritual aspects. Only then can we understand the unity of a human being and study him as an expression of that fundamental unity.

3. Classification: The entire data about a unit should be divided into suitable classes.

4. Temporal Study: The study of a case must be dynamic. It should not merely attend to the present structure of a unit but must consider it in its developmental aspects. Therefore, the case study must range over the past, present and future time.

From the above discussion it is clear that in the case study method, a subject is studied both horizontally and longitudinally that is, we study it in breadth as well as in depth.

Postulates of Case Study

The case study method is not merely a technique but is a belief, a viewpoint and an outlook in modern sciences. Spelled briefly, this outlook is an expression of a belief that various social phenomena, inspire of their apparent diversities, are fundamentally expressions of underlying unities. This belief is not demonstrable but is based on certain basic assumptions. These are :

1. Fundamental Unity of Human Nature: Until and unless we grant the basic fact that no two men are totally different but all men share a common nature and are fundamentally alike in some crucial matter, there is no sense in the case history method. For example, if some persons are totally rational and others totally impulsive and emotional, we shall have two species of men and there will be no element or essence like human nature. But the scientist assumes that there is something like essential human nature and that this is same in every man. Moreover, the social behaviour of men is a result of interaction between external and internal forces. In a more or less similar circumstances human beings show same type of behaviour. A social scientist grants that men are basically same and that the causes for differences in their behaviour are to be thought in their social milieu.

2. Resources or Circumstances: Besides believing in the fundamental sameness of human nature, the research scientist also believes that the marginal changes. For example, the family environment has definite influence on the development of a child. Now, this family environment is more or less same for two children whose parents are similar in economic and social status and the number and order of whose children is same. That is to say an only child is liable to be impaired whether it is 19th Century French Society or 10th Century Indian Society. The fundamental sameness of human nature and the tendency for social conditions to recur are as a matter of fact interrelated phenomena. The studies of various cultures and various times prove the fact that all cultures and all times display many similar patterns of social conditions and behaviour.

3. Effect of Temporal Order: It is a common knowledge that human persons, institutions, groups etc., are dynamic entities which undergo change with time. Accordingly, the study of these cannot be worthwhile unless it is long range and over considerable period of time so that institutions and groups in their various aspects may become well known.

4. Similarity of Responses in Human Beings: The perusal of personal memories, diaries, confessions and autobiographies reveals that whereas each human being shows his peculiarities and eccentricities, the fundamental responses are more or less the same. The diaries of a period when sex was freely indulged, the personal feelings and responses of people are more or less same. It is estimated that the quantum of sexual outlet does not vary greatly from time to time. Similarly, there have always been family feuds, murders, love triangles, practice of prostitution etc. All these go to show that there is a basic similarity in human responses.

Case Study and Statistical Techniques

There are some fundamental differences between the case study method and statistical techniques. The major points of differences are :

1. **Qualitative Study**: Whereas statistical techniques are formal and quantitative, the case study method studies its subject matter qualitatively.

2. **Depth Study**: Whereas the statistical method study particular aspects of numerous units, the case study method covers all aspects of a single unit.

3. **Lack of Sample:** This follow from the above point. In as much as the case study method studies everything in a single unit; therefore the question of sample study does not arise. In statistical methods, on the contrary, some representative units or some representative aspects of the units may be studied.

4. **Emphasis on Emotional Aspect**: The statistical method give no place to emotional aspects of the subject matter, since these are not quentifiable. Their approach to their subject matter is formal and generalised. The cases study method, on the contrary, studies a unit in all its aspects and the emotional factors have special importance in the case study in as much as the emotions factors have special importance in the case study in as much as the emotions and statements are the real foundation pillars of human beings as well as institutions and without due emphasis on these we cannot have insight into the working of any social phenomenon.

5. **Conclusions Based on General Knowledge**: In the statistical methods, the conclusions are drawn by strictly mathematical techniques of quantification. But in the case study method the conclusions are drawn on theoretical basis. The conclusions of case study method cannot obviously be quantative; they are qualitative.

The above differences between the statistical and qualitative methods notwithstanding, there are important points of agreement between the two. As Kimball Young puts it: "As a matter of fact many of the basic problems of case history method are not unlike those of statistics." According to Kimball Young following important points of agreement are to be found in the two methods :

1. In order to remove the possibility of error in generaliztation, the case study method also makes sample survey of other units.

2. In the case study method the experiments of the same nature as in statistical techniques are made to measure the central tendency.

3. As in statistical methods, the range of deviation is measured, in the same way the change of actions and reactions in the individual are measured in case study method.

4. As in the statistical techniques we try to know about correlations, co-deviations, in the same manner, we try to determine the agreement or similarity and differences in the case studies.

Keeping in view the above similarities between the statistical techniques and case study method, L. T. Bernard rightly observes, "The real source of methodological error (in case study) is in supposing that statistical generalisations can proceed from case data without some sort of statistical method." Accordingly, the two techniques are interdependent. Without the use of some statistical techniques no generalized quantitative conclusions having reliability are possible. Therefore, every wise research worker skillfully combines the techniques of case study and quantitative analysis.

Sources of Case Study

In the case study we make use of personal documental diaries, confessions, autobiographies and memoires. The sources of case study maybe divided into two categories: Personal documents and Case History. They are discussed below :

1. **Personal documents**: These include all those materials which throw light on the feelings, moods and reactions of an person to his social milieu. The diatries usually include reflection of a person regarding other people and things. The same is the case with memories, autobiographies, etc. These are goldmines of invaluable information and insight for the social historian and social scientist. In the words of P.V. Young: "Personal documents also tend to represent a continuity the experience of which helps to illuminate the writer's personality; social relations and philosophy of life, often expressed in terms of subjective appreciation as if it were so." Diary is a perennial and continuous record of personal reflections. It contains the emotional and intellectual responses of the writer to his multiform experiences. The diaries contain very personal and intimate items. This provides in many cases new lights and new insights hitherto veiled. The personal correspondences also are free, frank and intimate. Ordinarily, it is considered boorish and uncivilized to read the correspondence of other people. But after a lapse of sufficient is very interesting and provocative. Similarly, memoires and autrobiographies are extremely useful sources of information in the cast study method.

2. **Case Study**: In the case study method, besides personal documents detailed above, the case history is another important sources of information. This case history is collected detailed information about the life of a person and talks to him, whenever needed, to collect and verify the information gathered. For example, if we wish to collect information about the childhood of a man; we shall interview parents of that person, his neighbours, playmates and other individuals who watched him as a child or participated with him in various

childhood activities. Besides personal interview the information about a person can be gathered in various other ways. He may be watched while doing his routines or giving a public lecture or engaged in conversation and test his to visit a nigh-club, sex show or a famous personality. His reactions will tell us all about his moral qualities. Sometimes a person is hypnotized in order to bring to surface hidden memories. In short, all available socio- psycho- medical methods may be used to collect an authentic case history.

Major Importance of Case Study

1. **Formation of Valid Hypothesis**: In as much as it is a fundamental assumption of the case study method that human nature is uniform, very many valid hypotheses can be constructed on its basis. For example, granting uniformity of human nature we may validly assume that inspite of total sexual permissiveness of the Western Society, sexual jealously will not cease althogether and that there will continue to be cases of marital strife, divorces and sexual vindictiveness.

2. **Aid of Sampling**: The case studies help in classifying the units in a much better and efficient manner. A case study helps to fix defintely the character of a particular unit, and this, in turn to classify it and similar units under a well determined head.

3. **Aid to forming Questionnires and Schedules**: The greatest obstacle in the way of forming a useful and efficient questionnaire is the selection of queries which will yield the desired response. The case studies are of immense value in this regard.

4. **Discovering Deviant Units**: The cases which do not fit in the general pattern of an assumption are call deviant. Normally, these deviant cases are not accorded very great importance, because they are marginal and do not compare with the amount of information yielded by general cases, but sexuality is primarily due to the study of deviant cases. The homosexual and the sade-masochist tell us more about sexual behaviour than a normal heterosexual individual. The case study method is very useful in the study of deviations.

5. **Study of Process**: A stabilized material can be studied by a technique; but the effective study of dynamic and mobile material requires intensive and genetic approach possible only in the case study method.

6. **Gain in Experience**: Since in the case study a researcher undertakes an intensive as well as extensive study of a definite unit for a long period, he gains many new insights into human behaviour and becomes emotionally mature. The researcher studying a prostitute may learn more about human behaviour than researchers using different techniques and studying 1000 female delinquents.

7. Appreciation of Quantitative analysis in actual situations: The reserchers who do not come in contact with the actual situations and individuals would not quiite appreciate the various statistics about delinquency, prostitution, larceny, gangesterism, etc. A researcher doing actual case work can appreciate these far better.

Major Limitations of Case Study

From the above it becomes quite clear that the case study method is a useful technique of studying social material. But like all other methods, it has its own defects. These defects and limitations are as follows :

1. False Self confidence: Whereas a social researcher using all other techniques is constantly aware of the limitations of his knowledge, the researcher using case study method, on account of his deep and long acquaintance with a social subject, is liable to develop a false conviction that he knows all about his subject. He thinks that he needs learn nothing more about it. But this is untrue in the nature of the case. No one can claim that he knows anything so fully that no new fact will possibly be known about it by any body. As a matter of fact, the claim to know all is foreign to a scientific temper.

2. Chaotic and Unorganized: Since there is consideration given to representative character of a unit and the researcher is free to choose arbitrarily a case of study, a mistaken choice of the case will yield no reliable information.

3. Small-Unit-based Conclusions: However deep and penetrating a study may be, its conclusions will not be generally valid if the unit chosen for study is very small. For example, if a researcher studies a single prostitute and comes to the conclusion that prostitution is an art, the conclusion may have some validity in cases of highly sophisticated prostitutes but will be generally untrue, because to become an artist one needs total dedication to one's career but it is quite untrue to think that most prostitutes are highly enamored of their profession.

4. Highly Expensive and Time Saving: For a deep research study of a number of units the cost and time factor is prohibitive. It may take year to study some units. Of course, time and money spent is worthwhile if some grasp strides in knowledge become possible, but usually much effort is exhausted in routine things.

5. Possibility of Error: There are high chances of making errors in the selection of case, observation, noting and interview. Since the concentration is on a single subject one is less likely to become aware of the mistake and the mistake may become compounded in the absence of countervailing checks. Therefore, case study method is error-prone, and only a judicious and cautions researcher can avoid these.

6. Ad-hoc Theorizing: In the case study, instead of rational explanation deductively derived, *ad hoc* theorizing is very likely. Again, in the absence of checks on errors, theories are likely to appear quite sound and satisfactory.

7. Other Defects: Besides the above defect, eminent social scientists have pointed out many other drawbacks. Firstly, since the research worker in case study is dealing with a single case over a long time and in all aspects, he is liable to develop deep support and sympathy with his subject. This may affect the researcher emotionally and he may report conclusions which appeal to him. This may be seen in a number of case studies of prostitutes which tend to glorifyand praise them from their capacity of suffering, self effecement, etc. Secondly, the subjects of study themselves are so distinct facts as not to fall in the esteem of the scientist. Instead of giving a true narration of events, the subject laces his narration with a heavy does of imagination and tries to prove himself better than he actually is. He is lekely drop those facts which are vicious and immoral and would show him in poor light. Moreover, since all narration is done by a single individual there is on scope for cooperative study in their method.

Suggestion for Improvement

Inspite of above defects, the case study method is widely used in modern research. As we have already mentioned in the discussion of the defects, judiciousness and caution can remove many of these. Relative to the development of false confidence, it may be observed that this defect is not so much due to the method as due to a weakness of human nature. As a matter of fact, over-confidence is foreign to scientific temper and, therefore, in the selection of a case, this can be well-planned. And if the respondent's replies are light-keyed, their veracity can be checked by other sources. If the researches are classified according to general principles the scope for comparative study can be provided for.

As a matter of fact the greatest necessity in the case study method is to make it well-organized and the collection of facts should be made according to definite aim and principle so that they may not degenerate into fanciful tales. The classification must be well done and precisely defined. The amount of caution and judicious approach will repay rich dividents in the case study method.

The eminent researcher like Goode and Hatt, Carl Rogers, Mirra Komarovsky, Alfred C. Kinsey and John Dollard etc. have offered useful suggestions for effecting improvements in the case study method. By implementing above suggestions a lot of improvement can be made in the collection of data, its organisation and editing. By integrating the sampling technique with case study method and prearranged interviews, the effectiveness of case study, is multiplied manifold. These can render case study a fullfledged scientific technique. By not taking the subject matter of study as a single unit but taking it as a representative of its class the study can yield general principles. The study of each case should range over long period and should cover all aspects of the case including genetic or developmental. The material gained through the study should follow standard rules of organisation and classification. For the derivation of conclusion, the statistical technique should be use. For this purpose, Mertion, Kelly and others have offered uusful suggestions. By the incorporation of the above suggestions the case study method can be improved.

******

Chapter - 14

Questionnaire

Questionnaire is a printed list of questions sent through mail to respondents to be returned by the respondents after filling up the questionnaire. According to G.A. Lundberg, "Fundamentally, the questionnaire is a set of stimuli to which literate people are exposed in order to observe their verbal behaviour under these stimuli." In the questionnaire, as the name show, there is a set of selected questions whose answers, the researcher seeks from respondent in order to gain knowledge about certain specified matter. Since the questionnaire can be addressed only to literate people. A second feature of the mailed questionnaire which has been emphasized by W. J. Goode and P. K. Hatt is the fact the responses to a mailed questionnaire have to be made by respondents themselves. According to them, "In general, the word questionnaire refers to a device for securing answers to questions by using a form which the respondent fills in himself." The exchange of questions and answers by mail is the most economical of all other research methods of data collection. Writing about this aspect, C. A. Moser observes : "Without doubt the mailed questionnaire is generally quicker and cheaper than other methods." Since the questionnaire is sent to a restricted number of individuals, its scope is rather limited; but within its limited scope it can prove to be the most effective means of eliciting information, provided, however, that it is well formulated and the respondents fill in their genuine responses.

Criterion of Appropriateness

Regarding the qualities and features which make a research questionnaire an effective instrument of research and help to elicit maximum information, W.J. Goode and P.K. Hatt have pointed out the following factors :

1. **The type of the information required** – In the field of modern research, the usefulness and effectiveness of the mailed questionnaire is fired by the kind of the information sought. Not every type of information can be

elicited through it. A research questionnaire which will consume more than 10 to 20 minutes is unlikely to be responded well. Therefore, an appropriate questionnaire should contain only that number of questions which can be easily filled in 10 to 20 minutes. Moreover, the questions should be explicit and capable of clear-cut replies. Some research workers have found that if the information sough through a questionnaire is of personal and intimate nature the responses are better if the names of the anonymous, the information regarding sex and income can be had. If the questionnaire of this type is prepared with proper, the respondents disclose their identity.

Thirdly, if the information asked is not very complex and deep, the mailed questionnaire is suitable. However, the information sought through it is not so deep as in the case of an interview. The main reason for this is that in an interview a close rapport can be established between the interviewer and the interviewee. This interviewer can coax and cajole the interviewee to come out with the requisite information. For this, the interviewer has to be very skilled, tactful and amiable person who can inspire confidence and work very diligently as well as intelligently. For example, in studying the sexual habits and love relation of university students, it can be known only with great tact and resourcefulness as to how many students, it can be known only, how many have causal sex relation with their classmates and how many indulge in group sex. A questionnaire cannot elicit such information.

Here the replies are likely to be fake. But in an interview, if a girl is asked does she masturbate and she replies no, immediately another query is made do you neither masturbate nor sleep with boys, you must be sleeping with girls. To avoid being considered lesbian she will tell the truth. The main difference between an interview and questionnaire is that in our civilized society many acts are considered vicious, unlawful and against the spirit and ethos of the society. Yet there is strong temptation to do them. The conflict between personal desire and social conscience makes us feel guilty in doing those acts; and we try our best to conceal them from public view lest our social image be destroyed. Consequently, no one would fill up in the questionnaire positive responses to questions like; Do you make love to women other than your wife? But in an interview a casual remark may give the interviewer with a clue to probe the secrets of the interviewee, and if the interviewer tackles the issue delicately and with a finesse, he may succeed in ferreting out the desired responses. From this discussion it becomes quite clear that the questionnaire technique is suitable only where the emotionally-charged material is not used in formulation of questions.

1. **The type of the information reached**: A good deal depends upon the types of respondents covered by the questionnaire. The experience tells us that

all types of individual cannot be good respondents. There are many who would rather consign the questionnaire to w.p.b. than waste their time over it. Only literate and socially conscious individuals would give may consideration to questionnaire. Every body does not realize the importance and usefulness of modern research. Only those who appreciate the value of modern research are likely to be good respondents.

Secondly, since the researcher is not present when the questionnaire reaches the respondents he can do little to motivate them to fill up the questionnaire. Therefore, to respond or not to respond is a sweet discretion of the respondent.

Most of all, the respondents must be of the type who is competent to answer the kind of questions contained in a particular questionnaire. For example, if a questionnaire is about the experiences of third-class railway travel, a government secretary or a business man can hardly be expected to fill up such a questionnaire. It can be answered only by those who travel frequently and travel usually by the third class. Moreover, those who experience hardships of travel would be quite willing to fill up the questionnaire because their informations may help removal of hardships.

Besides literary persons, the persons belonging to upper strata of society are unlikely to be good respondents. They are either too preoccupied or are too sophisticated to feel any interest in the filling up of a questionnaire. However, certain types of questionnaire are filled up by all concerned. For example, if a person receives a questionnaire about his bio-data for inclusion in who is who, every one receiving such a questionnaire will promptly fill it up.

2. **The Accessibility of Respondents**: The major merit of the mailed questionnaire is that by its means a large number of scattered respondents are contacted easily and cheaply. If the researcher were to interview 5 persons each in Delhi, Mumbai, Kolkata, Mysore, Chennai, Kanpur, Secunderabad and Nagpur, he may take few months to reach them all but by a mailed questionnaire they can be reached in only one week time. Moreover, if the problem is of international significance and we want to have a cross-section of opinion from all over the world, it is well-high impossible to collect the required information except by means of a mailed questionnaire. Therefore, the mailed questionnaire may be considered the best method for surveying the opinion of people living far and apart.

3. **The precision of the hypothesis**: Whether the mailed questionnaire is appropriate for the research in a particular problem depends upon how realistic is the hypothesis in the mind of the researcher which he wished to verify. The researcher must frame his questions in such a manner that they

elicit responses needed to verify the hypothesis. As a precaution, the realism of the hypothesis should be tested by interview before mailing the questionnaire.

Formulation of Questionnaire

From the above discussion it is clear that the success depends largely on the skill and insight with which the list of questions are formulated. These questions must be unequivocal and easily intelligible. The following considerations should be kept in mind while formulating a questionnaire :

1. **Appeal**: Attached with every questionnaire is an appeal in which the aim and purpose of the enclosed questionnaire is set forth and sincere cooperation of the respondents is sought. The appeal should be short, clear and direct, establishing the genuineness of the research and its utility for all concerned. The long and wordy appeals tax the patience of the respondents. Though the appeal must be short, it must cover the following points without fail :

(i) The appeal must state clearly the individuals or organizations undertaking the research. If the research is government aided the fact should be clearly mentioned. The quality of paper and printing is quite an important consideration. If the paper is of superior quality and printing and get up of high order, respondents feel inclined to take interest in it. Shabby and defective printing act as disincentive.

(ii) The appeal should set forth in clear terms the aim and purpose of the proposed research study and also the benefits likely to accrue from it. Usually the heading or title of research is self explanatory. As, for example. "The breakdown of Joint Family in urban areas:, but it some further explanation is necessary it must be given.

(iii) The appeal should make clear, why is it important for the respondents to fill it up. The respondents should be motivated and made to realize the validity and utility of the research project. Sometimes some monetary incentive is also given. But as a rule is not enough to produce a real interest. The wording of appeal should be such that an interest is created among the respondents. It may be helpful if the respondent is told that his contribution is likely to make difference in the world of knowledge and he can feel proud to be a factor in the promotion of knowledge. Depending upon the nature of research and the availability of funds, many ways can be found to motivate the responded.

(iv) Another method of making the appeal effective is an offer to the respondents that their names will be kept anonymous, and that all steps will be taken to ensure that one comes to know anything about them. The precaution is necessary where information about private life or income is required.

2. **Instruction for filling up the Questionnaire**: Besides an appeal, the questionnaire must carry a list of instructions for filling it up and dispatching it.

The respondent must not have to pay for the return postage. It should either be pre-paid or stamps for the required amount should be enclosed.

3. **Form of the Questionnaire**: The get up and appearance of the questionnaire should be attractive. It must be tastefully printed on high quality paper. The sentences by which the questions are asked should be direct and forceful. Lacking these qualities, the questionnaire will be consigned to w.p.p.

4. **Clarity of Questions**: For the desired responses, it is of utmost importance to formulate the questions clearly and precisely. There should be no ambiguity and no dubiousness about them. They should lend themselves to a single interpretation. The best method is to ensure that our questionnaire does not have any misleading or confusing question, it should be first tried on a selected group of individuals and suitable modification should be made in questions in the light of the experience with the selected group.

5. **Serial order of questions**: The questions should be broken up into classes and each class should have a number of questions which are mutually interrelated. The order of questions should be such that the first should seem naturally to lead to the second. The second may depend upon the first, but the first should not depend upon the second; otherwise the order of questions will cease to be systematic and will become chaotic.

6. **Attractiveness**: Upon the attractiveness of the questionnaire depends to a large extent the success of the questionnaire. The attractiveness of a questionnaire is determined by the prestige of the researcher, of research organization and the form and style of the questionnaire. Besides, if the research project is aided by the government its prestige increases. If the above qualities are present the respondents are likely to take interest in the questionnaire.

Preliminary test of Questionnaire

As discussed above about the formulation, form and style of the questionnaire, it is advisable to try out questionnaire on a select group before making it final. This calls for preliminary testing of the questionnaire. In this connection, the following points should be borne in mind :

1. The questionnaire to be tested should be complete in all respects.

2. If, as a result of the preliminary test, some drastic changes are made in the questionnaire the revised questionnaire must be re-tested. The questionnaire which is shown by the preliminary test to be free from every blemish is worth sending through mail.

3. The respondents, to whom the questionnaire is mailed, must be representative of the class whose problems are discussed in the questionnaire. For example, a questionnaire about prostitution may not be sent to housewifes.

4. If a questionnaire on a preliminary test shows the following responses it should be considered defective :

(a) If it is unreturned.

(b) If the majority of questions are wrongly answered.

(c) If the majority of questions remain unanswered.

(d) If different persons are giving varying answers to the same questions.

(e) If the answers are mutually contradictory.

Methods of Getting Response

1. **Self Addressed Envelope**: Having formulated the list of questions, the next problem is the get these filled up properly in due time by respondents. This depends, in turn, on how faithfully the methods of getting response have been applied. Normally, the respondent has little incentive to return the questionnaire, and the cannot be expected to suffer any monetary loss whatever. Therefore, the questionnaire must be accompanied by a self-addressed and prepaid envelope. Unless these courtesies are observed, the questionnaire may never be returned.

2. **Incentives**: In order to ensure the return of the questionnaire, various researchers prefer offering of various incentives. Some believe that monetary incentive must be given. The success with monetary incentive is possible only if the remuneration offered is adequate and proportionate to the labour involved in filling up of the questionnaire. It its more advisable to send the money in advance than to promise payment on return of the questionnaire. Inclusion of stamps is also a type of monetary incentive. Another method of ensuring the return of the questionnaire is the offer of prizes by lottery. For example, one may offer books worth Rupees Fifty each to 50% of the respondents. This will also ensure quick response because entitlement to prize can be made subject to return of the questionnaire by a particular data. A convincing explanation about the value of the research project can go a long way to ensure response. This will have to be included in the 'Appeal'.

3. **Reminders**: The most popular method used to ensure response is the issue of reminders. The reminders must be issued at adequate intervals. The adequacy of interval is determined by the time taken in transit by letters and two to three days are considered permissible for filling up of the questionnaire. This means that the adequate interval will be about 10 days. Moreover, the interval between first and second reminders should be more than between the original letter and the first reminder. For instance if the first reminder is sent after 10 days, the second should go 15 days subsequent to the first reminder. Similarly, the third reminder should be sent 20 days after the second and so on. Some research workers are of the opinion that as many as six reminders may be sent. If the first reminder is sent on a mere post card, the second should be sent

by registered post with the questionnaire attached with it. This is to ensure that the questionnaire has reached the respondent. All steps have to be taken to neutralize the negative effect of postal vagaries. It has been learnt from experience that about 90% of respondents send back the questionnaire by the third reminder.

4. **Mediation**: Another method of ensuring replies is to send the questionnaire through mediators. Usually it is sent through the head of the institution but such a procedure has the drawback of creating some misunderstanding among the respondents. They may take ill or feel slighted for not having been approached directly.

5. **Sufficient Interval**: The interval allowed between the receipt and return of the questionnaire should neither be too long nor too short. If it is too short the respondent may feel by the time he receives the questionnaire that it is too late to send the reply. But if the interval is very long, the respondent may feel relaxed and put off the reply to a more convenient time. Meanwhile many things may happen and he may forget all about it or misplace the questionnaire.

6. **Repetition**: To counter the postal vagaries and to allow for the absence of the respondent at the time of receipt of the questionnaire, the reply should be patiently waited. And if, unaccountable time has lapsed, the questionnaire and reminder may be sent again by the registered post.

7. **Good Questions**: The successful return of the questionnaire depends upon the fact as to how far the research worker succeeds in enlisting the cooperation of the respondents. Some circumstances and conditions which determine the attitudes of respondents towards the questionnaire are : (i) In comparison with higher strata people, the respondents belonging to the middle strata are more cooperative. (ii) The amount and kind of cooperation received also depends to a great extent on the prestige and reputation of the research worker or research organisation sponsoring the questionnaire. (iii) The importance and worth of the problem involved is a very important factor in influencing the attitudes of the respondents. (iv) The form and style of the questionnaire is very important. A simple, direct and brief questionnaire is better received than the complicated and lengthy questionnaire. (v) An attractive appearance also facilitates the response. The well-sequenced list of questions improves the changes of response. (vi) The use of unfamiliar, technical and abstruse terms baulks the response, whereas easy to understand language facilitates it. (vii) Lastly, an adequate and appropriate reward by way of advance payment or lottery system greatly improves the changes of response. The forceful and convincing appeal attached with the questionnaire enhances the chances of response.

Factors Vitiating Reliability

After receiving the filled-up questionnaire, the next main problem is that of determining whether the answers are reliable or not. As a matter of fact some social scientists are so skeptical about the reliability of answers in a mailed questionnaire that they have remarked that the maximum a replied questionnaire proves is that the that the respondent is cooperative. However, the majority of social scientists do not share this view and are prepared to regard the answers reliable, provided strict measures have been taken to avoid the general the reliability of answers. If these are present the reliability of the answers is greatly vitiated.

1. **Confusing questions**: If the questions are not easily intelligible or they are capable of being interpreted in more than one way, the answers are unreliable, because the answer may be due to an interpretation of the question not intended by the researcher. In the methods of Schedule and Interview, the investigator is present to explain the meaning of terms and questions, but this being not the case, confusing questions in a questionnaire will cause distortions in the replies.

2. **Prejudice regarding sample**: This point can be best understood by an example. Suppose, a questionnaire is mailed to 100 Ph. D's and more qualified; to 100 M.A.'s; 100 B.A.'s., 100 Intermediates and 100 High Schools. Thus 500 persons are on the list of respondents. Now suppose 80% replies are received: The replies will be considered representative of all education-level group if 0 to 85 replies from each category are received. But actually, 95 High Schools, 100 Intermediates, 95 B.A.'s and only 20 Ph. D's and better qualified, may have replied. Therefore, the conclusions will not be representative of the ideas and views of highly qualified individuals.

3. **Lack of coverage of illiterates**: In the nature of the case, the questionnaire method is inapplicable to illiterate and semiliterate. But in a country like India where the bulk of population is constituted by these two categories, the responses received through questionnaire can have little application and relevance to a vast majority. Therefore, many social problems cannot be studied by mailed questionnaire, particularly in Asian and African countries.

4. **Response selectivity**: The respondents of mailed questionnaire belong to a select group, that is, educated middle class. The individuals belonging to other groups are either unwilling to reply or are unable to do so, because of little or no education. Therefore the mailed questionnaire's conclusions lack the kind of objectivity and representativeness essential for its validity.

The biggest difficult in the questionnaire method is to make it representative and reliable. One measure which can help in this matter is to break up in two classes the prompt and late respondents. It should be observed if they belong to separate classes, and if so, whether the percentage of observed if the belong to separate classes, and if so, whether the percentage of responses by both classes is high or is it low for one of them. If it is equally high in both the cases, the responses will creep in. Another measure for increasing the efficiency of this method is to undertake follow-up studies. These will reveal a hard-core which is altogether unresponsive. This class should be persuaded by various means to become responsive. If the researcher can succeed in this his responses will become quite representative.

In order to increase and diversify the number of representatives, the questions should be such as can be answered easily and quickly. For this purpose a may be divided into sub-questions. It should be remembered that anything which taxes the patience of the respondent will be rejected by the respondent. Furthermore surveys may be learnt if there are some especial reasons which prevent a group from responding. If they can be rectified, the steps to do so should be taken.

If the researcher feels skeptical about the particular section, he should send the same questionnaire after a lapse of sufficient time. If there is variation in responses his skepticism is justified. The time gap should not be so long that the respondent's mental make-up may have undergone some change. Another method to determine the reliability of answer is to try them on a sample group. There are some inherent draw-backs on account of which the responses cannot be literally accepted. Most people would reply casually and may give different answers in different trials. These defects are the natural limitations of the questionnaire method; and, as we have noted above, all methods have their strong and weak points. The questionnaire method is no exception.

Limitations of Questionnaire

As a method of modern research, the questionnaire method is, like all other methods, limited in value and application. This means that it can be used in every situation and that its conclusion are not always reliable. Following, briefly, are the limitations of this method-

1. **Limited response**: This method cannot be used either on illiterate ore semi-literate persons. Furthermore, very preoccupied, travelling and aristocrat individuals do not reply. Therefore, the number of persons who cooperate and respond to the questionnaire is very small. The percentage of such persons is extremely low in the underdeveloped countries.

2. **Lack of personal contact**: There is no provision in this method for coming fact to fact with the respondents. However much a researcher may try to simplify and rationalize his questionnaire, it is not possible to avoid each and every technical term. Even if this can be done the aim and purpose of the

questionnaire can be much better explained personally than through the appeal. Lastly, in the absence of personal contact, very little can be done to persuade the respondents to fill up the questionnaire.

3. **Useless in depth problems**: If a problem requires deep and long study, it is obvious, it cannot be studied by the questionnaire method.

4. **Possibility of wrong answers**: A respondent may not really understand a question or may give the answer in a casual manner. In both cases there is strong like lihood of misleading information being given.

5. **Illegibility**: Some persons write so badly that even they themselves find it difficult to read their own hand.

6. **Incomplete responses**: Some persons give answers which are so brief that the full meaning is incomprehensible.

Considerations in Questionnaire

1. **Spontaneity and Flow**: The design of a questionnaire needs a deliberate planning from the very Ist question onwards so that the respondent is brought from one point to another without any reasons to shrink back from the effort of answering the questions. The respondent must feel that the progression of question is natural, that the transition from subject to subject is easy, that he is not merely being quizzed but is actually taking part in an interesting and useful process. This feeling aids the study, in that co-operation leads to more *valid* data. But the *spontaneity and flow* of the questionnaire also aid in the better execution of the job by an interviewer.

2. **Basic Qustions**: Some researchers begin their questions with the most central and pressing issues, the more usual and apparently more natural introduction is a series of emotionally neutral, objective questions which are rather basic for later cross tabulation like age, sex, marital status etc. Many of these items have the double advantage of being basic to most sociological questions and at the same time amenable to demographic checking by the use of census data. Even where such questions are not to be tabulate, it may be useful as "stage setting" ones. The flow of the questionnaire should be smooth and involve easy transitions for the respondent and terminate with a socially appropriate ending. Sometimes the final questions may be a request for an evaluation of the self administered questionnaire.

3. **Comparability**: The essence of an adequate scientific method is not merely accuracy in result the accuracy that can be proved. It is quite true that a good journalist may often capture more completely what is happening in a group than a poor sociologist. On the other hand, the journalist, like the person who has "actually seen it", is in the scientifically weak position of being unable to prove that what he says is accurate. What is necessary is that the techniques to so formalized that the final results can be checked. A set of unique

observation is of little scientific importance. Other scientists must be able to repeat them under similar circumstances and conditions.

As the research becomes more focussed, then the necessity of obtaining standard data, this is cooperable information about each case in a given class, increases substantially. If the information obtained about each case does not deal with somewhat the same details of items, no dependable statements about the cases can be made. If the age of some respondents is obtained but not of others, income from some and not of others, a mass of data results, but none of them can be used for analytical purposes.

4. **Reliability**: Given a definite hypothesis the simplest way to assure such comparability is to formalize the questions. This relates directly to *reliability*, that is, the extent to which repetition of the study would result in the second data conclusions. We are not now discussing whether the questions elicit "the truth" from the respondents, but the simple problem as to how far another sociologist repeats the results by repeating the study.

The immediately pragmatic answer to this problem is that the sociologists actually can and do repeat each other results. Merely repetition of a study is not common, but some studies repeat particular questions, allowing a check on reliability. This is predictable enough that those who are interested in research can actually test *sampling designs*, using the same questions, instructions, etc. but varying the design of sample. Research experience has shown that, within a known range or error, the answers are stable enough so that differences can be ascribed to the differences in sample.

It is assumed that this pragmatic reliability of answers is part of the underlying order to be found in all natural phenomena whenever they are systematically studied. In the development of any science there are innumerable cases, in which there is no apparent reliability. However, in all these cases, once the underlying problem of technique was worked out, the results become considerably more predictable. Another competent sociologist can obtain the same results by repeating the operations if he follows the same sample design, interviewing instructions and many of the questions as understood by the respondent in both the studies are the same.

There is nothing mysterious about the last point. Minor differences in wording sometimes create major differences in meaning, and the answers of the respondents will reflect these differences.

5. **Recognition for poor question through pretests**: Perhaps it is useful at this point to suggest a few signs which indicate that something is wrong in the early drafts of the questionnaire like lack of order in the answer. All-or-none responses, a high proportion of "Don't know" or "Don't understand" answers, a great number of qualifications, or irrelevant comments, a high proportion of

refusals to answer, and substantial variation in answers when the order of questions has been changed.

6. **Technique Validity**: Questions must not only elicit stable or reliable answers, but they must also provide a kind of information which the researcher wants. A first question raised here, then, is whether or not the respondents answer questions truthfully. More often, the problem of truth is a much more complex one, for it involves that dim sphere, in which the respondent is not giving the facts but is not really certain that these are not the facts. All of us reconstruct our personal history to some extent, especially in areas of our self-conceptions. Only very careful probing can ever separate fact from fiction and for some respondents even this will not be adequate. This is not a cause for despair but a simple recognition of present limitations upon this technique of data collection. The answer to such dissimulation is not only good interviewing but also a good understanding of the kind of answers which might be given by the respondents on the part of the researcher, so that additional alternatives will also be asked. This technique rests upon the greater knowledge which the respondent has about the total situation. If the researcher asks a series of questions without adequate prior research, many of them will miss the mark. The respondent will be able to tell the truth without telling the facts.

A good questionnaire will contain some *check question* on crucial issues, variously placed within the document designed to conform each other.

Personal Documents

Meaning Personal Documents

Personal documents come in the category of secondary data or data which is not immediately observable but which help substantially in enriching the results of research by providing under the heading of documents in the array of research in social sciences. They contain written material composed by the subject himself such as authobiographies, diaries, letters etc. Personal documents are extensively used in clinical and case studies and small scale surveys undertaken with an intent of amelioration such as counseling.

Personal life records as complete as possible constitute the perfect type of sociological material and if social science has to use other materials at all it is only because of the practical difficulty of obtaining at the moment a problems and of the enormous amount of work demanded for an adequate analysis of all the personal meterials to characterize the life of a social group. Thomas and Znaneicket used personal documents extensively in their study of the polish peasant.

Utility of Personal Documents

In its narrow sense the personal document is a spontaneous first person description by an individual of his own actions, experiences and beliefs.

However, the personal documents, by themselves are of limited utility to the sociologist as his aims are to be objective and to study the actions and beliefs of an entire group. Blumer has brought our clearly the limitation of the use of personal documents in sociological research in his criticism of their use in the *Polish Peasant*. He found that while these documents had been highly illuminating and tended to strengthen or support the plausibility of the hypothesis put forward there was no sense in which they could be claimed as proving these hypothesis. While scientists agree that subject to the necessary safeguards, the use of personal documents is not only permissible but indispensable, they systematically analyse the attendant hazards of their use.

Limitation of Personal Documents

Two crucial issue have to be faced: 1. This is the methodological question of how far distortions enter during the process of translating private thoughts into permanent records. 2. Then there is a more practical problem as to how to amass and analyse the number of persons documents needed for derivation of general laws or hypothesis. There limitations are as follows :

1. **Possibilities of distortion by the information**: Allport distinguishes 12 motives that may induce individuals to record details about themselves, such as self justifications, exhibitionism, literary delight, relief from tension; monetary gain, scientific interest etc. In some cases the underlying motive may influence the document's content. For example, some authors have a deliberate propagandist intention. In such documents distortion is inevitable. Literary dishonesty which compels the writer to idealize his experiences to form an aesthetically structural whole may either be deliberate or result unconciously from the tricks of memory. This motive may lead to suppression of unpalatable or undramatic sequences, to an over emphasis on the continuity of a career and to a displacement of the moments of climax.

(i) Autobiographies: It must never be forgotten that every autobiographer is a prisoner of his own culture. Hence his thought processes are largely determined by the society in which he lives. Autobiographies which are intended for publication can be expected to suffer from conscious stylization, from propagandist intentions and from a tendency to rationalize.

(ii) Diaries: Although diaries are most revealing as personal data, as a source material they are of restricted use. They may exaggerate the conflicts and dramatic phases of life while leaving gaps during the calm periods. They are liable to take much for granted often failing to describe persons or situations whose existence and character the diarist merely assumes. Finally, they are not free from posing.

(iii) Letters: Letters have been extensively used by historians and biographers and little used by sociologists. Most letters have some

propagandist intentions in the sense that they try to create an "impression" to the receiver of the letter. They lack continuity and assume much.

2. **Distortions introduced by the investigator**: Many of the personal documents which have actually been used in social science have been recorded not by the informant but by the investigator. This has sometimes been necessary because the informant was illiterate, sometimes because of language difficulties and generally because the investigation has had definite preconceptions as to the form and content of data needed. This limits the validity of data procured.

Objections to the validity of generalization founded on personal document material are generally aimed at the representativeness of the size of the samples. There is further a general belief that those people whose personal documents become available tend to be suffering from frustrated emotional lives.

If this is a fair surmise, generalizations based on personal documents clearly refer to such people and not to the population as a whole.

One means of overcoming this objection is to solicit the co-operation of a more representative cross section such as class of students. However, the fact that they have been solicited will affect both the matter presented and the manner of presentation.

It is further, very difficult to obtain a fairly large sample of documents to permit fine analysis and an adequate statistical analysis which is the key note of contemporary sociology demands an exceptionally large sample. Thomas and Znaneicki used not only the full autobiography of some polish immigrants, but also a number of fragmentary autobiographies and over 7000 letters. Thus, personal documents on the whole, are of limited utility in general sociological research.

Importance of Questionnaire

Owing to the above-mentioned limitations of the questionnaire method, it is unsuitable in many social problems and if used, the conclusion will be highly unreliable. As a matter of fact, this method has application in a very narrow field. It can be used only if the respondents are educated and willing to cooperate; this makes its application very narrow. However, if the problem concerns mainly the educated middle class, 100% success is possible through the use of this method. In brief, inspire of limitations, the mailed questionnaire is an important research tool. Following are its merits :

1. **Economical**: The questionnaire needs paper printing and postage only. There is no need in it to visit the respondents personally or continue the study over a long period. Accordingly, in comparison with other methods, the mailed questionnaire is by far the cheapest and quickest research method.

2. **Time saving**: Besides saving money, the mailed questionnaire also saves time. Simultaneously, hundreds of persons are approached through it whereas if they are to be interviewed it may take a very long time.

3. **Most reliable in special cases**: As noted above, in certain problems the mailed questionnaire is not only suitable but a preferred technique of research. For example, if we study the problem of 3rd class railway passengers or the housing needs of teachers, the respondents will cooperate willingly and give true information because, upon it, depend the relief measures badly needed by them.

4. **Research in wide area**: When we have to make research about people living at great distances, the mailed questionnaire can be the only means of research if a researcher can undertake to travel the whole world, but by mailed questionnaire, people living in all countries can be approached.

5. **Suitable in special of response**: The information about certain problems can be best obtained through questionnaire method. For example, the research about sexual habits, marital relations, dreams etc. can be easily obtained by keeping the names of respondents anonymous.

From the above it is clear that through not many, yet in some cases the method in question is most suitable.

******

Chapter - 15

Experimentation

As a matter of fact, a number of methods are used in modern investigation, but experimentation is the most scientific technique and through it we get most accurate and precise data and conclusions. The major feature of this technique is that the observer exercises control over the observed. Such control over the materials to be observed can be done in a laboratory or open conditions. The conclusions derived from experimental data can be re-checked by another experiment. This feature of experimentation are known as reversibility. The scientific character of any modern science and the reversibility of its data conclusion depend upon openness of its subject matter to experimental method; greater the use of experimentation, greater is the reliability of its conclusions. In the physical sciences the experimental method is very widely used; but in the modern sciences, due to complexity and changeability of their subject matter, it not possible to use experimental method on amide scale. But with the increasing sophistication of techniques and improved methods of control, the use of experimental method daily becomes more and more extensive.

Meaning of Experiment

According to Garret, an experiment is a question which has been asked, i.e., it is a query the answer for which is being consciously sought for. In each case of experimentation, the experimenter has before him a problem whose solution he seeks by conducting an experiment. Marie Jarhead and other social scientists have described experiments as a means of verifying the hypothesis. An experiment is based on a hypothesis and this hypothesis is a product of rational thinking. The hypothesis is either proved; or disproved by an experiment. We can repeat the experiment at different times and places to assure that our results are not due to some error in the experiment. According to Greenwood, an experiment cal is a means of providing the hypothesis whereby the causal relation between two facts is studied. To study this relation save create contradictory situations in which all but one fact is controlled. The "free" fact is either a supposed cause or an effect. Therefore, in an experiment the free or independent factor is of most crucial importance. Explaining the fact that in an experiment we study a subject matter under controlled situations, John R.P. French writes: "We shall define a field experiment as a theoretically oriented research project in which the experimenter manufactures an independent variable in some real social setting in order to test some hypothesis."

Independent and Dependent Variables

The different factors in an experiment are divided into two groups: independent variables and dependent variables. The first set of factor or factors is called an Experimental Group and the second set of factors is called Controlled Group. An experimental or independent factor is sacra cause which is freely changed in an experiment; usually, an independent variable consists of a single factor only because an experimenter wishes to study the effect of a cause independent of all other influences. If such a variable consists of more than one cause, it becomes very difficult to determine the effect of each of them independent from operations of other causes. In the statistical evaluation, it is quite possible to have two or mom independent variables because statistical analysis separates the effects of each of them. The dependent variable, as is dear from the term, depends upon the independent variable. An experimenter tries to stabilize and control all the factors in an experiment; and then takes one of these for study. He varies it to see the effect of variations upon other factors. The variations of an independent variable produce responses in other factors and these responses are actually dependent variables. These responses are subject to the cause which is being studied. According to Greenwood, by control in an experimental situation, we mean all those manipulations by which we keep under thick the movement and behavior of various causes and are able to make changes in anyone of them at will. For example, if we wish to study the effect of a particular system of education, we have to stabilize all the factors except the system of education. We must keep the average level of intelligence; economic and social status, conditions of study unchanged during the experimental period. Having achieved this, we can't now make variation in the educational system and observe its effect upon the students. According to Loon Fastener, "A laboratory experiment may be defatted as one in which the investigator creates a situation with the exact conditions he wants to have and in which he controls some and manipulates other variables."

Kinds of Research Experiment

According to Greenwood, following five kinds of research experiments are made in the modern sciences:

1. Pure Experiment or Laboratory Experiment.
2. Uncontrolled or Natural Experiment.
3. Ex. Post Facto Experiment. In this type of experiment the experimenter tries to reach the cause via effect.
4. Trial and Error Experiment.
5. The Controlled Observation Study.

According to John R.P. French, the peculiarity of a social experiment lies in the design or research, its planning and outlay and its purpose. in a social experiment, first of all we become conscious about a problem band then try to think of various means by which it may be solved and out of them choose one as being most appropriate. This is hypothesis. Then we make explicit the aims and purposes of research. After having gone through the above processes, we plan and arrange for actual experimental conditions.

Difficulties in Experimental Method

In comparison with physical sciences, the use of experimental method is severely limited in modern sciences due to extreme complexity and mobility of the social phenomenon. Following are the main obstacles in the way of the use of experimental method in the social sciences.

1. **Complexity of Research Events**: In research events various causes are interwoven. In other words, a number of variables are simultaneously at work in these events, and it is well-nigh impossible to entangle and straighten out the network of causes. For example, juvenile delinquency is a social occurrence which has a multiplicity of causes, psychological, social, economic, etc., behind it. It is not possible to determine precisely the role of any of these factors because various factors always operate in unison. The smoker of pot may be sexually promiscuous and be engaged in such unnatural behavior as anal and oral sex. But it cannot be maintained that hashish by itself causes sexual looseness. A youth may turn to hashish smoking because he is abnormally interested in sex and wants to explore newer vistas of sexuality by smoking pot. This is why it is not quite possible to make use of experimental method in the study of juvenile delinquency. Social occurrences are as a rule of highly complex nature.

2. **Lack of Homogeneity**: As the subject matter of physical science is homogeneous it is easy to make experimentation. But the subject matter of modern sciences is-so heterogeneous that it is not easily traceable to experimentation. As a matter of fact, no two similar social phenomena are exactly alike. No two married couples have identical experiences. Therefore experimental studies of marital relations, as have been made by Masters and Masters, can have limited value only. If some marriages get broken because of inadequate sexual expression amongst couples, this will not hold good for

other couples. Because of socio cultural factors some people may regard sex very low in importance and among them breakage of marriages may be due to economic causes. Thus we sec that due to lack of homogeneity in the .social phenomena, the use of experimental method is severely limited.

3. **Consciousness in Research Phenomena**: The subject matter of physical sciences is inert and unconscious. Accordingly, it can be treated in any way one likes in the laboratory. But the social facts consist of human beings in their mutual relations. Now, obviously, human beings are not like matter or gas which can be treated in any manner one likes. So many experiments are impossible in case of human beings because of moral considerations. A social scientist is unable to transgress certain definite limits. A marriage counselor cannot give a practical demonstration of sex techniques. Many examples can be given to show the limitations of experimental research on human beings; but the point here is obvious and so well accepted that we need not dilate any further on it.

4. **Lack of Control**: As the subject matter of the physical sciences is material and stable, it can be easily controlled; but the subject matter of modern sciences is conscious and fluid and it cannot be easily controlled. We cannot create artificially, conditions in which husband and wife will sue for divorce. Similarly, we cannot take children out of their family environment to study the influence of family upon them. Mrs. P.V. Young has quite rightly emphasized the fact that a social scientist must observe scrupulously the mere dictates of the social conscience. It is open to a social scientist in America, Britain or Sweden to show pornographic films to students, family people etc., to see their effect upon their behavior. All important questions like, is pornography harmful to an individual, can be experimentally answered to some extent in the West. But in India a social scientist must not expose his subject to supposedly immoral things like films portraying sexual activity. Thus we conclude that in every society there are some moral considerations which come in the way of controlling social facts.

5. **Lack of Direct Observation**: The subject matter of physical sciences, being gross and relatively immobile, can be directly observed with the help of electronic and mechanical apparatus. But the fluid and conscious subject matter of modern sciences cannot be so observed. We cannot possibly observe directly the thoughts of a man. The Electroencephalogram (EEG) which records thought-waves indicates only the variation in the thought-waves consequent upon thinking; from the recorded patterns of thought-waves, we can only infer the thought patterns and not observe them.

Laboratory Experiment

The above mentioned hurdles in the way to experimentation in the social sciences notwithstanding, a number of important experiments have been made in social sciences. A noteworthy experiment on the formation of "social norms" was performed under strict laboratory condition by M. Sherif in 1935 and 1936. He performed the same experiment on one individual and then on the group. His experiments are widely known as experiments to determine influence of social factors in perception. Subjects were brought into a dark room and were instructed to regard a stationary point of light filtering through a small hole in a box with a lighted bulb. Under such circumstances an effect called auto-kinetic phenomenon occurs. The subjects report that the point of light is moving when, as a matter of fact, it is stationary. The light is seen to move erratically in all directions.

Sherif studied the reported extent of the auto. Kinetic effect which subjects tested singly and in groups of three or four. The conditions of experiment were kept constant in both instances. Among the single subjects the extent of variation was reported to differ very widely from subject to subject. But when the individual subjects were grouped in two's, three's or four's the data of each individual tended to approach the average of the group. In other words, the social factors influence our perception in such a way as to level the differences and bring it near to a 'norm'. This is known as social norm.

From the above experiment, the fact emerges that when an individual does not have any other individual to compare his perception; he tends to form arbitrary standards which differ widely from each other. But when the individual is in a group the range of variation becomes narrow and his perception tends towards a social norm. In other words, the standards arrived at in group situation tend to be objective.

In experiments on 40 students in group situations, Sherif discovered some new facts. His aim in group experimentation was to learn about the following fads:

1. How does the membership of a group influence the decisions of the individuals;
2. Does the capacity of an individual to form norms diminish in group situation?
3. Do the members of group level up their individual reactions to form an average?

If the individual is reverted back to the position of loneliness alter exposure to group situation he tries to regain his subjective norm.

In a group situation the individual tends towards an average but the differences are altogether ironed out. Of course, the social factors influence the individuals to lean towards a social norm.

From Sherd's experiments it becomes clear that in the absence (IL any comparative norms the individuals form arbitrary norm but when such norms arc before them they try to bring their own norms more or less in conformity with the group norm. The importance of social factors in our perception thus becomes evident from laboratory experiments of Mr. Sherif.

Experiments in Natural Conditions

Besides making experiment in laboratory conditions, Sherif also made some important experiments in natural circumstances and conditions.

For example, in an extensive experimental study of the social tensions and conflicts between certain groups. Sherif and his colleagues could pinpoint the causes of tension and conflict and could discover effective ways of removing these. This study is well known by the name 'Robbers Cave Study.

In the supervision and direction of Mr. and Mrs. Sherif, Harvey, White and Hood the eminent social psychologists, an experimental study under natural conditions was carried out on the group rivalries and tensions in an area known as Robbers Cave State Park, 150 miles away from Okhalahoma district of U.S.A. In this experimental study 22 children were lodged together at a particular place. All children were aged one year. These children were divided into two equal groups. The two groups of 11 children each were brought to Robbers Cave State Park in separate vehicles. The two groups were allowed no contact with each other. They were put up in separate camps and this separation was so well maintained that for a long time the campers in one camp did not know the existence of the other camp. This remoteness and distance was maintained so that the children in each camp could develop independent of the other group and so that the children in each group would develop mutual relations and togetherness and would come to have a separate idea not it and could develop their own leadership etc. And this is what actually happened. Each group was given tasks which would encourage group life. By this theory soon developed communal life. They also came to have their own leaders. The status of every member was determined and so was his prestige. The groups were given separate names. One group we called Eagles and the other was called Rattlers.

Once each group had developed its own communal life, they were introduced to each other and this gave rise to tension between them. Now, competitive games were arranged. In the first game of tug of war the Rattlers defeated the Eagles. This led to great rise of tension and this simmering tension took the form of burning down the flag of Rattlers by the Eagles. In the morning when Rattlers found their flag burnt and came to know that this was the mischief of Eagles, they immediately burnt the flag of Eagles. This led to hot exchanges and cache group hurled scurrilous abuses on the other. The tension was increased and the two groups came to blows. The situation took a serious turn. This affected the Forges so much that they began to consider themselves unfit and out of disgust changed their name. There was also great amount of mutual recrimination and heart-burning. Each blamed the other, in the atmosphere of tension certain stereotypes which are characteristically used in such situation were passed on to the group by the psychologists. The rust set was brave, tough and friendly and the second set of stereotypes was, sneaky, lazy, stinking. Each group used the first set for itself and the second for the opposite group. Each considered itself brave, tough and friendly and the other sneaky, lazy and stinking. This goes to show that in an atmosphere of tension each group showered words of praise-in its member& and blameworthy words were used for the opposite party. In India the communal tension between Hindus and Muslims also takes the form of stereotyping each other. Hindus call Muslims Malech (unclean) and Muslims call Hindus Kefir (Infidel). Both studied their own traditions and morals superior and those of the other inferior. Not only in different religions, but in different castes and communities, the scenes of great communal tension are witnessed. Brahmin's consider Sudras untouchable but some militant low-castes hate the Brahmins and consider them unworthy. The upper castes consider it a sport to violate the modesty of low caste women. The landlords used to subject their agricultural labour to much physical abuse. But the low castes also think of high caste women in no other terms but pleasure-dolls. In South, weepers live in separate quarters far off from other castes. But there are instances where if a higher caste man slipped into their area he was greeted with brooms and cow-dung paste.

So far two aspects have come to light in the Robbers cave experiment, first the development of communal identity and second, the development of communal tension. The feeling of mutual tension, suspicion and hate soon takes form of a permanent mood of mistrust. Once this stage is reached, an icy wall of tension comes up between the groups. To melt the ice and unfreeze the tension is no joke. Many efforts towards this end were made. The groups were invited to common dinner; they were made to talk to each other. They were taken together to cinema. In many other ways the group Members was brought into contact. But this contact programmed did not succeed in releasing the tension: on the contrary, the tension became worse. Whenever the groups were given the opportunity to make contact there occurred bitter exchanges between them. This shows that once the tension develops between groups contact programmers between them only have negative effects.

However, the experiment was not closed. The main purpose of the experiment was to pinpoint the causes of conflict and tension and to devise ways and means to remove these. Some projects were studied for removing the tension. These, however, demand co-operation from both sides. First of all the tap through which the boys fulfilled their water needs was sealed by a gunny bag and the boys were told that due to leakage lathe water storage tank, the water supply had to be suspended. This led to water scarcity and both the groups needed water very urgently. Both groups were thirsty. Accordingly, both had a common problem and its solution became a common goal and needed common efforts. As a consequence of the development of comm.= goal the two groups chose to solve the problem by a joint effort. The ladder by which they could climb to the top of the tank was already removed by the psychologists. Both groups made frantic search for the ladder and succeeded in finding it. Some went to the top of the tank and removed the lid. They round the tank full. They thus concluded that the fault must lie with the water tap. Soon they cut the gunny bag to piece suith their knives and removed the dirt from the tap. Soon water started to flow. Both groups were satisfied with their achievement and were less tense. But when an hour later they met for lunch, bitter exchanges took place and tension erupted again. This goes to prove that small snatches of cooperation are not effective in removing the: tension.

Now another device was tried. It was planned that a cinema reel should be bought from the market; the 50% of its cost would be. Borne by the psychologists. This was done in order to provide incentive to children to buy the cinema reel No single group was authorized to make good the other half of the cost. Obviously, the purpose was to raise funds from both groups and thus give them a cause to make joint effort. The cooperation in the raising of funds was forthcoming; both groups made their respective contribution. Yet when the film was screened both groups occupied separate seastrand did not mix up. This shows that the state of tension persisted though tension did not take the form of conflict.

The psychologists made some more effort. At a distance of six miles from Robbers Cave there was a lake in the hilly tract. Both groups were taken to the lake to camp there. Each group was brought to the camp in a separate truck and the food was also cooked separately for them. The utensils were at one place, but each group picked up its own pieces. But, however, the vegetables and other necessary things had to be brought from the city in a common truck for both the groups. Perchance, the truck did not start inspire of repeated efforts by the driver. The truck could not even be pushed forward because it was facing ascent. The only course available was to pull it with the help of a rope tied to the truck; but this needed at least 20 persons. Therefore, the two groups had no option except to cooperate and make a joint effort. This cause was common, so they did make a joint effort. Both groups combined forces to pull the truck. The truck began to move and this sent a wave of cheer in their hearts. With their cooperation, it became possible to bring the raw food. When the food arrived, they began cooking it in common; this feature encouraged in them a sense of cooperation. Once again they had to pull the truck jointly. This time their cooperation was enthusiastic. They did not pull the truck by taking the ends of rope in separate batches but to the contrary, allowed to mix themselves up for this purpose. In this manner the sense of cooperation and frit idleness increased so much that when they were asked to pick up a friend breach member, they did not pick up their own member but a member of the opposite group. Thus a feeling off friendliness and good will displaced the old feeling of tension and hatred.

From his detailed description of experiment on communal tension, few salient facts emerge: 1. the feeling of tension tends to harden and become permanent: 2. exposure of one group to the other in comparative activities worsens the state of tension: 3. exposure and mutual contacts between group members increase when faced with a common problem and therefore their immediate goals overlap, tension becomes less and even cooperation takes place, but only temporarily and 4. a prolonged contact between groups when they share common problems and common goals, the tension starts giving way to friendly feeling and if this state of affairs is maintained for some length of time the tension disappears totally.

In the field of psychology, the experimental method is in use since 1920. Experimental studies of public opinion, public likes and dislikes, the problems of propaganda and advertisement and also leadership have been frequently made with good results. Nonetheless, it must be contended that so far the use of experimental method in social science is confined to a very limited field. The reason for this is not far to seek. It is not possible to recreate social situation artificially in a laboratory. Moreover, there are definite ethical limits to manipulation of human beings. In certain cases experiment is impossible, whereas in others it is not desirable from moral point of view. To illustrate both: it is not possible to experiment on social situations like war, riots and mob behavior. Obviously, these conditions cannot be stimulated in a laboratory. As for second type we may refer to the undesirability of drugging human beings to watch reactions of drugs, also, to persuade prostitutes etc., to allow them to be photographed in various forms of sexual stimulations. Masters and Masters have recorded with precision instruments the configuration of responses of the body in such diverse situations as digital and artificial masturbation, oral and anal penetration etc. But there is bitter controversy about the moral correctness of such experiments.

Possibilities of Laboratory

From the above discussion it may not be concluded that it is not possible to use the experimental method or construct a laboratory in the social science. Stuart Chapin has made some notable experiments in the field of sociological research. The psychologists, of course, have their own laboratories. As a rule, in sociology, the entire society itself is a kind of laboratory because in sociology we have to study human behavior under natural conditions. Boards has offered the following suggestions for the construction of a sociological laboratory. According to him the following apparatus are needed in a sociological laboratory:

1. Type-writer, Calculating Machines and Computers.
2. Special admiral for storage of files.
3. Special type of room for Interview.
4. Drawing-boards etc.
5. A Specialized Research Library.
6. Rooms for holding conferences and seminars.
7. Regional Map or Chart giving details about various communities living in that region.

Functions of Sociological Laboratories

In accordance with the suggestions made by Boards, various sociological laboratories have sprung in the western countries. These laboratories arc well organized and they perform the following functions :

I. Collection and organization of data. In the sociological laboratories, a cumulative record of various types of data collected by individual researchers is maintained. These are collected and organized and the permissible new generalizations are made or their basis.

2. Training. In the sociological laboratories, students arc trained in the u.se of research techniques and methodology.

3. Improvement of Research Method. Another function of sociological laboratories is the constant review of research methods. They examine the efficacy of these actual practice and try to improve them in the light of practical experience.

4. Provision of Apparatus for Research. In as much as it is not possible for the individual researchers to arrange for various types of equipment needed for research, the sociological laboratories function as pools from where the individual researcher can loan the equipment needed by him.

5. Convening Conferences and Seminars. For progressive and healthy conditions of research, it is imperative that the workers in various fields of research mast meet from time to time to exchange ideas and acquaint each other about their experiences in their respective fields of work. For this purpose they must meet from time to time. This is made possible by organizing conferences and seminars. This is done by sociological laboratories which maintain records of researches and have necessary equipment and accommodation for seminars and conferences.

6. Providing Library facilities. One of the important functions of sociological laboratories is to maintain specialized research libraries. From these libraries, researchers can loan books.

7. To conduct or finance expensive Researches. It is not within the resources of individual research workers to conduct elaborate and complex research projects, involving huge expense. Such research projects are undertaken on their own or helped by way of finance and manpower by the sociological laboratories. The research project is divided into many departments and the conduct of each is entrusted to an individual researcher or a group. The information gathered by each department is collected at the head quarter and it is sifted and harmonized there. In the laboratories there arc computer and other facilities which enable quick disposal of great bulk of information. This enables speedy preparation of report on the research project.

From the above discussion, it is evident that a sociological laboratory functions as a research centre. Nevertheless it has to be admitted that it is feasible to make very extensive use of experimental method in sociological research. The chief reason for this is the fact that very many social vectors or forces are not amenable to measurement. Secondly, in the artificial laboratory conditions fret and natural behavior is not possible. Many attempts are being made nowadays to overcome these limitations. An attempt is made to create natural social conditions in the laboratories and the subjects are persuaded by various means to believe that all is normal but still it is not quite possible to transfer actual social conditions to the laboratory and an artificial touch persists in the laboratory. Accordingly, most of the sociological laboratories direct and supervise research in natural conditions of the society at large. According to Leon Festinger, "The laboratory experiment is a technique for basic and theoretical research and is not the goal of an empirical science."

******

Chapter - 16

Observation

Observation is the most important and popular technique of making new discoveries and conducting researches in the field of science. Even an infant in the very early stages. of his life observes and is curious about the persons and things and recognizes them as being various and different from each other. The observation enhances the knowledge of the child and this increased knowledge, in turn, helps him in making fruitful adjustment with his environs. The observant behavior is not confined to childhood. In the field of scientific knowledge and discovery the man makes new discoveries and learns new facts through observation, first of all. Gradually, the cumulative observation leads to invention and manufacture of scientific apparatuses and aids which, in turn magnifies manifold man's power of observation. But in social science observation retains its original connotation of being seeing things with naked eye.

Definition of Observation

According to Mrs. P.V. Young, "Observation is a systematic and deliberate study through the eye, of spontaneous occurrences at the time they occur. The purpose of observation is to perceive the nature and extent of significant interrelated elements within complex social phenomena, culture patterns or human conduct,"

As per Young's definition, observation is carried out with the help of the eye, and the main purpose and aim of observation is to discover significant mutual relations between spontaneously occurring events and thereby pinpoint crucial facts of a situation. It is quite plain from these remarks that observation is not just equivalent to perceiving; observation is not random perception but a close look at crucial facts. It is not in the sense of random perception, but in the sense of a deliberate effort to pinpoint significant fact, that observation is considered to be a scientific method. The observation can be of two types:

participant observation and nonparticipant observation. In the former the observer is himself a part of the events, that is, he is an active onlooker; and in the latter, he is remote from the events and is a passive onlooker.

According to Oxford Concise Dictionary, observation means "Accurate watching, knowing of phenomena as they occur in Nature with regard to cause and effect or mutual relations." This meaning of observation highlights two points. Firstly, in observation an attempt is made to discover causal and other relations between facts of a phenomenon; secondly, phenomenon is watched realistically and precisely and the facts written down.

Main Features of Observation

Following are important features of observation:

1. Observation, an affair of eyes: By and large, observation in social sciences is done through the medium of eyes. The fact that observation inn affair of the eyes has been stressed by C.A. Moser. According to him. "In the strict sense, observation implies the use of eyes rather than of the car and the voice."A trained observer never trusts the heresy. He puts his trust only in that which he has seen with his own eyes, and only if a report is a first-hand evidence of the eyes it can merit to be called "Observation" in the scientific sense of the term. It is said, half believe what you see and do not believe at all what you hear. The implication of this wise statement is that even eyes arc liable to mistake an illusion and that only a trained person, who takes all precaution against possible error, is a competent observer. His report is worthy of scientific status. The evidence of eyes as a rule is most trustworthy of all evidences.

2. Definite Aim: Before making scientific observation, it is imperative to define and make clear the aim and purpose of observation, because aimless seeing is not tantamount to observation. Without knowing to watch we cannot watch anything fruitfully. Every scientific observation has its peculiar aim. The aim can be verification of hypothesis, discover of certain facts or the knowledge of causal relations inherent in a phenomenon. Accordingly, observation is always purposeful and mostly the purpose is discovery of causal relations between various facts of a phenomenon.

3. Planning: Besides being purposeful, observation needs to be a well-organized and systematic effort. In the planning of an observation, we need at times certain equipment and instruments. In physical and social sciences different types of apparatuses arc made use of. Sometimes we need to control the subject matter of an observation; bur, however, control is not an essential feature of observation; becau.se observation can be made even when no control over the subject matter is exercised.

4. Noting: In no scientific method much reliance on memory is placed because memory is proverbially deceptive. We forget a great deal of what we learn and even most vivid impressions are blurred with the passage of time. Therefore, all impressions are suitably recorded simultaneously or immediately after. The general means of keeping record is writing down the impressions. But nowadays wherever possible the actual impressions are tape recorded. The greatest benefit of tape recording is that the possibility of making error is zero. Moreover a tape is a permanent record in which actual words are recorded and there is no interpretation and no possibility of prejudicial reporting. Moreover a tape is free from all the illusions and errors to which our eyes are liable. As far as the problem of erroneous seeing is concerned, even this is obviated by the use of powerful cameras; which also like a tape cannot lie.

Moreover a camera can record more truthfully than even human eye. Besides, cameral photo is a fairly permanent record, which can be multiplied ad lib, and a battery of scientists can interpret the meaning of the photo. Again, photo observation, unlike the eye, is repeatable. The delineation of moods of man, topography of a physical feature, movements of a ballerina and many other phenomena require considerable amount el observation for proper interpretation. This is not quite possible by human eye when the events are unfolding themselves; but a photo record of such things can be watched at leisure and the extensive in it studied carefully. In the modern social research extensive use of tape-recorder, camera and similar other devices is being made. This helps very greatly in COTICCI observation and maintenance of fairly reliable records. The powerful movie camera of modern days penetrates into depths of the subject.

Major Kinds of Observation

From the stand-point of the observer an observation can be of following two kinds: Participant or Active observation and, second, Non-participant or Passive observation. In the participant observation, the observer himself takes part in the events he is to observe and in non-participant type he remains remote and passive. In America, a number of sociological reports on group sex activity are being published. In certain cases the scientist is allowed to be present on the scene without any obligation to participate in the activities; but in certain cases he actually becomes a member of such a group and takes part in their activities. Many an observation is a mixture of participant and non participant types. Both types of observation arc made on uncontrolled subject matter. Accordingly, an uncontrolled observation will be either participant uncontrolled or non-participant uncontrolled observation. In controlled observation the subject-matter of an observation is manipulated or controlled. Mostly, controlled observation is done in the field of social psychology.

Uncontrolled Observation

The uncontrolled observation, as the name makes quite plain, is an observation in which no attempt is made to control, manipulate or influence the observed subject matter. The subject matter happens in natural course and the observer leaves it free. He watches it without in any way interfering with it. In order to make it more realistic, the use of a variety of equipment is made in the controlled observation; but there is no such thing in uncontrolled observation. Defining uncontrolled observation, Mrs. Young say, "In non-controlled observation we resort to careful scrutiny of real life situations making no attempt to use instrument of precision or to check for accuracy of the phenomenon observed." As in most cases it is not possible to control the phenomenon in social sciences, observation in social science is, by and large, uncontrolled.

However, an uncontrolled observation cannot compete with controlled observation in the matter of precision and accuracy. The chief characteristic of scientific laboratory is the possibility of controlled observation. And where experiment in laboratory is not feasible we cannot hope for accuracy and precision comparable with controlled observation. The main drawback of uncontrolled observation is that it is not easy to untangle the complex facts as we cannot control any factor in these. Accordingly, we usually fail to distinguish the causes of a social phenomenon and many an elements which may be crucial are overlooked or missed in uncontrolled observation. Therefore, when we believe that we have observed every important element of a situation we may have actually missed crucial facts, and, due to this our belief in the accuracy of our observation maybe a deception. Jessie Bernard has drawn pointed attention to this danger. According to him, "There is a danger that non-controlled observation is likely to give us the feeling that 1st know more than we actually do about what we have son." It is a common plate that even when a phenomenon is highly complex, it does not appear so at first sight : and even a trained observer is misled to believe that the phenomenon is really simple. Mostly, this belief and accompanying self confidence are chimerical. Therefore most social scientists arc of the opinion that along with observation, other methods should be used to supplement the evidence of observation.

However, on account of many limitations, uncontrolled observation cannot be rejected as a valid method of study. As remarked earlier, in most of the cases in social phenomenon control is simply out of question and that uncontrolled observation is inescapable if we wish to study these cases. Moreover, social events cannot be artificially induced into materialization and we shall do our best to watch them carefully as and when these occur. Mrs. young has forcefully brought this fact home. According to her, "Life situations which can be adequately studied under controlled and artificial conditions are relatively few. Often, we have to observe while 'the observing is good' and in the exact social and cultural setting in which the situations occurred."

Uncontrolled non Participant Observation

The uncontrolled observation is of following two kinds: (1) Participant uncontrolled observation and (2) Non-participant uncontrolled observation. In the uncontrolled non-participant observation, the scientist watches the events and activities from a distance, passively he makes no effort to influence them or take part in the events and activities he observes. He, of course, tries to go to the heart of the matter and watch with a penetrating eye. Without a deep penetration and a capacity to unveil the superficial layers of a phenomenon, the observation is not more than a casual survey. An observer must be deeply interested in what he watches and must possess an overall view of the situation. However, if we really wish to study a phenomenon deeply, we cannot do SU effectively unless our observation is of controlled type. As W.J. Goode and P.K. Hatt have remarked, "As our ideas grow in depth and sharpness, we wish to rely much less on uncoil-trolled observations. Accordingly, a non-participant observation tends to become participant because one cannot penetrate into the heart of a matter without participation." A remote and passive observer cannot feel the reality as acutely as can an active observer. That is why autobiographical accounts have more depth and reality than the objective reports. Therefore, a true scientist tries to observe a situation by becoming part of it and doing the watching from inside.

Major Demerits of non-Participant Observation

An uncontrolled non-participant observation does not yield very reliable data, because, generally, many personal beliefs and ideas in the mind of the observer affect his observation and interfere with true and objective appreciation of the observed phenomenon. To illustrate, we may refer to many researches and surveys, by means of uncontrolled nonparticipant observation, into the slum conditions. Most of the observers in these surveys had a preconception that slum-dwelling is a hot-bed of corruption and that all imaginable vices flourish there. Accordingly, they reported evidence of crime and deviant behavior far in excess than the actual state of affairs. This happens because our actual observation is influenced greatly by our preconceptions. We, for example, start with a belief that children in slums must have observed all kinds of sexual behavior. Therefore, if we find some children playing with their sexual parts, we may like to conclude that all slum children masturbate or indulge in other forms of sex. This may not be quite so. Though we can safely infer a great deal 'about people's attitudes from their overt behavior, but inferences after all, are not as reliable as actual observation. By living in a slum for a number of years, a scientist can form more adequate opinion about these people. Following are the defects of non-participant observation.:

1. **Subjectivity**: In an uncontrolled non-participant observation, a scientist haste interpret and understand what he sees. This interpretation and understanding is liable to be colored by his personal predictions, beliefs and preconceptions.

2. **Inadequate Observation**: In as much as the observer in the nonparticipant types of observation does not take part in the activities or events, he observes many aspects of a situation which escape his attention; and, therefore, his observation remains incomplete. Besides, he is unable to conned properly one situation with the other.

3. **Unnatural attitude of the subject matter of observation**: P.V. Young and other noted social scientists have drawn attention to a very grave handicap of mm-participant observation. According to them, an observer, who is completely neutral and objective, has usually a critical outlook towards his subject of study; therefore he is unable to win the confider= of the group he wishes to study. The members of the group become suspicious of the intention of the observer and behave unnaturally in his presence. P.V. Young could not gain the confidence of Molokan people till she herself participated in their activities.

4. **Inconvenience to the observed**: Any group of people would feel inconvenienced if they learn that among them there is a person who will be critically noting their behavior. It upsets a cohesive group participating in any type of activities. That is why not many clubs and societies would allow outsiders. Particularly, such an absent would be very much resented on informal occasions. Not many primitive people would allow an outsider to watch their dances and love making. As a matter of fact unless one becomes some sort of a member of a group and begins to take uninhibited pan in the activities of the group he cannot learn much about it.

Major Merits of Non-Participant Observation

From the above discussion of defects of non-participant observation it is not to be concluded that non-participant observation is without any merit. As a matter of fact the merits of non-participant observation are found lacking in the participant observation and similarly the merits of participant observation are missing in the non-participant. Therefore, it would be correct to say that these two types of uncontrolled observation are mutually complementary. Following are the merits of non-participant observation:

1. **Objectivity and neutrality**: In as much as an observer, in a nonparticipant observation, is remote from the actual happenings he can watch them with a scientific objectivity not easily attainable in pa participant

observation. If an observer is himself participating in the events he is liable to be swayed by them and, therefore, fail to absent things with neutrality and objectivity available in non-participant observation.

2. Gain of respect and cooperation of the group: Whereas, many a time, it is possible to gain the confidence and co-operation of a group by sympathetic participation in their activities, there are, of course, situations in which the reverse of this holds true. In certain situations, for example, communal disharmony, an observer can gain real respect and co-operation of group by not participating in the actual happenings.

3. Advantages of being new: It is observed in many situations that people are reluctant to discuss their problems with familiar persons. But they easily reveal their inner feelings and thoughts to strangers.

4. Subtle observation: The people who are actually involved in happenings fail to note many things because these appear ordinary to them. Therefore a spectator is better placed to notice subtle movements and 'names of a situation than a participant. This will be easily understood if we think of a game or sport. In every game the umpire or referee is a person who merely watches the players and does not himself take part in the game.

5. Freedom from factionalism: If a scientist tries to study a group by becoming its member, he is liable to get involved in factionalism. As we know, even a fairly homogenous group has within it sub-groups which pull against each other and try to dominate the whole group. In such a climate, the scientist is very liable to develop positive and negative attitudes towards these groups. He may even identify himself with one sub-group. Under these circumstances his objectivity and neutrality will be thrown to winds. Willingly or unwillingly his outlook will be partisan and his observation will be unscientific.

The above discussion of merits and demerits of uncontrolled nonparticipant observation clearly shows that inspire of numerous drawbacks, non-participant observation is worthwhile and under certain circumstances it is a better tool of study than participant observation. Warner and Lund have drawn a list of situations where non-participant observation is to be preferred. As a general rule it may be said that before undertaking participant observation, non-participant observation should be used, and that its results should be borne in mind while making participant observation.

Uncontrolled Participant Observation

The participant observation, as the name implies, means watching events and activities from inside by taking part in those events and activities which are to be observed. W.J. Goode and P.K. Hatt have defined participant observation in the following terms: "The procedure is used when the investigator can so disguise himself as to be accepted as a member of the group." In this kind of observation, the researcher lives as a member of the group he wants to study. Mrs. P.V. Young puts the matter in this way, "The participant observer using non-controlled observation, generally lives or otherwise; shares in the life of the group which he is studying." The example of studies using the method of participant observation, is provided by the studies by Charles Booth of Londoners, William F. White': study of Cornville Social and Athletic Club and P.V. Young's study of Molokan people. The famous studies of Margaret Mead and Abraham Kardiner of primitive societies were also based on participant observation. As GA. Lundberg and Margaret Taw sing say, "In the application of the techniques it is essential to realise that it is not only the investigator himself but also the members of the group being studied who are to regard him as a participant."

It is obvious that in order to live as or authentic member of a group a researcher must be accepted by the other members of the group. P.V. Young has very elaborately described her experiences while she studied Molokan people. In the beginning, as a non-participant observer, she failed to evoke any response from these people. But gradually, with great task, resourcefulness and sympathetic behaviour she succeeded in winning the confidence of both young and old. Thus she came lobe accepted as a scientist member of Molokan people. Once she built up confidence in people for her, her task was greatly facilitated and she started getting invitations for formal and informal occasions. Thus she should study these people naturally and as an insider. It is imperative for the success of participant observation that the members of the group being studied should not have even slightest doubt about the bona fide of the research worker. Success in participant observation is directly dependent upon the fact and resourcefulness of the research worker. The personal charm, suave manners and wit is what counts in participant observation.

Major Merits of Participant Observation

1. Observation of neutral behavior: As the participant observer is a member of the group, he is in a position to watch the behavior of the group members in neutral circumstances; this is not possible for the non-participation observer. For example, if one wishes to study the behavior of hostel students, it will be easier to study the students in their natural and unfeigned circumstances if one enrolls himself as a member of the hostel.

2. Proximity to the Group: As the participant is very close to the group, he comes in frequent contact with its members. This affords him an opportunity to study the customs and traditions of the group by being able to participate in their joys and sorrows.

3. Insight into Behavior: In order to gain insight into the behavior of any group it is necessary to observe it from close quarters and as actual experiences of the moods of the group. The social scientist undertakes to live in slums, and jails with hoodlums, gangsters and prostitutes in order to penetrate into the underlying causes of their behavior. Recently a woman sociologist, doing Ph.D. thesis on the behavioral patterns of the sis it ors to blue films, nude shows etc., worked as a nude waitress in a restaurant catering pornographic thrills. By this she could gain insight into the real character of such people.

4. Ease in Exchange of Ideals: By living with the group, the scientist can talk frequently with the various group members. This enables him to understand their feelings and ideas, not only superficially but in depth. He can share their hopes and fears. All this helps him to gain an intuitive understanding into the behavior.

Major Demerits of Participant Observation

Inspire of above advantages of participant observation, it lacks the advantages of non-participant observation. In order to gain a correct perspective we shall study the major drawbacks of participant observation:

1. Lack of Objectivity: By becoming 3 member of the group, the observer tends to lose his objectivity and his approach to issues becomes subjective and sentimental. As a member of a group he develops fascination of hi nags which arc of objectionable nature. For example a scientist studying slums, if he starts living in slums he may be fascinated by raw, racy and sexy talks of slum dwellers; and though the language used by slum dwellers is objectionable and obscene, he may justify it as being frank and expressive. Again, he may justify unsanitary habits of slum dwellers because these may fulfill his voyeuristic impulses. Therefore, membership of a group leads to too close identification with it and this blurs the perspective of the scientist.

2. The Defect due to Social Status: Some scientists have objected to participant observation on account of the fact that as a member of the-group, the scientist comes to occupy a special status in the group and he views the whole situation from his vantage point rather than in an objective manner. But as the examples of researches made by P.V. Young, Margaret Mead and Malinowski CAC., have shown the membership of a group does not necessarily prejudice objectivity. As a matter of fact the membership of the group and the special status help the scientist learn many aspects of group life which remain inaccessible to nonparticipant observer.

3. Oversight of Important Issues due to Familiarity: Some scientists are of the opinion that in as much as a participant activity is involved in the occurrences of events many crucial facts appear to him to be of little or no significance. Therefore he misses many important points. This objection may be valid in some cases, but on the whole, an observer is able to understand the importance of small points by little effort t. As a matter of fact an inside observer is in a much better position to assess the importance of issues. To an outside observer, a loud conversation may signify quarrel, whereas an inside observer would know that the members of his group generally talk loudly.

4. Limited Range of Experience: Another objection brought forward against participant observation is that in as much as the observer becomes confined to a particular are group, his experience of this group may be deep, but, on the other hand, the range of his experience becomes very narrow. This is of course true in certain cases, and if the observer is not very mature and experienced he may know little yet think very high of his experience. A person who spends some time in jail carries the impression of having become a great criminologist. However, this defect is due to personal foible and not due to any defect is the method. An experienced and mature observer does not tie down himself to a narrow range of experience. He knows that there is no final and ultimate knowledge and one can always learn.

5. Involvement in Groups: One more objection raised against participant observation is that because of proximity and propinquity with the group, the observer is likely to involve himself in factionalism prevalent in the group. As a matter of fact there are always factions in a group and it is only human to prefer one side to the other. However, a judicious observer can keep himself aloof from factionalism. It may not be always easy to do so; but as remarked earlier, the success in participant observation demands a great store of tact and wisdom and suave Behavior. Moreover, though a scientist becomes an active member of group he should never forget the fact that be is in the group for a specific purpose.

6. Limits of Participant Observation: In practical life there can be certain situation in which the participant observation is not possible. For example, it is not possible to observe dacoits and criminals in this way. Again, the orgies indulged by rapists, sadomasochists etc., cannot be observed in this manner. It has to be admitted that there are situations in which the participant observation is not possible. But young social scientists of today have opened many fields to participant observation which were hitherto not accessible. Some scientists have allowed themselves to become members of groups specializing in sexual thrills. Many have temporality become nude waitresses or call girls to study this group. In India many persons have lived with Chambal valley deceits and watched their activities from inside.

From the above discussion we learn that like other methods, participant observation has its limitations and did an backs. However in many cases these have been exaggerated. If we look into the matter carefully, we shall find that the above-stated objections apply to those researchers who will allow themselves to forget the purpose of research and the in to various temptations.

A researcher, for example, may develop drug addiction, alcoholism or voyeurism by remaining in the group of drug addicts and people who do not mind exposing their bodies. But these defects arc due to personal factors and do in no way affect the scientific status of participant observation. A researcher should never lose sight of his aim and should not become excessively free with members lest be be dragged into partisan disputes. Though as a human being the researcher is subject to all kinds of temptations but by constantly reminding himself that his purpose in being member oldie group is not revelry and orgies but an objective and scientific aim to seek knowledge of facts he may remain objective. Some prisons in the garb of social scientists and reformers live in slums not out of scientific curiosity but merely to have cheap-sex. But such charlatans are in every profession. Similarly, if some social scientists indulge in cheap thrills, the whole of social research need not be blamed. It is at times profitable to disclose to other members that the purpose of social research is scientific study of the group and not uninhibited indulgence in their ways of life. This can earn him the respect of the members. A woman sociologist who recently worked as a nude bargirl in an American restaurant tells that the visitors to that restaurant 'asked her many a time to sleep with them; but when she disclosed her real purpose, they respected her and sought her sincere advice in their sexual and family problems. Similarly, instead of taking part in feuds and quarrels, one can be instrumental to their resolution. In conclusion, we may observe that though there are some situations where we have to be satisfied with non-participant observation, in majority of the situations participant observation is the preferred method.

Mixed or Quasi Participant Observation

As a matter of fact there can be no pure non-participant observation. In some or the other way, the observer finds himself involved in the observed situation. According to W.I. Goode and P.K. Hatt, "As the student can understand, purely non-participant observation is difficult." In the same sway there can be no pine participant observation. Though the researcher can become a full fledged member of a group, wt he cannot afford to. Identify himself completely with the membership of a group. Unless be keeps himself a little remote and maintain a safe distance, his purpose as a scientific investigator will be utterly defeated Accordingly, as a deliberate mixture of the good points of both participant and nonparticipant observations we get them mixed, and this mixed methods is superior to either of the above two. As Goode and Hatt have rightly observed "systematic observation controls over observer and the observed." In this mixed method, the observer does not declare. The nature and purpose of research. As a matter of fact the scientific nature of research depends upon this concealment of the purpose of research.

As Goode and Hatt have correctly observed, in the beginning, for some days the researcher should remain a member of the group and later on should quasi-participate in the main activities of the group and simultaneously carry on his observation programmer. In this way, the study of the modern scientist will become reliable and at the same he will not have to waste a lot of his time in the activities of the group.

Controlled Observation

The greatest drawback of uncontrolled observation is that in it the observer has no control over the factors or circumstances operating in a situation; and, therefore, he cannot easily distinguish and determine the nature and quality of these. Accordingly, he is unable to disentangle and extricate one cause from the other and the situation usually appears to him as a plethora of mixed up inclined etc ram innate patterns. It is for these vital reasons that social scientists as a class frown upon the method of uncontrolled observation and prefer the controlled observation. However, there are innumerable social situations where the control of circumstances is neither feasible nor desirable. No one can condone inducing drug-addiction in human beings simply for the sake of determining the quantity and frequency of drug taking productive of addiction. Therefore, in situations where the control of circumstances is either not feasible or not desirable, we have no option to studying them by the method of uncontrolled observation. In their struggle to overcome the limitations and defects of uncontrolled observation, social scientists have made relentless efforts during the past two or three decades to devise new and improved techniques to study behavior of social organizations, social groups and their members. The greatest benefit of the techniques of controlled observation is that by its means it becomes possible to arrive at definite conclusions because the researcher knows full well which factor is the cause and which is the effect.

Major Types of control

In the technique of controlled observation, two types of control is exercised; firstly the control of subject matter of investigation and secondly control over the observer. In the words of WJ. Goode and P.K. Hatt, "Systematic observation controls over the observer and the observed."

1. The control of the observed: In certain social investigations the subject matter of the observation, i.e., and the observed is controlled For example, the behavior of children is observed by exposing them to various types of stimuli. Similarly the difference in the behavior of employees and workers is noted by exposing them to controlled conditions of work, that is, controlling the working conditions.

2. The Control of the Observer: According to WJ. Goode and P.M. Hatt, "It is rather difficult to control the object under investigation but he (the observer) must at least put control on himself." As we have seen earlier, there are numerous social situations which duty controls of any son. Under these circumstances the advisable course open to e social scientist's, as suggested by Goode and Hatt, the exercise of control by the observer upon his own activities.

As a matter of fact both types of control are exercised in the controlled observation. Before applying controlled observation, many relevant facts are discovered by uncontrolled observation. This lets us know the situation in which controlled observation is possible and where it is necessary. Now before undertaking the actual observation, the hypothesis which is meant to be tested in the observation is made explicit. Having clarified the hypothesis, the observation is planned. The controlled observation following the above procedure is common to all scientific investigations. Many an important observations of this type have been made in Child Psychology. In USA., Dorothy S. Thomas made important controlled observations on Nursery Schoolchildren, In these observations, the observers were teachers and they created such conditions as would cause minimum inconvenience to children. In the result, children would behave naturally and would not be knowing the fact that they are being observed. Dr. Thomas and, her associates were primarily concerned with the social behavior and read ion-pat terns of nursery school children to a multiplicity of objects like wooden blocks, dolls, picture books and also their behavior towards other children and their teachers. Many kinds of reactions, some active and some passive, like laughing, crying and playfulness were noted. Dr. Thomas prepared a sketch of the observation and she instructed different investigators to fill up the sketch by noting the behavior of 5 children for IS minutes. These observations were carried out in three places: (i) Before going to bed; (ii) After getting up; and (iii) Before lunch. A clinical psychologist of Loss Angeles General Hospital, Charlotte Buhler also made important studies about the personalities of small children in schools by means of controlled observation. The main lacuna in the controlled observation technique is that in order to exercise control over circumstances, artificial conditions have to be created and this interferes with the natural behavior. Accordingly, for the success of controlled observation, conditions have to be so controlled as not to affect the natural behavior of individual.

Techniques of Control

In modern research, various sophisticated techniques of control are used in the controlled observation. These are:

1. Planning of Observation: In the controlled observation, the scientist must first of all fix up and determine all the details: otherwise the observation will not be successful. In as much as the controlled observation is made to test some hypothesis, it is not necessary to attend all the factors or causes operative in a situation. Therefore he should know beforehand the factors and causes which pertain to his hypothesis and should investigate these only. The entire situation which is object of an observation should be broken up into small coherent units and those should be studied one by one. This economizes time and also aids precise observation.

2. Use of Schedules: In the social research, such schedules as have many blank columns arc used. In these blanks the investigator can record his findings as a result of his observations. According to Mrs. P.V. Young, 'Me construction of observation schedules involves many procedural difficulties. The schedule mug he so devised as to provide an optimum of verifiable quantifiable data and to. Avoid selective biases and misinterpretation of observed behavior. The units of observation must be simple, minute and meticulously worded by several observers, at different times." An illustration of scientifically constructed schedule is provided by Dorothy and Thomas. She prepared a schedule complete enough to record facts about various types of reactions given by children in a 15 minute observation of their behavior, before sleep and lunch and after sleep. The schedules can give important inform at ions about the behavior of a group but these inform actions are by no means exhaustive. The investigator m any perceive reaction not mentioned in the schedules. Such important observation must also be accommodated and this can be done by trial and error use of schedules as was done by Dorothy and Thomas.

3. Use of Mechanical Appliances: The modern social research has become very sophisticated. In order to make it more reliable movie cameras, tape-recorders and other scientific devices are widely used. By the photo camera, important events are photographed and these stills can be carefully studied at leisure. While the events arc occurring it is not humanly possible to see each and every de tail of these; but if we can photograph these the photos can be minutely studied. A movie camera is even better than the photo camera, though far more expensive, because with a movie camera we can record the entire sequence of events and can later on study these on a projector or as stills. The advantages of movie camera for research are the same as those of photo camera. However, the movie camera has an additional advantage; it reveals clearly the dynamic characters of happenings which is not quite possible in the photo camera. By the help of tape recorder we can keep a permanent record of various sounds of a phenomenon. Moreover, if an investigator is using tape recorder, he need not keep paper and pencil in his hand and this avoids unnaturalness in a situation. A tape-recorded speech or interview, can be heard again and again to remote any possible doubts in understanding of the material. Moreover a tape records not only the contents of speech but also the manner of speech.

4. Maps: In modern research various types of maps are used. These illustrate graphically the social situations. These also illustrate the various aspects of a social situation and the mutual relationship between these aspects. The maps represent various aspects of social organization and the various factors in their respective relationship. This can provide us an idea about the fields in which controlled observation is possible.

5. Detailed Note: In a number of situations in modern research, maintenance of detailed impressions of the observer recorded in a personal notebook in shorthand or personal symbols is the best means of precise and reliable observation. For this purpose the observer must maintain a personal notebook. These notes should as far as possible be complete. It is most unscientific to rely upon memory for detailed facts élan observation. The best safeguard against this is the habit of daily note taking. In note besides description of the observed a word of explanation to this description should be added wherever possible. A noting having both description and explanation is considered authentic.

6. Sociometric Scales: Sociometric scales are widely used in modern research to measure such factors as serial attitudes, morale, status, home environment, adjustment, participation etc. Sociometric scales have the same role and importance in social observation as the role and importance of thermometer and stethoscope in medical observation. These help to bring into relief the entire picture of a social research and the crucial facts get highlighted. In this connection it is of utmost importance to bear in mind the fact that the more complex a situation, more there is need for scrutinizing research by many and varied types of measurement norms. This checks and cross check of the data obviates the source of error.

7. Formulation of Hypothesis: In the controlled observation, before the start of actual observation, a hypothesis is formulated on the basis of controlled observation. It is for the sake of verification of this hypothesis that the controlled observation is undertaken.

8. Group Observation: In as much as the observation of any single scientist is liable to be vitiated by what is known as personal equation, that is, effect of personal likes and dislikes on what he sifts, an attempt is made to overcome this limitation by letting a group of scientific workers to observe the self same situation severally and their notes compared to make a general deduction. The great benefit of group observation is dissolution of personal equation in the results of an observation. If someone has bias in favour of something it will not be observed. Again, there are many situations whose full meaning cannot be appreciated unless they are viewed from many angles : political, economic, biological, anthropological etc. In such cases a team of experts is used to undertake the task of observation. These concerted efforts arc highly productive of reliable conclusions. In the complex social structures and functions of today, we generally need the services of a team of experts to study any situation.

9. Controlled Group: In modern-research when we need to know the operative strength and value of any particular factor, we try to stabilize all other factors and keep changing this particular factor. The factor which is being changed is technically known as the controlled group, because it is by varying this factor, sometime letting it operate, sometime reducing its strength and at other times blocking its operation, that we learn the effects of this factor. By this we learn the actual fact about it. In this way the various interwoven causes operating in a situation can be separately studied. For example, if we wish to know about the effect of pornographic films on individuals, we can expose some individuals to these films and compare their post-film behavior with non-viewing individuals having same rank and status as that of viewing group.

Organisation of Field Observation

In organizing a field observation, we have to proceed step by step and in a systematic manner. Following is the main sequence of steps encountered in the organization of the field observation :

1. Determination of the Method of Study: Once we have decided upon the problem of our research, we have taken the next decision about the method of study-whether we are going to use participant or non-participant observation etc. The choice of the method has to be in accordance with the nature of the problem, but this requires extreme care as the wrong choice of the method would be disastrous.

2. Determination of the nature and limits of observation: Depending upon the nature of the research and the hypothesis of research an outline of research project is prepared. This helps to-guide the observer as to-what should be observed and what may be left out. The preparation of notes is also determined by this outline or guide-line of research.

3. Determination of Time, Place and Subject of Study: Now a decision regarding the time, place and the subject of the research has to be taken. A project can be short or of long duration; it may be studied under laboratory conditions or in the open. Along with the determination of the time and place, we must also decide whether the subject of research needs subdivision or must be studied as a whole and whether we shall observer the behavior of a group as a whole or of the individuals in relation of the group.

4. Determination of investigators: For actual field-work the research usually requires a team of trained persons. In many cases we have to enlist the help of experts from other sciences. For example, the study of the effect of climate on social behavior would require the help of expert physiologist and ecologist. Again, to study the effect of vegetarianism on social behavior we shall have to enlist the help of medical experts. Moreover, certain situations are studied better by a single researcher while in other we must use a team.

5. Provision of Mechanical Appliances needed: Now various, mechanical aids of research are the photo camera, movie camera, tape recorder etc. The various schedules, graphs and socio-metric scales required for research should also be arranged beforehand. The research worker CRUSE be well trained to make use of the mechanical aids.

6. Data collection: Having arranged all the necessary equipments needed for research, the researcher should now collect through observation and other means at his disposal all possible data needed to test the hypothesis. In this connection, ins should be always remembered that the data collected should be thorough and no detail must be left out, if it has any bearing whatever on the hypothesis.

7. Classification and Tabulation: Once all the relevant data are at hand, these should be classified and tabulated in accordance with the nature of the subject matter. As a matter offset the collection of data and the work of classification and tabulation goes on simultaneously.

8. Generalization: When we have classified and tabulated our data, it becomes possible to draw general conclusions on its basis in generalizing, the laws of logic and statistical methods must be kept in mind and the trend in research is towards quantification and for this purpose sophisticated statistical techniques arc used.

When the work of drawing conclusions is complete, a report on the research project is prepared and committed to writing. The research worker must be very careful and vigilant at every step in research and he should examine everything most carefully to work as one step before proceeding to the next.

Major Limits of Observation

1. Some events cannot be objects of observation: Explaining the limits of observation, Mrs. P.V. Young writes, "Not all occurrences are, of course, open to observation, can be observed when an observer is at hand, not all occurrences lend themselves to study by observational techniques." There are may occurrences which a social researcher encounters, but which cannot be observed for one of the following reasons: these maybe microscopic, these maybe indefinite; these may not occupy any definite space or occur at any definite time; or these may be of future, Moreover, it is not feasible for social researchers to be present wherever a new event occurs. For example, it is not possible to observe all the factors responsible for marital discord, because many of these take plats in the utter privacy in which observers cannot be present.

There arc of course some primitive people who permit observation of marital privacy by some authorized persons. But on the whole it remains true that many important aspects of marital adjustment are not quite open to observation.

2. Observation and observable are neither extensive nor coeval: It is not the case that whenever a scientist chooses to absent, all relevant facts and events exhibit themselves. If these events occur in the absence of the observer the question of their being of served is irrelevant and if the scientist is unable to exercise control over the circumstances he cannot produce them at will, but he cannot at the same time afford to wait indefinitely for these to occur. Pro example, we cannot induce people to quarrel and light simply to watch their behavior. We cannot bombard a town to make a firsthand aunty of the behavior of people affected by this. All these clearly show that the observation and the observable are not synchronous.

3. Certain things are non-observable: There are some mental and emotional factors which, though cases of social phenomenon, are in the nature of things not perceivable and, therefore, unobservable. The examples of such factors are sentiments and prejudices, likes and dislikes, sets and orientations. These emotional and intellectual factors have definite role in the shaping social phenomenon; but these can be inferred and not observed.

4. Low Reliability or Conclusions: The conclusions based on observation are not very reliable, because in observation we have to depend upon human tact and resourcefulness alone. And though man's capacity for accurate perception and understanding is great, it is far from perfect. That is why we have the proverb, "to an is human." According to Mrs. P.V. Young, in observation, no attempt is made to use instruments of precision to check the accuracy of the phenomenon observed. According to Goode and Hatt, with the increase in the self confidence in a research worker and as his ideas become mature and sharpened, be looses confidence in observation.

5. Illusory Observation: In as much as we have to depend upon our eyes for observation, we can never be sure if what we are observing is the as e as it appears to our eye-s. Eyes are prone to deception. We see a mirage in the desert at noon. This fact is forcefully brought into relief by the following interesting example: An eminent chemist used to bring his small son to his laboratory where he carried out a variety of experiments. He saw something deep and meaningful in his colored test tubes, whereas to his son there were merely different colored waters in glass tubes. A literary man and a scientist may perceive a gold mine in an old tattered MSS, whereas to others it may not have even the value of scrap paper. A shrewd observer knows how to perceive truthfully and avoid pitfalls common to ordinary perception. But most persons are liable to deceptions which characterize visual perception.

6. Self-Consciousness in the Observed: Dr. Thomas, in discussing the limits of observation, points out that the atmosphere tends to become artificial and that this leads to a sense of self consciousness among the individuals who are being observed. This hampers their naturalness in behavior and thus the o purpose of observation which is to know the behavior of individuals under normal conditions gets defeated. In the artificial atmosphere, the language, style and behavior are affected. If a person is given a tough task to perform, which under normal conditions he may not quite fulfill, he may work harder than usual to achieve k because he knows that he is being observed. Some persons cannot give out their true behavior if they are, observed and they know this fact. A candidate stops writing or falters lithe investigator stands before him and starts reading what he is writing. However, this defect is not unavoidable, shrewd observer can overcome this by either concealing the fact from the observed individual or by creating absolute confidence in him.

7. Subjective Explanation: In as much as the final results of observation depend upon the interpretation and understanding of the observer, the defects of subjectivity in the explanation creep in Ms description and elucidation of the observed. Moreover, the observers are liable tube carried away by unreal and extraordinary elements in the field of their observation. Deleting upon this fact, Mrs. Young writes; "It is easy to become attracted by the conspicuous, dramatic and interesting factors. Because of the above mentioned tendency, the observers tend to attach undue importance to factors which have not much value. For example, if we see a man wining out of wine shop, quite drunk, and start ruing at random, we may believe that liquor induces irrational violence in man, which of course, is not quite the case.

8. Slow Investigation: As Mrs. P.V. Young says, the valid observation cannot be hurried; we cannot complete our investigation through observation in short periods. The slowness of observation methods leads to diminution of interest among both the observer and the observed.

9. Expensiveness: Being a long-drawn process and at times requiring group observation, the technique of observation is very expensive. Moreover, in order x to reach the observed and establish a rapport with them requires great amount of money and time.

10. Inadequate: As Mrs. Young puts it, "The full answer cannot be obtained by observation alone." Observation must be supplemented by other methods of study.

Major Merits of Observation

Inspire of the above limitations and drawbacks in the method of observation, it is still a worthwhile technique on account of the following positive qualities, characteristic of observation techniques:

1. **Common Method**: The method of observation is common to all social sciences.

2. **Simplicity**: As compared with other techniques used by social sciences, observation is by far the simplest. It is quite easy and requires relatively less training to become trained observer.

3. **Realistic**: In as much as observation is based on actual and first-hand experience, its data are more realistic than the data of those techniques, which use indirect and secondary source of information.

4. **Formulation of Hypothesis**: In all social sciences, the method of observation is the basis of formulating hypothesis.

5. **Verification**: For verification of a hypothesis we have to depend upon observation. It is correctly said that the problem presents itself and resolves itself through observation. Only by actually seeing the phenomenon can we know the nature of the c problem and form a guess about the possible means of resolving it. Now this guess or hypothesis can be known to be true to false by observation.

6. **Greater reliability of conclusions**: The conclusions of observation are more reliable than non-observation conclusions because they are based on first-hand perception by the eyes and can be verified by anyone by visual perception.

On account of the above qualities, observation is a classic technique of investigation in social science. In the words of CH. Moser, "Observation can fairly be called the classic method of scientific inquiry." in social sciences, the technique of observation is becoming progressively sophisticated with the use of camera, tape recorder and other mechanical appliances. The addition of mechanical appliances in observation has rendered it more scientific and reliable than before and it may fairly be hoped that in future, observation will become completely more scientific.

******

Chapter - 17

Simulation and Modeling

Continuous Systems: Systems in which the state changes smoothly or continuously with time is called continuous systems. Systems such as the aircraft, in which the changes are predominantly smooth is an example of continuous system. In continuous systems, the state or the variables vary continuously with time; can generally be described by means of differential equations. If the set of (simultaneous) differential equations describing a system are ordinary, linear, and time-invariant (Le have constant coefficients). An analytic solution is usually easy to obtain.

Example: Simulator of a chemical reactor

At any time t, if a, b, and c are the quantities of the chemicals A, B and C present, respectively, then their rates of increases are described by the following three differential equations:

$\frac{da}{dt}=k_2c-k_1\ ab, \frac{db}{dt}=k_2c-k_1\ ab, \frac{dc}{dt}=2k_1\ ab-2k_2\ c,$

Where k_1 and k_2 are rate constants. These constants will vary with temperature and pressure, but do not allow the temperature or pressure of the reaction to vary.

A straight forward method of simulating this system is to start at time Zero and increment time in small steps of At.

Other examples of continuous systems:

1. An aircraft system
2. Numerical integration
3. Rungc-kuttaintegration formulas
4. Simulation of a servo system
5. Simulation of a water reservoir system

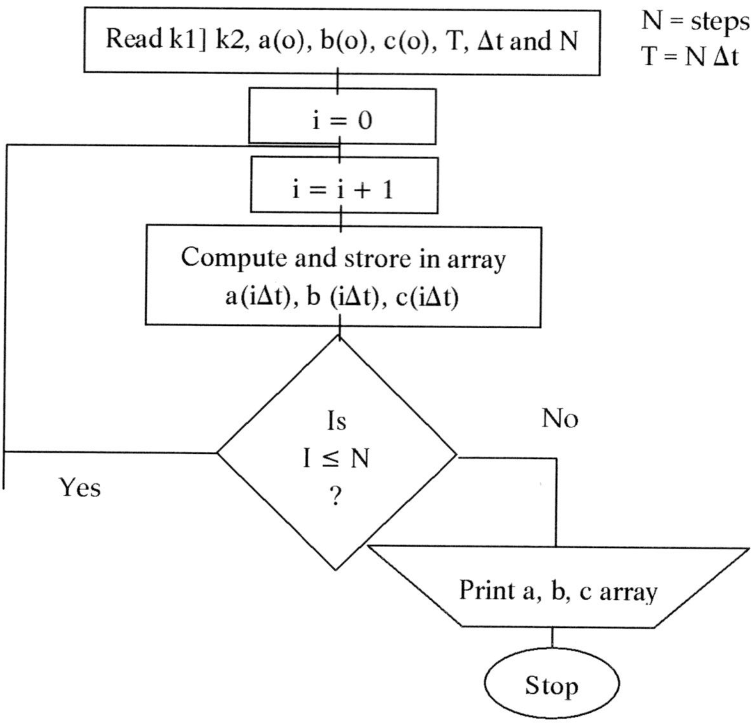

Fig. Flowchart of a Chemical Reaction Simulater

Discrete Systems : Systems like the factory, in which changes are predominantly discontinuous, will be called discrete systems. In a factory system, the ordering of raw materials or the completion of a product occurs at specific points in time. The complete aircraft system might even be regarded as a discrete system. If the purpose of studying the aircraft were to follow its progress along its scheduled route, with a view, perhaps, to studying air traffic problems, there would be no point in precisely how the aircraft turns.

In addition, in the factory system, if the number of parts is sufficiently large, there may be no point in treating the number as a discrete variable. Instead, the number of parts might be represented by a continuous variable with the machining activity controlling the rate at which parts flow from one state to another.

Discrete-event simulation is commonly used by operation research workers to study large, complex systems which do not lend themselves to a conventional analytic approach. Discrete system simulation is more diverse and has less of a theory than continuous system simulation. There is no overall sets of equations to be solved in discrete-event simulation..

In simulating any dynamic system continuous or discrete there must be a mechanism for the flow of time, determining the state of the system at the new point in time by keeping track of the total elapsed time. In the simulation of discrete systems, there are two fundamentally different models for moving a system through time the fixed-time step model and the event-to-event (or next event model).

(a) Next Event Simulation: In a next event simulation model, the computer advances time to the occurrence of the next event. It shifts from event to event. The system does not change in between. Only those points in time are kept track of when something of interest happens to the system.

Flow charts for those two methods of simulating a discrete system in their most general forms are shown below:

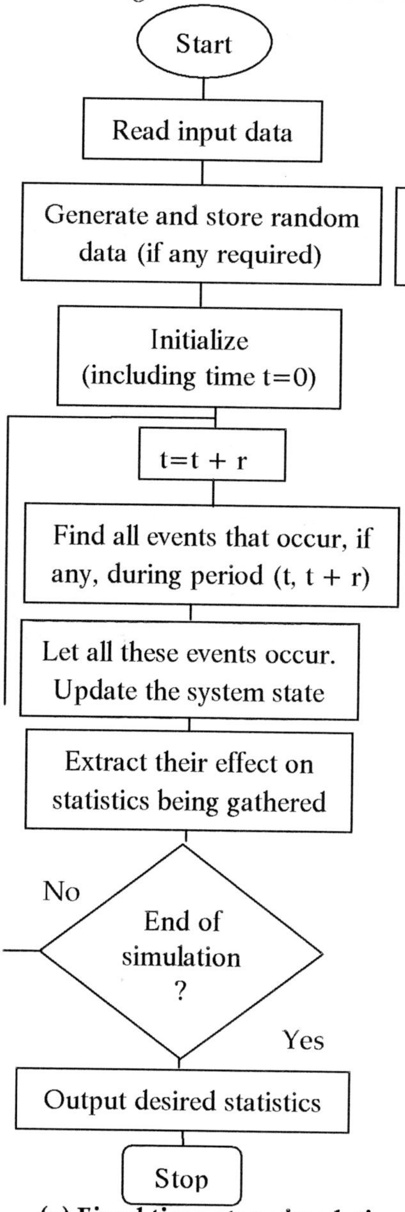

(a) Fixed time-step simulation

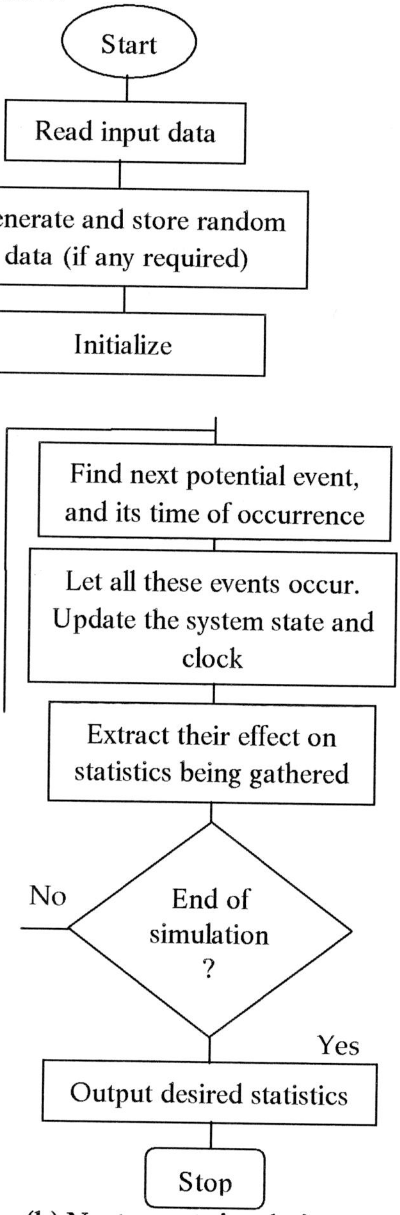

(b) Next-event simulation

(b) Fixed Time-step Model: In a fixed time-step model a timer or "clock" is simulated by the computer. This clock is updated by a fixed time interval and the system is examined to see if any event has taken place during this time interval. All events that take place during this period are treated as if they occurred simultaneously at the tail end of this interval.

Examples of discrete systems

(1) Changes in a factory system. the ordering of raw materials or the completion of n product occurs at specific points of time.

(2) Generation of random numbers

(3) Chi-Square test

There are also systems that are intrinsically continuous but information about them is only available at discrete points in time. These are called sampled-data systems. The study of such systems includes the problem of determining the effects of the discrete sampling, especially when the intention is to control the system on the basis of information gathered by the sampling.

We define a model as the body of information about the system gathered for the purpose of studying the real system. The purpose of the study will determine the nature of the information that is gathered.

There is no unique model of the system. Different models of the different persons/designers interested in different aspects of the system or by the same designer as his understanding of the system changes.

So we can say that with the help of model data we can study the real system.

For e.g.: ALU circuit

Arithmetic and logical unit, first we design this circuit at software level with the help of **Ultraman Software**.

Then we just put the input/information/collected data according to expected output then we compare the received output with the real or actual output, if these both output match then WC just convert this model or software design into hardware model.

The task of deriving a model of a system may be divided into two sub tasks.

(1) Establishing the model structure and supplying the data.

(2) Establishing the structure and determining the system boundary and identify the entities, attributes and activities of the system.

The data provides the values, the attributes can have and define the relationship involved in the activities.

The No jobs of creating a structure and providing the data are defined as parts of one task rather than as two separated tasks because that are usually so intimately related that neither can be done without the other.

Collect and Process Real System Data : Collect data on system specification (e.g. bandwidth for a communication network) input variables, as well as performance of existing system. Identify sources of randomness in the system. I.e. the stochastic input variable. Select an appropriate input probability distribution for each stochastic input variable and estimate corresponding parameter.

Although most simulation software packages include many distributions as a standard feature, issues relating to random number generators and generating random variants from various distributions are pertinent and should be looked in to.

Verify that the simulation model executes as intended. Verification techniques include traces, varying input parameter over their acceptable range and checking the output substitution constant for random variables and manually checking results and animation.

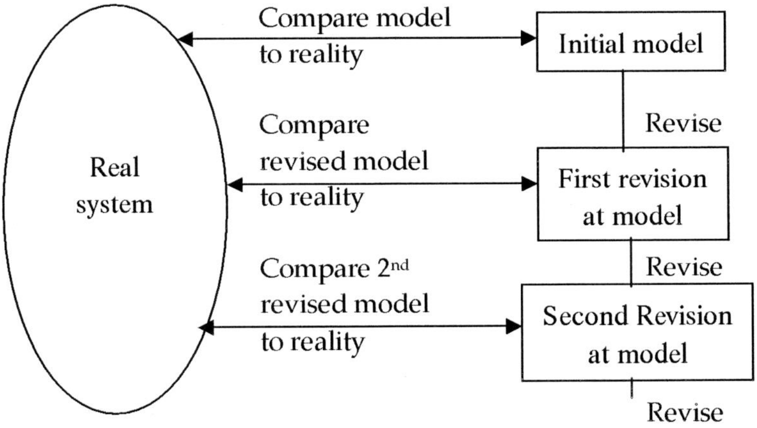

Simulation is the imitation of the operation at a real world process or system over time. It involves generation at an artificial history of a system and the observation of that artificial history to draw interference concerning the operating characteristics of the real system. Simulation is used before an existing system is altered or a new system is built in order to reduce chances of failure, to meet specifications, to prevent under or over utilization of resources and to optimize the system performance.

Conditions that make a problem suitable for simulation:

A system of explicit functional forms [e.g.,$y=f(\pi,t)$]

A system of difference equations [e.g.,$y_{n+1} = ay_n + b\pi_n$]

A system of differential equations [e.g.,$dy/dt=f(\pi,t)$]

The independent variable is time.

A particular numerical computation method, called the Monte Carlo method, consists of experimental sampling with random numbers.

Suppose the function f(x) is positive and has lower and upper bounds a and b respectively. Suppose, also, the function is bounded above by the value c.

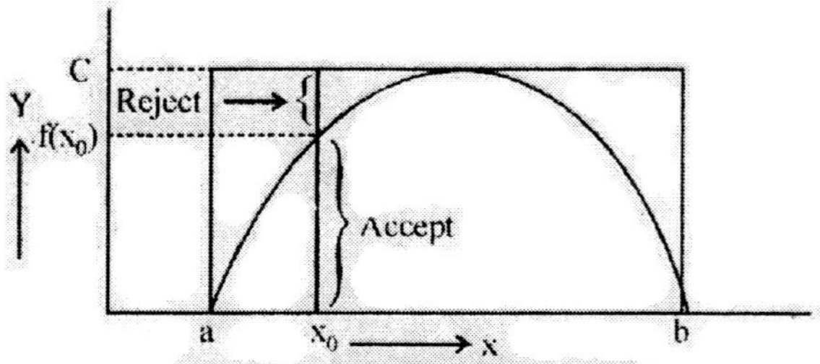

Fig. The Monte-Carlo Method

In the graph, the distribution of selected points is uniformly spread over a rectangle, the fraction of points falling on or below the curve is approximately the ratio of the area under the curve to the area of the rectangles if N points are used and n of them fall under the curve ,the approximately,

$$\frac{n}{N} = \frac{dy}{dx}\oint_{a}^{b} \frac{f(x)dx}{c(b-a)}$$

The accuracy improves as the number N improves.

Steps for Simulation Process

(i) Select the measures of effectiveness

(ii) Decide the variables, which influence majorly the effectiveness and significance.

(iii) Determine the cumulative probability distribution for each variable defined in step no.2.

(iv) Choose a set of random number.

(v) Choose each random number according to decimal value of the. cumulative probability distribution

(vi) Insert the simulated values so generated into the formula derived from the chosen measure of effectiveness.

(ii) Repeat step (v) and (vi). Until sample is large enough for satisfaction of the decision maker.

Time-sharing system is a logical extension of multiprogramming. In a time-shared systems, the CPU executes multiple jobs by switching among them, but the switching occurs so frequently that the users can interact with each program while it is running.

A time-shared system allot many users to share the computer simultaneously: Since each action or command in a time-shared system tends to be short, only a little CPU-time is needed for each user. As the system switches rapidly from one user to the next, each user is given the impression that the entire computer system is dedicated to his use, even though it is being shared among many users.

Model of Time-shared Computer System: Time-shared computer system has three events :

(i) Arrival of request (ii) CPU run (iii) End of simulation

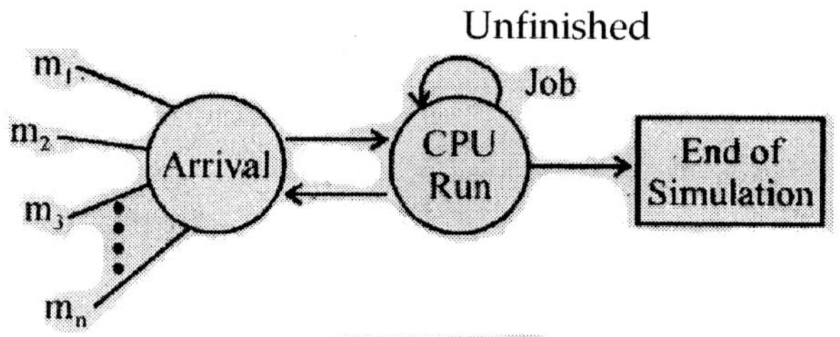

Fig. Event Graph

m1, m2, m3 ....mn = N number of jobs/processes the model uses CPU scheduling to provide each user with a small portion of a time-shared system. A program loaded into memory and executed is called a process. When a process executes. it typically executes for only a short time before it either finishes or needs to perform I/O, thus CPU sit idle as this I/O takes place, but in time-shared it rapidly switch the CPU to the next program in queue.

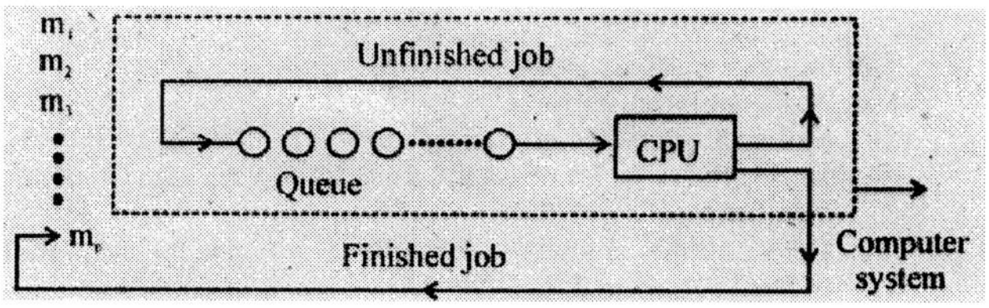

Discription of Events

(i) Arrival Event

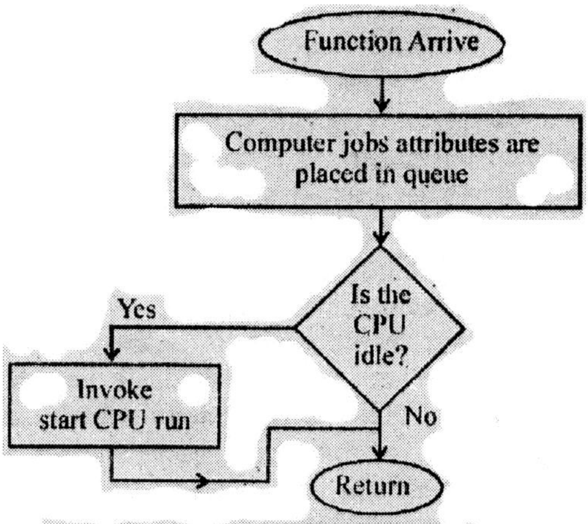

Fig. : Flow Chart for Arrival Function

Attributes for Arrival Event

- Time requirement
- CPU requirement
- Device requirement
- I/O requirement

(ii) DPU Run

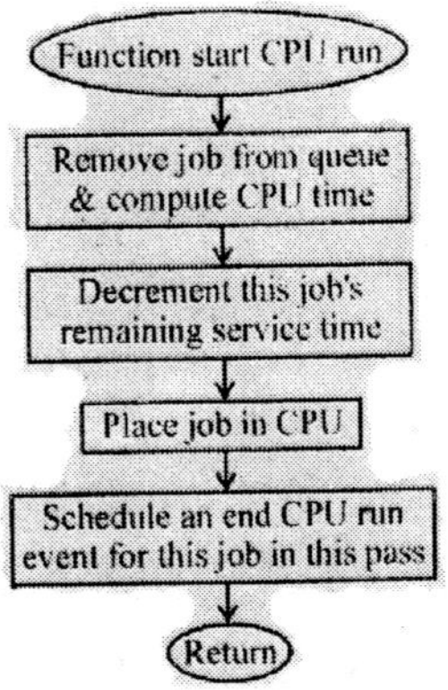

(iii) End of Simulation

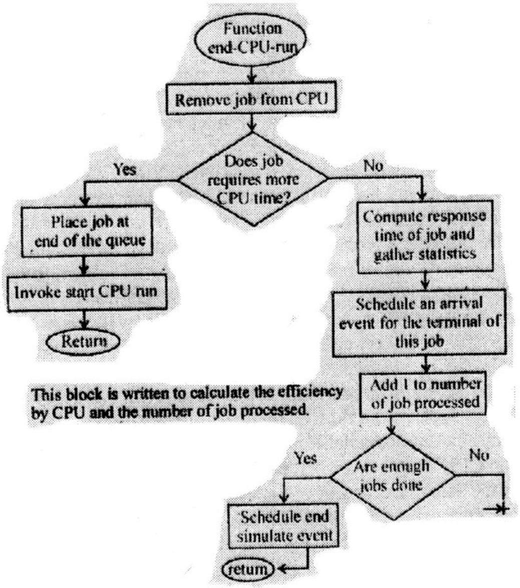

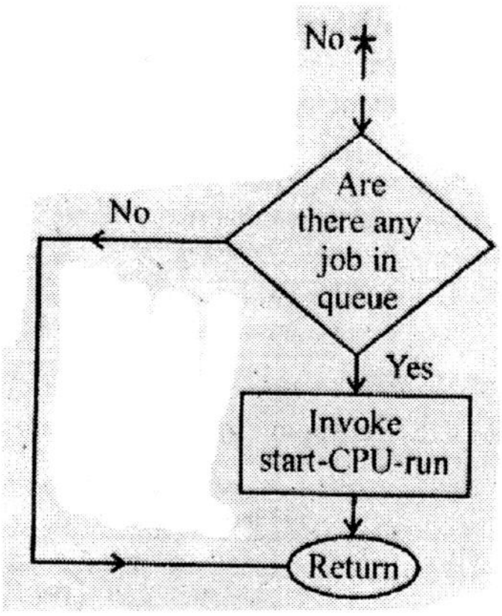

Multitasking: A instance of a program in execution is called a process or task. A multitasking operating system is distinguished by its ability to support concurrent execution of two or more active processes.

Multiprogramming: A multiprogramming operating system provides sophisticated forms of memory protection and concurrently control when processes access shared 110 devices and files in addition to supporting multitasking.

Multiprogramming does not guarantee that a program will run in a timely manner as one program can run uninterrupted for hours without needing access to a peripheral. The presence of independent jobs guarantees that the CPU and 1/0 activities are independent of each other. Some of the popular multiprogramming operating systems are UNIX, VMS. Windows NT etc. The significant advantage of multiprogramming operating systems was a drastic reduction of waiting times for various jobs. Multitasking is a technique, in most of today's operating systems, in which a computer's microprocessor is able to safely and efficiently run several independent tasks (such as the execution of many application programs), and at the same time there is no noticeable delays faced by the user. Multitasking operating systems are also called -Time sharing systems", as they divide the processor cycles between multiple user applications.

The number of programs that can be effectively multitasked, depends on various things such as the type of multitasking performed, the speed of the CPU and the amount of available main memory. Multitasking is accomplished because the CPU is able to switch from one task to another so quickly that it appears to the user that all programs are executing at the same time. Programs can be run concurrently within the computer because of the differences between the speed of l/0 and processing. The time of CPU is divided between multiple processes which are in execution concurrently. Most systems use time-slicing (round robin) scheduling for sharing CPU time between processes. In this approach, programs are executed with routing priority that increases during waiting and drops after the service is granted. Each process is given a system defined time period, called time-slice, for execution. After completion of this time period, the operating system interrupts the executing process and places it at the end of the queue of waiting programs. The ability or performing multitasking does not mean that an unlimited number of tasks can be indefinitely switched back and forth. Each task consumes a certain amount of system storage and other resources, and as more tasks are started, the operating system slows down or begins to run out of shared storage.

Dynamo: It is one of the most widely used simulation language among economist and social scientists

It uses first order differential equation to approximate the model process. The basic function of compiler of Dynamo is:

(a) Error Control

(b) Sequencing equations according to the structure and concept of system dynamics.

(c) Compilation of the program and generation of O/P in a tabular one graphical form.

(d) Weakness of these language is to very primitive and inaccurate integration scheme (Euler% method)

(e) Latest version of DYNAMO is DYNAMO II which has additional features of an array.

Classification Chart for Classification of Simulation Language: Simulation language often serves other very useful purposes. It provides a conceptual framework in which the system analyst can work while building a model of the system it also provides a terminology for describing a complex dynamic system

Classification of Simulation Language

1. **Continuous Language:** These are designed for simulating continuous models:

(a) Block-structured Continuous Language: They were designed to simulate only those system that could be represented as analog block diagram and thus their application area is restricted.

(b) Expression based Continuous Language: They do not need to follow block-structures of the analog patch boards but directly implement the differential equations of the model.

2. **Discrete System Simulation Language:** they are designed for discrete models. Models that change their state abruptly at discrete points in time!' provides streams of pseudo-random numbers for any desired statistical distribution.

Categories of Discrete System Languages

(a) Event -Oriented Language: Each event is represented by an instantaneous occurrence in simulated time and must be scheduled to occur (in advance) when a proper set of conditions exists.

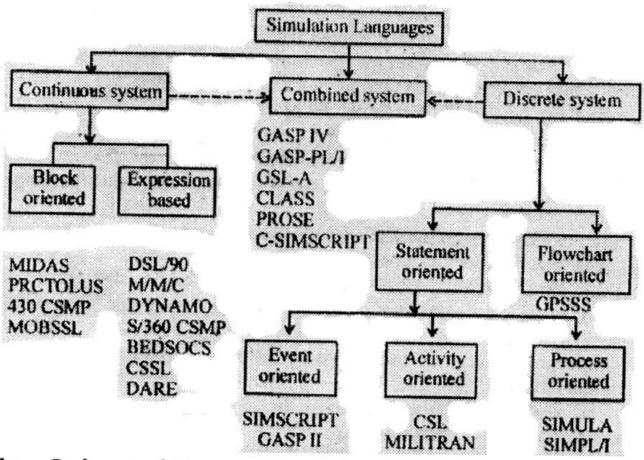

(b) Activity Oriented Languages: In this, the discrete occurrences are not scheduled in advance. They are created by a program which contains descriptions of conditions under which any activity can take place.

(c) **Process Oriented Languages:** Key feature is that of a single process routine, composed of a number of segments describing a sequence of activities. Each segment behavior as an independently controlled program.

Patton in Selection of a Simulation Language

I. **Language generality and programming power** : The language should be able to handle a wide area of application. It should offer strong algorithmic capabilities as well as special simulation oriented features.

2. **Ease of Use** : It includes the natural translation of the system under study to a corresponding computer program reduction is debugging effort, convenient documentation.

3. **Machlne Efficiency:** It is to a large extent a property of the equality of compiler implementation, which in turn depends on the language structure and content Two usual measures are execution time and memory requirement.

4. **Availability:** The language must be available and supported on the most important type of computers in order to be useful.

A bakery keeps stock of popular brand of bread. Previous experience indicates the daily demand as given below :

Daily Demand	Probability
0	0.01
10	0.20
20	0.15
30	0.50
40	0.12
50	0.02

Study the following sequence of random numbers:

48, 78, 19, 51, 56, 77, 15, 14, 68, 9

Using above sequence, simulate the demand for the next 10 days

(i) Find out the stock situation if the owner of the bakery decides to make 30 breads every day.

(ii) Estimate the daily average demand for the bread on the basis of simulated data.

Sol. The relative frequency table can be constructed as follows :

Demand	Probability	Cumulative Probability	Random Number Internal
0	0.01	0.01	00
10	0.20	0.21	01-20
20	0.15	036	21-35
30	050	0.86	36-85
40	0.12	098	86-97
50	0.02	1.00	90-99

The simulated demand for 10 days is shown below:

Day Number	Generated Random Demand	Generated Demand	Stock Level
1	48	30	0
2	78	30	0
3	19	10	20 (30 - 10)
4	51	30	20
5	56	30	20
6	77	30	20
7	IS	SO	40 [20 4- (30 - I 0)]
8	14	10	60 [40 - (30 - 10)]
9	68	30	60
10	09	10	80 [60- (30- 10)]

As the bakery owner makes 30 bread everyday and the demand on day 1 and day 2 is 30 each, the stock level is zero on both the days. Stock on day 3 will be 20 as he has made 30 bread but demand only of 20. Similarly on day 7. there was a stock balance of 20, he has made 30 and demand is only 10, so stock level 15 20 + (30- 10) = 40. Expected demand 220 bread per day and on an average stock of 30-22 = 8 will be available in the bakery.

Following is a model of corporation to illustrate the interaction that occurs in a system.

Corporate Model : Figure below shows corporate model and is used in various aspects of planning these operation.

Let corporation is a manufacturing unit and plan to produce and market some new products.

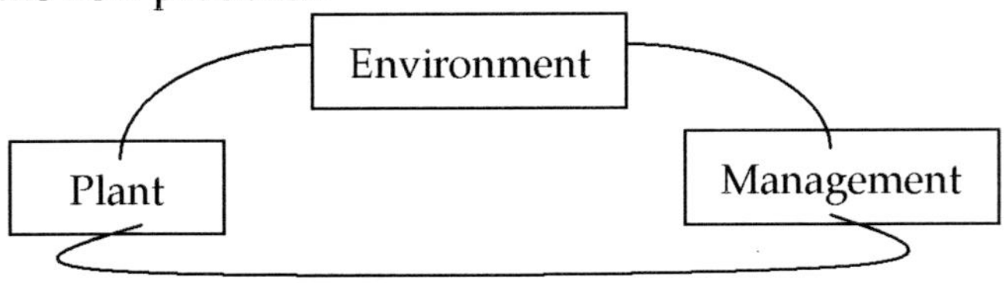

Context Diagram of DED Representing Model (system) in Short

Initially we can divide our system into three important subsystem namely plant, management and environment.

Corporation operates within an environment and it includes the factor influencing the corporation that is not under its direct control.

Plant provide the means for production.

Management is policy maker of the corporation.

Environment : It includes that entities entities which are not in our control.

E.g. customer, market.

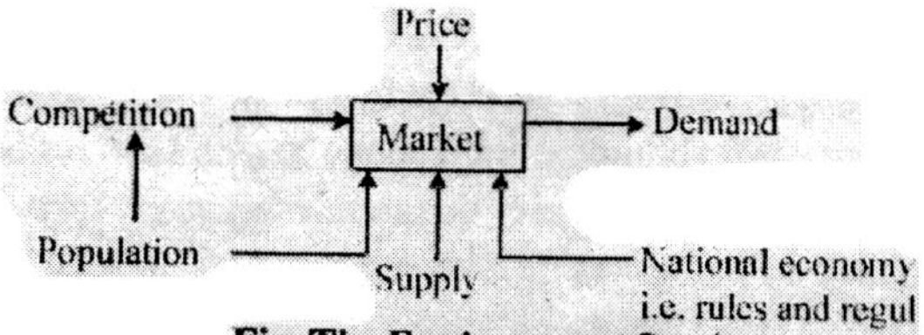

Fig. The Environment Section

No demand will be there if there exists no market or customers.

1. Environment Segment : Major component is market

The main output of market is demand, price and supply are the input for this model.

Other features are :

National Economy: it effect the market by influencing the amount of money available to consumer or customer.

Population: It should be divided regionally for forceful and efficient marketing.

Competition: From the other product. Competitive model is lightly to interact with the population model.

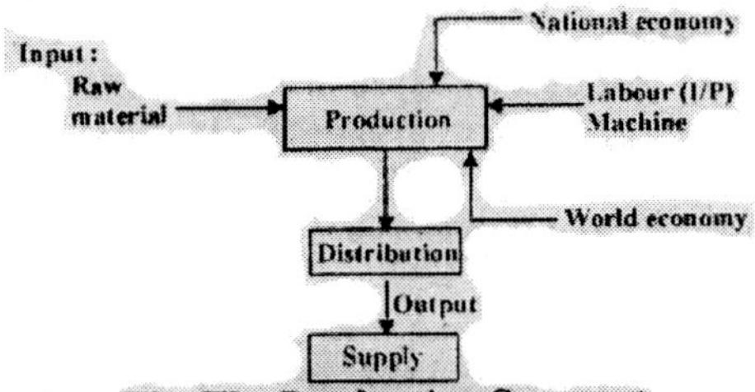

Fig. The Production Segment

2. Plant Segment: It can be further divided into:

(i) Main input is amount of labor. machinery, assign for production and raw material.

(ii) Main output is supply of the product.

(iii) Its subsystems arc distribution sub-system

Distribution sub-system : How the location of warehouse matched with the population.

Another Subsystem are

(i) National Economy : Wages effects the production (either due to more number of labour or hider salary to the labour) hence there are important aspects of national economy.

(ii) World Economy: If imported raw material is required incur production unit or product is sold in overseas market. The world economy effects the production segment.

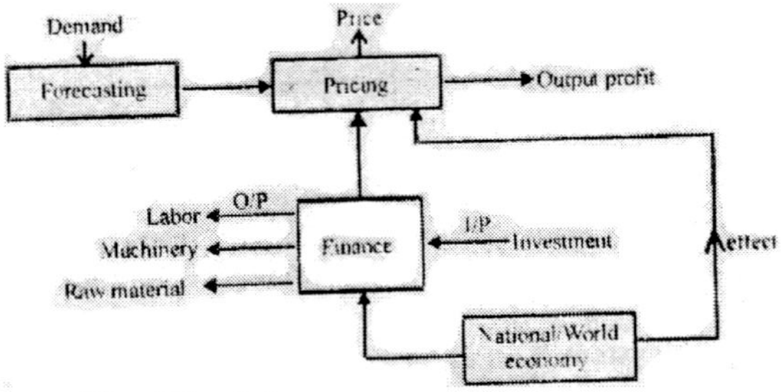

Fig. The Management Segment

Main input are demand and capital invested.

Main output are profit and price. (to be expected)

(i) Pricing subsystem: It is used to decide the price of the product.

(ii) Financial subsystem: Decides how the invested capital is to be divided into various subsystems (department).

(iii) Forecasting subsystem: It is used to predict the future demand of the product.

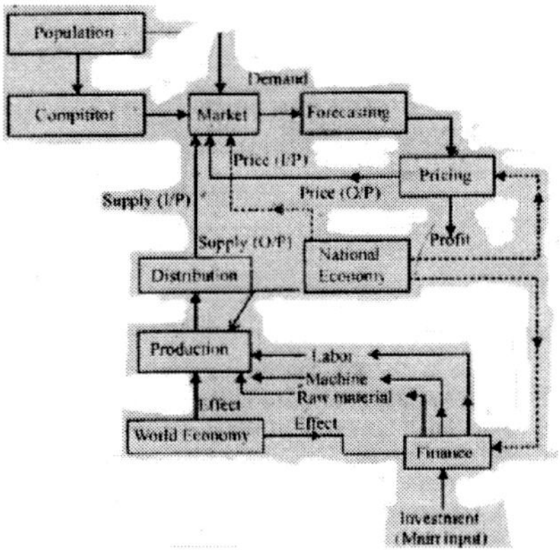

Input = Investment

Output = Profit

▭ → Entities

Fig. The Full Corporate Model

System	Entitles	Attributes	Activities
Petrol Pumping Station	1. Vehicles	1. Vehicle type	1. Checking in
	2. Customers	2. Balance	2. Payment
	3. Fuel	3. Fuel type	3. Fueling
	4. Staff	4. Category	4. Managing

Entity - The term entity is used to denote an object of interest in the system.

Attribute - The term attribute will denote a property of an entity.

Activity - My process that causes changes in system will be called an activity.

System - A system is an aggregation or assemblage of objects joined in some regular interaction or interdependence.

System Analysis: Aim of system analysis is to understand how a existing system or proposed system operates.

It helps in :

(1) Construction of a model

(2) Investigate the behavior of the model

(3) The result obtained or interpreted in terms of system performance

E.g. System involves four variables denoted by the following variable :

K Capital Investment

L. Labor.

M Machinery

S Supply

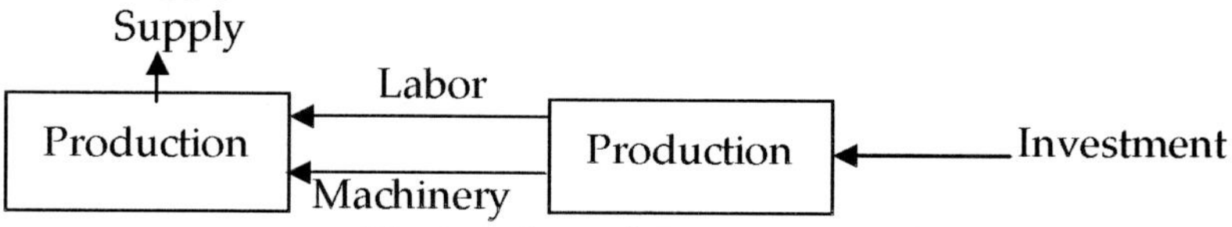

Fig. Portion of Corporate Model

(ii) System Design : The aim of system designer is to produce a system that meets the specifications.

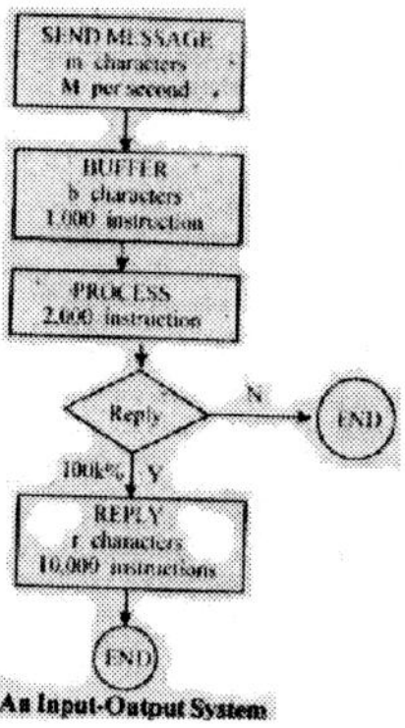

Fig. An Input-Output System

Certain system parameters or components are related and are used to combine to construct the system.

The proposed system is modeled and its performance predicted from the behavior of the model.

If the performance is acceptable, then the system is acceptable. Otherwise it is re-designed and the process is repeated.

(iii) System Postulates : System postulates is the characteristics of the way the model are employed in social, economic, political and medical studies where the behavior of the system is labium but the process that produce a behavior are not. Hypothesis are made to explain the behavior.

These behavior arc compared spirit known behavior. If matches, leads to the assumption that the structure of the model been the resemblance to the actual system and allows a system structure to be postulated.

Ex. Mathematical Model

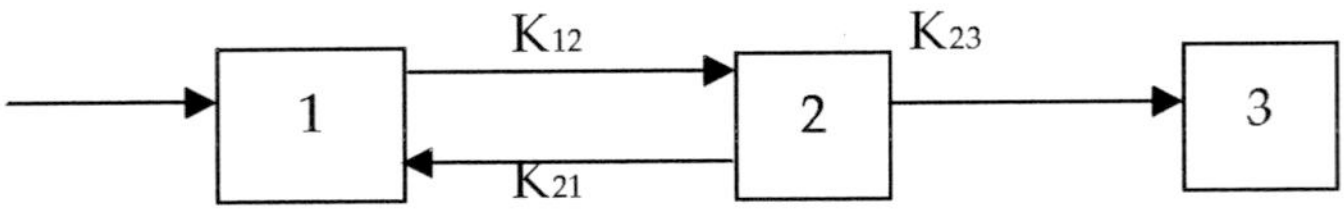

For Verification and Validation Steps in Modeling Process are:

(i) Real world problem
(ii) Defile the goal
(iii) Characterize the system.
(iv) Formulate the model
(v) Solve or simulate
(vi) Analyze Not adequate
(vii) Validate the model
↓ Adequate
(viii) Problem solved or goal achieved

Verification and Validation (Valid V) Activities :

Verification is concerned with the building of the model (product) right : It is utilized for the comparison of the conceptual male to the computer representation that implements the concept.

Validation is concerned with building the right model (product). It is utilized to determine that model is an accurate representation of the real system. Validation is achieved through calibration of the model. It is an iterative process of comparing the model with the-actual system behavior or model. This process is repeated until the model is accepted.

Goals of Validation: To produce a model that represent a Omni system behavior. To increase an acceptable level, the readability of the model. Successive calibration leads to validation of a Model.

Purpose of Verification: To assume that the conceptual model is reflected accurately in the computerized representation (operational model) i.e. verification ask the question:

Is the conceptual model (Assumptions on the system component and system structure, values of the parameters and simplification) accurately represented by the operational model.

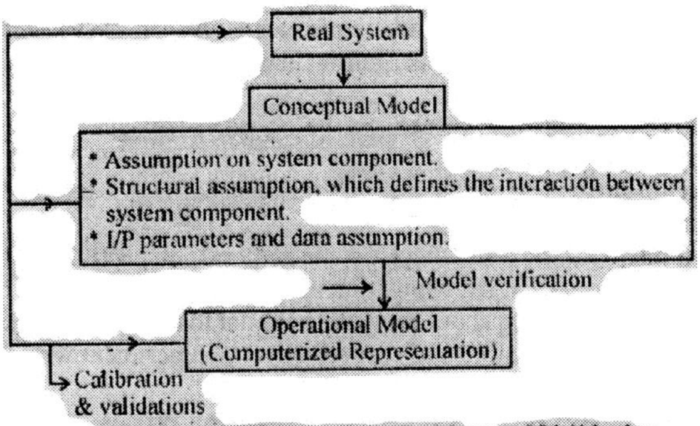

Fig. Model Building, Verification and Validation.

Steps of Verification:

(i) Computerized representation must be checked by someone other than the developer.

(ii) Prepare a flow chart/other relevant diagrams which include each logical action, which a system can take when an event occurs and follows the logic behind the model.

(iii) Check the model output under a variety of input data set.

(iv) Make a computerized representation as self explanatory. Every variable must tie preciously defined and purpose of every section in code mist be mentioned.

(v) If the computerized fermentation is animated: stay that what is appearing on screen is the actual/desired.

Verification and Validation Modeling Procedure : One of the most difficult problem facing a simulation analyst is that of trying to determine whether a simulation model is an accurate representation of the actual system being studied it whether the model is valid or not.

Technique for verifying a simulation computer programs are as follows:

Technique 1 : In developing a simulation program/model, write and debug the computer program in module or sub program.

Technique 2 : 11 is advisable in developing large simulation model to have more than one person review the computer program.

Technique 3 : Run the simulation under a variety of setting of the input parameter and check to see that the output is reversible.

Technique 4: One of. the most powerful technique that can be used to debug a discrete event simulation program is a trace.

Technique 5 : The model should be rim, when possible under simplifying assumption for which its true characteristics arc known or can be easily computed.

Technique 6: With some types of simulation model it may be helpful to observe an animation attic simulation output.

Technique 7: Compute the sample means and sample variable for each simulation input probability distribution and compare them with the desired e.g. Historical mean variance.

This suggests that values are being correctly generated from the distribution.

Technique 8: Use of commercial simulation package to reduce the amount of programming required.

Validation: The following are some general perspective on validations.

(1) Conceptually. if a simulation model is 'valid' then it can be used to make decision about the system similar to those that would be made if it were feasible and cost effective to experiment with the system itself.

(2) The ease or difficulty of the validation process depends on the complexity of the system being modeled and on whether a version of the system currently exists.

(3) A simulation model should always be developed bra particular set of purpose. Indeed a model that is valid for one purpose may not be for another.

(4) The measure of performance used to validate a model should include those that the maker will actually use for evaluating system design.

(5) Validation is not something to be attempted after simulation model has already been developed.

Calibration: Calibration is the iterative process of comparing the model to the real system. Making adjustments to the model, comparing the revised model to reality making additional adjustments, comparing again and so on.

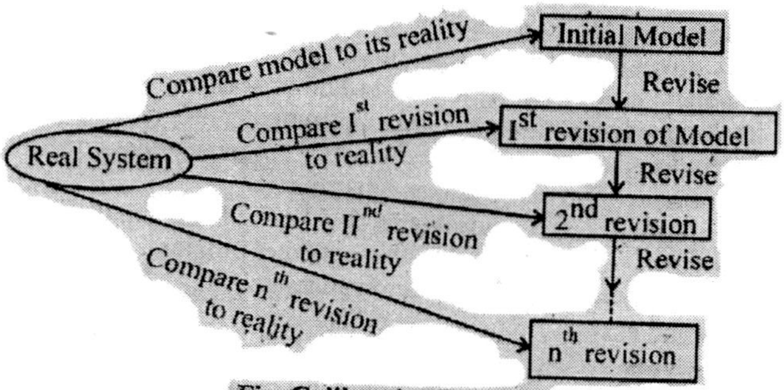

Fig. Calibration Process

Comprising of model to reality is carried out by following test

1. **Subjective test**: It involves people, who are knowledgeable about one or more aspect of the system, making judgment about the model and its output.

2. **Objective test**: It require data on system behavior and the data produced by the model

3. **Statistical test**: These test are performed to compare some aspects of the system, data set to some aspects of the model data set. Hence. it is an iterative process of comparing model and system and revising both test model becomes sufficiently accurate.

Naylor and Finger : suggested a three step approach as an aid in the validation process

(i) Built a model that has high face validity

(ii) Validate model assumptions

(iii) Compare the model input output transformation for the real system

(a) Face Validity: Model must appear reasonable on its face to model users and others who are knowledgeable about the real system.

(b) Validate Model Assumptions

1. **Structured Assumptions**: It involves questions like how the system operates and involves simplification and extraction of reality (system).

2. **Data Assumptions:** These are based on collection of reliable data and correct statistical analysis of the data.

3. **Validating I/o Transformation** : The structure of the model must be accurate enough to make good predictions not just for one input data set, but for the validity of input data set.

A simulation is an imitation of some real thing, state of affairs or process. The act of simulating something generally entails representing certain key characteristics or behaviors of a selected physical or abstract system.

Simulation is also known as management laboratory which determines the effect of an alternate policy without disturbing the real world system.

Simulation is the representative modal for real situations:

For example

(i) Children's cycling path with various signals and crossing in an exhibition is a simulated model of city traffic in real world.

(ii) The combination of computer and simulation results as a video / TV Games.

(iii) Chess playing is a non-probabilistic simulation of a fight between the black and white armies.

(iv) Game of snake and ladder simulates the moral process of the players, who moved up ladders when they were good and MI down snakes, indicating temptation, when they were bad.

Conclusion : Thus, representation of reality which may be either in physical form or in a mathematical equations form is known as simulation.

Definitions Proposed for Simulation : According to Naylor Et al, "Simulation is a numerical technique for conducting experiments or a digital computer, which involves certain types of mathematical and logical relationships, necessary to describe behavior and 'structure of a complex real world system over extended periods of time".

According to Churchman:

X simulates Y is true if:

(a) X and Y are formal systems

(b) Y is taken to be a real system.

(c) X is taken to be an approximation to the real system i.e.?.

(d) The rules of validity in X are non-error free. Other wise it becomes real system.

Simulation is a representation of reality through the use of a model or other device, which will react in the same manner as reality under the set of given conditions.

Classification of Simulation

(i) Physical Simulation: It refers to simulation in which physical objects are substituted for the real thing. The physical objects are often chosen because they are smaller or cheaper than the actual objects or system.

(ii) Interactive Simulation: it is a kind of physical simulation often referred to as a human in the loop simulation on in which physical simulations include hum art operators. Such as a flight simulator or, a driving simulator. Human is the loop simulations and can include a computer simulation as a so-called synthetic environment.

(iii) Computer Simulation: It is formulated into a mathematical model for which a computer program can be developed and the problem is solved using the computers. Such type of simulation is known as system Simulation or computer simulation

Simulation Models: Simulation models are of following four types:

(i) Deterministic Model: In this model input and output variables are not permitted to be random variables and the model arc described by exact functional relationship.

(ii) Stochastic Model : In these models at least one of the variables or functional relationship is given by the probability function.

(iii) Static Model : These models do not take variable time into consideration.

(iv) Dynamic Models : These models deals with the time varying interactions.

Process of Simulation

1. Simulation cannot produce optimum results since model deals with the uncertainties, hence the result of simulation is a reliable approximation having statistical errors.

2. Variable which affect the behavior of the complex real world system cannot be quantified.

3. To solve the very complex problem it is difficult to make computer program having large number of variables and the function,' dependencies between them.

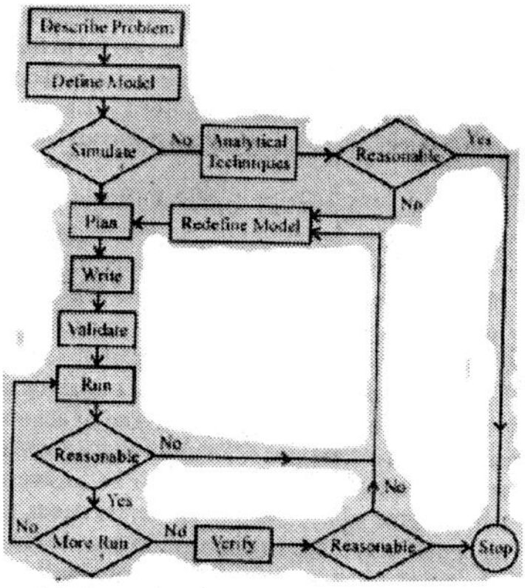

Major Limitations of Simulation

1. Simulation cannot produce optimum results since model deals with the uncertainties, hence the result of simulation is a reliable approximation having statistical errors.

2. Variable which affects the behavior of the complex real world system cannot be quantified.

3. To solve the very complex problem it is difficult to make computer program having large number of variables and the functional dependencies between them.

Major Advantages of Simulation

1. Simulation model are comparatively flexible and can be modified to adjust the variation in the event of real situation.

2. It is an easier technique to use than the mathematical model, hence it is Superior to the mathematical analysis

3. It gives solution through. experiment on a model of the. System without interfering the real system.

4. Peoples can be trained on simulated model before patting into their hands to the costly real system.

Compared with analytical solutions of problems, the main drawback of simulation is apparent: it gives specific solution rather than general solution. In the study of the automobile wheel motion, for example, an anal" cal solution gives all the conditions that can cause oscillation. Each execution of a simulation tells only whether a particular set of conditions did or did not cause oscillation to try to find all such condition requires that the simulation be repeated under many different conditions. The mathematical solution is obviously preferable, particularly when the solution being sought is some maximizing condition. A single mathematical solution might give such condition, whereas many simulation nuts maybe needed to find a maximum, and yet still leave undecided the question of whether it is a local or global maximum.

The range of problems that can be solved mathematically is limited, however mathematical technique requires that the model be expressed in some particular format.

Ex. In the form of linear algebraic equation or continuous linear differential equations. The system must be approximated or abstracted in order to derive a model that fits the format of a mathematical technique. All too often, the process-amounts to making the problem fit the solution rather than the other way Found.

In approaching a system study, it is essential to consider first what mathematical technique might be applied to derive analytical solutions. It is a matter of judgment to decide whether the degree of abstraction required to apply analytical methods is too severe. To make that judgment it is necessary to consider carefully what questions needs to be answered in the system study, and to what degree of accuracy the answers needs to be known.

When the decision is made to simulate in order to use a more realistic model, it is still important to limit the amount of detail in the model to the

Minimum level necessary. The step by step nature of the simulation technique means that the amount of computation increases. very rapidly as the amount of detail increases coupled with the need to make many run to explore the range of conditions, the extra realism of simulation model can result in a very extensive amount of computing.

In many ways, the ideal nay of using simulation is an extension of mathematical solutions that might have been obtained at the cost of too much simplification. There are many simple limitation on a system, such as physical stops finite time delay or non linear forces, which render what would otherwise be a soluble mathematical model insoluble. Simulation easily removes these limitations and it can then provide a powerful extension of known mathematical solution.

Even when a model with a known solutions is considered adequate, there are still times when a simulations will provide a quicker or more convenient way of deriving results. Many analytical results occur in the form of complex series or integral that still require extensive evaluation.

It is often more convenient to use simulation to obtain results directly from a model with specific values rather than to perform the numerical evaluation of analytical solutions.

Cobweb Model

A particularly Simple but la g model can be constructed from static market model. The related supply 'S' and demand 'Q', the market price The supply should be made dependent upon price (The price will lower more supply) from the previous marketing period. The demand will respond to current price.

The equations are

$$Q = a\text{-}b\ P$$

$$S = c\text{+}d\ P\text{-}1$$

Assume Q =S (Equilibrium State)

Given an initial value of price P the value of S at the end of first interval can be

Po=1, a=12.4. b= 1.2. c = 1.0,d=9

Models of this type are called cobweb models because of a particular way they can be solved graphically. Two straight lines represents supply and demand. Beginning from the initial price of I, a horizontal line to the supply line determines the supply that will be produced at that price level that is about 1.9 units. A venial line to the demand line reflects the fact that demand. equals to the supply then supply price immediately rises to about 8.7 units. This supply is too big, then drop to about 3.5 units, continuing in this manner, we will get the spiral pattern.

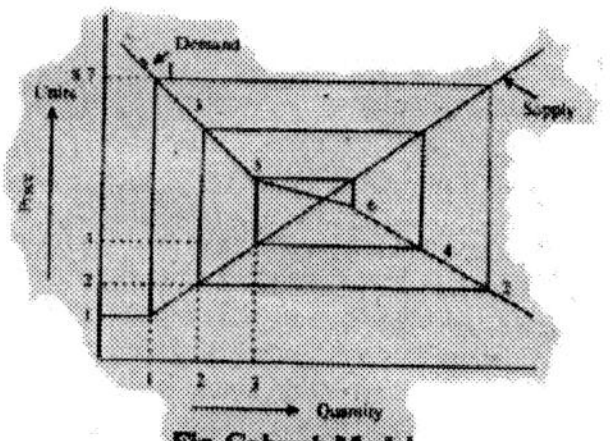

Fig. Cobweb Model

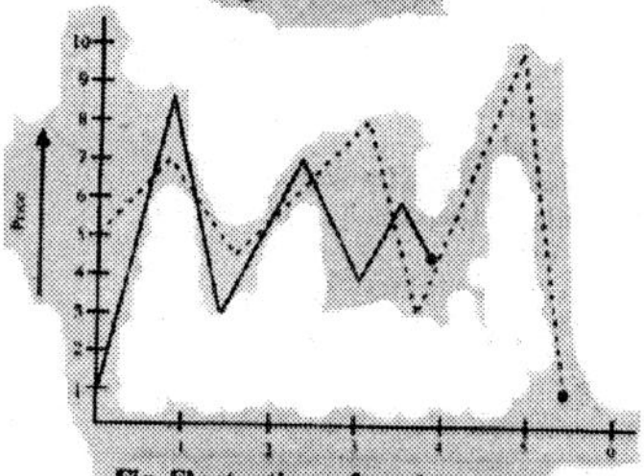

Fig. Fluctuations of market-price

Pseudocode : Pscudo code (derived from pseudo and code) is a compact and informal high level description of a computer programming algorithm that uses the structural conventions of programming languages, but omits detailed subroutines, variables declaration and language specific syntax. The programming language is augmented with natural language descriptions of the details, with convenient or with compact mathematical notation. The purpose, of using pseudo code as opposed the language syntax is that it is easier for humans to read. This is often achieved by making the sample application independent so more specific items can be added later. Pseudo code resembles, but should not be confused with, skeleton programs including dummy code, which can be compiled without errors. Flowcharts can be thought of as a graphical form of pseudo code.

Syntax: As the name suggests pseudo code generally does not actually obey the syntax rule of any particular language there is no systematic standard form, although any particular writer will generally borrow the appearance of a particular language. Pseudo code may therefore vary widely in style, from a near exact limitation of a real programming language at one extreme, to a description approaching formatted prose at the other.

Examples of pseudo code

```
If   credit card number is valid o
     execute transaction based on number and order
else
     show a generic failure message end if
```

Algorithm: An algorithm is a procedure or formula for solving a problem. A computer program can be viewed as an elaborate algorithm. In mathematical and Computer science, an algorithm usually means a small procedure that solves a recurrent problem. It is a definite list of well-defined instructions for completing a task; that given an initial state, Will proceed through a well-defined series of successive states, eventually terminating in an end-state. The transition from one state to the next is not necessarily deterministic. The concept of an algorithm originated as a means of recording procedures for solving problems.

Example of Algorithm

Largest Number

Input : Anon-empty list of number L

Output : The largest number in the List L

largest 4 Lo

for each item in the list L>l, do

If the item > largest, then

largest 4- the item

return largest

Describe role of GPSS in simulation.

Sol. (a) GPSS (General Purpose Simulation System) language was developed principally by the IBM corporation published in 1961.

The system which Is to be simulated in GPSS is described by a blocks diagram in which the blocks represent the activities, and lines joining the blocks indicate the sequence in which the activities can be executed. Where there is a choice of activities, more that one line leaves a block and the condition for the choice is stated the block.

Features of GPSS

1. Restricted to simple queuing problem.
2. Poor computational Facilities.
3. Inflexible input and output.
4. No language extension possible.
5. Easy to learn and use.
6. Good debugging facilities.
7. Machine efficiency is often poor.
8. Interpretative system

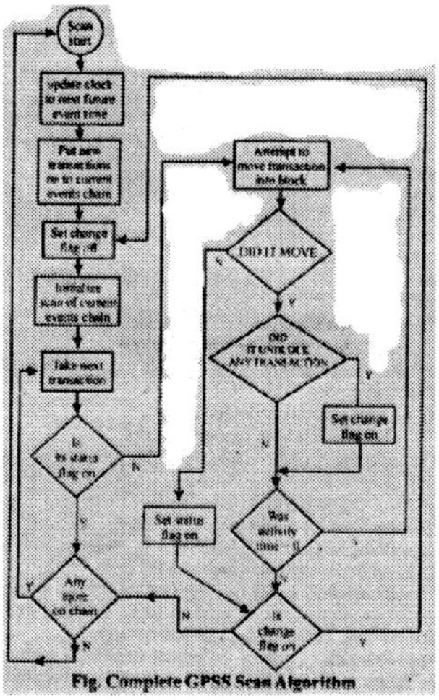

Fig. Complete GPSS Scan Algorithm

Aggregation: Aggregation is the extent to which the number of individual entities can be grouped together into larger entities.

The general manager of Me factory may be satisfied with the description that has been given. The production control manager, however will want to consider the shop of the department as individual entities.

In some studies, it may be necessary to construct artificial entities through the process of aggregation.

Example: An economy on research study will usually treat a population as a number of social classes and conduct a study as through each research class were, indistinct entity.

Similarly consideration of aggregation should be given to the representation of activities.

e.g. In studying a missile defense system. It may not be necessary to include the detail of computing a missile trajectory for each ruing: It may be sufficient to represent the outcome of many firings by a probability fiction.

Types of aggregation:

(1) Static aggregation : In a static aggregation number of sub objects , cannot vary.

e.g. (i) A rectangle has a point and dimension

(ii) A customer has a name and an address

(2) Dynamic aggregation : In a dynamic aggregation number of sub objects may vary.

(i) A catalog has many catalog items

(ii) A host list has been changing entries

The consideration in developing and using computer singular ion model will naturally depends upon the system being studied and on the scope of the study. The Way a simulation experiment proceeds will vary from system to system. I low ever, there are certain basis of basic steps which can be identified as common to all digital simulation which may be summarized as follows :

I. Problem definition and planning of the study.

2. **Model building** : Including identification of those aspects of systern performance that are of interest to us and data collection for detcnnining, values of the system parameter.

3. **Flowcharting** : To show the logical steps to be performed by the computer in simulating the mathematical model obtained in step 2 above.

4. **Choice of a Programming Language** : There are usually two operations available at this point. The first option is to use a high level general purpose language such as FORTRAN, (or AIGOL, PL/I, BASIC).

The second option is to use a special purpose simulation language such as GPSS (or SIMSCRIPT, SIMULA etc). Both of these approaches are extensively based in simulation studies.

Use of a simulation language can save time and drudgery for the programmer. If the system being simulated is very complex.

On the negative side, he would have to learn a new language and the program written in a special purpose language would usually tat up more computer time and memory.

5. **Program Writing:** While converting the flowchart into a running program (in the language chosen in step 4) special attention should be paid to modularization.

The "simulator should consist of a number of natural and simple module (sub program) which can be listed independently and allow changes in the model conveniently.

Intermediate print statement should also be included for diagnosis in mediating the debagging stages.

These statements may be removed before running the validate program. The format of the final output should be designed for easy interpretation.

6. Validate the model.

7. **Design of Experiment** : Including removal of unwanted transients, determination of run length, initial condition and number of replications.

8. Execution of simulation run, analysis and interpretation of results. Some of these steps have to be performed iteratively till acceptable results are obtained.

Principles used in Modeling : there are mainly four principles used in modeling :

- Block building
- Relevance
- Accuracy
- Aggregation

Block Building : Description of system must be organized in a series of blocks, to simplify the specification of the interaction within the system.

Each block describes a part of the system that depends on few input variable and result in few output variables.

System. Is the interconnection of these blocks.

Block diagram is the diagrammatic representation of the system.

Relevance : The model must include those aspects that are relevant to the study objectives.

E.g. lithe factory system study aims to compare. the effect of different operating rules on efficiency, it is not relevant to consider the hiring of employee as an activity. While irrelevant information in the model may not do any harm. It should be excluded because it increases the complexity of the model and causes more work in solving the model.

Accuracy : The accuracy of the information gathered for the model should be considered.

E.g. In the aircraft system, the accuracy with which the movement of the aircraft is described depends upon the representation of the air frame. It may suffice to reared the airframe as a rigid body and derive a very simple relationship between control surface movement and airframe heading or it may be necessary to recognize the flexibility of the airframe make allowance for vibration in the structure.

An engineer responsible for estimating the final consumption may be satisfied with the simple representation.

Another engineer, responsible for considering the comfort of the passenger, need to consider vibration and will want the detailed description of the airframe.

Aggregation : Extent to which the number of individual entities can be grouped together into large entities

Modeling Process:

(i) Real world problem
(ii) Defining the goal
(iii) Characterize the system
(iv) Formulate the model
(v) Solve or simulate
(vi) Analyze
(vii) Validate the model Note
↓ Adequate
Problem solved goal achieved

Simulation Solfware

Specitic (For special kind of need)

General Purpose (For common need)

Comparison of simulation 'package with the programming language:

• Simulation package automatically provides most of the features needed to build a simulation model, resulting in a significant decrease in programming time and a reduction in overall project cost.

• They provide a natural framework for simulation modeling. These basic modelling construct are more closely akin to simulation then. are those in a general purpose programming brigade like C.

• Simulation models are generally easier to modify and maintain when written in s simulation package.

• They provide better error detection because many potential types of error are checked for automatically. Since fewer modeling constructs need to be inclined in a model, the chance of making an error will probability be smaller.

Following Two types of simulation software are as follows:

Simulation Software

Simulation Language

Application Oriented Simulation Software

(General Purpose)	(Specific)
1. General in nature panicular application.	Specific or oriented towards a
2. Model development is done by writing code. pull down menus etc.	Model development is done by using gniphics, dialog boxes,
3. Provide modeling flexibility	Not flexible
4. Often difficult to use	Easy to learn and use

General purpose software can be used for any application. but migh have special features for certain ones like manufacturing communication process reengineering etc.

Specific purpose is designed to be used for certain class of application such as call centre, health care etc.

Advantages of General Purpose Programming Language:

1. Models may know a programming language which is not to as in the case of simulation pack.

2. A simulation model written in C ore.; * may require less execution time than a model developed in simulation package. (Because program written in C with specifically for the model under consideration).

2. Programming language may allow greater programming flexibility than simulation software on package.

4 Software cost is lower, but overall simulation project cost may not be

Features : Discrete simulation software (package)

1. Facility for random no. generations.

2. Facility for generating random variants from a specified probability distribution.

3. Advancing simulated time.

4. Facility to determine next event from the event list and passing control to the appropriate block of code.

Continuous Simulation Software

1. Facility to handle any order differential equation.
2. Can handle log and exponential (mathematical operation).
3. Facility for integration and differentiation.

Artificial Intelligence (Al) is the study of how to make computer to do things which at the moment people do better. Computers can perform the task like game playing chess, theorem provintwell by being fast at exploring a large number of solution path and then selecting the best one.

AI includes perception (vision, speech) natural language understanding and problem solving in specialized domain such as medical diagnosis and chemical analysis.

Perception of the world around us is crucial to our survival animal, with much less intelligence than the people are capable of more sophism incited visual perception than arc current machines. Perceptual tasks are difficult because they in volves analog signals.

The signals are typically very noisy and usually a large numbers of things must be perceive at once. o

The ability to use language to communicate a wide variety and ideas is. exceptional thing with the human.

The problem of understanding spoken language is again a perceptual problem but if restrict it to 'smitten language only then to understand the sentence on a topic, it is necessary to know about the language itself as well as the knowledge of the topic also.

Al domain is the domain that require lily specialized expertise without the assistance of common sense knowledge e.g. voice, synchronization language, robots.

Artificial intelligence is the simulation of human intelligence processes by machines especially computer systems. These processes include learning (the acquisition of information and rules for using the information), reasoning (using the rules to reach approximate or definite conclusions) and self correction. Particular applications of AL include expert systems, speech recognition and image recognition.

The ability of a digital computer or computer controlled robot to perform tasks commonly associated with intelligent beings. The term is frequently applied to the project of developing systems endowed with the intellectual processes characteristic of humans, such as the ability to reason, discover meaning, generalize or learn from past experience. Some programs have attained the performance levels of human experts and professional in performing certain specific tasks, so that artificial intelligence in this limited sense is found in applications as diverse as medical diagnosis, computer search engines and voice or handwriting recognition.

1. Healthcare (clinical) Simulators: Medical simulators are increasingly being developed and deployed to teach therapeutic and diagnostic procedures as well as medical concepts and decision making to personnel in the health professions. Simulators have been developed for training procedures. They are also important to help on prototyping new devices for biomedical engineering problems. Currently, simulators are applied to research and development of tools for new therapies, treatments and early diagnosis in medicine.

2. Military Simulations Evaluating military weapons system or their logistic requirements: Military simulations, also known informally as war games, are models in which theories of Welfare can be tested and termed without the need for actual hostilities. They exist in many different forms, with varying degrees of realism. In recent times, their scope has widened to include not only military but also political and social factors. While many governments make use of simulation, both individually and collaboratively, little is known about the model's specifics outside professional circles.

3. **Finance**: Determining ordering policies from inventory system. In finance, computer simulations are often used for scenario planning. Risk-adjusted net present value, for example, is computed from well-defined but not always known (or fixed) inputs. By imitating the performance of the project under evaluation, simulation can provide a distribution of NPV over a range of discount rates and other variables.

4. **Evaluating**: Designs for science organization such as call-centers, Fast-food restaurants, Hospitals and Post-offices.

5. **Flight Simulators**: A flight simulator is used to train pilots on the ground. It permits a pilot to crash his simulated -aircraft" without being hurt Flight simulators are often used to train pilots to operate aircraft in extremely hazardous situations, such as landings with no engines. or complete electrical a hydraulic failures. The most advanced simulators have high-fidelity visual systems and hydraulic motion systems. The simulator is normally cheaper to operate than a real trainer aircraft.

6. **Robotics Simulators**: A robotic simulator is used to create embedded applications for a specific (or not) robot without be dependent of the 'real' robot. In some case, these applications can be transferred on the real robot (or rebuilt) without modifications. Robotics simulators allow to reproduce situations that we cannot `create' in the reality because cost, time, or the 'unique' resource. Also, the simulator can be used to create fast robot pent typing.

7. **Marine Simulators**: Bearing resemblance to flight simulators, marine simulators train ships personnel. The most common marine simulators include :

Ship's bridge simulators o Engine room simulators

Cargo handling simulators o Communication simulators

Simulators like these are mostly used within maritime colleges and training institutions. They often consist of a replication of as hip's bridge, with operating desk(s), and a number of screens on which the virtual surroundings arc projected.

8. **Engineering, Technology or Process Simulation**: Simulation is an important feature in engineering systems or any system that involves many processes. For example in electrical engineering, delay lines may be used to simulate propagation delay and phase shift caused by an actual transmission line. Similarly, dummy loads may be used to simulate impedance without simulating propagation, and is used in situations where propagation is unwanted. A simulator may imitate only a few of the operations and functions of the unit it simulates. Most engineering simulations entail mathematical modeling and computer assisted investigation.

9. **Designing and Operating Transportation Systems:** Airports, Freeways parts and Subways. City simulators are generally agent-based simulations with explicit representations for land use and transportation.

10. Determining hardware and software requirements for a common system or protocols for communication networks.

Pmb.0 (a) Customers arrive at a milk booth for the required service. Assume that inter arrival and service times are constant and given by 1.8 and 4 time units respectively: Simulate the given by hand computations for 14 time units. What is the average time per customer? What is the percentage idle time of the facility ?

(Assume that the system starts at t 0)

How will you simulate a time sharing system? Explain.

Milk Booth Problem

It is given in the question that :

Inter arrival time.. 1.8

Service time = 4 unit (constant)

We have to calculate service time up to 14 units for 1st customer, waiting time -0

Since queue is empty that's why customer will not wait for the service. Let CA stands for customers arrival and CD stands for customer departure.

******

Chapter - 18

Sample Size Decisions

Once the simple design is final the next step is to the sample size. When a survey is undertaken and it is not possible to study the entire population the researcher has to deal with some basic problem. For example: How large should be the sample? There are two basic approaches to the problem of sample size:

(1) The Ad-hoc or Practical approach.

(2) The Statistical approach.

(i) Ail-hoe or Practical Approach: In this approach a sample size of less than a few hundred units is not chosen. That is the reason that when a field survey is undertaken, interviewers are appointed, trained and asked to conduct field investigations. This will cost very high, it would not be wise for the researcher if only a small sample is chosen. A survey confined to a relatively small number of units would mean a relatively high cost per interview. Another consideration in favor of selecting a reasonable size of sample is that it enables the researcher to test several hypotheses. This is especially true for simples in the sub-groups. Such hypotheses can be tested with a high degree of statistical significance when the sample size is reasonably large. Another practical consideration in case of a stratified sample is that the overall sample size is so fixed that the sample size within each stratum is not less than 30. A common practice in this regard is to deterine the sample size of each stratum first and then add up the samples of all the strata to obtain the overall sample size.

(ii) The Statistical Approach: The statistical approach is based on statistical principles. A good researcher is expected to follow it rather than the rule-of-thumb approach. According to the statistical approach, the problem of sample size involves several aspects such as the type of sample design, the homogeneity in the population from which a sample is to be chosen and the availability of finance, personnel and time for the conduct of the field survey. In view of all these considerations, the question of sample size becomes difficult. Since a comprehensive discussion of all these aspects would need a good deal of space, only some basic principles for determining sample size are discussed.

Thus, it is necessary to have some idea of sampling distribution, which forms the basis for any problem on sample size.

Sampling Distribution of the Mean

According to the central limit theorem, the various arithmetic means of a large number of random samples of the same size will form a normal distribution. If an arithmetic mean of all possible sample means is calculated, it will coincide with the population mean. To illustrate this point, the following example will serve the purpose-

There are six persons A, B, C, D, E and F constituting the population. Each one of them has some money. Assume that A has rupee one, B rupees two, and so on. Then, the population mean and standard deviation will be as follows:

Identity of persons	Amount (X)	X2
A	1	1
B	2	4
C	3	9
D	4	16
E	5	25
F	6	36
	21	91

Mean or μ= Rs.$\frac{21}{6}$ = Rs. 3.5

Standard deviation $\sigma = \sqrt{\frac{1}{N}S(X-\mu)^2} = \sqrt{\frac{SX^2}{N} - \left(\frac{SX}{N}\right)^2}$

$$= \sqrt{\frac{91}{6} - \left(\frac{21}{6}\right)^2} = \sqrt{15.1667 - 12.2500} = Rs. 1.71$$

Suppose two persons are selected as a sample. The number of possible sample size 2 that can be selected is :

$$\binom{N}{n} = \binom{6}{2} = \frac{6!}{2!\,4!}$$

$= \frac{6\times5\times4\times3\times2\times1}{2\times1\times4\times3\times2\times1} = 15$ (Total number of samples without replacement)

The following table gives all the 15 samples along with their respective means.

S. No.	Sample	Sample Mean
1	A, B	1.5
2	A, C	2.0

3	A, D	2.5
4	A, E	3.0
5	A, F	3.5
6	B, C	2.5
7	B, D	3.0
8	B, E	3.5
9	B, F	4.0
10	C, D	3.5
11	C, E	4.0
12	C, F	4.5
13	D, E	4.5
14	D, F	5.0
15	E, F	5.5

Again the table shows the distribution of sample means, as also some other calculations.

Sample Mean	Frequency	Deviation from assumed mean	d ÷ 0.5	fd	d²	fd²
1.5	1	-2.5	-5	-5	25	25
2	1	-2.0	-4	-4	16	16
2.5	2	-1.5	-3	-6	9	18
3	2	-1.0	-2	-4	4	8
3.5	2	-0.5	-1	-3	1	13
4	2	0	0	0	0	0
4.5	2	1.5	1	2	1	2
5	1	1	2	2	4	4
5.5	1	1.5	3	3	9	9
	15			-22	69	85
				7		
				-15		

$$\overline{X}= \text{A}+\frac{\Sigma fd}{n}\text{x C} = 4.0+ \left(\frac{-15}{15}\text{x } 0.5\right)= \text{Rs. } 3.5$$

$$\sigma_{\overline{X}}=\sqrt{\frac{\Sigma fd^2}{n}-\left(\frac{\Sigma fd}{n}\right)^2} \times C = \sqrt{\frac{85}{15}-\left(\frac{-15}{15}\right)^2} \times 0.5$$

$$= \sqrt{5.6667 - 1} \times 0.5 = 2.16 \times 0.5 = \text{Rs.} 1.08$$

It will be seen that standard deviation of the population, as arrived at , is 1.71, while the standard deviation (called standard error) of the sample distribution as given in is 1.08.There is a certain relationship between the two. This is best explained by the following formula :

$$\sigma_{\overline{x}} = \frac{\sigma}{\sqrt{n}}\sqrt{\frac{N-n}{N-1}}$$

where $\sigma_{\overline{X}}$= standard error of the sample distribution

σ = standard deviation of the population

n = sample size

N = Number of units in the population

Applying the different values in the above formula,

$$\sigma_{\overline{x}} = \frac{1.71}{\sqrt{2}}\sqrt{\frac{6-2}{6-1}} = \frac{1.71}{1.41}\sqrt{0.8} = \frac{1.71\times0.89}{1.41}$$

$$= 1.08 \text{ (same as obtained earlier)}$$

The term $\sqrt{\frac{N-n}{N-1}}$ is called the finite population correction *(fpc).*

It may be noted that in case of an infinite population, the term $\frac{N-n}{N-1}$ approaches 1.00 and hence the finite population correction also approaches 1.00. In such a case, the formula becomes $\sigma_{\overline{x}} = \frac{\sigma}{\sqrt{n}}$ In the case of sampling with replacement, there is an infinite population and as such, the seduced version of the formula may be used. In other cases too, if the sample is relatively too small vis-a-vis the population. fpc need not be used as it will approach 1.00. In other words, when N is large relative to n, the formula $\sigma_{\overline{x}} = \frac{\sigma}{\sqrt{n}}$ may be used, The question is: how to decide that N is relatively larger than n? Different people may take different values but the general practice is to use this formula (which excludes the correction factor) when n is less than 5 per cent of N.

Characteristics of the distribution of sample means

1. Although the population shows a rectangular distribution, the distribution of sample means shows a symmetrical distribution and thus only one mode, i.e. it is unimodal.

2. The mean of the sample distribution coincides with the mean of the population. In the example given above, the population mean is Rs 3.5 (Table 1) and the mean of the distribution of the sample means too happens to be Rs. 3.5 (Table 3).

3. The standard deviation of the population, and the standard deviation of the sample means, σx related, as is indicated by the formula given earlier. If the finite population correction is to be ignored, then the standard deviation of the distribution of sample means $\sigma_{\overline{x}} = \frac{\sigma}{\sqrt{n}}$

It may be noted that σx (Table 3) was 1.08 it whereas σ (Table 1) was 1.71. In other words, the standard deviation of the sample means turns out to be smaller than that of the population. Further, it may be noted that the former tends to be smaller as the sample size, n, increases. This is because of the fact that as the sample size increases, the mean of the sample distribution tends to be closer to the population mean which, in turn, makes the scatter of the sample means narrower.

Since the formula for the relationship between the standard deviation of the population and the standard error of the sample is $\sigma_{\bar{x}} = \frac{\sigma}{\sqrt{n}}$ we find that $n = \frac{\sigma^2}{\sigma_{\bar{x}}^2}$ ignoring the finite population correction. Thus, to determine n, the size of the sample, both the numerator and the denominator should be known to us.

Main considerations for sample size decisions

There are three considerations required to be checked when determine the sample size necessary to estimate the population mean. These are :

1. The extent of error or imprecision allowed.
2. The degree of confidence desired in the estimate.
3. Estimate of the standard deviation of the population.

The first two considerations involve the judgment of the researcher. The third consideration is the responsibility of the researcher. Sometimes, estimates of standard deviation are available, from earlier studies. Even when standard deviation is not available, it can be calculated from the summary tables containing the data. However. If this too is not possible, the researcher may choose a Mall sample from which the standard deviation is calculated. He then uses the sample standard deviation as an estimate of the population standard deviation and then determines the final sample size. 'F he initial sample need not be discarded afterwards and can be used as a part of the final sample. However, some additional time is needed to carry out this exercise.

One may consider the problem of determining sample size in two different situations, namely when (0) the standard deviation of the population is known and (ii) when it is unknown.

(i) Determination of Sample Size when Standard Deviation is Known

Extent of Error: The first consideration relates to the extent of error allowed. This is indicated by the standard error (i.e., the standard deviation of the sample means). The researcher himself has to decide the magnitude of the standard error that he can tolerate. Although this is a difficult question, it is necessary to fix the limit of the standard error beyond which it should not exceed The fixation of standard error should not be confined to overall results but should also be applied to various sub-groups. One way is to first determine the size of each sub-group on the basis of a given degree of precision. The total of the size of each sub-group could then be taken as the overall Size of the sample, though it may turn out to be too large and on considerations of time and money, it may not be acceptable to the researcher.

The Degree of Confidence: A second consideration is the degree of confidence that the researcher wants to have in the results of the study. In case he wants to be 100 per cent confident of the result, he is left with no option but to cover the entire population. However, as this is often not possible on account of cost, time and other constraints, the researcher should be satisfied with less then 100 per cent confidence. Normally, three confidence levels, namely. 99 per cent, 95 per cent and 90 per cent are used. When a 99 per cent confidence level is used, it implies that there is a risk of only 1 per cent of the true population statistic falling outside the range indicated by the confidence interval. In the case of a 95 per cent confidence level, such a risk is of 5 per cent and in the case 01 90 per cent confidence level, it is of 10 percent. In marketing research studies, the most frequently used norm is the 5 per cent confidence level.

It should be noted that there is a tradeoff between the degree of precision and the degree of confidence. For a given size of a sample, one can specify one of these two not both of them at the same time. To illustrate this point, let us assume that in a survey of households in a certain territory, the average income per household has turned out to the Rs. 1000 per month. As this is a point estimate, it is not associated with any bounds of error and therefore, it is regarded as a precise estimate. At the same time, such an estimates likely to be wrong, i.e. one can associate a very low level of confidence unit it, in contrast if we say that the average monthly income per household varies from Rs. 500 to Rs. 2500, we are associating very high degree of confidence in this estimate, although it tends to be far less precise than the earlier one. An estimate of this type, having a very wide range, will not be of much help to the researcher.

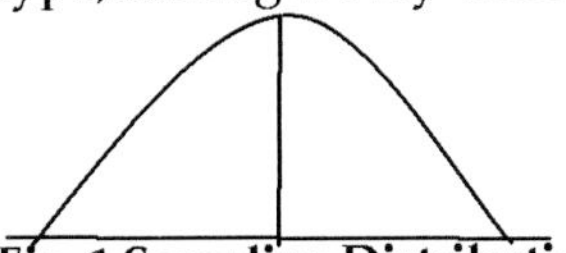

Fig. 1 Sampling Distribution of Sample Means

The above basic considerations involved in determining the sample size can be better understood with the help of some examples. We have earlier seen the sampling distribution of sample means will be normal regardless of the distribution of population. Figure 1 gives the normal distribution. First take the case where the population variance is known. Suppose in our previous example of average monthly income per household, we find that the standard deviation is Rs. 100. Further, we suppose that the estimate is within Rs. 40 of the true population mean. This means that the total precision is 80 and half precision is 40. One shall use the latter values one shall work out the calculations on the basis of one-half of the curve. In this way, certain calculations can be implified as we know that (he population mean μ divides the normal curve into two equal halves.

Another point that needs to be decided relates to the degree of confidence in the result that one would like to have. Suppose that this degree of confidence is 95 per cent which would imply that Z is approximately 2. Strictly speaking, the 95 per cent confidence interval gives Z = 1.96 which can be taken as 2 so as to simplify the calculations.

The formula to determine the size of n 9s:

$$H = Z\sigma_{\bar{x}}$$

$$= Z\frac{\sigma}{\sqrt{N}}\left(\because \sigma_{\bar{x}} = \frac{\sigma}{\sqrt{n}} as\ given\ earlier\right)$$

Where H is half precision which is 40 in the above example: Z = 2 approximately and a is 100. Hence

$$H = 2.\frac{100}{\sqrt{n}}$$

$$or \qquad 40 = \frac{200}{\sqrt{n}} or\ 1 = \frac{200}{\sqrt{n}} \times \frac{1}{40} or \sqrt{n} = 5$$

This calculation gives the sample size as 25. This indicates that when the standard deviation of population is Rs. 100 and the extent of precision is Rs. 40, a sample of 25 households needs to be chosen.

Additional Examples

There are some more examples. making certain variations in the original values. Suppose that we are interested in making our estimate twice as precise; as the earlier one, then H becomes 20 instead of 40. Taking Z = 2 and standard deviation as 100, as in the earlier case, and applying the formula $H = Z\frac{\sigma}{\sqrt{n}} we\ get$

$$20 = 2.\frac{100}{\sqrt{n}}$$

$$or\ 20 = \frac{200}{\sqrt{n}}$$

$$or\ 20\sqrt{n} = 200$$

$$or\ \sqrt{n} = 10$$

$$\therefore\ n = 100$$

One find that the value of n now arrived at is 100, i.e., foretimes of the original value. In other words, when precision is doubled, the value of n increases four times. This result can be generalized as follows : When the precision is increased by a factor x, sample size increases by a factor x'.

Sec what happens to the sample size n if the degree of confidence undergoes a change. Suppose that the degree of confidence is 99 per cent instead of 95 per cent, then Z is equal to 3. Thus

$$H = Z\frac{\sigma}{\sqrt{N}}$$

$$40 = 3.\frac{100}{\sqrt{N}}$$

$$or\ \ 40 = \frac{300}{\sqrt{n}} or\ 40\sqrt{n}\ = 300$$

$$or\ n = \left(\frac{300}{40}\right)^2 \ = 56.25$$

If Z is reduced to 1, than

$$H = Z\frac{\sigma}{\sqrt{N}}$$

$$or \qquad 40 = 1.\frac{100}{\sqrt{n}}$$

$$or \qquad 40\sqrt{n} = 100$$

or $\sqrt{n} = \frac{100}{40} = 2.5$

∴ $n = (2.5)^2 = 6.25$

Notice the changes in the value of *n*.

In the first case, when Z is increased from 2 to 3, there is an increase of 3/2 times in its value. When Z is increased 3/2 times, the value of *n* increased $\frac{3}{2} \times \frac{3}{2} = \frac{9}{4}$ times as $2.5 \times \frac{9}{4} = \frac{225}{4} = 56.25$ Likewise, when the value of Z is reduced from 2 to 1, there is a fall in its value by 1/2 . When Z is reduced by 1.2, the value of *n* reduces to $\frac{1}{2} \times \frac{1}{2} = \frac{1}{4}$ th of its original value $\left(n = 25\frac{25}{4} = 6.25\right)$ To generalise the above results, when Z is increased by a certain factor *y*, sample size increases by a factor y^2.

(ii) When Standard Deviation of Population is Unknown

Many times the standard deviation is not known. In such cases too, the method followed is the same except that an estimate of the population standard deviation in place of its previously known value is taken. Sometimes, the researcher may undertake a pilot survey to ascertain the standard deviation. If this is not possible, the researcher may have to use some alternative approach. As we know, the entire area under the normal curve falls within μ+ 36. This means that we should have some idea of the range of variation, i.e.. the difference between the highest item and the lowest item. This range needs to be divided by six in order to get an estimate of the standard deviation.

Suppose in our previous example, the minimum monthly income amongst households is Rs. 500 and the maximum is Rs. 2000. This giver a range of Rs. 1500 which divided by 6 yields a figure of 250. This is the estimated value of σ. Taking other values as earlier, the sample size can be determined as shown below :

$H = 2.\frac{250}{\sqrt{n}}$

or $40 = \frac{500}{\sqrt{n}}$

or $\sqrt{n} = \frac{500}{40} = \frac{25}{2}$

∴ $n = \frac{25}{2} \times \frac{25}{2} = \frac{625}{4} = 156.25$

This shows that a sample of 156 households should be taken.

Suppose a sample of 156 households gives a sample mean $\overline{X} = 1000$, and a sample standard deviation S = 200. then the confidence interval would be $\overline{X} \pm ZS_{\overline{X}}$

or $1000 \pm 2\frac{\hat{s}}{\sqrt{n}}$

or $1000 \pm 2\frac{200}{\sqrt{156}}$

or $1000 \pm \frac{400}{12.5}$

or 1000 ± 33 or $968 \leq \mu \leq 1032$

This shows the precision as ± 32 as against ± 40 in the earlier example. Thus the interval has become narrower than earlier envisaged. This is because the sample standard deviation (200) is less than the estimated population standard deviation (250) in the earlier 'example. In other word, as the population standard deviation at over-estimated as judged by the sample standard. Deviation, the confidence interval became narrower. Conversely, if the population standard deviation turns out to be under-estimated vis-a-vis sample standard deviation, the confidence interval will become wider.

Relative Precision.

So far the discussion was concerned with the basis of absolute precision measured in terms of specific units. We now introduce another dimension, namely, the relative precision. It can be defined as the extent of precision relative to level. Suppose the mean is 200 and a relative precision of 10 per cent is aimed at. This would mean a confidence interval from 186 to 220. In case the mean- is 100, the confidence interval will be from 90 to 110.

When applying relative precision instead of absolute precision, the usual formula $H = Z\frac{\sigma}{\sqrt{n}}$ is transformed to $r\mu = Z\frac{\sigma}{\sqrt{n}}$ where r = the relative precision and μ is the mean of the population. This, too, can be changed as shown below :

$$\because \quad r\mu = Z\frac{\sigma}{\sqrt{n}}$$

$$or \quad \frac{r\mu}{r\mu} = Z\frac{\sigma}{\sqrt{n}} \times \frac{1}{r\mu}$$

$$or \quad 1 = \frac{Z\sigma}{\sqrt{n}.r\mu} or\ 1 = \frac{1}{\sqrt{n}}.\frac{Z}{r}.\frac{\sigma}{\mu}$$

Multiplying both sides by $\sqrt{n}$

$$\sqrt{N} = \frac{Z}{r}.\frac{\sigma}{\mu}$$

$$or \quad n = \frac{Z^2}{r^2}\left(\frac{\sigma}{\mu}\right)^2 = \frac{Z^2}{r^2}C^2 \ (Since\ \frac{\sigma}{\mu}\ is\ the\ coefficient\ of\ variation)$$

In the above form of the formula, it is necessary to have values of three variables namely, Z, r and C. Since Z relates to the desired level of significance, it will be known. So also r sill be known as it indicates the level of precision which has to be decided in advance. It is only C that is not known and which needs to be estimated. The researcher has to very carefully use his judgment regarding the magnitudes of the population mean and the population standard deviation. If there are some earlier studies available for his guidance, he should draw upon them in order to make his judgment as realistic as possible. it may be noted that if the coefficient of variation C turns out to be higher than that actually given by the ratio of the sample standard deviation to the sample mean, then this could show that the sample size should have been larger and vice versa.

Cost as a Factor in Determining Sample Size

So far cost is not considered which is an important factor ht determining sample size. Suppose a firm has earmarked a sum of Rs. 50,000 for a research study involving field survey. It has also decided to choose a sample of 1200 respondents for a specified level of precision and 95 per cent confidence of the results. The study would involve many aspects such as training to interviewers, designing of questionnaires, supervision of field work, coding, editing and tabulation of collected data, analysis of data and report writing. Suppose further that the fixed costs are likely to be Rs. 30,000 and the field survey would cost Rs. 20 per interview. In such a case, a sum of Rs. 20.000 (Rs. 50,000 - Rs. 30,000) is available for the field survey. Since one interview costs Rs. 20, the field survey can covers i.e., 1000 respondents only. Thus the firm finds that the sample size of 1200 would not be possible. Now, the sample size of 1000 respondents would yield a lower degree of confidence, say, 90 per cent instead of 95 per cent as originally envisaged. The firm should, therefore, decide whether it would really serve its purpose.

Another alternative before the company is to increase the size of the allowable error. A lower degree of precision would need a lower sample size than the 1200 determined earlier. Thus, one would notice that there could be several combinations of the extent of confidence and precision which can be thought of by the firm. It has to choose one of these feasible combinations, within the financial resources available. It may as well find that lowering of the degree of confidence or precision or both may considerably reduce the utility of the study. In such a case it may even go to the other extreme and drop the idea of undertaking it.

Important Objectives

One should be serious about that a marketing research study is seldom conducted to estimate a single parameter. Generally some objectives are involved in a single study. Now, a sample size may vary from one objective to another on account of the expected variance. It is not necessary to go through the process of determining sample size for all objectives. The general approach is4o choose a few crucial questions on the basis of which the sample size is determined. The researcher should especially include objectives that arc likely to have greater variability as their inclusion will be more crucial for sample size.

Suppose that in a study three parameters are to be estimated each with a 95 per cent confidence and with desired precision the sample size required has been determined as 40 units 80 units and 25 units respectively. The most conservative approach in such a case would be to select a sample of 80 units, which is the largest However. If the second parameter where sample size required is 80 is not crucial, it is advisable not to choose a sample of 80 units. Taking a sample of this size would involve additional expenditure which could be saved. In such a case a sample size of 40 would be most appropriate. Thus, the marketing researcher should be guided by the relative importance of the parameters and the one which is most crucial should be taken into consideration. The sample size should then be determined for the desired precision and confidence with respect to that parameter. The sample size thus determined should be applicable to the entire study, covering all tile parameters.

In previous example. If a sample of 80 is chosen, then the degree of confidence as also precision ill be higher than the desired degrees, as envisaged earlier. Conversely, if a lower sample size say, 25 units is chosen, then in case of the other rue parameters, the demurs of confidence and precision would be lower than the corresponding values 'envisaged earlier. The researcher has to exercise his judgment vary carefully in such cases.

Sample Size Decisions When Estimating Proportions

The previous discussion was carried out in relation to sample size for estimating mean values. At times, it is the proportion or population with a particular attribute that becomes more relevant to the marketing researcher than the mean value. For example, one may be more interested in knouting the proponed of households having a monthly income of say, Rs. 1000 and less or of Rs 2500 and above rather than in knowing the average income of the households.

The formula for the standard error of a proportion// based on a simple random sample of size,/ is

$$S.E.(p) = \sqrt{\frac{\pi(1-\pi)}{n}}$$

Where π is the proportion of units with 3 particular attribute.

The above formula can be transformed as follows:

$$[S.E.(p)]^2 = \frac{\pi(1-\pi)}{n}$$

$$or \quad \frac{1}{n} = \frac{[S.E.(p)]^2}{\pi(1-\pi)}$$

By inverting the above. we get

$$n = \frac{\pi(1-\pi)}{[S.E.(p)]^2}$$

Conclusion: It is clear that the values of π and the standard error of a proportion should be known in order to determine the sample size, n. However, one finds that π is generally not known, which necessitates its estimation. Suppose the value of π is estimated so also the extent of the standard error is chosen, then one can arrive at the sample size. Further suppose that the sample size thus determined turns out to be a sizeable proportion of the population. In that case it is necessary to use the finite population correction (fpc). This can be done with the help of the following formula :

$$n' = \frac{n}{1+\frac{n}{N}}$$

where *n'* is the revised size of the sample, n is the earlier size of the sample and N is the population size. Let us illustrate this.

Suppose one is interested in estimating the proportion of households having a television set. We believe that this figure is about 26 per cent. Further. we decide that a standard error should not be more than 2 per cent. We now apply the earlier formula, namely.

$$n = \frac{\pi(1-\pi)}{[S.E.(p)]^2} = \frac{20(100-20)}{(2)^2} = 400$$

This gives the sample size of 400 households. This could be regarded as the desirable sample provided that the population is relatively large, if, however, population is only 1600 households, then the revised sample size can be worked out. as follows :

$$n = \frac{n}{1+\frac{n}{N}}$$

$$= \frac{400}{1+\frac{400}{1600}} = \frac{400}{\frac{5}{4}} = \frac{400\times 4}{5} = 320$$

This shows that a sample size of 320 households should be taken instead of 400 households.

From the formula

$n = \frac{\pi(1-\pi)}{[S.E.(p)]^2}$, it should be clear that

the value of a $(1-\pi)$ would influence the size of n. The smaller is this value, the smaller will be the sample size required for a given standard error. It may also be noted that *n* will be at a maximum when $\pi\,(1-\pi)$ is at a maximum. When π I= 1/2, $\pi\,(1-\pi)$ is at a maximum. This also shows that if a small standard error is to be preferred, than a relatively large sample size is required.

Another point that needs to be emphasized is that in the initial stage when an estimate of π is made, it may not be right. Let us take an example. Suppose the proportion of households earning Rs. 1000 or less per month has been estimated as 0.40.

This means that

$$n = \frac{\pi(1-\pi)}{[S.E.(p)]^2}$$

$= \frac{40\times 60}{4}$ (on the assumption that the S.E. is not more than 2)

$$= \frac{2400}{4} = 600$$

Suppose that when the survey is undertaken and the 600 sampled households arc contacted, the sample proportion p turns out to be 0.30. With this revised proportion, the standard error is determined

$$S.E.(p) = \sqrt{\frac{p(1-p)}{n}} = \sqrt{\frac{0.30 \times 0.70}{600}} = 0.0187$$

and the confidence interval will then be

$$p \pm Z\,\text{Sp} = 0.30 \pm 2\ (0.0187)$$

$$0.263 \leq \pi \leq 0.337$$

The interval is narrower than desired as the sample proportion (0.30) turned out to be less than the population proportion (0.40).

Relative Precision

As was discussed earlier, while determining sample size when estimating means, here too the same approach is applicable in respect of relative precision. The term 'relative precision' signifies that the size of the interval will be within a certain per cent of the value, regardless of its level. For example, if the sample proportion is 0.40 and if the relative precision is to be within 10 per cent, then the interval would be 0.36 to 0.44.

Statistical Efficiency

The term 'efficiency or 'statistical efficiency' is frequently used in discussions of sampling. A sample, design is considered statistically more efficient than another if its standard error of the mean is smaller, given the same sample size. Conversely, a more efficient sample design will yield as precise a result as in alternative sample design but with a smaller sample. Thus, efficiency implies a comparison of two Or more sample designs. Symbolically.

$$E_A = \frac{\sigma_\mu}{\sigma_A}.100$$

where E_A = the statistical efficiency of sampling design A, expressed as a percentage

σ_μ = the standard error of the appropriate statistic, e.g., mean produced by an unrestricted single-stage sample of size II

σ_A = the standard error of the appropriate statistic, produced by sampling design A of size n.

In the degree of precision required is specified in advance, regardless of the sample design, then the relative size of the sample required would indicate efficiency. Symbolically,

$$E_A = \frac{n_\mu}{n_A}.100$$

where E_4= the efficiency or sampling design A. based on relative sample size and expressed as a percentage.

n_A a the size of the sample, using sampling design A

n_u = the size of the Sample, using the unrestricted single-stage sampling design.

It may be noted that when a comparison is made of standard errors of the mean of different sample designs requiring the same rupee expenditure, it sill indicate relative economic efficiency. In other words, economic efficiency is measured in terms of the precision of results per rupee of cost. Marketing researchers are generally concerned with economic efficiency of sample designs and aim at obtaining maximum efficiency of this type.

Determining the Size of Non-Probability Samples

Generally, two approaches are followed in respect of probability samples. However, non-probability samples are used, perhaps more frequently, in marketing research than probability samples. The questions is : How should the size of a non-probability sample be determined ? In this case, there is no theoretical basis for estimating sampling error. We have seen how important the concept of sampling error is in determining size when the sample is based on probability.

Generally, two approaches are followed in respect of non-probability samples. One approach into determine the size as if it were a probability sample. Another approach is to take as large sample as possible within the constraints of time and money. For example, if a sum of Rs. 50,000 has been earmarked for a research project, the estimated fixed costs of sampling and the non-sampling costs are Rs. 30,000, and sampling costs are Rs. 25 per element, the sample size (n) should be $\frac{\text{Rs.50,000} - \text{Rs.30,000}}{\text{Rs.25}}$ = 800. There are two limitations of this approach. It fails to take into consideration the difference in value of information of the sample of 800 as compared to that of other sample sizes. Second, unlike the probability sample, it usually fails to consider trade-offs between sampling and non-sampling errors.

Conclusion: Here the focus on sample size were discussed by taking several factors that are relevant in determining sample size on the basis of the traditional approach have been briefly discussed. Quite distinct from the traditional approach is the Bayesian approach which is sometimes used by researchers. It introduces the conditional costs of wrong decisions into the model and determines the optimal sample size. Although its main strength is that it incorporates the cost of sampling which the traditional approach fails to do, it is not widely used. The main reason for its infrequent use appears to be its being relatively complicated.

✱✱✱✱✱✱

Chapter - 19

Simple Sampling

In order to examine a large data with respect to a specified characteristic much time, energy and money would be needed for its statistical analysis. From the big mass of data a part or parts may be taken to represent the whole. This small mass selected from the big mass is called a sample. The process of such a selection is called sampling. The big mass is called population or parent universe or simply universe from which samples are taken.

There are three kinds of population. The first, includes finite and actually existing populations which, although large, can be enumerated if necessary. For example the total number of persons living in India forms a finite population.

The second type of population is a generalization from experience and is indefinitely large, such as, for instance, the total number of throws that might conceivably be made in unlimited time with a particular pair of dice. Any actual set of throws, however numerous can be regarded as a sample from this practically infinite population.

A third kind is purely hypothetical population which can be described mathematically. That is, the distribution of values in the population is given by a mathematical formula. This type of population is used in the prows known as curve-fitting or graduation, in which an actually occurring distribution is replaced for the purposes of further discussion by a mathematically described distribution which seems to have similar characteristics.

Consequently a major theory of sampling is concerned with the evaluation of the constants of the parent universe on the basis of the samples. To avoid confusion R.A. Fisher has given the name of statistic to a statistical measure calculated from the actual frequencies given by a sample while parameter is the name given to the statistical measure of the patent universe.

Fundamental to the theory is the incept of random sampling. This is defined by the property that, in the selection of an individual from the population, each member of the population has the same chance of being chosen. Sampling is random sampling with the further provision that the probability of success is the same at each trial. Thus p is constant in the process, and the probability of success at any trial is independent of the success or failure of the preceding trials. Hence, for the sampling to be simple, either the population must be very large, or the individual selected must be returned to the population before the next trial, after the success or failure having been noted in the first trial. As an example of a large population, production of wheat may differ from place to place, owing to the scarcity of rains, the visit of floods, or some other cause, the total production of the world as a whole remains fairly constant.

The descriptive term "random" is often misunderstood. It does not imply that the sample has been chosen in an off hand, careless, or haphazard fashion. Instead it means that we rely upon a certain method of selection (called "random') to provide an unbaised cross section of the larger group or population.

Randomness in a sample is assured when we draw similar and well shaken-up slips out of a hat; or numbers in a lottery (provided it is honest); or a hand from a easefully shuffled dick of cards. In each of these eases 'election is made in terms of some mechanized process and is not subject to the whims or biases (if any) of the experimenter.

A random sample is not the same as a representative sample. A representative sample is one in which the distribution of scores in the sample closely parallels that of the population. Experience has shown that if one is asked to get representative samples from a population he will for various reasons often draw samples which exhibit, consistent biases of one sort or another. The most trustworthy way of securing representativeness, therefore, is to make sure that sampling is random.

We may take every third or eighth name etc. from a catalogue provided names have been arranged in alphabetical order and are not arranged according to some differential factor, such as age, income, or education. A better plan in such cases is to assign numbers to the members of the population and draws sample. By this method an approximately random sample of telephone users may be obtained by reference to the telephone directory; of fourth grade children from attendance rolls; of automobile owners from the licensing bureau; of workers in a factory from pay roll list; etc.

But if a firm which manufactures dish-washing machines wants to know what percentage of the population uses their machines and they do this by selecting people at random from a telephone directory, then the sample obtained will not be random because the sample will ho biased towards a certain social class.

Or, if we want to know how popular our Prime Minister, is and for this purpose we go to the Super Baser at 11 a.m., on a working day and interview people, our sample will be far from being a random one because we are most likely to meet housewives doing the shopping.

The theory of sampling can be studied under two heads: (1) the sampling of attribute., and (2) The sampling of variables. The sampling of attributes' is concerned with qualitative data or hypothetical universe. In such cases the observer can only study the presence or absence of a particular quality in a group of individual. For instance we cannot measure blindness or honesty in magnitude. All that we can do is to count 'the number of persons who are blind or who are honest. Such data are called statistics of attributes.

A hypothetical universe may he defined as the aggregate of all conceivable ways in which a specific event can happen. For example, the throw of a die where each event may be taken as an individual event is a case of hypothetical universe, where infinite possible throws can be made with a die. Actually all these possible throws may never take place; hence the word hypothetical.

In sampling of variables we come across such individuals which can assume any value of a variable. Thus in a series relating to heights we are no more concerned with the question whether a particular individual is comparatively tall or not but we have before us individuals who can have any height ranging from the lowest to the highest. Under these circumstances we cannot classify the items of a sample in two groups-one possessing the attribute and the other not possessing it.

The sampling of variables is concerned with such data as heights, weights. marks, etc., in which quantitative measurement of the magnitude is possible. The universe connected with the sampling of variables is called existent universe as it is a universe of concrete/objects.

First of all we shall take up sampling of attributes.

Mean and Standard Deviation in Simple Sampling: The problem connected with the drawing of a simple sample of n members is thus identical with that of a aeries of it independent trials, with constant probability p of success. The probabilities of 0, 1, 2.......... successes in a simple sample of n members are thus the term of the binomial expansion $(q+p)^n$. The binomial probability distribution thus determined is called the:

Sampling distribution of the number of successes in the sample. Thus Table is an example of the sampling distribution.

The expected value, or mean value of the number of successes

$$= n\,p$$

The standard deviation = $\sqrt{npq}$

If instead of recording the number of successes we record the proportion of successes, we get.

$$\sigma = \sqrt{\frac{npq}{n}} = \sqrt{\frac{pq}{n}}$$

And the mean of the proportion of successes = $\frac{np}{n} = p$.

The precision of the proportion of successes observed in the sample is regarded as inversely proportional to the standard deviation of this proportion. Hence the precision of the observed proportion varies as $\sqrt{n}$, and therefore the larger the sample the greater the precision.

Standard Error: The standard deviation is usually called the standard error (S.E.) of the number of successes in a sample of site n, the deviation from the expected value n p being looked upon as 'error'.

If the difference between the number of successes in the sample and the expected number n p is 3 times or more than. This means that an event has happened which, on the hypothesis of simple sampling, is very improbable and therefore the 'sample is certainty biased. Considerations of the aspects of the problem will then lead us to suspect either that the value of p employed is incorrect, or eke the conditions of simple sampling were not observed.

Alt the results discussed above have been derived from the fact that for large values of n, the binomial distribution approximates to a normal distribution which has been described briefly in Art.

If we know the probability of the happening of the event in the universe we can find very easily, by comparing with the probability of the happening of the event in the sample, how far the latter approximates the former. In many cases it is not taken. In such cases usually the proportion of a success in the sample (or the value of p) is taken as an estimate of the proportion of a success in the universe. The assumption is justifiable only if the size of n is large and neither p nor q is very small. Another course open to us in such cases is to take the highest value of pq. It is clear that the value of pq for normal distribution cannot exceed $\frac{1}{2} \times \frac{1}{2} = i.e. \frac{1}{4}$. As such if we do not know the value of p in the universe and if the value of p in the sample is very small or very large then instead of taking the values of p and q the value of pq may be taken as $\frac{1}{4}$ which is the maximum value.

Ex. 1. Certain crosses of pea gave 5321 yellow and 1804 green seeds. The expectation is 25% of green seeds on a Mendelian hypothesis. Can the divergence from the expected value have arisen from fluctuations of simple sampling only?

Sol. The total number of pea seeds examined

= 5321+1804=7125.

The expected result of green seeds

$$\frac{25}{100} \times 7125 = 11781$$

But the observed result is 1804 green seeds, and so it is in excess of the expected result by 1804-1781, i.e., 23.

$$\sigma = \sqrt{npq} = \sqrt{7125 \times \frac{25}{100} \times \frac{75}{100}} = 11781$$

The divergence from the expectation is thus only

$$\frac{23}{\sigma} = \frac{23}{36.6},$$

i.e., .6 times σ and hence may very well have arisen due to fluctuation of simple sampling.

Ex. 2. 12 dice are thrown 3086 times and a throw of 2, 3, 4 is reckoned as a success. Suppose that 19]142 throw of 2, 3, or 4 have been made out. Do you think that this observed value deviates from the expected value? If so, can the deviation from the expected value be due to fluctuations of simple sampling?

Sol. The total number of throws=3086X12=37032.

∴ The total no. of throws with one die=37032

The chance of success, that is of throwing 2, 3, or 4 with one die in one throw= $\frac{1}{6} + \frac{1}{6} + \frac{1}{6} = \frac{1}{2}$

Hence the expected value of successes

=np=37032X$\frac{1}{2}$=18516

The observed value of successes=19142

Difference between the observed and the expected values of successes

=19142-18516=626

$$\sigma = \sqrt{npq} = \sqrt{37032 \times \frac{1}{2} \times \frac{1}{2}} = 96.2$$

$$\text{Now } \frac{626}{\sigma} = \frac{626}{96.2} = 6.5$$

$$\therefore 626 = 6.5 \times \sigma$$

∴ Deviation is highly significant and thus the event is most improble. It is, therefore, not due to fluctuation of simple sampling. This means that the conditions of simple sampling were not observed.

Ex. 3. A group of scientific men reported 1705 sons and 1527 daughters. Do these figures conform to the hypothesis that the sex ratio is $\frac{1}{2}$?

Sol. The total number of observations
=1705+1527=3232.
The number of sons is 1705.
∴ The observed male ratio

$$\frac{1705}{3232} = 0.5275$$

On the given hypothesis the male ratio ought to be 0.5. Thus the observed male ratio is in excess of the theoretical ratio by .0275 (=·5275-·5).

$$\sigma = \sqrt{\frac{pq}{n}} = \sqrt{\frac{1}{2} \times \frac{1}{2} \times \frac{1}{3232}} = \cdot 0088$$

Now $\frac{\cdot 0275}{\cdot 0088} = 3 \cdot 31$

∴ The divergence from the hypothesis is most improbable that it arose as a sampling fluctuation.

Hence it can be definitely said that the figures given did not conform to the given hypothesis.

Ex. 4. 400 children are chosen in an industrial town of Northern India and 150 are found to be underweight. Assuming the conditions of simple sampling, estimate the percentage of children who are underweight in that industrial town and assign limits within which the percentage probably lies.

Sol. Taking the observed values of p and q in the sample we have p, that is the chance of getting an underweight child,

$$\frac{150}{400} = \frac{3}{8},$$

and q that is the chance of failure=6.5 - $\frac{3}{8} = \frac{5}{8}$

n=total number of children=400

Standard Error of the proportion of children

$$= \sqrt{\frac{pq}{n}} = \sqrt{\frac{3}{8} \times \frac{5}{8} \times \frac{1}{400}} = \cdot 0088 = 2 \cdot 4\%$$

Whatever may be the percentage of children who are under-weight in the population, a simple sample should give a percentage within three times this standard error.

Hence taking $\frac{3}{8}$ (or 37·5%) to be the estimate of the number of children who are underweight, we have the limits

37·5%±3X2·4%,i.e., 30·3% and 47·7% approx.

If, however, we feel that the value of p in the sample should not be taken as its value in the population we can proceed in a different manner. We take pq= $\frac{1}{4}$ and hence the standard error cannot exceed

$$\sqrt{\frac{1}{2} \times \frac{1}{2} \times \frac{1}{400}} \text{ or } \cdot 025 \text{ or } 2 \cdot 5\%$$

On this basis the limits would be 37·5±(3X2.5)% or 30% and 45%.

Ex. 5. A life insurance company founded upon the Indian Experience Table has a thousand policies averaging Rs. 2000 on lives at age 25. From the experience table it is found that of 89032 alive at age 25, 88000 are alive at age 26. Find the upper and lower values of the amount that the company will have to pay out in insurance during the year.

Sol. The chance that a man of age 25 will not be alive at age 26 is

$$p = 1 - \frac{88000}{89032} = \frac{1032}{89032}$$

∴ The expected number of deaths out of 1000 insured persons is $1000 - \frac{1032}{89032} = 12$ approx.

The S.E. of simple sampling= $\sigma = \sqrt{npq}$

$$\sqrt{1000 \times \frac{1032}{89032} \times \frac{88000}{89032}} = 3.4.$$

The actual number of deaths would lie between (12 ±3x3.4) or 1.8 and 22.2.

The average amount of a policy is Rs. 2000. Therefore the upper and lower values of the amount that the company will have to pay out in insurance during the year are Rs. 2000x1.8 and Rs. 2000x22.2 or Rs. 3600 and Rs. 44400.

Ex. The weights of packets of cereals were checked by examining 100 samples of 12. The results were as follows :

No. of underweight per sample of 12,	0 1 2 3 4 5 or more
No. of samples	59 30 8 2 1 0

Use the formula $\overline{x}$=np to estimate the percentage of underweight packets in the output being tested.

Sol. Total no. of packets=12x100=1200

No. of underweight packets=59x0+30x1+8x2+2x3+1x4+0

=30+16+16+4=56

∴ The probability of getting underweight packets

$$= \frac{56}{1200} = \frac{7}{150}$$

∴ The expected value or mean value of the number of successes, i.e., getting underweight packets

$$= np = 1200 \times \frac{7}{150} = 56.$$

This means that in a lot of 1200 packets we can expect 56 underweight packets, and this is

$$\frac{56}{1200} \times 100, i.e.\ 4\frac{8}{3}\% \cdot$$

Sampling of Variables: After studying the sampling of attributes we take-up the sampling of variables. As stated before here we shall come across such individuals which can assume any value of a variable like heights, weights, marks, etc.

The aims of sampling studies in statistics of a variable are the same as in case of statistics of attributes. Here also we compare the actual observed frequencies with those expected under certain assumptions any try to find out whether the difference can be attributed to chance. As in sampling of attributes here too we try to obtain one or two constants of the universe --mean or standard error because if they are obtained, an idea about the type of parent, distribution is easily formed. In sampling studies 'relating to variables also out third aim is to assess the reliability of our estimates.

Sampling Distribution: In statistics of variables generally the question of finding the values of p and q does not arise and as such it is very difficult, to obtain the expected ire, mammies. If, however, we take a large number of samples from the same universe and calculate any function (wean or standard deviation, etc.) then we shall have a series relating to the values of the function. If, say, 100 samples are taken and if the mean value of each sample is found we shall have a series relating to the means of 100 samples. Similarly, we can have a series relating to standard deviation of 100 wimples. Such series relating to the values of a statistic are called Sampling Distributions of the statistic measured. There is one very important characteristic of all sampling distributions and it is that they give more or less normal distribution. If the number of samples used in the sampling distribution is large, almost invariably the sampling distribution would be a normal distribution even though the parent distribution from which the samples have been taken may not be normal. This is very important and useful characteristic which helps in the analysis of samples relating to variables.

It should also be remembered that in actual practice all sampling distributions ore based on simple sampling. Thus the conditions of simple sampling discussed before are assumed to hold good here also. In particular we can safely presume that (mean$\pm$3 σ) would corer almost all cases and that 'the value of the parameter would not be outside the limits. On the other bandit the mean M of the universe is known, than the means of the samples will lie between M-3 σ and M+3 σ.

Sample Means: It we consider not the distribution of the values of individual items but the distribution of the average value of individual items but the distribution of the average value (Mean) in a sample of items, what shall we expect ? To make the matter concrete, let us suppose that we were to consider the distribution for the average weight in samples of eight men. One thing is quite clear that these averages will be much nearer the average of the universe than will the weights of the Individual men, for the sampling

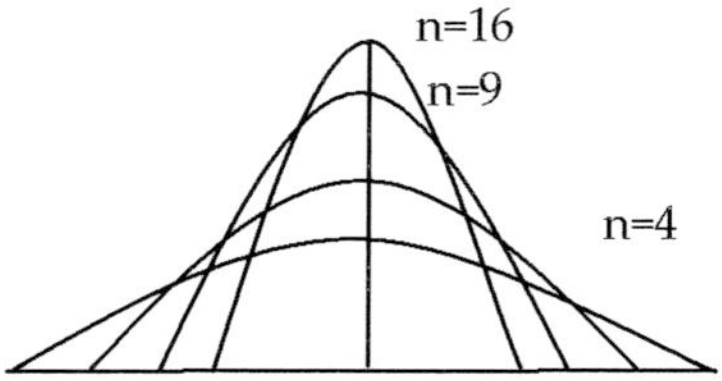

Fig.

Distribution of Means simple reason that when eight men are chosen to form a random sample the chances are that some will be lighter than the average of the universe and some will be heavier. It. will be a very rare thing to get eight men either all above the average weight or all below the average weight. The larger the sample the closer will be the average weight in the sample to the average of the universe.

This means that the sampling distribution of the means will have a smaller spread (or S.D.) than the distribution for the weight of the individual men. Or, in other words the standard deviation of a random sample is smaller than the corresponding standard deviation of the universe.

Above Fig. illustrates the point mentioned above.

Standard Error of the Mean : if is the standard deviation of the universe and n is the number of items in the sample under consideration then

* Standard Error of the Mean = $\frac{\sigma\text{ (universe)}}{\sqrt{n}}$

It should be noted that the standard deviation given in the numerator of this fraction is the standard deviation of the universe. This is usually unknown. We can calculate the standard deviation of the sample but there is no way of knowing the facts relative to the universe. As a matter of practice, in the absence of the necessary data describing the universe, we du assume that the standard deviation of the universe is equal to that of the sample. It is known empirically that the error made in *lamming this is not great. It does, however, make our conclusions approximate rather than exact. Thus

Standard Error of the Mean=$\frac{\sigma\text{ (sample)}}{\sqrt{n}}$

where n is the number of items in the sample and a is the standard deviation of the sample.

Our present line of reasoning started with the assumption that, we know the facts concerning the universe, and were trying to predict the variations which might occur in samples drawn from this known universe. Actually, the statistician works the other way around. Ho bas a known sample, and wishes to Infer from the characteristics of this sample the facts about the universe. Since he has not investigated every ease in the universe he cannot describe the universe with complete precision. He can, however, make boom estimates on the basis of his sample if he assumes that the standard deviation which he found in his sample is the same as the standard deviation in the universe. It is at this point that he introduces an element of error. He has already used up one of the samples which could be drawn from his universe, and to this extent has influenced his conclusions. We shall say that he has lost one -degree of freedom" in his work. Consequently now that. we are to work backward, from sample to universe instead of from universe to sample, we must divide by the square root of n-1 instead of by the square root of n. The formulas that we have given so far are formulas for estimating the characteristics of samples drawn irons known universes. If we are to turn now to the much more important problem of drawing influences about unknown universes from known samples we should give our formula as follows :

Standard Error of the Mean= $\frac{\sigma}{\sqrt{n-1}}$

where n is the number of items in the sample and σ is the standard deviation of the sample.

Or, we can argue like this:

The standard deviation of a random sample underestimates is smaller than the corresponding standard deviation of the universe. To correct this tendency towards underestimation we reduce the denominator from n to (n-1) so that $\frac{\sigma\text{ (sample)}}{\sqrt{n-1}}$ is a good approximation to $\frac{\sigma\text{ (universe)}}{\sqrt{n}}$. From this it follows that in the formula $\sigma = \sqrt{\frac{\sum fdx^2}{n}}$ obtained in Art. 4.05 we should always use (n-1) instead of n whenever the standard deviation eta sample is to be an estimate of the standard deviation of the universe, unless the sample is large enough.

If n is large, there is negligible difference between the values of $\frac{\sigma}{\sqrt{n}}$ and $\frac{\sigma}{\sqrt{n-1}}$. But if n is small the difference becomes important, and the student will be wise to fall into the habit of using the formula in die precise form.

It should be observed that the above formula is derived without any reference to the form of the parent distribution and that this standard error depends on the number of items in the sample and the standard deviation of the sample. It is also clear that largo samples are more reliable and dependable than small ones and that we can draw conclusions concerning the universe from large samples with more certainty than from smell ones.

Fluctuations from sample to sample-the so called "errors" of sampling-are not to be thought of as mistakes, failures or the like, but as variations arising from the fact that no two samples arc over exactly alike. Means or σ's from random samples are estimates of their parameters, and the standard error (S.E.) formulas measure the goodness of this estimate, i.e., they show whether the difference between the statistics and the parameters is significant or not.

We have seen above that the sampling distributions of the number and the proportion of successes in a simple sample of size n are binomial distribution& It was also shown in the previous chapter that, for large values of n, the binomial distribution approximates to a normal distribution in the sense that the probabilities for the corresponding intervals in the two distributions tend to be equal as is increases indefinitely. Now, we know that the probability that a random value of a normal score, of a, will lie outside the interval is only 0.0027. Similarly, the probability that the value will deviate from the mean by more than 2σ is 0.0456 or about 4.5%. We may, therefore, conclude that, for large values of n, the probability that the number of successes in a simple sample of n numbers will differ from the mean by more than three times the standard error is also very small; and that a deviation of more than twice the standard error is rather unusual.

Note: If a is the S.D. of the sample and or the S.D. of the universe, then

$$\sigma^2 = \sqrt{\frac{\Sigma(dx)^2}{n}} \text{ and } \sigma^2 = \sqrt{\frac{\Sigma(dx)^2}{n-1}}$$

$$\therefore \frac{\sigma^2}{\sigma^2} = \frac{n}{n-1}$$

$$\text{or } \sigma = \sigma\sqrt{\frac{n}{n-1}}$$

where n is the number of items in the sample.

If m is the mean of the sample of n items, then m$\pm$3. $\frac{\sigma \text{ (universe)}}{\sqrt{n}}$ would cover almost all means and the mean M of the universe would also lie in this range. Also, if the mean M of the universe is known, then the means of the samples would be between M- $\frac{3\sigma}{\sqrt{n}}$ and M+ $\frac{3\sigma}{\sqrt{n}}$ where is the S.D. of the universe.

Like the standard error (S.E.) of the mean, the S.E. of the standard deviation for a sampling distribution of the standard deviations is given by $\frac{\sigma \text{ (universe)}}{\sqrt{2n}}$. In other words, if s is the S.D. of a sample, then s$\pm$3 $\frac{\sigma \text{ (universe)}}{\sqrt{2n}}$ would cover almost all standard deviations.

Ex. 7. Suppose that for tyres of a certain factory, the mean milage is 15,180 and the standard deviation is 1248 miles.

Suppose further that a sample of 900 tyres shows a mean milage of 15,232 miles with a standard deviation of 1210 miles. Ascertain if the sample mean represents a significant divergence from the mean of the universe.

Sol. S.E. of the sample mean=$\frac{\sigma \text{ (universe)}}{\sqrt{n}}$

$$\frac{1248}{\sqrt{900}} = 41.6 \text{ miles.}$$

The observed difference between the two means of milage

= 15232-15180=52 miles=1.25x(S.E.)

So the difference being less than 2x(S.E.) could have arisen due to the fluctuntions of sampling. Hence it own be said that the divergence of the sample mean from the universe is not significant.

Note: When the standard deviation of the universe is given. the standard deviation of the maple should not be used as the latter la only a substitute for the former.

Ex. 8. .4 large population cons (sting of N Ojeda has a mean if and a standard deviation a. If a number of random samples of the or ore taken from this population, state dearly what you would expect to observe with regard to the means m_1, m_2, m_3, .., of these samples.

The daily maxima,* temperature at a given place was read cc-cry fifth day over a 60-day period as follows v

59°, 63°, 66°, 65°, 69', 60°, 64°, 71°, 66', 85°, 84°, 88'.

Find the mean and standard deviation of this sample. The actual mean maximum temperature over this period was 68.5°. State whether you consider the Oren sample was representative or not giving reasons for your answer.

Sol. We would expect to observe that each of the means m_1 m_2.............should lie within the limits M± $\frac{3\sigma}{\sqrt{n}}$If the means lay within these limits the standard error would not be significant and the samples would be representative.

$$\text{Mean}=\frac{840}{12} = 70$$

$$\sigma = \sqrt{\frac{\Sigma(x-M)^2}{12}} = 9.617$$

(This can be verified by the student)

Standard Error of the mean

$$= \frac{\sigma}{\sqrt{n}} = \frac{9.617}{\sqrt{12}}$$

$$\frac{9.617}{12} \text{x} \sqrt{12}$$

$$= .801\text{x}3.46$$

$$= 2.77146.$$

The parameter mean is expected to range within (70±3x2.77), 7.e., within 78-31 and 61-60.

Since the actual mean68.5° lies in the range, therefore, the given sample was representative

Ex. 9. The mean of a population and its standard deviation arc 17-0 and 2 7 respectively. Use these estimates to calculate the range of wines within which 99% of the sample means, based on samples of 26 members, may be expected to lie.

Sol. The mean M of the population=17.0

σ (population)=2.7, and n=25

σ_m (S.E. of the mean)= $\frac{\sigma\,(\text{Pop.})}{\sqrt{n}} = \frac{2.7}{5} = 0.54$

Since the sampling distribution of the means is always normally distributed, therefore, from Table 6.04 we find that 99% of the sample means lie in the range within 2.6 σ_m of their mean M.

The lower end of the range=17.0-2.6 σ_m =17.0-2.6x0.54

= 17.0-1.404=15.596.

The upper end of the range-17.0+2.6 σ_m=17.0+1.404=18.404

Hence 99% of all sample means lie within the range 15.6 to 18.4.

15.6 and 18.4 are called the 99% confidence limits of M, the mean of the population, and the level of confidence is 0-99.

Confidence Intervals for the Population Mean

We know that 95% of the cases in a normal distribution fall within the limits ±1.1.96 σ and 99% of the cases fall within the limits ±2.59 σ. In the case of a sampling distribution also 95% of the sample means will lie in the interval M±1.96 σ_m and 99% of the sample, means in the interval 14±2.58 σ_m, where M. is the mean of the population and σ_m is the standard error of the mean. The respective levels of confidence for the above intervals are 0.95 and 0.99 respectively and the limits are called confidence limits.

The limits of the confidence interval of a parameter have been called by R.A. Fisher fiduciary limits and the confidence placed in the interval defined by the limits as containing the parameter is called the fiduciary probability. In terms of fiduciary probability, the 0.95 confidence interval would be described as follows:

"The fiduciary probability is 0.95 that the sample means Ho within the interval M±1.96 σ_m, and 0135 that they fall outside of these limits."

Or, if m is a sample mean, it can be described alternatively as follows:

"The fiduciary probability is 0.95 that M lies within the Interval m ± F96 σ_m, and .05 that it falls outside of these limits."

Ex. 10. If the standard deviation of the weights of a particular species of bird is estimated to be .5 lb., find the probability that as mean weight of a random sample of 100 such birds will differ by more than 1 lb. front the mean weight of all such birds.

So. σ (population)=5)

n=100

σ_m (S.E. of the mean)= $\frac{\sigma\,(\text{Pop.})}{\sqrt{n}} = \frac{5}{10} = 0.5$

Thus, 1 Ib.= $\frac{1}{0.5}\sigma_m = 2\sigma_m$

Since the sampling distribution of the means is normally distributed, therefore from Table 6.04, the probability of the mean weight of the crimple not differing by more than 1 lb. is 2 x0.4773, i.e., 0.9546.

Hence the probability of the mean weight of the sample differing by more than 1 lb. is 1 -0.9346, i.e., 0.0454 or 0-05.

Comparison of two samples

In questions done so far we have tried to study the difference between actual proportions of successive as observed and the expected proportions in the universe. There may be ewe where two samples have been taken from distinct materials or different populations and they give pi and p, as the proportions of successes, the number of observations in the two samples being n1 and n2, respectively. The question that may arise here is whether the difference in the two proportions disclosed by the two samples is significant, or there is no real difference between them and the observed difference is due to fluctuations of sampling, the two populations being similar so far as the proportions of successes in them are concerned, In such eases we do not have any idea about the proportions of successes in the universes from which the samples have been taken. We may combine the samples and find the weighted mean proportion in the two samples taken together, which will give the estimate of the common value of the feistiest frequency of the successes in the populations. This estimate is then

$$p_1 = \frac{p_1 n_{1+} p_{12} n_2}{n_{1+} n_2}$$

Where p is the proportion of successes in the populations.

The standard errors of the proportions of successes in samples of and members are

$\sqrt{\frac{p_0 q_0}{n_1}}$ and $\sqrt{\frac{p_0 q_0}{n_2}}$ respectively. The standard error of the difference of p_1 and p_2 is given by

$$\sqrt{\frac{p_0 q_0}{n_1} + \frac{p_0 q_0}{n_2}}$$

$$\sigma_{1-2} = \sqrt{p_0 q_0 \left(\frac{1}{n_1} + \frac{1}{n_2}\right)^*}$$

If the observed difference between p_1 and p_2 is more than 3 σ_{1-2} it is highly significant; if it is 2 σ_{1-2} or more than 2 σ_{1-2} it is said to be significant and if it is less than 2 σ_{1-2} it is not significant. Generally, if the abserced difference between p_1 and p_2 is more than 3 σ_{1-2} it is thought to be significant. In all other cases it is assumed to have arisen due to fluctuation of sampling and as such can be ignored.

Ex. 11. In a simple sample of 600 men from a certain large city, 400 are found to be smokers. In one of 900 from another large city, 450 are smokers. Do the data indicate that the cities are significantly different with respect to the prevalence of smoking among men ?

Sol. Here, $p_1 = \frac{400}{600} = \frac{2}{3}$

$$p_2 = \frac{450}{900} = \frac{1}{2}$$

So that $p_1 - p_2 = \frac{1}{4}$. On the assumption that the cities are alike with respect to prevalence of smoking among men, we have as our estimate of the common value of p_0 as

$$p_0 = \frac{\frac{2}{5}X600 + \frac{1}{2}X900}{600+900}$$

$$= \frac{850}{1500} = \frac{17}{30},$$

$$\text{And } q_0 = 1 - \frac{17}{30} = \frac{13}{30}$$

$$\text{and } \sigma^2{}_{1-2} = p_0 q_0 (\frac{1}{n_1} + \frac{1}{n_2})$$

$$= \frac{17}{30} x \frac{13}{30} (\frac{1}{600} + \frac{1}{900})$$

$$=0.000682$$

$$\therefore \sigma_{1-2} = 0.026$$

$$\text{Now } \frac{p_1 - p_2}{\sigma_{1-2}} = \frac{1}{6} x \frac{1}{0.026} = 6.4$$

$$\text{Or} = p_1 - p_2 = 6.4x\, \sigma_{1-2}$$

Thus the observed difference is greater than 6 σ_{1-2} and is therefore highly significant. Our assumption that the populations are similar is therefore certainly wrong.

Standard Error of the Difference of sample Means: Suppose we have two sample which give us two means We have to find whether there is a significant- difference between the two mean values, or whether they could have come from one universe or from different universes having the some mean and standard deviation. Here we shall calculate the standard error of the difference of the two sample means. If the difference between the two means is more than thrice the standard error of the difference it is said to be highly significant, if it is twice or more than twice the standard error it is said to be significant and if it is loss than twice the standard error it is not significant.

Now, the formulas for the standard error of the difference of two sample means are as follows :

(1) * $\sigma_{Dilff.} \sqrt{\frac{\sigma_1 2}{n_1} + \frac{\sigma_2 2}{n_2})}$

Where σ_1 and σ_2 are standard errors, of the two samples, and n_1 and n_2 are respectively the number of items in the samples.

(2) Where standard deviation of the universe is known, $\sigma^2\, \sigma_1$

$$\sigma_{Dilff.} = \sqrt{\sigma^2 (\frac{1}{n_1} + \frac{1}{n_2})}$$

Where is the standard error of the universe and, n_1 and n_2 are the numbers of items in the samples.

Ex. 12. A random sample of 1000 farms in a certain year gives an average yield of barley of 2000 lbs. per acre with a standard deviation of 192 lbs. a random sample of 1000 farms in the following year gives an average yield of 2100 lbs. per acre with a standard deviation of 224 lbs. Show that the data are inconsistent with the hypothesis that the average yields in the country as a whole were same in the two years.

Sol. Here $\sigma_1 = \frac{\sigma}{\sqrt{n_1}} = \frac{192}{\sqrt{1000}}$

And $\sigma_2 = \frac{\sigma}{\sqrt{n_2}} = \frac{224}{\sqrt{1000}}$

$\therefore \quad \sigma_{Dilff.} = \sqrt{\left(\frac{192}{1000}\right)2 + \left(\frac{192}{1000}\right)^2} = \sqrt{87.04}$

=9.33 per acre.

Now, observed difference=2100-2000=100 lb. per acre

=10x $\sigma_{Dilff.}$=10 times its S.E. approx.

Hence the difference cannot be due to fluctuations of sampling. Hence the data are inconsistent with the assumption that the average yields in the country as a whole were same in the two years.

✶✶✶✶✶✶

Chapter - 20

Random Samples and Random Numbers

Frequently in this book we have talked about 'random' samples and 'random' selection. The word 'random' has been used in a more or less intuitive way to imply the purely haphazard and unbiased collection of measurements or allocation of treatments to the experimental material. At the same time, it has been hinted that it is often necessary to ensure that the events in question are sufficiently random by appealing to some special technique. Although one can easily get into deep philosophical waters over questions of the 'true meaning of randomness', it is unnecessary to broach such difficulties here. So far as the experimenter is concerned, he wants to avoid the sort of bias that will lead him to infer, for instance, real differences between treatments, when the observed differences are due merely to some heterogeneity in the test material. We shall therefore discuss randomness only in relation to avoiding various forms of conscious and unconscious bias. The use of tables of random numbers is the chief means of achieving this object. It is, however, worth mentioning in passing that randomization in properly designed experiments, like those with randomized blocks, for example, does in fact make the usual significance tests approximately valid even when the assumption of normally distributed residual variation does not hold.

The possibility of simple forms of bias will of course occur quite naturally to the competent experimenter. If you are testing the effect of two different types of diet on two groups of rats, then obviously the two groups of rats ought to be in some sense equivalent in all relevant features. What features are relevant can be decided only by experience and general background knowledge. It would clearly be unwise to feed animals from one inbred strain on the first diet and animals from another inbred strain on the second diet; we know that different strains may easily have different metabolic characteristics, and so an observed difference in growth-rates might be due to the effect of strain rather than diet. Similar remarks apply to other ways of classifying experimental animals, such as by age, sex, size, weight, previous diet, state of health and so on. We may be prepared to dismiss some of these factors as unimportant. There are two main ways of dealing with those that remain.

First, we can allot the whole set of rats available at random to the two treatments, without making any distinction in the factors we regard as influencing the effect of diet, and then use a t-test for comparing the mean growth-rates of the two groups. The idea is that any factor like strain or sex will have an equal chance of falling to either treatment, and so the variation entailed by such factors is absorbed in the residual variation. This reasoning is perfectly valid. The snag is that if the animals are a rather heterogeneous collection the residual variation will be large and will therefore render the experiment insensitive to differences between the two treatments. Mention has already been made of this disadvantage, where we saw how two drugs could be tested more efficiently on a set of heterogeneous subjects by applying both drugs at different times to each patient, and then examining the series of differences of pairs of corresponding responses. Similarly, it was pointed out how large natural variations could be reduced by means of a randomized block design as compared with a completely randomized arrangement.

A better plan in the dietary experiment would therefore be to divide up the rats into pairs, each of which were comparatively homogeneous. That is, the two members of each pair would be, so far as possible, similar with regard to strain, age, sex, weight, etc. We could then allot (at random to be on the safe side) the two members of each pair to the two diets, and analyze results by means of the paired-comparison test. With more than two diets we should require small groups each large enough to provide as many animals as there were diets to be tested. This would then lead immediately to a randomized block design, in which the diets were the treatments and the blocks were the homogeneous groups of rats. More generally, we may choose as blocks any groups of experimental units that are homogeneous with regard to characters possibly affecting the results.

A more ambitious scheme would be to attempt a factorial experiment in which age, sex, weight-class, etc., constituted the various factors. This would certainly be more informative about the general effect of diet under varying conditions, but it would also be more difficult to obtain a balanced arrangement in which all combinations of factor levels were represented.

As an alternative and with a view to keeping the design simple, we might consider using only two groups of rats, one for each of the two diets, specially chosen to match each other in the relevant factors instead of being decided at random. Thus each group would contain, so far as possible, the same proportion of animals of each strain, age, sex, weight, etc. This procedure is not to be recommended. Compared with purely random allocation the residual variation would be somewhat reduced, although, as with quota-sampling in social surveys, the proper residual variance is difficult to assess. In general, the method leading to a paired-comparison test or randomized block lay-out is much superior.

Such considerations apply equally well to any form of experimental design, whether we are allocating treatments to animals, plots of land, bacterial colonies, fruit trees, etc. It may also happen that the experimental units are not under quite such strict control. We might have to rely on raging observations under specified conditions. This sometimes occurs in the study of insect or animal populations, for instance, when we want to observe behavior against a range of meteorological or other environmental conditions. We might have a factorial 'experiment in which the factors involved were sunshine, rain, humidity and temperature. Although we cannot go into details here, the same principles apply. We first try to imagine all reasonable sources of possible bias, and then try to choose some system of random sampling that will overcome the bias.

Suppose now that we want to take a representative sample of plants from a strongly growing field of wheat. How should this be done? By 'representative' one means, of course, a sample in which ideally an variations in quality are present in the proper proportions. In practice one must naturally be satisfied with something that is only an approximation to this. Nevertheless, one wants to avoid bias towards any particular type of plant. If, for example, we cast a hoop into the field, it would be more likely to come to rest in or near a patch of plants that were taller than average. Moreover, we should probably tend to aim somewhere near the centre of the field and away from the border where growth is likely to be poor. With practice we might hope to do better, though it has usually been found in many different spheres that even experienced observers tend to produce heavily biased samples: e.g. the plants selected are on average too tall, too short, have too many large ears, show too much or too little variation and so on. No matter how reasonable and honest one tries to be, there is always a strong likelihood of being influenced by purely subjective factors causing unconscious bias. A mentions was made of the tendency of some laboratory technicians to obtain repeats of differential white-cell counts that were much closer to the original one than would be expected, unless special steps were taken to eliminate unconscious bias by means of a mechanical method of scoring the results.

In the case of the field of wheat we want to be able to select a number of points in it at random, perhaps collecting all plants within some specified radius of each point. With a rectangular field we shall achieve our object if we take points whose distances, measured say to the nearest foot, from two adjacent sides are selected at random.

Each individual problem may have its own special difficulties with regard to random allocation or selection, and some ingenuity may be required to choose a method that will avoid known types of bias with a reasonable economy of effort. In the next section we consider in detail the technique of using random numbers to achieve the desired result.

The use of random numbers

Various sources of random numbers are available, but the most convenient and accessible for ordinary statistical purposes is Table in Fisher & Yates' Statistical Tables. The first six pages of the table contain 15,000 numbers arranged in pairs. These numbers have been generated so as to be an effectively random or haphazard series of digits. Without embarking on any detailed logical analysis, we can loosely define what we mean by 'random' in this context as follows. Each of the digits 0, 1, 2, ..., 8, 9 ought to appear in a long series with approximately equal frequencies; so should all possible pairs 00, 01, 02, ..., 99, and all possible triplets, etc. In fact, any specific pattern of digits ought to appear with approximately its calculable chance of occurrence. The tables have been tested to make sure that they have the elementary properties expected of them. It is obvious, however, that if one looks carefully enough at any given series one will always discover some pattern or property which could be regarded as evidence of non-randomness. This need not worry us in ordinary biological experimentation: we only want to avoid the kinds of bias mentioned in the last section, and so long as the random numbers available will do this for us they are good enough.

The main problem is how to use an effectively random series of digits to allocate experimental units at random to a number of specific treatments. Suppose we have 45 rats on which to test three kinds of diet. If they are all fairly similar in age, sex, weight, etc., we may decide that the best thing is simply to divide them at random into three groups. We could do this by earmarking the first 15 that came to hand (either physically as we moved from cage to cage, or theoretically by going through a litter-book) for treatment by the first diet, the second 15 for the second diet, and the rest for the third diet. Such a procedure is always liable to be somewhat suspect even if we cannot see any possibility of bias. Some unconscious or environmental bias might creep in with regard to the cages we approached first, or the order in the litter-book might be related to some unsuspected genetically trend. Moreover, hostile critics could always assert the possibility of bias, and might even discover it after the experiment was over.

The best plan is to label the animals with the numbers 1 to 45; then use the table to arrange these numbers in random order. We can then assign the first 15 rats to the first treatment, the second 15 to the second treatment and the rest to the third treatment. In this way we shall avoid the risk of subsequent allegations of hidden bias.

To carry out the randomization we first read across the lines of random numbers writing down those that are 45 or less and rejecting 00 and any repetitions. Starting at the beginning of Fisher & Yates' Table, we obtain 03, 43, 36, 33, 26, 16, having rejected numbers like 47, 73, 86, ... because they are greater than 45, and also ignoring 36 when repeated after 47. The required random order therefore starts off with 3, 43, 36, 33, 26, 16, ..., and the rats with the first 15 identification numbers to appear are all allotted to the first treatment. Rats with the next 15 numbers are assigned to the second treatment and the remainder to the third treatment.

The above process entails rejecting, on average, 55 numbers in every 100 selected from the table, not counting repetitions, namely 46-99 and 00. Again, if we were arranging 30 numbers in random order we should be rejecting 70 in every 100. This is an unnecessary waste of time, as most of the rejected numbers can be brought into service as follows. Take the case of the 45 rats. Suppose we accept every number thrown up by the table at face value lift is 45 or less, and subtract 50 from it if it is greater than 50. The numbers 51-95 would then yield 1-45, and the only numbers in the table which we should have to reject would be 00, 46-50 and 96-99, i.e. only 10 in every 100.

If we had, say, 35 rats to be put in random order, we could subtract 40 from numbers over 40. This would still mean rejecting 30 in every 100. It might be thought that we could use numbers over 80 by subtracting 80 (r2 x 40) from them. This would not, however, be correct, because 81-99 would yield only 1-19, and the remaining numbers 20-35 would not be supplied from this source. Thus all numbers between 1 and 35 would not have an equal chance of being chosen to fill a given place in the final series; we should be more likely to find numbers between lath 19 towards the beginning.

There are many modifications of the above ideas that can be used to suit particular circumstances, but it is better to use a simple method known to be correct rather than a more elaborate procedure which, though quicker, may introduce some unsuspected bias.

In order to aid the random arrangement of small sets of numbers, Fisher & Yates also give, in their Table 1, random permutations of the 10 numbers 0-9, and, in Table XXVII 2, random permutations of the 20 numbers 0-19. These tables avoid some of the difficulties mentioned above, such as large random numbers having to be modified by subtraction of a suitable constant or the rejection of repetitions.

In a simple factorial lay-out of type 23 there are eight basic treatment combinations per block, i.e. '1', a, b, at', c, cc, be and abc. If we are applying this to an agricultural experiment, each area of land making up a block has to be divided into eight plots. And to avoid bias it is advisable to allot the eight treatments at random to the eight plots of each block, using different randomizations for the different blocks.

Suppose we label the eight treatments, as written in the order shown above, with the numbers 1 to 8. We then take a random permutation from the tables, dropping out 0 and 9. The first one given in the tables thus yields 3, 5, 2, 8, 4, 7, 6, 1. Taking the plots of the first block in some systematic order, we therefore assign to them the treatments b, c, a, abc, ab, bc, cc and '1'. For the next block we take a new random permutation and so on.

If we are carrying out only an occasional experiment requiring some deliberate randomization, we can start reading the numbers from any haphazardly chosen point or can take a permutation from anywhere on a page. But when a series of experiments is involved we should be more careful, and should work through a section of the table systematically so as to avoid any sequence being used twice (except in so far as it may reappear by chance in the random numbers themselves)

Surreys and censuses

The subject of surveys is one in which problems of random sampling loom very large. This topic is a rather specialized one, and it would take us too far afield to discuss it in any detail. Nevertheless, it is worth while drawing attention to some of the main uses of surveys in biology and medicine, and pointing out the importance of obtaining adequately representative samples of data by means of an appropriate method of randomization.

Some surveys are intended more for the preliminary investigation of a problem rather than for the precise testing of specific hypotheses. Suppose we want to make an ecological study of a particular geographical region and plan some preliminary inquiries to find out the main features of the area. A fairly cursory inspection may show that there is a considerable variety in the landscape: moorland, bog, grassland, rivers and so on. Each of these items may appear in several distinct types. Initially, at any rate, all these various aspects of the terrain may appear to have roughly equal claims to one's attention. In this case we should consider a small pilot survey in which approximately equal amounts of information were collected from each main aspect. Later we may decide that some aspects are unimportant and will therefore concentrate more attention on the remainder

Having reduced the main features of the region to a number of more or less homogeneous items, we are faced with the problem of surveying each of these in more detail. An area of woodland or grassland can perhaps be divided up on a map into a number of small squares. We then select squares at random for individual investigation. Using the methods of the last section, we simply number the squares in some standard order and then refer to a table of random numbers. If there were 15 squares in a particular area and we thought that we had time to examine only 3, then the first 3 pairs of random numbers (lying between 1 and 15) obtained from the table would tell us which squares to look at in detail.

A similar technique can easily be applied in other contexts. If we want to make a broad clinical survey of a particular disease, we may prefer to start by selecting, say, 10 patients at random from each sex and age-group, the latter berg in 5- or 10-year intervals. We should do this even if the majority of cases occurred in men between 45 and SO. The reason is that for scientific purposes we want to obtain data over a good range of possibly relevant conditions. In the study of a disease we should probably want to extend the basic classification to include the Registrar-General's main social classes, the distinction between town and country, etc.

Obviously there is a limit to the extent to which we can introduce additional classifications and still obtain sufficient data in each sub-class. This is largely a question of judgment. The main point being made here is the importance of giving adequate weight to relatively uncommon combinations of factors, and not allowing these to be swamped by excessive quantities of information about the commoner situations.

If, on the other hand, we were primarily concerned with a census rather than a survey, then a different attitude would be adopted. In a census we want to obtain an inventory of the material in question, say the timber in a forest. Since we are unlikely to be able to catalogue each tree separately, we must adopt a suitable sampling scheme. But now we want the sample to reflect the character of the forest in a representative way. The main subdivisions of the forest should appear in the sample in the same proportions. A small group of larch trees in an oak forest may be of no economic consequence, and would hardly be represented at all in, say, a 1 per cent sample.

******

Chapter - 21

Presentation of Data

There is hardly any problem in business or industry, which cannot be reasonably answered with the help and use of statistics. All businessmen and industrialists, accountants and cost accountants are to a certain extent statisticians in that they frequently base their decisions on an analysis of a set of figures. Statistics may be defined as the collection, presentation, analysis and interpretation of numerical data. When applied to business or industry, it deals with analysis, measurement and presentation of facts and provides information upon which judgments can be based and often snap decisions taken by executives at all levels of administration. Comparative figures of sales, output, overheads, costs and profits are typical examples of business statistics. Compilation of comparative figures of production is of great importance for purposes of control and measurement of efficiency, when the activities of a unit are divided into departments and responsibility over each delegated to different individuals. Loss in production, loss in process, waste, rejections, costs, overheads, wages, idle time of both men and machines are measures of efficiency and have a great bearing on the success of an undertaking, its progress and its profits, the last which in the ultimate analysis is the sine qua non of its existence. Similarly, for the successful planning of any business, trade or industry or for that matter the utilization of a nation's resources in men and material comparative statistics play a vital role and provide a useful base. The lack of it has frequently resulted in losses and failures.

For purposes of control, it will become evident, that management of business or industry requires statistical information. Normally, such information comprises of:

(1) Statistical statements of production, of purchases of raw materials and of expenses under different heads of services.

(2) Statistical statements of orders received, of sales in categories or over geographical areas. Sometimes relationship of sales to stocks or to advertisement expenditure.

(3) Statistics pertaining to employees, their earnings, their output, their efficiency, absenteeism and the extent of labour turnover and its effects on costs.

(4) Numerous statements for budgeting and budgetary controls.

(5) Graphical planning of sales by area or by item, of work in factory and the degree of accomplishment.

(6) Statements showing balance available in cash, with banks and investment accounts'; anticipated realizations from debtor's commitments in regard to wages and salaries and purchases.

Statistical data is usually obtained and collected from existing published sources such as Publications of the Department of Commerce and Industry, or periodicals of trade associations, research bureau or from unpublished sources such as records of activities kept by business and industry for its own use or by personal investigations. Whatever be the source for gathering the requisite information the data available is usually in a jumbled form, and entails considerable investigation of a variety of records. In fact, it is necessary to examine all available sources of information before launching on the collection of data and at the same time maintain an approach free from bias.

In the matter of compilation of data, though there is much, which could be taught, there is much more which can be learned only through experience. No two sets of records of any two companies or factories arc alike, and even if the basic method of keeping these records may be the same in the same industry, each unit of industry is bound to have its own peculiarities and its set of circumstances, which make the adoption of an identical procedure practically impossible.

In the process of compilation and analysis, it is necessary to classify the data into useful or pertinent categories. These categories must be considered carefully, when the procedure for collection of the data is decided. For instance, never attempt to compare data that have nothing in common. Do not reject a number that is contrary to what is expected merely because it shows grit deviation from the average. Weigh and record all possible causes of an event or occurrence and do not attribute to one event or occurrence what is indeed the result of several. A working knowledge of the processes of collection as well as the ability to evaluate the reliability of data is essential to ensure adequate and accurate conclusions.

The data once collected requires suitable form of expression. This is presentation. For the statistical presentation of a given data two methods are in general vogue. Of these the most accurate and factual is presentation in tabular form. The other method which has greater appeal for laymen is known as the method of graphical presentation or graphical expression. The method of graphical presentation, though not as accurate as tabular presentation, has the capacity to illustrate a trend in broad outline immediately and more effectively than a table.

Once given a problem it is necessary to study the information required, the person by whom it is required and the purpose for which it is required. The next step is to determine the sources of information and then to decide on the mode of treatment. In between, it is essential to define the most suitable unit of measurement and ascertain whether figures available are a goad estimate or indication of die thing to be measured. The unit must of necessity be specific and unmistakable. It must be homogeneous, i.e. it should not be possible to apply different meanings or different features or characteristics at different times or places. It should be stable and capable of correct ascertainment. Then determine the degree of accuracy that will be sufficient. It is a well defined law of statistics that a moderately large number of items chosen at random from a very large group are almost sure to have, on the average, the characteristics of the group. Large groups or aggregates of data show a higher degree of stability than small ones. Also, when large numbers are involved changes are likely to be more gradual and regular than when relatively small numbers or aggregates are considered. If comparison is made over a period of time, it should be long enough to give a true insight of the trend and to overcome seasonal or exceptional variations.

Table

The table is designed to exhibit the results of classification or grouping and the effectiveness of the tabulation depends on its success in conveying a clear impression. Its construction should be as simple as possible so that it could be easily understood. Tables arc of two kinds. In the first place there arc general or reference tables, which are merely repositories of information and are therefore known as general or reference or informative or classifying tables. A factory pay roll or tables of orders received are tables of this category. Both these contain considerable information and from these useful statistics can be compiled. In the second place there are summary or text tables, which are small in size. These are designed to set forth one finding or a few closely related sets of findings as effectively as possible. These are generally known as summary or text or interpretative or derivative tables. Interpretative tables are analytical and are prepared to convey significant aspects of data and to show definite conclusions. Interpretative tables arc prepared by boiling down information contained in one or more informative tables, by omitting data which are nor important or relevant to the problem. Sometimes, data may be combined in groups and sometimes it may be advantageous to use averages, ratios, percentages or other computed measures in substitution of or in addition to original absolute figures.

Part of Table

A Table is usually composed of seven parts: (1) The title; (2) The stub, by which is meant the left-hand column and its heading; (3) The caption, in which are included the headings of the remaining columns of the table; (4) The body, in which is given the classified data for purposes of comparison or illustration of trends, which is the main aim of the use of the table; (5) Prefatory note providing an explanation concerning the entire table; (6) One or more foot-notes explaining the various details, when such details are not very obvious to the reader or the observer; and (7) A source note, if the figures or details given in the table are not original.

Layout

As the tabular method of presentation is invariably used to disclose a set of data closely connected with each other, its layout must be such as to ensure that it attracts immediate notice. It should be simple anti easy to understand. Generally too many columns or rows would make a table obscure and may even defeat the purpose for which it is constructed. When data to be presented is complicated, it is advisable to prepare subsidiary tables to precede a summary table. In practice it would be found more convenient to arrange lengthy headings vertically than horizontally. The size of a table is of vital importance and this can be kept to a minimum by keeping horizontal captions brief and providing explanations in foot-notes, if the meaning is not very clear. Large numbers have a tendency to confuse. Avoid this by dropping the last three or five digits and add a note to that effect in the caption. The layout of a table can be made more effective by varying rulings. Principal divisions should be separated by heavy or double lines and sub-divisions by light or single lines.

Comparisons

If comparison is the main aim of constructing the table, place the figures to be compared in contiguous columns and rows to facilitate this comparison. Sometimes, in the same table, a series of two or more sets of figures are required to be compared. In such cases, it is better to prepare two or more tables with the same classified data, hut containing a different arrangement of columns so that each table will lay emphasis on one set of comparisons only. This interchange of columns and/or rows is most important, as it enables the reader to focus his attention on the single set of conclusion or trend at a time

Table 1

Sales, Costs and Percentage of Costs to Sales of Milk Products Ltd.
2013-2014 (Rupees in Lakhs)

Products		**Sales Price**		**Section Price***		**Costs /Sales**	**Costs / Sales**
		2013	2014	2013	2014	2013	2014
I	Fresh Milk	1.82	1.98	1.62	1.72	89.00%	86.90%
II	Condensed Milk	4.38	4.02	4.01	3.62	91.60%	90.10%
III	Fresh Butter	3.28	4.06	2.65	3.39	80.80%	83.50%
IV	Tinned Butter	29.26	33.06	23.18	26.55	79.20%	80.10%
V	Cheese	2.38	3.68	2.32	3.6	97.50%	97.80%
VI	Casein	12.52	18.63	10.11	15.08	80.70%	80.80%
	Total :	53.64	65.43	43.89	53.96	80.10%	82.50%

without creating confusion. Tables I and 2 illustrate this principle. Two or more sets of figures can be more easily compared when placed in adjacent columns than when arranged in two adjacent rows, and figures of a series are more easily compared when placed in a column than when set in a row.

The Roman figures at the left of the names of products represent the division of company's activities in six sections.

* Section price is the nomenclature adopted by the Company to represent the total cost of a product of a section.

Table 2

Sales, Costs and Percentage of Costs to Sales of Milk Products Ltd.
2013-2014 (Rupees in lakhs)

Products		2013			2014		
		Sales Price	**Section** Price	**Costs** Sales	**Sales** Price	**Section** Price	**Costs** Sales
I	Fresh Milk	1.82	1.62	89.00%	1.98	1.72	86.90%
II	Condensed Milk	4.38	4.01	91.60%	4.02	3.62	90.10%
III	Fresh Butter	3.28	2.65	80.80%	4.06	3.39	83.50%
IV	Tinned Butter	29.26	23.18	79.20%	33.06	26.55	80.10%

V	Cheese	2.38	2.32	97.50%	3.68	3.6	97.80%
VI	Casein	12.52	10.11	80.70%	18.63	15.08	10.80%
	Total :	53.64	42.27	80.10%	65.43	53.96	82.50%

The Roman figures at the left of the names of products represent the division of Company's activities in six sections.

* Section price is the nomenclature adopted by the Company to represent the total cost of a product of a section.

TABLE 3

Comparison of the various Elements of costs to Total Sales

Percentages	Years					Average Standard per Cent
	2010	2011	2012	2013	2014	
Factory Cost Total Sales	79.9	79.2	78.1	77.8	80.1	78.5
Manufacturing Expenses Total Sales	34.4	35.2	36.1	34.6	36.8	34.2
Direct Labour Total Sales	45.5	44	42	43.2	43.3	43.3
Indirect Labour Total Sales	25.1	24.9	24.6	23.8	25.4	25
Fixed Overheads Total Sales	5.2	5.3	5	5.4	5.6	5
Variable Overheads Total Sales	8.3	8.4	8.1	7.8	7.5	8
Manufacturing Profit Total Sales	6.3	6.6	4.3	6.2	4.8	5.3
Administration Expenses Total Sales	20.1	20.8	21.9	22.2	19.9	21.5
Selling Expenses Total Sales	4.5	4.3	4.8	5.2	4.9	4.8
Net Profit Total Sales	4.5	4.7	4.2	3.8	4.1	4.2
Working Capital Total Sales	11.1	11.8	12.9	13.2	10.9	12.5
Working Capital Total Sales	35.1	34.8	35.5	34.2	33.1	35
Stocks **Total Sales**	20.1	19.8	17.2	15.6	13.2	18

When absolute figures to be compared are large, it is difficult to gauge the relative strength or the increase or decrease between each at a glance. In such cases, it is better to make use of ratios, percentages, averages, means, etc. Table 3 shows the fundamental operating ratios of elements of costs, which are the various factors of production, to total sales, and illustrates the trend of these elements of costs over a period of five years. It will be realized that if absolute figures in rupees were placed in this table instead of percentages, it would be practically impossible to make out the increases or decreases in the various elements of costs to total sales.

Emphasis

To give suitable emphasis to a particular item in a table, the place where this item should appear is the most important. It would, therefore, be well to remember that, in the stub, the most prominent position for this purpose is at the top and the least prominent is at the bottom. Similarly, the most prominent position in the caption is at the right while the least prominent is at the left. It will be noticed that in accordance with this rule, in Table 3, the ratio of factory cost to total sales is placed at the top, as this ratio is of paramount importance to a manufacturing concern. The other ratios of the other elements of cost are shown subsequently as these go to make the total factory cost. The ratio of working capital and the ratio of stocks to the total sales are alternatively of lesser importance and have therefore been placed at the bottom. The average standard percentage, which is placed at the extreme right, is of the greatest importance, as it enables comparisons with the results of various years and has, therefore, been placed in this position.

Totals should always be placed in either the most prominent or the least prominent position according to the emphasis it is desired to place on them. Table 4 is an illustration of this point, where the total taxes paid by the Company arc shown at the top in the body of the table.

Use Italicized figures or ink of another colour or pencil as the case may be, to emphasize individual figures, columns or rows of figures where such emphasis is necessary to distinguish prominent conclusions, prominent findings or prominent trends. It will be absented that in Table 4 a certain row of figures to which it is necessary to give prominence is so placed.

Table 4

Various Contributions made to Government Revenues by the Tata Iron & Steel Co. Ltd.*

(in 00,000 Rs.)

Year	2008-09	2009-10	2010-11	2011-12	2012-13	2013-14
Total Taxes	534.35	651.08	647.99	661.39	547.36	572.69
Income Tax	274.65	382.6	412.83	311.47	213.7	127.38
Excise Duty	43.69	38.19	40.6	41.23	36.07	36.25
Customs Duty	4.28	6.39	13.63	7.52	10.66	11.73
Rly. Freight	201.8	199.86	139.73	257.09	249.42	336.45
Miscellaneo us Taxes	9.93	24.04	41.2	44.08	37.51	60.88

* Source : The Report of the Tata Iron & Steel co. Ltd. For the year ended 31-3-2014.

When monthly, yearly or other periodic fluctuations in sales, costs, employment or such other factors are to be shown, it may become necessary to give prominence to the highest and lowest variations in each: column or row. To give emphasis to the lowest in this set of figures, set them in bold face while placing the highest in italics as in Table 3.

Arrangement of Data

As stated earlier, the arrangement of data is of primary importance in the work of presentation. Ill-arranged sets or sequence of figures, however accurate or carefully compiled, could convey no meaning unless the method by which these figures are arranged makes the implications of the conclusions, the findings or the trend immediately obvious. There are a few recognized methods of arranging items in the stub and the caption and these are described below.

Alphabetical

This method is most suited when the table is large and unwieldy and is used merely as a repository of information for ready reference. Such tables' are usually called reference tables. In such type of tables, it is not necessary to make an effort to arrange the data very carefully, us the table is not created to bring out any comparisons of periodic trends or conclusions or findings, as is usually the case in the other category of tables, which are composed after careful compilation and shifting of data. The sole purpose of a reference table is to present the data in such a form that individual items could be found readily and therefore the: alphabetical method of presentation is the most suitable in such cases, as it makes reference very easy. Tables of this category arc usually published periodically by the Department of Commercial Intelligence and Statistics or by Census Departments or by die Central Banking authorities of every country for ready reference of traders, industrialists and persons engaged in import and export trade. One of the most prominent table usually to be found in the periodic publications of the Department of Commercial Intelligence and Statistics is the per port exports and imports of a large variety of goods, which go to make the seaborne trade of the country. These varieties of goods are placed in alphabetical order under categories such as automobiles, boilers, carbon rods, diesel engines and so on, arranged in a sequence.

Geographical

When established usage has set its mark on geographical divisions and the mention of each such division leaves no doubt in the mind of the reader of the exact location and extension of such a division, the geographical method of classification could be employed. Table 5 showing the sales of various products distributed by Standard Stationery Manufacturers Ltd. in the various parts of India is one such, illustrating the point.

Table 5

Sales of Standard Stationery Manufacturers Ltd. During 2014

(in 000 Rs.)

Section	Stencils	Carbon Pater	Type writer Ribbons	Duplicating inks	Ink Tablests
Bombay State	82	4,62	69	15	72
Bengal	36	3,84	94	8	49
Bihar, Assam and Orissa	12	2,62	36	3	82
Punjab,U.P and Delhi	26	3,56	48	5	96
Madhya Pradesh and Rajasthan	3	86	15	1	15
Madras, Mysore	10	1,52	36	3	35
Andhra and Kerala	2	38	18	....	18
Kashmir	6	12	8	1	6

Magnitude

A very useful method of arranging data in a summary or interpretative table is by listing items according to magnitude. Usually the largest item is placed first but sometimes the order is reversed. This method can be employed only when the importance of a certain set or series of figures is determined by magnitude alone, i.e. by its size, its volume, its weight, etc.

Historical

Any data which is classified historically and revealed in the form of a time-study is arranged in this form. The most recent date, the month, the year or whatever other element of time is used, is placed at the top or bottom, first or last, depending upon whether the emphasis is to be placed on the nearest or the latest event. Table 3, Table 4 and Table 7 are illustrations of this method of presentation. While Table 3 affords an understanding of the trends of various elements of costs in a given company over a period of five years, Table 7 gives an interesting study of the trend of index numbers of various commodities, which enter into production. Table 6 shows a case where the years are shown in the stub.

Table 6

Hindustan Petroleum Co. Ltd Employees and their Wages

Year	No. of Employees	Total Wages	Average hours worked/week	Average weekly Rate
		Rs		**Rs**
2009	12,639	35,764,589	38	55.86*
2010	11,616	34,663,373	43	57.62*
2011	11,451	37,329,794	45	61.20*
2012	12,964	36,319,923	42	52.08
2013	12,482	30,901,934	39	45.24
2014	11,761	24,997,633	39	38.22

- Excluding strike period.
- Includes allowances for wage inequities.

Table 7

Index Numbers of Wholesalw Prices

Year ended August 2014=100

Average of Weeks		Food Articles 1	Industrial Raw Materials 2	Semi-manufacturd Articles 3	Manufactured Articles 4	General Index 5
	2012-13	383	445	327.3	346.1	376.2
	2013-14	391	472	331.6	347.2	385.4
April	2013	374	463	325.2	3247	376.1
May	"	377	464	324.5	347.1	377.1
June	"	382	460	326.3	349.2	378.3
July	"	396	449	326.7	344.7	380.6
August	"	411	461	330.8	348.6	389

September	"	403	469	335	351.4	389.8
October	"	407	478	332.2	352.6	393.3
November	"	405	472	333.9	344.2	390.2
December	"	374	478	334.1	343.8	381.3
January	2014	379	486	335.5	344.6	384.7
February	"	395	493	338.1	346.5	392.3
March	"	396	490	338.2	347.4	392.4
April	"	399	484	332.7	347.8	391.3
May	"	402	486	335	348.3	393.6

Source : Office of the Economic Adviser to the Government.

Progressive

According to this method, the items arc arranged in such a way that the final figure or some of the other intermediary figures develop logically, king the resultant of the figure-s preceding either column-wise or row-wise. Table 8 is an illustration of such row-wise arrangement. Total additions of the assets shown in the sixth row arc the sum total of the various assets added during the year, such as net income, depreciation, changes in debenture capital, proceeds front sale of properties and. Other Additions. Similarly, in the 10th row are given the total of all deductions, which arc the sum of figures shown in rows 7, 8 and 9 and which represent the outgo. The last row shows the net increase or decrease in the working capital during each year and is derived by deducting the figures in row 10 from the figures in row 6. In order to distinguish these rows, which arc the results of the figures given in the preceding rows, the figures in the body of the table pertaining to these rows are in italics.

Table 8

Changes in Working Capital

(Rupees in lakhs)

Average of Weeks	2010	2011	2012	2013	2014
Net income accruing	192	190	212	321	467
Depreciation	119	138	120	143	168
Changes in debenture capital	18	12	6	15	12
Proceeds from sale of prosoerties	23	13	13	29	17
othe additions	46	28	-	7	0
Total Additions	362	357	339	515	664
Additions to Fixed assets	163	186	279	425	530
Investments in subsidiaries	..	..	..	..	74
Dividends paid	88	88	101	139	91
Total Deductions	251	274	380	564	695
Net increase or decrease in work ing capital	111	83	41	49	31

Numerical

It is the usual practice in large workshops and factories to divide the various activities of the organization into small units, sections or departments. Each unit, section or department is fairly composite in itself with a quasi-independent organization of its own. In some cases it is the practice to identify these units by means of specific technical names such as spinning department, weaving department, dyeing department, bleaching department and carding department in a textile mill. It is, however, not possible to give a specific name in

TABLE - 9

Facts at a Glance

	2010	2011	2012	2013	2014
FINANCIAL POSITION (Dollars in lakhs)					
Investments in railway equipment and properties	1025	992	1004	1018	1072
Investments in subsidiary companies	451	451	454	464	466
Current assets	296	266	214	214	188
Current liabilities	194	113	108	130	126
Debentures	561	557	556	565	590
INCOME (in lakhs)					
Operating revenues	715	654	616	703	780
Operating expenses	532	581	558	607	667
Taxes	98	6	24	52	54
Net Rly. Operation income	66	50	15	25	37
Fixed Charges	46	44	41	42	43
Net income	36	24	10	2	15
Operating ratio	74.40%	88.70%	90.50%	86.20%	85.40%
Return on depreciated property investment on net operation income	3.80%	3.00%	0.90%	1.40%	2.10%
Profit in relation to Total	4.90%	3.60%	Nil	0.30%	1.80%
Dividend per share	$1.50	$1.50	Nil	Nil	$0.50
SIGNIFICANT FREIGHT FIGURES (in lakhs)					
Revenue Freight tons	196	180	171	188	185
Revenue ton-miles	51921	44363	40215	43570	41926
Revenue Per ton-mile	0.90*	0.94*	1.02*	1.14*	1.34*
SIGNIFICANT PASSENGER FIGURES (in lakhs)					
Revenue Passengers	82	79	78	73	69
Revenue Passenger-miles	9292	8787	7046	6079	5526
Revenue Per Passenger mile	1.95*	1.93*	2.10*	2.19*	2.46*

EMPLOYEES AND WHAT THEY RECEIVED (in lakhs)

Number of employees	12276	12446	11984	11999	11972
Total wages	337	337	373	394	433
Average wage per employee	2748	2711	3109	3282	3616
Provident funds and other benefits	20	20	23	32	24
Total average wages and benefits per employee	2912	2874	3300	3548	3819

• In cents.

all cases and hence alternatively the practice is to assign numbers to various sub-divisions for purposes of identification and quick reference. The numbers assigned serve as a label to identify some specific underlying activity or a particular department. Where data for such sections or departments is to be shown, a numerical arrangement could be conveniently followed. For instance, in a shoe factory, department (1) may be the cutting department, department (2) may be the fitting department, department (3) the lasting department and so on. Another illustration would be in the case of a canning factory in which department (1) may be the flaying department, department (2) may be the de-boning department, department (3) may be the slicing department, department (4) may be the brining department and so on.

To sum up these methods, it needs be remembered that in a table the arrangement should be such that important conclusions, comparisons or trends are properly emphasized except in the case of a reference table, where the greatest case of reference is the sole and prime consideration.

Useful Hints in Construction of Tables

(1) There should be a brief and clearly worded title to every table placed at the top of the table. Where a title is long and necessitates the use of more than one line, arrange the lines in the form of an inverted triangle. On the other hand, if brevity is likely to distort the meaning and significance of the title, use some convenient catch expression and explain the purpose of the table in a clearly worded prefatory note in smaller type just below.

(2) Avoid a complicated table. It is better to construct a number of simple tables instead of one large table from which it may be difficult to extract the information, it is desired to convey. When more than one table is contained in a given study, it is usually advisable to number the tables for identification and easy reference.

(3) Foot-notes are placed always at the bottom of the table. If the foot-notes relate to details in the stub, use numerical to indicate them. But if the foot-notes

relate to the figures in the columns, use symbols for the purpose of identification.

(4) Source notes are usually placed below the foot-notes, and it needs be remembered that it is not necessary to indicate the source for the purpose of acknowledgment alone, as the indication of a source besides serves the purpose of enabling the reader to gauge for himself the degree of reliability of the information contained in the table.

(5) When percentages are used in the table in either the stub or the caption, the entry should indicate clearly the figures to which the percentages relate, if such is not very obvious. Table 3 and Table 9 clearly indicate the proper use of headings in connection with percentages.

(6) When the table involves the use of a variable such as wages between certain limits, it is advantageous to use group intervals to distribute data adequately. In doing so, no gaps should be left out or the limit of one group interval allowed overlapping the limit of preceding or succeeding group interval. For instance:

Rs. 100 and under Rs. 125	Rs. 100-125
Its. 125 and under Rs. 150 and not	Rs. 125-450
Rs. 150 and under Ks. 175	Rs. 150-175

(7) To avoid confusion, it is usual to round up several digits of numbers. For instance, if the number 6, 84,384 is to be rounded up to the nearest thousand, it would become 6, 84 (thousand), whereas 20, 84,500 would become 20,85 (thousand). In any case, when numbers are rounded up, an indication of this should be given either in the prefatory note, the stub or the caption. It should, however, be borne in mind -that when percentages, ratios or averages are shown in a table, where the figures have been rounded, these values should be in any case calculated on the basis of the original figures and not on the basis of the rounded figures.

(8) Comparison is made more effective if the numbers in the same column are so arranged that the decimal paint and the figures to its right and left in any row lie in a vertical line with the decimal point and corresponding figures in any other row. Spacing and type can be varied with advantage to give prominence to important facts.

(9) When the units of measurements of figures shown in columns or rows are not self-explanatory, the correct nature of the unit should be made clear either in the stub or the caption but if, the same unit applies to the entire table as a whole; it could be indicated by a single prefatory note.

(10) A table should neither be too long and narrow, or too short and wide. If it is too large either way, recast it into several tables of smaller size. This remark of course cannot apply to reference tables. Rut, when reference tables are to be spread over several pages, they should be split either horizontally or vertically, and in either case, the complete stub or caption entries should be made to appear on each page. The horizontal breadth of a table should always be determined by calculating the width of the longest entry in the stub, the width of the longest entry in each column and the apportionment of reasonable space for ruling and margins for purposes of elegance. Similarly, the vertical length of a table could be determined by roughly calculating the space needed for the title, the prefatory note, foot-notes, source notes, the number of lines required by caption and stub headings, the number of rows required for the body, and reasonable space for ruling and margins for the sake of elegance.

Graphs & Charts

Some people find it difficult to understand the statistical relationship from rows and columns of figures and have therefore a tendency to skip a table. For such people charts and graphs will be found more useful. On the whole, charts or graphs are more effective in attracting attention and on top of that are definitely more easy to understand than is a table.

There are few limitations to the use of methods of graphical presentation and it is necessary to point them out at the very outset. The most important among them all, is that, graphs or charts cannot show as many set of conclusions, comparisons or trends as can be shown by tables. As such, while charts and graphs are useful for giving a quick picture of the general situation, these cannot give much detail, and arc only useful for presenting a limited amount of information at a time. The other limitation to the use of graphs and charts is that these can show only approximate values, unlike tables, which can show exact and accurate data to any required degree of accuracy. The third limitation, if at all it can be so called, is that graphs and charts require more time to con-struct and while most people can understand the method and manner in which the construction should be undertaken, one and all will not be adept at the drawing portion of it. This necessarily requires considerable elegance and neatness.

Otherwise, graphs and charts are by far the best and most effective methods of presenting a quick picture of conclusions, comparisons or trends, and in this respect stand no comparison with the method of tabular presentation or tabular analysis.

Curves

Readers will be familiar with the use of graph paper and the ordinary school methods of constructing graphs. The resume of the method of drawing graphs given below is mainly for the purpose of making them familiar with the technical expressions used in the body of this chapter so that there may be no confusion in a proper understanding of the methods discussed.

When two straight lines X'OX and YOY' are drawn at right angles to each other, the line X'OX is called the X-axis, the line YOY' is called the Y-axis and the point 0 is called the origin. For our purpose, we shall call the point 0 as the zero point and measurements made along OX towards the right as positive and measurements along OX' towards the left as negative, 0 being the barricade between the positive and negative values. Similarly, measurements made along OY in the upward direction are to be considered as positive, whereas those made along OY' in the contrary direction arc to be considered as negative, 0 once again acting as the barricade between the positive and negative values. The four quadrants into which the plane of the lines X'OX and YOY' is divided are called the first, the second, the third and the fourth quadrants in anti-clockwise direction. Thus, XOY is the first quadrant, YOX' is the second quadrant, XOY' is the third quadrant and Y'OX is the fourth quadrant. Any point in the plane of the two axes can be determined by measuring the horizontal and vertical distance of the point from the X and Y-axis. Thus, any point P in the plane is located by the length of its abscissa, which is the horizontal distance of the point along the X-axis from the zero point, and its vertical distance along the Y-axis from die zero point, which is called the ordinate. Accordingly, the points Pa, Ps and Ps in Figure 1 are (2, 3), (-2, 3), (-2, - 3), and (2,-3).

It will thus be perceived that any point in the plane of X'OX and YOY' can be determined by its abscissa and its ordinate, which arc the two factors, that determine the whereabouts of a point in the given plane. These factors are technically known as variables. One of these variables is usually dependent on the other. That variable, which is independent, is called the independent variable and the other variable is called the dependent variable.

Statistical data, it will be recalled, are composed of several variables or factors, some of which are dependent on the others and some of which are mutually related to each other. But the use of graphs can only be made when there are two and only two factors to be represented. In the case of such representation, it is the usual practice to plot the independent variable along the X-axis and the dependent variable along the Y-axis. In Figure 2, for example, it is apparent that time is the independent variable and therefore shown along the X-axis. Raisings or output of coal is the dependent variable and shown along the Y-axis. It is very rare that the two variables are mutually dependent on each other, or dependent on an altogether different third variable, in which case the choice of allocating the one or the other of the axis to any one of the variables is purely arbitrary.

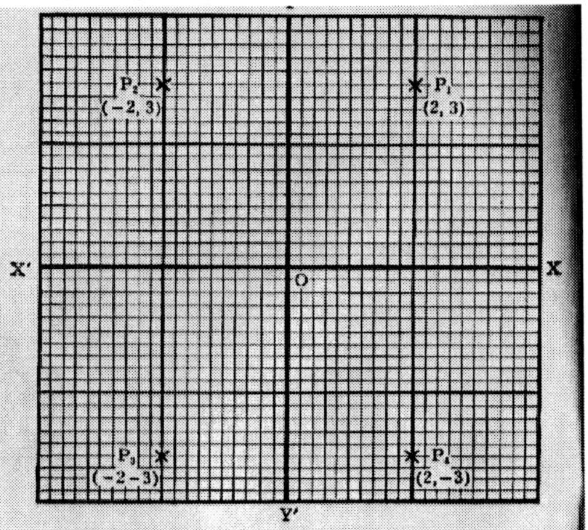

Figure 1—Construction of Graphs.

TABLE 10

COAL MINE ' A '

Raisings 1992-2014 (In Lakh Tons)

Year	Raisings	Year	Raisings
1992	13.95	2004	11.80
1993	14.05	2005	11.90
1994	13.80	2006	12.30
1995	13.75	2007	11.40
1996	14.00	2008	12.05
1997	14.25	2009	11.95
1998	18.05	2010	11.30
1999	12.90	2011	11.15
2000	13.00	2012	10.95
2001	11.60	2013	10.80
2002	11.80	2014	11.00
2003	12.10		

Generally, both the variables involved are positive and the use of the first quadrant only is necessary. As such, when a table of statistical data is given and it is desired to represent this in the form of a graph, allocate the X-value, i.e. abscissa to the independent variable. In Table 10 are given the raisings of Coal Mine 'A' over a period of 23 years. The data in this Table are plotted in Figure 2.

The years are plotted along the X-axis and the raisings or the output of coal along die Y-axis. The year 1992 which is the starting point of the Table is identified with the zero point in Figure 2. A unit of distance from the Zelli point represents a period of four years. The unit distances are indicated by fine vertical lines and each unit of distance is sub-divided in four equal parts and such sub-divisions indicated by small vertical marks on the horizontal axis to provide further guidance. The raisings or quantity of coal produced arc plotted along the Y-axis. The zero point on the Y-axis is identified with zero output and each unit along the Y-axis represents two laky tons of coal. After plotting the points represented in the data in Table 10,

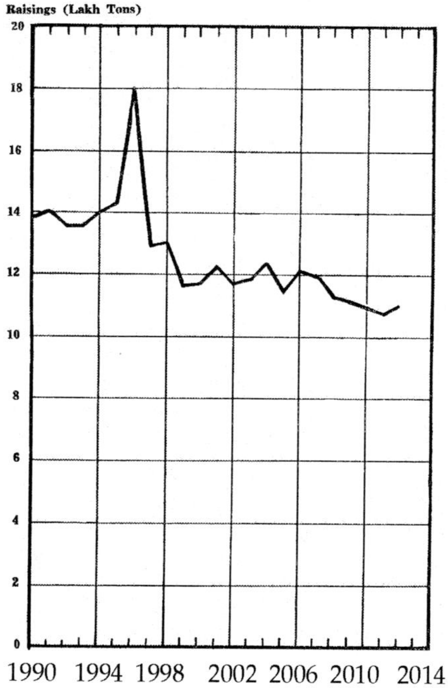

Figure 2- Curve showing Raisings of Coal Min 'A', 1990-2014. (Data Table 10.)

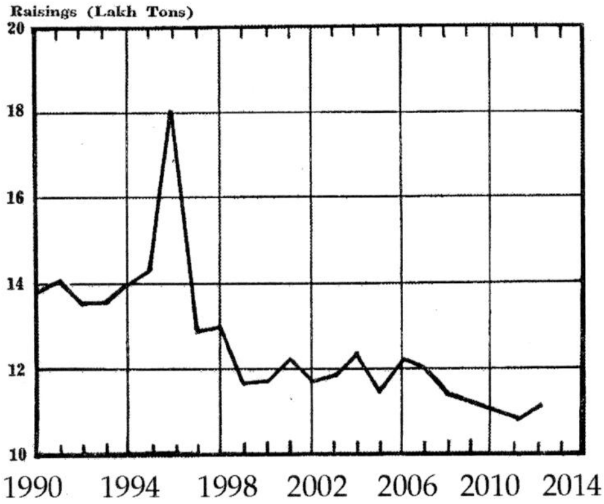

Figure 2(a)-Curve showing Raisings of Coal Mine 'A'. This curve in incorrectly drawn, since vertical scale begins with 10 and no indication of omission of zero is given. (Data Table 10.)

each two consecutive points are joined together by straight lines; which is the curve showing the raisings of Coal Mine 'A' over the period 1935 to 1957 as detailed in Table 10.

Generally when connecting points, it is necessary that the lines joining the same should be drawn heavier than the co-ordinates or guide lines to emphasize the curve. When drawing the curve for data that is not cumulative the points may be connected by straight lines, but when the data represents cumulative totals or a continuous series, it would be advantageous and also appropriate if the points plotted are connected in as smooth a curve as possible. This method of connecting the points by a smooth curve should not be confused with 'Smoothing Curves' described later.

The inclusion of a zero on the vertical scale of a curve is very essential and very frequently this principle is overlooked with the result that die curve gives a misleading impression. The data of Table 10 has been plotted in Figure 2 in accordance with this principle with reference to a vertical scale beginning with zero. In Figure 2(a) the same data has been plotted with vertical scale beginning with 10 (ix. 10 lakh tons) with the result that Figure 2(a) gives the impression that the sales were doubled between 1939 and 1941. This is not the case as the output increased from 14 lakh tons to 18.05 lakh tons, i.e. approximately 29 per cent, 35 will be seen from the table and as is apparent from Figure 2. Few persons are able to notice the omission of zero from the vertical scale and fewer still arc able to make due allowance for this omission while interpreting the curve. On the other hand, implicit use of a scale beginning with zero is apt sometimes to place the curve high up on a chart and thereby distort its effectiveness. This kind of distortion can be avoided in one of the few ways indicated below. Figure 2(b) shows one method of breaking the chart on the vertical scale by drawing notched parallel lines (with the use of a bread knife). Notice that

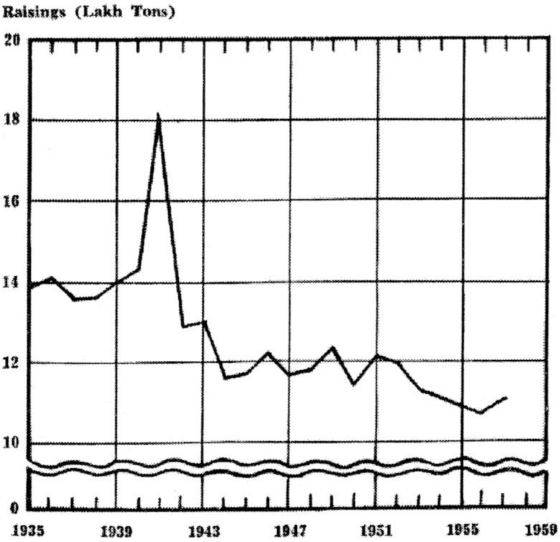

Figure 2(b)-Raisings of Coal Mine A '. (Data Table 10.)

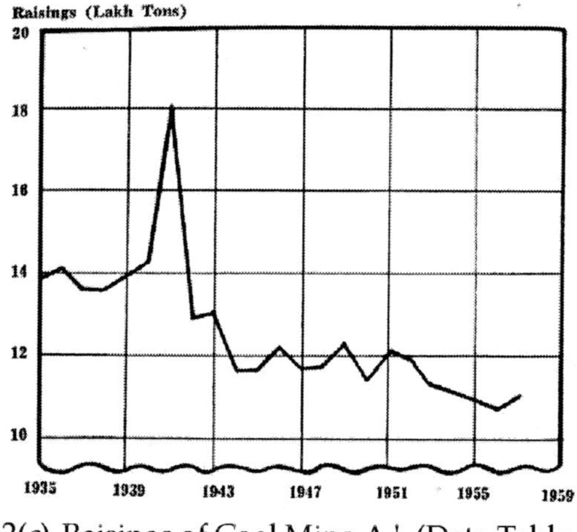

Figure 2(c)-Raisings of Coal Mine A '. (Data Table 10.)

Figure 22 shows another method of drawing attention to the break in the vertical scale by couple of notches on the vertical scale itself very near the base. Figure 2(c) shows yet another method of indicating that the scale does not begin with zero and is incomplete.

Curves are frequently used to present data of such kind where one of the variables is time. On account of this main characteristic, such curves are commonly called TIME SERIES CURVES or HISTORIGRAMS. The method of plotting this kind of curves is the same as for other curves, i.e. it will depend upon the type of data. However, there is one important feature about the time curves, and that is the data may be periodic data or may be point data. Total output per week, total sales per month, average price during a year are instances of periodic data, as the variable factor, related to the time element is for a specific period of time and is therefore called periodic data. The value of stocks, cash balances of bank, investments of insurance companies refer to a particular point of time and are therefore classed as point data. Figure 2 is an instance of periodic data. As in this case, the output of coal refers to a period of time, viz, a year. Figures 4 and 5 are cases of point data, as the variables railway freight, raw material costs, wage rates, wholesale price index, cost of electricity and cost of living index number, all relate to a point of time.

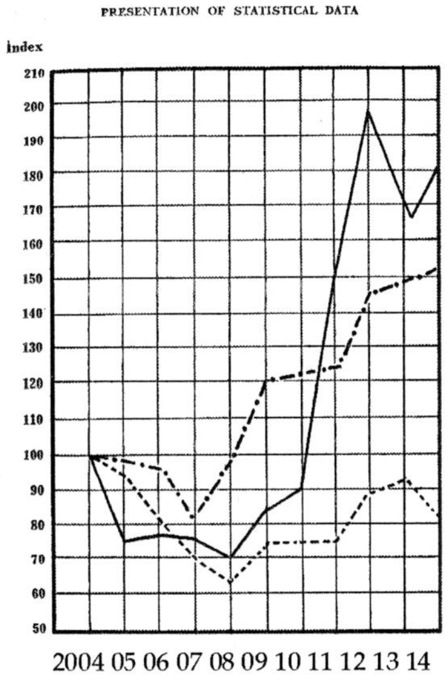

-------- Taxes

------ Average Sheet Steel Price

-·--·--- Average Monthly Wage Rate

Figure 3-Sheet Steel Prices, Wage Rates, Tax Burden Comparative Study, 2004 to 2014. (2004=100.)

It is customary to use the horizontal scale for denoting period or point of time. When annual data of any type are plotted, the dates on the horizontal scale may be placed below the vertical lines, as in Figures 2, 3, 4 and 7. When monthly, daily or weekly data are plotted over a comparatively long period of time, it would be advisable to label the space representing each year and the sub-divisions of the year by small marks as in Figure 11 or as in the right-hand part of the Figure 15.

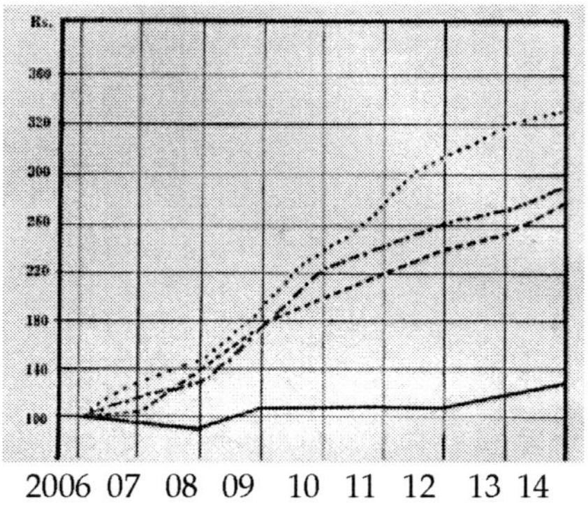

———Freight Rates ---------- Wage Rates

.... Raw Meterial .... Wholesale Price Indix

Figure 4

While there are no set rules which govern the procedure of construction and presentation of curves, there are a few hints, which it may do well to bear in mind. A. curve or curves representing any data should he so drawn that the outline of the curve or curves stands out clearly and perspicuously from the background of the chart. This could obviously be achieved by drawing the curves more heavily than the coordinates which form the background. When more than one curve is used in the same chart, use different categories of lines to indicate each curve as distinct from the others, at the same time labeling the different -curves. It is not usual to show the various points plotted from the given data in the body of the chart itself, since the purpose of the curve is to show the general situation rather than give individual readings.

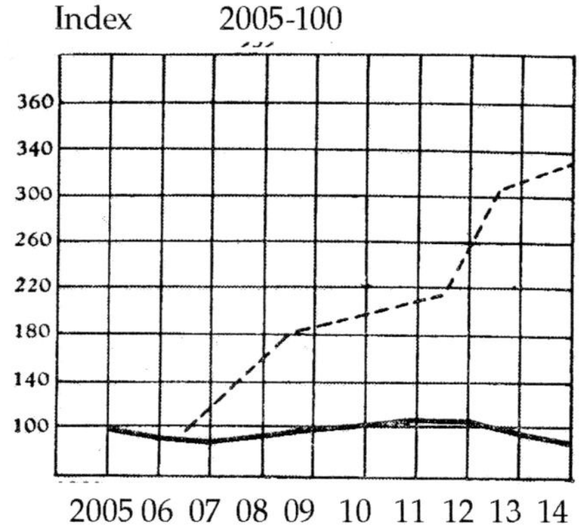

——— Cost of Electricity ---------- Cost of Living Index

Figure 5

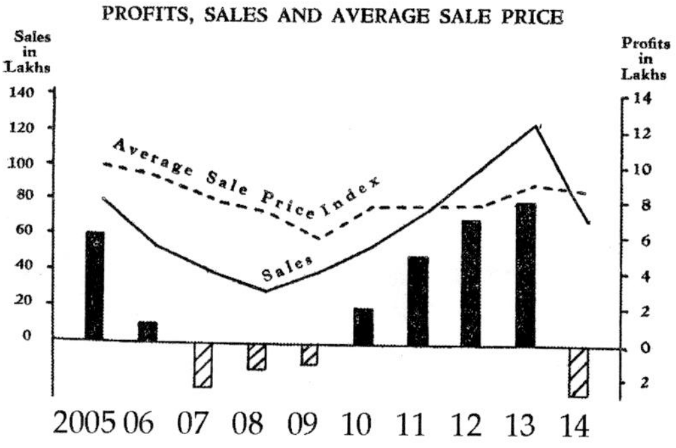

Figure 6

Occasionally curves will be seen without a zero on the vertical scale because it is hardly conceivable that the variable plotted along the vertical scale will ever approach zero as in the case of index numbers, where l(X) is the norm and deviations from this norm arc only of interest. See Figures 4 and 5.

In the normal course, it is very rare to find a chart containing more than two or three curves. Particularly if curves cross and re-cross any too often, there is bound to the confusion. In such cases, there are other methods of presentation, which could be used and which arc discussed later.

The axes or the zero lines are usually drawn heavier than co-ordinates and the marginal, vertical and horizontal lines are usually drawn slightly heavier to distinguish them from the normal co-ordinate lines, which are drawn very lightly. More co-ordinate lines than are necessary to assist the reading of a chart will create a gaudy impression and as such, keep the number of co-ordinate lines to as few as possible. Sometimes, co-ordinate lines arc entirely omitted. Sometimes, the zero lines or axes are also omitted, if they serve no useful purpose.

When more than one scale is used, it is necessary to clearly label the nature of variables indicated and the units of measures adopted, if these are not so obvious. For instance, in Figure 6, the vertical axis represents two different scales. The scale to the right indicates profits in lakhs of rupees, whereas the scale to the left indicates sales in millions of rupees, i.e. the sale on the left is one-tenth of the scale on the right and each scale is for a different purpose, the scale on the right being for the profit bars and the scale on the left for the sales curve.

Though it is impossible to give any recognized rules, which could govern the proportions of a curve, it is necessary to realize that undue expansion or exaggeration or undue contraction of a scale may create an impression entirely contrary to the one that it should convey as indicated by the data from which the curve is plotted. Figure 7 shows the population of a country over a period of several years plotted on a scale, which is reasonably appropriate. Figure 8(a) has been drawn by plotting the same data with a horizontal scale exaggerated in comparison to the vertical scale whereas Figure 8(b) has been drawn with the same data with the vertical scale exaggerated in comparison to the horizontal scale. Accordingly, Figure 8(a) gives the impression that over a period of years, the growth of population of the country was extremely slow. Figure 8(b) on the other hand conveys the impression that the growth was very fast and rapid and the fluctuations were tremendous. Such Undue

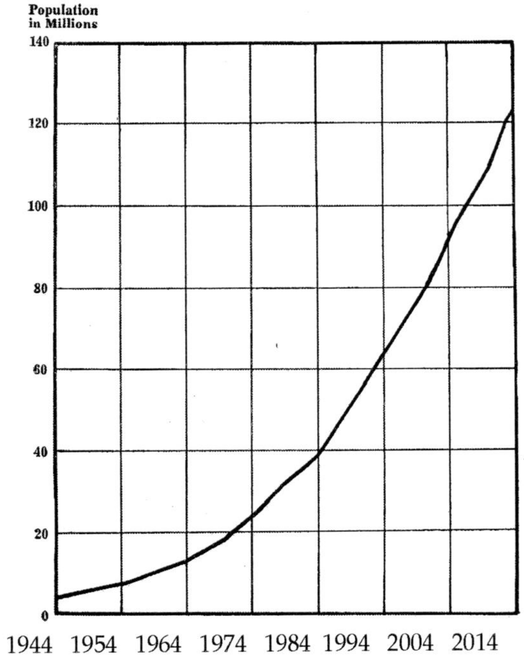

Figure 7-Population of a country-1944 to 2014

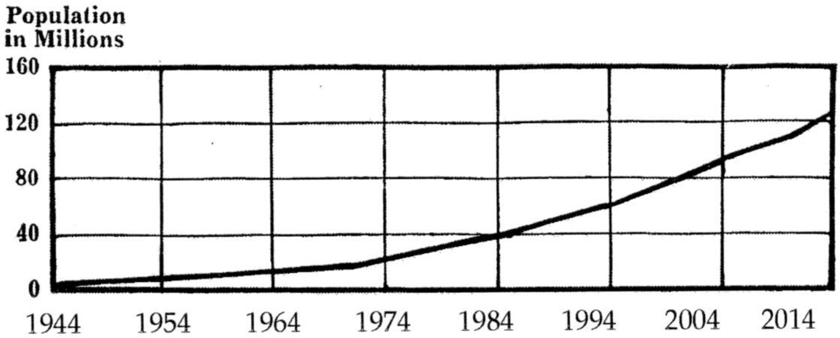

Figure 8(a)-Population of a country. The horizontal scale is exaggerated in comparison to vertical scale. (Data from same source as in Figure 7.)

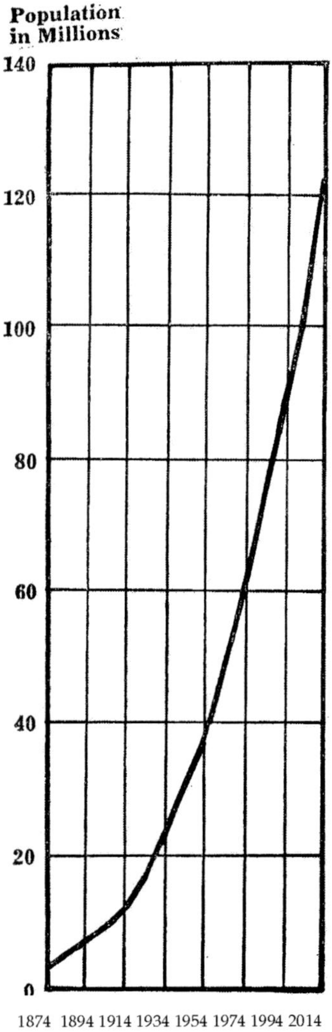

Figure 8(a)-Population of a country. The vertical scale is exaggerated in comparison to horizontal scale. (Data from same source as in Figure 7.)

exaggeration of scale is therefore capable of completely distorting results. Rut as said earlier, there are no specific rules, which one could be asked to follow in the selection of scales except perhaps for one general rule according to which a scale, which gives angular Actuations of more than 45 degrees at any turn of the curve would show results in a distorted formation. By following this rule, it is possible to avoid too flat or a too sharp curve.

While it is invariably the practice to put the title of the Table at the top, the title of a graph or a chart can be placed either at the top or at the bottom, whichever is convenient.

Silhouette Charts

At the outset, it was broadly stated that statistical data arc usually positive and it is generally necessary to use the first quadrant only in presenting statistical data. Of course, this is usually the case, but then there are charts, where negative values are required to be plotted. An instance of such a case is shown in Table 11 and Figure 9. Table 11 gives the total income of a bank A' in two different categories. That portion of the income derived from the normal trading activities of the bank in its day-to-day working is shown as distinct from the profit or loss made by the bank in the sale and purchase of investments. There were occasions, it will be seen from Table 11, when the bank incurred huge losses in its investment activity, whereas there were years during the course of which it made fair to large gains. The losses incurred on sales of investments are plotted by negative values below the X-axis and the profits are plotted by positive values above the X-axis. In order that profits and losses in the investment activity of a bank can be more clearly emphasized and made absolutely perspicuous to the render, the portion of the curve above the X-axis is left blank and the portion of the curve below the X-axis is shaded black. This is an instance of a. Silhouette Chart.

Table 11

Incomes of Bank 'A'

(2006 to 2014)

Year	Trading Income in Lacs of Rs.	Gains or Losses on Investment in Lacs of Rs.
2006	27.51	7.52
2007	35.00	10.06
2008	37.46	7.36
2009	42.48	12.44
2010	47.39	7.49
2011	32.61	-14.40
2012	10.06	-9.07
2013	14.93	2.62
2014	24.97	-4.91

Incomes of Bank 'A'

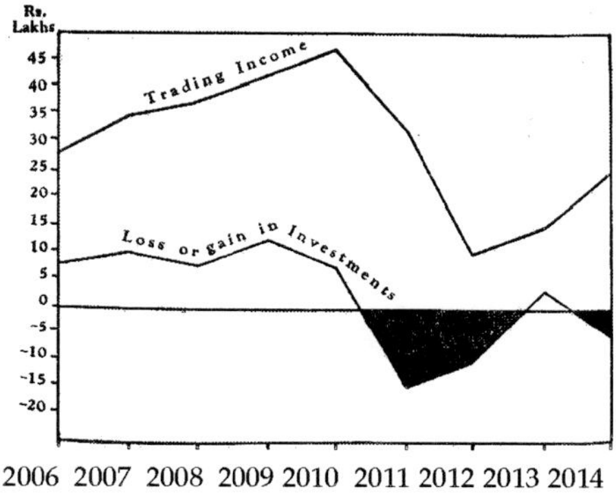

Figure 9

'Z' Charts

When it is desired to show the monthly figures of production or sales with the cumulative figures from the beginning of the year, with the totals for the previous twelve months at the end of each month, the 'Z' Chart is the most convenient device, which could be brought into play for depicting these three categories of data. This type of chart enables the observer to visualize (1) the figure for any given month; it may be of output, it may be of cost, it may be of salts or any other periodic data; (2) the total figure for all the months that have elapsed from the beginning, or for any set of consecutive months from the start of the accounting year; and (3) the total for the last twelve months ending each given month. The figure showing the total cumulative results of the operations over the last twelve months at the end of each consecutive month is commonly known as the rolling average or the moving annual total. In Figure 10 will be found the three curves showing (1) sales of Company ' B' for each month commencing with January; (2) the cumulative sales for the period ending with any given month from the commencement of the accounting year or the operating year; and also (3) the total sales for the period ending twelve months ending with any given month of the period for which the data is shown. It will of course be seen that such charts require the use of two distinct vertical scales as in Figure 10, in which the scale on the left covers smaller magnitudes showing sales per month and the scale on the right showing the rolling average or the moving annual total for the period ending twelve months ending with any given month and the total sales for any set of consecutive months from the start. Accordingly, the scale on the right will show magnitudes several times bigger than the scale on the left.

Sales of Company 'B', Monthly, Cumulative and Moving Annual total

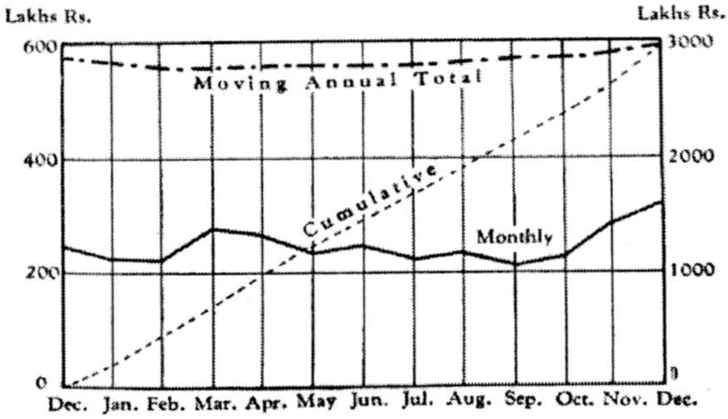

Figure 10

'Z' Charts could be used for any similar kind of data, where such three categories of results are required to be shown.

The advantage of the 'Z' Chart is that it shows on the same chart all the information a business would require to judge the progress of its trade. Actual results are shown monthly while the cumulative results show the achievement as the year progresses enabling a comparison to be made with the target fixed for the year. Finally, the rolling average or the moving annual total indicates the movements in the annual turnover. With these three curves in front, it is possible to forecast whether the actual results at the end of the year will come up to expectations. I.e. achieve the target, fall short of the target or over-reach the target. If such charts arc prepared for a number of consecutive years and compared with each other, definite information can be obtained about the normal fluctuations in the working of the business. It should, however, be noted that this type of chart is not of much use if monthly or periodic fluctuations arc abnormally wide as in such cases the curves would become distorted and consequently the results are difficult to grasp.

A detailed analysis of any activity of business invariably gives ample reward. For example, the company manufacturing inks and also ink tablets can obtain from its statistics department accurate information of the relative selling power of inks and ink tablets in any city of the country with the result that it can control the distribution of these items without stocks accumulating with wholesalers in lines which do not move fast in a particular town. It can amend its selling policy to suit the taste or requirements of the market in any year and push its products to its ultimate benefit.

In comparing sales over a series of years, it is better to compare the sales for the accounting year to-date, it. Cumulative total and for the twelve months just ended, i.e. moving annual total instead of just comparing sales of isolated months. In reviewing performance or achievement and estimating tendencies, it is usually more appropriate to compare the volume instead of value because the same value, particularly these days, does not always represent the same volume of sales owing to fluctuations in price. As further aid to comparison it is profitable to use index numbers. For example total sales of a certain year may be taken as a basis and expressed as 100. Sales for the subsequent years are reduced to this denominator by expressing them as percentages of this basis. Suppose that the basis year chosen is 2012, and that total sales of that year were 1, 03, 0(X) units, this figure would represent the index number 100. If in 2013, the sales improved to 1, 02,000 units, the index of sales for 2013 would be 102 and if in 2014 the makes declined to 97,000 units, the index would he 97. Where sales are voluminous and reach unwieldy figure:, this method of reducing them to index numbers goes a long way in facilitating comparison. Similarly, if the total output of the given product, say vegetable ghee, throughout the country is known and similarly reduced to index numbers, a comparison of two sets of index numbers when illustrated on a chart would give a clear indication of the trend of the company's sales as compared with the trend of output in the country.

If it is realized that the function of charts and graphs is not in any way to add to the information disclosed by the actual data but simply to illustrate or demonstrate the information in a manner good enough to attract attention, it will he evident that whilst bar charts, described later, are satisfactory for comparing quantities, a curve is definitely more useful for showing changes in quantities over a period of time.

For comparing sales and studying the trend, three particularly useful forms of curves arc the monthly total curve, the moving total curve and the cumulative total curve. The following example is meant to show the relative importance of these three curves from various points of view.

Table 12 shows the sales in tons of soda ash manufactured by company 'X' over a period of three years:

Table 12

		2012	**2013**	**2014**
		Tons.	**Tons.**	**Tons.**
January	.. .. ..	200	250	300
February	.. .. ..	250	250	400
March	.. .. ..	250	300	450
April	.. .. ..	300	350	45
May	.. .. ..	400	450	600
June	.. .. ..	500	500	450
July	.. .. ..	550	600	800

August	.. .. ..	600	850	950
September	.. .. ..	700	600	700
October	.. .. ..	450	500	550
November	.. .. ..	350	450	500
December	.. .. ..	250	350	400
Total :		4,800	5,450	6,145

The curve in Figure 11 indicates the seasonal fluctuations in the sales, hut at the saint time it is unable to show with any degree of clarity the long term of trend of the company's sales.

The curve in Figure 12 is plotted by taking the moving total of sales for 12 months ending December 2013, January 2014, and February 2014 and so on in succession. This curve eliminates seasonal fluctuations in sales and therefore gives a clear indication of the progress made by the company.

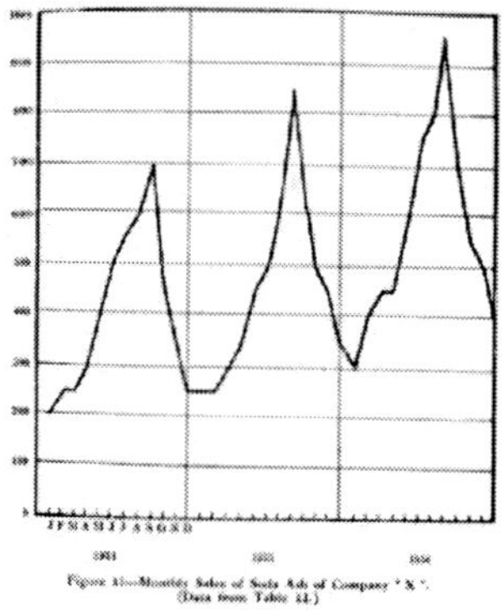

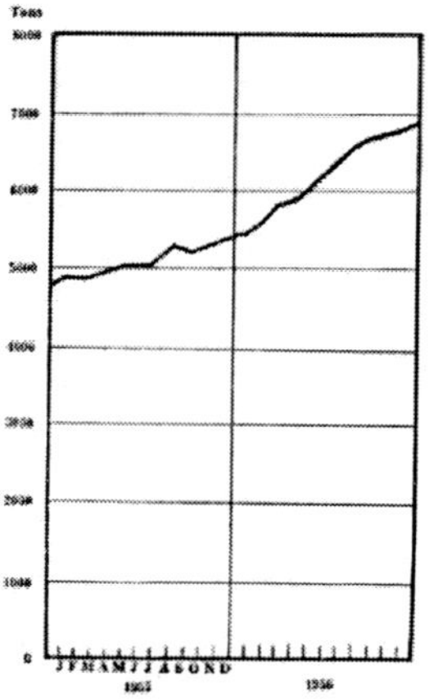

Figure 12-Twelve Month Total of Sales of Soda Ash, 2013-14.
(Data Table 12.)

The curves in Figure 13 are plotted from cumulative monthly totals for each year, i.e. 200 for January 2014, 450 for February 2014 (total of sales in

January 200 and February 250), and 700 for March 2012 (total of January 200, February 250 and March 250) and so on for each of the years 2012, 2013 and 2014. "This enables comparison with previous working. It is also useful in determining achievement in relation to a target if one is fixed.

When adopting such methods for charting sales, it would be advisable to note on the body of the chart every change in policy such as a special advertising campaign, or a change in the formulae which would make the product more effective in use, or an event of national significance such as a railway strike which is likely to affect sales so that while comparing the trend of sales, these can be borne in mind and their effects taken cognizance of.

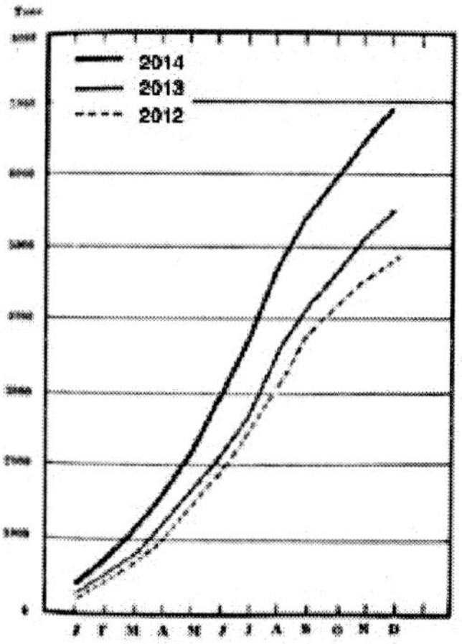

Figure 13-Cumulative Sales of Soda Ash 2012-14. (Data Table 12.

Component Parts Charts

It is sometimes most necessary to study the variations, that is, the increases and decreases in the components which go to make a whole or a total of any given data. For instance, it may be the elements of costs of a given article over a given period or it may be the increases and decreases of the various categories of assets and liabilities shown in the yearly balance sheet of a company over a period of years, in order to enable the observer to study the financial growth or otherwise and the financial stability or othenvise of any given company. Figure 14 shows the various categories of assets and liabilities of a company over a period of ten years. The width of each band indicates the extent of each class of assets and liabilities at the end of each year over a period of ten years. The position of the assets and liabilities of the company at the end of any particular year could be very easily ascertained from the various guide lines, horizontal and vertical, horizontal showing the strength of the assets and liabilities and vertical showing the year to which they relate. It is very easy to observe from such a kind of chart the increases and decreases in the various components and also the increases and decreases of the total of all components not only at the cad of any given year, but also over a period of any number of years shown in the chart.

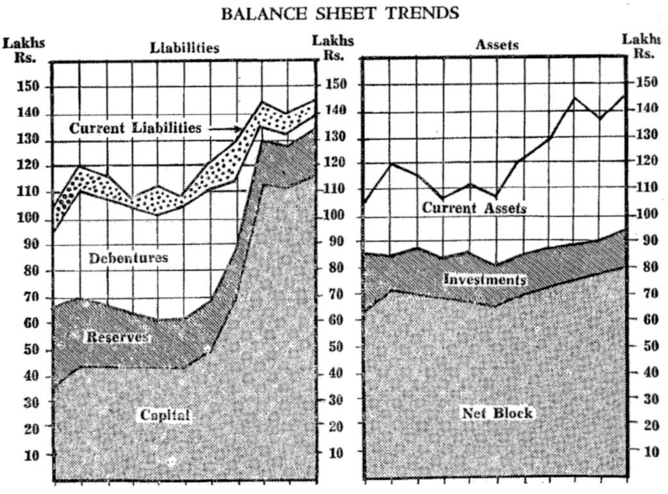

Figure 14

Another method of presenting the same data shown in Figure 14 would be to convert the absolute figures of each of the assets and liabilities, that is converting each of the components which go to make the total or whole, into percentages of the total or the whole. Then plot these percentages into similar curves instead of the absolute figures. This will show the relative increases and decreases of the various components of the whole or the total more clearly.

Thus, for studying the general trend of various components in relation to their total over a period of years "this method of presentation will he found most suitable as, such a chart would clearly show the decrease or increase in the proportion of each component over a period of time.

Charts with Variable Horizontal Scales

Sometimes, it may become necessary to show the annual sales or output or any other periodic data of similar nature over a number of years, and the monthly data in a more detailed form for one or two of the latest years. This could be done by breaking up the chart into two separate divisions. The first part of the horizontal scale in such a chart would show the years, whereas the second part of the horizontal scale would show the months. This is done by expanding the right-hand half of the horizontal portion of the chart by adopting a scale approximately twelve times or multiple of twelve times of that used in the left-band half of the chart. Figure 15 shows the index of output of coal over a period of eighteen years with the index over the last two years shown month wise (according to months).

INDEX OF OUTPUT OF COAL
2004 to 2014

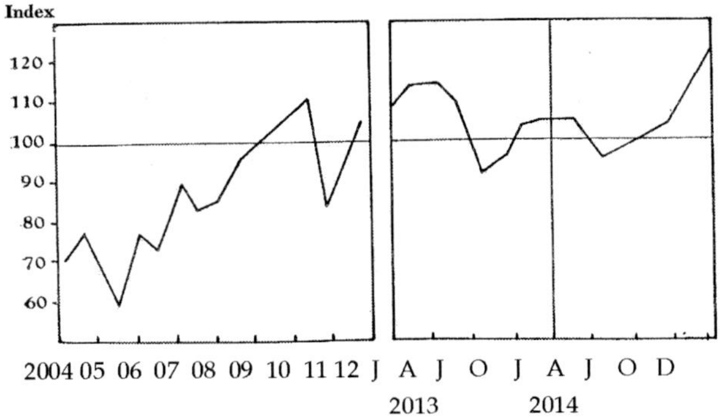

Range Charts or Zone Curves

It is common knowledge that the load of electricity supplied by any generating station varies over the period of the day. For instance, during the day when all the factories are working at full capacity, the load may be heavy. But it may be heavier still towards the evening, when the factories are about to close, but have not yet closed and lights and fans arc switched on in the streets and houses towards sunset. The load will decrease between 11 and 12 p.m., when most of the lights and fans in houses would have been switched off and almost all the factories would be invariably closed. If it is desired to depict the range of this load over a period of day's showing the maximum and minimum load of each day, the method depicted in Figure 16 will be found most suitable. In such a presentation, the top of each bar will represent the highest load of the day, while the bottom of each bar will represent the lowest load of the day. The line connecting the bars will represent the load at the commencement of the day, that is, say at 8 a.m. in the morning. Charts like these are also utilized to show the variations in. commodity prices of major raw materials like jute and cotton along with their fluctuations over the day over a period of time. Figure 13 shows the trend of raw rubber prices over a period of two months in this style. Range charts or zone curves can be wed to show prices of materials, wage rates, interest rates, output per man or machine or sales per person over a period of time.

Range Charts of Price of Raw Rubber

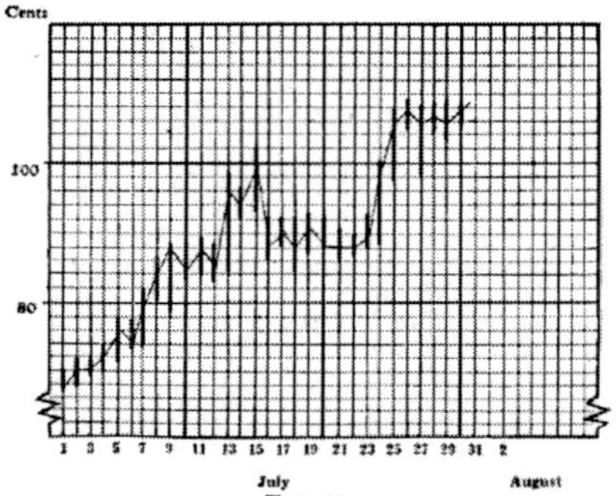

Figure 16

Smoothing Curves

Whenever there are frequent. Fluctuations up and down in a curve, there is quite often a broad general movement or trend of the whole curve, quite apart from the occasional irregularities in the line connecting the various points. Accordingly, when it is obvious that the data lie fairly and regularly and there is enough ground for a presumption that the data follows a more or less regular law or discloses a more or less regular pattern, it is advantageous to resort to the process of drawing a free hand curve through or near the points plotted instead of merely connecting them with straight lines. This is known as smoothing a curve. Smoothing is particularly appropriate in case of a continuous series, where it suggests the existence of infinitesimal gradation or minute variations and is based on the fact that many classes of phenomena tend to yield regular distribution according to a law and that the larger the sample the more regular is the distribution. The smoothed curve will therefore represent what is believed the distribution would be if every example in existence had been taken. Smoothing eliminates accidental fluctuations and shows what is believed to be the correct tendency or trend of data.

Sometimes, it is advantageous to smooth the data instead of the curve. This is done by taking a series of averages or a series of totals and these computed figures are plotted instead of the original accurate figures. Figure 17 shows a curve of actual sales as well as curve drawn by using smoothed data of five weeks moving average.

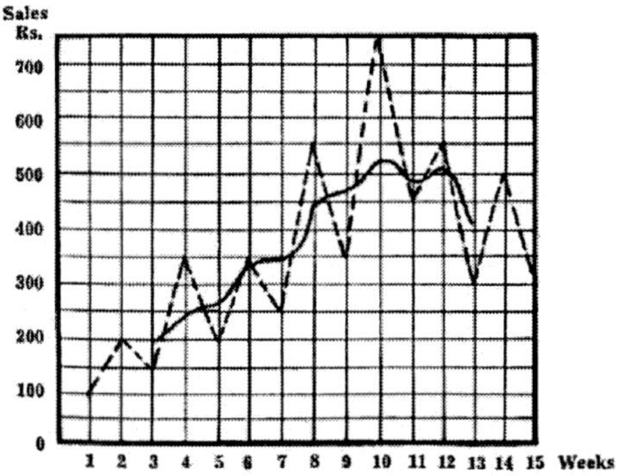

Figure 17-Curve of Actual Sales (dotted curve) smoothed by using five weeks' moving average (dark curve).

Semi-Logarithmic or Ratio Charts

Frequently while comparing the development of a series of data; it is necessary to present a visual indication of relative growth or rate of change as distinct from absolute increases or decreases. Charts and graphs described so far have all been plotted on what is known as natural-scale or arithmetic-scale, arc useful primarily in showing the actual increases or decreases, i.e. absolute changes. Such graphs art nor able to give any definite indication visual or othenvise of the relative change or the rate of change.

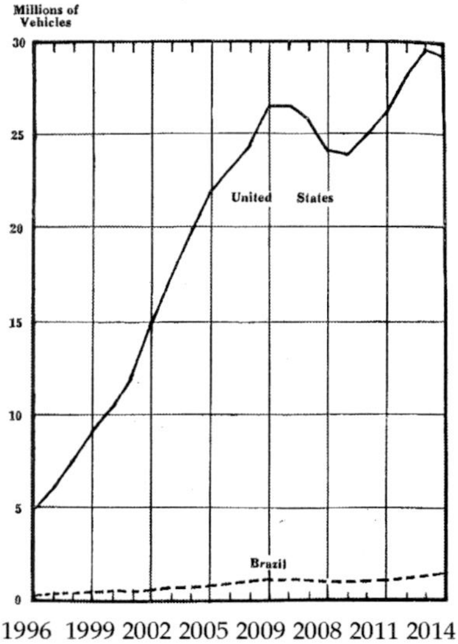

Figure 18-Motor Vehicles Registered in U.S.A. and Brazil, 2013-14.
(On natural scale graph.)

Figure 18 shows the growth of motor vehicle registrations in U.S.A. and Brazil from 1996 to 2014. It can be seen from the chart that the use of motor vehicles in U.S.A. increased rapidly between 1996 and 2008, then was fairly constant from 2008 to 2014, dropped in 2011, 2012 and 2013 and then again began to show an increase from 2014. On the other hand, changes in the registration of motor vehicles in Brazil are difficult to see for the simple reason that the scale which must be used to accommodate the data of registrations for U.S.A. causes the curve for Brazil to be shown near the bottom. The faith is obviously not with the method of presentation but with the use of the natural or arithmetic scale, because if the data from which the curves are plotted is studied, it will be apparent that relative growth of motor vehicle registrations in U.S.A. and Brazil over a period of time is more or less similar as will be seen later from Figure 19.

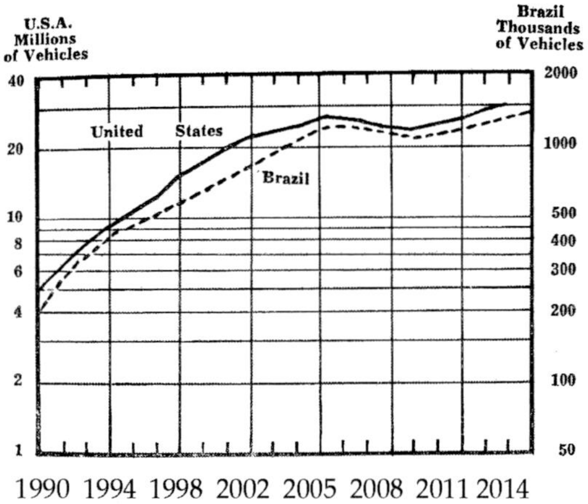

Figure 19-Motor Vehicles Registered in U.S.A. and Brazil, 2013-14. (On ratio ruled scale graph.)

It would serve no purpose to re-plot the data of Figure 18 by using one vertical scale for U.S.A. and another for Brazil to magnify the movements of the curve for Brazil. Because if two different scales are used there will be merely two distinct curves hut still no visual comparison of the size of the two series plotted, or the amount of change that has taken place in one series in comparison to the amount of change in the other, or of the rates of change of the two series.

Similarly, if it is necessary to compare the output Nr week of two departments of a factory it is not possible to present a comparison of their proportional rates of increases or decreases by using a natural-scale graph. Suppose that Department ' A ' of the factory has an output of 2,000 units per week at the beginning of a period and Department B ' has an output of 1,000 units per week. If both the Departments increase their output by 200 units in the following week, the output of Department '13' has increased at a rate twice as fast as that of Department o A', for the rate of increase in case of Department 'B' is 20 per cent while that in case of Department 'A' of 10 per cent, even though the absolute increase in output in case of both is the same. On a natural-scale graph, the actual increases being equal, these will be shown by the same vertical distance and it will be only by calculation that the proportional rates of changes in output can be determined.

This deficiency or inadequacy to show relative movements or rate of change can be overcome by the use of semi-logarithmic or ratio stile graphs. Instead of plotting the actual output of the two Departments, plot the logarithms of the numbers from which the graph is to be drawn. On such graphs equal vertical distances will represent equal proportionate movements, irrespective of whether the output increases from 1,000 to 1,200 or from 2,(X)0 to 2,400 or from 20,000 to 24,000. When the logarithms of the actual figures of output arc plotted, slopes of lines joining the points will indicate the proportional rate of increase or decrease as the case may be. From such a graph it will be possible to tell at a glance not only whether there is an increase or decrease but also whether the rate of change is faster or slower at one period or another, or when two sets of figures are plotted whether one is changing at a greater rate than the other.

Such graphs can also be drawn on a ratio-ruled paper or logarithmic paper, in this case directly from the original data. The ruling of such paper can be obtained by marking off logarithmic scale from a slide rule instead of from an arithmetic rule.

The difference in plotting actual figures and their logarithms are clearly revealed by the following examples:

Table 13

Averge weekly Earnings of ' A ' and ' B '

Year	Earnings of ' A '		Earnings of ' B '	
	Amounts	Logs	Amounts	Logs
	Rs		Rs	
2004	10.50	1.02120	50	1.6990
2005	13.50	1.13030	65	1.8129
2006	15.50	1.19030	75	1.8751
2007	18.00	1.25530	95	1.9777
2008	21.00	1.32221	105	2.0212
2009	22.50	1.35220	115	2.0607
2010	25.00	1.39790	125	2.0969
2011	28.00	1.44720	140	2.1461

2012	31.00	1.49140	155	2.1903
2013	33.50	1.52500	175	2.2430
2014	36.00	1.55630	185	2.2672

Figure 20 does not at all show that the earnings of both 'A' and 'B' are increasing at the same proportional rate, but Figure 21, which is drawn by plotting the logarithms of the numbers, shows this fact very clearly. Similarly, while Figure 18 gave no idea of the relative growth of motor vehicle registrations in either U.S.A. or Brazil, Figure 19 which is drawn on a ratio-ruled paper with two different vertical scales, one for U.S.A. and another for Brazil, shows that the general rates of increase and decrease are similar throughout the period even though the two series are of dissimilar size.

Table 14

Earnings of ' A and B '

Year	Earnings of ' A '		Earnings of ' B '	
	Amounts	Logs	Amounts	Logs
	Rs		Rs	
2009	50	1.69990	100	2.0000
2010	70	1.84510	120	2.0792
2011	90	1.95420	140	2.1461
2012	110	2.04140	160	2.2041
2013	130	2.11390	180	2.2553
2014	150	2.17610	200	2.3010

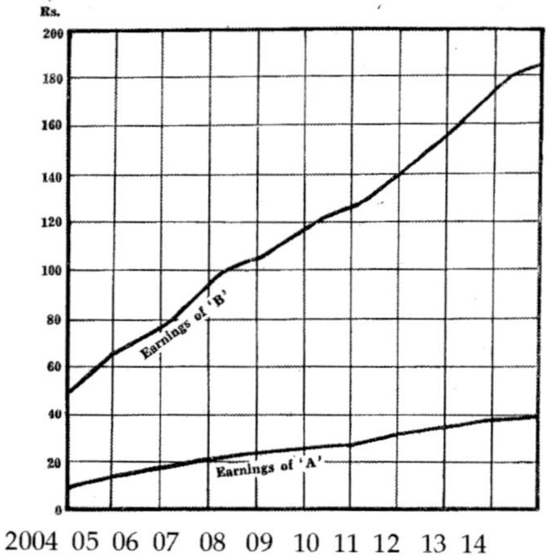

Figure 20-Average Weekly Earnings of 'A' and 'B', 1938-1948.
(On natural scale graph.)

Table 14 shows a hypothetical case of two workmen whose earnings have increased by Rs. 20 per week each year. Since the earnings of both ' 'A' and "B' are increasing by the same amount, Figure 22 in which the data is plotted on a natural-scale shows both graphs as two parallel straight lines. It would therefore appear at a glance that earnings of both 'A' and B' are increasing in the same proportion. This is clearly shown to be a fallacy when ratio-scale is used as in Figure 23, which shows two graphs rising at a diminishing rate and tending to come closer together. It is due to the fact that each annual proportional increase is smaller than the previous one and that the annual proportional increase in case of 'B' is smaller than that in case of ' A '.

On a ratio chart there is no zero base line. Only the slope of the curve has a meaning and consequently in ratio charts curves can be placed anywhere on the diagram according to convenience. Thus, two Curves can be brought into close

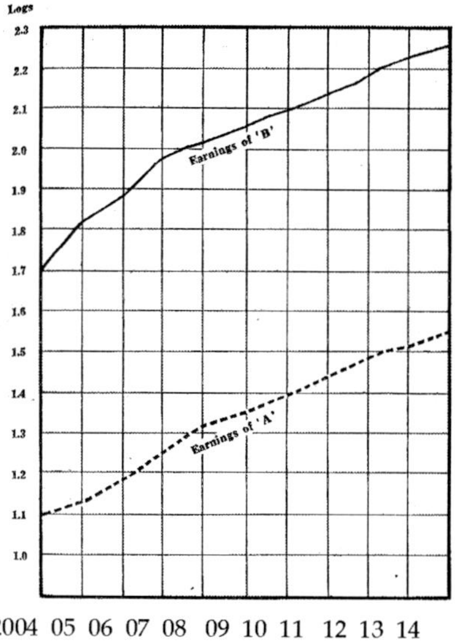

Figure 21-Average Weekly Earnings of 'A' and 'B', 2004-2014.
(On semi-logarithmic scale graph.)

proximity even though they are not plotted from actual numbers which diner widely or there is no common unit of measurement. This is because the ratios are the same at whatever points the curves are plotted. As a result, curves showing fluctuations in commercial failures in lakhs of rupees, volume of trading on the stock exchange in numbers of shares traded, coal production in tons, petroleum production in 42 gallon barrels, cement production in bags of 1 cwt., electric power in Kilowatt hours, gas manufactured in 1,000 cubic feet can all be shown in close proximity, whereas in a natural scale graph the wide disparity in figures and the different units of measurement would necessitate different scales if this had to be shown close together.

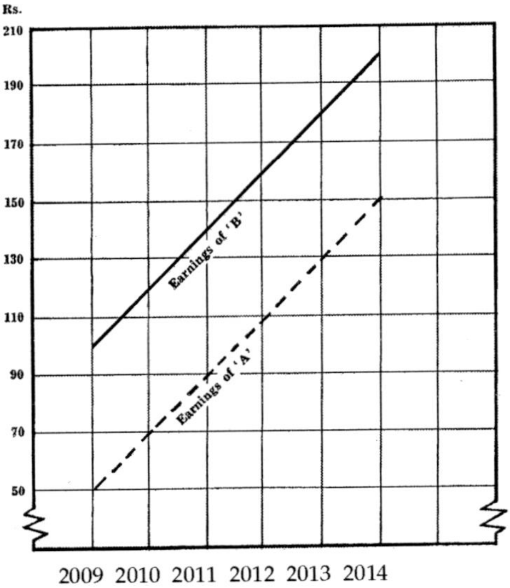

Figure 22-Annual Earnings of 'A' and 'B'-2009-2014.
(On natural scale graph.)

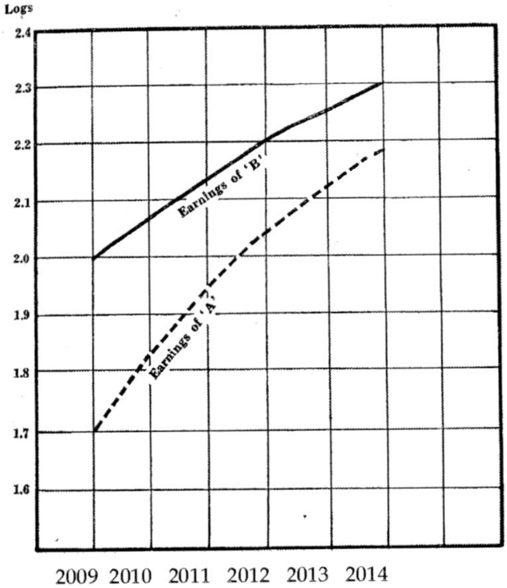

Figure 23-Annual Earnings of 'A' and 'B'-2009-2014.
(On semi-logarithmic scale graph.)

Some Hints

1. If two curves plotted by using actual figures show resemblance, there is correspondence in absolute change, hut if two curves plotted by using

logarithmic scale show resemblance, there is correspondence in proportional change.

2. The logarithmic scale is particularly important where the original numbers themselves represent ratios and not actual numbers as in the case of index numbers.

3. If the curve is ascending and is nearly a straight line, it means that the variable plotted is increasing at a nearly uniform rate and vice versa.

4. If the curve bends upward, the rate of growth is increasing and if downward, the rate of growth is decreasing.

5. If the direction of the curve in one portion is the same as in some another portion, the percentage rate of change in both parts is identical. If the curve is steeped in one portion than in another, the rate of change in the former is more rapid than in the latter.

6. If the two curves on the same ratio chart arc parallel, the percentage rates of change are equal; if one is steeper than another, the steeper curve is changing faster than the other.

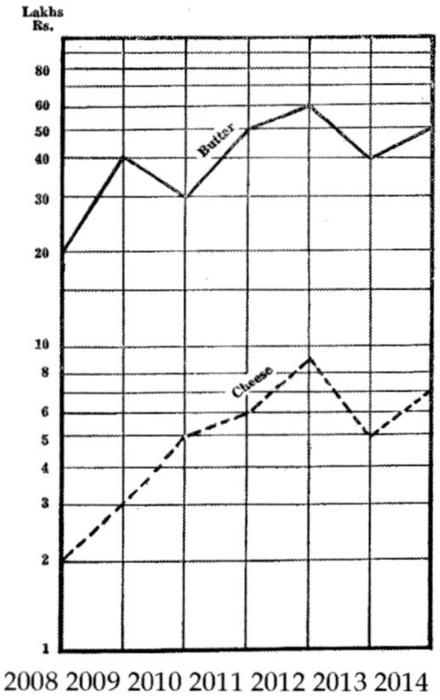

Figure 24-Ratio-scale Graph comparing Sales of Butter and Cheese.

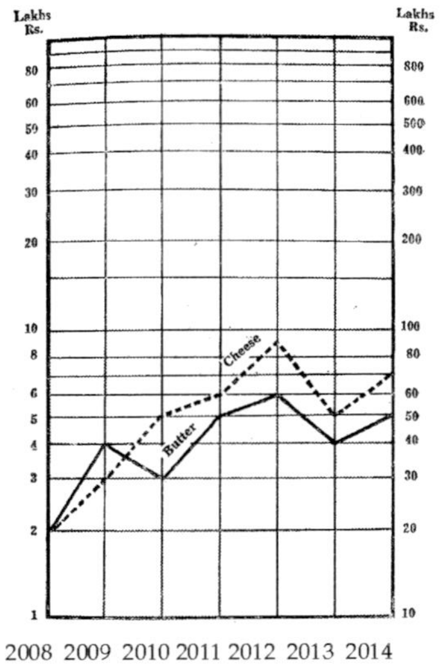

Figure 25-Ratio-scale Graph comparing Sales of Butter and Cheese. Comparison facilitated by bringing curves closer together.

7. Zero and negative values cannot he shown on semi-logarithmic or ratio charts. As no base line is necessary, the whole graph or different curves on it can be moved up or down without changing the meaning. (See Figure 24 and Figure 25.)

8. A series showing a very wide range can be plotted admirably on semi logarithmic scale hut cannot he plotted conveniently on a natural-scale Two or more scales can be used in semi-logarithmic or ratio charts. Two or more series with entirely different units of measurements can be compared on the same semi-logarithmic or ratio charts to show rates of change.

We now come to the remaining three methods of graphic presentation, viz, bar charts, area diagrams and volume diagrams.

Figure 26 shows the number of dynamos manufactured by a factory utilizing the abovementioned three methods of graphic presentation. Figure 26A shows a bar chart, where the output of dynamos is related to the height of each bar and involves only one dimensional comparison.

Figure 26B shows circle; where the output is compared by means of the area of each circle involving two dimensional comparisons.

Figure 26C shows squares where the output is compared by means of the volume of the cube represented by the squares, involving three dimensional comparisons.

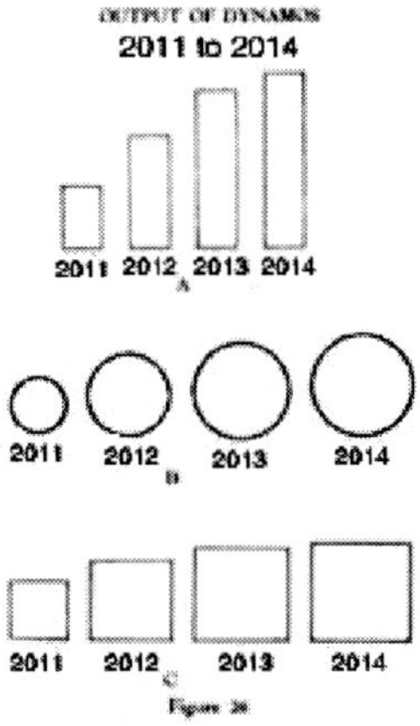

It will he immediately obvious that an observer will get the most accurate idea of the size of the output, when the data is presented by means of bars involving mere comparisons of heights as in Figure 26A. The observer will. However, get the least accurate impression, when the same data is presented pictorially by means of the volume diagram as in Figure 26C. The area diagram of Figure 26B will give a more accurate impression than a volume diagram, but less accurate impression than a bar chart. Secondly, in the case of Figures 26B and 26C the observer may be in doubt as to whether he should compare the heights or areas in the case of the former and the areas or volumes in the case of the latter, whereas in the ease of the bar chart in Figure 26A, it is obvious that the height alone could be the criterion of comparison, the base of each bar being the same. As such, when area or volume diagrams are used, it will be necessary to provide guidance for the observer by stating in the foot-note the basis on which the diagram has been drawn. In the case of Figure 26A no such mention of basis will obviously be necessity and, therefore, bar charts are preferable to area and volume diagrams.

Bar Charts

Figure 27 shows the net sales of a Company 'D ' over the period 1939-48 with a scale on the right giving a clear indication of the extent of sales during each year. As the data is for consecutive years, the space between each bar is uniform. In ease, the data shown in bar

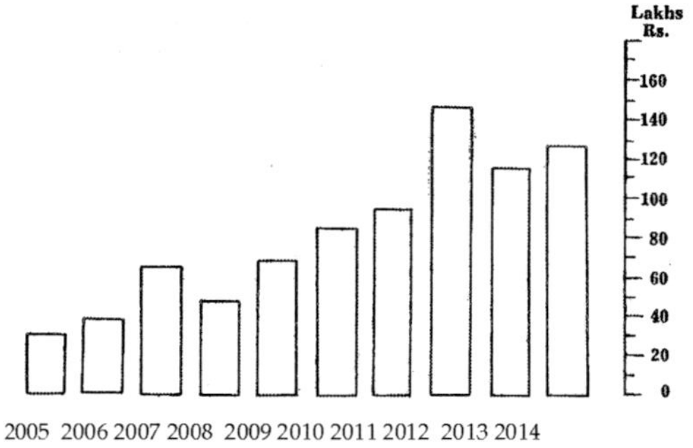

Figure 27

charts arc not for a period of consecutive years or for a period of years where the interval between each period is not uniform, it is suggested that the spacing between the bars should be graduated or kept varying so that the observer may at the first glance realize that the data does not refer to periods, which are at a uniform distance from each other.

Figure 28 shows the capital of the Company E ' between the years 1945-48 and also the dividend paid on the prevailing capital during each year. The capital is depicted by plain bars, while the dividend is depicted by bars, which arc placed adjoining the bars for capital and are shaded black. This chart shows two categories of data at a time.

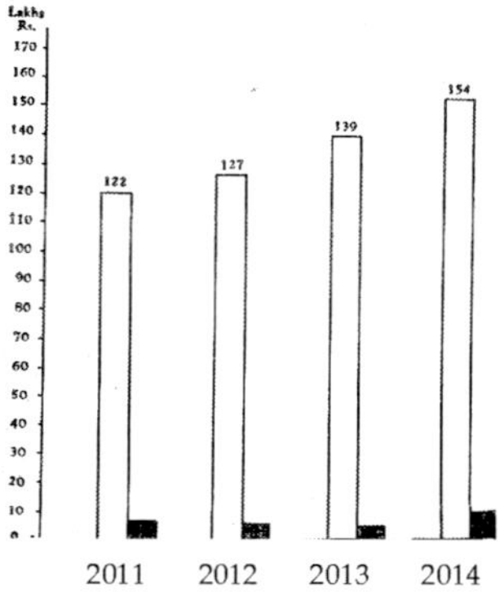

Figure 28

Figure 29 shows useful information about a steel company and illustrates very clearly (1) The average income of the employees of the company per person during the years 2004 and 2014, (2) The average cost of labour per ton of steel produced in 2004 and 2014, and (3) The average output of steel per employee during 2004 and 2014. From this chart, the observer will learn at a glance a few salient (claims, viz, that while the average income of an employee of the company increased from Rs. 768 in 2004 to Rs. 1,513 in 2014, i.e. nearly doubled over the period of 10 years, the output per workman declined from

24.3 tons CO 16.3 tons with the result that the average labour cost per ton of steel produced trebled to Rs. 93 per ton in 2004 from Rs. 31.5 in 2014.

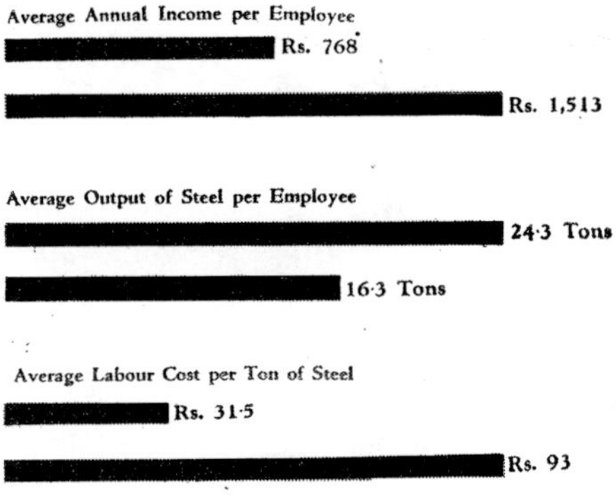

Figure 29

There is no better method of showing the various conclusions depicted in Figure 29, as a table would hardly attract enough attention to give these salient features so effectively.

It will be observed that in Figure 29 the bars have been drawn horizontal instead of vertical, as is usually the cast with bars, obviously because the horizontal placing in this case is more convenient.

While drawing bar charts, it should be remembered that as in the case of curves, co-ordinates are an aid to the reading of the chart. Sometimes, the scale alone is drawn on one side and this is all that is necessary to guide the observer. Sometimes, coordinates arc drawn in the body of the chart itself, as in the case of Figures 30, 31 and 32.

Whether bars should be shown horizontal or vertical will depend on the purpose for which they are drawn. However, when the data reduced to a bar chart is with reference to time, it is usual to employ vertical bars with the time scale along the horizontal as in Figure 27 and Figure 28. When such charts are used for comparison, it is imperative that the scale must begin with zero as otherwise the impression created will be misleading. The scale should be so selected that the individual bars are neither too long nor too short. The numbers on the scale should not be too numerous. If plain paper is used, it is sometimes useful to insert a few thin guide lines. If the bars are shaded or black the guide lines should not run through the bars. The bars should be so separated from each other that on the whole the chart looks elegant.

Bar charts are useful for illustrating business data of many kinds, such as:

Volume or value of products bought, sold, produced or in stock. Various data concerning employees.

Expenses by items, departments, depots, branches.

Profit by departments, depots, branches or by product. Progress of work in. Movement of stock.

Comparison of budget with actual.

Two Directional Bar Charts

Sometimes it becomes necessary to illustrate data where both positive and negative values have to be shown. Figure 6 showing profits, sales, and an average sale price index is a MSe in point. The profits and losses alone are indicated by bars in this Figure. The other relevant data are shown by means of curves, as that is a more appropriate method for showing the variations in the sales and the average sale price. The losses have been shown below the axis by means of bars shaded by diagonal lines, whereas profits have been shown by bars above the axis shaded black. Such types of bar charts are called two directional bar charts.

Component Parts Bar Charts

As explained while discussing curves, it is sometimes very necessary to study the fluctuations in various components, which go to make the whole or the total. The parts of the whole can be shown by means of curves as in Figure 14 where the various categories of assets and liabilities of a company over a period of year's arc shown. The same kind of data can also be presented by means of bar charts. Figure 30 is an instance of a two directional component parts bar chart. In this chart arc shown the estimated reserves, the proved reserves and the actual raisings of coal from the mines of a Colliery Company. The black shaded bars show the estimated reserves of the colliery year by year. It will be perceived that that have gone on increasing and that may have been partly due to die acquisition of more coal-bearing land or may have been due to more extensive and intensive survey of existing coal-fields, or both. The bars shaded by diagonal lines show that on actual exploration, that much quantity of coal reserves had been proved Meaning that the rest of the estimated

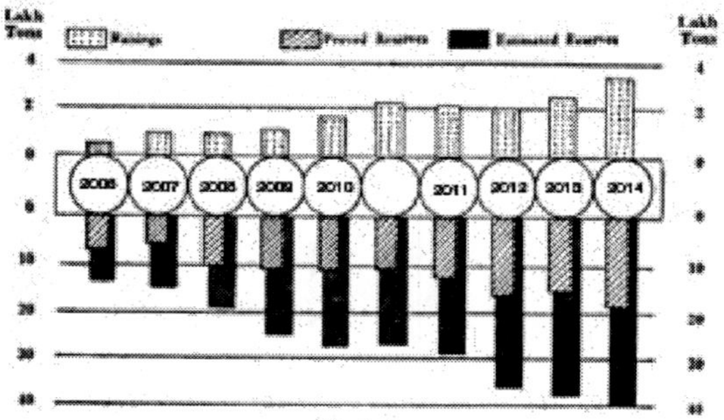

Figure 30

reserves had yet to be explored before proof of their actual existence could be established. The bars containing dots shown above the axis finally show the quantity of coal extracted from the mines during each of these years. In the case of Figure 30 bars showing the estimated reserves and the proved reserves have been shown below the axis and the raisings have been shown above the axis. Thus, the two directional method is used here, not because the values shown are positive and negative, but bemuse the bars below indicate at a glance that, that much coal remains underground, whereas the bars above indicate that which has been brought above ground, i.e. extracted.

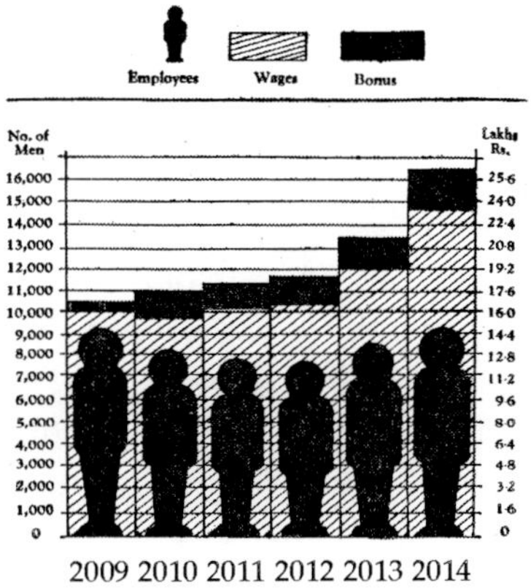

Figure 31

Figure 31 is another instance of a component parts bar chart. Here the total emoluments of workmen have been split up into two distinct classes, such as wages which arc the reward of work and paid weekly or monthly, and bonus or other benefits, which are the reward to workmen for producing bigger or better output and paid or calculated over a year usually after the profits of a company are determined at the end of each accounting year. The height of bars shaded by diagonal lines shows the wages component of the employees' total remuneration. The height of bars shaded black shows the bonus or other benefits component of the employees' total emoluments. The combined height of the two bars shows the total emoluments. It will be at once apparent from this chart that in 2009 the employees received approximately Rs. 16.8 lakhs by way of total remuneration, the bonus or other benefits paid amounted to a small sum of Rs. 80,000, which was hardly '4.76 per cent of the total emoluments, whereas in 2014 during which year the work men received a little over Rs. 25 lakhs by way of total emoluments, bonus or other benefits amounted to as much as, a little over Rs. 3 lakhs and formed nearly 11.6 per cent of the total emoluments.

The pictures of men shown in outline in each of the bars relate to the number of employees during each year and its significance would be explained later, when pictographs are discussed.

Analysis of a Railway's total operating Expenses

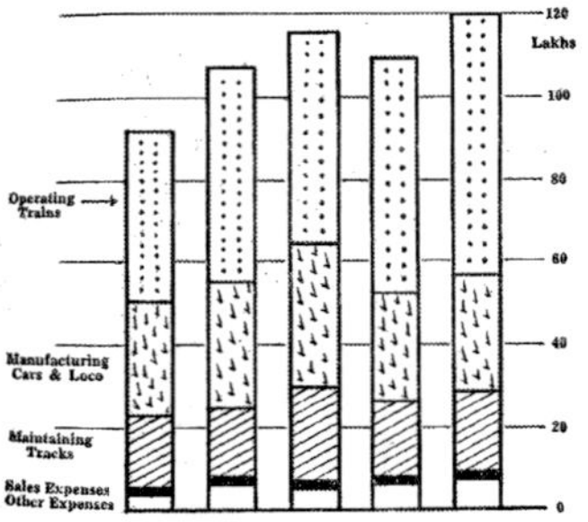

2010 2011 2012 2013 2014

Figure 32

Figure 32 is yet another illustration of component parts bar chart. In this figure are shown the components of the total operating cost of a Railway Company over a period of years. A few co-ordinate lines giving indications of the amount of expenses in lakhs are shown awl they arc. It is believed, sufficient to guide the observer in his examination of the chart.

Figure 33 is an illustration of another category of component parts bar chart more usually known as a cylinder bar chart here two cylinders are drawn of lengths proportional to the revenues of a Company 'F'. The cylinder to the left represents total revenue of Rs. 146.5 akin for the year 2005, and the cylinder to the right represents total revenue of Rs. 216.7 lakhs for the year 2004. The total revenue for each of these years has been split up into various components, such as Wages to employees, Cost of materials, Taxes to Government-Central and State, Freight on materials, Repairs to plant and machinery, Cost of Administration, Reserves ploughed back into the business and finally the Dividend paid to the shareholders. Parts of die cylinder proportional to the various components of revenue have been cm off from the cylinder and shown with a little artistry in Figure 33. 'This Figure gives a very useful comparison between the components of total revenue for the two years shown in the chart. It will at once be perceived from Figure 33 that between the year 2005 and 2014 changes of major importance took place in the strength of each component of the total revenue. Thus, while the wages and salaries to workmen shot up from 19.1 per cent in 2005 to 32.2 per cent in 2014 and cast of materials rose from 17.1 per cent to 23.5 per cent, contribution by way of taxes to the Government (Central and State) declined from 122 per cent to 7.8 per cent and the dividend to the shareholders came down from 15.1 per cent to 4.8 per cent despite a much larger revenue. The allocation to revenue suffered equally and decreased to 2.2 per cent from 6.7 per cent. There was no material change in freight costs, but cost of repairs was higher at 89 per cent or Rs. 22, lakhs against 5.8 per cent or Rs. 83 lakhs showing that the plant has either been getting worn-out, thus needing more frequent repairs or that spare pans anti replacement costs had gone up and so repairs became a more costly affair

Gantt Cigars

The Gantt chart is a device originated by Henry L. Gantt for purpose of keeping a watch on the progress of work in factory, of sales, of expenses, of performance of labour, all of which are vitally important to a business executive. For example, a schedule of work to Ix: done in a department is prepared for a number of weeks in advance after taking into consideration the orders in hand, raw materials available and on order, the number of workmen in the department, the capacity of the machines and various other factors that may be applicable in a given case in preparing such a schedule. Table 15 gives an example of such schedule. The data of Table 15 is shown in Figure 34. The schedule of work in number of units for each week is shown by fine horizontal lines with quantity of units for each week shown below. As the work in

How Revenue was Split

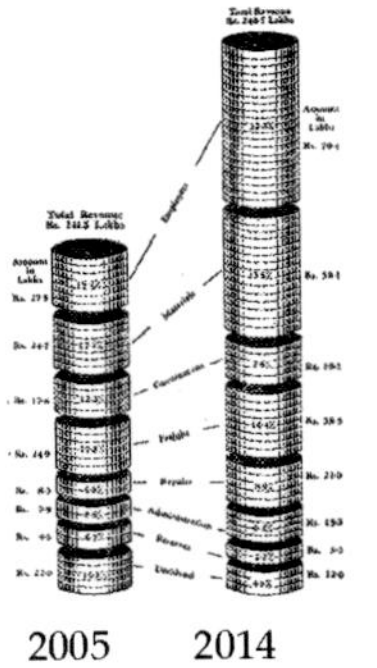

Figure 33

department proceeds, a thick bar is drawn parallel to the fine line showing the schedule. If the number of units produced are less than the units shown in the schedule the bar will fall short of the line showing the schedule.

Table 15

	Scheduled	Completed
1st Week ..	160 Units	140 Units
2nd Week ..	140 "	160 "
3rd Week ..	200 "	260 "
4th Week ..	180 "	160 "
Total : ..	680 Units	720 Units

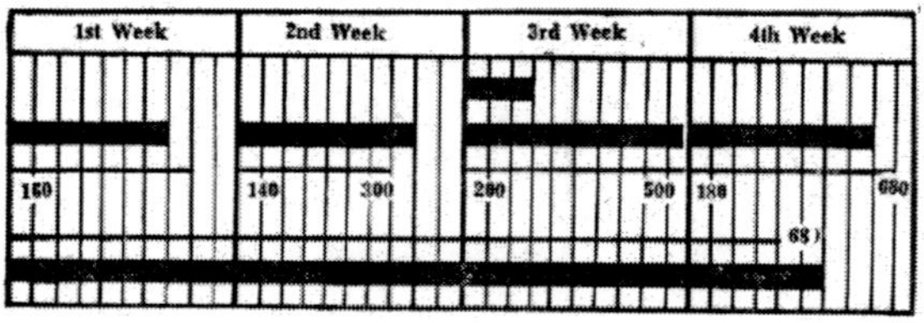

Figure 34—Progress Chart from facts shown in Table 15.

When the number of units produced is greater. the bar will over-reach the fine line showing the schedule. The continuous fine line and the continuous thick bar represent the total units scheduled and produced for a period of four weeks in question. This kind of chart enables the person in charge of getting the work done to keep track of the performance in his department. The width of the daily space in such chart usually represents the standard task or schedule of work rather than time because spaces on the chart representing time can be converted in the ultimate analysis into work units or represent amounts that can be produced in that time.

The principle of Gantt chart can be applied to any human activity. Gantt charts are most extensively used in industrial production. A few broad classifications of Gantt charts arc:

Progress Charts.
Layout and load charts.
Man and machine record charts.

The purpose of the progress chart is to show what progress is being made in the execution of a pre-determined schedule as shown before. If performance is below the standard fixed, the cause can be investigated, and the bottlenecks removed. Progress charts can be used as well for controlling sales, budgeted expenses, total factory overheads actual and applied and actual and applied overheads and budget for each department, where the method of standard costing is employed.

The man and machine record charts provide a mechanism to show the relation between what is done and what should have been done by the man or machine, for the gap between the actual and the standard derived represents idleness, which could be either voluntary or compulsory, or both, and which in any case is injurious to the company.

The layout chart provides a mechanism for advance planning of work in order of its importance. The load chart is intended to show the amount of work ahead in quantity of time for a given machine. With the issue of such charts, it becomes possible to determine the cost of idle capacity and translate it in terms of money so that it can be shown separately to advantage in the profit and loss account.

Pie Diagrams

Yet another method of presenting component parts of a total or a whole is by means of a Pie Diagram, in which only one dimensional comparison is involved. The measure of comparison in the case of a Pie Diagram is either the arcs of a circle or the angles subtended by the arcs at the centre. As for the accuracy of judgment, it is more or less the same in the case of Pie Charts, as in the case of the other two methods of presentation of components such as cylinder bar charts in Figure 33 or bar charts as in Figures 31 and 32, with the only exception that 4 and are more perspicuous in Pie Diagrams than in the other two cases.

The centre inset of Figure 35 is an illustration of a Pie Diagram and shows the locations of the shareholders of a company area-wise.

From this figure it will be observed that a very large majority of the shareholders of the company resided in the State of Bombay, \Vest Bengal anti Madras, meaning that outside these States the public had little confidence -in the integrity, the prospects and other features of joint-stock enterprise. It may also mean that the company and its products enjoyed greater popularity in these States or probably salesmanship of shares in these areas was better on account of well-established firms of brokers in these areas. Or, for that matter, it could be construed that the surplus of savings with individuals in the remaining provinces was insignificant, or if it was significant, it was employed in other channels. The bars to the right and the left of the centre inset show the various classifications of shareholders. It is very revealing to learn that there were nearly as many female shareholders as male. That joint holders were few and that institutional investors like banks and insurance companies held a good few shares and possibly held the shares in large quantities. Secondly, front the bars on the right, it will be perceived that a little more than half of the total shares issued were held by what are called small investors or middle class salaried persons, whose holdings did not exceed 100 shares. A study of this kind showing the spread of investors class-wise and strength-wise is indeed very revealing especially during these days when the rich are getting poorer and the poor arc getting better, with the transfer of wealth from one class of people to another in most countries of the world, which have come under a lighter or darker shade of socialistic influences.

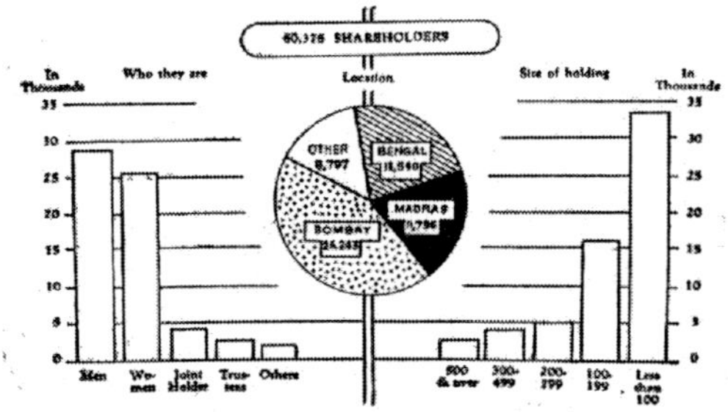

Figure 35

Figure 36 on the other hand, shows the splitting of total revenue into various components such as materials, wages, salaries, reserves, repairs, dividends, contingencies and taxes. This is an instance of a Pie Diagram, which gives at a glance the relation of every component to each of the others and also to the total revenue.

After studying Figures 31 to 33 and 35, it will be apparent that between the MO methods of presentation, Piz, presentation by Cylinder Bars and Pie Diagrams, the former is more suitable when two sets of components are too he compared, and the latter is more suitable when a single set of components is to be compared.

For the presentation of Pie Diagrams, it is usual to use the tail piece imprint of a rupee, a pound or a dollar coin. In the background of such an imprint a Pie Diagram looks unique and impressive.

When components arc very small and very many, k is advisable not to use Pie Diagrams, as sections of circles will be difficult to place and therefore not so obvious for purposes of comparisons. A vertical bar chart in such cases would be more easy M draw and less difficult to read.

How 2014 Revenue Rupee was spent

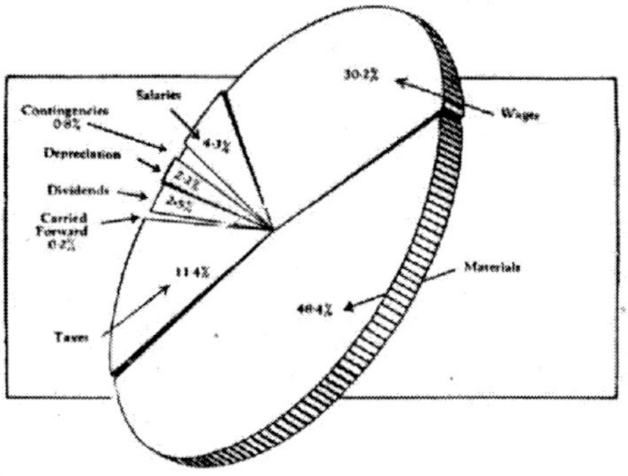

Figure 36

Pictographs

Figure 37 shows the manufacturing capacity of Standard Wagons Ltd. over a period of 20 years by means of pictures of wagons for which the data arc shown. This method of presentation is more attractive and is more likely to catch the eye of an observer, though fundamentally there is no difference between a bar chart and a pictograph. In a pictograph, there is no necessity for a scale or coordinate lines or guide lines in the body of the chart itself, though it is necessary to mention in the foot-note the quantity each picture is supposed to represent by way of guidance. From this figure an observer will require a little imagination to conclude that the manufacturing capacity of the Standard Wagons Ltd. had become fivefold during its existence of 20 years and that the rate of growth had been well sustained.

The only difference between a bar chart and a pictograph is that a bar chart is usually vertical and its height is the usual criterion of measurement, whereas in a pictograph, the pictures are presented in horizontal fashion and the criterion of measurement is the number of pictures.

Manufacturing Capacity of Standard Wagons Ltd. (1995-2014)
Each Symbol represents 1,000 Wagons

ss

The major details in connection with Figure 31 have been explained earlier without the explanation of the significance of the outline of the figure of men shown in the body of the bars. This Will now become apparent. The actual height of each man represents the total labour strength of the company during each of the six years. Thus, during 2014 it was little over 9,000 as indicated by the scale to the kit and went on decreasing till it reached 7,500 in 2012 from whence onward the labour strength grew to reach the strength prevailing in 2014 at a little over 9,000 workmen. As such, the final analysis of Figure 31 shows that though the number of workmen during 2009 and 2014 was equal, their total emoluments increased during the period of six years from Its. 16.8 laths to a little over its. 26 lakhs and that bonus and other benefits increased from a nominal figure of its. 80,000 to a link over its. 3 lakhs during the period under review.

While presenting pictographs it will do well to remember the following few hints :-

(1) The symbols used for pictures should be absolutely self-explanatory and obvious.

(2) Pictographs can only give approximate comparisons and not minute details as in the case of tables.

(3) Larger quantities in pictographs are shown by a larger number of symbols and not by the use of a larger symbol, i.e. to say a wagon five times bigger

instead of five wagons shown in the last figure would not be an appropriate method of showing that die capacity had increased five times. It would be difficult for an observer to say at a glance whether the bigger picture shown is five times bigger or six times bigger.

(4) Pictographs can only be used when comparisons are to be shown and not for showing isolated statements or details, where no comparisons are involved.

Statistical Maps

The last and the least of the statistical devices employed in presenting any given data is the use of statistical maps. Most students will be familiar with maps shown in school atlas, wherein shading devices are utilized in order to present areas with varying range of rainfalls. Thus, for instance, an area in which the rainfall is the heaviest will be shown by the darkest shade of a given colour. As the rainfall goes on decreasing, the shade of the colour goes on becoming lighter. - Similarly, in statistical presentation also, colored maps are employed to show the concentration of a given event in a particular area by means of various shades of colour after the event has been analyzed and grouped into several required categories. No particular illustration is necessary to expound this device of presentation and as such none is shown. Beyond this type of statistical maps, which are usually called hatched maps, there are others which are known as dot maps. The only difference between the former and the latter is that, whereas in the former, shades arc utilized to show the intensity of an event in a certain area, in the latter, dots are utilized to show the frequency of an event in a given area. Here again, an analogy of a school map will hold. It is the usual practice in the school maps to show wet areas and dry areas in any country, by showing the greatest number of dots in an area where rainfall is the highest and by means of most spare dots, where the areas are most arid and dry. For instance, if it is desired to show the distribution of textile mills in the country of India, the areas surrounding Ahmedabad, Mumbai, Cawnpore and Nagpur besides Madura, Chennai and Coimbatore will be spread over with small dots approximately equal to the number of mills in that area. The observer will be able to perceive at a glance that the maximum numbers of mills are to be found in Ahmedabad and Bombay and a few other places shown in the map.

However, these are not the types of maps, which one usually comes across in factories and offices, as these are mostly used in agricultural departments and various other places, where geographical conditions or analysis of broad statistical data over large fields or areas are required to be shown.

Similar to the dot maps, there are pin maps, which consist of maps mounted on backing of cork, cardboard or plastic material. On these maps information is recorded by means of pins carrying flags. It is usual in large organizations to show the tour programmers of a salesman and an organizer by pinning the places to be visited by means of such pins carrying flags and connecting the various places by means of a string to give an idea of the route being followed by the salesman or the organizer. One important feature of pin maps is that it could be readily altered as facts undergo change. It is because of this flexibility and the wide use that could be made of this device that pin maps are found to be popular amongst business executives and Government officials.

Bar Maps

Occasionally in order to depict the intensity of an event or the frequency of an event, bar maps are used. Figure 38 is an illustration of this point, where the various towns of India are divided into three main categories. In the first category arc included towns with a population of more than 2 labs and these are shown by means of dark black dots. In the second category are included towns with populations' between one and two lakhs, and these are depicted by

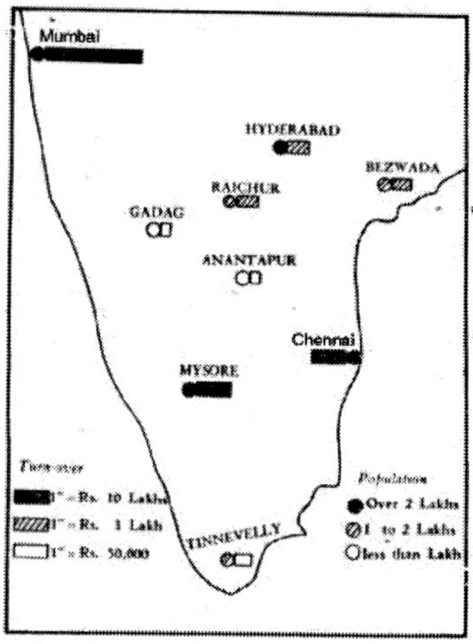

circles containing diagonal lines, whereas towns with populations of less than one lakh form the third category and are shown by means of mere circles. The sales turnover of a company is then classis field into groups. Turnover in a town of more than Rs. 10 lakhs is shown by horizontal bars, which are dark black in colour and are extended from the margin of the dot representing a particular town. Similarly, Turnover of more titans Rs. 50,000, but less than Rs. 1 lakh is represented by means of horizontal bars carrying diagonal lines, whereas turnover of less than Rs. 50,000 is depicted by means of plain bars having an outline. Of course, bars are drawn on different scales for each category of turnover, but of lengths proportional to that of the turnover. In Figure 33, only a few such bars and a few such towns arc shown, as it would be appreciated that for of statistical presentation, a wall map of large size would be necessary, and in a map of the size of a page, such data cannot be conveniently shown. Sometimes, it is the practice to mention the population of the town in fine handwriting towards the left-hand side of the bar and the number of customers and the actual turnover separated by a stroke on the right-hand side of the bar, if mentioning these figures does not make the map confusing or gaudy.

Index numbers of selling Price, Wages, and rates of Iron ore and Coal

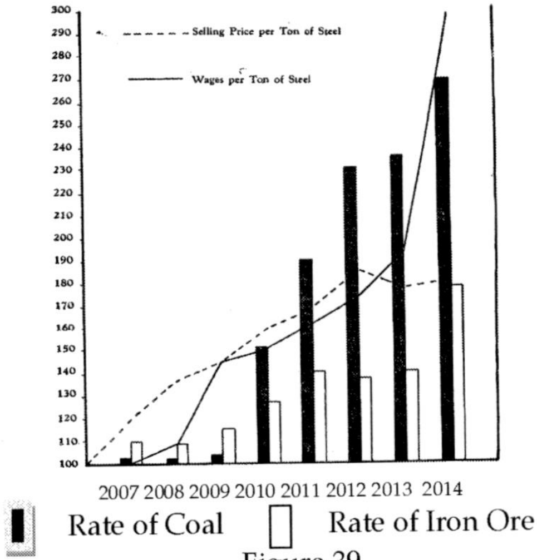

Figure 39

Now that readers have been made familiar with the various methods of statistical presentation, it would become obvious that it is not necessary, that one and one method alone could be used at a time. In fact, a combination of methods could be used for a given presentation.

******

Chapter - 22

Interpretation of Data and Report Writing

The interpretation of data which has been collected, classified and analyzed is of crucial importance. This task has to be done very carefully, otherwise a wrong interpretation may undermine the research purpose completely.

The interpretation may be for the purpose of testing some hypothesis which if proved may lead to some generalizations. If the research was exploratory or descriptive to begin with, the interpretation of data will lead to new questions leading to further research.

Meaning of Interpretation

Interpretation means drawing inferences, from the collected facts after an analytical and or experimental study. Inferences may be of two types - induction and deduction.

Inferences

Inductive | Deductive

An inference is the process of forming judgment or opinion on the ground; of other judgments or on the evidence of observation.

Induction : It is a process of reasoning from particular cases to a whole group of ideas, phenomenon or situations e.g. exploration of generalization from observed data is induction.

Induction is exploration of generalizations from observed data.

Deduction : It is a process of reasoning from given premise to a necessary conclusion. -ALL MATHEMATICAL REASONING IS DEDUCTIVE. It is the process of applying general truths to suitable instances. It serves scientific research by :

(1) Detecting questionable assumptions.
(2) Logically deducing consequences gives clarity to hypothesis.
(3) The process of rigorous deductions helps to steer clear of irrelevancies.

All progress in science and knowledge is facilitated by supplementing the simpler inductive methods by deductive reasoning.

When the sequence is

(i) Deduction precedes induction- Physical Method.
(ii) Induction precedes deduction- Historical Method.

Verification

If observed facts are used to generate a theory consistent with the facts the process is called induction.

When we ask-what are the consequences of the theory? What specific implications does our general theory reflect-it is deduction.

The act of collecting new facts which permit us to decide whether the theory is supported by these new facts or refuted is called VERIFICATION.

Major Importance of Interpretation

The use of research is only possible if the results are interpreted correctly. Its importance emerges out of the following reasons:

(i) Through interpretation the researcher shall be able to link the results of research to other studies in the same or related field.

(ii) Interpretation helps to establish new concepts which will guide future research.

(iii) Only through interpretation can research become significant.

(iv) The interpretation of the findings of exploratory research helps in creating hypothesis which will result in further research.

Inputs to Interpretations

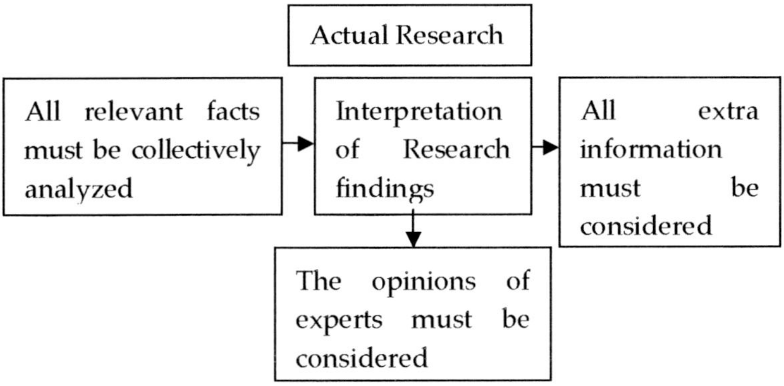

Important Precautions to Be Taken During Interpretation

(1) The data which is going to be interpreted must be appropriate, reliable and adequate. Proper statistical analysis must have been performed on the data.

(2) The researcher must avoid errors in interpretation which may arise due to false generalizations or wrong interpretation of the findings.
(3) The relationship between analysis and interpretation must not be undermined as the correct interpretation will depend upon a proper analysis of the data.
(4) The researcher must look beneath the surface and beyond obvious interpretations to find the real cause of the problem.
(5) While interpreting the results the researcher must remember the link that should run through the study binding the hypothesis to the observations and finally to the interpretations. The interpretations must retain the focus of the research.

Report Writing

The importance of a well-written report cannot be ever-emphasized! The research report contains findings, analysis of findings, interpretations and conclusions, and sometimes recommendations. Because the research report is an authoritative one-way communication, it imposes a special obligation on the researcher to provide a complete, comprehensive, clear and confident report.

Writing a report is the last step in a research study but it is a very significant one because the results of research have very little value unless they are communicated effectively to the right person, at the right time and in the right manner.

The Writing Process

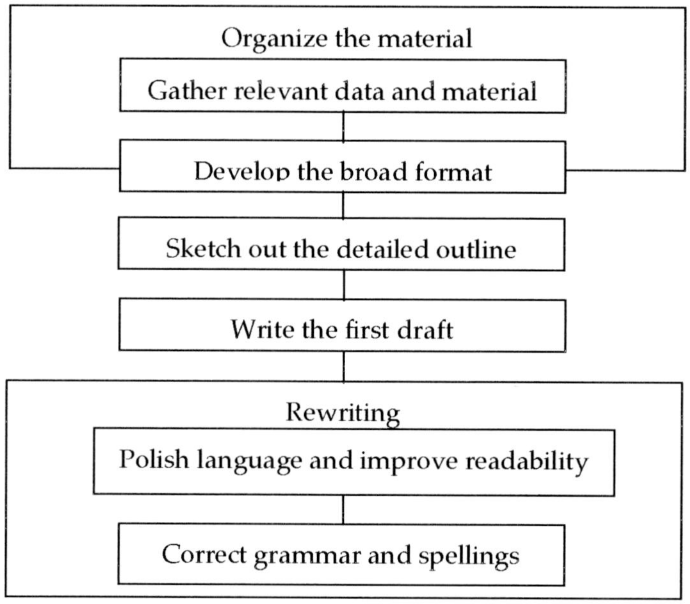

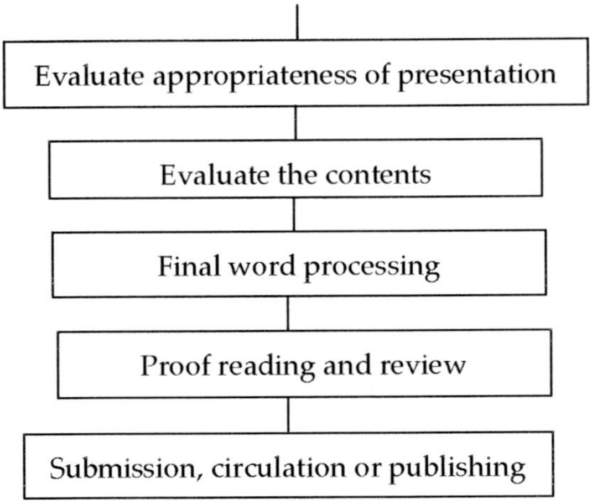

Types of Reports

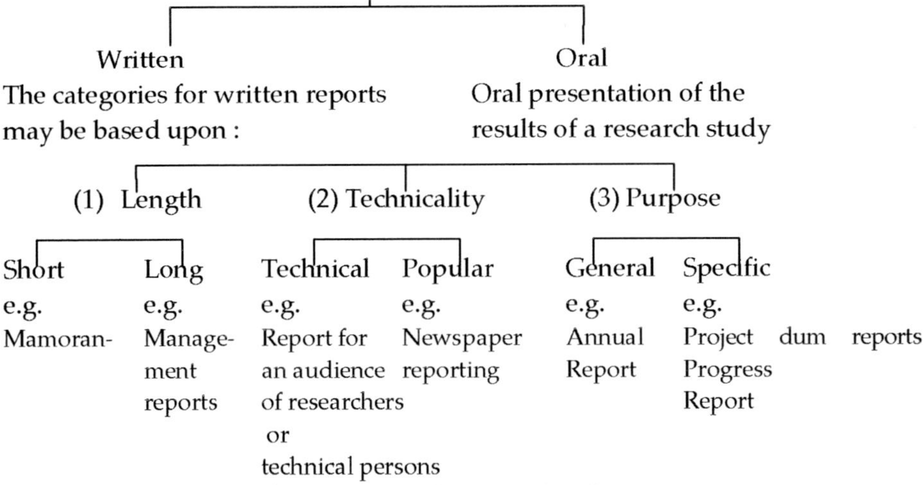

Main Contents of The Research Report

The layout of the report must be appropriate. A comprehensive report will include-

(A) The Preliminary Pages

(B) The Main Text

(C) The End Matter.

(A) The Preliminary Pages :

These should Include:

(i) **The Title Page**

The title page should carry the title of the research study, the organization for which the research is being done and the name of the researcher. The date of research being completed should be also given.

(ii) **Acknowledgements** :

The researcher will acknowledge any person or persons who have contributed in completing the research.

(iii) **Any Certification Required** :

If any certificate/s regarding the research are necessary these may be attached at this point.

(iv) **Preface** :

The preface is a brief one or two page general introduction to the topic of the research and why the researcher took up the research.

(v) **Table of Contents / Index** :

The table of contents or Index is a vital part of the report and must include the page numbers for each of the contents.

(vi) List of tables and illustrations and List of Graphs and/or Charts:

These may be given on the following pages as a ready reference.

(B) Main Text;

Introduction : This should introduce the research to the reader.

Nature and Scope of the Study : Why the study was undertaken and what geographical area and time frame it occupies.

Research Methodology: The methodology involved in the study, the research design, data collection techniques, analysis techniques and methods of interpretation should be mentioned.

Hypotheses: If the study involves the testing of hypotheses. These should be clearly stated.

Supporting Theoretical Background: Any secondary research, or theories that may be relevant for our studies should be discussed.

Results of the Primary study: A detailed presentation of the findings of the study with supporting data in form of tables and charts should be given.

Analysis of Data : The analysis of the data which has been statistically treated should be made and noted.

Interpretation of Results : The researcher should then note down his / her interpretation of the results derived from the analysis of data.

Recommendations, Suggestions, Conclusions : This forms, what is perhaps, the most important part of the research report. Any decisions taken on the basis of the research will be based upon the recommendations, suggestions and conclusions.

Summary : The summary helps to present the results briefly and presents all the information about the research in a capsule form.

(C) End Matter :

(i) Appendices : All technical data such as questionnaires, sample information. mathematical derivations etc. should form a part of the appendix. These should be numbered Appendix A. B and so on.

(ii) Bibliography : The sources consulted must be given. The correct way to give entries in the bibliography is:

1. Name of author, last name first.
2. Title, underlined or in italics.
3. Place, publisher and date of publication.
4. Number of volume.

Notes and References : Any additional information may be given here.

(iii) Glossary : This includes a list of special terms used in the research along with their definitions.

(iv) Subject Index: Sometimes a subject Index given alphabetically works as a guide to the reader for the contents of the report.

Points to Remember While Important Writing a Research Report

(1) The report should be lengthy enough to cover all the points but short and crisp enough to hold the interest of the reader.
(2) The report should provide relevant and important information leaving out winding, extra information.
(3) Technical terms used in the report should be explained in the glossary and jargon should be avoided.
(4) Charts, graphs, statistical tables and figures should be used for both readability, interest and a quick grasp of the research.
(5) The layout of the report should be as per the format discussed earlier.
(6) The report should be free of grammatical mistakes and should contain sound sentence construction. Use of quotations. footnotes, etc. should be done in the correct manner and context.
(7) The research report should be an original work.
(8) The analysis of data must he done in a logical manner.
(9) A detailed bibliography must be given.
(10) Appendices must be numbered and attached if needed.
(11) The index should be clear and the pagation should be done correctly.
(12) The report must be neat and attractive in appearance.
(13) The summary must be given in the end of the report.
(14) The objective of the study, nature and scope of the study must be mentioned in the beginning of the study and the conclusions, recommendations and suggestions must justify in the end.

Case-1
Interpretation of Data

Penta Media's business model includes projects, products and services, all housed under one roof at the Software Park, near Chennai. The scrip of Penta Media Graphics was listed during 2010 when the stock market was in the grip of bears. After opening at Rs. 21, the scrip moved sideways for some time. During the 2011 bull-run, it touched a high of Rs. 171. After retracing half of its upward movement, the scrip moved sideways between Rs. 60 and Rs. 110. During 2012: it moved upward very sharply to touch a high of Rs. 557. During the bearish phase which gripped the stock market after the nuclear blasts, the scrip touched a low of Rs. 240; followed by a high of Rs: 621. The scrip witnessed very, strong upward movements during the last quarter of 2013 to touch a new high of Rs: 2,341. After this, the correction wave set in and the scrip witnessed fourteen weeks of continuous downward movement. The financial statements stood as follows:

As a business researcher, draw inferences from this case study and answer the following two parts of the question in about 200 words each:

(i) What is the long-term trend of Penta Media Graphics- Upward, Downward or Sideways I Discuss.

(ii) What is the short-term trend of Penta Media Graphics- Upward, Downward or Sideways? Discuss.

Case - 2
Century Textiles and Industries Ltd.

Century's principal areas of business include textiles and yarn, cement and paper and pulp. It is also engaged in the shipping business and leads a consortium of companies who manufacture types. Century's performance was adversely affected during list-al 2010 by difficult market conditions in cement. (capacity utilization 81%) and paper (capacity utilization 72%). as also by steep decline in shipping freight rates. Century's biogases-based plant also encountered serious teething problems leading to heavy inventory pile-up of inferior quality paper. The cement division faced problems of severe power cuts, shortage of wagons for transport and poor quality of coal which affected production. Overall, the company's diversification into capital Intensive businesses financed through debt, led to heavy outflow by way of interest charges. The net profit per employee rose from Rs. 69,000 in fiscal-2012 to Rs. 85,000 in fiscal-2013, thereafter, it suddenly fell to Rs. 2,000 in fiscal-2014. In this light, it is proposed to cut down the strength of employees from 23,000 to 13,000 through:

(i) Compulsory retirement of workers above 50 years of age.

(ii) Voluntary retirement scheme for employees between 40 and 50 years of age.

As a business researcher, draw inferences from this case study and answer the following two parts of the question In about 200 words each :

(1)What is wrong with the Company ? Present your own diagnosis.

(2) Comment on the company's solution of the malady. What are your suggestions in this regard?

******

Chapter - 23

Laboratory Result

At one time, research institutes grew up under the impetus of an original idea or around an individual specialist. They might have also been set up with the more general aim of carrying out a series of researches in a given field. Their evolution might be continuously in response to the development of science and technology or, more generally, to the pressure of events.

Research organizations are no longer small units built around a few outstanding scientific personalities who use them principally for their own research Modern research laboratories and particularly those working on directed and applied research are part of the country's economic life and are, therefore, subject to the exigencies which govern today life of modern industrial firms. In as much as it is an essential factor in industrial development and prosperity, research can no longer be carried on anarchically, at the whims of individuals. It must be conducted on the lines likely to ensure maximum efficiency and output.

A large R & D laboratory is a complex of scientific equipment and brain-power. A laboratory supplies the organization, motivation and talent and facilities to produce the best results. Even from the standpoint of increased production and better quality products, the laboratory is the nursery of men and ideas for industry, and a large research staff may well be a real stimulus to the fruitfulness of the production department.

Some of the important factors in setting up a research laboratory are:

The extent of industrial activity.

The scope of research and development.

Different departments, such as, basic research, applied research, process research, product development, and user investigations.

Future expansion.
Mechanization.
Finance.
A laboratory management has the following expects:
A modern office and its management;
Physical facilities;
Automation and management information;
Systems and procedures;
Services;
Controls;
Staffing.

Location :

The location of a research laboratory vis-a-vis that of the production unit is very important. In the early years of industrialization, the more or less universal practice was to have the laboratory as a part of the production unit or as an adjunct to it. In those days, the laboratory mainly functioned as a testing organization which also applied itself to solution of day to day production or other problems. The extent of applied research that was handled was limited.

With the prioress of industrialization and the increase in complexity and magnitude of the demands on the laboratory, it ceased to be a mere adjunct to production and assumed independent status. The laboratory ceased to be a service organization and in addition to relating to its vitality began to develop more. Yet, the problem of location of the laboratory in relation to the production unit remained.

There are three possible locations for an R & D laboratory near the production factory, some distance away from it, and at a long distance from it. In the first case, research and production could be linked provided the size of the industry and geographical location permit. There are considerable differences of opinion on the relationship between research and production. Continual personnel contact between the research staff and plant operators will enable the research men to be in touch with reality and the operators to be in touch with research work. If the research organization is geographically 'located near the production department, the best production and research efficiency is obtained by having the research department self-contained. An important difficulty, however, is that it may not be possible to keep research away from the pressure of day to day of the factory. There has to be continuity in scientific and investigational work and scientists would like to concentrate on specific problems and find solutions, without being asked to out a side their projects and undertake other urgent problems of day to day operation. Also, planned R & D work will then not be systematically carried out. Priorities of work must not be altered, except in special case.

There are some advantages in having the research laboratory in one place, a development laboratory in a second place, and a production unit in a third place. In this case, there could be a testing and instrumentation section in the production unit for day to day work. Research and development could function on a planned basis, without being rushed to tackle problems of production, to the detriment of programmed work. In this setup, the idea and design evolved by the research laboratory can be critically examined and improved upon in the development laboratory. Similarly, what is done in the development laboratory can be improved upon in the production unit before commercial production is undertaken.

In large industries with a number of factories spread all over a country, there may he several research and development laboratories located at various centers.

Communications have to be very good for this system to succeed. A very great advantage in locating a large laboratory in close proximity to universities, libraries, learned societies, and so on, is that it is easy to recur at good scientists. Some of the greatest industrial laboratories of the world are located thus, far from production units they serve in certain cases functional specialization has been resorted to.

Setting, Layout and Design:

Where a new laboratory is to be built, it may be feasible to pay special attention to the setting. The setting may conceptualize literally and peace and solitude for the scientists and technologists to concentrate on their problems without distractions of any kind.

The layout and design of a large R & D laboratory is a specialized task. It has to take into account the current needs and the likely requirements in the conceivable future. Layout drawings have to be prepared by specialists in various fields. A master plan showing also the likely requirement of land is a must. Phased expansions keeping pace with expansion of business have to find a place.

No survey of the structure and management methods of research institutes would be complete without a consideration of the 'dynamic' aspects of the problems involved. Two aspects call for special attention; the first is the institute considered as an entity, and in particular what has been called its critical size, and the other is the human side, which constitutes the daily pattern of life in the research institute and of the lives of its research workers. The minimum size of a research institute is determined partly by the economic cost of its overheads and partly by the staff needed to carry out the prescribed tasks in the available time. It is, moreover, impossible to lay down a maximum size for a research institute, although it may be recognized that when the total staff is more than about 2,000, fresh problems arise inherent in the numbers. It then becomes difficult to maintain unit of control, human relations lose the personal touch which is their very essence, and it is hard to preserve informal contacts between departments and general services. The danger is that these difficulties may result in the formation of isolated groups without the contacts, which constitute both the sources of their own work and their contribution to that of the institute as a whole. The concept of critical size is not absolute. There is only an optimum size at any given moment and under any circumstances, which is itself, in any event, difficult to determine. From the time of its creation and through all its successive modifications, the most delicate function of the institute undoubtedly is to adapt itself and to approach constantly nearer to this optimum.

Generally, an applied research institution is larger in size as there would be several lines of investigation.

Facilities :

(i) Equipment : On the question of facilities there are wide differences of opinion. Some hold that it is the brilliance of the scientist that matters and not the amount of facilities provided to him. Others think that in modern science and technology, equipment, machinery and instrumentation are the determinants of the level and extent of R & D work. If a balanced view is taken, it seems that the amount and sophistication of facilities required would depend on the nature of research. In certain types of R & D, modest facilities may do, but in others, sophisticated facilities would be essential.

In general, a good laboratory should have adequate equipment, information and ready communication between individuals. Salary of scientists cannot be a total substitute for good research facilities. On the other hand, equipment cannot replace creativity and skill, but equipment may be essential for a creative scientist.

(ii) Information:

Introduction: With growth in complexity in modern management, top managers have become increasingly dependent on information. Information is produced with mechanical and manual aids. The information system in an organization is like the nervous system of an animal. The components of an information system perform functions, such as, sensing, classification, transmission on, storage, transformation, retrieval and display. The main purpose of an information system is to enable decision-making and coordination. When an organization is big and the problems it deals with are diverse in nature and large in scope, regular information services will be required.

The demand for information increases with the demand of problems and their solutions. Management information has vital implications for management. Information to the extent to which the manager has need for it. Information and knowledge should be accumulated, not as a luxury but for effective use.

In an information system, information is stored and it is located and recovered when needed. The collection of information should be systematic so that it can be stored and recovered without difficulty. Scientific information comprises dissemination, organization, translation, travel, scientific information comprises dissemination, organization, translation travel, scientific conferences, and symposia. A research scientist should keep himself fully posted with all the work that is being done in his field in other laboratories not only in his country but also in other countries of the world, otherwise he might be wasting his time in duplicating.

Information is an important common denominator for all organizational planning and control. Information economicis the study of the allocation of certain scarce resources of an organization to achieve the best decisions for that orga-nization. It concentrates on the allocation of resources for storage of knowledge, for obtaining information through data processing and for effective utilization of both stored knowledge and processed information by scientists and technologists in the firm.

The demand for information relates directly to the attitude towards progress. The strength of a nation lies in this healthy curiosity to see what more can be done. In an industrial economy motivation leads to progress, and self satisfaction weakness of men, industry and nations alike.

Scientific and technical information has been steadily expanding in volume and the number and diversity of user groups and user needs as also creation of new disciplines are urgent aspects of the information problem. New science and technology are built on the basis of information accumulated in the past. The efficiency of information transfer determines to a significant extent the future work in universities, laboratories, and industry. Computer aids are being increasingly used by large institutions.

In U.S.A., great progress has been made since the late in organizing scientific and technical communication on scientific lines. The U.S. Senate and House of Re-presentatives carried out a number of major studies in this field. Some of the outstanding examples are the Senate Committee on Government Operations, the Home Committees on Science and Astronautics, Education and Labour, and Government Research. There were a number of task groups appointed by the executive branch to carry out short-term analyses and assessments of scientific and technical information problems and to recommend solutions. Some of these are Reports of the Raker Panel, Crawford Task Group, the Weinberg Panel and Licklider Panel. Out of these efforts came the creation of an office of Science Information Service in the National Science Foundation (NSF), acceptance of a Presidential Reorganization Plan to establish the office of science and technology in the executive office of the President and the organization of the Committee on Scientific and Technical Information of the Federal Council of Science and Technology, which endeavored to develop standard practices and procedures among the information handling activities of Federal agencies and to foster greater coordination among them. Large scientific and technical lobrieties and libraries took steps to enhance the effectiveness of their communication programmers. Strong science and technology care to be recognized as a national necessity, and adequate communication as a prerequisite for strong science and technology.

There is ever growing need to sift, evaluate, compile and consolidate the rapidly increasing store of scientific and technical information. The most effective means of coordinating and focusing scientific and technical communication efforts were recommended by the Weinberg Panel. The basic element of strength in a country's overall scientific and technical communication effort is the participation of the members of the scientific and technical community. These activities should be responsive to the needs, desires and innovative ideas of the scientific and technical groups. They must be flexible enough to adapt to changes in user deeds and communication techniques. The administration of scientific and technical information programmers should represent logical and efficient division of functions. Information activities should be planned so that they evolve constant attention to simplification and consolidation of existing knowledge.

New information handling technology offers scope for promising advances, but it also throws up difficult problems. The application of advanced technologies is a challenging problem.

Systems: Information is the basic requirement in decision making. The growth in size and complexity of companies has emphasized the need for improved information systems in recent years. Some aspects are information system theory and design., man-machine relationships, language data processing, artificial intelligence, mechanization of library process, non-numerical applications of digital computers, storage and retrieval, automatic publishing, command and control, information display, and so on.

In a complex organization, the net work approach to planning is essential for improvement of management planning, and control effectiveness as development programmers are rapid and contain many uncertainties.

Qualitative and quantitative data are required in various forms for decision making. Although decisions cannot be made by the instruments of management they are essential aids to management. Try an age of dynamic changes unless a manager is skilled in understanding and utilizing the systems planning methods that are available by way of advanced management information and control systems, he cannot optimize time, cost and man-power o utilization. The elements of the system had to be understood by utilizing information systems and then only can result a sound mature system designed and implemented. The manager needs a master plan with an up-to-date picture of the operation at all times. General types of information systems are:

Product-related systems;

Operations-related systems;

Administrative-related systems.

Some specific types are the following information systems :

Programmed Evaluation and Review Technique PERT);

GANTT Chart;

Network Planning,

Critical Path Method (CPM) ;

Minimum Cost Expediting (MCX) ;

Resources, Planning and Scheduling Method (RPSM)

Network planning can be adapted to electronic data ,processing and this makes it possible for a computer to be used. A computer can perform the time analysis calculations and relate cost and man-power data to the detailed plan linking these with management information to the calendar scale and predicting when actions must occur and the resources must be available. The computer is to do the job less expensively and in a shorter time than is possible by human efforts. These are not only the direct benefits that are conferred by the computer but also the indirect benefits, such as, making available real time information which enables and promotes correct decisions being taken by management. The benefits of a computer are :

Safety;

Economy;

Accuracy;

Capacity to handle large volumes
of' information;

Partial interpretation;

Legible, uniform results.

The problems of a computer are :

The aura of mystery;

Discipline and accuracy;

Administrative problems;

Access to the proper computer with the proper programme;

Cost of developing new or modifying programmers;

Difficulties in using a poorly designed programme.

Physical storage of information is effected by the following means:

Ultra high speed; diodes, read-only-storage;

High speed immediate access: magnetic core thin film;

Bulk immediate access: magnetic core;

On-line direct access: magnetic drum, disc, cartridge;

Off-line magnetic tape, removable disc or cartridge.

The need for a national information policy and for government support for storing, retrieving, and supplying scientific and technical information is growing. The expenditure involved is likely to be large. Science has an international character, and economies are possible by international division of labour between disciplines and by collaboration between various information centers.

Computer-aided printing has recently made possible an integration of two functions of communication ; primary publication and secondary retrieval. The introduction of automation to duplicate printed material quickly has proved of great use, but this appears to be only the beginning of further innovations.

The computer which was invented at the end of the Second World War, has worked wonders in the scientific and technological world. It may in future be the main information processor. Computer speeds may increase to a level of 1,000 million operations per second in the next 10 years. The future computers may be small, powerful and inexpensive.

In U.S.S.R., the entire processing of world literature and dissemination of the information to branches of science and of the national economy has been centralized. The information disseminated is in the form of newsletters, reviews of technical and economic aspects of the most important problems, abstract cards, and so on. It is a descending flow of information.

The satellite is a fantastic addition to man's alternatives for communicating with his fellows. A worldwide network of communication satellites will make it possible to transfer information across oceans with clarity and ease. Image transmission over communication channels will become common place in the next few years. Raid copying may change office routines.

Library : There is an enormous amount of published information concerning science and technology. If all or even a significant part of this information is made use of, it can be of inestimable value. The library and documentation department of the organization should be charged with the responsibility of locating and making available whatever knowledge and experience may advance its activities. A library and documentation service is sometimes called "Information Service." The library service secures, assembles, and presents in usable form all the information that relates to specific subject areas.

A general library serves the general public, whereas a special library provides specific information. A special library should be able to produce information which may not even be published. A special library for science and technology maintains a regular and systematic information service for the immediate and foreseeable future needs of the enterprise. In the last few years, the rate of growth of scientific literature has been phenomenal. Traditional methods of filing and indexing have given place to mechanical devices, such as notched or punched cards sorted by electro-nice computers.

Scientific and technical libraries have been established by government agencies, research institutes, professional societies, trade associations, hospitals, and so on. An ideal library is planned and established as an integral part of an organization. The library should be an independent department of the research organization and its head should rank with the heads of the other departments. The chief of the library must be given strong support to enable the library to serve its purpose. The main functions of a scientific-technical library are:

Collection of books, periodicals, and other publications;
Special subject references, files and indices;
Supply of currently published information by personal notifications, library bulletins, special service publications, etc;
Circulation of books and routing of periodicals;
Piling and indexing of internal reports and technical correspondence;
Reference services;
Compilation of bibliographies and organization of reports;
Editorial assistance with publications;
Translation of foreign language publications;
Personalized service..

Perhaps the best set-up is a central library with supporting units in other locations, such as, the concerned specialized departments.

Laboratory research should be preceded by an adequate library research. Important discoveries are often made in the library and subsequently tested in the laboratory. A discovery is often .a combination of old ideas which come to a person in a library.

The humidity and temperature of a library should be controlled and should be between 30 and 50 per cent, and 18 and 24°C respectively. A library should be air-conditioned.

The following is a suggested list of equipment in a scientific-technical library :

Duplicating equipment;
Microfilm reading machines;
Hand viewers;
Microfilm cameras;
Micro text reading machine;
Stenciling or mimeographing equipment; Hectograph;
Multiline.

A science-technology librarian has to handle a heterogeneous mass of specialized materials. He should be familiar with the experience of others in dealing with similar problems. The planning of a library service is a challenge. Books should he selected systematically so that the broad burnoose and interest of the organization are served. The types of books that are included in a science-technology library are texts, monographs, handbooks, encyclopedic works, dictionaries, and treatises on scientific works.

A translation section capable of translating from modern language to English is a must. A library service is to ensure that nothing worthwhile in a particular field is missed. Periodicals contain the latest developments in science and technology. Many libraries spend a larger part of their budget for subscription to Periodicals than on our-'chase of books. A thorough knowledge of the principles of cataloguing, classification, and subject headings form a firm foundation for indexing in a library. Indexing of published information may be carried out by automated Procedures on a national or even an international scale. It should be possible to find the required information easily.

Given a responsive organization structure and a consultative corporate management culture within the laboratory, consideration of total resources and total finances will prevail. The information, storage and retrieval system should function like a bank. A modern library is not a passive repository of printed material. It has -to be a live and dynamic institution. An extensive library is a great asset to any laboratory. Scientists should be encouraged to spend a significant part of their time in the library. The library is a store-house of information.

The tremendous increase in scientific journals and technical literature that is a feature of science and technology today makes information retrieval extremely important. That is why library service is vital. Three to five percent of the research budget is recommended to be spent on the library.

Documentation Service: Documentation service is the name given to reference service when the emphasis shifts from macro to mascent-micro thought and from the generalist to the specialized reader. An applied research library with a small number of specialized readers should have a documentation service including a good translation service. The documentation centre may have the following sections:

Documentation Prope;
Translateon service;
Duplicating machines;
Printing.

List of current scientific literature should reach the hands of scientists before the periodicals covered by them arrive from foreign countries.

Publications : An R & D laboratory should issue publications for internal and ext renal information. The annual report, research and development reports, project reports, scientific and technical reports, and bulletins are some of these. A useful system is that of reciprocity between R & D laboratories in the same country and in other countries in respect of exchange of publications.

Environment:

Environment is one of the most important factors in human behavior. Environment is undergoing continuous change and requires continual adaptation. Environment determines to a great extent the effectiveness of utilization of the skill of scientists and the results of research. The effectiveness of the work of a scientist is sensitive to the environment and to working relationships. A high morale can be maintained in a favorable environment. There has to be an atmosphere of confidence and a spirit of helpfulness. True, great discoveries and inventions and theories have sometimes come out from under deplorable conditions, but modern industry cannot plan on such a basis.

Environment affects morale, team spirit, loyalty, dedication and productivity. Young scientists should work in an atmosphere of discipline but not regimented freedom. The environment must be adequately stimulating. An individual may be creative but this creativity has to be nursed by the environment. What is wanted is refreshing lack of formality in the relation s between scientists.

Work environment must be made more effective in releasing the creative powers of scientists. Involvement in the common cause and adequate communication and compensation are key motivating factors. A good laboratory is characterized by bright scientists producing good research. A good laboratory administration is essential, but by itself it will not produce ideas; it only establishes an environment in which ideas can grow and thrive. A laboratory management may not be creative by itself but it should enable creative scientific work being done. R & D should have a stimulating atmosphere. R & D organizations provide not only facilities for their members but also an environment which may either stimulate or inhibit the performance of scientists. The director should ado Pt techniques which increase the achievement its of his laboratory.

The physical and physiological factors in the environment of a laboratory are - temperature, light, humidity, noise, air-flow, color decor, atmosphere, and safety, each forming a specialized field.

The research laboratory of the General Electric Company near Schenectady in U.S.A. is a scientist's dream. Located in sylvan surroundings in an ideal setting, it has some of the best physical facilities for research and some of the most brilliant scientists of the world. If a laboratory can be a heaven, it is the one at Schenectady.

Relations with Other Bodies:

A laboratory does not exist in isolation. It should have good relations with competitors, non-competitive groups, trade associations, technical societies, scientific publishers, etc.

******

Chapter - 24

Electronic Mail (E-Mail)

The conventional mailing by post can take several days to travel across the country and weeks to go around the world. That is why nowadays it is referred to as 'snail mail'. In recent times, e-mail or electronic mail is being used to send and receive messages. It saves time and money, is fast, easy to use and less expensive than the post. We can send e-mail practically to anyone with an e-mail address, anywhere in the world. So what is e-mail? In its simplest form, e-mail is an electronic message sent from one computer to another. We can send or receive personal and business-related messages with attachments like pictures or other documents.

Just as a letter or document stops at the different postal stations along its way, e-mail is passed from one computer to another as it travels along the network. Each computer reads the email address and routes it to another computer until it eventually reaches its destination. It's then stored in an electronic mailbox. With the Internet, this whole process usually takes just a few minutes, allowing us to communicate quickly and easily with millions of people around the world anytime of the day or night, for the cost of a local phone call.

Until recently, e-mail on the Internet was good only for short notes. We couldn't send attachments like formatted documents or graphics. With the advent of MIME (Multipurpose Internet Mail Extension) and other types of encoding schemes, like UUencode, not only can you send messages electronically, but we can also send formatted documents, photos, sound files, and video files as attachments.

Email Messages

E-mail messages are a lot like letters. There are two main parts: header and body. The header contains our name and address, the name and address of the person it's being sent to, the name and address of anyone who is being copied, the date of the message and what the message is about (subject). Just like with regular' mail, we need the correct address. If we use a wrong address or mistype it, our message will get bounced back to us - the old 'Return to Sender, Address Unknown' routine. When we receive an e-mail from someone, the header tells us where it came from, what it is about, how it was sent, and when. It acts like an electronic postmark.

The body is the meat of the message where we write the content of what we want to communicate. The key to make people read our messages are simplicity, directness, and brevity. Our E-mail says a lot about our values, the attention to detail, and the reputation of the organization we represent. Here are some guidelines which will improve the quality of our e-mail writing style:

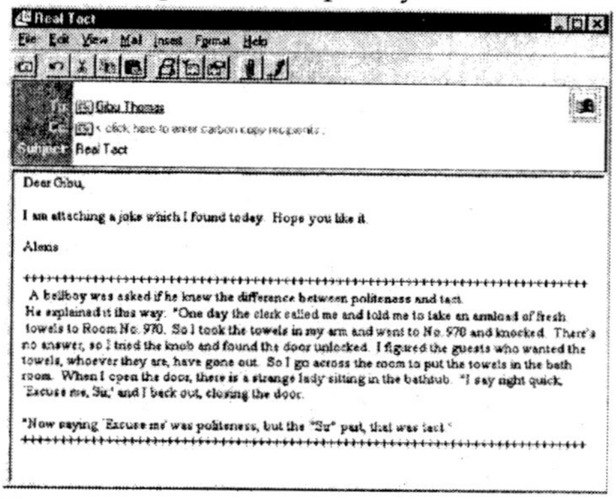

Figure 1. Structure of an e-mail message

- Sound human.
- Write it the way we would say it - use everyday language.
- Vary the length of our sentence.
- Be friendly, and use humor to break up the tension of what we have to say.
- Look sharp. Good writing is 90% clarity, and half of clarity is appearance. No one likes facing a long unbroken block of text characters. Put a blank line between paragraphs to help us organize our thinking. If we have six points to make, number them as such and indent each one.
- Use the technology. A memory-resident spellchecker or thesaurus will help we avoid the embarrassment of a misspelled word or a word used incorrectly.
- Compose our messages off-line. A regular word processor is much more powerful than the text editors used on most e-mail systems. Read the message before sending it, we will be amazed by the numbers of mistakes that have crept in.

- Most e-mail programs these days let we insert what's called a signature at the bottom of the message. This can be anything from a clever quote to some additional information about us, like our title and company name or other e-mail addresses we have.

Customizing our E-Mail Programs

If we have a TCP/IP dial-up access then we can use many of the available e-mail programs, like Microsoft Internet Mail, Netscape Mail, Eudora, etc. But if we have a Shell account then we can use the e-mail software that is available with VSNL, called Pine.

Most of the e-mail programs, like Microsoft Internet Mail, Netscape Mail, Eudora, etc. have a lot of things in common, even though there will be slight differences. But if we know how to customize one, then it is a child's play to do the same with others. We will treat Pine separately since it is quite different from the other programs.

The Microsoft Internet Mail program is shown in Fig. 2.

As we can see, the mail program toolbar contains the icons for the most frequently performed tasks, like composing a new message, replying to a message, forwarding a message, deleting a message, etc. Below that we can see the current folder's name And if we press the combo box bottom, we can see the

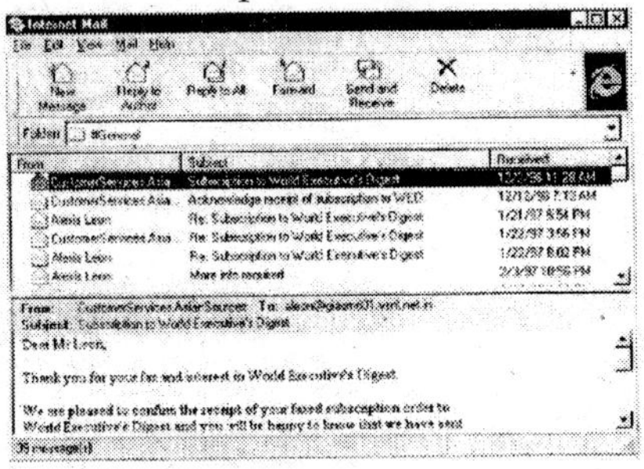

Figure 2. Microsoft internet Mail program

list of all available folders. Most mail programs will have four folders as default - the inbox, outbox, sent items and deleted items. The exact names may vary from program to program but they perform the same functions. The inbox is where all the incoming mail are downloaded to, the outbox contains those that we have composed and are ready to be sent, and once sent they will be moved to the sent items. The mails, which are deleted, will be moved to the deleted items folder. The deleted items folder has to be emptied to permanently delete the mail items.

Managing our Mail

We can organize our mails into different folders, so that managing them will be much easier. If we keep all the incoming mails in the inbox and the outgoing mails in the outbox, soon the number of mails in these folder will become unmanageable. We can create as many folders as we want and we can move the mails between the various folders. To create a folder in the Internet Mail, click on the 'Folder' menu item in the 'File' menu and we will be presented with three options: Create, Delete and Compact. We can click on the 'Create' item and a dialog box will appear asking us to enter the name of the new folder.

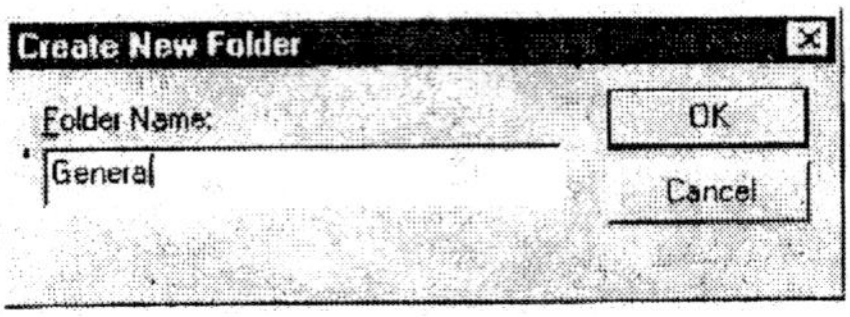

Figure 3. Creating a folder

We can enter the folder name and press the OK button; the folder will be created. Similarly, to delete a folder click on the 'Delete' item and the list of the existing folders will be shown to you. Select the folder you want to delete and press the OK button. When we delete an existing folder, all the contents of the folder will also get deleted. We can only delete the folders that we have created; in other words, we cannot delete the four default folders. It is a good practice to compact the folders once in a while, to free up unutilized space and thus increase the available disk space.

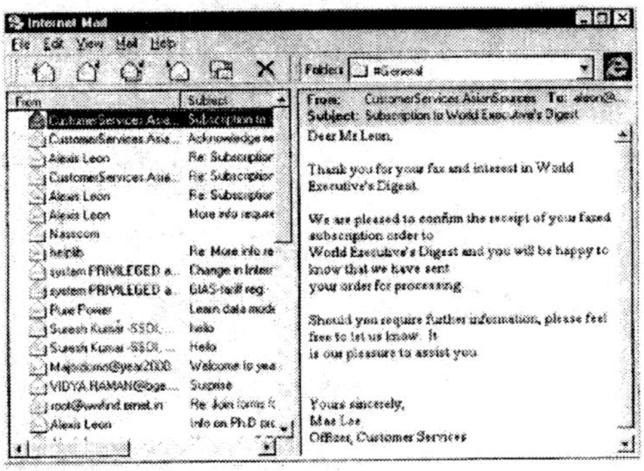

Figure 4. We can customize the mail program to suit our needs

We can customize the look of the mail program. We can remove the toolbar, or hide the text of the toolbar icons, change the preview pane to split the screen vertically, sort the mails in each folder by received/sent date, address, subject. Etc. Figure 4 shows the same mail program with a different look.

We can access all the frequently performed functions by right-clicking (context sensitive menu) the mouse. For example, if we want to move a mail to a folder, select that mail, right-click on the mouse and choose the folder from the pop-up menu, as shown in. Fig. 5.

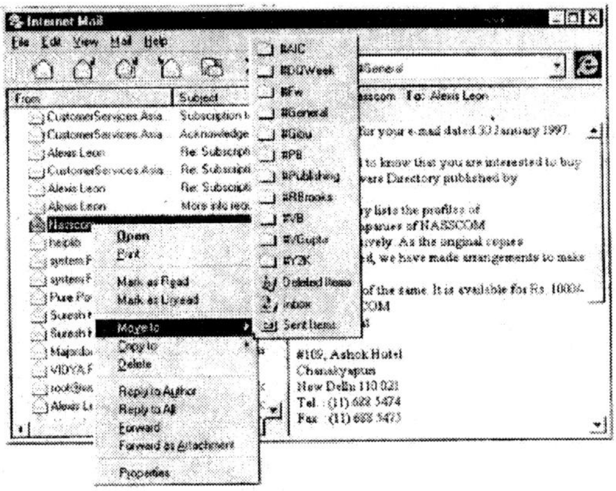

Figure 5. Frequently performed functions can be accessed by accessed by right-clicking the mouse

We can use the same method to copy or delete the mails, reply to the mail, forward, etc. -The functions that are available on the toolbar can be accessed by this method also.

The Zen of 'E-Mailing'

Just like us send and receive letters, we consigned and receive electronic mails also. But e-mail programs give us many more options. We can reply to the author of a, message by pressing a button-we need not type in the address or the subject, the programs are intelligent enough to automatically put the electronic address of the person whose mail we are replying to and prefix the subject with 'Re:' to indicate that it is a reply. The programs will also include the original mail (if we set that option) as part of the reply, which is a great help in identifying the mail, especially when a person receives hundreds of mails a day. We have two options for replying to a mail: 'Reply to Author' and 'Reply to All'. The difference between the two is that, in the first case, the reply mail will be sent only to the person who has sent the mail to you. In the second case, your reply will be sent to all persons, to whom the copy of the original mail was sent. If the mail was sent to us only then using 'Reply to Author'; here, 'Reply to all' does not make any difference at all.

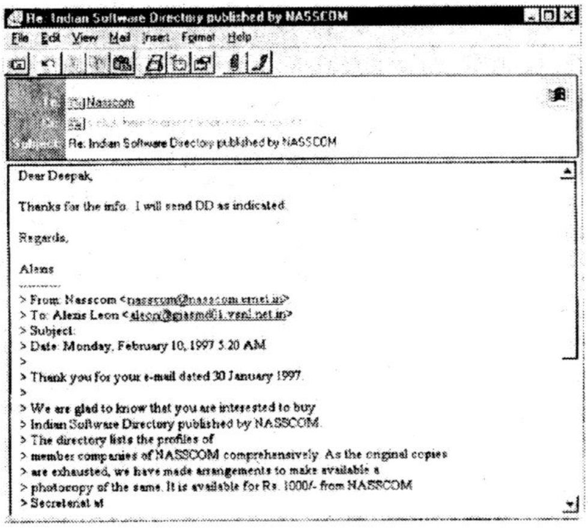

Figure 6. Replying to a mail

For example, if we want to reply to the mail that we have received from NASSCOM, we will highlight the mail by clicking on it and then, will press the reply button. The 'To' address, the 'Subject' (with Re :) and the original message will automatically appear. We just have to type in our reply and send the mail. Notice that the original message is marked with a '>' sign this is to indicate that it is part of the original message and the message is being replied for the first time. If we receive a mail from NASSCOM again then the message that we have just typed in will have a '>' sign and the first message will be marked with '>>' Thus the number of '>' signs will get incremented by one as the mail is sent back and forth. But it is better to limit the previous message to the last one or two; otherwise, the length of the mail will keep on increasing which, in turn, will increase the time taken to send the message because of the increase in the file size.

Some programs allow us to use other symbols 'instead of '>'. But the '>' symbol is the most commonly used one. -

Another task that we can accomplish with considerable ease while using the electronic mail is forwarding a message that we have received. The difference between replying and forwarding is that we reply to the person who have sent the mail, but we can forward a message to anybody we like. Most e-mail programs will let we add any message we want. The message that is being forwarded will be indented with '>' symbol as in the case of replying. We will have to enter the e-mail ID of the person(s) to whom the message is forwarded. Most e-mail programs will prefix the subject of the forwarded message with 'Fw:' In the case of forwarded messages also, the number of '>' will indicate the number of times the message was forwarded. Figure 7 shows the same message from NASSCOM being forwarded to another person. Notice the different 'To' address and the 'Fw:' prefix to the subject line.

Figure 7. Forwarding a message

We should configure the mail program before we can start-sending and receiving the message. We should give the IP ad-dress of the mail server (we will have to contact our service provider for more details), our name and e-mail ID (which will be used for replying to us), etc. as shown in Fig. 8.

If we are the only person using the mail program, then we can key-in our username and password, and ask the program to save or remember it so that every time we connect to the mail server we don't have to enter the password and username, One Problem with this is that anybody who has access to our machine can access our mailbox. The previous figure shows the options dialog box where we will have to enter our details like name, e-mail ID, server details, username and password, etc. If we press the 'Advanced Settings ...' button we will be shown the Advanced settings dialog box where we set options like the server timeout duration (for how many minutes should the pro-gram try to send or receive a message), whether to leave a copy of the mail that we have downloaded on the server and, if yes, for how many days should it be kept on the server, etc.

We can customize the way in which we send the mail. In the options dialog box in the 'Send' tab we set all the necessary options. We can do this by simply checking the options that we want.

We have seen that the usual practice is to include the original message in the reply. If we don't want that, then we can uncheck that option. We can decide whether to send the mail in Text format or in HTML format. The new

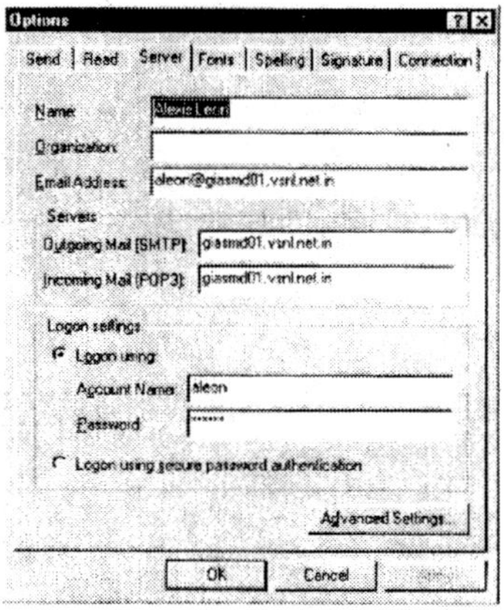

Figure 8. Configuring the mail program

mail programs are capable of reading the mail in HTML format. The advantage of using HTML format is that we can add colour and other formatting like bold, italics, bulleted or numbered lists, etc. The disadvantage is that not many mail programs are capable of reading the mail in the HTML format, so if the person who receives the mail does not have a program which is capable of reading the mail in HTML format, then he will get a lot of HTML tags, which can be quite annoying. So it is better to select text format, at least for a while. We can also decide whether to indent the original text with a symbol like '>' when replying or forwarding.

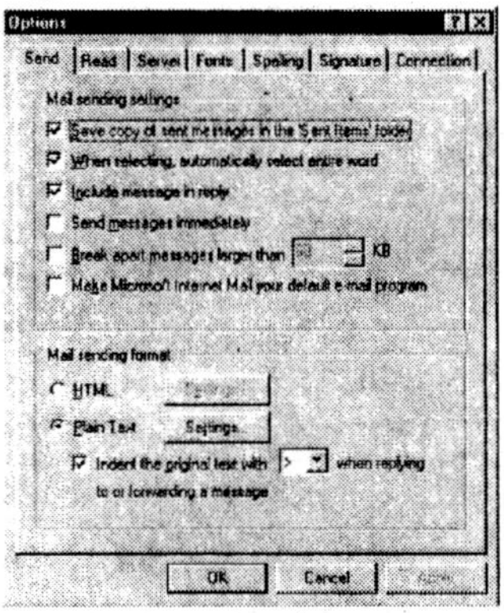

Figure 9. Options menu to customise the way in which you send the mail

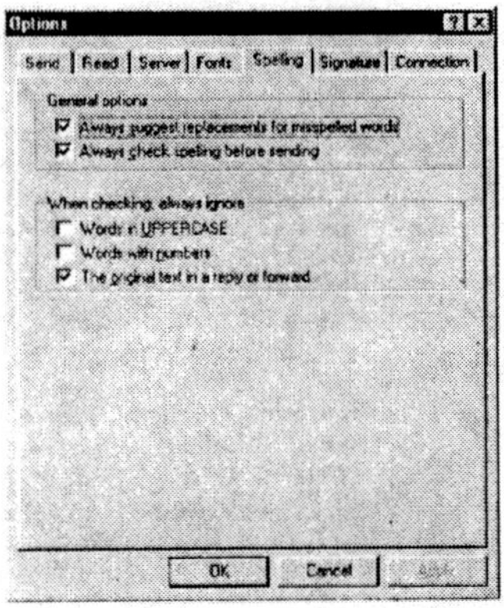

Figure 10. Enabling automatic spell checking

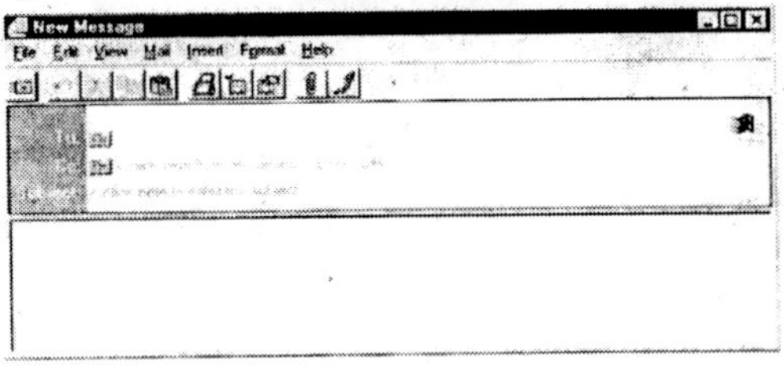

Figure 11. Composing a new message

We can use the spell checking feature of the e-mail programs so that spelling errors can be avoided. Some programs will allow us to set the option in such a way that spell checking is done for all the outgoing messages. If our mail program has these features then do enable it. It is a very useful feature because it will prevent any mail from being sent without a spell check. We can enable this feature by checking the appropriate boxes as shown in Fig. 10.

We have seen the guidelines to be followed in composing a mail message. Now we will see how to compose a message. Click on the 'Compose new message' button on the toolbar. We will get an empty mail form, which will have the following parts as shown in Fig. 11.

- 'To' - enter the e-mail address of the person(s) to whom the message is sent.
- 'Cc' - enters the e-mail address of the person(s) to whom the copy of the message is sent.
- 'Subject' - enters a brief description as to what the message is about.
- 'Body' - enters the actual message here.

Some mail programs have the facility to send blind copies. If this feature is available, the other recipients of the mail will not know that we have sent a blind copy to another person. Almost all e-mail programs have the following features: address book, signature feature, and attachment facility. Now we will see how to make use of these features.

Address Book

An address book is a place where we can store the information about the people with whom we correspond. The advantage of having a person's details in the address book is that we don't have to key in those details each and every time we send a message. We just have to select the person's name and the e-mail ID will automatically get inserted. A typical address book will look like the one shown in Fig. 12.

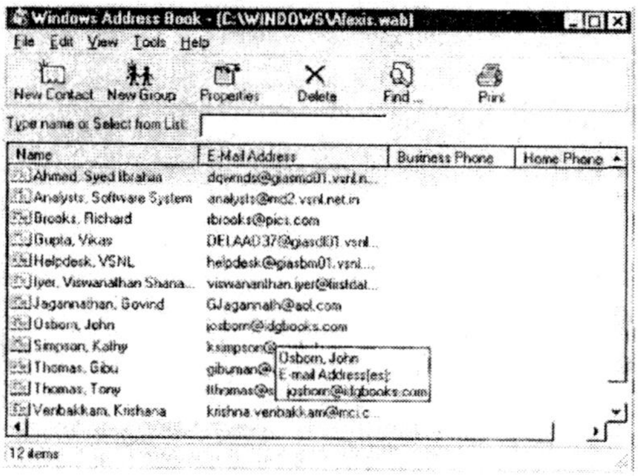

Figure 12. Address book

We can add new addresses to it, create groups (so that when we want to sent a mail to all members of a group, we need only to select the group instead of adding each person's ID), modify the details, and delete a person's name form the book, if a person has more than one e-mail ID then we can set one among the m as the default ID.

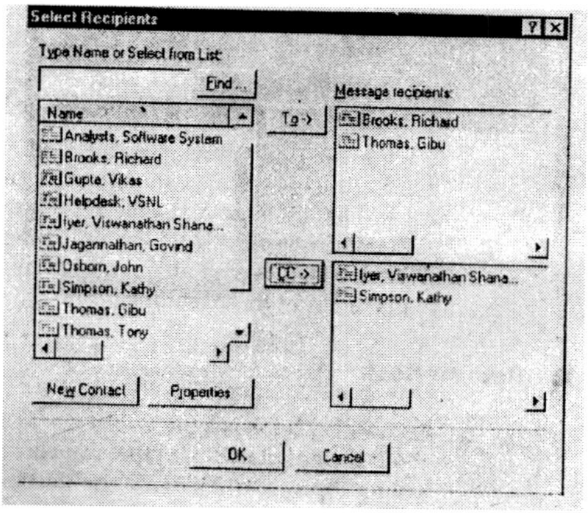

Figure 13. Selecting the Recipients

When we went to insert the e-mail ID of a person, press the small icon by the side of the 'To' or 'Cc' columns and the contents of the address book will pop-up.

We can select the names and it will appear in the respective columns as shown in Fig. 14.

Figure 14. Entering values for the 'To' and 'Cc' fields

Signature Feature

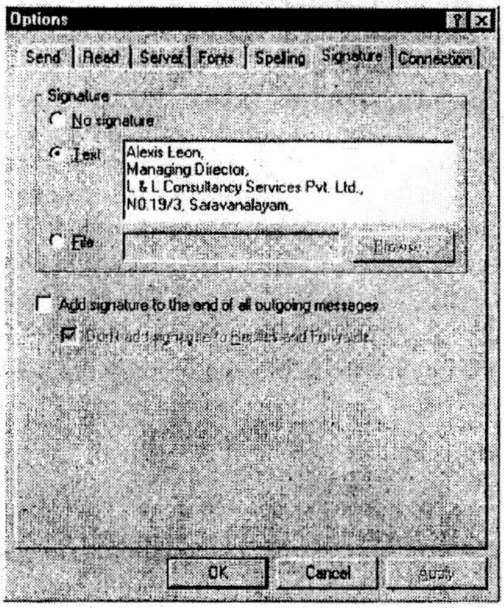

Figure 15. Creating the signature

Are we tired of typing in our name and address at the end of each message that we send? Then we can make use of the signature option provided. We can store the information that we want to attach at the end of the message as our signature. Then we can configure our system in such a way that all the outgoing messages will have our signature at the end of the message. If we don't want to have our signature on all messages, we can uncheck the option. When we need to include the signature to a message, click on the signature icon (the icon with the picture of a pen on it) and the signature will be appended to the message. The signature can be anything from our name and address, to our URL or contact information. It can also include a good quotation or even our geek code (for more information on geek codes, visit the site http://krypton.mankato.msum.edu/-hayden/.codes/geek3.1html). We can specify your signature in the options dialog box as shown in Fig. 15.

File Attachment Facility

One major drawback of e-mail is that we cannot send formatted text. For example, if we want to send a word document which contains pictures, bulleted lists, etc. and if we do a cut and paste, all the formatting, pictures, etc. will be lost. We will get only the ext. the solution is to send the file as an attachment to the mail. We can attach any file to a mail. It is a good idea to compress the file we are attaching using utilities like pkzip, which will reduce the file size and save time and money during transmission. We can attach the file we want to send by clicking on the icon with the picture of the paper clip. A dialog box will appear asking us to specify the name and location of the file we want to attach. Once we have given the necessary information, the file will be attached to the mail. A mail with an attachment will have a paper clip icon by the side of tot indication that it has an attachment.

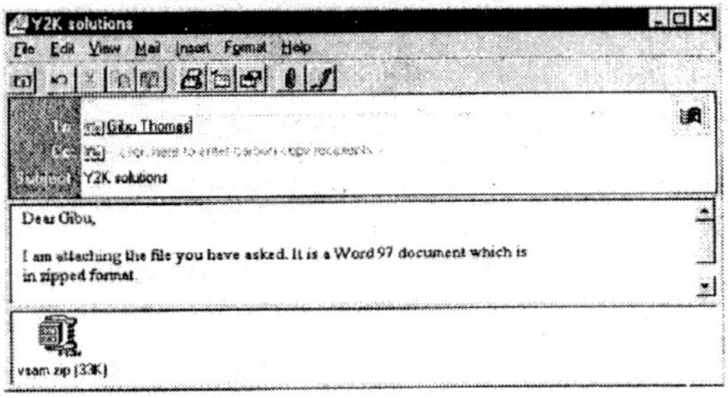

Figure 16. Attaching a file to a mail message

When we browse through a folder, we can easily indentify the files with attachment form the paper clip sign b the side of it, as shown in Fig. 17.

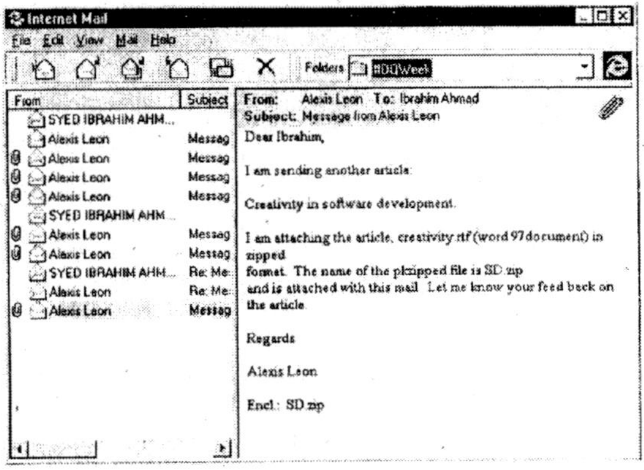

Figure 17. Sample folder

Setting Priority

We can set priority to a mail message that we are sending .the usual values are' Low', 'Normal' and 'High'. When we set the priority of a mail as 'High', we are indicating that he message requires immediate attention. High-priority message will be marked in red to indicate that it needs immediate attention. It is not a good practice to set the priority of the entire message as 'High'. Use this option only when required. The default priority is 'Normal'.

We have now seen how to compose a mail, reply and forward a mail, how to customize your mail program, how to add the signature, how to attach a file, etc. Now we can explore on our own what additional features our mail program has.

Pine

Pine is a mail program developed at the University of washing ton. It has easy-to-remember single character commands and an interface, which displays those available at each point.

Figure 18 sows Pine's opening menu. We can choose commands using the arrow keys and pressing enter for the highlighted choice, or by pressing the letters '?','C', 'I', 'L', 'a', 'S' and 'Q'. The 'FOLDER INDEX' is where we'll go to read a message. The 'COMPOSE MESSAGE' Screen is where we'll go to send a message. The 'ADDRESS BOOK' can be used to keep a list of people our mail frequently.

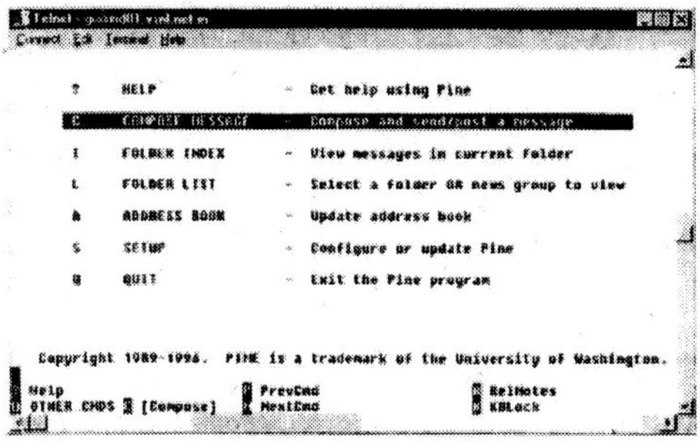

Figure 18. Pine menu

Pine use the bottom of the screen to show us what keys we can press to issue commands. Looking over these commands is very important of us don't know what to do next. Frequently, there will be more commands available than Pine can tell us about on the screen. Press the O key for 'OTHER CMDS' to display more of them.

In some of Pine's screens, as shown in Fig. 19, the list of commands may show a caret ('^') in front of a letter. This means to press and hold the control key while typing the letter. For example? C exits the editor when we're composing a message.

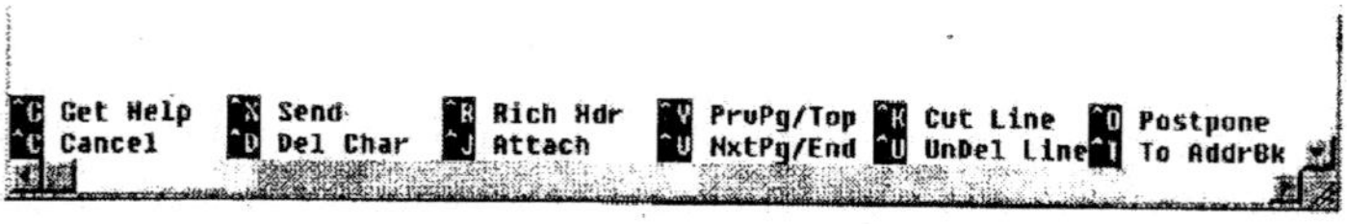

Figure 19. Pine commands

Here are some pointers to using Pine:

1. Choosing Option 1 (e-mail) form VSNL menu will start the Pine e-mail system
2. Press the O key to quit Pine (this will not disconnect from VSNL).
3. Always look at the menu at the bottom of the screen of we don't know what to do next.
4. Check our e-mail frequently - people expect we to reply quickly, and e-mail cans easily "pile-up".
5. Delete old e-mail message or move them to folders rather than keeping them in our inbox.

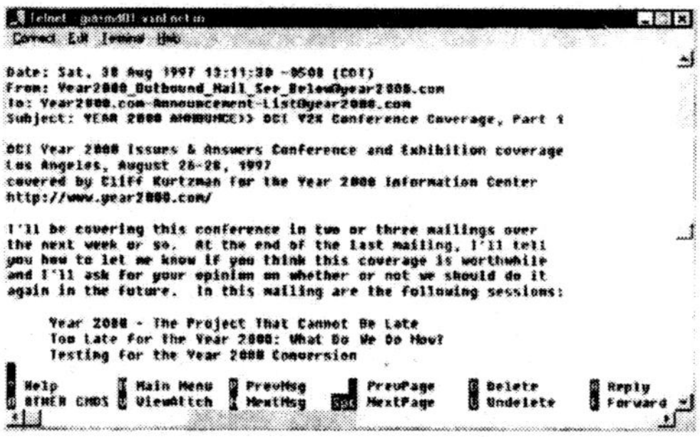

Figure 20. Sample message as seen in pine

- Select a message to read by moving the arrow keys and pressing the <Enter> key
- The list of message shows us the status of message.'+' means a message was sent just to us. 'A' means a message has been answered. 'N' means it is a new message. 'D' means the message will be deleted when we leave Pine.
- We can delete a message from this list by pressing the 'D' key. We can also delete a message while reading it.
- The save command places the message in a folder-not in file that we can this command form the list or while reading a message.
- To EXPORT the message to a file for transferring to your PC, use the Export command.
- We may receive message with attachment. Attachments are another file that comes with our mail message (like a picture included with a letter.) Use the 'V' key to view the attachment (if it's viewable on our terminal.)
- We can print a message by pressing 'Y' for 'pYrnt'.

- We can reply to a message by pressing the 'R' key. If the message is from a list, we'll be asked if we want to reply to everyone. It's our choice. We'll also be asked if we want-to include text from the message in our reply it's usually a good idea to do so.

Sending (Composing) Messages

We can go to the compose screen from anywhere in Pine by pressing 'c'.

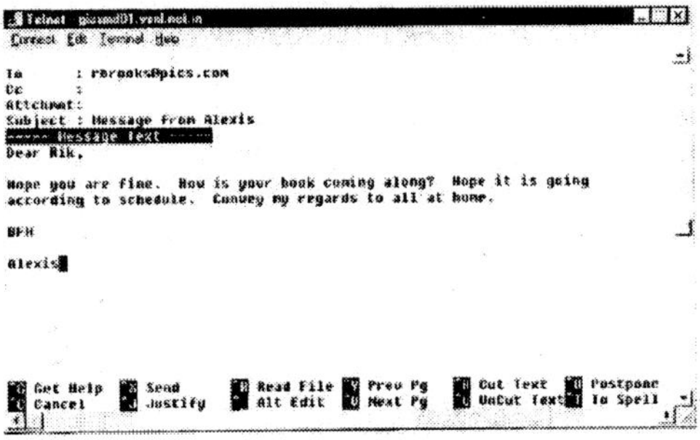

Figure 21. Composing a message in Pine

In the to: field, type the E-mail address of the person we are mailing. If we have created an entry in our address book, we can type the short name. We can send the same message to several people by listing their addresses on the to: line separated by commas. Press the down arrow key to move off the to: line to other fields.

Move to the Subject: line and type the subject for our message. Always put a subject on our messages. When we move the cursor below the line "-message Text-", you are actually using the editor Pico. The menu at the bottom of the screen describes the commands you can use in Pico. When we-are finished editing our message. Press ^x (that's control and the x key) to send our message. If we have another file we want to send with this message, moves the cursor to the "Attachment:" line. The file we want to send must be on the server, not your PC. If you know the name of the file, just type it on the line. If we don't know the name of the file, press AT for a list of files that we have on server. If the file we want to attach is not on the server in our directory, we will have to upload the file before attaching and sending it. The attached file can be a text file or a binary file. Pine will take care of encoding and decoding binary attachments. Examples of binary attachments are spreadsheets and Word Perfect files. And always read our e-mail messages before we actually send them.

Working with Folders

Pine allows us to store our messages in folders. We've already used one folder, our INBOX. New messages are automatically placed in our INBOX. Whenever we are reading a message, we can also save them to another folder.

When we choose Save, we will be prompted for the name of the folder. We can type the name for a new or existing folder. If the folder doesn't exist, it will be created for us. We can also press AT to go to a list of our folders. Using folders is an effective way to organize our messages. All of the commands for reading, replying to, deleting, and printing messages work in folders.

Our Address Book

The address book in Pine is a convenient way for us to keep up with the e-mail addresses of our friends (even enemies!). Once we've set up an entry in our address book, we can use the short name in the first column instead of typing in the long e-mail address in the third column. When we are reading a message, we can press AT to take the address from the current message into our address book.

Finding an E-Mail Address

Here's a question for us: how do we go about finding someone's e-mail address? Even though there are many directory services available, there is not comprehensive and reliable directory assistance for the Internet - at least yet. Because these directories contain the listing of the people who have registered their names, so we can find a person only if he has taken the pains to register his details.

Although there is no comprehensive directory of e-mail or Internet addresses, there are several search and reference tools we can consult. Some of them are Lookup! Directory Services (www.lookup.com), Inter NIC Directory Services (www.internic.net), NetFind (www.nova.edu), Net Pages (www.aldea.com), OKRA: net. Citizen Directory Service (okra.ucr.edu), Four11 Directory Services (www.fourlicom), Internet Address Finder (www.iaf.net), etc.

Mailing Lists

A mailing list is a way to share information via electronic mail with many people, usually on a specific topic or for a specific purpose. People' choose to be part of a mailing list by subscribing to the list.

This is how a mailing list works:

- A message is sent to a single e-mail address, which is referred to as the mailing list address.
- This same message is then re-distributed or "reflected" to all subscribers to the list.

The single, central e-mail address for the list is also referred to as a mail reflector. Mailing lists originated on a network called BrTNET. BITNET was created to connect universities in the United States, and now connects over one thousand institutions throughout the world.

Because mailing lists have their origins in the academic community, many mailing lists address academic and research oriented topics. However, many mailing lists exist for non-academic topics as well.

Managing a mailing list can be tedious; for example, keeping track of all the messages that are received and sent, and keeping track of the subscribers to the list and people who quit the list. Frequently, software is used that automates the management of hiese mailing list functions. Some of the more common mailing list management programs are:

- Lsoft's LISTSERVTm
- majordomo
- ListProc by CREN (Corporation for Research and Educational Networking)

Working with mailing lists involves several e-mail addresses. Administrative requests, such as a request to be added to the list, dropped from the list, or asking for an index of 'messages that have been sent to the list are sent to the list's administrative address. There may be a person on the other end of this address, but most often administrative requests are received and interpreted by mailing list management software.

The other address is for the mailing list itself. This is the address to which messages are sent for dissemination to the entire mailing list. Subscribers can send a reply either directly to the author of the message, or to the entire list.

Some lists are moderated. This means that each message is reviewed by a human (list owner) to ensure that it is appropriate and in keeping with the purposes of the list before it is redistributed to the list's subscribers. Some lists are restricted - subscriptions to the list are not available to the public. Still other lists are completely open: they are not moderated, open to anyone, and a person does not have to subscribe in order to send messages to the list.

A mailing list is a way to communicate and share information with many people via electronic mail. People join mailing lists by subscribing, which allows them to receive all messages sent to that list. Mailing lists may be moderated, restricted, or open and unmediated. Working with mailing lists usually involves at least two e-mail addresses: an administrative address for subscription requests and other administrative functions, and the list address, where subscribers send messages for distribution and sharing. In most cases, the administrative actions are handled by list management software.

Smileys

When we talk with people face-to-face, our body language, the tone of our voice and our facial expressions impart great meaning to what we say. On-line, we can personalize our messages using smileys or emoticons (on-line emotions). We create smileys by typing characters from our keyboard. We'd be amazed at the range of emotions these little characters can express. Some of the very popular ones are given below, but we can get a comprehensive list of smileys from the Ernoticon's Home Page at wwws.enterpriseenetifortknox/emoticon/.

:-) Happy
:-(Sad
:-o Surprised
:-@ Screaming
:-I Indifferent
:- e Disappointed
>:< Mad
:-D Laughing
;-) Wink

In addition to smileys here are a few common abbreviations we can use :

< BFN> Bye for Now
<BFN> By the way
<G> Grin
<Hth> Hope This Helps
<UJWTK> I JUST WANT TO KNOW
<IJWTS> i just want to say
<IMHO> IN MY HUMBLE OUT LOUD
<OTOH> ON THE OTHE HAND
<ROTFL> ROLLING ON THE FLOOR LAUGHING
<TIA> THANKS IN ADVANCE

E-Mail Ethics (Netiquette)

Like in any other form of communication, there are certain manners that we should follow when using the e-mail: Here are some guidelines which will help in getting the most out of our electronic mailing system:

- Know our recipient. Different people have different ideas of what is acceptable. Find out and respect each person's wishes.
- Avoid sarcasm, unless we're sure it will work, and think very carefully before using e-mail to express anger. With e-mail, once it's sent, it's gone.
- Be careful about our use of irony or even some forms of humor, which can be misinterpreted. Unlike face-to-face meetings or phone conversations, there are no visual or oral clues to provide a sense of what is going on.
- Be succinct and considerate of the recipient's time and online charges, especially with services that charge by the hour or by the size of messages. E-mail messages work best if they're short and to the point.

- If we are sending large files as attachments, use some compression utility like pkzip before sending them.
- Don't send copies of e-mail to people unless they need to be copied. In addition to cluttering up their mailboxes, it can place them in an awkward position, making them feel as if they have to do something with the information it also can be intimidating to the main recipient.
- Stay on the topic if we're posting to a public bulletin board, forum or news group. Most ate focused on a specific topic, and messages that stray too far from the topic can be annoying. Briefly describe who we are if the recipient doesn't already know. Be aware that e-mail can be archived and, under certain circumstances, may not be secure. On-line services and public e-mail providers protect the confidentiality of their subscribers' e-mail, but some companies consider employee e-mail sent over the office network to be company property and subject to scrutiny.
- Avoid "Urgent" or "Priority" unless it really is.
- Employ capital letters sparingly. Using them for an entire
- Message is the electronic equivalent to SHOUTING, and it is also harder to read.
- We should check our mail regularly unlike a fax or normal mail, an e-mail message in most cases is not automatically delivered to our desk. We have to log on to check our mail.

E-Mail - Advantages And Disadvantages

It is difficult sometimes to comprehend all the benefits and values of electronic-communication technology. There is now access 24 hours a day from anywhere in the world to endless amounts of data and information. Global communication is easier. The technology also has opened the door for more types of professionals to work at home, because they can still tap into corporate information. Thus, work can now be done anywhere a computer can be plugged in.

But there is a dark side to the technology. First, it has created an information overload. People are swamped by junk mail and finding what is relevant and need to be read from the-hundreds of mails that one receives can become a daunting task.

Second, the very existence of electronic communication has perpetuated the myth that it will lead to better communication. But that's not true, if we are not a good communicator without Electronic technology, we won't become a good, communicator just because we use the technology. Technology improves our ability to communicate, it extends the reach of our communications, and it can reduce long-distance communications timelines, but it is the individual using the technology that makes the communications better or worse.

Another disadvantage of the e-mail is that it can become a distraction and can prevent people from doing any productive work. To work more productively and to prevent e-mail interruptions, we can do the following:

- If the mail is automatically delivered to our mailbox, shut off the computer beep that alerts we when we have an incoming message.
- If our mail does not come to our in-box and we have to check for our mail by connecting to the mail server, and then do it during non-peak hours, when we will get connected immediately.
- Compose our messages off-line, this will save on-line time and we will get a chance to review the mail.
- Organize the mails in different folders, so that it can be tracked easily and efficiently.
- Keep the e-mail IDs of all the people with whom we correspond in the address book, so that each times we don't have to key it in. This will reduce the chances of error and will save time.
- Tell our friends and colleagues what type of documents we want to receive and what we don't.
- And remember; don't let technology wipe out oral communication!!!!

Some Useful E-Mail Services

Have we ever wanted our personal e-mail ID? We can have our personal e-mail account free of cost. All we need to access our mailbox is an Internet connection. There are several companies which offer this service, absolutely free, all we have to do is register, choose an e-mail ID, and give a password. We can access these mailboxes from anywhere, provided we have an Internet connection. Some of the sites, which offer this service, are www.hotmail.com, www.lema.com, www.rocketmail.com, etc. Figure 22 shows the screen of Hotmail, which offers an absolutely free service.

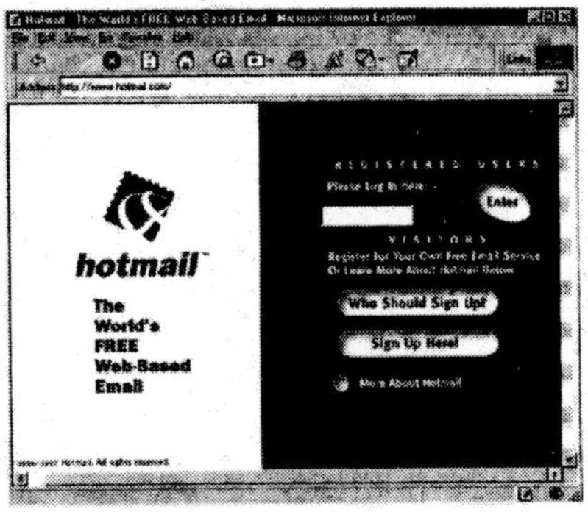

Figure 22. Hotmail Home page

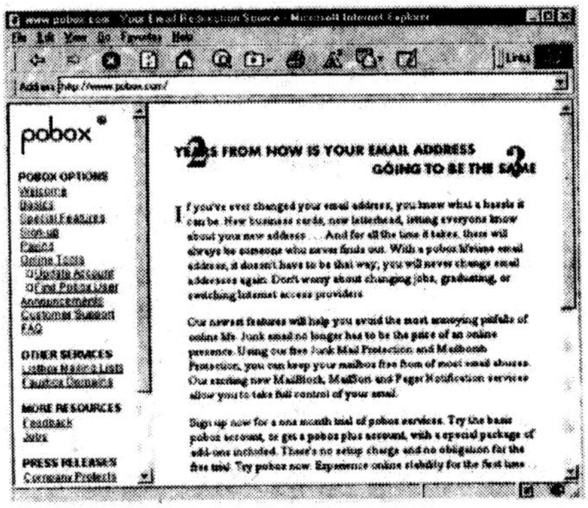

Figure 23. Pobox home

Another useful service is a permanent e-mail address. This is for the people who need to change their e-mail IDs frequently. The service is basically a message forwarding facility. We can choose an e-mail address and specify the address to which the messages are to be forwarded. So whenever our e-mail ID changes, we go to the site of the service provider and change the forwarding address. Some of the sites which offer this facility are www.poboxes.com www.pobox.com, www.iname.com, etc.

Yet another service which is useful is the e-minder (e-mail reminder) facility. We just have to give our e-mail ID and when we want a reminder e-mail sent. We will be reminded automatically. This is also a service, which is absolutely free. We can avail this service from www.netmind.com, www.conklyns.com, etc.

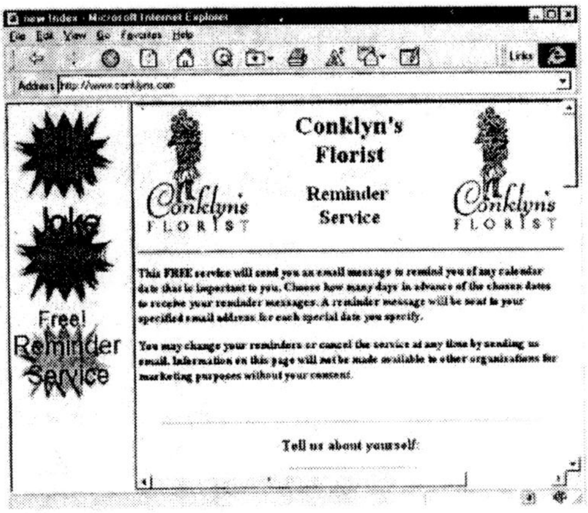

Figure 24. Reminder Services at Conkiyn's florist

Net Sport

1. Customize our e-mail program to suit our individual taste; for example, change the fonts, colour, toolbar, etc.
2. Compose and send mail to some of our friends.
3. Create an address book and signature file in our mail program.
4. Try reply to author, reply to all and forwarding of an incoming mail.
5. Send a mail to aleon@giasindOl.vsnl.net.in, telling me how we like the book. Put "Internet for everyone" in the subject line.
6. Create an account with any -one of the free e-mail service providers.
7. Use the net minder facility and create reminder requests for the birthday of all our family members.
8. Subscribe to the weekly newsletter at hap: // www.shareware.com.

******

Chapter - 25

Understanding Internet

These days the internet seems to be everywhere Web addresses appear on television ads and billboards. There are TV shows and magazines devoted to the internet. And every new computer program that comes out has some internet features. The next thing we know, our computer desktop will connect us just as easily to internet resources as it does to the files on our hard drive.

We know, you're raring to go. You want to start sending and receiving e-mail, browsing the Web, and exploring the global library of fun stuff out on the internet. Well, we don't want to hold you back. Feel free to skip to *Sending and Receiving E-Mail,* and start right in on e-mail (or even jump to *Browsing the Web* to start messing around with the World Wide Web). However, if you've got some questions about what the internet actually is, how you get access to it, and what you do once you're there, we'II try to answer those questions here.

We'II also try to explain most of the jargon you hear when people start babbling about the Net, so you can figure out for yourself what you want to learn about and what you'd like to ignore. Notice that we just used the word Net and not internet. For the most part, the words are synonymous, although some people will use the word Net to refer to just about any aspect of the global inter-networking of computers.

Note. If you want a more thorough compendium of internet jargon, terminology, and culture at your fingertips, try our internet Dictionary, also from Sybex.

What is the internet?

In this chapter, there are no dumb questions. Everybody talks about the internet these days, but most people don't really know what it is. One reason for this is that the internet looks different depending on how we come across it and what we do with it. Another reason is that everyone talks about it as if it's actually a network, like a local network in someone's office or even a large global network like CompuServe. Fact is, it's something different. A beast unto itself. The internet is really a way for computers to communicate.

As long as a computer or smaller network can "speak" the internet lingo (or protocols, to be extra formal about it) to other machines, then it's "on the internet". If the internet were a language, it wouldn't be French or Farsi or Tagalog or even English. It would be Esperanto.

Having said that, we might backtrack and allow that there's nothing wrong with thinking of the internet as if it is, in fact, a single network itself. It certainly behaves like one in a lot of important ways. But this can be misleading. No one "owns" the internet. No one even really runs it. And no one can turn it off.

E-mail and a Whole Lot More

The internet is also a collection of different ways to communicate or store information in a retrievable form. Take e-mail, for example. If we work in an office with a local-area network, then chances are we have an e-mail account and can communicate with people in your office by sending them messages. This is not the internet. Likewise, if we have an account at America Online and we send a message to someone else at AOL, we're still not using the internet. But, if our office network has a gateway to the internet, and we send e-mail to someone who does not work at our office, then we're sending mail over the internet.

Note. A gateway is a computer or the program running on it that transfers files (or e-mail messages, or commands) from one network to another.

Likewise, if we send a message from our AOL account to someone at CompuServe, or elsewhere; then, again, we are sending messages over the internet.

Figure 1 The internet carries e-mail from one network to another.

But, from our point of view, the internet is not just a collection of networks all talking to-each other. A single computer can also participate in the internet by connecting to a network or service provider that's connected to the internet. And while the local office network we described and the big commercial online services are not themselves the internet, they can and often do provide access through their gateways to the internet.

This can be confusing to first-time internet users (universally reterred to as newbies). Say we have an AOL account and we join one of the discussion groups (bulletin boards) there. It may not be obvious to us right away whether we're talking in an internal venue, one only accessible to AOL members, or in a public internet newsgroup. One of the benefits of an online service is the seamlessness that makes everything within our grasp appear to be part of the same little program running on our computer.

Note: A bulletin board is a public discussion area where people can post messages-without sending them to anyone's e-mail address-that can be viewed by anyone who enters the area. Other people can then reply to posted messages and ongoing discussions can ensue. On CompuServe, a bulletin board is called a forum. On the internet, the equivalent areas are called newsgroups.

The Web is not the Net, or is it?

Nowadays, most of the hype about the internet is focused on the World Wide Web. It's existed for under ten years now but it's been the fastest growing and most popular part of the Net for many of those years (except, perhaps, for the voluminous flow of e-mail around the globe). But what is the Web (also called WWW or WWW) and is it the same thing as the internet? Well, to answer the second question first: yes and no. Technically, the Web is just part of the internet-or, more properly, a way of getting around part of the internet. But it's a big part, because a lot of the internet that's not (strictly speaking) part of the Web can still be reached with a web browser.

So the Web, on one level, is an interface. A window onto the Net. A way of getting to where we're going. Its appeal derives from three different benefits:

1. It disguises the gobbledygook that passes for internet addresses and commands.
2. It wraps up most of the different features of the internet into a single interface.
3. It allows you to see pictures, and even hear sounds or watch movies (if our computer can hack it), along with our helpings of text.

Tip: To play sounds, our computer needs a sound card, speakers, and some kind of software (such as MS Sound Recorder or Sound Machine for the Macintosh, but there are many others); to play movies, our computer needs software (such as Media Player for Windows or QuickTime for the Macintosh or Windows) and a lot of memory (or else the movies will play real herky-jerky).

It helps to know a little bit about the history of the Net to understand why these three features of the Web have spurred on the internet boom. First of all, before the Web, to do anything beyond simple e-mail (and even that could be difficult, depending on your type of access) used to require knowing weird Unix commands and understanding the internet's systems for numbering and naming all the computers connected to it. If we've ever wrestled with DOS and lost, then we can appreciate the effort required to surmount this type of barrier.

Imagine it's 1991 and we've gotten ourself an internet account, solved the problems of logging in with a communications program to a Unix computer somewhere out there, and mastered the Unix programs needed to send and receive mail, read newsgroups, download files, and so on. We'd still be looking at lots of screenfuls of plain text, reams and reams of words. No pictures. Well, if we were dying for picture and then were encoded as plain text so they could be squeezed though the text-only pipelines that constituted the Net. Next we'd have to decode the files, download them onto our PC or Mac, and then run some special program to look at them. Not quite as easy as flipping through a magazine.

The Web used a method called hypertext to disguise the actual commands and addresses we use to navigate the Net. Instead of these commands and addresses, what we see in our web browser (the program we use to travel the Web) is plain English key words highlighted in some way. Simply select or click on the key words, and our browser program talks the internet talk, negotiates the transaction with the computer at the other end, and brings the picture, text, program, or activity we desire onto our computer screen. This is how all computer functions should work (and probably how they will work one day).

Note: We may have already encountered a form of hypertext on our desktop computer. If we have a Macintosh, think of hypercard stacks-the cards in those stacks are hyperlinked to one another. If we have Windows running on a PC, think about the Windows help system, where clicking on highlighted words connects we to definitions or tangentially related help topics.

Early, Unix-based web browsers such as WWW (developed at CREN, the European particle physics laboratory where the web was invented) and Lynx (developed at the University of Kansas) were not especially attractive to look at, but they did offer the "one-step" technique for jumping to a specific location on the Net or downloading a file or piece of software. Figure 2 shown Lynx, running on a Unix machine in a terminal window and connected to a PC by a modern.

The next advance on the Web was the development of graphical web browsers that could run on a desktop. PC or Macintosh, permitting the user to employ the familiar point-and-click techniques available for other programs on the computer and incorporating text formatting and graphics into the browser screen. The first program of this type was NCSA Mosaic, which was developed at the National Center for Supercomputer Applications and distributed for free.

Furthermore, the various web browsers can more or less substitute for a plethora of little specialty programs (such as Gopher clients, newsreaders, FTP programs, and so on) that you had to assemble and set up yourself "in the old days." The browsers all have their own little idiosyncrasies, but they're still remarkably uniform and consistent compared to the zoo of different programs and rules you had to follow just a few years ago. These days, the most popular browser is Netscape Navigator.

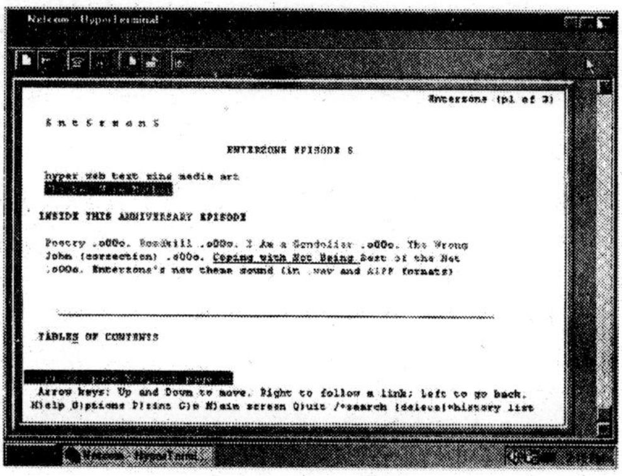

Figure 2 : In Lynx, you can press Tab to get to and highlight a link, and then press Enter to execute the link and follow it to a file or another part of the internet.

Note: "Just a few years ago" is the old days on the internet. Changes happen so rapidly in the online world that time on the internet is like "dog years," something like seven years go by for each one in the real world.

The Web has made it possible for browsers to display pictures right there in the midst of text, without your having to know how to decode files. A picture's worth a thousand watchamacallits, and pictures look better in newspaper articles and on TV than scads of typewritten text. So, this final ingredient made the Web seem both accessible and interesting to people who'd never in a million years care to learn what a Unix "regular expression" is.

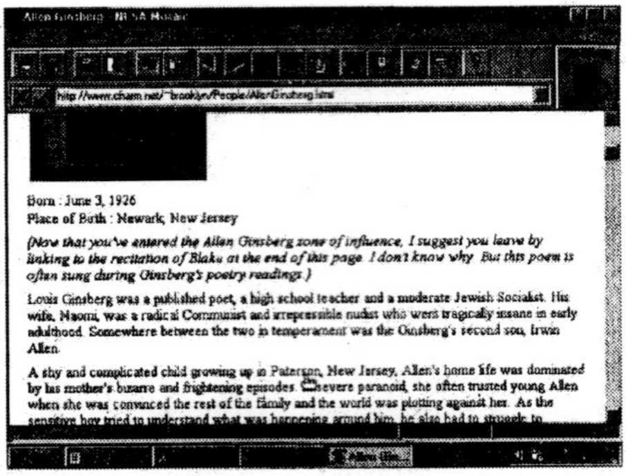

Figure 3 : Mosaic made it possible to point to a link and click on it, making the internet much more accessible to non-technical users. It also pioneered the use of in-line graphics (meaning illustrations mixed in with text).

We haven't tally answered the question that heads up this section: Is the web the internet? Technically it's not exactly the same thing, but for all intents and purposes, it is. And web browsers are the must-have programs that have made the internet what it is today.

What's New on the Net?

These days, the latest internet development are mostly being driven by the access tools. Browser makers Netscaps and Microsoft are each trying to develop all-in-one solutions that make their own products the "platform" for everything you do on the Net. New companies are offering free internet accounts with a Web-based e-mail interface. The catch? We have to keep the ad window open on the screen. There are even internet solutions that don't even require we to have a computer, such as WebTV (our TV plus a modern plus a keyboard plus a remote), or a modem, such as DirectPC (we computer plus a special satellite hook-up).

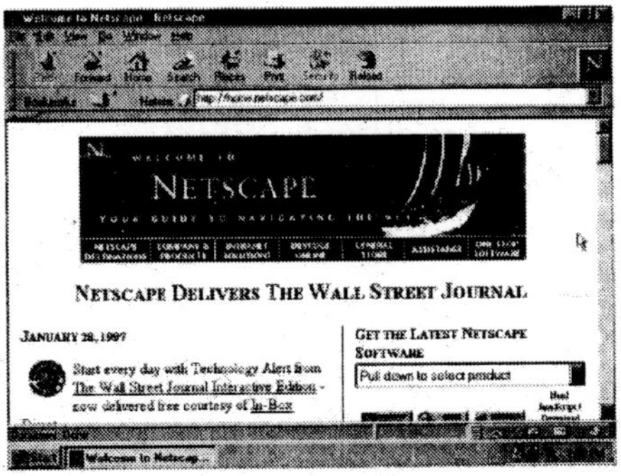

Figure 4 : Netscape Navigator is hands-down the most popular World Wide Web browser program. It words very much the way Mosaic does but with a number of additional features and improvements.

The web on our Desktop

From the user's point of view, the biggest changes planned for day-to-day internet use are in the way net-access is being built directly into computer operating-system desktops (as well as directly into many new applications). Both Netscape and Microsoft are trying to turn their browsers into substitute desktops, more or less equating our view of the internet (out there) and our own computer (in here).

Netcasts Aimed at our Screen

The popularity of PointCast, a program that displays news on our screen and automatically connects to the internet for updates, has demonstrated a market for "netcasting" software (programs that "broadcast" over the internet directly to our computer screen). This use of the internet is more passive, more like TV than the interactive, web-browsing model, but it's possible to do both. The new internet Explorer will offer various netcasting "channels" and Microsoft has already made a special deal with Pointcast to make their offerings one of those channels.

Figure 5 : The PointCast Network (shown here in screen-saver mode) automatically downloads news from the Net displays it on our computer screen.

Internet-Savvy Applications

The growth of the internet, coupled with the advent of smaller, local intranets running on internet principles, has led users to expect their everyday business software to help them deal with retrieving remote documents, collaborating with colleagues over network links, and save or publish documents to web and intranet servers. To meet this demand, software publishers are adding internet features to their programs left and right. We can expect our next upgrade of various programs to include the ability to transfer files (open and save them to remote computes) and probably create documents and reports in HTML (web format) as well.

Getting on the internet

So what exactly does it mean to be "on the internet"? Generally, if someone asks you, "Are we on the Net?" it means something like, "Do we have an internet e-mail address?" That is, do we have e-mail and can our e-mail account be reached over the internet? With the popularity of the Web what it is, another common interpretation of what it means to be on the Net is, "Do we have the ability to browse the World Wide Web?" Often these two features-internet e-mail, and Web access-go hand in hand, but not always. We're also getting to a time when being on the internet will also entail having our own home page, our own "place" on the Web where information about us is stored and where we can be found.

Accessing the Net a Work

More and more companies these days (as well as schools and other organizations) are installing internal networks and relying on e-mail as one of the ways to share information. E-mail messages are starting to replace interoffice memos, at least for some types of announcements, questions, and scheduling purposes. The logical next step for most of these organizations is to connect their internal network to the internet through a gateway. When this happens, we may suddenly be on the Net. This doesn't mean that anything will necessarily change on our desktop. We'll probably still use the same e-mail program and still sent and receive mail within our office in the same way we always have.

What will change at this point is that we'll be able to send mail to people on the internet outside of our office, as long as we type the right kind of internet address. (Generally, this means adding @ and then a series of words separated by periods to the username portion of an address, but we'll explain more about addresses at the end of this chapter.) Likewise, people out there in the great beyond will be able to send mail to us as well.

Depending on the type of internet connection our company has, e-mail may be all we get. Then again, it might also be possible for us to run a web browser on our computer and visit internet sites while sitting at our desk. Of course, our company will only want we to do this if it's relevant to our job, but it works the same way whether we're researching a product our company uses or reading cartoons at the Dilbert site.

Accessing the Net at Home

If we're interested in exploring the internet as a form of entertainment or for personal communication, then a work account is not really the way to do that. (An account minimally consists of a username and an e-mail in box; it may also provide storage space on a computer or access to a web server). We'll need our own personal account to really explore the internet on our own time, without looking over our shoulder to make sure nobody's watching.

Tip: If our office is quite sophisticated, we may actually be able to dial into a company network from home via a modem to check our e-mail messages or even browse the Web, but again, this might not be an appropriate use of our boss's resources.

Our best bet is to sign up for an account from a commercial online service or a direct-access internet service provider. What's the difference between those two choices? Will, an online service (such as CompuServe, America Online, Prodigy, Microsoft Network, and so on) is first and foremost a private, proprietary network, offering its own content and access to other network members. An internet service provider (also called an ISP) offers just access to the internet and no local content (or only very limited local information and discussion groups). Figure 6 will help illustrate this distinction.

Online services have only recently begun offering full (or somewhat limited) internet access. Because they are trying to do two things at once (sell we their own content and connect we to the internet), they are usually an expensive way of exploring the Net. On the other hand, they tend to offer a single, simplified interface, we often recommend to people who just want to get their feet wet before plunging whole-heartedly into the Net, to sign up for a free trial account at one of the online services. If they like what the internet has to offer or if they start using the Net so much they run up an expensive bill (after that first free month), then we recommend that they switch to a direct-access internet service provider.

ISPs can be much cheaper than online services, especially if we can find one that offers a flat rate-a monthly charge that doesn't vary no matter how much time we spend connected to the Net. They also don't try to compete with the internet by offering their own content and sponsors. Instead, they function as a gateway, getting us onto the internet and letting we go wherever we want.

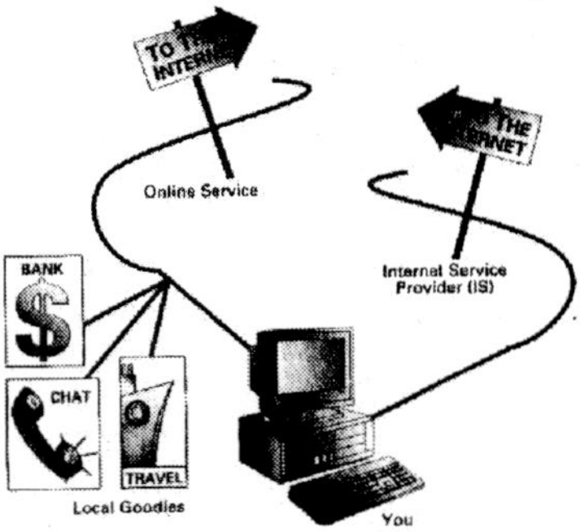

Figure 6: Online services connect we to the internet but encourage us to explore their own offerings, whereas ISPs just connect us to the internet and let we fend for ourself.

What kind of ISP Accounts are there?

An ISP account generally includes, along with the e-mail address, an account with some storage space on a computer somewhere on the Net, usually in a directory (a folder) with the same name as our username. As account is also a billing entity, and our account will be billed monthly, sometimes with a surcharge based on the amount of time we spend connected that month (depending on the provider) or the amount of space we used on their hard drive.

But how do we use an account? Well, we need a computer with a modem, and we need software that knows how to use that modem to call up (dial up) our provider and allows we to log in to our account. If we want more than simply a connection to a Unix command-line and a plain text account (and we suspect that you do), then nowadays you need something called a PPP or SKIP account. (The other kind is usually called a shell account or sometimes a Unix shell account.) Again, we'll explain more about these distinctions, if we're really interested. A PPP (or SLIP) account lets our computer behave like it's connected directly to another computer on the internet-when it's really connected over a phone line whenever we dial in-and it enables we to run software, such as graphical web browsers like Mosaic and Netscape Navigator, that functions in our computer's native environments (for example, text programs like the text-only browsers Lynx and Unix.

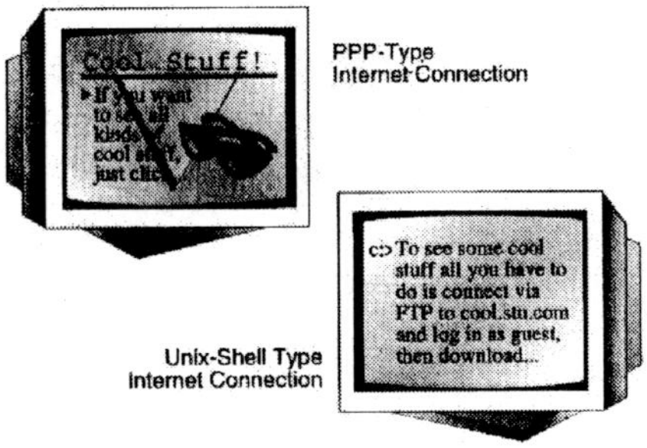

Figure 7 : If we can get a PPP (or SLIP) account, then our connection to the internet will be much more seamlessly integrated into our computer's normal environment.

Once we're set up, we won't have to think much about whether we have a PPP or SLIP account or any other kind of account, but we just wanted to introduce the terminology so we'll know what we are talking about when we mention it again.

Warning: By the way, the speed of our modem-and that of the modem at the other end of the dial-up line, that is, our provider's modem-determines the speed of our internet connection, and even the fastest modems these days are still slower than a direct network connection to the Net, such as we might enjoy at our office.

The internet doesn't Care what kind of Computer we use

One of the nice things about the internet is that it makes some of the seemingly important distinctions between types of computers a lot less important. Sure, if we use a Macintosh, we have to run Macintosh software, and if you use Windows 95, we have to run Windows software, but the information out on the internet, the public discussion areas, and the World Wide Web look and act more or less the same, no matter what kind of computer we use.

In fact, the Web is quickly becoming a sort of universal computer platform now that certain types of programs and services are being designed to run on the Web, rather than to run on one specific type of computer. In this book, most of the screen shots show Windows 95 screens, because that's the kind of computer we do most of our work on, but many of the programs featured also exist for the Macintosh, and when they do, we'll be sure to fill we in on the Macintosh equivalents and where to find them. Figure 8 shows a Netscape window on a Macintosh. Notice how similar it looks to the Windows 95 version shown in Figure 4.

Part of the elegance of the internet is that much of the heavy duty processing power and storage of large programs and dense information takes place "out there," not on our computer. Our computer-whether it's a PC, a Mac, or a Unix work-station-becomes just a convenient beanstalk to climb up to the land of the internet giants. We'll sometimes refer to this common structure of internet facilities as client-server (sorry for the jargon). In this scenario, we are client (or our computer or the program running on it is) and the information source or World Wide Web site or mail-handling program is the server. Servers are centralized repositories of information or specialized handlers of certain kinds of traffic. All a client has to do is connect to the right server and a wealth of goodies are within our reach, without our having to overload our machine. This is a major reason why it doesn't matter kind of computer we prefer.

Figure 8 : Netscape for the Mac works almost exactly the same way as the PC (and for that matter, Unix) version of the program, except for the normal Macintosh user-interface features, such as the menu bar being at the top of the screen instead of below the title bar.

What we can do on the Net

We've touched on the most popular facilities on the internet-e-mail and the World Wide Web-but we'll run down some of the other useful features covered in this book. All of these things are interrelated, and we may notice me mentioning something before we cover it in detail. We don't want to leave we scratching our head when we are forced to sputter terms of the trade, such as FTP, Telnet, and Gopher.

Once we start exploring the Web we might get tired of its disorganization (imagine a library where every card-carrying member worked part-time as a librarian for one of the shelves, and each micro-librarian used their own system for organizing their section) or with not knowing for sure where anything is on the internet. Fortunately, there are a lot of useful search engines available on the Net, and we'll show we where to find them and how to use them. Not as thorough as a card catalog, perhaps, but easier to use.

Note: A search engine is a program or web page that enables we to search an internet site (or the entire internet) for a specific key word or words.

The Web itself is becoming more of a whiz-bang medium with some of the bells and whistles we've come to expect in television advertisements and big budget movies. To take full advantage of some of the more dynamic Web offerings, though, we have to learn how to plug special tools into our browser. We'll show we where to find the tools and how to plug them in.

Those newsgroups we alluded to before, the internet's public message boards, are organized (to use the term loosely) into a system called Usenet.

We'll tell us how Usenet works, how to get and install a newsreader, and how to start participating in this public forum without getting called a jerk. If we plan to join in on the public discourse of the Net, we have to learn a thing or two about something called netiquette-the traditional rules of civilized behavior online.

If we prefer the idea of communicating with people "live" rather than posting messages and waiting for people to reply later, then we'll want to know about the various chat facilities available on the internet, particularly IRC (internet Relay Chat).

If we're willing to get our hands a little dirty and want to start tunneling our way around the internet, connecting to computers all over the globe and moving files hither and we, we might be able to do all that from our web browser, or we may want to pick up the basics of FTP (File Transfer Protocol) and Telnet, a system that allows us to log into remote computers over the Net.

Finally, if we want to join the ranks of people with their own some pages on the Web, so we can create a "presence" on the Net or publicize our favorite internet sites, we'll show us how to do that as well.

A few words about internet addresses

One of the confusing things to internet newbies is that the word "address" is used to mean at least three different things on the internet. The most basic meaning-but the one used least often-is the name of a computer, also called a host or site, on the internet in the form something, (to really use the lingo properly we have to pronounce the periods "dot" we'll get used to it and it saves a lot of time over the long haul). For example, we publish a magazine (or 'zine) on the internet called Enterzone; it's stored on a machine at Vassar that's part of the American Arts and Letters Network. The address that machine is:

ezone.org

Reading from right to left, we first have the domain, org, which stands for (non-commercial) organization. Next we sometimes have a subdomain. Finally we have the hostname, ezone, which is the name (or a name) of the specific computer the magazine is stored on.

Another type of address is an e-mail address. An e-mail address consists of a username (also called a login, a log-on name, userID, an account name, and so on), followed by an "at sign" (@) and then an internet address of the type just described. So, for example, say we want to sent mail to Ram in our capacity as editor of Enterzone. We could address that e-mail message to a special username created for that job (it will stay the same even if someone else takes over in the future):

editor@ezone.org

The third type of address is the kind we see everywhere these days, on billboards, on TV commercials, in the newspaper, and so on-a web address, also called a URL (Uniform Resource Locator). We'll explain more about how to read (or ignore) URLs, Browsing the Web. For now, it's enough just to know what one looks like.

http://ezone.org/ez

Fortunately, we often can avoid typing in web addresses our self and can zip around the Web just by clicking pre-established links. Links are highlighted words or images that when clicked or selected take we directly to a new document, another part of the current document, or some other type of file entirely.

✶✶✶✶✶✶

Chapter - 26

History of Internet

The Internet is an outgrowth of a network established in the 1960s to meet the needs of the researchers working in the defense industry in the USA then called the ARPANET. From a handful of computers in 1971, the ARPANET or Internet grew to 10,000 computers by 1987 and to more than 100,000 by 1989. In 1990 ARPANET ceased to exist, but the Internet continued to grow to an estimated: 1 million computers in 1992, 10 million in 2014. The Internet now offers both information access and a fast and inexpensive means of communication to the public.

Many people have helped in the development of Internet. The initial phase began way back in the 50s. In order to regain the space supremacy from USSR (which they stole from US by launching Sputnik in 1957) the US government created an agency called ARPA (Advanced Research Projects Agency), with J.C.R. Likelier as the head of the computer department. The history of Internet is chronicled below:

1960's

In 1969 the Department of Defense Advanced Research Projects Agency (ARPA) created an experimental network called ARPANET. ARPANET stands for Advanced Research Projects Agency (ARPA) Network. The network was developed in 1969 by ARPA and funded by the Department of Defense. The network was chiefly experimental, and was used in research, and to develop and test networking technologies. The original network connected four host computers at four separate universities throughout the United States, enabling users to share resources and information.

By 1972, there were 37 host computers connected to ARPANET. Also in this year, ARPA's name was changed to DARPA (Defense Advanced Research Projects Agency). In 1973, ARPANET went beyond the boundaries of the

United States by making its first international connections to England and Norway.

One objective of ARPANET was to devise a network that would still be operational if part of the network failed. The research in this area resulted in a set of networking rules, or protocols, called TCP/IP (Transmission Control Protocol/Internet Protocol).

TCP/IP is a set of protocols that govern how data is transmitted across networks. It also enables different "types of computer operating systems, such as DOS and UNIX to share data across a network.

ARPANET functioned as a "backbone" network - allowing smaller local networks to connect to it. Once these smaller net works were connected to the backbone, they were in effect connected to each other.

In 1983, DARPA decided that TCP/IP would be the standard set of protocols used by computers connecting to ARPANET. This meant that any smaller networks (for example, a university network) that wanted to connect to ARPANET also had to be using TCP/IP. TCP/IP was available for free and was increasingly used by networks. The spread of TCP/IP helped create the Internet as-we know it today - the network of networks that either use the TCP/IP protocols, or can interact with TCP/IP networks.

The ARPANET grew slowly from a handful of computers in 1971 to more than 1000 in 1984. After working with the ARPANET, researchers came to regard high-speed computer networks as an indispensable tool for academic research in all fields.

1970's

The Networking tools developed in the 1970's include:

♦ In 1972, the telnet application was developed by the National Center for Supercomputing Applications (NCSA) for remote login, making it easier to connect to a remote computer.

♦ In 1973, FTP (file transfer protocol) for standardizing the transfer of files between networked computers was introduced.

1980's

Several significant events occurred in 1983, including:

♦ The TCP/IP suite of networking protocols, or rules, that became the only set of protocols used on the ARPANET. It set a standard for other networks, and generated the use of the term "Internet" as the network of networks, which either use the TCP/IP protocols or are able to interact with TCP/IP networks.

♦ The split of Arpanet into two networks namely Arpanet and Milne in order to keep military and non-military network sites separate.

♦ 1982 and 1983, the first desktop computers began to appear. Many were equipped with an operating system called Berkeley UNIX, which included networking software. This allowed for relatively easy connection to the Internet using telnet.

♦ The personal computer revolution continued through the eighties, making access to computer resources and networked information increasingly available to the general public.

♦ In 1986 the National Science Foundation (NSF) connected the nation's six supercomputing centers together. This network was called the NSFNET, or NSFNET backbone. To expand access to the Internet, the NSF supported the development of regional networks, which were then connected to the NSFNET backbone. In addition, the NSF supported institutions, such as universities, in their efforts to connect to the regional networks. Here is a diagram of the NSFNET backbone, as it appeared in 1993:

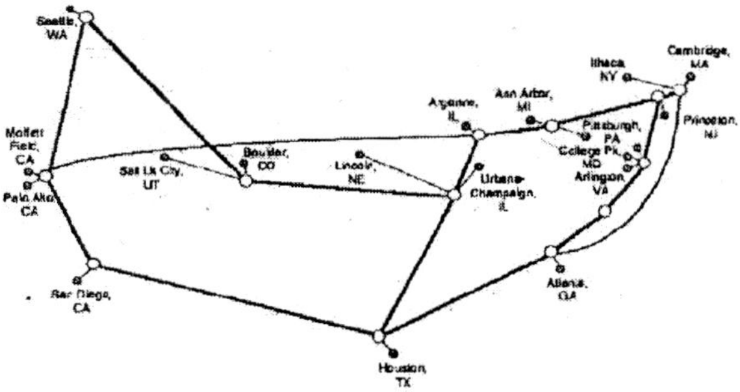

♦ 1987 - The NSF awards a grant to Merit Network, Inc. to opt irate and manage future development of the NSFNET backbone. Merit Network, Inc. collaborates with International Business Machines (IBM) Corporation and MCI Telecomminactions Corporation to research and develop faster net-working technologies.

♦ 1989 - The backbone network is upgraded to "Ti" which means that it is able to transmit data at speeds of 1.5 million bits of data per second, or about 50 pages of text per second.

1990's

♦ 1990 - The ARPANET is dissolved.

♦ 1991 - Gopher is developed at the University of Minnesota. Gopher provides a hierarchical, menu-based method for providing and locating information on the Internet. This tool makes using the Internet much easier.

♦ 1993 - The European Laboratory for Particle Physics in Switzerland (CERN) releases the World Wide Web (WWW), developed by Tim Berners-Lee. The WWW uses hypertext transfer protocol (HTTP) and hypertext links, changing the way information can be organized, presented and accessed on the Internet.

♦ 1993 - The NSFNET backbone network is upgraded to "T3" which means that it is able to transmit data at speeds of 45 million bits of data per second, or about 1400 pages of text per second.

♦ 1993-1994 - The graphical web browsers Mosaic and Netscape Navigator are introduced and spread through the Internet community Due to their intuitive nature and graphical interface; these browsers make the WVVW and the Internet more appealing to the general public.

♦ 2014 - The NSFNET backbone is replaced by a new network architecture, called vans (very high speed backbone network system) that utilizes Network Service Providers, regional networks and Network Access Points (NAPs).

******

Chapter - 27

Creating Our Presence on the Web

We have products to sell and services to offer.

We are a professional, an expert in our field, we what to share our expertise with others, and we want to earn professional recognition.

Our are hunting for a job and we want to market our self.

We're an educational institution and we want to let people know about our courses and other training facilities.

We are a consultant and we want to advertise our services.

We are an employer and we want to attract the best talent available.

Now, it is possible for all of the above people and organisations to find an inexpensive, yet highly effective medium which cuts across language and geographical barriers, which can be used 24 hours a day, 365 days a year. The internet or the World Wide Web (or simply web or WWW) provides an ideal medium for all these people to create their presence.

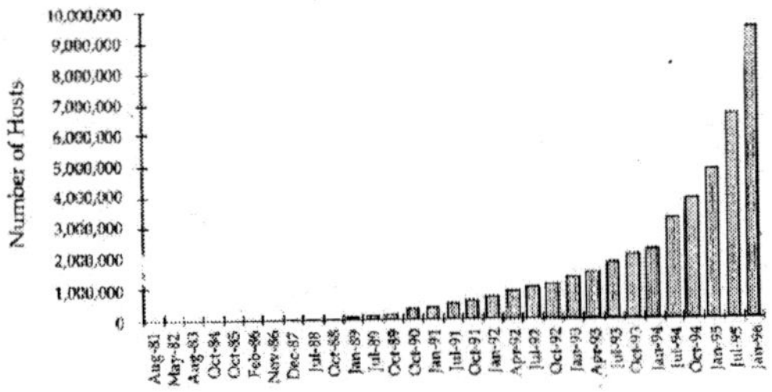

Figure 1: Number of Hosts

The web has grown very fast. In fact, the web has grown substantially faster than the internet at large, as measured by the number of hosts. Figure 1 and 2, and Table 1 (source : Matthew Gary of the Massachusetts Institute of

Technology) show the growth in the number of hosts and number of users from 1981 to 1996.

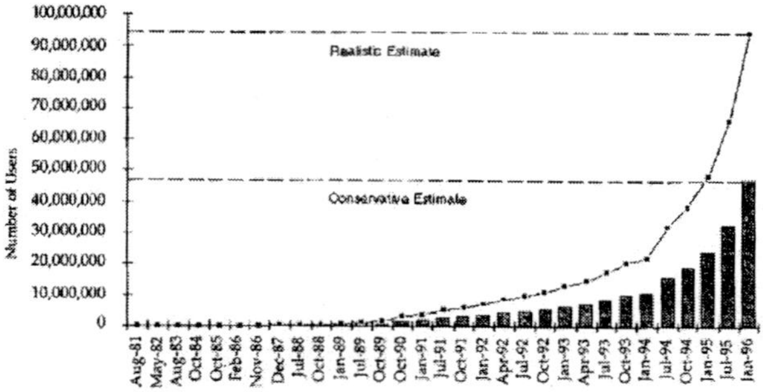

Figure 2 : Internet users

Table 1 : shows the growth in the number of web sites from 1993 to 1997.

Month	Number of Web sites	%.com sites
6/93	130	1.5
12/93	623	4.6
6/94	2,738	13.5
12/94	10,022	18.3
6/95	23,500	31.3
1/96	100,000	50.0
6/96	230,000 (est)	68.0
1/97	560,000 (est)	62.6

Source : Matthew Gray of the Massachusetts Institute of Technology

No other medium has this big an audience. More than 100,000,000 potential educated people access the net. Nearly Hal of the audience is composed of professionals, more than half are in the 25-35 age group, which means that the literacy and income levels are much higher than any comparable group.

So, if we want to survive, thrive and compete, then we n longer can ignore the web. Our marketing strategy, may it b personal or organisational, should include plans for creating our presence on the web. There is a profitable place on the internet for everyone – everyone with the right strategy. It is one thing to understand the potential of the internet for breaking down barriers to international electronic commerce and quite another to establish a competitive, profitable business on the global network. Six fundamental capabilities of the internet or the WWW give it the competitive advantage over other media. They are :

- Global dissemination – With connectivity in over 100 countries, international communication is a fundamental facet of the Web.

• Customisation-Information can be maintained centrally on a network server and still be displayed, accessed, and disseminated on an individual basis.

• Interaction-Two-way or multi-channel communication is possible on the net. We can get immediate and focused feedback from customers and forwards the on-line customer queries to appropriate internal resources so that necessary action can be taken.

• Collaboration-Seamless access to shared data, project coordination, and coordinated information management resulting in enhanced opportunity for joint development and innovative products and services.

• Electronic commerce-Support for on-line ordering, purchase orders, inventory, and delivery tracking.

• Integration-We can link on-line activities with internal, bookend processes for maximum impact, distribute information and customer interaction across functions, and promote new business applications.

The is a lot of difference between just establishing connectivity and gaining competence. As the internet connectivity soars all over the world, it becomes ever more challenging just to attract attention on the Web. With well over 100,000 World Wide Web servers vying for visitors and the number of home pages doubling every few months, commercial ventures without a clear strategy risk being lost in the crowd. In this chapter, we will be discussing how to create web presence, the resources you will be requiring, how to go about creating your home page or web site etc. However, we will not be discussing the web design concepts or the strategies and techniques to make your web site stand out, which is a topic that is beyond the scope of this book.

If we want to set up our home page or our organisation's web site, there are many options. The charges can range from zero upwards. There are many internet Service Providers (ISPs) who offer an individual or a non-profit organisation the necessary infrastructure free of cost. We can create a simple one-page site to a full-fledged site occupying 5-6 megabytes of disk space. We will see more about these ISPs later in this chapter. One thing with these free services is that, we should know how to create our own pages, which means that we should have knowledge of HTML or its more sophisticated cousins like Java, CGI, Pearl, etc. Although some of these free ISPs have automated facilities which allow even a layman to create simple sites, but to create sites with reasonable pedigree, you need to know at least one of the many web authoring languages.

If we don't believe in going in for these free web hosting services or we are a commercial organisation, then we need to have a place where we can put up our site. The place where we physically store the pages that make up our site is called a server, more precisely a web server. The server will have all our web pages, graphics, and other programs that are needed to host our site. It goes without saying that our server needs to be connected permanently to the internet.

Once we have the server and internet connection, we need an address or a URL. In order to facilitate others to connect to our site, or for us to tell others that we have put up a site at such and such a place, we need to have this address or URL. We have seen what an IP address and domain name is. As there are two kinds of domina names, country-specific ('in' for India 'sg' for Singapore) or global ('com for commercial, 'edu' for educational, etc), we will have to register with the appropriate authority to get the domain name. If we want a country-specific domain name (ending with 'in') we will have to register with the National Center for Software Technology (NCST), Bombay. If we want a global domain name then we will have to register with the InterNIC, USA.

Now that we have the internet connection, a web server and a domain name, the next step is designing our site. The site will have pages, images, and other programs. If we are planning to design and develop the web pages by ourself, we can add an HTML editor to our shopping list. With the HTML editors, we don't have to remember the HTML tags, we just have to type-in the text, place the graphics, formal the text and graphics, and the HTML editor will do the job of putting the HTML tags. Some of the HTML editors are Microsoft FrontPage, Netscape Hotmetal, etc. If we want to have feedback forms, access counters, shopping carts, search engines, etc. in our page HTML alone is not enough. We will need CGI (Common Gateway Interface) on your web server and the programming languages and tools to implement the CGI programs, like C, C++, Pearl, Java, etc. We can also seek the help of a professional consultant or agency, which specialises in web design and development. But the charges can vary anywhere from Rs. 500 to Rs. 10000 per page depending on the complexity of the page, scope of the work (whether it is development alone, or whether it is design and development, whether images are supplied by us, whether the text is in soft copy, etc.), and the reputation and competence of the consultant/agency.

Now comes the million-dollar question. Where will we put up our web server? Actually, we have many options. The easiest way is to get the services of an internet Service Provider (ISP). An ISP is a company that provides access to the internet (in our case VSNL). Their customers can be individuals or ogranisations. In this option we will rent a specified amount of disk space on the server of the ISP as well as a shared or dedicated bandwidth on its internet connection. The ISPs will configure their machine (virtual hosting) so that their computer will respond to your domain name. The users will not know whether our site is hosted on our server or an ISP's machine. The ISP will be handling hundreds of clients like us and will have many web sites on their computer. Most ISP's will give we an URL, which will be an extension of their domain name. For example, suppose we have taken the service of an ISP whose domain name is 'www.isp.com' and our company name is, say, 'xyz'. Then the ISP will assign we a URL, which will be something like 'www.isp.com/xys' and for which we won't have to pay anything extra. But if we want a domain name like 'www.xyz.com' then the only way is to get the name from InterNIC, that is if it is not already given to somebody else. Almost all ISP's will have web design and development services. They will do the domain registration for us if we want. Each activity will have separate rates and we can decide which activities we want to do and which we want to give to the ISP. The summary of the charges for hosting a site with an ISP is given in the following table:

Activity	Approximate charges (Rs.)	Payable to
Domain name registration	3600 (US$ 100 for 2 years)	InterNIC
Setup charges	5000	ISP
Disk space and other connection	Variable, depending on required disk space (10,000/year for 5MB)	ISP
Web design and development	Variable	
Internet Connection	15,500 for TCP/IP account	VSNL

The advantage of having an ISP is that we can leave most of the day to day activities like server management and housekeeping to the ISP. But we should be careful when we choose an ISP. Choose the ISP which has a reputation in the business and a good technical support team. If we are doing the design and development, then we should have FTP access to our sites to make the updations. Ask for what other values added services that the ISPs offer. For example, many ISPs offer services like free domain registration, daily/weekly/monthly statistics of the number of hits, free site counters, etc. If we can directly deal with an ISP in the US, the rates will be much lower there. Many US service providers have their agents in India, who offer all the services and we need to pay only in rupees.

The second option is setting up our own computer on the internet through a dedicated connection from VSNL. For this we need our own web server, a leased line connection from VSNL and the technical support staff for setting-up, configuring and maintaining the system. But the costs for this option can be prohibitive and for small business and personal home pages, we strongly recommend going in for the first option. For example, a 64 kbps leased line connection from VSNL alone can cost you 12 lakhs.

Now we will see some of the free web presence providers. As mentioned earlier, there are a lot of companies who will host our home page free of cost.

But this facility is, in most cases, available only for individuals and non-profit organisations. There are free web presence providers who offer a late of facilities free, for which we have to spend a fortune otherwise. Many of these providers will give us FTP access to our site (a must if we want to update the files from our PC), CGI access (a must if we want to have site counters and feedback forms), free e-mail accounts, and other facilities. The amount of disk space will vary depending on the provider, but most of them will give disk space as high as 5-6 MB per individual/organisation, which is more than enough to host a reasonably large site. In fact, most individual home pages will require less than 1 MB of space. Most of these providers will have facilities like wizards and templates which will allow even novices, who do not know anything about the HTML or web authoring, to host their sites. For experts, the provider will give the disk space and FTP, and in most cases CGI access, so that one can do the design and development and then upload the files to the providers server.

Figure 3 : Tripod home page

In most cases, the service provider will have a technical support team. So in case of any problem, we can contact the technical support team or the webmaster of the site. Almost all the free web presence providers will put advertisements and banners in our page; that is how their revenue comes, which enable them to provide us the free service. But there are a few providers who do not put the advertisements, so if we are very particular that our site should not have any advertisements then we can choose a provider who does not put banners in our site. Many providers will delete the site if it is inactive or does not have any hits for a specified period of time (usually 2 to 3 months). Also, most providers will not allow pornographic or illegal material or links to it and there will be additional restrictions depending on the provider. So it is a good idea to read the 'rules and regulations', FAQ and support guide before we sign-up.

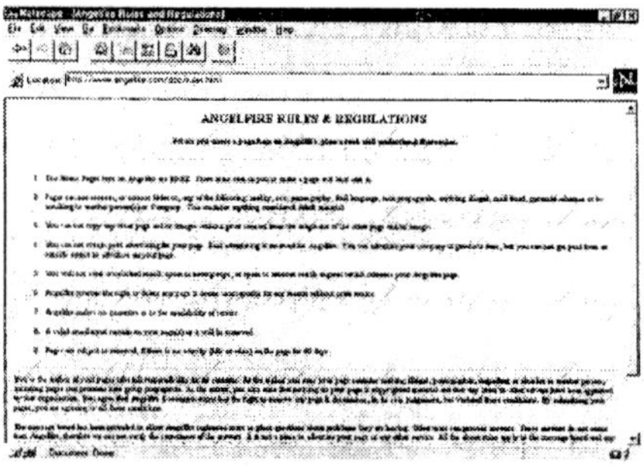

Figure 4 : Angelfire home page

Given below are some of the most popular free web presence providers:

1. Tripod (http//www.tripod.com)
2. Geocities (http//www.geocities.com)
3. Cybercity (http//www.cybercity.hko.com)
4. Achievement International (http//www.achiever.com/design freehmpg.html)
5. Tool-box (http//www.tool-box.com)
6. Aparker (http//www.aparker.org)
7. Joe's Cyberpost (http//www.joes.com)
8. Phrantic Web (http//www.phrantic.com)
9. SpiderCity (http//www.spidercity.com)
10. Fortune City (http//www.fortunecity.com)
11. USA online (http//www.usaonline.com)
12. Howdy Neighbor (http//www.howdyneighbor.com)
13. Friend's World (http//www.friendsworld.com)
14. Web Spawner (http//www.webspawner.com)
15. Top Town (http//www.toptown.com)
16. EZpage (http//www.ezpage.com)
17. Angelfire (http//www.angelfire.com)

Figure 9.5 shows the home page of Geocities.

Now we have our web site up, but that is not enough. The world has to know that such a site exists. Or in other words, we will have to market our web site or announce our web presence. To successfully market our web site we need to run an on-going campaign, just as we would for a product or service. We've identified the following major areas that you should con-centrate during the ad campaign. All of them may not apply to our web site, and the emphasis on each area may vary according to our situation.

Figure 5 : Geocities home page

1. Announcing our web site with the internet search engines and directories
2. Issuing a press release
3. Announcing in newsgroups
4. Participating in e-mail lists
5. Obtaining links from other web sites
6. Purchasing ad banners on other web sites
7. Running on-site events
8. Issuing an e-newsletter
9. Conducting a direct e-marketing campaign
10. Using our letterheads, brochures, annual reports, visiting cards, etc.

• Announcing our web site with the internet search engines and directories. The objective here is to get our web site listed in the internet's equivalent to the yellow pages. This is probably the most cost effective way of reaching prospects who otherwise may not be aware of our company. Once listed, prospects who search on these directories can find our site. There are several "tricky" things we can do to try to get our URL listed higher or more times on a search engine results page. We are listing these alternatives, but are in no way recommending them as these alternatives, but are in no way recommending them as these web site promotion methods may be viewed as "cheating" by some members of the internet community. In fact, some members of the engines penalize people who use these tricks. The reason why we list these tricks is to help us understand why some sites always show up multiple times or always at the top.

1. Placing mass amounts of hidden keywords <!publishing company, publishing company,....> at the bottom of our document. Search engines calculate keywords by how many times they appear on a page. It is important to be aware that search engines may penalize us for excessively repeating keywords. At present, InfoSeek and Lycos are two examples and other may adopt similar policies in the future.

2. Changing our name to A1 Enterprises or !Rob's restaurant in order to appear at the top. Our suggestion is that we pick something descriptive instead. We might appear at the top by changing our name, but will be skipped over because the new one does not evoke a professional or trustworthy company image.

3. Changing our <TITLE> regularly so when robots revisit our site to refresh their information, they will interpret the new title to mean the existence of a new site. The result being our page will be listed more than once in a search.

There are hundreds of sites where we can announce our site. Each typically falls into one of the following six categories:

1. Search engines
2. Announcement sites
3. General directories
4. Geographic sites
5. Specific-interest sites
6. Selective sites.

Always announce our site the day it's published as it will take from a day to several weeks for the search engines to include it in their database. It's best to not announce before our site is published, however, as prospects who click to a site still under construction are unlikely to return. As our Web site changes and grows we may want to announce additional Web pages to the search engines. For example, if we create a new section of our site for a new product, we may want to announce the main page of that section.

• Issuing a press release : a press release allows us to reach prospects through publications that cover our topic of interest. A release needs to be coordinated with the launch of our site (or it's not news) and may be distributed by e-mail, newswire, fax or mail. The four keys to a successful press release are:

1. Having newsworthy content
2. Targeting interested editors
3. Matching distribution method with editor preference
4. Properly formatting the release for each method of distribution.

• Announcing in newsgroups: A newsgroup is an electronic bulletin board where people with shared interests can communicate. There are over 20,000 newsgroups on the internet with millions of daily participants. Done right and with care, posting to a newsgroup can generate tremendous, almost instant, word-of-mouth. If we want to post, target only those newsgroups that cover topics associated with our product. First determine if the newsgroup accepts postings. If it does, monitor the postings and participants' response. When we post, provide useful advice or information, not an advertisement for our product. Be specific and keep it short. We can end with a mention that our site has useful information on the topic we are posting. If possible, become a known participant by posting frequently with both advice and questions. And, don't forget to include our signature on every e-mail or posting. If we have an announcement be sure to post it to the "announcement newsgroups" which are designed for announcements. Finally, if there's sufficient interest, we may even want to create our own newsgroup.

• Participating in e-mail lists: An e-mail list is much like a newsgroup. The key difference is that messages go directly to a participant's e-mail box rather than the participant going to the newsgroup to read the postings. For that reason, posting to an e-mail list requires even more caution than a newsgroup. Otherwise, newsgroup' rules apply.

• Obtaining links from web sites: There are two types of links:

1. One-way links to our web site
2. Two-way links where we provide a return link to the other web site.

Getting a link simply requires finding sites that have a reason for pointing to us, then asking for the link. If a site acts as a resource for information that resides on our site, the owners of the site will probably want to point to us. If we can't get them to point to our main page, then ask for a link to that page which contains the specific information. Seek out partners for trading links including vendors, suppliers and providers of complimentary products.

• Purchasing ad banners on other web sites: As more links appear on any given page, advertising increasingly becomes a way to stand out from our competition. We can sponsor another site through barter or direct payment. In either case, we can find appropriate sites to sponsor ourself or have another company find them for us. Join LinkExchange for free internet advertising.

• Running on-site events: Running events on our site is an excellent way to encourage repeat traffic. We'll want to begin running events once traffic from our site launch begins begins to fade. Examples include contests, games, on-line interviews, chat sessions and audio broadcasts.

• Issuing an e-newsletter: We can ask site visitors to sign up for a newsletter, then distribute it by e-mail. An e-newsletter allows we to keep visitors up-to-data on site changes and new offerings. It also serves as a channel for delivering valuable information related to your products that can help convert prospects into customers.

• Conducting a direct e-marketing campaign: Direct e-marketing on the Internet is in its formative stages. We can send our message in e-mail or HTML format; solicited or unsolicited. We do not recommend using unsolicited e-mail as the receiver bears the cost.

• Using our letterheads, brochures, annual reports, visiting cards, etc: This is another inexpensive, but a very effective way of advertising our site. Each time an employee gives his/her card to somebody, we are getting free advertisement. Same is the case with annual reports and brochures. Because the web is dynamic in nature people will want to visit our site for the lastest information that might not be available in the brochures or product catalogues.

So now we know how to create and announce our web presence. If we want to thrive and succeed in todays competitive companies in particular should care about their web. Small companies in particular should care about their web presence strategy, because for the first time they have a real and accessible way to level the playing field with larger competitors. We can communicate more efficiently through e-mail and newsgroups. We can access more information through research online. Our online presence can look as polished and professional as that of a Fortune 50 company. Also, the internet is a low-cost technology that is accessible to even the smallest micro-business and easier to use. So, there is virtually no reason not to advantage of this powerful tool!

Net Sport

1. Visit the site of at least four free web presence providers and find out the various services offered.
2. Find out the name of the providers who offer templates and wizards to create your web page.
3. Create our web page in any one site.
4. Visit some of the cool sites such as 'Lycos Top 5% sites' (www.lycos.com) and find out what makes them cool.

******

Chapter - 28

Network Interconnection Issues & Internetworking

Internetworking means connecting two or more distinct computer networks or network segments together to form an internetwork (often shortened to internet), using devices which operate at layer 3 (Network Layer) of the OSI Reference Model (such as routers or switches) and bridges to connect them together to allow traffic to flow back and forth between them. The layer 3 routing devices guide traffic on the correct path (among several different ones usually available) across the complete internetwork to their destination.

An internetwork is a collection of individual networks, connected by intermediate networking devices, which function as a single large network. Internetworking refers to the industry, products, and procedures that meet the challenge of creating and administering internetworks.

As single computer network may be converted into an internetwork by dividing the network into segments and then adding routers or other layer 3 devices between the segments.

The original term for an internetwork was catenet. Internetworking started as a way to connect disparate types of networking technology, but it became widespread through the developing need to connect two or more local area networks via soapier sort of wide area network.

The most notable example of internet, working in practice is the Internet, a network of networks running different low-level protocols, unified by an internetworking protocol, the Internet Protocol (IP). IP only provides an unreliable packet service across an internet. To transfer data reliably, applications must utilize a Transport layer protocol, such as TCP, which gives a reliable stream (These terms do not mean that IP is actually unreliable but instead that it sends packets without contacting and establishing a connection with the destination router beforehand. The opposite applies for reliable). Since TCP is the most widely used transport protocol. TCP and IP are referred together, as "TCP/IP". Some applications occasionally use a simpler transport protocol (called UDP) for tasks which do not needed absolutely reliable delivery of data, such as video streaming.

Following figure illustrates an internetwork.

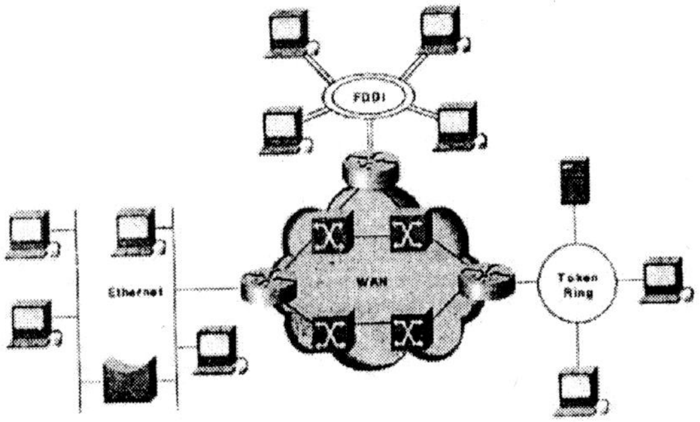

Figure: 1

Internetwork, Connecting Different Network Technologies

History of Internetworking

The first networks were time-sharing networks that used mainframes and attached terminals. Such environments were implemented by both IBM's Systems Network Architecture (SNA) and Digital's network architecture.

Local-area networks (LANs) evolved around the PC revolution. LANs enabled .multiple users in a relatively small geographical area to exchange files and messages, as well as access shared resources such as file servers and printers.

Wide-area networks (WANs) interconnect LANs with geographically dispersed users to create connectivity. Some of the technologies used for connecting LANs include Ti, T3, ATM, ISDN, ADSL, Frame Relay, radio links, and others. New methods of connecting dispersed LANs are appearing every day.

Today, high-speed LANs and switched internetworks are becoming widely used, largely because they operate at very high speeds and support such high-bandwidth applications as multimedia and videoconferencing.

Internetworking evolved as a solution to three key problems: isolated LANs, duplication of resources, and a lack of network management. Isolated LANs made electronic communication between different offices or departments impossible. Duplication of resources meant that the same hardware and software had to be supplied to each office or department, as did separate support staff. This lack of network management meant that no centralized method of managing and troubleshooting networks existed.

Network Interconnection Issues (Internetworking Issues)

Implementing a functional internetwork is no simple task. Many challenges must be faced, especially in the areas of connectivity, reliability, network management, and flexibility. Each area is key in establishing an efficient and effective internetwork.

The challenge when connecting various systems is to support communication among disparate technologies. Different sites, for example, may use different types of media operating at varying speeds, or may even include different types of systems that need to communicate.

Because companies rely heavily on data communication, internetworks must provide a certain level of reliability. This is an unpredictable world, so many large internetworks include redundancy to allow for communication even when problems occur.

Furthermore, network management must give centralized support and troubleshooting capabilities in an internetwork. Configuration, security, performance, and other issues must be adequately addressed for the internetwork to function smoothly. Security within an internetwork is essential. Many people think of network security from the perspective of protecting the private network from outside attack- However, it is just as important to protect the network from internal attacks, especially because most security breaches come from inside. Networks must also be secured so that the internal network cannot be used as a tool to attack other external sites.

Early in the year 2000, many major web sites were the victims of distributed denial of service (DDOS) attacks. These attacks were possible because a great number of private networks currently connected with the Internet were not properly secured. These private networks were used as tools for the attackers.

Because nothing in this world is stagnant, internetworks must be flexible enough to change with new demands.

Bridges

A bridge is a LAN interconnection device, which operates at the data link layer (layer 2) of the OSI reference model. It may be used to join two LAN segments, constructing a larger LAN. A bridge is able to filter traffic passing between the two LANs and may enforce a security policy separating. Different work groups located on each of the LANs. Bridges were first specified in IEEE 802.1D (1990) and later by ISO (in 1993).

We can also define the bridge as a device that connects two local-area networks (LANs), or two segments of the same LAN. Unlike router, bridges are protocol -independent. They simply forward packets without analyzing and re-routing messages.

Moreover, a bridge is a LAN connection device with two or more ports that forwards frames from one LAN (local area network) segment to another. In the past, the bridge was a small box with several LAN connectors or a server with several network interface cards. Today, bridges are more likely to appear in the form of switching devices, which are technically multi-port bridges. Each port provides a separate LAN connection that is bridged to the other ports.

On Ethernet networks, collisions occur when two nodes attempt to transmit at the same time. As more nodes are added to a network, collisions increase. A bridge can be used to divide a network into separate collision domains while retaining the broadcast domain. A broadcast domain is basically a LAN as compared to an internetwork, which is multiple LANs connected by routers. In a broadcast domain, any node can send a message to any other node using data link layer addressing, while a routed network requires internetwork addressing.

A bridge reads the outermost section of data on the data packet, to tell where the message is going. It reduces the traffic on other network segments, since it does not send all packets. Bridges can be programmed to reject packets from particular networks. Bridging occurs at the data link layer of the OSI model, which means the bridge cannot read IP addresses, but only the outermost hardware address of the packet. In our case the bridge can read the Ethernet date, which gives the hardware address of the destination address, not the IP address. Bridges forward all broadcast messages. Only a special bridge called a translation bridge will allow two networks of different architectures to be connected. Bridges do not normally allow connection of networks with different architectures. The hardware address is also called the MAC (media access control) address. To determine the network segment a MAC address belongs to, bridges use one of:

- Transparent Bridging - They build a table of addresses (bridging table) as they receive packets. If the address is not in the bridging table, the packet is forwarded to all segments other than the one it came from. This type of bridge is used on ethernet networks.
- Source route bridging - The source computer provides path information inside the packet. This is used on Token Ring networks.

Major Functions

The bridge gives many important functions:

- It allows a single LAN to be extended to greater distances.

- We can join different types of network links with a bridge while retaining the same broadcast domain. For example, we can bridge two distant LANs with bridges joined by fiber-optic cable.
- A bridge forwards frames, but a filtering mechanism can be used to prevent unnecessary frames from propagating across the network.
- They give a barrier that keeps electrical or other problems on one segment from propagating to the other segment.
- A bridge isolates. each LAN from the collisions that occur on other LANs. Thus, it creates separate collision domains within the same broadcast domain.

Types of Bridges

Bridges can be grouped into categories based on various product characteristics. Using one popular classification scheme, bridges are either local or remote.

Local bridges provide a direct connection between multiple LAN segments in the same area.

Remote bridges connect multiple LAN segments in different areas, usually over telecommunications lines. Following figure illustrates these two configurations.

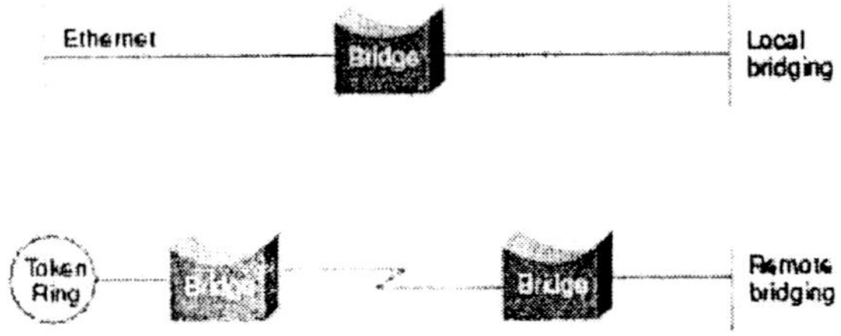

Figure: 2

Local and Remote Bridges Connect LAN Segments in Specific Areas

Remote bridging presents several unique internetworking challenges, one of which is the difference between LAN and WAN speeds. Although several fast WAN technologies now are establishing a presence in geographically dispersed internetworks, LAN speeds are often much faster than WAN speeds. Vast differences in LAN and WAN speeds can prevent users from running delay-sensitive LAN applications over the WAN.

Remote bridges cannot improve WAN speeds, but they can compensate for speed discrepancies through a sufficient buffering capability. If a LAN device capable of a 3-Mbps transmission rate wants to communicate with a device on a remote LAN,' the local bridge must regulate the 3-Mbps data stream so that it does not overwhelm the 64 kbps serial link. This is done by storing the incoming data in onboard buffers and sending it over the serial link at a rate that the serial link can accommodate. This buffering can be achieved only for short bursts of data that do not overwhelm the bridge's buffering capability.

Operation of a Bridge

The simplest type of bridge, and that most frequently used is the Transparent Bridge (meaning that the nodes using a bridge are unaware of its presence). The bridge therefore has to forward (receive and subsequently transmit) frames from one LAN (e.g. LAN A below) to another (e.g. LAN B). Obviously, the bridge could forward all frames, but then it would behave rather like a repeater; it would be much smarter if the bridge only forwarded frames, which need to travel from one LAN to another. To do this, the bridge need to learn which computers are connected to which LANs. More formally, it need to learn whether to forward to each address

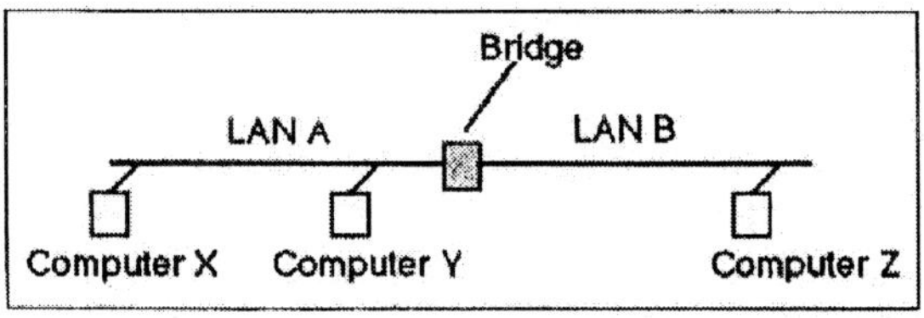

Figure : 3

A bridge connecting two LAN segments (A and B).

To learn which addresses are in use, and which ports (interfaces on the bridge) theory are closest to, the bridge observes the headers of received Ethernet frames. By examining the MAC source address of each received frame, and recording the port on which it was received, the bridge may learn which addresses belong to the computers connected via each Dort. This is called "learning". In the figure above, consider three computers X,Y,Z. Assume each sends frames to the other computers. The source addresses X,Y are observed to be on network A, while the address of computer Z will be observed to be on network B.

The learned addresses are stored in the an interface address table associated with each port (interface). Once this table has been setup, the bridge examines the destination address of all received frames, it then scans the interface tables to see if a frame has been received from the same address (i.e. a packet with a source address matching the current destination address). Three possibilities exist:

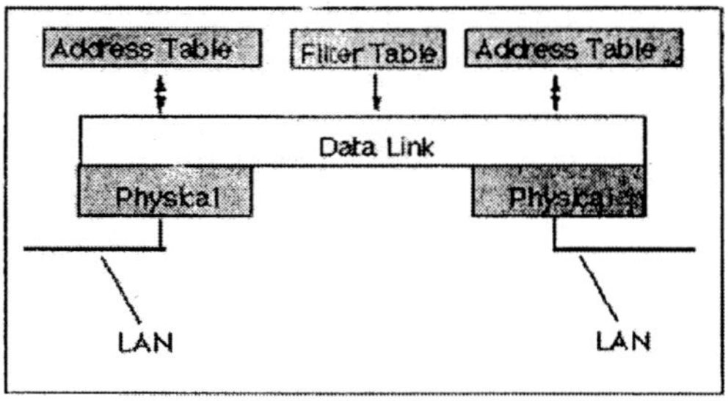

Figure : 4

A bridge stores the hardware addresses observed from frames received by each interface and uses this information to learn which frames need to be forwarded by the bridge.

1. If the address is not found, no frames have been received from the source. The source may not exist, or it may not have sent any frames using this address. (The address may also have been deleted by the bridge because the bridge software was recently restarted, ran short of address entries in the interface table, or deleted the address because it was too old). Since the bridge does not know which port to use to forward the frame, it will send it to all output ports, except that on which it was received. It is clearly unnecessary to send it back to the same cable segment from which it was received, since any other computer/ bridges on this cable must already have received the packet. This is called flooding.
2. If the address is found in an interface table and the address is associated with the port on which it was received the frame is discarded. (It must already have been received by the destination.)
3. If the address is found in an interface table and the address is not associated with the port on which it was received, the bridge forwards the frame to the port associated with the address.

Packets with a source of X and destination of Y are received and discarded, since the computer Y is directly connected to the LAN A, whereas packets from X with a destination of Z are forwarded to network B by the bridge.

Managing the Interface Tables

A bridge may implement an interface table using a software data structure or use a Contents Addressable Memory (CAM) chip. In either case, the size of the table is finite, and usually constrained to 1000's - 10 000's of entries. In a large LAN this may be a limit. To help keep the table small, most bridges maintain a check of how recently each address was used. Addresses, which have not been used for a long period of time (e.g. minutes) are deleted. This has the effect of removing unused entries, but if the address is again used, before a frame is received from the same source, it will require the frame to be flooded to all ports.

A useful side effect of deleting old addresses is that the bridge interface table records only working MAC addresses. If a NIC stops sending; its address will be deleted from the table. If the NIC is subsequently reconnected, the entry will be restored, but if the connection is made to another port (the cable is changed) a different (updated) entry will be inserted corresponding to the actual port associated with the address. The bridge always updates the interface table for each source address in a received MAC frame, therefore even if a computer changes the point at which it is connected without first having the interface table entry removed, the bridge will still update the table entry.

Filter Tables

In some bridges, a system administrator may override the normal forwarding by inserting entries in a filter table to inhibit forwarding between different work groups (for example to provide security for a particular set of MAC addresses). The filter table contains a list of source or destination addresses. Frames, which match entries in the filter table, will only be forwarded to specific configured ports.

Routers

Like bridges, routers are devices whose primary purpose is to connect two or more networks and to filter network signals so that only desired information travels between them. For example, routers are often used to regulate the flow of information between school networks and the Internet. However, routers can inspect a good deal more information than bridges, and they therefore can regulate network traffic more precisely. They also have another important capability: they are aware of many possible paths across the network and can choose the best one for each data packet to travel.

Routers determine some possible routes to the destination network and then choose the one that promises to be the fastest. As network traffic patterns change during a day, routers can adjust their route recommendations. There is a good deal of jargon associated with the art and science by which routers select paths, and a whole host of protocols that define their methods (for example, OSPF [Open Shortest Path First], RIP [Routing Information Protocol], or RTMP [Routing Table Maintenance Protocol] etc.)

Routers are internetworking devices that connect similar and heterogeneous network segments into internetworks. It may be used to connect two or more IP networks, or an IP network to an Internet connection. Routers are layer 3 networking devices designed to take incoming packets, analyzing the packets and then directing them to the appropriate locations, moving the packets to another network, converting the packets to be moved across a different type of network interface, dropping the packets, or performing any other number of other types of actions.

The device may be a stand-alone dedicated router from a vendor such as Cisco Systems, or a computer with network interface cards (Ethernet, token ring, and so on) running a network operating system like Novell NetWare, Sun Microsystems's Solaris, or Microsoft Windows 2000.

A router has a lot more capabilities than other network devices such as a hub or a switch, which are only able to perform basic network functions. For example, a hub is often used to transfer data between computers or network devices, but does not analyze or do anything with the data it is transferring. A network router, however, may take the data being sent over a network, change how it is packaged, and send it to another network or over a different type of network. For example, routers are commonly used in home networks to share a single internet connection with multiple computers.

Routers store and forward datagram's and process network layer information. Routers also run routing protocols that discover and gather information about the network topology calculate routes to other networks, and build routing tables. Some management functions are also required. This requires one or more processors and memory to store routing tables and other information.

A router consists of a computer with at least two network interface cards supporting the IP protocol. The router receives packets from each interface via a network interface and forwards the received packets to an appropriate output network interface. Received packets have all link layer protocol headers removed, and transmitted packets have a new link protocol header added prior to transmission.

Characteristics

- Routers transmit packets across different types of data link layer networks.
- Since different networks have different frame sizes, routers must be able to fragment packets so they fit in the frame size of the underlying network.
- Store a packet temporarily to read its routing information and then forward it. Store and forwarding causes some delay, but newer switching and multi-layer switching techniques improve performance.
- Allow routers to drop packets in an overflow situation, but rely on TCP running in end systems to determine that packets have been dropped (or lost).

- Routers do not maintain state information, which is information that can be used to track packet delivery between end systems and detect errors, or reserve bandwidth for flows as is done with RSVP.
- Routers also discover, collect, and assemble information about routes on the network that can be used to perform route selection when forwarding packets. This is handled by routing protocols that run in the router, such as RIP, OSPF, or BGP.
- A router may perform "firewall-like" functions such as packet filtering and discard. For example, packets may be dropped if they do not match a range of IP addresses or if they are for applications other than those allowed.

Interfaces of a Router

A modern router is a complex piece of equipment. The outside of the equipment is usually very simple, consisting of a number of network interface ports (shown on the left in the figure below) to which cables may be connected and a few indicator lights to indicate that the router is functional.

Most routers also have a serial connector to which a terminal (or a modem) may be connected, known as the "Console Port" (shown to the right in the figure below). This port is usually used to control the router configuration when the router is first installed. It may be the only port, which is allowed to configure the filter table (used to prevent unauthorized access between the connected networks).

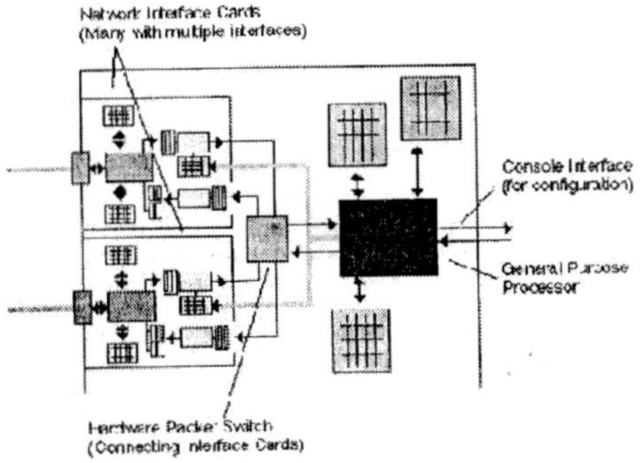

Figure: 5

Block diagram of a complete router showing the interfaces to the network

In the simplest case, the processing of packets is implemented in the general purpose processor, which implements all the algorithms. More advanced routers may separate "forwarding" (the tasks of moving packets from one interface to another) from "routing" (the task of determining the best path through the network) and include a number of processors capable of performing these tasks. A router interface card resembles the LAN Network Interface Cards (NICs) used in PCs except that the card is normally of a higher specification (faster packet processing). The very first routers were designed used standard network interface cards, but modern high performance routers use special high performance interface cards and may also include a "Forwarding Engine" on-board the card which speeds the operation.

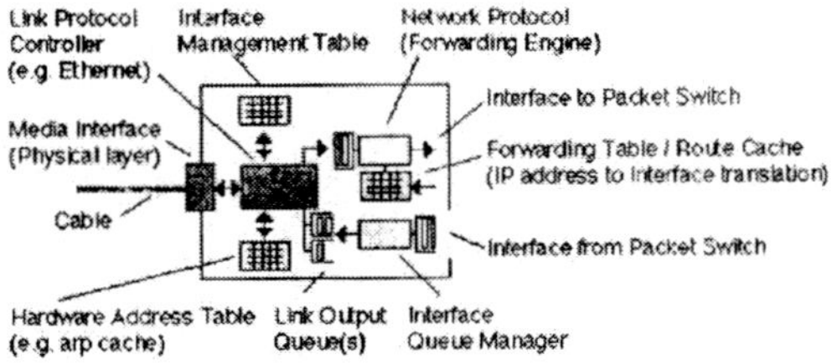

Figure: 6

Router Network Interface Card

Received packets are processed by the link layer protocol controller, which handles the link layer protocol (e.g. HDLC, Ethernet) used over the physical link (cable). This also checks the received frame integrity (size, checksum, address, etc). Valid frames are converted to packets by removing the link layer header and are queued in the receive queue. This is usually a First-In-First-Out (FIFO) queue, often in the form of a ring of memory buffers.

The buffers are passed (drained) into the input to the forwarding engine. This takes each buffer, one at a time, and removes it from the interface receiver. The packet is then forwarded to an appropriate output interface, corresponding to the "best" path to the destination specified in the destination address of the IF packet header.

At the output interface, the packet (together with a new link layer header) is placed into a transmit queue until the link layer processor is ready to transmit the packet. This, like the receive queue, is a FIFO queue, and usually also takes the form of a ring of memory buffers.

Each out-going packet requires a new link layer protocol header to be added (encapsulation) with the destination address set to the next system to the receive the packet. The link protocol controller also maintains the hardware address table associated with the interface. This usually involves using the Address Resolution Protocol (ARP) to find out the hardware (Medium Access Control) addresses of other computers or routers directly connected to the same cable (or LAN). The packet is finally sent using the media interface with the hardware address set to the next hop system. When complete, the buffer (memory) allocated to the frame, is "freed", that is, it is returned as an empty buffer to the receive queue, where it may be used to store a new received packet.

Route Processor

The routing processor is responsible for configuring each network interface card (including the forwarding table), and collecting management information (from the management table associated with each interface) for the Router Management Table. The processor is also directly connected to the packet switch which allows the configuration to be (optionally) accessed and modified by establishing a connection form an End-System connected via the network. All configuration data and all performance data collected from the network interface cards are stored in the central router management table. Iii large routers, a backup routing processor may be provided, in case the main processor fails.

The route processor also processes all packets destined to the router itself (see below).

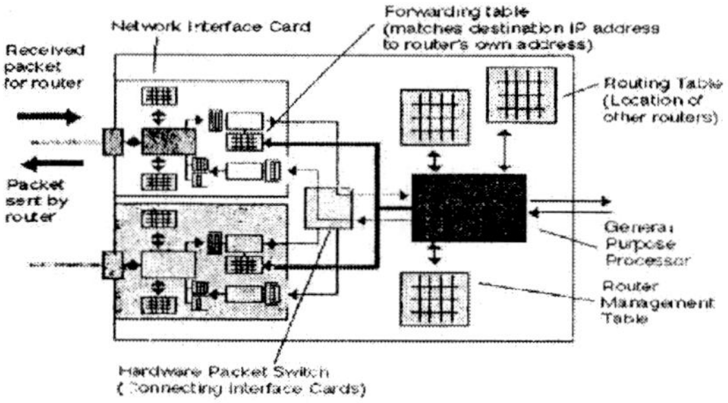

Figure: 7

Sending and receiving packets which have address which match the routers own IP address. These packets may simply be ICMP echo request messages (to check the router is working) or may be packets directed to the router itself (e.g. indicating routing information from other routers or accessing the information held in the router management table).

Packets Destined for the Router (Route Processor)

When the router responds to received packets (with one of the router's own IP addresses) it will behave as an End-System, rather an Intermediate-System (where it forwards packets between interfaces). The router general purpose processor will also respond to any ICMP messages it receives (e.g. sent by the "Ping" program), and may generate ICMP error messages when error events are detected (such as a packet received which cannot be routed because the address is not known).

The processor first performs any necessary checks on the packet header and will then determine whether the packet should be discarded, logged (in the router management table) or forwarded. The general purpose CPU is also responsible for configuring the Forwarding Tables used by the switching process. The router computes the forwarding tables by processing two local tables: The Routing Table and the Filter Table.

The "Routing Table" contains lists of internet addresses and their corresponding location in the network. A router connected to the Internet will need to be able to identify which interface is to be used to reach every other connected end system. Routers near the centre of a network generally have very large routing tables, those nearer the edges have smaller tables.

The routing table is constructed by using information supplied when the router is configured (installed) by the manager, which it stores in the routing table. Although the routing table may be configured by hand, it is usually configured automatically using a "Routing Protocol". The routing protocol allows routers to periodically e.g. every few tens of seconds exchange information about the contents of their own routing tables. After a period of time, the router becomes aware of all the possible ways to reach each end system connected at any point in the network. It therefore adds information to its own routing table about the other routers to which it is connected, building a picture of how to reach other parts of the network. This is achieved by periodically sending packets to all neighboring routers.

The filter table is usually manually configured, and contains a list of addresses and other packet header details, which, if they match a received packet, will cause the packet to be examined in detail and possibly rejected. This may be used to prevent unauthorized packets being forwarded (e.g. to act as a firewall). When a packet is detected by a network interface card (i.e. it matches an entry in the forwarding table), it may be either discarded by the network interface immediately, or forwarded directly to the general-purpose processor for further processing. This table is often called an Access Control List (ACL), and may become very complex in some applications.

As the router discovers changes in the routing tables and filter tables it may either

I. Invalidate the forwarding cache, causing the fast switching process to start build a new forwarding cache.
2. Constructs a new forwarding information base for each network interface card, with the appropriate modifications.

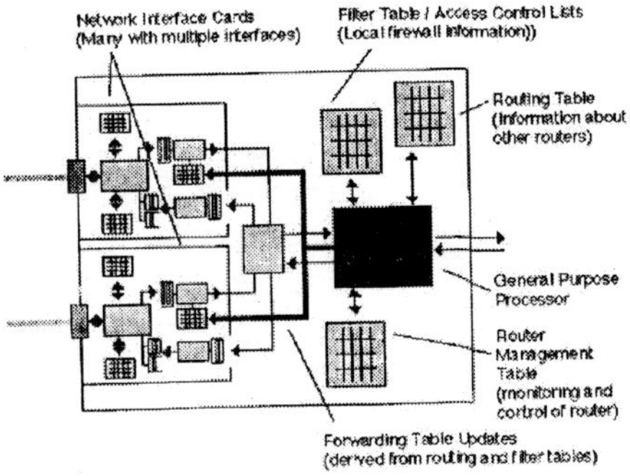

Figure: 8

This ensures the forwarding engines (switching processors) to be updated. The forwarding information base is optimized for speed (since it needs to be consulted for each received packet), in contrast, the routing table is optimized to ease updating, since received packets received via the routing protocol may require many changes to be made to the routing table (e.g. after the network topology changes following a failure of a communications link).

Figure: As required, network interface cards must be reloaded with new forwarding information, which reflects any changes to the network topology. This information is based on the information configured in the filter table and collected from the network and stored in the routing information base.

Important Functions of a Router

When a packet arrives at a router port, it is placed in an input buffer to await processing. Buffers are blocks of memory that temporarily hold packets until they can be processed. Note that each interface has input and output buffers. The switching fabric may also have its own buffers. Buffers are a key part of a router. The size of the buffers is critical. Network traffic may burst into the router faster than the router can process the traffic. Buffers temporarily hold packets until they can be processed. If there are too few buffers, the buffers will fill quickly and incoming packets will be dropped. Dropped packets require retransmission, which affects network performance. Too many buffers can cause excessive delay.

An incoming packet may be addressed to the router, but most packets will require forwarding, as described here:

1. Strip off the frame information and retrieve the datagram. Check for errors and forward the datagram to the appropriate protocol forwarding process in the router (for multiprotocol routers).
2. Get the IP network address (the host portion is irrelevant until the datagram reaches the destination network).

3. Look up the address in the routing table to determine how to forward the packet. Find the best match in the table by finding the longest match, meaning that the network address with the most number of bits that match the destination address is used. If no match is found, generate an ICMP error response ando send it to the source.
4. Update the IP datagram Time-To-Live field (TTL). If the TTL decrements to zero, discard the datagram (assumes it is in a loop).
5. Make sure the datagram will fit in the MTU (maximum transmission unit) of the next hop network. MTU is the size of the data area for the frame. Datagrams may be fragmented to fit the MTU.
6. Send the packet to the output queue of the appropriate interface. If the queue is full, drop the packet and send an ICMP message to the sender that indicates congestion.

******

Chapter - 29

Correlation

Correlation means a relation between two series or groups of data. If two or quantities vary in sympathy so that movements in the one tend to be accompanied .responding movements in the others, then they are said to be correlated. Prof. Y defines "when two quantities are so related that the fluctuations in one are sympathy with the fluctuations in the other, so that an increase or decrease of one series has connection with an increase or decrease or inversely of the other and the magnitude of the changes in the one, the greatest the magnitude of the changes in the other, the two quantities are said to be correlated "

In the words of Prof. W.I. King "If it is proved true that in a larger r of instances two variables tend always to fluctuate in the same or in inverse directions, we consider that the fact is established and that a relationship established. This relationship is called correlation."

Methods of Determining Correlation

A. Graphic Methods: (i) Scatter diagram, (ii) Simple graph.

B. Mathematical Methods: (i) Karl Pearson's Coefficient of Correlation

(ii) Spearman's. Rank Coefficient of Correlation

(iii) Coefficient of Concurrent Deviations.

(iv) Least Squares Method.

We are concerned here with Mathematical methods only. Therefore, Karl's coefficient of correlation is popularly denoted by r (Small r)

(i) Direct Method. Deviations from Actual average.

(Karl Pearson's coefficient of correlation)

1. Positive and Negative Correlation: When both the variables change in same direction, that is when both increase or decrease the relationship between the two series is called positive or direct. But when the change is in opposite directions one is increasing and the other is decreasing, the correlation is negative.

For determining the direction of change average values are taken.

For example :

(I) Positive Corelation				(II) Negative Correlation			
(a) Both variables increasing		(b) Both variables decreasing		(a) One variable incrasing the other decreasing		(b) One variable decreasing the other increasing	
x	y	x	y	x	y	x	y
	100	7	147	25	125	75	110
	150	60	140	30	110	60	180
	160	40	135	35	90	40	190
	190	30	130	40	80	30	200
	200	15	120	45	75	20	240
	255	10	90	50	60	10	250

We find that in I (a) the values of X series are increasing so also of the Y series. In I (b) values in X and Y are decreasing. Thus, they are both instance of positive correlation. On the other hand, in II (a) the values of X are increasing and the values of Y are decreasing, similarly in II (b) the values of X are decreasing and the values of Y are increasing. Thus, they are both examples of negative correlation.

Examples : (Positive Correlation)

1. Age of husband and age of wife.
2. Price of commodity and amount of supply.
3. Increase in rainfall up to a point and production of rice.
4. Increase in heat affects temperature.
5. Increase in cost of advertisement and sales.
6. Increase in height and weight.

Examples : (Negative Correlation)

1. Demand of a commodity may go down as a result of rise in prices.
2. Increase in the number of television sets and number of cinema goers.
3. Sale of woolen garments and day temperature.

2. Linear and Curvilinear Correlation: If the ratio of change between two variables is uniform then there exists linear correlation between them. Linear and non-linear correlation is based upon the consistency of the ratio of change between the variables. Their relationship is described by the straight line. If the variables under study are graphed, the points will form a straight line. In Case of non-linear relationship (curvy-linear), the amount of change in one variable does not bear a constant ratio to the amount of change in the other variable. Such relationship will form a curve on graph.

3. Simple, Multiple and Partial Correlation. Simple, multiple and partial correlation is based upon the number of variables under study. When only two variables are involved, the analysis of relationship between them is called simple correlation. When more than two variables are studied; the relationship can be either multiple or partial. Simultaneous effect of two or more dependent variables are one independent variable is a study of multiple correlation. For example if we study relationship between agricultural production, rainfall and the amount of fertilizers used, it will be a multiple correlation. In partial correlation, the relationship of two variables is studied by eliminating the effect of other variables from the both. Partial correlation is a study of relationship of more than two variables. For examples, Mathematical study of combined effect of both the amount of rainfall and temperature on the yield of wheat is a problem of multiple correlation. But the correlation analysis of amount of rainfall and yield of wheat in a certain constant temperature, is a problem of partial correlation.

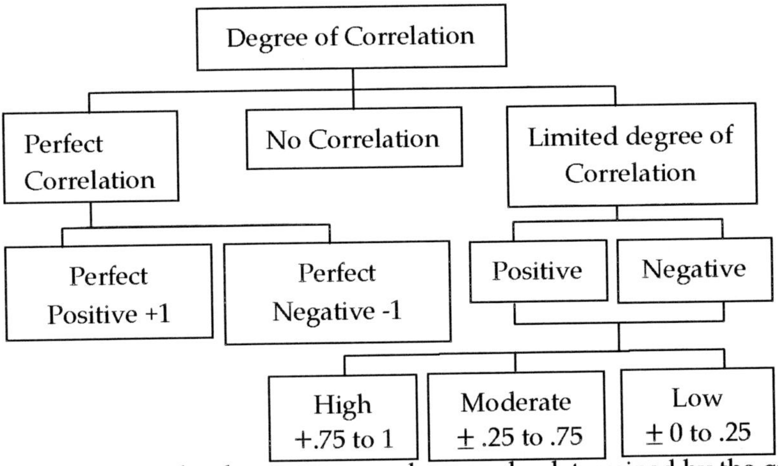

The relationship between two values can be determined by the quantitative value of coefficient of correlation, which is obtained by calculations.

Perfect Correlation: Perfect correlation is that 'Where changes in two related variables are exactly proportional. If equal proportional changes are in the same direction, there is perfect positive correlation between the two values described as +1; and if equal proportional changes are in the reverse direction, there is perfect negative correlation described as - 1. For example; the .circumference of a circle increases in the equal proportionate ratio with an increase in the equal proportionate ratio in the length Of its diameter, the amount of electricity bill increase in a perfectly. definite ratio with an increase in the number of unit consumed; the volume of a gas varies inversely with the pressure at constant temperature, etc.

No Correlation: When there exists no interdependence between the two variables or no relationship is found between the change in them, there is no correlation or absence of correlation; described as .0 (zero).

Limited Degree of Correlation: In social .science, the variables may be correlated, but an increase in one variable need not always be accompanied by a corresponding or equal increase (or decrease) in the other variable. Correlation is said to be limited positive when there are unequal changes in the two variables in the same direction; and correlation is limited negative when there are unequal changes in the reverse direction. The limited degree of combination can be high (between ± .75 to I); moderate (± .25 to .75), or low between (between ± 0 to .25).

Thu, the calculated result of correlation must vary between - 1 to + 1.

Limitations of Correlation or Assumptions of Correlation

The following are the limitations or assumptions of correlation:

(i) Normality: Correlated series are affected by numerous causes thus, there may arise a possibility of normality.

(ii) Causal Relationship: Cause and effects are responsible for Positive and Negative correlation between two independent variables. If there is no evidence of such cause and effect reason, then the existence of correlation is doubtful.

(iii) Linear Nature: This is also a limitation that while knowing correlation it is to be assumed that there exists a linear relationship if these are plotted on a graph-paper then the picture will be like a straight line.

(iv) The existence of correlation always moves between + 1 or - 1, it can not 'exceeds in any case more than + I.

(v) Difficulty in Calculation of Probable Error: Calculation of 'y' is not easy, yet for drawing reliable result probable error be calculated which is again a difficult task.

(vi) Calculation of Standard Errors: It is always .6745 in normal distribution 50% values are covered in it, thus, it is a test of significance of 'y'.

Methods of Studying Correlation

There are various methods of finding correlation. Some of them are :

(a) Scatter Diagram

(b) Karl Pearson's Coefficient of Correlation

(c) Coefficient of Correlation by Rank Differences

(d) Regression Lines and Regression Coefficients.

Scatter Diagram

Scatter diagram is a simple visual method for getting some idea about the presence of correlation. It is obtained by plotting value on a graph paper. When the plotted points show some trend: upward or downward, we know that there is some correlation between the variables. When the trend is upward the correlation is positive, when it is downward the correlation is negative. Let 'us study the scatter diagrams on following page.

Figure (a), (c) and (e) show an upward trend, they show positive correlation. Figure (b), (d) and (f) show a downward trend, they show negative correlation. However, there are differences between (a), (c) and (e) and similar differences between (b), (d) and (f).

We find from the plotting on the scatter diagrams that there is a certain similarity between (a) and (b), (c) and (d), and (e) and (f). In (a) and (b) the plotted points are almost in a straight lines, this indicates perfect correlation. In (c) and (d) the plotted points are not in a straight line but if we draw a straight line in a middle of their points (regression line) we will find, the points are near about the line. This kind of scatter diagram shows high degree correlation. In (e) and (f) if we draw a similar line (regression line), we will find that the plotted points are very much scattered around the line-not as near as in the case of (c) and (d). This kind of scattered diagram shows low degree correlation. Finally, diagram (g) shows such a vast scatter of points that it is impossible to see any trend, this shows no correlation or zero correlation.

SCATTER DIAGRAM AND CORRELATION

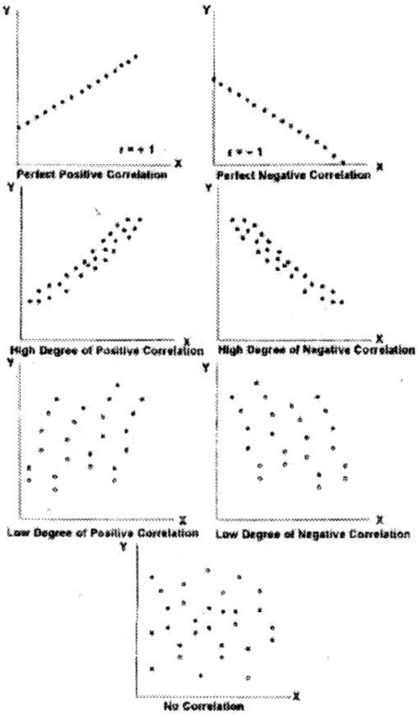

$$r = \frac{\sum dxdy}{N\sigma_x\sigma_y}$$

Here $\sum dxdy$ = Total of the products of the deviation of values from the respective arithmetic means in both the series.

N = Number of items

σ_x = Standard deviation of X series

σ_y = Standard deviation of Y Series

(ii) Short Cut Method

Deviation from assumed average

$$r = \frac{N\sum dxdy-(\sum dx)(\sum dy)}{\sqrt{N\sum d^2x-(\sum dx)^2}\sqrt{N\sum d^2y-(\sum dy)^2}}$$

Here N= Number of items d^2

$\sum dxdy$ = Total of the products of the deviations of value from the respective arithmetic means in both the series.

$\sum dx$, Edy = Sum of the deviations from the assumed mean in X and Y respectively.

Σd^2x, Fd^2y = Sum of the squares of the deviations from the assumed mean in X and Y series respectively.

(iii) Probable Error (P.E.) or r=.6745 $\frac{1-r^2}{\sqrt{N}}$

Where 0.6745 is a constant Number

N = Number of items

r = Karl Pearson's Coeff. of correlation.

(iv) Spearman's Rank Difference Method.

'ρ'(Pronounced as rho) $= 1 - \frac{6\sum d^2}{N(N^2-1)}$

Where P stands for rank coeff. of correlation,

Ed^2 = Total of squares of rank differences.

N = Number of pairs of items

Correction for tied ranks

$$\rho = 1 - \frac{6[\sum d^2+1/12\,(m^3-m)]}{N\,(N^2-1)}$$

Where m=represents the number of items having tied ranks.

(v) Concurrent Deviation Method.

$$r_c = \pm\sqrt{\pm\frac{2C-N}{N}}$$

Where = coefficient of concurrent deviations

C = Number of concurrent deviations

N = Number of pairs of deviations.

The use of + or – sign will depend upon the sign of

$$\left(\frac{2C-N}{N}\right)$$

Practical Problems

Example : Calculate Karl Pearson's coefficient of correlation from the advertisement cost and sales as per the data given below :

Advertisement Cost (in Rs.)	39	65	62	90	82	75	25	98	36	78
Sales (in Rs.)	47	53	58	86	62	68	60	91	51	85

Solution: Calculation of Coeff. of correlation.

Advertisment Cost (in (Rs.) (x)	Dev. From Mean (65) dx	Square of Dev. d^2x	Sales (Rs.) y	Dev. From Mean (66) dy	Square of Deviatition of d^2y	Product of deviation dxdy
39	-26	676	47	-19	361	494
65	0	0	53	-13	169	0
62	-3	9	58	-8	64	24
90	25	625	86	20	400	500
80	17	289	62	-4	16	-68
75	10	100	68	2	4	20
25	-40	1600	60	-6	36	240
98	33	1089	91	25	625	825
36	-29	841	51	-15	225	435
78	13	169	84	18	324	234
$\sum x$=650 N = 10	98-98 $\sum dx = 0$	Σd^2x = 5398	Σy= 660	Σdy =0	Σd^2y = 2224	$\Sigma dxdy$=2704 (2772 - 68)

$$Mean\ of\ x\ series\ x = \frac{\Sigma x}{N} = \frac{650}{10} = 65$$

$$Mean\ of\ y\ series\ y = \frac{\Sigma y}{N} = \frac{660}{10} = 66$$

$$r = \frac{\Sigma\, dxdy}{N\sqrt{\frac{\Sigma d^2x}{N}}\sqrt{\frac{\Sigma d^2y}{N}}} = \frac{2704}{10\sqrt{\frac{5398}{10}\times\sqrt{\frac{2224}{10}}}}$$

$$= \frac{2704}{10\sqrt{593.8}\times\sqrt{222.4}}$$

$$= \frac{2704}{10\times 23.23\times 14.91}$$

$$= \frac{2704}{3464.31} = 0.78$$

$$r = 0.78\ Ans.$$

Example : The following table gives indices of industrial production of registered employed (in thousand hundred.) Calculate the value of the coefficient so obtained.

Year	2007	2008	2009	2010	2011	2012	2013	2014
Index of Production	100	102	104	107	105	112	103	99
Number employed	15	12	13	11	12	12	19	26

Solution. Calculation of Karl Pearson's coeff. Of correlation.

Year	Production X	dx	dx2	unemployed Y	dy	dy2	dxdy
2007	**100**	**-4**	**16**	**15**	**0**	**0**	0
2008	102	-2	4	12	-3	9	6
2009	104	0	0	13	-2	4	0
2010	107	3	9	11	-4	16	-12
2011	105	1	1	12	-3	9	-3
2012	112	8	64	12	-3	9	-24
2013	103	-1	1	19	4	16	-4
2014	99	-5	25	26	11	121	-55
	832	**0**	**120**	**120**	**0**	**184**	**-92**

$$X = \frac{\sum x}{N} = \frac{832}{8} = 104 \qquad Y = \frac{\sum y}{N} = \frac{120}{8} = 15$$

$$r = \frac{\sum dxdy}{\sqrt{\sum x^2 \times \sum y^2}}$$

$$r = \frac{-92}{\sqrt{120 \times 184}} = \frac{-92}{\sqrt{22080}} = \frac{-92}{148.5934} = -0.619$$

$$r = -0.619 \; Ans.$$

Short cut Method

Example : Calculate Karl Pearson's coefficient of correlation between price and supply of a commodity from the following data :

Price (Rs.)	17	18	19	20	21	22	23	24	25	26
Supply (Kg.)	38	37	38	33	32	33	34	29	26	23

Solution: Calculation of Coeff. Of Correlation.

price Rs. X	Deviation from As. Av. 20 dx	d2x	Supply (Kg) y	Deviation form As. Av. 32 dy	d2y	dxdy
17	**-3**	**9**	**38**	**6**	**36**	**-18**
18	-2	4	37	5	25	-10
19	-1	1	38	6	36	-6
20	0	0	33	1	1	0
21	1	1	32	0	0	0
22	2	2	33	1	1	2
23	3	9	34	2	4	6
24	4	16	29	-3	9	-12
25	5	25	26	-6	36	-30
26	6	36	23	-9	81	-54
N=10	Σdx=15	Σd^2x =105		Σdy=3	Σd^2y = 229	Σdxdy = -122

$$r = \frac{N\sum dxdy - (\sum dx)(\sum dy)}{\sqrt{N\sum d^2x - (\sum dx)^2}\sqrt{N\sum d^2y - (\sum dy)^2}}$$

$$= \frac{10(-122) - 15 \times 3}{\sqrt{10 \times 105 - (15)^2}\sqrt{10 \times 229 - (3)^2}}$$

$$= \frac{-1220-45}{\sqrt{1050-225}\sqrt{2290-9}} = \frac{-1265}{\sqrt{825}\sqrt{2281}}$$

$$= \frac{-1265}{28.7228 \times 47.7598} = \frac{-1264}{1371.7956} = -0.922 \quad r = -0.922 \; Ans.$$

Example : The following table gives the soil temperature and the germination time at various places. Calculate the correlation coefficient and interpret its value.

Temperature	57 42 40 38 42 45 42 44
Germination Time	10 26 30 41 29 27 27 19
Temperature	40 46 44 43
Germination Time	18 19 31 29

Take 44 and 26 as assumed mean.

Solution. Let temperature be denoted by X and germination time by Y.

Calculation of coeff. Of correlation

x	dx (x=44)	dx^2	y	dy(Y - 26)	dy^2	dxdy
57	13	169	10	-16	256	-208
42	-2	4	26	0	0	0
40	-4	16	30	4	16	-16
38	-6	36	41	15	225	-90
42	-2	4	29	3	9	-6
45	1	1	27	1	1	1
42	-2	4	27	1	1	-2
44	0	0	19	-7	49	0
40	-4	16	18	-8	64	32
46	2	4	19	-7	49	-14
44	0	0	31	5	25	0
43	-1	1	29	3	9	-3
n = 12	Σdx = 16-21 = -5	255 Σdx^2	N = 12	Σdy = - 6 - 38 + 32	Σd^2y 704	Σdxdy = -339 + 33 = - 306

$$r = \frac{N\sum dxdy - (\sum dx)(\sum dy)}{\sqrt{N\sum dx^2 - (\sum dx)^2}\sqrt{N\sum dy^2 - (\sum dy)^2}}$$

$$= \frac{12 \times (-306) - (-5)(-6)}{\sqrt{[12 \times 255 - (-5)^2]}\sqrt{[12 \times 704 - (-6)^2]}}$$

$$= \frac{-3672-30}{\sqrt{[3060-25][8448-36]}} = \frac{-3702}{\sqrt{3035 \times 8412}}$$

$$= \frac{-3702}{55.0908 \times 91.7169} = \frac{-3702}{5052.7635} = -0.7327 \; Ans.$$

Thus, there is a high degree of negative correlation between temperature and germination time.

Example : Find Karl Pearson's correlation between temperature and germination time.

Age	15	16	17	18	19	20
No. of Students	250	200	150	120	100	80
Regular Player	200	150	90	48	30	16

Solution: Here we will compute the correlation coefficient between the age (X) and percentage of regular players (Y).

No. of Students	No. of Regular players	Percentage of Regular Player (y)
250	200	$\frac{200}{250} \times 100 = 80$
200	150	$\frac{150}{200} \times 100 = 75$
150	90	$\frac{90}{150} \times 100 = 60$
120	48	$\frac{48}{120} \times 100 = 48$
100	30	$\frac{30}{100} \times 100 = 30$
80	16	$\frac{16}{80} \times 100 = 20$
We see that we can take the factor 5 common from each of the y values		

X	dx (X-17)	dx^2	y	$dy\left(\frac{y-40}{5}\right)$	dy^2	$dxdy$
15	-2	4	80	8	64	-16
16	-1	1	75	7	49	-7
17	0	0	60	4	16	0
18	1	1	40	0	0	0
19	2	4	30	-2	4	-4
20	3	9	20	-4	16	-12
n = 6	dx = 3	Σ dx^2=19	n = 6	Σ dy=13	149	-39

$$r = \frac{n\sum dxdy-(\sum dx)(\sum dy)}{\sqrt{n\sum dx^2-(\sum dx)^2} \times \sqrt{n\sum dy^2-(\sum dy)^2}}$$

$$= \frac{6\times(-39)-3\times13}{\sqrt{[6\times19-(3)^2]}\times\sqrt{[6\times149-(13)^2]}}$$

$$= \frac{-234-39}{\sqrt{114-9}\sqrt{894-169}} = \frac{-273}{\sqrt{105\times\sqrt{725}}}$$

$$= \frac{-273}{\sqrt{105\times725}} = \frac{-273}{\sqrt{76125}} = \frac{-273}{275.907}$$

$or\ r = 0.989\ Ans.$

Example (i) Find Karl Pearson's coefficient of correlation from the following series of marks secured by 10 students in a class test in Mathematics and Statistics :

Marks in Maths 45 70 65 30 90 40 50 75 85 60

Marks in Statistics 35 90 70 40 95 40 60 80 80 50

Also Calculate its probable error. Assume 60 and 65 as working means.

(ii) Hence discuss if the value of r is significant or not. Also compute the limits within which the population correlation may be expected to lie.

Solution: (i) Let the marks in mathematics be denoted by the variable X and the marks in statistics by the variable Y. It may be noted that we can take out the factor 5 common in each of the X and Y series. Taking 60 and 65 as working means for X & Y.

Calculation of correlation coefficient.

x	dx(60)	dx^2 (5)	dx^2	y	dy(65)	dy^2 (5)	dy^2	dxdy
45	**-15**	**-3**	**9**	**35**	**-30**	**-6**	36	18
70	10	2	4	90	25	5	25	10
65	5	1	1	70	5	1	1	1
30	-30	-6	36	40	-25	-5	25	30
90	30	6	36	95	30	6	36	36
40	-20	-4	16	40	-25	-5	25	20
50	-10	-2	..	60	-5	-1	1	2
75	15	3	9	80	15	3	9	9
85	25	5	25	80	15	3	9	15
60	0	0	0	50	-15	-3	9	0
$n = 10$		2	140			-2	176	141

$$r = \frac{n\sum dxdy - \sum dx \times \sum dy}{\sqrt{n\sum d^2x - (\sum dx)^2}\sqrt{n\sum d^2y - (\sum dy)^2}}$$

$$= \frac{10 \times 141 - (2) \times (-2)}{\sqrt{10 \times 140 - (2)^2}\sqrt{10 \times 176 - (-2)^2}}$$

$$= \frac{1410 + 4}{\sqrt{1400 - 4}\sqrt{1760 - 4}} = \frac{1414}{\sqrt{1396}\sqrt{1756}}$$

$$= \frac{1414}{37.3 \times 41.90} = \frac{1414}{1565.51} = 0.903$$

$$\text{P. E. or Probable Error } = 0.675\frac{1 - r^2}{\sqrt{n}}$$

$$= 0.6745\frac{1 - (.903)^2}{10} = 0.6745\frac{1 - 0.8154}{3.16}$$

$$= 0.6745\frac{0.1846}{316} = 0.6745 \times 0.0584$$

$= 0.0394$

(ii) Significance of r, we have

$r = 0.9$ and 6 P.E. of r = 6 Xo. 0.394 = 0.2364 since r is much greater than 6 P.E. of r, the value of r is highly significant. Means higher the marks of a candidate in maths, higher is his score in statistics and vice-versa.

Limits of Population correlation coeff. are

$r \pm$ P. E. or 0.903 ± 0.0394

Limits are therefore between 0.8626 and 0.9424 Ans.

Example: The following are the results of B.Com examination.

Age of candidates	Candidates appeared	Successful Candidates
13-14	200	124
14-15	300	180
15-16	100	65
16-17	50	34
17-18	150	99
18-19	400	252
19-20	250	145
20-21	150	81
21-22	25	12
22-23	75	33

Calculate the coefficient of correlation between age and successful candidates in the examination.

Solution: In this problem two points have to be noted.

(a) The class intervals of age have to be represented by their mid-values.

(b) No. of successful candidates have to be calculated on a common base *i.e.* percent or per thousand any other such value.

Age-group	Mid value	% Successful Candidates
13-14	13.5	$\frac{124}{200} \times 100 = 62$
14-15	14.5	$\frac{180}{360} \times 100 = 60$
15-16	15.5	$\frac{65}{100} \times 100 = 65$
16-17	16.5	$\frac{34}{50} \times 100 = 68$
17-18	17.5	$\frac{99}{150} \times 100 = 66$
18-19	18.5	$\frac{252}{400} \times 100 = 63$
19-20	19.5	$\frac{145}{250} \times 100 = 58$
20-21	20.5	$\frac{81}{150} \times 100 = 54$
21-22	21.5	$\frac{12}{25} \times 100 = 48$
22-23	22.5	$\frac{33}{75} \times 100 = 44$

Calculation of coefficient of correlation

Age Group	M.V. (X)	dx (17.5)	dx²	% of Successful candidate (y)	dy (59)	dy²	dxdy
13-14	13.5	-4	16	62	3	9	-12
14-15	14.5	-3	9	60	1	1	-3
15-16	15.5	-2	4	65	6	36	-12
16-17	16.5	-1	1	68	9	81	-9
17-18	17.5	0	0	66	7	49	0
18-19	18.5	1	1	63	4	16	4
19-20	19.5	2	4	58	-1	1	-2
20-21	20.5	3	9	54	-5	25	15
21-22	21.5	4	16	48	-11	121	-44
22-23	22.5	5	25	44	-15	225	-75
	$n = 10$	5	85	$n = 10$	-2	564	-168

$$r = \frac{n\sum dxdy - \sum dx \times \sum dy}{\sqrt{[n\sum dx^2 - (\sum dx)^2]} \times \sqrt{[n\sum dy^2 - (\sum dy)^2]}}$$

$$= \frac{10\times(-168)-(5\times-2)}{\sqrt{[10\times85-(5)^2]}\times\sqrt{[10\times564-(-2)^2]}} = \frac{-168+10}{\sqrt{850-25}\sqrt{5640-4}}$$

$$= \frac{-1670}{\sqrt{825\times5636}} = \frac{-167}{28.7228\times75.0733}$$

$$= \frac{-1670}{2156.3152} = 0.7745$$

$$r = -0.7745 \ Ans.$$

Concurrent Deviation Method

In this method deviations are calculated not from the arithmetic mean, but from the preceding items and it considers only the direction of the deviation and not its extent. Deviations are marked '+' in the case of increase; (-) in the case of decrease and '=' when there is no rise or fall. i.e. if the item values remain the same. All the pairs are then carefully observed and those having the same signs for both the items of the pair, known as Concurrent Deviations; are marked '+' in the column of Concurrent Deviations. The formula for calculating coefficient of correlation is.–

$$r_c = \pm\sqrt{\pm\frac{2C-N}{N}}$$

Where r_c = Coefficient of concurrent deviations

C = Number of concurrent deviations

N = Number of pairs of deviations which will be naturally one less than the total observations.

The use of + or – sign will depend upon the sign of $(\frac{2C-N}{N})$. If it is in minus then a minus sign is placed. If it is plus, then plus sign is placed.

Example : Following are the marks scored by a group of 11 students in Commerce and Economics.

Students	A	B	C	D	E	F	G	H	I	J	K
Marks in Commerce	65	40	35	75	63	80	35	20	80	60	50
Marks in Economics	60	55	50	56	30	70	40	35	80	75	80

Calculate the coefficient of correlation by the method of Concurrent Deviation.

Soluation: Calculation of coeff. of correlation by method of concurrent Deviations.

Students	Marks in Commerce	Dev. From Preceding students (dx)	Marks in Economics	Dev from Preceding Students (dy)	Concurrences	Disagreements
A	65		60			
B	40	-	55	-	+	
C	35	-	50	-	+	
D	75	+	56	+	+	
E	63	-	30	-	+	
F	80	+	70	+	+	
G	35	-	40	-	+	
H	20	-	35	-	+	
I	80	+	80	+	+	
J	60	-	75	-	+	
K	50	-	80	+		
				N = 10	C = 9	1

Putting the values in the formula

$$r_c = \pm\sqrt{\pm\frac{2C-N}{N}}$$

$$= \pm\sqrt{\pm\frac{2\times 9-10}{10}}$$

$$= \pm\sqrt{\pm\frac{18-10}{10}} = \sqrt{\frac{8}{10}} = \sqrt{.8} = +0.8944 \qquad r_c = +\,0.8944 \text{ Ans.}$$

Spearman's Rank Difference Method

In this method the biggest items get the first rank, the next to it gets second rank and so on. But difficulty may be encountered where two or more items are of equal value. In such a case all items with equal ties are assigned the average of ranks assignable to all the them. The next is assigned the usual rank.

$$\rho\ (rho) = 1 - \frac{6\sum d^2}{N(N^2-1)}$$

Correction for tied ranks

$$\rho = 1 - \frac{6[\sum d^2 + {}^1/_{12}(m^3 - m]}{N(N^2-1)}$$

when two or more items are of equal value, they are assigned average rank. An adjustment is required for each group of tied ranks. Here m = number of items having tied ranks.

Example : The ranks of the same 15 students in two subjects A and B are given below; the two numbers within the brackets, denoting the ranks of the same students in A and B respectively. (1,10), (2, 7), (3, 2), (4, 6), (5, 4), (6, 8), (7, 3), (8, 1), (9, 11), (10, 15), (11, 9), (12, 5), (13, 14), (14, 12), (15, 13).

Use Spearman's formula to find the rank correlation coefficient.

Solution: Calculation of Spearman's Correlation Coefficient.

Rank in A (x)	**Rank in B (Y)**	**D (difference of ranks (X-Y)**	**D²**
1	10	-9	81
2	7	-5	25
3	2	1	1
4	6	-2	4
5	4	1	1
6	8	-2	4
7	3	4	16
8	1	7	49
9	11	-2	4
10	15	-5	25
11	9	2	4
12	5	7	49
13	14	-1	1
14	12	2	4
15	13	2	4
		d = 26-26 = 0	272

$$\rho = 1 - \frac{6\sum d^2}{n(n^2-1)}$$

$$= 1 - \frac{6 \times 272}{15(225-1)} = 1 - \frac{1632}{15 \times 224}$$

$$\rho = 1 - \frac{1632}{3360} = \frac{3360-1632}{3360} = \frac{1728}{3360} = 0.514$$

$\rho = 0.514$ *Ans.*

Example: Ten competitors in a beauty contest are ranked three judges in the following order.

1 st Judge :	1	6	5	10	3	2	4	9	7	8
2 nd Judge :	3	5	8	4	7	10	2	1	6	9
3 rd Judge :	6	4	9	8	1	2	3	10	5	7

Use the rank correlation coefficient to determine which pair of judges has the nearest approach to common tasts in beauty.

Solution: Let R_1, R_2, and R_3 denote the ranks given by the first, second and third judge respectively.

Calculation of Rank Correlation Coefficient.

R_1	R_2	R_2	d_{12} R_1-R_2	d_{13} R_1-R_3	d_{23} $R2$-R_3	d_{12}^2	d_{12}^2	d_{23}^2
1	3	6	-2	-5	-3	4	25	9
6	5	4	1	2	1	1	4	1
5	8	9	-3	-4	-1	9	16	1
10	4	8	6	2	-4	36	4	16
3	7	1	-4	2	6	16	4	36
2	10	2	-8	0	8	64	0	64
4	**2**	3	2	1	-1	4	1	1
9	1	10	8	-1	-9	64	1	81
7	6	5	1	2	1	1	4	1
8	9	7	-1	1	2	1	1	4
			$\sum d_{12} = 0$	$\sum d_{13} = 0$	$\sum d_{23} = 0$	200	60	214

$$\rho_{12} = 1 - \frac{6\sum d_{12}2}{N(N^2-1)} = 1 - \frac{6\times200}{10(100-1)}$$

$$= 1 - \frac{120}{10\times99} = \frac{990-1200}{990} = \frac{-210}{990} = -0.212$$

$$\rho_{13} = 1 - \frac{6\times60}{10\times99} = 1 - \frac{360}{990} = \frac{630}{990} = 0.636$$

$$\rho_{23} = 1 - \frac{6\times214}{10\times99} = 1 - \frac{1284}{990}$$

$$= -\frac{294}{990} = -0.297$$

Since ρ_{13} is maximum, the pair of first and third judges has the nearest approach to common tastes in beauty. Ans.

Example : Obtain the rank correlation coefficient for the following data :

X	68	64	75	50	64	80	75	40	55	64
Y	62	58	68	45	81	60	68	48	50	70

Solution: Calculation for Rank Correlation Coefficient

X	Rank (X)	Y	Rank (Y)	D (X-Y)	dy^2
68	4	62	5	-1	1
64	6	58	7	-1	1
75	2.5	68	3.5	-1	1
50	9	45	10	-1	1
64	6	81	1	5	25
80	1	60	6	-5	25
75	2.5	68	3.5	-1	1
40	10	48	9	1	1
55	8	50	8	0	0
64	6	70	2	4	16
Total				$\Sigma d=0$	$\Sigma d^2=72$

In X series 75 occurs 2 times and 64 occurs thrice. Similarly in Y series 68 occurs twice. So we have to add in E d^2,m(m^2-1)/12 for each value repeated.

$$\rho = 1 - \frac{6\left[\Sigma d^2 + m\frac{(m^2-1)}{12}\right]}{N(N^2-1)}$$

$$\rho = 1 - \frac{6\left[72 + \frac{2[4-1]}{12} + \frac{3[3-1]}{12} + \frac{2[4-1]}{12}\right]}{10 \times 99}$$

$$= 1 - \frac{6\left[72 + \frac{1}{2} + 2 + \frac{1}{2}\right]}{990} = \frac{990 - 6[75]}{990}$$

$$= \frac{990 - 450}{990} = \frac{540}{990}$$

$$\rho = 0.545 \; Ans.$$

******

Chapter - 30

Regression Analysis

The literal or dictionary meaning of the word 'regression' is "stepping back or returning to the average value" or to 'revert'. The term was first introduced by Sir Francis Galton in 1877. He used the term regression in connection with some studies he made on estimating the extent to which the stature of the sons of tall parents reverts or regresses back to the mean stature of the population. He studied the relationship between the heights of about one thousand fathers and sons and published the results in a paper. The interesting features of his study are:

(1) The tall fathers have tall sons and short fathers have short sons.

(ii) The mean height of the sons of tall fathers is less than the mean height of their fathers.

(iii) The mean height of the sons of short fathers is more than the mean height of their fathers.

(iv) Gallon found that the deviations in the mean height of the sons from the mean height of the race was less than the deviations in the mean height of the fathers from the mean height of the race. When the fathers move above the mean or below the mean, the sons tended to go back or regress towards the mean.

Definition of Regression

"Regression is the measure of the average relationship between two or more variables in terms of the original units of the data." **-Blair**

"Regression analysis attempts to establish the 'nature of the relationship' between variables- -that is to study the functional relationship between the variables and thereby provide a mechanism for prediction or for casting".

-Ya-Lun-Chou

"One of the most frequently used techniques in economics and business research, to find a relation between two or more variables that are related carnally. Is regression analysis." **-Taro Yamane**

Simple and Multiple Regression

In our day to day life we come across many variables which are interrelated. For example. with a rise in price the demand of a commodity goes down, or with better monsoons the output of agricultural product increases, or the effect of expenditure on publicity may lead to a rise in the volume of sales. With the help of regression analysis we can estimate or predict the effect of one variable on the other e.g., we can predict the fall in demand when the price rises by a particular amount. However, in modern sciences there is multiple causation which means that a large number of factor affect various variables. The regression study which confines itself to a study of only two variables is called simple regression. The regression analysis which studies more than two variables at a time is called multiple regression.

Dependent and Independent Variable

While dealing with the practical problems related with the regression, we often come across two terms 'dependent variable' and 'independent variable.' Naturally, we are required to pre-assess the. meaning and significance of these.

Suppose the values of two series. X and Y are given. If for a particular value of X the corresponding value of Y is to be ascertained, then X is the independent variable and Y is the dependent variable.

Regression Curve and Regression Line

If we plot all the original values of the two variates, X and Y, on a graph paper to obtain a scatter diagram, a peculiar tendency that is found to be present in it is that the points mostly concentrate either in the form of a curve or that of straight line.

So, taking "most of the points as the normal route, if we draw a curve then it is known as a curve of regression" However, if the points concentrate in such a way that ultimately the concentrations gives a straight line, then it is known as a line of regression. The nature of this type of regression is known as a linear.

In this connection also we must remember that if the variates X and Y are related to each other, only then we can have the regression curve or line. If there is no correlation between X and Y, we can neither have a regression curve nor a regression line.

Methods of Studying Regression

Broadly speaking regression can be studied either:

(i) Graphically, or (ii) Algebraically

We shall study these methods now in detail

(i) Graphic study of Regression. When !egression is studied with the help of graphic methods we have to draw a scatter diagram. A scatter diagram contains one point for one pair of values of X and Y variable. When all related pairs of values have been plotted on a scatter diagram, we have to draw two regression lines to predict the values of X and Y variables. The regression line which is used to predict the values of Y for a value of X is called the Regression Line of Y on X. Similarly the regression line which is used to predict the value of X for a value of 'Y is called the Regression Line of X on Y. If the coefficient of correlation between X and Y is perfect i.e., its value is either +1 or -1 there will be only one regression line as the variations in the series in such cases always increase or decrease by a constant figure.

Regression lines can be drawn by:

(i) Free hand curve method or by (ii) The Method of Least Squares.

Free Hand Curve Method

In the free hand curve method we first plot the pairs of the values of X and Y in the front of a scatter diagram one point for one pair of values. After this we draw two free hand straight lines. One of these lines is drawn in such a way that the positive deviations of Y- series from its mean are cancelled by the negative deviations. The sum of the deviations on one side of the line is equal to the sum of deviations on the other side. This will be the regression line of Y on X. The other regression line would be drawn in such a way that the positive deviations of X- series from its mean would cancel the negative deviations. This regression line would be called the regression line of X on Y. The two regression lines would cut each other at the point of means of the series. Once these lines are drawn we can predict or estimate the values of Y from the Regression line of Yon X and similarly the values of X can be predicted from the regression line X on Y.

Method of Least Squares

In order to avoid the difficulties associated with the drawing of regression lines by the free hand curve method, a mathematical relationship is established between the movements of X and Y series and algebraic equations are obtained to represent the relative movements of X and Y series.

One such method is the method of least squares. In this method we minimize the sum of squares of the deviations between the given values of a variable and its estimated values given by the line of the best fit. Line of regression of Y on X is the line which gives the best estimate for the value of Y for a specified value of X and similarly the line of regression of X on Y is the line which gives the best estimate for the value of X for a specified value of Y.'

If the values of Y are plotted on Y axis (or the vertical axis) then the regression line of Y on X will be such which minimizes the total of the squares of the vertical deviations. Similarly if the values of X are plotted on the X-axis (or the horizontal axis) the regression line of X on Y will be such which minimizes o the total of the squares of the horizontal deviations.

The line of best fit is obtained by the equation of straight line

$$Y = a + bX$$

and that in the method of least squares this line is obtained with the help of two normal equations.

$$\Sigma(Y) = na + b\ (\Sigma X)$$

$$\Sigma(XY) = a\Sigma X + b\Sigma(X^2)$$

If the values of X and Y variables are substituted in the above equations we get the values of a and b and thus get the regression line of Y on X. Here Y is the dependent variable and X the independent variable.

To get the regression line of X on Y

$$\Sigma(X) = na + b\ (\Sigma Y)$$

$$\Sigma(XY) = a\Sigma(Y) + b\Sigma(Y^2)$$

Here X is the dependent variable and Y is the independent variable.

Thus we will get two equations for the two regression lines.

Why Two Regression Lines?

Very often this question is asked as to why there should be two regression lines to obtain the value of Y and X and why one regression line does not serve the purpose. The answer is simple, and it is that one regression line cannot minimize the sum of squares of deviations for both the X and Y series unless the relationship between them indicates perfect positive or negative correlation. In case of perfect correlations one regression line is enough because X and Y series have the same type of dominations. Ordinarily in modern sciences perfect correlation is very rarely found.

Why Least Squares Fit is The Best?

Suppose there are 'N' number of points, each point representing a pair of observations (X_1,. Y_1) (X_2, X_2) ..... (X_n, Y_n). We want to fit Y + b X equation. Thus there are two values of Y for each value of X. One is the observed value of Y paired with the observed values of X, and the other is the Y co-ordinate to the corresponding point on the line, which is obtained by substituting the given observed value of X into the above equation. For X_1 the observed value of Y_1 is one value of Y and Y coordinate of the point on the line (or a + bX_1) is the other. For X_2, the observed value Y_2 is one value Y, and the Y co-ordinate of the point of the line of (or a + bX_2) is the other and so on. Since there are N number of' points, we have N deviations between the two Y-values for the N number of observed X values. They are Y_1 - (1 + bX_1), Y_2 - (a + bX_2) Yn - (a + bXn). If there are N pairs of observations in the sample, the least squares criterion requires that $\Sigma[Y - (a + bX)]^2$ must be the minimum sum. Thus any line that minimizes this quantity is called the least squares lines. That is why the least squares fit is considered the best, it minimizes the sum of the squared deviations from the point to the line.

This can be explained with the help of the following diagram:

No.	1	2	3	4	5	6	7	8	9	10	11	12
X	23.0	19.0	26.0	31.0	25.0	23.0	18.0	23.0	18.5	19.5	28.5	21.5
Y	22.5	23.5	23.5	25.0	25.0	25.5	19.0	21.5	22.0	19.0	26.0	24.0

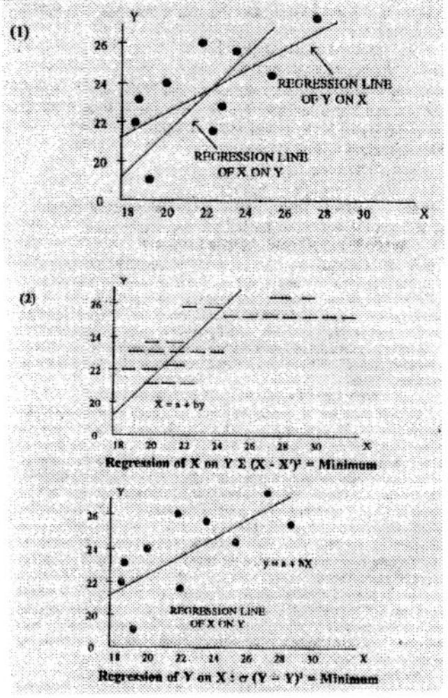

Use: Regression analysis is of great practical use even more than the correlation analysis The following are some uses :

(1) Regression analysis helps in establishing a functional relationship between two or more variables. Once this is established it can be used for various advanced analytical purpose.

(2) With the use of electronic machines and computers the medium of calculation of regression equation particularly expressing multiple and a non-linear relations has been reduced to a great deal.

(3) Since most of the problems of economic analysis are based on cause and effect relationship, the regression analysis is, a highly valuable tool in economic and business research.

(4) The regression analysis is very useful for prediction purposes. Once functional relationship is known, the value of the dependent variable can be predicted from the given value of the independent variables.

Correlation and Regression

Both the correlation and regression analysis helps us in studying the relationship between two variables, yet they differ in their approach, and objectives.

(1) Correlation studies are meant for studying the co-variation of the two variables. They tell us whether the variables under study move in the same direction or in reverse directions. The degree of their co-variation is also reflected in the correlation coefficient, but the correlation study does not study the nature of relationship. It does not tell us about the relative movement in the variables under study and we cannot predict the value of one variable by taking into account the value of the other variable. This is possible through regression analysis.

(2) Correlation between two series is not necessarily a cause and effect relationship. A high degree of positive correlation between price and supply does not mean that, supply is the effect of price. There may be no cause and effect relationship between the variables under study and yet they may be correlated. Regression on the other hand presumes one variable as a cause and the other as its effect. The independent variable is supposed to be affecting the dependent variable and as such we can estimate the values of the dependent variable by projecting the relationship between them.

(3) The coefficient of correlation varies between ± 1. The regression coefficients have the same signs as the correlation coefficient, If r is positive, regression coefficients would also be positive and if r is negative the regression coefficients would also be negative.

(4) Further whereas correlation coefficient cannot exceed unity of the regression coefficients can have a value higher than unity but the product of the two regression coefficients can never exceed unity because r is the square root of the product of the two regression coefficients.

Calculation of Regression Equations and Coefficients

Regression Equations: The regression equation of Y on X expressed as follows.

$$Y = a+bX$$

It may be noted that in this equation Y is a dependent variable. i.e., its value depends on X. 'X' is independent variable, i.e., we can take a given value of X and compute the value of Y.

'a' is "Y-intercept" because its value is the point at which the regression line crosses the Y-axis, that is, the vertical axis 'b' is the "slope" of line. It represents change in the Y variable for a unit change in X variable.

'a' and 'b' in the equation are called numerical constant because for any given straight line, their value does not change. -

The following Regression Equation will yield values of the parameters a and b such that the least squares requirement is fulfilled:

$$\Sigma Y = Na + b\Sigma X$$

$$\Sigma XY = a\Sigma X + b\Sigma X^2$$

These equations are usually called the normal equations. In the equations ΣX, ΣXY, Σx^2 T indicate totals which are computed from the observed pairs of values of two variables X and Y to which the least squares estimating line is to be fitted and N is the number of observed pairs, of values.

(ii) Regression Equation of X on Y: The regression equation of X on Y is expressed as follows :

$$X = a + bY$$

To determine the values of 'a ' and 'b' the following two normal equations are to be solved simultaneously :

$$\Sigma Y = Na + b\Sigma Y$$
$$\Sigma XY = a\Sigma Y + b\Sigma Y^2$$

(iii) Deviations taken from Arithmetic Means of X and Y: The above method of finding out regression equation is tedious. The calculations can very much be simplified if instead of dealing with the actual values of X and Y we take the deviations of X and Y series from their respective means. In such a case the two regression equations are written as follows:

(a) Regression Equation of X on Y.

where X is the mean of X series, Y is the mean of Y series

$$\bar{X} - X = r\frac{\sigma_x}{\sigma_y}(\bar{Y} - Y)$$

Where $\bar{X}$ is the mean of X series,

$\bar{Y}$ is the mean of Y series

$r\frac{\sigma_x}{\sigma_y}$ is the regression coefficient of X on Y.

The regression coefficient of X on Y is denoted by the symbol bxy or b_1. It measures the change in corresponding to a unit change in Y. When deviations are taken from the means of X and Y the regression coefficient of X on Y is obtained as follows :

$$bxy \text{ or } r\frac{\sigma_x}{\sigma_y} = \frac{\Sigma XY}{\Sigma Y^2}$$

$$r\frac{\sigma_x}{\sigma_y} = \frac{\Sigma XY}{N\sigma_x\sigma_y}\frac{\sigma_x}{\sigma_y}$$

$$= \frac{\Sigma XY}{N\sigma^2}$$

$$= \frac{\Sigma XY}{N\frac{\Sigma Y^2}{N}} = \frac{\Sigma XY}{\Sigma Y^2}$$

(b) Regression Equation of Y on X

$$Y - Y = r\frac{\sigma_y}{\sigma_x}(X - X)$$

Here all the notations mean the same as already explained

$r\frac{\sigma_x}{\sigma_y}$ is the regression coefficient of Y on X. It is denoted by byx or b_2.

It measures the change in Y corresponding to a unit change in X. When deviation are taken from actual mean, the regression coefficients of Y on X can be obtained as follows :

$$r\frac{\sigma_y}{\sigma_x} = \frac{\Sigma XY}{\Sigma X^2}$$

It should be-noted that the under root of the product or two regression coefficients gives us the value of correlation coefficient.

Symbolically,

$$r = \sqrt{bxy + byx}$$

Deviations Taken From Assumed Means

When actual means of X and Y variables are in fractions the calculations can be simplified by taking the deviations from the assumed means. When deviations are taken from assumed means the entire procedure of finding regression equations remains the same -the only difference is that instead of taking deviations from actual means, we take the 'deviations from assumed means. The two regression equations are :

$$\bar{x} - x = r\frac{\sigma_x}{\sigma_y}(\bar{y} - Y)$$

The value $r\frac{\sigma_x}{\sigma_y}$ will now be obtained as follow :

$$r\frac{\sigma_x}{\sigma_y} = \frac{\Sigma dxdy - \frac{(\Sigma dx)x(\Sigma dy)}{N}}{\Sigma dy^2 - \frac{(\Sigma dy)^2}{N}}$$

Similarly the Regression Equation of Y on X is

$$\bar{y} - Y = r\frac{\sigma_y}{\sigma_x}(\bar{x} - X)$$

$$r\frac{\sigma_x}{\sigma_y} = \frac{\Sigma dxdy - \frac{(\Sigma dx)x(\Sigma dy)}{N}}{\Sigma dx^2 - \frac{(\Sigma dx)^2}{N}}$$

Practical Problems

Example : Fit a straight line regression of Y on X from the following table :

X	0	1	2	3	4	5	6
Y	2	1	3	2	4	3	5

Solution: Fitting straight line regression equation:

X	X^2	Y	Y^2	XY
0	0	2	4	0
1	1	1	1	1
2	4	3	9	6
3	9	2	4	6
4	16	4	16	16
5	25	3	9	15
6	36	5	25	30
$\Sigma X=21$	$\Sigma X^2=91$	$\Sigma Y=20$	$EY^2=68$	$\Sigma XY=74$

Regression line of Y on X

$Y = a + bX$

The corresponding normal equations are

$\Sigma(Y) = Na + b\Sigma X$

$\Sigma(XY) = a\Sigma X + b\Sigma X^2$

Putting the value in Eq. No. 1 & 2 and solving these equations

$20 = 7a + 21b$

$74 = 21a + 91b$

Multiplying Eq. No. 1 by 3 we get

$60 = 21a + 63b$

$74 = 21a + 91b$

- - - By Subtracting

$-14 = -28b$

or $b = 0.5$

Putting the value of b in Eq. No. 1

$20 = 7a + 21(0.5)$

or $20 = 7A + 10.5$

or $7a = 9.5$

$a = 1.357$

Regression Equation Y on X

$Y = 1.357 + 0.5X$ Ans.

Short cut Method

Example : From the following data, obtain the two regression equations.

Sales	91	97	108	121	67	124	51	73	111	57
Purchase :	71	75	69	97	70	91	39	61	80	47

Solution: Let us denote the sales by the variable X and purchase by the variable Y.

Calculations for Regression Equations

X	dx (x*=90)	dx^2	Y	dy (y=70)	dy^2	dxdy
91	1	1	71	1	1	1
97	7	49	75	5	25	25
108	18	324	69	-1	1	-18
121	31	961	97	27	729	837
67	-23	529	70	0	0	0
124	34	1156	91	21	441	714
51	-39	1521	39	-31	961	1209
73	-17	289	61	-9	81	153
111	21	441	80	10	100	210
57	-33	1089	47	-23	529	759
$\Sigma X=900$	$\Sigma dx=0$	$\Sigma dx^2=6360$	$\Sigma Y=700$	$\Sigma dy=0$	$\Sigma dy^2=2868$	$\Sigma dxdy=3900$

We have

$X = \frac{\Sigma X}{N} = \frac{900}{10} = 90$

$Y = \frac{\Sigma Y}{N} = \frac{700}{10} = 70$

$byx = \frac{\Sigma XY}{\Sigma X^2}$

$= \frac{3900}{6360} = 0.6132$

and

$byx = \frac{\Sigma XY}{\Sigma Y^2}$

$= \frac{3900}{2868} = 1.3598$

Equations of the line of regression of Y on X is :

Y – Y = byx (X-X)

or Y-70 = 0.6132 (X-90)

or Y-70 = 0.6132 X- 55.188

or Y = 0.6132X+70 - 55.188

or Y = 0.6132X+14.812 Ans.

Equations of the line of regression of X on Y is :

$x - x$ = byx (Y-Y)

or x -90 = 1.3598 (Y-70)

or x -90 = 1.398Y - 95.186

or x = 1.3598Y+90 - 95.186

or x = 1.3598Y-5.186 Ans.

Example : Calculate the two regression equations and the coefficient of correlation from the data given below :

Marks in Statistics (out of 50) 40 38 35 42 30

Marks in Mathematics (out of 50) 30 35 40 36 29

Solution: Let marks in Statistics be denoted by X and marks in Mathematics by Y.

Calculations of Regression Equations

X	dx (x= x)	dx^2	Y	dy (y=34)	dy^2	dxdy
40	+3	9	30	-4	16	-12
38	+1	1	35	+1	1	1
35	-2	4	40	+6	36	-12
42	+5	25	36	2	4	10
30	-7	49	29	-5	25	35
ΣX=185	Σdx=0	Σdx^2=88	ΣY=170	Σdy=0	Σdy^2=82	Σdxdy=22

Regression equation of X and Y.

$X - X = r\frac{\sigma_x}{\sigma_y}(Y-Y)$

$X = \frac{\Sigma X}{N} = \frac{185}{5} = 37$

$Y = \frac{\Sigma Y}{N} = \frac{170}{5} = 34$

$r\frac{\sigma_x}{\sigma_y} = \frac{\Sigma XY}{\Sigma Y^2} = \frac{22}{82} = 0.268$

X-37 = 0.268 (Y-34)

or X-37 = 0.268Y - 9.112

X = 0.268Y+37 - 9.112

or X = 0.268Y+27.888 Ans.

Regression Equations of Y on X.

$Y - \overline{Y} = r\frac{\sigma_y}{\sigma_x}(X-\overline{X})$

or $r\frac{\sigma_y}{\sigma_x} = \frac{\Sigma dxdy}{\Sigma dx^2} = \frac{22}{88} = 0.25$

Y - 34 = 0.25 (X – 37)

or Y – 34 = 0.25X - 9.25

or Y = 0.25X + 34 - 9.25

or Y = 0.25X + 24.75

$r = \sqrt{byx \times bxy}$

$\sqrt{0.268 \times 0.5}$

$\sqrt{0.067}$

r = 0.259 Ans.

Example : Calculate the coefficient of correlation from the following by the least square method.

X	1	2	3	4	5
Y	338	180	142	184	166

Solution: By the least square method the coefficient of correlation can be calculated as follows :

$r = \sqrt{byx \times bxy}$

Calculation of Regression coefficient

X	dx X=3	dx^2	Y	dy Y=202	dy^2	dxdy
1	-2	4	338	136	18496	-272
2	-1	1	180	-22	484	22
3	0	0	142	-60	3600	0
4	1	1	184	-18	324	-18
5	2	4	166	-36	1296	-72
ΣX=15	Σdx=0	Σdx^2=10	ΣY= 1010	Σdy=0	Σdy^2=24200	Σdxdy=340

$bxy = r\frac{\sigma_x}{\sigma_y} = \frac{\Sigma dxdy}{\Sigma dy^2} = \frac{-340}{24200} = 0.014$

and byx or $r\frac{\sigma_x}{\sigma_y} = \frac{\Sigma dxdy}{\Sigma dx^2} = \frac{-340}{10} = -34$

$r = \sqrt{byx \times bxy} = \sqrt{(-0.014) \times (-34)}$

$= -\sqrt{0.477683}$ or = r = -0.691 Ans.

Example : Write down the equation of the line of regression of Y on X.

X	78	89	97	69	59	79	68	61
Y	125	137	156	112	107	136	124	108

(You may use 69 as the working mean for X and 112 for Y)

Solution: Calculation of Regression Line of Y on X.

X	dx (A=69)	dx^2	Y	dy (A=112)	dy^2	dxdy
78	9	81	125	13	169	117
89	20	400	137	25	625	500
97	28	784	156	44	1936	1232
69	0	0	112	0	0	0
59	-10	100	107	-5	25	50
79	10	100	136	24	576	240
68	-1	1	124	12	144	-12
61	-8	64	108	-4	16	32
ΣX=600	Σdx=48	Σdx^2=1530	ΣY= 1005	Σdy =109	Σdy^2=3491	Σdxdy =2159

Regression line of Y on X

$Y - \overline{Y} = r\frac{\sigma_y}{\sigma_x}(X - \overline{X})$

or $\overline{Y} = A + \frac{\Sigma dy}{N} = 112 + \frac{109}{8} = 112 + 13.625$

$\overline{Y} = 125.625$

$\overline{X} = A + \frac{\Sigma dx}{N} = 69 + \frac{48}{8} = 75$

$$r\frac{\sigma_y}{\sigma_x} = \frac{\Sigma dxdy - \frac{(\Sigma dx)x(\Sigma dy)}{N}}{\Sigma dx^2 - \frac{(\Sigma dx)^2}{N}} = \frac{2159 - \frac{(48)x(109)}{8}}{1530 - \frac{(48)^2}{8}}$$

$$= \frac{2159 - 654}{1530 - 288} = \frac{1505}{1242} = 1.2117$$

$\therefore Y - 125.625 = 1.2117 (X - 75)$

or $Y - 125.625 = 1.2117 X - 90.8775$

or $Y = 1.2117X + 34.75$ Ans.

Example : From the following data obtain the two regression equations and calculate the correlation coefficient.

X:	1	2	3	4	5	6	7	8	9
Y:	9	8	10	12	11	13	14	16	15

Estimate value of Y which should correspond on an average to X = (6.2)

Solution: Calculation of Regression equations and correlation coefficient.

X	dx (A=5)	dx^2	Y	dy (A=112)	dy^2	dxdy
1	-4	16	9	-4	9	12
2	-3	9	8	-3	16	12
3	-2	4	10	-2	4	4

4	-1	1	12	0	0	0
5	0	0	11	-1	1	0
6	1	1	13	1	1	1
7	2	4	14	2	4	4
8	3	9	16	4	16	12
9	4	16	15	3	9	12
$\Sigma X=45$	$\Sigma dx=0$	$\Sigma dx^2=60$	$\Sigma Y=108$	$\Sigma dy=0$	$\Sigma dy^2=60$	$\Sigma dxdy=57$

Regression line of *x* on y

$X-\overline{X} = r\frac{\sigma_x}{\sigma_y}(Y-\overline{Y})$

or $\overline{X} = A + \frac{\Sigma dx}{N}$

$= 5 + \frac{0}{9} = 5$

or $\overline{Y} = A + \frac{\Sigma dx}{N}$

$= 12 + \frac{0}{9} = 12$

$r\frac{\sigma_x}{\sigma_y} = \frac{\Sigma dxdy - \frac{(\Sigma dx)x(\Sigma dy)}{N}}{\Sigma dy^2 - \frac{(\Sigma dy)^2}{N}}$

$\frac{57 - \frac{(0)x(0)}{9}}{60 - \frac{(0)^2}{9}}$

$= \frac{57}{60} = 0.95$

$\therefore X - 5 = 0.95\ (Y - 12)$

or $X - 5 = 0.95\ Y - 11.4$

or $X = 0.95Y - 6.4$ Ans.

Regression line of Y on X

$Y-\overline{Y} = r\frac{\sigma_x}{\sigma_y}(X-\overline{X})$

$r\frac{\sigma_x}{\sigma_y} = \frac{\Sigma dxdy - \frac{(\Sigma dx)x(\Sigma dy)}{N}}{\Sigma dx^2 - \frac{(\Sigma dx)^2}{N}}$

$= \frac{57-0}{60-0} = \frac{57}{60} = 0.95$

or $Y - 12 = 0.95\ (X - 5)$

or $Y - 12 = 0.95X - 4.75$

or $Y = 0.95X + 7.25$

When X = 6.2 than the value of Y is

$Y = 0.95\ (6.2) + 7.25$

$= 5.89 + 7.25 = 13.14$

Correlation coefficient (r) = $\sqrt{byx \text{ x } bxy}$

or $r = \sqrt{0.95 \text{ x } 0.95}$

or r = 0.95 Ans.

Example : Following are the marks in Malayalam and English in an annual examination :

	Malayalam (X)	English (Y)	
Mean	40	50	
S.D.	10	16	r= 0.5

Estimate the score of English when score in Malayalam is 50 and score in Malayalam when score in English is 30.

Solution. Regression Equations of X on Y.

$X - \overline{X} = r\frac{\sigma_x}{\sigma_y}(Y - \overline{Y})$

or $X - 40 = 0.5\frac{10}{16}(Y - 50)$

$X - 40 = 0.3125\ (Y - 50)$

or $X - 40 = 0.3125Y - 15.625$

or $X = 0.3125Y + 24.325$

or $X = 9.375 + 24.375 = 33.75$ Ans.

Regression line of Y on X

$Y - \overline{Y} = r\frac{\sigma_x}{\sigma_y}(X - \overline{X})$

or $Y - 50 = 0.5\frac{16}{10}(X - 40)$

$Y - 50 = 0.8\ (X - 40)$

or $Y - 50 = 0.8X + 18$

When X = 50 then Y will be

or $Y = 0.8\ (50) + 18$

or $Y = 40 + 18 = 58$ Ans.

Example : The following calculations have been made for prices of twelve stocks (X) on the Calcutta Stock Exchange on a certain day along with the volume of sales in thousands of shares (Y). From these calculation find the regression equation of prices of stocks on the volume of sales of shares.

$\Sigma X = 580,\ \Sigma Y = 370,\ \Sigma XY = 11494,\ \Sigma X^2 = 41658,\ \Sigma Y^2 = 17206$

Solution: We have to fit a regression equation of X on Y

$X - \overline{X} = r\frac{\sigma_x}{\sigma_y}(Y - \overline{Y})$

$\therefore X = \frac{\Sigma X}{N} = \frac{580}{12} = 48.333$

$Y = \frac{\Sigma Y}{N} = \frac{370}{12} = 30.833$

$r\frac{\sigma_x}{\sigma_y}$ or $bxy = \frac{\Sigma XY - N(X)(Y)}{\Sigma Y^2 - N(Y)^2}$

(When figures are given in original values)

$= \frac{11494 - (12)(48.333)(30.833)}{17206 - (12)(30.833)^2}$

$= \frac{11494 - 17883.208}{17206 - 11408.086} = \frac{-6389.208}{-5797.914}$

$r\frac{\sigma_x}{\sigma_y} = -1.102$

Now

$X - 48.333 = 1.102 (Y - 30.833)$

or $X - 48.333 = 1.102Y + 33.977$

or $X = -1.102Y + 48.333 + 33.977$

or $X = -1.102Y + 32.31$ Ans.

Example : Fit a straight line to the following data by the method of least squares :

X	0	1	2	3	4
Y	1	1.8	3.3	4.5	6.3

Solution: Calculation of Straight line equation.

X	X^2	Y	Y^2	XY
0	0	1	1	0
1	1	1.8	3.24	1.8
2	4	3.3	10.89	6.6
3	9	4.5	20.25	13.5
4	16	6.3	39.69	25.2
N=5 Σx=10	30	16.9	75.07	47.1

X on Y is

Y on X is

Two normal equations are:

$\Sigma x = Na + b\,\Sigma Y$

$\Sigma xy = a\,\Sigma + b\,\Sigma y^2$

Y on X is

$Y = a + bx$

Two normal equation are:

$\Sigma y = Na + b\,\Sigma x$

$\Sigma xy = a\,\Sigma x + b\,\Sigma x^2$

Putting the value and solving these equations as simultaneous equations :

$10 = 5a + 16.9b$

$47.1 = 16.9a + 75.7b$

Multiplying equation on. 1 by 16.9 and Eq. no. 2 by 5, we get.

$169 = 84.5/1 + 285 - 61b$

$-235.5 = 138.5a + 375.35b$

$- 66.5 = - 89.74b$ By subtracting

or $b = 0.74$

Putting the value of b in eq. no. 1, we get $10 = 5a + 16.9 (0.74)$

or $10 = 5a + 12.5234$

or $5a = -2.534$

or $a = -0.505$

The equation of X on Y is

$X = a + by$

or $X = -0.505 + 0.74Y$. Ans.

Y on X

$\Sigma y = Na + b\,\Sigma x$

$\Sigma xy = a\,\Sigma x + b\,\Sigma x^2$

Putting the value and solving these simultaneous equations :

$16.9 = 5a + 10b$

$47.1 = 10a + 30b$

Multiplying Eq. on. 1 by 2

$33.8 = 10a + 20b$

$47.1 = 10a + 30b$

$- 13.3 = - 10b$ By subtracting

or $b = 1.33$

Putting the values of b in Eq. no. 1

$33.8 = 10a + 20 (1.33)$

$33.8 = 10a + 26.6$

or $10a = 33.8 = 26.6$

$10a = 7.2 = 0.72$

∴ The normal equal of Y on X is

$Y = a + bx$

or $Y = 0.72 + 1.33 X$ Ans.

Example : From the following data obtain the two regression equations.

Sales (x)	91	97	108	121	67	124	51	73	111	57
Purchase (y) :	71	75	69	97	70	91	39	61	80	47

Solution: Calculation of Regression Equation

X	dx	d^2x	Y	dy^2	d^2y	dxdy
91	1	1	71	1	1	1
97	7	49	75	5	25	25
108	18	324	69	-1	1	-18
121	-31	961	07	27	729	837
67	-23	529	70	0	0	0
124	34	1156	91	21	441	714
51	-39	1521	39	-31	961	1209
73	-17	289	61	-9	81	153
111	21	441	80	10	100	210
57	-33	1089	47	-23	529	759
		6360			2868	3900

$$\overline{X} = \frac{\Sigma X}{N} = \frac{900}{10} = 90, \overline{Y} = \frac{\Sigma Y}{N} = \frac{700}{10} = 70$$

$$byx = \frac{\Sigma XY}{\Sigma d^2 Y}$$

$$= \frac{3900}{6360} = 0.6132$$

and

$$byx = \frac{\Sigma XY}{\Sigma d^2 Y}$$

$$= \frac{3900}{2868} = 1.3598$$

∴ X on Y

$X - \overline{X} = byx\ (Y-\overline{Y})$

or $X-90 = 1.35\ 98\ (Y-70)$

$X = -5.186 + 1.3599$ (1) Ans.

Y on X

$Y-\overline{Y} = byx\ (X - \overline{X})$

$Y - 70 = 0.6132\ (X - 90)$

or $Y = 14.81 + 0.613\ X$ (2) Ans.

Find r if bxy – 0.8 and byx = 0.46

Solution: Calculation of r.

$r = \sqrt{byx \times bxy}$

$= \sqrt{0.8 \times 0.46}$

$= \sqrt{0.368}$

$= 0.67$

r = 0.67 Ans.

Problem : Given that variance of X = 9 and regression equations are

$8x - 10y + 66 = 0$

$40x - 18y = 214.$

Find the correlation coefficient between the two variables.

Solution:

$8x = 10y - 66$

$x = 1.25y - 8.25$

or $bxy = 1.25$

$40x - 18y = 214$

or $18y = + 40x + 214$

or $y = 2.22x + 11.89$

or $byx = 2.22$

Now $r = \sqrt{byx \times bxy}$

$= (2.22 \times 1.25)$

$= 2.775$

$r = 1.666$

Since the value of r is greater than one, it is not possible and we interchange the equation.

Y on X

$-10y = -8x - 66$

$y = .8x - 6.6$

or $bxy = 1.25$

Similarly X on Y

$40x - 18y = 214$

or $40x = + 18y + 214$

or $x = 0.45y + 5.35$

or $byx = 0.45$

$\therefore$ $r^2 = bxy \times byx$

$= 0.8 \times 0.45 = 0.36$

or $r = 0.6$ Ans.

******

Chapter - 31

Range Deviation

Range = L S

Where L = Largest item,and

S = Smallest item.

The relative measure corresponding to Range, called the Coefficient of Range, is obtained by applying the formula

Coefficient of Range = $\frac{L-S}{L+S}$

Example : The following are the prices of shares of AB Co.. Ltd., from Monday to Saturday :

Days	**Price**
Monday	200
Tuesday	210
Wednesday	208
Thursday	160
Friday	220
Saturday	250

Calculate Range and its coefficient.

Solution: Range = L-S=250-160=90 Rs.

Coefficient of Range = $\frac{L-S}{L+S} = \frac{250-160}{250+160} = \frac{90}{410} = 0.2195$ Ans.

Example : Suppose we are given the incomes of 10 persons in two localities A and B as follows :

Income per month

Locality A :	Rs.	70,	100,	50,	130,	140,	150,	90,
Locality B:	Rs.	1250,	1350,	1600,	1450,	1550,	1700,	1750,
Locality A:	Rs.	60	110, and 600.					
Locality B :	Rs.	1800,	1400 and 1650.					

Calculate Range and Coefficient of Range.

Solution:

Range (A) = L-S=600-50=550

Range (B) = L-S=1800-1250=550

Coefficient of Range (A) = $\frac{L-S}{L+S} = \frac{600-50}{600+50} = \frac{550}{650} = 0.846$

Coefficient of Range (B) = $\frac{L-S}{L+S} = \frac{1800-1250}{1800+1250} = \frac{550}{3050} = 0.1803$

Ans. (i) Range (A) = 550

Range (B) = 550

(ii) Coefficient of Range (A) = 0.846

Coefficient of Range (B) = 0.1803

Example : The weights of 11 forty year old men were 184, 154, 158, 160, 161, 162, 166, 170, 182, 195 and 236 pounds. Calculate the Range and Coefficient of Range. If the heaviest man is omitted what is the percentage change in the range?

Solution. Array: 148, 154, 158, 160, 161, 162, 166, 170, 182, 195, 236.

Range = L-S=236-148=88

Coefficient of Range = $\frac{L-S}{L+S} = \frac{236-148}{236+148} = \frac{88}{384} = 0.229$

When the heaviest man (236 Ibs) is omitted the Range will be= 195-148=47.

Change in Range = 88-47=41

Percentage change in the Range= $\frac{41}{88}$X1000 = 46.59%

(i) Range = 88

(ii) Coefficient of Range = 0.229

(iii) % Change in Range = 46.59% Ans.

Range-Discrete series

Example : Find the Range and its coefficient of the following data :

Size	5	7	9	11	13	15
Frequency	1	5	3	9	4	2

Solution: We have to calculate the differences of size, not of frequencies.

Range=L-S=15-5=10

Coefficient of Range =$\frac{L-S}{L+S} = \frac{15-5}{15+5} = \frac{10}{20} = 0.5$

Range-Continuous Series (Exclusive)

Example: Find the Range and its coefficient of following:

Size	0-10	10-20	20-30	30-40	40-50
Frequency	1	3	12	6	3

Solution: We have to calculate the differences of size, not of frequencies.

Range=L-S=50-0=50

Coefficient of Range = $\frac{50-0}{50+0} = \frac{50}{50} = 1$

Range-Continuous Series-Inclusive Series

Example: Calculate the Range and its coefficient.

Size	0-10	10-20	20-30	30-40	40-50
Frequency	3	7	20	15	6

Solution: First convert the series into exclusive series. The first class will then become 0.5 – 10.5 and the last class will become 40.5 –

Largest value = 50.5

Smallest value = 0.5

Range=L-S=50.5-0.5=50

Coefficient of Range = $\frac{50.5-0.5}{50.5+0.5} = \frac{50}{51} = 0.98$

Range = 50

Coefficient of Range = 0.98 Ans.

Quartile Deviation of Inter Quartile Range Individual Series

Example:15 students of a class obtained the following marks in statistics. Calculate the Quartile Deviation and its Coefficient.

15,20,20,21,22,22,24,25,28,28,29,30,32,33,and 35.

Solution: Arrage the marks in an ascending order.

S.N.	Marks	S.N.	Marks
1	15	9	28
2	20	10	28
3	20	11	29
4	21	12	30
5	22	13	32
6	22	14	33
7	24	15	35
8	25		

Q_1 = Size of $\{\frac{N+1}{4}\}$ th item

= Size of $\{\frac{15+1}{4}\}$ th item

= Size of 4th item

= 21 marks

Q_3 = Size of 3 $\{\frac{N+1}{4}\}$ th item

= Size of 3 $\{\frac{15+1}{4}\}$ th item

= Size of 12th item

= 30 marks

Quartile Deviation = $\frac{Q_3-Q_1}{2} = \frac{30-21}{2} = \frac{9}{2} = 4.5$ marks

Inter Quartile Range = Q_3-Q_1 = 30-21=9

Coeff. of inter Quartile Range = $\frac{Q_3-Q_1}{Q_3+Q_1} = \frac{30-21}{30+21} = \frac{9}{51}$

Coeff. of Q.D. = 0.176

or

Coeff. of I.Q.R.

Q_1= 21

Q_3= 30

Q.D.= 4.5

Inter Quartile Range = 9

Coeff. of I.Q.R. = 0.176

Quartile Deviation-Discrete Series

Example: Find the Quartile Deviation and its coefficient from the following data :

Size	15	16	17	18	19	20	21
Frequency	4	6	10	15	12	9	4

Solution:

Age in Years	**No. of Students (f)**	**c.f.**
15	4	4
16	6	10
17	10	20
18	15	35
19	12	47
20	9	56
21	4	60

Q_1= Size of $\{\frac{N+1}{4}\}$ th item

= Size of $\{\frac{60+1}{4}\}$ th item

= Size of $\{\frac{61}{4}\}$ th item

= Size of 15.25^{th} item

Which lies in c.f. 20 and value corresponding to this c.f. is 17. Therefore Q_1= 17.

Q_3 = Size of 3 $\{\frac{N+1}{4}\}$ th item

Q_3 = Size of 3 $\{\frac{60+1}{4}\}$ th item

Q_3 = Size of 45.75^{th} item

Size of 45.75 lies in c.f. 47 and value corresponding to this c.f. is 19. Therefore Q_3 = 19

Q.D. = $\frac{Q_3-Q_1}{2} = \frac{19-17}{2} =$

Coeff. of inter Quartile Range = $\frac{Q_3-Q_1}{Q_3+Q_1} = \frac{19-17}{19+17} = \frac{2}{36} = \frac{1}{18}$

Coeff. of Q.D. = 0.056 Ans.

Example : From the following table giving height of students calculate the Semi-Interquartile Range and the Coefficient of Quartile Deviation.

Heights (in cms)	153	155	157	159	161	163	165	167	169
No. of Students	25	21	28	20	18	24	22	18	2

Solution: Computation of Semi-Interquartile Range

Heights (in cms)	No. of Students (f)	Cumulative Frequency c.f.
153	25	25
155	21	46
157	28	74
159	20	94
161	18	112
163	24	136
165	22	158
167	18	176
169	23	199

Q_1 = Size of $\{\frac{N+1}{4}\}$ th item

= Size of $\{\frac{199+1}{4}\}$ th item

= Size of $\{\frac{200}{4}\}$ th item

= Size of 50th item

= 157 cms.

Q_3 = Size of 3 $\{\frac{N+1}{4}\}$ th item

= Size of 3 $\{\frac{199+1}{4}\}$ th item

= Size of 3x50th item

= Size of 150th item

= 165 cms.

Sime Inter-quartile Range or Q.D. = $\frac{Q_3 - Q_1}{2} = \frac{165-157}{2} = \frac{8}{2} = 4$ cms.

Quartile Coeff. of Dispersion = $\frac{Q_3 - Q_1}{Q_3 + Q_1} = \frac{165-157}{165+157} = \frac{8}{322}$=0.025

Coeff. of Q.D. = 0.056

Q.D. 4 Ans.

Quartile Deviation Continuous Series

Example : Compute Quartile Deviation and its Coefficient from the following data :

Class Interval 10-15 15-20 20-25 25-30 30-40 40-50 50-60 60-70

Frequency 1 12 16 22 10 8 6 4

Solution: Calculations for Quartiles.

Class Interval	Frequency	c.f.
10-15	4	4
15-20	12	16
20-25	16	32
25-30	22	54
30-40	10	64
40-50	8	72
50-60	6	78
60-70	4	82

Q_1 = Size of $\{\frac{N+1}{4}\}$ th item

= Size of $\{\frac{82}{4}\}$ th item

= Size of 20.5th item

= Which lies in 20-25 class

Q_1 = Size of 3 $\{\frac{20.5+16}{16}\}$x5 th item

$Q_1 = 20 + \left\{\frac{4.5x5}{16}\right\} = 20 + 1.4$

Q_1 = 21.4

Q_3 = Size of 3 $\frac{N}{4}$ th item

= Size of 3x20.5th item

= Size of 61.5th item

Which lies in 30-40 Class

$Q_3 = 20 + \frac{61.5-54}{10} x10$

= 30+7.5=37.5

Q_3 = 37.5

Q.D. $= \frac{Q_3 - Q_1}{2} = \frac{37.5-21.4}{2} = \frac{16.1}{2} = 8.05$

Coeff. of Q.D. $= \frac{Q_3 - Q_1}{Q_3 + Q_1} = \frac{37.5-21.4}{37.5+21.4} = \frac{16.1}{58.9} = 0.273$

Q.D. = 8.05

Coeff. of Q.D. 0.273 Ans.

Example : Calculate quartile deviation and its coefficient from the data given in the following table.

Class	1	2	3	4	5	6	7	8	9	10
Size of item										
Frequency	2	9	11	14	20	24	20	16	5	3

Solution: We are given the central size. We are to form class intervals by adding and subtracting 0.5.

Class	Frequency	c.f.
0.5-1.5	2	2
1.5-2.5	9	11
2.5-3.5	11	22
3.5-4.5	14	36
4.5-5.5	20	56
5.5-6.5	24	80
6.5-7.5	20	100
7.5-8.5	16	116
8.5-9.5	5	121
9.5-10.5	3	124

Q_1 = Size of $\{\frac{N}{4}\}$ th item

= Size of $\{\frac{124}{4}\}$ th item

= Size of 31th item

= lies in 3.5-4.5 class

Therefore the Q_1 $= 3.5 + \frac{1}{14}(31 - 22)$ th item

$= 3.5 + \frac{9}{14} = 3.5 + 0.64 = 4.14$

Q_3 = Size of $3\left\{\frac{N}{4}\right\}$ th item

= Size of (3x31)th item

= Size of 93rd item

Which lies in 6.5-7.5 group.

$Q_3 = 6.5 + \frac{1}{10}(93 - 80)$

$= 6.5 + \frac{13}{20}$

$= 6.5 + 0.65 = 7.15$

Coeff. of Q.D. $= \frac{Q_3 - Q_1}{2} = \frac{7.15 - 4.14}{2} = \frac{3.01}{2} = 1.505$

Coeff. of Q.D. $= \frac{Q_3 - Q_1}{Q_3 + Q_1} = \frac{7.15 - 4.14}{7.15 + 4.14} = \frac{3.01}{11.29} = 0.266$

Q.D. = 1.505

Coeff. of Q.D. 0.266 Ans.

Example : Calculate Quartile Deviation and its measure

Variable	20-29	30-39	40-49	50-59	60-69	70-79
Frequency	306	182	144	96	42	34

Solution. Calculation of Quartiles.

Variable	f	c.f
20-29	306	306
30-39	182	488
40-49	144	632
50-59	96	728
60-69	42	770
70-79	34	804

Q_1 = Size of $\{\frac{N}{4}\}$ th item

= Size of $\{\frac{804}{4}\}$ th item =201

= 201th item lies in 19.5-29.5

Q_1 = $19.5\text{x}\frac{10}{306}(201-0)$

= $19.5+\frac{201\text{x}10}{306}$

= $4.14+\frac{2010}{306}$

= 19.5+6.5686

= 26.068

Q_3 = Size of $3\left\{\frac{N}{4}\right\}$ th item

= 3x201=603

lies in 39.5-49.5

Q_3 = $39.5+\frac{10}{144}\text{x}(603-488)$

= $39.5+10\text{x}\frac{155}{144}$

= $39.5+\frac{1550}{144}$

= 39.5+7.986

= 47.486

Q.D. = $\frac{47.486-26.068}{2} = \frac{21.418}{2} = 10.71$

Coeff. of Q.D. = $\frac{47.486-26.068}{47.486+26.068} = \frac{21.418}{73.554} = 0.29$

Q.D. = 10.71

Coeff. of Q.D. 0.29 Ans.

✶✶✶✶✶✶

Chapter - 32

Attitude Measurement

Attitude : Attitudes are evaluated statements or judgments either favorable or unfavorable - concerning objects, people or events.

According to Bern, "Attitudes are likes and dislikes."

According to Engel, "Altitudes are all overall evaluation that gallows one to respond in a consistent favorable or unfavorable manner with respect to a given object or alternative."

An 'attitudes' is the 'predisposition to respond to an idea or object.'

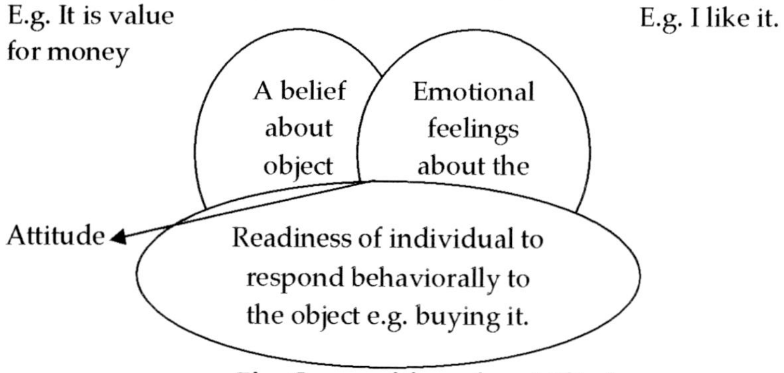

Fig. Composition of an Attitude

Functions of Attitude

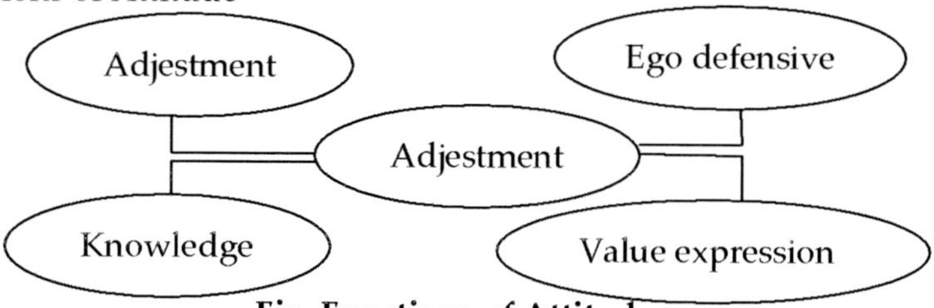

Fig. Functions of Attitude

(1) Adjustment Function: Attitudes help people adjust to their work environment. When employees are well treated. They are likely to develop a positive attitude towards management and the organization. When employees are berated and paid poorly, they are likely to develop a negative attitude towards the company and its owners. Their attitudes help employees adjust to their environment and are a basis for future behavior.

(2) Ego-Defenses Functions: People often form and maintain certain attitudes to protect their own self-images. For example workers may feel threatened by the employment or advancement of minority or female workers in their organization. These threatened workers may develop prejudices against the new workers. Such an ego defensive attitude is formed and used to cope with its feeling of guilt or threat.

(3) Expressive Function: It helps express to the individual's central valves and self identity. Consumers express their values in the products they buy. The shapes they penetrate and the lifestyle they exhibit.

It also helps individual define their self-concepts, adapt and internalize the values of a group they have recently joined.

(4) Knowledge Function: Attitudes provide the standards or frames of reference by which an individual judges objectives or events.

Attitude Theories and Models: 'The three classical theories based upon the consistency principal are congruity. Balance and cognitive dissonance.

(1) Congruity Theory

This theory was developed by CE Osgood and P.H.Tannenbaum. This theory is building on the notion of positive and negative attitudes and adds the concept of attitude strength. This theory helps to rate attitude towards an object from 3 (highly unfavorable) to +3 (highly favorable) with middle zero point.

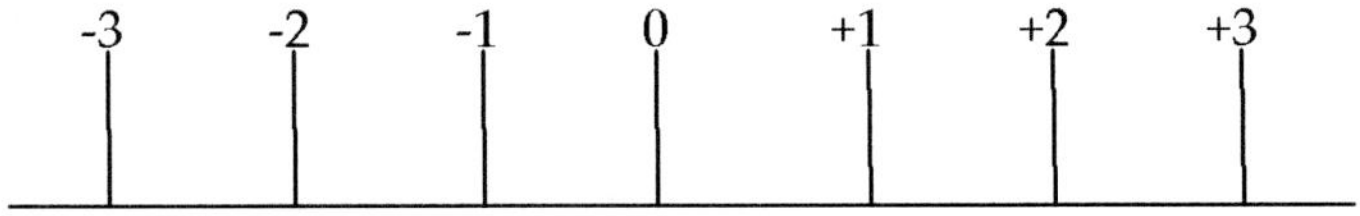

(2) Balance Theory

This theory has been developed by Fritz Heider. According to balance theory, a person perceives her or his environment in terms of trials. That is, a person views herself or himself as being involved in a triangular relationship in which all three elements (Persons. Ideas and things) have either positive (liking, favorable) or negative (disliking. unfavorable) relationships with each other.

There are no numerical values used to express the degree of unity between elements.

"I like large luxurious Cars."

The situation is described the triad shown in figure below:

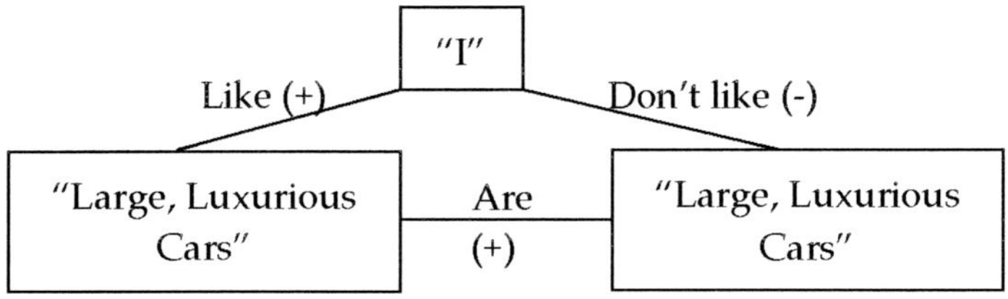

Graphical representation of an unbalanced attitude structure:

(3) Cognitive Dissonance:

It was developed in 1957 by Leon Festinger. Festinger describes cognitive dissonancy as a psychological state, which results when a person perceives that two cognitions (thoughts), both of which he believes to be true, do not 'fit' together, that is, they seem inconsistent. The resulting dissonance produces tension which serves to motivate the individual to bring harmony to inconsistent elements and thereby reduce psychological tension. For example, two pieces of information '1 like ice-cream' and 'ice-cream can make me fat are dissonant. 'This means, one does not want, to become fat and yet one wants to eat ice-cream. On the other hand 'I like green salad', and 'green salad is good for you' are consonant pieces of information. The aim of cognitive dissonance theory is to reduce the amount of dissonance often defined as mental discomfort'. This theory can be applied to marketing so as to reduce post-purchase dissonance in consumer purchase decision.

Method for the Measurement of Attitudes

General Methods

Questionnaire Methods
- Self reports
- Structured questionnaire
- Indirectly worded questionnaire e.g. respondents are asked about factual knowledge and their attitude is inferred from their knowledge.

Observation Methods
- Observing behavior
- Observing physiological reactions like sweating, dilation of eyes, change of voice pitch etc.

Specific Methods
- Non disguised, non-structured techniques
- Disguised, non-structured techniques
- Non-disguised. structured techniques
- Disguised, structured techniques

Methods/Techniques of Attitude: Disguised refers to whether the respondent knows the purpose of the research and structure refers in the formal procedure or structure for questioning.

(A) Non-Disguised, Non-Structured Technique

(i) Depth Interviews: Depth interviews do not try to hide or disguise the subject of interest and use no structural framework for getting the information. Depth interviews are conducted by highly trained interviewers who simply go the respondents talking about the subject.

(ii) Check-lists: this device allows the recording of whether a given behavior, structure or process is present or not.

Two types of check-lists

Static Checklist	Action Checklist
Such information as age, race, sex, may be recorded	It records actual behavior, appropriate behavior, etc. Which have a limited number of alternatives

Behavior

Sign system	Category system
Useful for studying infrequent Behavior uses questions about Behavior to be ticked.	Developing and using categories to be ticked.

(iii) Intensively- Extensively: This dimension deals with the degree of detail found in the system (checklist).

Other methods

(a) Physical Trace Analysis:

Erosion: Measures or signs of selective wearing of some material. (Library).

Accretion: Measures or sips of material deposits.

(b)Archival Record Analysis or Document:

Archival Record Analysis or Document

Public Records	Private Records
➔ Birth, death, Marriage records.	Sales Records, autobiography,
➔ Political and judicial Records.	Diaries, Letters.
• Government Documents	

(c) Content Analysis: This is the method of measuring attitudes and opinion from written and spoken language. The words and phrases are coded by category of interest.

(iv) Picture Frustration Test: This is an adaptation of Rozenweing test. It consists of 24 sets of cartoon pictures in pairs. In each pair there is a picture depicting a frustrating situation accompanied by verbal remarks. A blank space is provided for the respondent to write what the frustrated person would reply.

The responses are classified with reference to the direction of aggression and type of aggression.

The direction of aggression is scored its extra punitive, intropunitive and impunitive. This type of aggression includes obstacle dominance, emphasizing frustrating subject, ego defense, following siltation are the constructive solution of the frustrating problem.

(v) Holtzman Inkblot Test (HIT) : Developed by W. H. Holtzman. This consists of 145 cards based on color, movement, shading and other factors. Only one response per card is obtained from the respondent and his responses are interpreted at three levels of from appropriateness. From responses are interpreted for knowing the accuracy or inaccuracy of respondent's percepts shading and color for as certaining his affectional and emotional needs.

(B) Disguised, Structured Techniques

Sometimes catch questions may be added to a lengthy questionnaire. If the respondent answer three questions differently, the researcher shall know that the respondent is taking some responses.

Example: How many calories does one piece of chocolate contain?.

- 25 or less
- 25 to 50
- 50
- 100 calories

Interestingly, overweight people underestimated the number of calories and slim people overestimated the number of calories.

(C) Expressive Techniques

(1) Play Techniques: This is used often in studying children's attitudes through manipulation of dolls. A set of dolls representing a miniature life situation is given to children who are allowed to play with them freely.

(2) Finger Painting: A set of pots of a special type of paint is given to the respondents who is told to draw what he likes with paints. Using his fingers and hands. Sixteen aspects of finger painting were measured: time to begin painting. use of whole hand, fingertip approach, washing up, behavior and so on.

(3) Role Playing: It is the acting out of assigned specific roles for a brief period by two or more individuals. This is used in behavioral research.

(D) Non-Disguised, Structured Techniques

(1) Graphic Rating Scales: In these scales, respondents are asked to rate themselves a product or a concept by ticking the paint at which they or the item would fall on a scale running from one extreme of the attitude in question to the other:

(Please check (L) one box for each item)

	Extremely important	Very important	Some what important	Not Very important	Note at all
Price	☐	☐	☐	☐	☐
Configuration	☐	☐	☐	☐	☐
Brand	☐	☐	☐	☐	☐
After sales service	☐	☐	☐	☐	☐

Semantic Differential

Higher Quality	3	2	1	0	1	2	3	Lower quality
Lower Price	-	-	-	-	-	-	-	Higher Price
Higher Value	-	-	-	-	-	-	-	Lower Value

(2) Ranking Scales: In this method we ask respondents to rank the brands or other subjects of interests accordingly.

e.g. Rank the following In order of your preferences. Tooth Paste

Colgate----------Babool-----------Close-up------------Pepsodent--------

Provided with a empty speech balloon

(3) Multiple item scales: Multiple item scales develop a series of statements related to the attitude. Individuals are then asked to indicate agreement or disagreement to each statement and on the basics of the responses scores are determined and measures the attitudes.

(A) Thrust one scale (B) Likert's scale

(E) Verbal Projective Techniques

(1) Word Association Test

The interviewer administering the test rends list 25 to 100 words, one at a time, emotionally-tinged words are mixed up with neutral words. The respondent is asked to respond with the rust matching word that comes to his mind, in two or three seconds. As he reads the words, the interviewer records the response and the time taken by the respondent to react to each word.

If the respondent takes more than three seconds to respond with a matching word it is called hesitation. In some cases, the respondent may block and given no answers, because the test word or what is it symbolizes to him is highly charged with emotion.

(2) Story Completion Test

The interviewer provides the respondent with the beginning of a story and asks him to complete it; it is assumed that in completing the story, the respondent will reveal his own attitudes and other characteristics. This tact is of great help in identifying and evaluating specific psychogenic needs that cannot be uncovered by simple projective techniques.

(3) Sentence Completion Test

This is an extension of word association test. It is administered and interpreted in the same manner the respondent is exposed to the first parts of incomplete sentences and asked to complete them.

Attitude Measurement Scales

Attitude measurement scales art used not to rate individuals but to examine their views, agreement or disagreement with the subject. With different statement related to an issue, such as war, religion, God, family, planning, capital punishment etc.

Here, the individual is not required to directly express his position on the subject rather, he is required to express his agreement or disagreement along with its degree.

(1) Differential Scale - Thurston's Technique

In differential scale, associated with LL. Thin-stone scaling is done with the help of judges. It's a simple technique and is based on either equal appearing interval or on paired comparison. For differential scale, the investigator first draws a list of several hundred possible statements of individuals expressing their attitude about a particular issue, covering the entire range from most favorable to most unfavorable including sufficient number of neutral statement.

The statements are edited and given arbitrary numbers for identification. These may be written on different slips of paper for the sake of convenience. A large number of judges are then given complete sets or these statements unit are asked to classify these statements and several positions of responses, say from 1 to 11, representing graduate series of attitudes from extremely unfavorable to extremely favorable. Here, 1, 2, 3 may be favorable statements 4, 5, 6 neutral statements and 7, 8, 9, and 11 unfavorable statements. Statements with too broad scatter are discarded as ambiguous or irrelevant for the study. Finally 15 to 20 comparatively unambiguous and relevant statements are selected and scale value of each of these statements is fixed at the mean or median position assigned by the judges. This scale is used for measuring attitude of individuals towards objects under investigation. In survey subjects may be asked to check (V) either the statements, which are close to their attitude, or check (g) two or three statements, which are closest to their positions. Thurston's scale is most appropriate in case a single attitude k, sought to be investigated.

(2) Summated Rating Scale-R.C. Likerts' Technique

The object or summated rating scale is to place an individual somewhere on an agreement continuum of the attitude in question. Like Thurston's technique, in Likert's technique also the investigator takes a number of statements or items considered relevant to the attitude being investigated. The subjects are required to indicate their altitude to each of those statements ranging from clearly favorable to clearly unfavorable on it five-point scale as given here under:

I	II	III	IV	V
Strongly Approve	Approve	Undecided	Disapprove	Strongly Disapprove
5	4	3	2	1

(3) Commutative Scale - Guttmann's Scalogram Technique

Guttmann has used a technique known as scalogram in test whether the attributes being studied actually involve only a single dimension. In Guttmann's method, perfect commutative scale implies that a person who answers a given question favorably will have higher total score than a person who answers it unfavorably.

The scalogram technique is a simple method of testing the scalability of the statements, for this the responses of all the individuals are reproduced on a scalogram as shown in following, table:

Score	Say 'Yes' to Item			Say 'No' to Item		
	3	2	1	3	2	1
3	X	X	X			
2		X	X	X		
1			X	X	X	
0				X	X	X

If the pattern in table holds well then a given score or a particular series of items always has the same meaning. i.e., the score of the respondent is known without consulting the questionnaire and it can be slated which items he has endorsed and which he has opposed.

Guttmann has developed another technique where the respondents are required to give not only their views (Agreement or disagreement) but also indicate the intensity (Degree) classified into five categories. Thus two scores are obtained for each respondent, content score and intensity score, which can be plotted adjoined to each other on graph

The plotting on the graph is 'U' 5hapcd as the extreme views have high intensity. The content score at the lowest point of the curve may be regarded as the dividing line between favorable and unfavorable responses.

(4) Semantic Differential Scale - Osgood's Technique

In this technique, like Likert's scale, each respondent is required to make his rating on the given scale. Osgood and his colleagues, for their studies, developed the semantic differential technique to evaluate the 'meaning of certain concepts A group of subjects were required to mark their views regarding the concepts. The two ends by the scale were described by adjectives, which were polar opposite as shown below:

Good	Bad
Kind	Cruel
True	False
Strong	Weak
Hard	Soft
Severe	Lenient
Active	Passive
Fast	Slow

The subjects were asked to place check mark on one of the seven spaces on the scale to indicate their rating of the concept. The semantic differences in respect of series of concepts were used by Osgood and others to calculate correlation between the scores given to a set of concepts through factor analysis. The semantic differential can be used in a broad group of studies. For example, in market research to compare the image of different car models- the adjectives like overpowered, underpowered, cheap-costly, ordinary-unique etc. may be used. Mean scores can then be used to give a comparative profile of different models.

Motivational Research

Motivational Research is a type of qualitative research that attempts to explain why people behave as they do. Motivational research seeks to discover and comprehend what people do not fully understand about themselves. Implicitly, motivational research assumes the existence of underlying or unconscious motives that influence human behavior. Motivational research attempts to identify forces and influences that consumers may not be aware of (e.g. cultural factors, sociological format. Typically these unconscious motives (or beyond awareness reasons) are intertwined with and complicated by conscious motives, cultural biases, economic variables, and fashion trends.

Motivational research in marketing, attempts to examine all of these influences and factors to unravel the mystery of consumer behavior as it relates in a specific product or service, so that the marketer better understands the target audience and how to influence that audience.

Definition: Motivation is the drive of an individual towards a goal. The motivation is caused because that person has a 'need' or a deprivation and is therefore driven inwards aspiring for fulfillment of his need and achieving satisfaction.

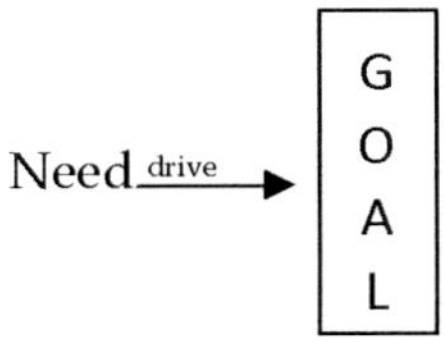

Any research that attempts to explore the area of motivation of people can be called motivation research.

Motivation research attempts to get below the surface of people's behavior as consumer of goods and services, so that a better appreciation of their needs can he fanned. For example, a lot of knowledge has been used in devising advertisements which project products in consumer attractive terms. The research technique can help in the development or new products, investigation of price, packaging and methods of distribution.

Scalograms

Guttmann proposed a method for scaling attitude items. It consists of series of statements to which a respondent expresses his agreement or disagreement. The special feature of this type of scale is that statements in it form a cumulative series.

Scalogram analysis refers to the procedure for determining whether a set of items from a unidimensional scale. A scale is said to be unidimensional, if the responses fall into a pattern in which endorsement of the item reflecting the extreme position results also in endorsing all items, which are less extreme? Under this technique, the respondents are asked to indicate in respect of each item whether they agree or disagree with it, and if these items form a unidimensional sale the response pattern will be as under:

Response pattern in scalogram analysis is :

Item Number				Respondent
4	3	2	1	Score
X	X	X	X	4
-	X	X	X	3
-	-	X	X	2
-	-	-	X	1
-	-	-	-	0

+ = Agree

– = Disagree

Problems

1	2	3	4	5	Score
+	+	+	+	+	5
+	+	+	+	-	4
+	+	+	-	-	3
+	+	-	-	-	2
+	-	-	-	-	1
-	-	-	-	-	0

A diagram in which the individual's response's are laid out as above is called a scalogram. If a set or attitude items is perfectly scaleable in the above sense, the scalogram contains only (n+1) response pattern which are known as scale types. One can infer from the individual's total score precisely which items he agreed and disagreed with.

Scores and Ranks of Respondents

Respondents	12345	Scores of Respondents	Ranks of Respondents
A	11111	5	1
B	01111	4	2
C	00111	3	3
D	00011	2	4
E	00001	1	5
F	00000	0	6

Assume that there are five attitude statements ranging from the most favorable to the least with respect to some psychological aspects. We rank this statement in such a manner that the most favorable statement is assigned Rank I. The next most favorable rank 2 and so on with the least favorable statement standing at rank 5. If he agrees with the statement he is given a weight of 1 and if he disagrees he is assigned weight of 0.

Internal Consistency Scale

Various Measures of the Internal Consistency Scale: Internal consistency measures estimates how consistently individuals respond to the items within a scale. Measures of internal consistence are not tests of the unidimensionally of items in a scale. For example, if the first half of an instrument is educational items which correlate highly among themselves and the second is political items which correlate highly among themselves, the instrument would have a high croubach's alpha anyway, even though two distinct dimensions were present. Measures of internal consistency are often called measures of "internal consistency reliability".

1. Cronbach's Alpha: Popularized in a 1951 article by Cronbach based on work in the 1940s by Guttmann and others, is the most common estimate of internal consistency of items in a scale. Alpha measures the extent to which item responses obtained at the same time correlate highly with each other.

Though widely interpreted as such study speaking alpha is not a measure of unidimensionality. Rather, alpha is a measure of level of mean intercorrelation weighted by variances, or a measure of mean intercorrelation for standardized data, stepped up for number of items. A set of items can have a high alpha and still be multidimensional. This happens when there are separate clusters of item which intercorrelate highly, even though the clusters themselves do not intercorrelate.

In addition to estimating internal consistency scale from the average correlation, the formula for alpha also takes into account the number of items on theory that the more items, the more reliable a scale will be. That is, when the number of items in a scale is higher, alpha will be higher even when the estimated average correlations are equal as the number of items rises, Alpha rises.

Congeneric V-tau-equivalent V-Parallel Indicators

The psychometric literature sorts indicator sets for latent variables into three types. Congeneric sets are those which are presumed to have passed some test of convergent validity, such as Cronbach's alpha.

Tau-equivalent sets also have equal variances for the indicators. Parallel sets arc tau-equivalent sets where the items have equal reliability coefficients.

When items are less than tall-equivalent, alpha is only a lower bound on reliability.

Standardized Item Alpha

Standardized item alpha is a variant of alpha designed to be used to test i.e. one-item parallel tests and is meant to be interpreted as the average Spearman-Brown-Corrected reliability estimate from all possible splits in a series of applications of split half reliability on a single test. It is also the value of computed alpha when all scale items are standardized to have an equal means and variances.

Factor Analysis

This is often used to establish internal consistency. Inter correlated items will sort themselves out an separate factors if the data exhibit a simple factor structure, and this is taken as evidence that the indicator items, "belong together" in a scale, and also an evidence of discriminate validity. That scales are different horn one another.

2. **Rasch Model**: Rasch logistic models are often preferred to Cronbach's alpha or factor analytic methods because Rasch models take into account not only additive relations among indicator items, as alpha and factor analysis does, but also relations where items exhibit an ordinal relationship. Even when correlations may not be high.

3. **Tarkkone's Measure of Scale Reliability**: This was introduced by Lauri Tarkkone and further studied by Kimmo Vehkalatir. As yet much less widely used than Cronbach's alpha, Tarkkone's measure has some statistical properties superior to it.

4. **Loviager's H**: this is another alternative to Cronbach's alpha. It is a better approximation to the classical reliability coefficient rather than Cronbach's alpha, which has been widely used to measure the internal consistency of a scale. Specifically alpha strongly underestimates when there is large variation in item difficulties.

5. **Kuder-Richardson Formula 20, KR 20**: This is a special case of Cronbach's alpha, for ordinal dichotomies. That is Alpha 0= KR 20 when the pair of items are both dichotomous.

6. **Spearman's Rho** : This is a form at rank order calculation. It is calculated with the same formula as for Pearson's correlation, but using rank rather than interval data. Since scales are ran-order data. This is often use in place of r when correlation is called for. As in inter-term correlations. The median Rho between all pairs of items in a scale is a classic measure of reliability in the sense of internal consistency. Rho values above 0.60 are considered necessary for an adequate scale.

Inter-item Correlation: This is used to spot-reverse-coded items. Seale items should correlate positively with one another. A negative correlation may well indicate, for instance, that an item was coded such that "1" meant the opposite direction (ex, low) from the measuring of "1" (ex, low, high) for the other items in the scale.

Process of work of Thurston's Scale

A type of attitude scale constructed by the method of equal appearing intervals, in which a large pool of candidate statements about an attitude object, ranging from strongly negative (Abortion is never, justified) through neutral (There are arguments both for and against abortion) to strongly positive (Abortion is every woman's right), are sorted by a group of judges into eleven categories. Assumed to appear equally spaced on the attitude continuum, according to how favorable the statements are towards the attitude object, and loans that yield the highest level of agreement among the judges as to their scale position, and that collectively represent an adequate range of contents and scale positions, are then selected for the final scale. Respondents to the scale endorse just those items with which they agree, and an individual respondent's score is calculated as the mean (or occasionally median) of the items endorsed, such scores being assumed to lie on an interval scale of measurement. Also called an equal-appearing interval scale.

Likert Scale

One of the most popular types of attitude scale. Constructed by the method of summated ratings in which a sample of respondents are given a large number of candidate statements about an attitude object (such as Homosexuality is acceptable in today's society, homosexuality, should he outlawed) to which they respond with their own attitudes by choosing one of the response categories attached to each item, for example, strongly disagree, disagree neutral, agree, strongly agree. Items that are worded positively towards the attitude object, such as the first of the examples above, are assigned positively increasing stores to their response categories such as 0. 1, 2, 3, and 4, respectively, and for negatively worded items such as the second example the scoring is reversed (4, 3, 2, 1, 0). Each respondent's scores on all the candidate items are summed to yield a total score, the candidate items are then subjected to item analysis, and those with the highest discriminating power are retained for the final scale.

Semantic Differential:-

A device for measuring the affective or connotative meaning of words, also widely used for measuring attitudes towards other concepts and objects. It consists of a variable number of seven-point bipolar rating scales, such as

Good .... Bad
Active .... Passive
Strong .... Weak

On which respondents rate the items under investigation. According to factor catalysis, there are three underlying dimensions of affective or connotative meaning, exemplified by the three core scales shown above, labeled evaluation, activity, and potency, respectively. Scores ranging from -3 at the negative end of each scale to +3 at the positive end are usually assigned. To illustrate how it works, research in the US has shown that average ratings of the word nurse tend to be towards the good, active, and weak poles, whereas the word policeman tends to be rated towards the good, active, and strong poles. The particular adjective pairs used depend on the items being evaluated: active versus passive could be included among the scales used to measure the activity dimension if the items being rated were political parties, for example, but this might be less appropriate if the items were types of food. The technique was developed by the US psychologist Charles E (gerton) Osgood (1916-91).

Guttmann Scale

A type of attitude the item, of which can be arranged in a hierarchical order such that agreement with any particular item implies probable agreement with all those below it in the hierarchy, as would apply to the following (non-attitudinal) items: I am over 5 feet tall; I am over 5 feet 6 inches tall; 1 am over 6 feet tall; I am over 6 feet 6 Inches tall. It is constructed by the method of scalogram analysis in which a large pool of candidate statements about an attitude object (such as Euthanasia is morally wrong; Euthanasia should be legalized, and so on) are administered to a group of respondents who mark just those items with which they agree, and from these responses a set of items is selected that can be arranged into a hierarchy with as few errors (deviations from a perfect linear hierarchy) as possible, a satisfactory Guttmann scale having relatively few errors as indexed by a reproducibility (Rep) of at least 0.90. Implying that the scale is one-dimensional, measuring only one major attitude variable. The process of constructing a Gutunann scale is called smlogram analysis. A simple example of a Guttmann scale is a social distance scale.

Sociometric Scale: Sociometric scales are used for measuring the change in institutional behavior and these similar to attitude scales; they present generally the same problems as are encountered in the construction of attitude scales, however, there is fundamental difference between the two scales. 'The attitude scales deal with favorable or unfavorable attitude, and may represent personal or group attitude. The sociometric scales are never personal as they deal with the behavior of the institution. The opinion as expressed in attitude scales may be dichotomous and may be divided into two clear cut class, but in measurement of institutional behavior the intensity of measurement is essential. It cannot be grouped into water-tight-compartments".

Characteristics of a Good Sothometric Scale

The following are the essential characteristics of a good sociometric scale:

1. **Reliability**: The sociometric scale must be reliable in the sense that it must give the same measurement or result in similar conditions. In case a scale gives different measurements, on being applied to the nine or a highly similar phenomenon, its reliability is doubtful.

2. **Validity**: The validity of scale Iles in the fact that it measures in some demonstrable way. What 'ii claims to measure'. The test of validity of a sociometric scale is an extremely complicated task and it is difficult to give a satisfactory criteria of the phenomena being measured and also no-objective measurement of-the validity of a scale have yet been evolved. 'Logical test of validity is generally used for this purpose and a scale is said to be valid if the measurements given by it stands to reas.

3. **Simplicity**: The sociometric scale should be simple and easy enough to he understood by a common man. A simple scale is capable of being frequently tried by persons and its constant use will make it more accurate and precise. In addition, simple scale also generates confidence in the minds of the people and the scale thus evolved Is more acceptable to the people at large.

4. **Universality**: A good sociometrie scale should he widely applicable. The most notable characteristic of physical scale is their universal acceptance, whereas, one of the limitations of sociometric scale is limited applicability. But the point bearing upon this limited applicability be cleared at this stage in the social phenomena is not 'as homogeneous as the physical phenomenal. The various attributes of social phenomena differ from place to place, according to difference in culture, religion and social values'.

5. **Practicability**: A good sociometric scale should be practicable and this implies that factors which are considered for the construction of the scale must be such as to be measured and gathered. If in a study, the Intangible behaviors of 'traits' are included in the scale, it would be difficult to introduce the scale as these cannot be measured.

6. **Based on norms**: A sociometric scale should be based on accepted norms since for all purposes of comparisons the researcher will use norms with which the measurement is to be compared.

7. **Proper weight age**: A sociometric scale should have proper weight age for each factor included in the scale. 'Every item included in the scale is not of some importance. Unless proper weights ale attached to various attributes their total measurement would not be a representative one'.

Motivational Research: It is a type of qualitative research that attempts to explain why people behave as they do. It seeks to discover and comprehend what people do not fully understand about themselves. Motivational research attempts to Identify forces and influences that consumers may not be aware of (e.g.. cultural factors, sociological forces.)

Major Motivational Techniques: The three major motivational research techniques are observation. Focus groups, and depth Interviews.

1. **Observation** can be fruitful method of deriving hypotheses about human motives. Anthropologists have pioneered the development of this technique. All of us are familiar with anthropologists living with the "natives" to understand their behavior; This same systematic observation can produce equally insightful results about consumer behavior. Observation can be accomplished in-person or sometimes through the convenience of video. Usually, personal observation is simply too expensive, and most consumers don't want an anthropologist living in their household for a month or two.

It is easier to observe consumers in buying situations than In their homes, and here the observation can be in-person or by video cameras. Generally, video cameras are less intrusive than an in-person observer.

Finding a representative set of cooperative stores, however. is not an easy task, and the installation and maintenance of video cameras is not without its difficulties, in-store observers can be used as tacit, so long as they have some - cover" that rakes their presence less obvious. But, observation by video or human eye cannot answer every question. Generally. Observation must be supplemented by focus groups or depth interviews to fully understand why consumers are doing what they do.

2. The Focus Group

The focus group in the hands of a skilled moderator can be a valuable motivational research technique. To reach its full motivational potential. The group interview must he largely nondirective in style, and the group must achieve spontaneous interaction it is the mutual reinforcement within the group (the group excitement and spontaneity) that produces the relations and behaviors that reveal underlying motives. A focus group discussion dominated by the moderator will rarely produce any motivational insights. A focus group actively led by the moderator with much direct questioning of respondents will seldom yield motivational understanding. But the focus group s a legitimate motivational technique.

3.The Depth Interview

The heart and soul of motivational research is the depth interview, a lengthy (one to two hours), one-on-one. Personal interview, conducted directly by the motivational researcher, much of the power of the depth interview is dependent upon the insight, sensitivity, and skill of the motivational researcher. The interviewing task cannot be delegated to traditional marketing research interviewers - who have no training in motivational techniques.

During the personal interview, the motivational researcher strives to create an empathic relationship with each respondent, a feeling of rapport. Mutual trust. And understanding. The researcher creates a ' climate in which the respondent feels free to express his feeling and his thoughts. Without fear of embarrassment or rejection. The researcher conveys a feeling that the respondent and his opinions are Important and worthwhile, no matter what those opinions are. The motivational

Researcher is accepting, none threatening, and supportive. The emotional. Empathy between motivational researcher and respondent the single most important determinant of an effective interview.

The motivational researcher relies heavily upon nondirective interviewing techniques. Her goal Is to get the respondent to talk, and keep talking. The researcher tends to introduce general topics, rather than ask direct questions. She probes by raising her eyebrows, by a questioning lock upon her face, by paraphrasing what the respondent has said, or by reflecting the respondent's own words back to the respondent in a questioning tone. Non-directive techniques are the least threatening (and the least biting) to the respondent.

Nominal Scale

A nominal scale consists of two or more categories into which individuals, objects or responses may he classified, Classification individuals as per their religion, residents, marital status, are examples of nominal scale.

It is more a way classification rather than an arrangements along a continuum. Even if numbers can be assigned to these classes, no meaningful calculation can be performed using them. The numbers are used only as labels or identification tags in a nominal scale.

Ordinal Scale

An ordinal scale defines the relative position of objects or of persons with respect to a characteristic without any implication regarding the distances between the positions. In ordinal scale objects are given. 1.2. 3 Ranks in continuum. The ranks are nut based on any measurements as such but Indicate the relative position such as greater than or less than etc. of different items/persons in the group under observation.

Interval Scale

This is a cardinal scale also. Herr the objects under observation are not only ranked on scale position as 1, 2.3.4.5.... etc. but the interval between these tanks is also taken as equal. thus, the order of position indicates the declining order with equal difference between the characters, not only the order of scores but also the distance between them. The position of zero may be a matter of convenience, but the successive positions are equally a part. i.e. I & 2 are as apart as 4 and 5. However, it certainly does not mean that 10 is twice as strong or large as 5.

Ratio Scale

A ratio scale is a highest level measurement. It combines. The property of interval scale, a fixed origin and equal interval with rank order as in ordinal scale and also equality of ratios. Thus, with a ratio scale the difference and the relative magnitude both can be measured this type of scales.

Likert's Summated Scale: A liken scale is a psychometric scale commonly used in questionnaires. And is the mini widely used scale in survey research. When responding to a Liken questionnaire item. Respondents specify their Intl of agreement to a statement. The scale is named after Reams Liken The Liken scale is the sum of responses on several Liken items, A liken hem is simply a statement which the respondent is asked to evaluate according to any kind of subjective or objective criteria. Generally the level of agreement or disagreement is measured. After live ordered response levels are used, although many psychometricians advocate using seven or nine levels a recent empirical study. Found that dots from 5 levels. 7 levels and to level items showed very similar characteristics in items of mean, variance. skewness and kurtosis after a simple transformation was applied. The format of a typical type five levels Liken item is:

1. Strongly disagree
2. Disagree
3 Neither agree or disagree
4 Agree
5. Strongly agree

Liken scaling is a bipolar scaling method. Measuring either positive or negative to a statement. Sometimes four point scale is used this is a forted choice method since the middle option of "Neither agree nor disagree" is not available.

Semantic Differential Scale

This is a type of a ruling scale designed to measure the connotative meaning of objects. Events and concepts. The connotations are used to derive the attitude towards the & sea object, event or concept.

Osgood's semantic differential was designed to measure the connotative meaning of concepts. The respondent is asked to choose when, his or her position lies, on a stale between two bipolar adjectives (for example, "adequate-inadequate" , "Good-evil" or "valuable-worthless") sermonic differentials can be used to describe not only persons, but also the connotative meaning of abstract concepts- a capacity used extensively in affect control theory.

The semantic differential today one of the most widely used scales used in the measlier-1mm of attitudes. One of the reasons is the versatility of the items. The bipolar adjective pairs can be used for a wide variety of subjects and as such the scale is nicknamed. The ever ready battery" of the attitude researcher.

Statistical Properties

Five items or 5 bipolar pairs of adjective and have been proven to yield reliable findings which highly correlate with alterative measures of the same attitude.

The biggest problem with this scale is that the properties of the level of measurement Is unknown. The most statistically sound approach is to treat it as an ordinal scale. But it can be argued that the neutral response serves as an arbitrary zero point, and that the intervals between the scale values can be treated as equal. Making it an interval scale.

Conditions of Using Multidimensional Scales

Multidimensional scaling is a set of data analysis techniques that display the structure of distance like data as a geometrical picture. It is an extension of the procedure discussed in scaling.

MDS has its origins in psychometrics. where it was proposed to help understand people's judgments of the similarity of members of a set of objects. MDS pictures the structures of a set of objects from data that approximate the distances between pairs of the objects. The data which are called similarities, dissimilarities, distances or proximities. Must reflect the amount of dissimilarities between pairs. In addition to the traditional human similarity judgment, the data can be objective' similarity measure or an index calculated multivariate data.

Coding: Coding involves assigning numbers or other symbols in answers so that the responses can be grouped into a limited number of categories. In coding, categories are the partitions of a data set of a given variable (Tor example, if the variable is gender. the partitions are male and female). Categorization is the proems of using rules to partition a body of data. Both closed arid free response questions must be coded.

The categorization of data sacrifices some data detail but is necessary for efficient analysis. Most statistical and banner; table software programs work more efficiently in the numeric mode. Instead of entering the word male or female in response to a question that asks for the identification of one's gender, we would use numeric codes (for example. 0 for male and 1 for female) Numeric coding simplifies the researcher's tusk in converting nominal variable, like gender, to 'dummy variables'. Statistical software also can use alphanumeric codes, as when we use M and F, or other letters, in combination with number and symbols for gender.

Coding of Data

Two types of coding: Deductive coding in which researchers derive codes from theory and Inductive coding in which researchers identify categories from the data collected. The number assigned to an observation called a code. This code should be consistent across cases or units of analysis when the same condition exists. Information on what a code means should be listed in a code hook and accompanies the data set.

Researchers can also Inc codes to group various classifications of a concept like for e.g., occupation being categorized into professional and managerial, technical and sales, service and skilled labows and unskilled labour. Systems of categories such as this once, used to classify responses or nets that relate to a single item or variable are referred to as coding schemes

Rules of Coding

Since coding is the process by which responses are classified into meaningful categories, the initial rule of coding is that the numbers assigned must make intuitive sense. For example. Higher scores on a variable should be assigned higher codes than lower stores. A person who is older than another should receive a higher code on age.

In an inductive coding scheme, the responses mentioned more frequently arc included in the coiling scheme used to analyze the data. The researcher's time h spent switching back and forth between the raw data and in evolving scheme until the categories arc applicable to and tied in with the general purpose of the study.

The chief advantages of inductive approach are its flexibility and its richness which enable the researcher to generate explanation from die findings. The shortcoming of this it method is that researchers may be bogged down by the mass of details as they try to explain the data Sometimes too little context preserved for the coder to determine which details are trivial and can therefore be eliminated

To Summarize

1. Code numbers should make intuitive sense for variables that can rank-ordered. For example, higher scores should be assigned higher code numbers

2. In deductive coding, categories should be linked to the theory from which the research hypothesis was derived. Deductive coding is most common with quantitative research. Qualitative researchers usually design the coding scheme inductively from the data in their effort to develop grounded theory.

3. The coding categories must tic mutually exclusive i.e. each unit of analysts should fit into one and only one category.

4. The coding scheme must be exhaustive i.e. every response must in into a category with few responses being classified as "other"

5. Categories must be specific enough to capture differences using the smallest possible number of categories i.e. the criterion of detail.

Coding Reliability and Data Entry Devices

Once the researcher has constructed the code book the data need to be 'coded or transferred to a form from which someone can enter them into a statistical computer programmer for storage and analysis. Raw data can he coded in a number of ways to facilitate efficient computer entry.

Coder Reliability

Studies with well constructed code book, preceded, closed-ended questions; and proper coder training rue prone to fewer problems with coder reliability than other studies, all things being equal, because coders do not have to exercise their own Judgment in deciding what code to give a response

It is standard practice to recheck or verify a sample of coder's Work to ensure that they have not become lax.

Code Book Construction

A code hook or coding of scheme, contains each variable in the study sad specifies the application of coding rules to the variables. It is used by the researcher or research staff to promote more accurate and more efficient data entry. It is also the definitive source for locating the positions or variables in the data file during analysis. In many statistical programs. The coding scheme is integral to the data file. Most code books arc computerized or not contain the question number, variable name location oldie variable's code on the input medium (SPSS data file) descriptions for the response options and whether she variable is alphabetic or numeric.

Coding Closed Question (Inductive)

The responses to closed questions include scaled items for which answers can be anticipated. Closed questions are favored by researcher's ever open-ended questions for their efficiency and specificity. They are easier to code. Record and analyze. When codes are established in the Instrument design phase of the research process, it is possible to precede the questionnaire the design urge with computerized survey design, and can-after assisted. Computer administered or online collection of data, precutting is necessary as the software tallies data as they are collected. Proceeding is particularly helpful for manual data entry (for example, from mail or self- administered surveys) bemuse it makes the Intermediate step of completing a data indirectly from the questionnaire. A participant. Interviewer field supervisor or researcher (depending on the data collection method) is able to assign the appropriate code on instrument in checking circling or printing it in the proper coding location.

Sample Questionnaire Items

1. What is the zip code of your residence?
2. What is the year of your birth?
3 Calder (I) Male (2) Female
4. What is your marital status?
   (1) Married
   (2) Widow
   (3) Divorced
   (4) Separated
   (5) Never married
5. Do you own or rent your primary residence?
   1. Own
   2. Rent
   3. Living quartets provided
6. What prompted you to purchase your most recent life insurance policy?

Coding Free-Response or Open Ended Questions

One of the primary reasons for using open questions Is that insufficient information or lack of a hypothesis may prohibit preparing response categories in advance. Researchers are forced to categorize responses after the data are collected. Other reasons for using open-ended responses include the need to need to measure sensitive or disapproval behavior, discover salience or importance or encourage natural modes of expansion. Whatever the reasons for their use. Analyzing enormous % atomic of open ended questions slow the analysis process and increases the opportunity for error. The variety of answers to a single question can be staggering, hampering post collection categorization. Even when categories are anticipated and preceded for open-ended questions. once data are collected researchers may find it useful to reassess the predetermined categories. In the above questionnaire the answer to "What prompted you to purchase your most recent life insurance policy?" was in be filled in by the participant as a short-answer essay, After preliminary evaluation. Response categories were created for that item.

Coding Rules

Three rules guide the pre and post coding and categorizations of a data set. The categories within a single variable should be.

- Appropriate to the research problem and purpose
- Exhaustive
- Mutually exclusive

Researchers address these issues when developing or choosing each specific measurement questions. One of the purposes of pilot testing of any measurement instrument is to Identify and anticipate categorization issues.

(i) Appropriateness

It is determined at two levels: (1) the best partitioning of data for resting hypothesis and showing relationships. (7) The availability of comparison data.

For example, when actual age is obtains-II (ratio scale) the editor may decided to group data by ranges to simplify pattern discovery within the data.

(ii)Exhaustiveness

Researchers often add another "option" to measurement question because they know they cannot anticipate all possible answers. A large number of "other" responses. however. Suggest the measurement scale the researcher designed did not anticipate the full range of information.

The editor must determine if "other" responses appropriately fit into established of these actions will be taken.

(iii) Mutual Exclusivity

Another important rule when adding categories or realigning categories is that category components should be mutually exclusive. This standard is met when a specific answer can be placed in one and only one cell in a category set. For example, in a survey. Assume that you asked participants for their occupation, One editor's categorizations scheme might include: (1) Professional (2) Managerial (3) Saks (4) clerical (5) Crafts (6) Operative (7) Unemployed.

Rating Scales: There are number of rating scales dam in in the fineness of the distinctions they permit and the procedures involved in assigning persons or objects to positions. One of the common features to all types of rating scales is that the rater places the person or object being rated at some point along a continuum or in one of an ordered series of categories. Some of the ratings scale graphic rating scale, graphic rating scales, comparative-rating scales and self-rating scales.

1. Graphic rating scales: In graphic rating scale, the rather indicates his rating by simple placing a check at the appropriate point on a line that rims from one extreme of the attribute to the other. The Seale point with brief descriptions may he indicated along the line; their function is to serve as a guide to the rater in localizing his rating. This scale is relatively easy to use though certain precautions like avoiding the use of end statements that are extreme. And making the descriptive statements as close as possible to the numerical scale.

2. Itemized rating scales: In itemized types of scale like the graphic scale, the niter selects one of the limited numbers of categories (usually five or seven categories) that arc ordered in terms of their scale position The scale also pros ides a central neutral point with equal number of categories on either side. This scale consists of a series of items describing a particular act or attribute of the object or person to be rated and the rater selects one which best described the act or the attribute or an object or person. One could obtain reliable rating if the categories are properly defined.

3. Comparative rating scales: In comparative rating scale unlike the other two scales the rater gives relative rating. The positions on the rating scale are expressly defined in terms of a given population or social group or in terms of people of known characteristic. Here the ruler ranks each one of the individuals in relation to one another on the characteristics being measured. Ranking is used in this way only when the rater is confronted with a limited number of rates. There is another technique known as forced choice technique where pain of items arc chosen which have equal popularity hut different discriminating power. Two such pairs arc combined in a retrial. The rater is required to say which item in the tonal is most like the individual and which is, the least like the individual. The major difficulty in this technique is that the - four item, in the team' may not be comparable

However, this is an attempt to overcome the halo-effect. It is well-known that some sets of specific items are not much better than an overall oiling seating scale, since all items can be rated on the basis of a general impassion of the impression In most or the investigations for want of rates who are familiar with the rates and also where information on some non-observable behavior is required.

4. Self-rating stoics: Self-rating technique is used where the individual himself gives oiling on the attribute measured. It has its advantages and limitations like those of self-reporting techniques. However. This method has proved useful in the measurement of social attitudes as the individual rater is in a better positions to report his beliefs, felling etc.

Advantages and Disadvantage:

There are certain disadvantages in the use of rating scales. There is room for systematic emirs in one's rating through the influence of personal bias of the rater or raters which is commonly referred to as "halo effect". In this if more than one characteristic or a person is to be rated, raters frequently carry over a generalized of the person from one rating to another. Another frequent types of constant error is the "generosity error" where the rater develops a tendency to overestimate the desirable qualities of the rater whom he likes. There are another types of error known as contrast error where there is a tendency on the pan or the rater to us: others as opposite to himself on a trait.

One of the ways of reducing constant error is to train the raters carefully and make them aware of the possibility of such biases in rating. The generosity error Ina) Sc reduced by using relatively neutral accomplished by setting cutting-points for the response categories of each statement. A cutting-point marks that place in the rank order of the subjects where the most common response shifts from one category to another. Gunman suggests two rules in locating culling points: 1. The cutting- points should be located as to minimize the error, 2. Nom category should base more error in it than non-error. On the basis of cutting-point, the errors in each category of response are located for each of the statements and they arc summed up. The total number of errors is exerts-oat as a proportion of the total in another method. As suggested by Good enough; the score metrics is prepared with rows corresponding to the subjects and columns to statements. The responses of the subjects to the various statements are recorded in the row of metrics in terms of 0 and 1 weigh.

The response patterns are recorded having subjects with the higher score assigned to the first row and the next row will correspond to the subject whit the neat higher score and so on The scares for each one of the rows is summed up down the rows and across the columns, which give the frequencies with which the I response has Scot made to catch of the variants statements Pie sums for each column or the metrics is divided by the total number of subjects to obtain the proportion of subjects giving the 1 response to each of the statements, and the proportion giving 0 response is found out for deducting the obtained proportion from the unity. For example, in a four-statement sale. The possible range ad score oft) to 4. The bar charts arc used to find out the predicted patterns of response to the statements corresponding to each total score. The errors can be located in the observed patterns of response based on the predicted pattern of response for each of the subjects These response errors are summed up and recorded, and, the coefficient of responsibility as mentioned earlier is found out.

Another simple method to find out the coefficient of reproducibility is based on the total frequency of the responses for each statement. The predictive patterns of response for each of the statements for a set of say, four statements with a total score of 4 or 0 can be easily assumed. The predictive patterns of response for the remaining total score of 3, 2 & 1 for a set of four statements 1 each which gives the predictive response for a total score of 3. Similarly, among the remaining total, frequencies, the lowest is given 0 and the next two, 1 each which gives the predictive response for a total score of 2. Thus, the predictive response pattern is found for a total number of 1 also using the same procedure. On the basis of this the predictive pattern of response for each total score is obtained and the response error are calculated for each subject to arrive at the coefficient of reproducibility.

Though commutative scales like cumulative scales are composed of monotone items, the additional property of item magnitude is taken into account by the scoring procedure. Clearly this procedure is cumbersome, arbitrary and difficult to specify analytically. There are other reasons besides analytical complexity for rejecting cumulative scaling procedure. Whether items are retained or discarded depends more cm variations in item popularities than on degree of inter-correlation or functional equivalence. The ideal model of cablegram analysis assiiidgs unidimensional items, which probably, do not exist. The kinds of items retained are typically those, which are widely spread in popularity. Generally, cumulative scales are not recommended for attitude measurement, descriptive terms for the scale positions rather than evaluative ones. Some random errors may also affect ratings because at' different frames of reference of the raters in describing Individuals in terms of the characteristics in question. Reliability of the rating scale can be increased by not only careful training of raters hut also by giving attention to the construction of the rating scale. Some of the factors that must be taken into account in constructing a scale are:

1. The discriminative ability of the judges or the raters including the extent to which they are trained and experienced.

2. The kind of characteristics to be judged.

3. The conditions under which the ratings are to be made whether it is based on extensive or limited date. The reliability of ratings is usually enhanced considerably by having several raters making independent rating that are the pooled or averaged to give a final score Validity of the rating scale their meaning would be uniformly understood by the raters using the scales, and the ratings were themselves obtained under optimal conditions, including carefully constructed scales, trained judges and specified common frames of reference. An attempt was made to briefly sketch some of the map or scaling methods for attitude measurement. Which are in use. Each one of the methods has its own advantages refinances of the procedure. Scoring and analytical natural but each of that has its own disadvantages in terms of times consumed, feasibility for certain measurements and complexity involved through cumbersome scaling procedure. The use of any particular technique very much depends on the nature of research and the type of data that individual researcher would seek to examine. As pointed out in the beginning it is a question of whether the interest is in the response or in the individual, which by and large decides the approach to be followed and the scaling method to be used.

Scale: Scale is a measure used in scaling techniques which are method of turning a series of qualitative facts i.e., 'attributes' into a quantitative series i.e. variable. A scale is a measuring unit which measures the relative importance and social attributes regarding a subject by converting them into 'quantitative variables' so that the same could be measured.

Types of Scale: Sociologists have emphasized only two types of scales:

1. Concerning 'behavior' and 'personality': These scales Include the Known 'attitude scales, moral scales. Character lest, social participation scales and psychoneurotic inventories'.

2. Concerning cultural and social environment: There is another type of scales used which measure certain other aspects of the cultural and social environment. Some of them scales are used to study 'socio-economic stalls, communities, housing conditions and social institutions'.

Attitudes Scales: A series of short but carefully formulated statements of propositions dealing with selected aspect of issues. Institutions or groups of people under consideration arc included in 'Attitude scales'.

In his life an individual reacts verbally with 'approval' or 'disapproval', to the items on the scale. These reactions quanta) his position on controversial issues. Thurston's technique of equal apprising intervals in an important contribution in tins area of study of scales.

Measurement of Attitudes: Given below sue various scales for measuring attitudes:

I. Opinion Scales: Opinion scales are based on 'opinions' as the basis of attitudes. A person's attitudes towards some specific person. Subject. Matter or object can be known by analysis of his opinions concerning them. On the premise psychologists evolve scales for discovering the opinions of individuals relating to various objects, problems raid persons. 'These standards differ in respect of the method of their construction and kind But the aim of every standard is to locate and determine the position of an individual upon a measure extending from one limit of acceptance to the other limit of refusal, We have had occasion to point out before that it is not possible to measure attitudes directly by means of any available standard. The opinion scales reveal the reactions of the Individual towards some particular things. and from these reactions his attitude can be deduced' It is advised that, die scale should be so formulated as to reveal to the maximum possible level the attitudes of the individual This requires u selection of statement.; which tam give expression to the concurrence of otherwise of the attitude of the person relating to a person, matter or object.

Opinion scales are many but the main among them are the following:

1. Turnstone Scale Construction Method
2. Liken Scale Construction Method.
3. Cullman Scale Construction Method.

In addition to these other important scales ate: the Bogardus Scales. Kant; Order Scale and Paired Comparison Scales

1. Turnstone Seale: In 1919 or 1931, scale, were constructed by Thurston and his colleagues for the measurement of 'opinions' and 'beliefs' of groups concerning varied questions such as war, church, negroes, capital, punishment, birth control, etc.

Constitution of the Scale: Turnstone scale constitution method was constituted of the neon mentioned below:

1. Collection of numerous scale opinions related to the question or subject presented.

2. Determination of the saint of the scale for these opinions by some definite determinant. This evaluation leads to the elimination of controversial statement. Leaving only those statements concerning which all specialists are unanimous. Opinions extend between a negative and a positive limit.

3. Determination of the medium point for every statement according to the opinion of the specialist judges.

Precautions in the Construction of the Scale: The following precautions arc observed:

1. It should he ensured that every statement of the scale should be distinctly- worded.

2. It must be seen that the number of determining specialists is large enough to indicate clearly the position which would be given to the opinion expressed by the 'subject'.

3. Only of those statement about which the judges are unanimous should he given place in the scale.

2. Liken Scale: Liken another sociologist constructed a scale in 1932 which differed from Thurstone's. Scale. This scale aimed at locating the attitudes of various human groups relating to "imperialism" 'internationalism' and 'Negroes'.

Constitutions of the Likert's Scale: The following items are included in the Liken scale constructions method:

1. To construct many statement related to the object to the object or problem the attitudes towards which are to be studied.

2. To show mace statements to the subject and to get they classified into the following groups:

Strongly approve, Undecided, Disapprove, Strongly Disapprove. Approve.

3. To award points to the above classification in the Wowing manner:

5 4 3 2 1

4. To find the correlation between the tonal score of the subject and the scores of the statements individually, and lastly.

5. To exclude those statements which tar a negligible correlation to the score.

3. Guttmann Scale: Guttmann constructed a scale to measure and study the Level of morale in American soldiers in 1941. This scale is comprised of following main elements:

1. To determine whether any statement Can be shim it upon the scale or not.
2. To prepare scalogram to test the consistency of any statement.
3. To vary the questions concerning the same problems in such a manner as in determine that the opinion of the subject is consistent.

After six years of its formulation, Guttmann's scale was severally criticized by Feininger pointing out many drawbacks present in the scale.

II. Rating Scales: Besides the opinion scales, another method is that of rating smiles the striking features of the rating scales lies in the fact that here the attitudes are evaluated not on the bath of the opinions of the subjects, but on the bath of the opinions and judgements of the experimenter. Himself. Thus in rating scales discretion of the experimenter comes into the picture of the measurement of attitudes.

Through the following means, the experimenter collects the data in the - Rating Scales":

1. Nun-verbal behavior.
2. Verbal behavior
3. Secondary expressive cues
4. 6. Clinical type interview.
5. Personal documents.
6. Projects techniques.
7. Intermediate experience.

Types of Rating Scales: In general, rating smiles are put under two classes: (i) Relative and (ii) Absolute. Both of these scales are being briefly discussed below:

(i) Rank Order Scale: The experimenter in this scale gives to individual's attitude, a placing in the scale extending from the highest to the lowest quantity. In studying the individual in the circumstances of the human grouts the position, of the individual relatively to the positions to other is considered. Thus. in the Rank Order method, the individual is allotted a relative position on a similar wale, which is Ids placing in comparison with other individuals,

(ii) The Percentage of Population Scales: This scale, gives position to more individuals Here a particular min to population is examined and then the opinion of an individual are analyzed. Following this examiner places the opinion of the individual on the scale, showing the percentage of the population 'concurring with his opinion as well as the percentage differing from him' this also gives the percentage of his opinions.

(iii) Indirect scales: After the Rating scales the third method for the measurements or attitudes is that of indirect scales. The methods so far discussed suffer from the defect thin the subject generally, realized dint he is being examined and he therefore, tries to conceal his real attitudes. Hence, psychologists have favored the indirect scales for the measurements attitudes, in which it cannot he guessed that tendencies are being examined.

Sociometry: Sociometry is the science and art of measuring relationships between social configurations or structures and psychological well-being. Sociogram is a systematic method for graphically representing individuals as points/nodes and the relationships between than as lines/arcs.

Sociometry is a broad term indicating a number of methods of gathering and analyzing data on the choice, communication and interaction patterns of the people in groups. In other words, sociametry is the study and measurement of social choice. It is the study through which we come to know about the attractions and repulsions of member, of groups.

Sociamerty is a study of group behavior in several social activities, particularly with regard to revealing individual choices. This has served as a useful technique in analyzing the choices of social groups with regard to acceptance or otherwise of a group leader or even in explaining individual choices with regard to each other.

Sociometry has been defined as "a method for discovering. Describing and evaluating social status, structure and development through measuring the extent of acceptance or rejection between individuals in groups." Socioinetric rest is undertaken to determine the degree to which individuals are accepted in a group or for discovering the relationship which exist among these individuals and for disclosing the structure of the group itself.

Sociometry is a method used for discovering and manipulation of social configurations by meaning the attractions and repulsions between individuals in a group. Criteria around which the group is organized such as roaming together. Eating together, working together or otherwise associating with persons in specific situations. The initial steps in socinmetry, therefore. Involve first ascertaining the fundamental criteria around which the group activities take place and second, testing for the attraction, repulsion patterns In terms of these criteria.

The main forms of sociometric analysis are the sociometric matrices and sociograms.

Sociometric Matrices

An important technique for portraying and analyzing soctometric data is the matrix. In soclometric studies, only square or n ii matrices are used. N being equal to the number of persons in a group. Rows of mains are numbered i, columns are labeled j. i and j can stand for any number and any person in a group. A, would mean any number In the I'm row and in column of the matrix.

The various entries, frequently represented by symbols, indicate each pawn's feeling towards every other member of the group.

Suppose we take an example that there is group of six members from six Indian communities (sections) viz. Hinduism. Buddhism, Christianity, Islam, Jainism & Sikhism, and ore asked to respond to the sociometric question." With whom would we like to associate among the group members for work?" We would give these names in order of preference. If a group members choose another member, his choice in the matrix is represented by the subscript 1 On the contrary, if a group member does not chooses another member. The negative choice is represented by subscript 0. The S matrix of this hypothetical example has been depicted below in the table:

Sociometric Choice Matrix : Six Member group, Three choice questions

Rows → Columns ↓	Hindu	Buddhist	Christian	Muslim	Jain	Sikh
Hindu	-	1	0	0	1	0
Buddhist	0	-	1	0	0	1
Christian	1	0	-	0	1	0
Muslim	0	1	1	-	0	0
Jain	1	0	1	0	-	0
Sikh	1	0	1	0	0	-
Total	3	2	4	0	2	1

In the above table there are three kind of choices, simple or one way, mutual or two way and no choice. A simple one way choice is made when i choose j but does not choose i. In the above table Hindu chooses Buddhist but Buddhist does not choose Hindu. We writes this kind of choice as i-j or Hindu-Buddhist. In case of mutual choice i choose j and j chooses i. This type of choice is written as i-j. In the above table Hindu chooses Jain and Jain chooses Hindu or Hindu-Jain.

The extent to which any member is popular in time group is seen by adding the columns of the matrix. In the above table, Christian is most popular. He is chosen by 4 other group members. Evidently Muslim is not at all popular Ibis con be a socio- metric scale for Indian society. Showing how close its different sections (communities) with each other are.

Sociogram

Sociogram is a technique by which the sociometric data is diagrammatically presented. In this technique, individuals are placed on paper and their choices arc marked with arrows. Target sociorgrams is drawn in circle shape and is most widely drawn for small and medium sin: groups having members not more than 30. While such sociorgrams, the most chosen individual is placed in the middle and the least chosen or the isolated individual on the outer circle. Other members get their positions in between according to their sociometric sums. The target sociogram of the above matrix of the group of six members from six Indian communities is shown below:

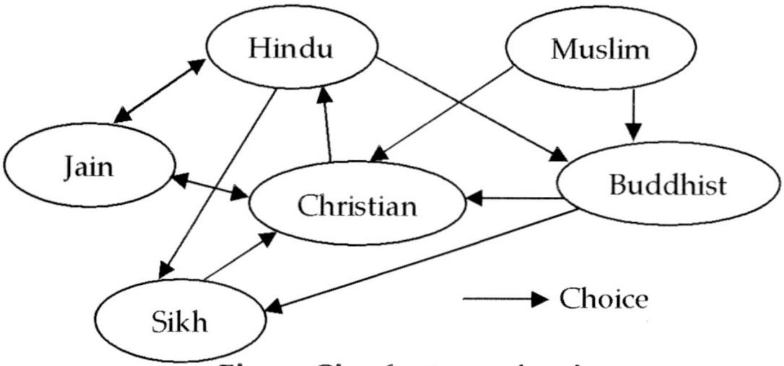

Figure Circular type of sociogram

Sociometric Analysis:

Sociometry is a number of methods of gathering and analyzing data on the choice, communication and interaction patterns of the people in groups.

Soclometry is the study and measurement of sac the choice. Sociometry has been defined as a method for discovering. Describing and evaluation social status, structure and development through measuring extent of acceptance or rejection between individuals in groups.

J.G. Franz has defined sociometry, a method used for discovery and manipulation of social configuration by measuring the attractions and repulsions between individuals in a group.

Helen Jennings defined, "Sociometry is a device for a graphic and straight forward portrayal of the total configuration of relations among the members of d group at some given point of time."

This technique has been applied in each widely diversified situation as Informal gimps. School classes, prisons and other organizations.

For example, there are A to P members and everybody can make three choices according to their own preferences, ranking the first preference, ranking the first preference as I. second preference as 2 and third preference as 3.

The form of the sociometric test as applied up to the present.

1. A specific number of choices are allowed according to the size of the groups tested.

2. A specific criterion for choice is used varying with the functional activity of the group.

3. Different levels of preferences arc designated for each choice.

Sociometry

Sociometric Matrix	Sociogram	Sociometric Indices
Tabulation of data. Also showing the frequency of being chosen.	Plotting the data from sociometric matrix to make clear the network of acceptance and rejection in a graphical way	

There are three main forms of sociometric analysis, sociometric matrices, sociograms and sociometric Indices.

(a) Sociometric Matrices: An important technique for portraying and analyzing sociometric data is the matrix. In sociomatrix studies, we are concerned only will square or n n matrices, n being equal to the number of persons in a group. Rows of matrix arc numbered i. columns are labeled j, i and j, of course, can stand for any number and any person in the group.

A would mean any number in the row and jth column of the matrix. The various entries, frequently represented by symbols, indicate each person's feeling towards every other member of the group.

Method of socio matrix will become clear by taking a hypothetical example:

Rows →	A	B		C	D	E
Columns ↓						
Buddhist	0	3	0	0	0	1
Christian	0	2	0	0	0	1
Muslim	3	0	0	0	2	1
Jain	0	0	0	0	0	3
Sikh	0	1	2	2	0	3

Sociometric Matrix

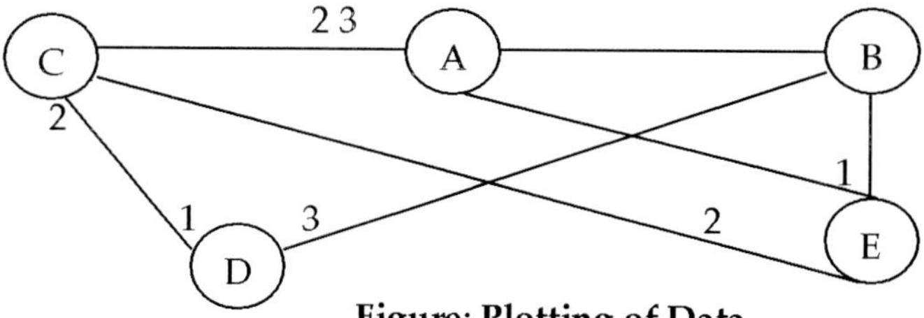

Figure: Plotting of Data

(b) Sociogram : Sociogram is a technique by which the sociometric data, is diagrammatically presented. Sociogram in discovers the relationship that exists among the members and discloses the structure of the group. In this technique, individuals are placed on paper and their choices are marked with arrows. We have two type of sociograms, target Sociogram which is drawn in circle and the other is in horizontal-vertical shape. Target sociogram is mostly drawn for small and medium size groups having members not more than 30, while preparing such sociagam, the most chosen individual is placed in the middle and die least chosen or the isolated individual on the outer circle. Other members get their positions in between according to their sociometric status.

Horizontal - vertical sociagam can be drawn to accommodate more members in a group. For small and medium groups and for descriptive purposes. Sociogram are excellent means of summarizing group relations. For larger groups and more analytical purposes. These graphs are not as suitable since they become difficult to construct and difficult to interpret.

(c) Sociometric Indices: If a review is made of writings in the field sociometry one finds that extensive application of various types of statistical techniques has been made by various authors. An useful index is:

$$CS_i = \frac{\Sigma C_i}{n-1}$$

Where CS_i = The choice status of person i

ΣC_i = The sum of choice in column i

n = Number of individuals in a group

Attitude: It is difficult to give a scientific and concise definition of attitude. It is really difficult to define correctly what everyone blows as a everyday matter and hits his own opinion about it. In the opinion of L.L. Bernard. "The behavior winch we define attitudinal or attitude is a certain observable 'set' organism or relative tendency preparatory Its and indicative of more complete adjustment".

According to La-Pirere them are four parts of human behavior.

(a) Overt symbolic, which includes the acts of speaking, writing and gesturing.

(b) Overt non-symbolic, which includes such directly significant acts as driving a car or closing a door.

(c) Coven symbolic or what is commonly designated as thought.

(d) Coven non-symbolic or what is usually described as feeling or emotions.

Importance of Attitude

The study of attitudes individual in well as of very significant importance in all sociological studies. Following are the main advantages derived from the study of attitudes:

1. **Knowledge of attitude helps in social control**: A controlled and planned social development Is aimed at, only when the knowledge of the attitude of the persons is acquired. It may be pointed out here the most of the social changes are only voluntary in nature and no amount of legal or (statutory) measure can make people to behave in a particular way.

The failure of totalitarian states had been bemuse of total disregard of the attitude of the people. 'The knowledge of the response mechanism is essential for the successful implementation of all such plans.'

2. **Study of attitude helps in formulation of idea types**: For successful classification of people according to 'types' its study is essential Since in all sociological studies the concept of ideal type holds a great significance, the basis of grouping is the attitude of a person towards certain aspects in life e.g., conservation and radical. A person may be classed conservative only on the basis of his attitude regarding social changes. Similar other types are also based upon the specific attitude of the people.

3. **Knowledge of attitude facilitates surveys**: For successful conduct of surveys framing the questionnaire of schedule the attitude of the people replying it must be kept in mind. It is cautioned that such questions as are to create offending influence have to be avoided cautiously. The investigator must know the weak points of the respondents. He must know when the respondents are likely to give a false reply, under what circumstances they are to be most non-cooperating and how can their cooperation be achieved, what are the types of queries and manners that are most offending to them.

4. **It helps in forecasting**: Knowledge of attitudes facilitates predictability as an analysis may result in a generalizations regarding the attitude of people in a given set of events and their attitudes may be predicted when the circumstances are known 'The quality of predictability is very useful in social control.

5. **It helps in maintaining social order**: For peaceful living in every sector of life we have to known the attitude of others, likes and dislikes, emotional reactions and behavior pattern in different circumstances. An indifference to these may result into clash. The same thing applies to groups. The tack of understanding of each other's attitude has resulted in much racial hatred, communal riots, class struggle? And a lot of human misery and unrest.

This discussion points out that study of attitudes in the field of social problems is of paramount importance.

1. **Attitudes are intangible**: The attitudes are intangible and thus not subject to visual observation. But intangibility is a relative term and changes with our knowledge of the phenomena and thus what is intangible and unmeasurable today may become perfectly tangible and may be measured precisely.

2. **Attitudinal behavior is complex**: The attitude of a person or a group is a complex and is subject to multiple influences, which am so large that It is very difficult to account for all of them. This is the reason why we cannot say with certainty how a person will react. At best we can only say that other things remaining unchanged a person or a group is most likely an behave in a particularly way, but in petrol practice these other things hardly ever remain unchanged and as such the prediction about the attitude have little practical validity.

3. **Absence of proper scale**: Lack of a well accepted and proper scale for measuring 'attitude' is yet another problem, whereas 'in case of physical sciences we have the proper instruments for the purpose. example, we have the thermometer that will gives us exact measurement of heat, the barometer would tell us exactly the pressure of the air and so on. In case of social phenomena no such instrument have been devised this can infallibly give a correct measurement of our attitudes.

4. **Dynamic nature of attitudes**: The attitudes are never fixed because of multiplicity' of factors influencing the attitude. The attitude of the same person may change with the change in time and circumstances. Making it difficult to lay down definite rules governing the attitude.

Case: Job satisfaction among women in educational institutions

A management scholar was assigned a protect that required conducting field investigations to determine 'Job Satisfaction. Among women working in educational Institutions the universe consisted of about 20,000 women working in schools colleges and other educational institutions A sample of 200 such women was selected which represented cross-section of the population. Resides 20 women and 20 snot in educational administration were also administered the questionnaires the data collected form respondents included information on employment fin school, college, profession institution or other institution), age (< 30) years., young -30 to 50, years, middle aged. >50 years, elderly) and education (up to degree. Postgraduate, professional degree or postgraduate +. The aspects of professional life covered to determine 'Job satisfaction included monetary benefits (Present monthly employment. perquisites and retirement benefits each classified separately (< Rs 50.000 Rs. 50,000 to Rs. 10.0000. Rs 1, 00.000 to Rs. 2, 00.000 or > Rs. 2, 00000), behavior of seniors, peer groups and juniors each rated as (highly, encouraging,

encouraging, 50-50, not encouraging or hostile), opportunities for promotion, arrangement for training and development each rated as (very good, good, adequate, inadequate or poor). Conditions at work (highly, satisfactory average, not satisfactory or highly unsatisfactory), self perception and social esteem (each rated as very High, High, Average poor or very poor).

Case Questions:

Q.1 Develop an appropriate framework for tabulation of informal on employment, age, education and monetary benefits of respondents, separately in each case.

Q.2 Develop a framework of Tabulation for relating (a) Age of respondents with self perception, (b) Education with social esteem.

Q-3 Suggest appropriate statistical techniques for analysis of data on:

(a) Behavior of seniors and peer group.

(b) Opportunity for promotion.

(c) Arrangement for training and development, separately in each case.

Q.4 Suggest what other information may be required for the achievement of research objective.

Q.5 State the Null Hypothesis.

Suggested Solutions:

Ans. (1) **Employment**

Respondents	School	College	Professional Institution	Other Institution
Respondent A			✔	
Respondent B	✔			
Respondent C		✔		
Respondent D				✔
Respondent E			✔	

(Sample of framework, which we can use to collect information from the respondents.)

In this case study we have taken the sample of 200 respondents front 20, 000 women populations, working in schools, colleges and other educational institution, For comparative analysis, we have also taken the respondents from mean.

Employment

Respondents	**School**	**College**	**Professional Institution**	**Other**	**Total**
Men	25	15	40	20	100
Women	25	5	40	30	100
Total	50	20	80	50	200

Age Responses

Respondents	Below 30 years	30-50 Years	Above 50 years
Respondent A		✔	
Respondent B	✔		
Respondent C		✔	
Respondent D	✔		
Respondent E			
Respondent F		✔	

Age

Respondents	Below 30	30-50	Above 50	Total
Men	20	30	20	70
Women	40	10	80	130
Total	60	40	100	200

Education

Respondents	Up to degree	Post graduate	Professional Degree	Postgarduate+	Total
Men	35	20	35	15	105
Women	35	30	25	5	95
Total	70	50	60	20	200

Monetary Benefits

Respondents	Presently Monthly Employment	Perquisites	Retirement Benefits	Total
Men	70	30	5	105
Women	50	30	15	95
Total	120	60	20	200

Ans. (2) (a)

Self Perception

Age	Very high	High	Average	Poor	Very Poor	Total
Below 30	5	20	15	30	10	80
30- 50	5	10	5	35	20	75
Above 50	10	10	10	5	10	45
Total	20	40	30	70	40	200

Table Description: The table (a) revealed the relationship between age group of the respondents (Male and Female) and their, self-perception. In below 30 age group, them are 80 responses where as 75 and 45 respondents given response in 30-50 and above 50 age group.

(b) **Social Esteem**

Education	Very high	High	Average	Poor	Very Poor	Total
Up to degree	5	5	15	20	10	55
Postgraduate	5	10	10	10	10	45
Professional	5	5	10	15	5	40
Postgarduate+	5	10	15	25	5	60
Total	20	30	50	70	30	200

The above table reveals the information on social esteem, which varies the relationship with education. Maximum respondents found in up to degree level education where maximum category of social esteem is 20 responses.

In the above tabulations, scales and variables are used for categorized the information. Ordinal sale is used to categorized the dam and relate the information between age and self-perception. Education and self-esteem.

Ans. (3) (a) **Behavior of Seniors and Peer Groups**

Respondents	Highly Encouraging	Encouraging	50-50	Not encouraging	Total
Men	10	20	30	15	75
Women	30	40	40	15	125
Total	40	60	70	30	200

In the table ordinal scale or attributes are used to discover the information from the respondents. For this we can use non-parametric test, which is appropriate for nominal or ordinal data We can use non-parametric zest, which is appropriate for nominal ordinal data. We can use here rank test, runs test or chi-square lest to analyze the information collected.

(b) **Opportunity for Promotion**

Respondents	Very Good	Good	Adequate	Inadequate	Poor	Total
Men	30	25	25	5	5	90
Women	40	35	15	15	5	110
Total	70	60	40	20	10	200

The above table is based on ordinal smile and numeric scale.

Highly Satisfactory ________________________ Highly Unsatisfactory

We can use here chi-square tint Ii, analyze the information. Because ordinal data is based on non-parametric test. Because chisquare test does not specify the! Tomtit' distribution perfectly.

(c) **Arrangement for Training and Development**

Respondents	Very Good	Good	Adequate	Inadequate	Poor	Total
Men	35	20	10	5	5	75
Women	35	40	30	15	5	125
Total	70	60	40	20	10	200

Again cross-sectional tabulation, reveal the information of men and women respondents on arrangement for training and development. Use chi-square, rank or runs test to analyze the information.

Ans. (4) Other information's which require research objective are:

1. Interpretation of data information.
2. Interpretation with graphs or charts
3. Correlate the factors
4. Analyzing the effect of variables
5. Coding and encoding of data
6. Receding of data

Ans (5). H_0: Women are not getting highly job satisfaction in educational institutions

H_1 : Women are getting highly job satisfaction in educational Institutions.

H_0 : There is no relationship between conditions at work and job satisfaction.

H_1 : Conditions at work is the significantly affecting factor of job satisfaction.

Thus we can make other Null Hypothesis like this to relate variables with job satisfaction of women in educational institutions.

★★★★★★

Chapter - 33

Report Writing

Writing a report is the last step in a research study and requires a set of skills somewhat different from those called for in respect of the earlier stages of research. This task should be accomplished by the researcher with almost care; he may seek the assistance and guidance of experts for the purpose.

Report Format

The outcome of research works are to be conveyed to end-users or recorded for future use. The research efforts will be useful to the end-users only when they are documented in the form of reports. So, a standardized format for the report will help to researchers in present their contributions and findings more systematically.

Cover Page

The cover page gives the title of the research, department to which the thesis is submitted, degree for which it is submitted, name of the researcher, name of the supervisor, department/organizational faculty, name of the university and as address, month and year of submission etc.

Sample of Cover Pace

Development of New Efficient Heuristic for Deterministic
Assembly Line Balancing Problem.
A thesis submitted to the Faculty of Management.
Rajasthan University in partial fulfillment of the
requirements for the award of the degree of
Doctor or Philosophy
By
J. Narayan, B.E., M.S.
Research Supervisor

K Panneerseham, M.E., PhD
Professor

University seal

School of Management
Rajasthan University
Jaipur 302004 (India)
November, 2014

Introductory Page

Vita: Brief Bio-data of the researcher

- Name of the researcher.
- Date of birth and place of the birth.
- Degrees already holding and the respective years of pass and Institution of study.
- Details of experience in chronological sequence.
- List of publications by the researcher which are classified as follows:

(a) Publications by the researcher from the current research.

(b) Publication by the researcher in other areas.

Acknowledgement: In the process of carrying out any research the researcher would have received help from different persons and organizations. So, all those helps should be acknowledged under this heading:

- Research supervisor
- Organizational head
- Colleagues of the department who rendered their valuable suggestion and criticism during the research period,
- The executives in different organizations who provided data and literature for the research.
- The computer setting office and personnel.

Abstract: Abstract gives the overview of the research report outlining the title of the research, objectives, shortcomings of exiting literatures, need for further research, proposed measure of performance and research methods, results of comparison and highlights of inferences and brief mention about a case study.

Table of Contents: Table or contents is the catalogue of the research report which summarizes every aspect of the report.

List of Tables: In reports, the data and results are presented in the form of tables for quick grasp. Each and every table must be numbered. 1 he numbering should be such that it is internal to each chapter. For example,. if the total number of tables in chapter 4 is 20, then the numbering should be from table 4.1 to table 4.20.

List of Figures: Each and every figure must be numbered. The numbering should be internal in each chapter. For example. If the total number of figures in chapter 5 is 30, then the numbering should be from fig. 5.1 to fig. 5.30.

Figures and charts help infer the relative comparison of result of a research study.

List of Variables: The researcher will be forced to use different variables and abbreviations in different chapter of the research report to discuss about the models, equations and results.

TEXT

Chapters: The text of the report should be divided into different chapters depending on the type of research:

1. Introduction
2. Literature Review
3. Objectives and hypothesis
4. Research Methodology
5. Data Analysis
6. Conclusions

1. **Introduction**: The chapter on introduction should begin with the background of the research topic and state of the art scenario in brier. The origin and the development of the research concept along with the most significant contributions in the past must be summarized in this chapter. At the end of this chapter, the plan of research in the form of flowchart should be presented. Further, this chapter should give a lead for literature search.

2. **Literature Review**: This helps the researcher avoid reinventing past contribution and results, this focuses on the past literature in the field of research and its classification under different angles. The critique comparison of the past literatures will narrow down the research topic and provide a base for selecting a research topic which will have more pay off. The outcome of the literature review gives a direction for future research.

3. **Objectives and Hypothesis**: Based on the direction of the literature review, the researcher should clearly spell out the objectives of the research and related hypothesis. Hypothesis is an assumption about the population where the truth of the assumption is not sure. Hypothesis is the tentative and a testable statement affirm the relationship between two or more variables.

This hypothesis will he tested under the chapter 'Data Analysis'.

4. **Research Methodology**: Research methodology aims to finalize the activities of research design and data collection procedure which are as follow :

- Selection or research approach
- Design of sampling plan
- Design of experiment

- Design of questionnaire
- Determination of sample size
- Design of sampling frame
- Execution of survey

Selection of the research approach includes importance of the study and research area. Design of sampling plan includes the source of sample, size of sample and type of sample.

Design of experiment, includes tools of analysis like map, chart, tests, statistical analysis etc. Profile can be included in this. All profiles are sample profiles, data of respondents.

5. Data Analysis: The data analysis can be classified into preliminary analysis and hypothesis testing. It deals with application of statistical tools for the analysis of data and making inferences.

In preliminary analysis, the data presented in the form of chart and graphs to have insight into the research problem. This helps the research come out with some inferences, but these are based on the observation form the charts and graphs.

The second type of analysis is the testing of hypothesis. The different hypothesis which have been formulated earlier are tested at this stage. In some cases, this section deals with mathematical models and regression models, in addition to the above items.

6. Conclusions: The chapter on conclusions summarizes research findings:

- Contribution of the study
- Limitations of the study
- Scope for the future research.

Recommendations

- **Contribution of the study**: Summarize importance, finding, with review of literature. references etc.
- **Limitations of the study**: The limitations should be clearly written, as it is helpful to the reader in forming his own opinion as to how far the results are reliable.
- **Recommendations**: These should be given only when study has been commissioned by the management. These will be found and recommended in future research.

Bibliography

Standard form of the Harvard System- the standard form for listing books in the bibliography is:

Author's surname, Initial, Title (Underlined or in Italics), Place of Publication, Publisher, Year of edition which are using.

For example, Mill, N.S.A., System of logic Ratiocinative and Inductive, Longmans Green, London, 2014.

The entries are then arranged alphabetically by author.

Standard form of a web bibliography entry:

Author's surname, rest of name, date of document, title of document. (web address). date accessed.

For example, Quinton, Michael N. 2014 citing online sources. Advice on online citations formats <http: //www.org/articles/citation.htm> (Accessed 10.1.1.2014).

References

Referencing is referring someone to the source. References/citations show the reader what different aspects of our work are based on. At point in our writing references can be inserted in brackets that lead the reader to intimation about the page of a book or other source that is evidence for what have been said.

A reference after an item or information tells the reader the source of the information.

The references must how what the writing is basal on, and this requires substantial referencing. Much of the writing, although of the researcher's owns, is based on books or articles, lectures, web pages or other sources. This should be shown, if for example: a paragraph has drawn ideas heavily from a book, the reference is put at the end of the paragraph.

In report writing it is required to interpret sources, making an argument or evaluating evidence. It is particularly important to reference the evidence for the interpretation, argument or evaluation.

The standard form for a reference is:

(Author's name, Year to match the one shown in the Bibliography, Page number)

For example the references like this:

"Mill. N.S. 2014 P. 238"

Appendices: Extra information of further details placed after the main body of the text.

- The work of any past research which is used in the current report as a module
- The format of the questionnaire
- Original data
- Taken while Writing a Report

Care taken while Writing a Report

While writing a report following points to be taken care of :

• **Objectivity** : The report has to be written objectively i.e. the researcher should not impose his view points on the reader.

• **Concrete Style**: This means that the report should contain necessary statistics to support the theses. One should avoid using vague words as 'several people', a large number of respondents, a few etc.

• **Organized and Coherent**: It should be logically from beginning to the end.

• **Impersonal Style**: Write for the reader use gender neutral language.

• **Clarity**: Clarity should be maintained in presentations of ideas so as to avoid chances of misunderstanding keep the language simple, use short sentences and paragraphs rather than longwinded constructions.

• **Neat and tidy** : It should be neat and tidy. The write-up should be divided into paragraphs with suitable headings.

Reference: In the Harvard system a reference looks like this:

"What is now called the nature of women is an eminently artificial thing" (Mill N.S. 2014 P 238)

The reference is the part that is in brackets. Because the reference is put within the text of the writing it can be called an in-text reference.

The reference relates to an entry in the list of books (called the bibliography) at the end of the piece of writing. The bibliography should match the above reference.

Bibliography: Mill, N.S. 2014 The Subjection of Women, Dent/Everyman edition 2014, London.

The reference acts as the key to unlock the Information in the bibliography. The short keyword/key number combination directs to the full information in the bibliography. The page number in the referent tells the whereabouts in the book (or whatever) to find what is being referenced.

Oral and Written Reports: The report can be (I) Oral and (II) Written, although research reports are mostly written ones. The oral reports as:

Oral Report: An oral report is any presentation of information through the spoken word. There are three major differences between oral and written reports. (Based on Lesiker, Raymond V., Report Writing for Business, Homewood, III, Richard D. Irwin, Inc. 2014. pp. 222-223.) First, oral reports lack visual advantages. No charts, diagrams or pictures can be used, though, to stress particular points in oral presentation, the reporter can use pauses and volume emphasis. Second, the pace of presentation cannot be controlled and regulated by any one from an audience, who is being presented an oral report. In contrast, whenever a certain point is not clear in a written report the reader can read it two or are times, if need be slowly and more carefully. This advantage is not available to one who is receiving the report through oral presentation. Third, since a written report is bound to receive considerable attention and scrutiny from the readers the report writer is likely to work hard to produce an accurate report of a high quality. In contrast, an oral report will not be so precise nor will the reporter give as much time in its presentation since it cannot be subjected to the some degree of scrutiny as written report because of the extremely limited time at the disposal of the audience for indicating its reaction. Also, established standards for oral presentation are far less rigid than for written reports.

Written Report: The marketing research can be in writing which is considered most authentic. These can be the reports could be daily, weekly, monthly, quarterly, or annually. However, all reports cannot regularly brought out. There are some which are prepared for a special assignment and we known as special report.

Considerations for Oral Reporting: Sometimes the researcher has been asked to make an oral presentation of his research finding, he should bear in mind a few major considerations, as:-

(1) He should know the audience to whom he is to report. If it has any special characteristics such as highly qualified or specialized in a certain subject, these must be noted down.

(2) In oral reporting he should be properly planned. To begin with, the reporter should be clear about the objectives of the report.

In each of these cases, the oral presentation will be different. After the reporter has decided the objective of his report, he should gather the necessary information. If he has not already done any research, he may be required to collect data uniformally. He may have to approach some people to get the requisite information or he may collect it on the basis of his own observations.

Once the information is ready, the reporter has to organize it in a logical manner. The subject matter should be divided into meaningful and comparable parts. Simple ideas should precede complex and difficult ones. There should be a logical and coherent approach in presenting the subject matter before an audience.

When an oral summary of a written report is to be presented, the reporter should exercise great care in the preparation of the summary. All major points must be covered and excessive details avoided otherwise the focus will be lost. The reporter should ensure that within the time allotted to him, he covers all major points including his recommends.

Bases of classifying Reports:

Reports are also classified on a functional basis, according to which there could be three types of reports-informational, examination and analytical (also known as problem-solving). The informational report is a factual report on a particular subject and it neither contains an analysis nor conclusion. The examination report goes a step further. In addition to giving facts on a subject-matter, it analysts these facts. It does not specify conclusions or recommendations though the reader can draw these on the basis of the factual information and analysis contained in the report. The analytical report goes a step further than the examination report. It not only presents and analyses data but it also draws conclusions and, if necessary, makes recommendations. This is, obviously, the most comprehensive report.

Reports can be classified on the basis of their subject matter or field. Since there are innumerable subjects, the types of reports within a certain subject will be different from those in another. For example, reports on economics could he classified by various subjects covered within its scope such as a report on monetary reforms.

Reports can he classified on the basis of their physical form or make-up. The two usual forms are short-form and long-form. For example, memoranda, knees and progress reports may follow a short-form whereas information examination reports may follow a long-form.

Reports have also been classified on the basis of the relationship between the reader and writer. Such reports are described as administrative, professional and independent. An administrative report is written within an organization, while professional report is submitted by an outside expert to an organization. Independent reports are generally prepared by non-profit research organizations and published for the benefit of the public. These reports are not written for any particular group.

Reports are sometimes classified on the basis of the employment status of their authors. Reports prepared in a business organization are known as private reports while those prepared in a government or public institution are known as public reports. Here, Too, there may be independent reports which are prepared by individuals without any authorization either by a public or private agency.

Yet another basis of classification of reports is their formally. On this basis, the reports may be either formal or informal. The dividing line between the two types is rather hazy. A formal report is written benefiting the requirements of a formal occasion. An informal report, on the other hand, may be worded to suit an informal occasion. A report prepared by one employee for the information of his colleagues may be an example of an Informal report. In contrast a report prepared by an executive for the top management may be a formal report.

Guidelines to Report: The following points will guide this process:

1. The style of the report should relate to the needs of clients. It may be desirable, for example, to have two (or more) editions of a report; one with detailed technical data for technical specialists. the other, principally for commercial management, might cover technology at less depth but concentrate

more on the commercial implications of survey findings. If only one edition is planned, technical terms should be carefully defined, perhaps in an appendix.

2. Clear grammatical language should be used in survey reports.

3. Diagrams and tables used in survey reports should be captioned, units of measurement clearly quoted and, if published material is used, the source should be given.

4. It is largely a matter of expediency and taste whether textual matter should be interspersed with diagrams and tables. Extracts from lengthy tables may be given in the text of a report, and the complete date printed in an appendix.

The type of printing and binding of survey report should be checked with researchers.

Components of a Technical Reports:

In the technical report the main emphasis is on (i) the methods employed. (ii) Assumptions made in the course of the study (iii) the detailed presentation of the findings including their limitations and supporting data.

A general outline of a technical report can be as follows:

1. Summary of results
2. Nature of the study
3. Methods employed
4. Data
5. Analysis of data and presentation of findings
6. Bibliography
7. Technical appendices
8. Index.

Preparation of the Report: Having decided on the type of report, the report writer should now concern himself with its preparation. This can best be done when he is clear about what aspects or points are to be covered by it. Let us first consider the format of the research report.

Research Report Format: A research report can be written in a number of ways. However, three formats are generally followed. First, the report may use a logical pattern, which implies that the findings are presented in inductive order i.e., moving from specific to general. Second, the report may follow a psychological pattern which is almost inverse of the preceding pattern. In this format, the most critical information, i.e., the conclusion, is provided first after which follow the findings supporting the conclusion. Third, the report may use a chronological format wherein information is given along the time dimension. i.e., things which happened earlier precede those which happened later. This form is generally combined with other formats. The chronological format is the least popular though in respect of problems of a historical nature, it is the most appropriate.

Having decided the format to be used in a research report the researchers has now to prepare the report outline in accordance with the format

Report Outline. Before attempting to write any report, the researcher must prepare a report outline. Without any outline his report is bound to be haphazard and clumsy. An outline is to the writer what the blueprint is to be construction engineer or what the pattern is to the dressmaker. The outline will not only guide the writer as to the order of presentation of ideas but will also enable him to think before writing. This will lead to clarity in his presentation.

While preparing an outline, it must be noted that it should not be restrictive and rigid. There should be flexibility built into it so that if subsequently a change is needed, it can be easily introduced. Too frequent changes should be avoided. If they seem to be necessary, they will only indicate that the task of outlining the report was not done properly. It should also be noted that a change of one point in the outline may involve one or more related changes elsewhere for that point may have a bearing. On one or more other points contained in the outline.

Changing one point may mean that other points are thrown out of sequence or out of context, so consider the relationship of a changed point to the rest of the piece and, where necessary, make changes in the other parts of the outline.

The writer should therefore, satisfy- himself that all related changes as a sequel to one particular change have been carried out in the outline.

A typical report outline based on the logical format is given below.

Outline

1. Title page
2. Letters of transmittal and authorization
3. Table of contents, statistical tables, charts and illustrations
4. Introduction
5. Methodology
6. Findings
7. Limitations
8. Summary and Conclusions
9. Recommendations
10. Appendices, bibliography and index.

(i) Title Page: the title page should indicate the topic on which the report has been prepared-the person or agency who has prepared it, the person or agency for whom it has been prepared and the date of submission (or completion) of the report.

(ii) Letter of Transmittal and Authorization: This indicates the official who has authorized or sponsored the research and the official to whom the report is addressed.

(iii) Table of Contents: Unless the report is extremely brief, it should contain a table of contents to guide the reader as to what it contains. The table of contents should indicate the main parts, divisions or sections of the report, the chapter headings along with the page numbers. When a report containing a number of statistical tables charts, figures or illustration, a separate table for each of these categories should be given immediately after the table of contents.

(iv) Introduction: The introduction deals with the genesis of the report. It explains why the study was undertaken, the statement and formulation of the problem, formulation of hypotheses, if any and the scope of the study. It is desirable to give a review of the related studies done earlier so that the reader may take the present report in the proper perspective.

(v) Methodology: The report should describe the methodology used in studying the problem. If a sample survey has been undertaken, the report should indicate the type of sample, design used, its size and the procedure used to draw the sample, the number of research workers employed in the field work, supervisors, the extent of precision achieved and the methods used for handling a special problems during the course of the study. It is necessary for the researcher not only to specify the method used but also its suitability vis-a-vis other methods. If the report are to be written for people not familiar with various statistical concepts, the researcher should explain the methodology in very simple language, confining himself only to the broader aspects, the more intricate aspects can be given separately in the form of an appendix. In a way, this is the most difficult part for the researcher as he has to communicate various concepts, methods and procedures to executives who are not deeply interested in research methodology and who are not familiar with the technical aspects.

(vi) Findings: This section of the report contains the results of the research and is perhaps the largest section of the report. The researcher should ensure that the findings are presented in proper sequence and in such a manner the reader has no difficulty in undemanding them. The researcher should also ensure that only the major findings are given as too many will be confusing to the reader. It is desirable to present the related data and exhibit as near the write-up on the findings as possible.

(vii) Limitations: The report should also point out the main limitations of the research reports therein. This will be helpful to the reader who can form his own opinion as to how far the results are reliable. In addition, it will be useful to researchers who subsequently undertake a study on the same or a related theme.

(viii) Summary and Conclusions: This section contains a summary of the reports as well as the main conclusions. The latter part is based on the findings given earlier. To facilitate the reader, the conclusions reported in this section should give references to pages, paragraphs or tables in the findings section.

(ix) Recommendations: It may not be necessary for all reports to contain recommendations. However, when a study has been commissioned by management which expects that the researcher will recommend certain measures, it is necessary that these be made in clear language.

(x) Appendices, Bibliography and Index: This is the Last section of the report. An appendix gives supplementary information which supports the body of the report but which cannot be given within it. If it is given within the main report. It may distort the focus on the main theme and confuse the reader. Generally, large and complex statistical tables, technical notes, copies of the questionnaires used, instructions to field staff and any other material used as supporting evidence for the write-up in the report are given in the form of appendices. Each append is should pertain to one particular aspect.

Further, most of the research reports also contain a bibliography showing the title of the books/reports used in the preparation of the reports. Name of authors, publishers, the year of publication and. if possible, the page numbers. In addition similar information is given in respect of' articles/papers. The bibliography should be arranged in an alphabetical order.

Finally, an index showing the various topics and the relevant page numbers in the report should also be given. It should be prepared on an alphabetical basis. However, an index may not be necessary in case the report is very short

Writing of the Report: Once the outline of report are prepared the researchers has to write it down. Repot-writing is a job that needs some skill which can he developed with practice. However, some board principles of writing a report may be as followed:

First, report must be written objectively.

Second, the report must be written in a concrete style. It must contain necessary statistics to support the thesis.

Third, the report must be organized and coherent, which can be ensured by formulating a research outline prior to writing the report.

Fourth, a research report or any formal report should be written in the impersonal style, avoiding the use of the first-person. This would also help full in writing, to remain more objective.

Fifth, that must be absolute clarity in the presentation of ideas. Clarity in writing is not possible in just one draft.

Sixth, the report should be neat and tidy. Wherever possible, charts and diagrams should be given. The write-up should be divided into different paragraphs and suitable headings should be provided if necessary, paragraphs may be numbered to facilitate easy reference.

Last but not the least is the question regarding the length of the research report. While a lengthy report may not be favored by busy executives, a short report may, on the other hand, omit some important aspects of the study.

A final advice to the researcher in this regard is 'Read, Think, Plan, Write and Re-writs". If he follows this advice and critically examines his earlier draft report, he will be in a position to write a good final report.

Feedback on the Report

After the report has been submitted by the researcher, he should try to get the feedback or the same, in a number of cases, this will be available to him without his asking while in other he may have to ask for it specifically. Feedback will enable him to know the deficiencies of his report, both in regard to the subject-matter and the write-up. He should receive the feedback with an open mind, especially, if he attempts a revision of the study later, or to avoid many shortcomings and pitfalls especially in regard to the presentation of the subject-matter, in subsequent research studies.

✶✶✶✶✶✶